QUEST
AND
RESPONSE

QUEST AND RESPONSE

Minority Rights and the Truman Administration

by

Donald R. McCoy

and

Richard T. Ruetten

The University Press of Kansas
Lawrence/Manhattan/Wichita

For

Earl Pomeroy and Ernst Posner
Gentlemen, Scholars, and Mentors

Preface

When most people talk about the civil-rights revolution, they speak of it as something that began in the mid 1950s or the early 1960s. They talk of its origins in terms of the Supreme Court's school desegregation decision, Dr. Martin Luther King, Jr., the sit-ins, or the Student Nonviolent Coordinating Committee. Yet the drive for minority rights in the United States had roots. It did not start from scratch.

These roots can be traced back to the early contacts between Indians and European settlers and the coming of black men to America; they are embedded in the subsequent development of relations among the races. Let there be no mistake, however. The quest of racial minorities for equal rights and opportunities for advancement has never been a smoothly growing, coordinated movement either in intensity or in success. Despite occasional excitements and successes, it was a scattered, scraggy movement until the beginning of the Second World War. It reflected the weaknesses of black-, brown-, red-, and yellow-skinned Americans, who were largely segregated and intimidated, poverty-ridden and undernourished.

We contend that this situation changed to an unprecedented extent during the years between 1945 and 1953. The change was inadequate in bringing equal rights and opportunities to the people of racial minorities, but it did bend patterns of thought and behavior and did confer tangible benefits. Under President Harry S. Truman, the executive branch of the federal government listened to minority groups as never before—and they spoke as never before—and often responded to their entreaties and pressures. Civil-rights victories were also won in the courts. Educational levels rose, and employment opportunities and the types of work undertaken increased. Legal segregation began to crumble, and the campaign for better housing inched forward. Leadership and individual accomplishment, political activity and organization, and pride and a sense of purpose grew markedly, at least among Negroes. Somewhat effective alliances were forged among racial minorities, Jews, organized labor, and political and religious liberals, in the search for ways to increase minority rights and opportunities in America.

Of course, the impact of these and other developments varied among and within minority groups. Oriental-Americans stood well in front of the racial minorities in all areas, and blacks forged ahead of the bulk of Indians and Spanish-speaking Americans. Within groups, the small middle class expanded and probably profited the most; but substantial segments of the lower classes experienced progress, and their aspirations heightened. In all, for the first time, sizable elements among racial minorities developed a modicum of economic power and political influence, and they often skillfully applied it for their own advantage. This rudimentary power—along with the frustration at not gaining more—and increasing pride, purpose, knowledge, and leadership were among the bases for civil-rights and racial developments after 1953.

Our goals are to detail and to analyze the advances and frustrations of the quest for minority rights and the response of American society, particularly the Truman administration, during the years 1945 to 1953. We view the civil-rights movement as one embracing a variety of minorities, because the problems, battles, successes, and failures were not confined to one group. They were often shared, sometimes in concert, by Negroes, Indians, Mexican-Americans, Puerto Ricans, Japanese-Americans, and Chinese-Americans—the major groups usually called racial minorities. Jews are included because they occasionally shared grievances with the racial minorities and because they played a key role in sparking the informal civil-rights coalition of the period. But this study emphasizes black Americans. They had the overwhelming strength of numbers and purpose among minority peoples and had generated and led the civil-rights movement since the 1930s. Of necessity, other groups are given less attention because of their smaller numbers and their lesser influence and impact on American life.

The list of people and organizations that we are indebted to is long. We might begin by mentioning the strong encouragement and generous financial support given by the Harry S. Truman Library Institute, the University of Kansas, and the National Endowment for the Humanities. Particularly noteworthy are the wise counsel and invaluable assistance tendered us by Philip C. Brooks, the former director of the Harry S. Truman Library, and former Vice-Chancellor Francis H. Heller of the University of Kansas, and the personal interest taken in this study by James B. Rhoads, the archivist of the United States, and his predecessor, Robert H. Bahmer.

A study such as this, based upon a wide range and massive amount of research material, documents in part the diligent and intelligent help of a large number of civil servants and librarians and especially archivists and manuscript curators, our brothers-in-arms in Clio's service. Among these we are particularly obligated to Benedict K. Zobrist, Philip D. Lagerquist, Mary Ann Blaufuss, Harry Clark, Jr., John Curry, Willie L. Harriford, Jerry Hess, Helen C. Luckey, Erwin Mueller, Anna Parman, and Cecil Schrepfer of the Harry S. Truman Library; Lois C. Aldridge, Mark Eckhoff, Thomas E. Hohmann, Joseph Howerton, Maria Joy, Richard L. Lytle, Richard Maxwell, Charles E. Neal, Harry Schwartz, and John E. Taylor of the National Archives; Reginald Winter of the Washington National Records Center; John C. Broderick and Paul T. Heffron of the Manuscript Division of the Library of Congress; Elizabeth B. Drewry and Jerome V. Deyo of the Franklin D. Roosevelt Library; Mildred Baruch of the Office of the Secretary of the Navy; D. C. Allard of the Naval History Division of the Office of the Chief of Naval Operations; H. Charles Hallam, Jr., librarian of the Supreme Court; Gerald Chopin of the Justice Department; Dorothy Sparks of the Treasury Department; Henry Greenberg of the Civil Service Commission; Idris Rossell and Eddie Williams of the State Department; Marion Howey and Terrence Williams of the University of Kansas; Alexander P. Clark of Princeton University; William B. Liebmann of Columbia University; Archie Motley of the Chicago Historical Society; Judith A. Schiff of Yale University; James C. Evans and Rudolph A. Winnacker of the Defense Department. We greatly appreciated assistance from Lucile Bluford, Oscar Chapman, Campbell C. Johnson, and Regina McGranery, as well as the insights and suggestions we received from a number of historians, including Joseph Boskin, David M. Chalmers, Richard M. Dalfiume, Constance M. Green, Flint Kellogg, Richard S. Kirkendall, Thomas A. Krueger, Ulysses G. Lee, Jr., Rayford W. Logan, August Meier, Morris MacGregor, Saunders Redding, Arvarh E. Strickland, and Robert L. Zangrando. John Hope Franklin of the University of Chicago and William Tuttle of the University of Kansas deserve a special vote of thanks for their patience and kindness in reading and commenting on the manuscript of this study. And, as in all things, we benefited from the forbearance, reactions, and intelligence of our wives, Vivian McCoy and Margaret Ruetten.

Donald R. McCoy
Richard T. Ruetten

Contents

1 THE STATE OF MINORITIES BEFORE THE TRUMAN YEARS

The United States, from its beginnings, has been a land of minorities, and one of its continuing challenges has been the adaptation of these minorities to the land and to each other. The nation's history is studded with struggles, by individuals and groups, to achieve civil rights. Colonists fought against royal and proprietary powers and against each other to establish fundamental rights to what the Declaration of Independence would call "life, liberty, and the pursuit of happiness."* Indians fought against whites, and whites against Indians. Many Negro slaves sought insurrection and the fugitive life as ways to attain rights enjoyed by other Americans. One religious group after another and wave upon wave of immigrants struggled to secure the rights promised them in charters and constitutions. These battles, as much as any other American phenomenon, can be considered the leitmotiv of the nation's development.

After World War I the fight for minority rights was considerably subdued because of postwar repressive attitudes and the restrictive immigration legislation of the 1920s. Yet new and great civil-rights contests were in the offing, if for no other reason than the continuing presence of minorities that had not achieved anything approaching equality or even the power to fight for it. These are the minorities to be dealt with in this study.

Indians, of whom there were 333,969 in 1940, were the nation's oldest minority and in many ways the most disadvantaged. As wards of the federal government, they had exchanged much of their freedom for a thin slice of government assistance. It was not until 1924 that all

---

* In quoted passages the stylistic conventions of the original have not been retained in minor matters such as capitalization.

Indians attained citizenship, although as late as 1938 seven states still forbade them to vote. The Meriam Report of 1928 called attention to the plight of America's Indians and suggested a program designed to develop their potentialities. Beginnings were made along that line during Herbert Hoover's administration with attempts to improve Indian schools, Indian Bureau personnel, and land policies.

Further change in the status of Indians came during the presidency of Franklin D. Roosevelt. Congress in 1934 repealed twelve laws that had virtually made the Indian Affairs commissioner a warden and Indian reservations prisons. That same year the Indian Reorganization Act was passed, which offered to reservation Indians some self-government, federal loans for economic improvement, protection against encroachment on their lands, and increased employment in the Bureau of Indian Affairs. The act implicitly repudiated the attempt to terminate reservations and to integrate Indians into white society. Indians also benefited somewhat from other New Deal programs, especially the Civilian Conservation Corps and various relief measures. Efforts after 1934 to improve their dire economic situation led to the addition of some four million acres to Indian lands by summer 1941 and low-interest loans of over $5.5 million by 1945. Indians were able to gain an additional four hundred thousand acres of crop lands and seven million acres of leased grazing land by war's end. Between 1932 and 1944 the number of beef cattle owned by Indians grew from 171,000 head to 361,000 and of dairy cattle, from 11,003 to 50,700 head.

During World War II, 24,521 Indians saw military service, on a nonsegregated basis, and some 50,000 others gained industrial employment. Also the National Congress of American Indians was organized to advocate their interests, which reflected their slowly mounting economic strength and political awareness. Yet it was clear in 1945 that those Indians who had left the reservations suffered from problems of segregation and "ghettoism," although not to the extent that other racial minorities did, thanks to the lack of uniformity of prejudice against them throughout the country. Those who remained on reservations were at an economic disadvantage because of the difficulties of making reservation resources yield even subsistence livings and because government paternalism was interpreted by most Americans as a sign of inferiority. Few reservation Indians could compete for jobs in nearby towns on the same footing as whites, and they did not have equal protection from the courts and police. There was no denying that most full-blooded red men suffered severely from discrimination and segregation despite the reforms and assistance of the Roosevelt period.[1]

A larger minority group was the Spanish-speaking Americans of Mexican and Puerto Rican origins. There are no reliable estimates of the number of Puerto Ricans resident in the continental United States in 1940, but that year there were 61,463 in New York City, where most of them had settled.[2] Yet during the Roosevelt years Puerto Ricans were so few and so quiescent that their problems were rarely discussed. That situation was to change somewhat after the war.

Mexican-Americans constituted the second-largest so-called racial minority in the United States well before the 1940s, with estimates of their numbers running from the 1,422,533 given in the 1930 census to about 3,000,000 indicated in 1938 by the National Resources Committee. (The 1940 census counted as Mexican-Americans only those who had been born in Mexico themselves or had one or both parents born in Mexico; they were numbered at 1,076,653, which was probably well below their actual number.) The 1930s were an unhappy time for Mexicans in the United States. Because of the depression, large numbers of Mexican-born Americans returned to their homeland, often under pressure in order to remove them from relief rolls and from job competition. Those who remained, including Mexicans born in the United States, experienced conditions similar to those of most American Negroes. Carey McWilliams observed: "Large employers of Mexican labor have consistently pursued a policy of isolating Mexicans as a means of holding them to certain limited categories of work. Systematically discouraging all 'outside contacts,' they have kept Mexicans segregated by occupation and by residence." Some Mexican-Americans did not submit unresistingly to this condition. From time to time they banded together in independent farm unions and struck for better wages and relief from discrimination. Success was rarely theirs, however, in the face of wholesale firings, and even violence and deportations.

World War II brought only small changes. Tens of thousands of young Mexican-Americans served in the military forces on an unsegregated basis, and some returned with greater skills and expectations. War-industry jobs, however, only slowly became available to Mexican-American civilians. Moreover, there was evidence of discrimination and segregation, and the Mexican-American leaders were unable to command respect in either their own or the Anglo communities. There is also the probability that Mexican-Americans served as substitute scapegoats for local problems after the evacuation of the Japanese-Americans from the West Coast.

Generally the public ignored the problems of Mexican-Americans. Yet the Coordinator of Inter-American Affairs, Nelson Rockefeller, encouraged public and private agencies to relieve tensions between Spanish-speaking peoples in the United States and the community at large. Mexican officials worked against exploitation of their brothers in the United States and were largely responsible for the actions of American officials to lessen the effects of prejudice against Mexican citizens and, indirectly, Mexican-Americans. Spanish-speaking people in the United States did benefit economically from wartime prosperity and Good Neighbor propaganda. Nevertheless, they were by 1945 still a repressed group, with little influence and few prospects for advancement outside of the few northern communities where they had been received with a modicum of tolerance.[3]

There were also the minorities of Asian origins, which in 1940 mainly included 126,947 Japanese-Americans and 77,504 Chinese-Americans. Like other racial minorities, Oriental-Americans could not move freely in American society. Segregation, discrimination, and economic disadvantages were common to their lives; although segregation, at least among the Chinese-Americans, stemmed as much from their cohesiveness as from the pressures of the general community. Racial tensions, where they surfaced, usually existed on the social frontiers between Japanese-Americans and whites, because of the former's high-paced striving for equality and opportunity.

Considerable change came with the war, for the worse for Japanese-Americans and for the better for Chinese-Americans. Japanese-Americans became America's scapegoat for the attack on Pearl Harbor. Early in 1942 the government herded 112,000 West-Coast Japanese and Japanese-Americans into camps located well inland. Their property losses were heavy, and the psychological toll was great in their shouldering of the burdens of questioned loyalty, ostracism, and confinement. It was tragic that Americans were subjected to life in concentration camps while the nation was mobilizing to combat persecution abroad. The best that was allowed to Japanese-Americans during the war was to prove their loyalty under ordeal by fire. Early in 1943 a volunteer combat unit was formed and was so successful that in November selective service was reinstituted for Japanese-Americans. Some 33,300 served in the army. The record of the two organizations identified with them—the 442d Infantry Regiment and the 100th

Infantry Battalion—was among the most distinguished in American military history.

Wartime civilian manpower needs also slightly softened the harsh treatment given the Japanese-Americans, and by spring 1943 significant numbers began leaving the relocation camps for resettlement over the country. In December 1944 the army even revoked the West Coast exclusion order. By 1946, when the last relocation camp was closed, almost 49 percent of the evacuees had returned to the Pacific Coast, with the remainder settling elsewhere in the country. The relocation and exclusion orders stemmed in large part from racial prejudice, but they slowly evoked a counterresponse, which in the long run bolstered strivings for equal civil rights by Japanese-Americans and even other racial minorities.[4]

The Chinese in America were in a different position. Not as motivated as Japanese-Americans in questing for equal rights, they had usually avoided those occupations jealously guarded by whites, which helped to reduce tensions. Thanks to increasing sympathy for China during the Japanese invasion and the wartime Sino-American alliance, discrimination lessened to the point where, as Shien-woo Kung wrote, "the Chinese enjoyed at least a temporary equality in the eyes of the American public." Chinese-Americans were allowed, sometimes even encouraged, to compete in small business, civil service, and professional undertakings. Many of the barriers to housing, union membership, and social activities were relaxed. Moreover, in 1943 Congress repealed the Chinese Exclusion Act of 1882. In 1944 a yearly quota of 105 was established for Chinese immigrants, and the right to naturalized citizenship, still denied the Japanese, was conferred. All this did not wipe out discrimination against Chinese-Americans. There were the instances of segregation in the military services and in the schools of several states as well as the fact that they were still among the first to be fired when jobs were cut back. The Chinese, however, had achieved substantial advancement during the war, almost without struggling for it, and were to keep most of their gains.[5]

There were minorities other than racial ones, but neither their needs nor demands seemed pressing enough to command major attention, at least during the 1930s. America's twenty million Catholics used the traditional methods of education, economic improvement, legal action, and especially political influence to progress toward equality. Although discrimination was occasionally evident, one could agree with Arnold and Caroline Rose that by 1940 "it was questionable whether Catholics could any longer be called a minority group."[6]

The nation's five million Jews had also found a substantial position in American life. Drawing on a strong sense of group identity and on traditions of accomplishment and cooperation, they had been able to make much of opportunities for advancement. By the 1930s Jews were found in prominent positions in business, law, medicine, the arts, science, literature, education, and even politics. This advancement continued during the 1940s, and it could be said by the 1950s that there had been a rapid and generally satisfying rise in the status and income of Jews. Yet during World War II they suffered to a certain extent from being "ghettoized" and from being barred from or admitted on a quota basis to many educational institutions, social groups, and public accommodations. They also found that anti-Semitism was growing in America, while the nation was fighting a war against Nazi anti-Semitism. Jews responded to this vigorously. Some of their most important organizations became defense groups, launching propaganda to counter anti-Semitism and working for laws against discrimination. Particularly noteworthy were the efforts of the American Jewish Committee, the American Jewish Congress, and the Anti-Defamation League of B'nai B'rith. Jewish organizations also sought allies in their quest for a tolerant nation, one in which they, and all men, could achieve advancement through merit.[7] They thereby formed a nucleus for a civil-rights coalition.

Yet the idea of minority-group cooperation went beyond Jews. Negroes were similarly reaching out for allies during the war. The black newspaper the *Chicago Defender* regularly carried a column by S. I. Hayakawa, and a number of prominent Negroes denounced the evacuation of Japanese-Americans from the West Coast in 1942. Congressman Adam Clayton Powell, Jr., sought for other participants in a minority front, appealing in 1945 for a Negro-Mexican coalition in California.[8] All this sowed a seed that was to sprout through the topsoil of racial discontent during the postwar period as minorities increasingly came together to work for common goals.

Negroes were, of course, central to the problem of securing civil rights in America. They constituted the largest racial minority in the continental United States, with 12,865,518 counted in the 1940 census. Indeed, at the most generous estimate, all the other racial minorities together did not amount to as much as one-third their number. Negroes were central for other reasons. One was that no other group was so restricted: For many minority people there was the possibility of return to a homeland; for some there were occasional refuges in America with opportunities for advancement; for all others the patterns of discrimination and segregation were less rigid than for black men. Another reason was that the Negro had been the cause of the nation's greatest civil-rights skirmish, during the Civil War and Reconstruction, which had led to the Thirteenth, Fourteenth, and Fifteenth amendments to the Constitution and various civil-rights statutes. Enforcement of the bright promises of the 1860s and 1870s had faltered as time passed, and the statutes had been drained of their vitality by contradictory administrative practices and unfavorable judicial decisions, which by Woodrow Wilson's presidency had reduced the mass of blacks to political impotence and social despair. Retrieval of the rights proclaimed in the 1860s was a goal for Negroes that other minority groups would share only with less fervor and symbolic significance. A last important reason was that blacks had not come to America voluntarily, or to escape anything, or to seek freedom and opportunity. What they found upon their arrival were slavery and discouragement. Moreover, even after emancipation, they had been afforded scant preparation and opportunity to make a decent place for themselves. Because of their color and their former condition of bondage, they were more conspicuous than other minorities and usually encountered the most insulting attitudes about their character and potential. And for Negroes there were too few tribunes at home and no consuls from abroad to intervene in their behalf.

Until the 1930s, blacks had not developed sufficient position in American society to contest discrimination and repression effectively. The 1930s brought some change. Franklin D. Roosevelt's promises of a new deal for Americans took on special significance for Negroes. For the first time, attempts, however often unsuccessful, were made to give them their share of government assistance. Increased numbers of blacks entered government service. President Roosevelt and especially his wife, Eleanor, listened to and talked with Negro leaders. In all, the tangible results were modest, but the psychological effect was impressive. Hope had dawned in the minds of blacks.

Hope is a fragile tissue, but it was reinforced by other developments. Black leadership and skills were increasing. Literacy among blacks rose from 83.7 percent to 90 percent between 1930 and 1940, and the percentage of Negroes in skilled and semiskilled occupations rose from 23.3 to 28.8. Health improvements were reflected in the extension of life expectancy at birth from 48 to 53 years of age. The percentage of young blacks attending school increased from 60.0 to 64.4. Outstanding Negro writers, such as Langston Hughes and Alain Locke, achieved national prominence. The National Association for the Advancement of Colored People reached a membership of some fifty thousand by 1940. Negroes were given a greater sense of pride and community, moreover, by such stirring events as the black nation Ethiopia's strenuous resisting of white Italy in the war of 1935–1936; Jesse Owens's Olympic victories in Adolf Hitler's Berlin; and Joe Louis's pugilistic triumphs. The successful use of black boycotts to increase job opportunities in New York, St. Louis, Washington, and other cities also contributed to their hope.[9] The importance of the developments of the 1930s, however, lay not in what they tangibly accomplished, for that was little, but in their being the overture to what was to come.

The outbreak of World War II in September 1939 marked the beginning of the end of economic depression for most American workers. Foreign war orders and American defense requirements swelled the job rolls throughout most of the country. Negroes found, however, that the new prosperity was not so all-encompassing as to embrace them. Some factories would not hire blacks, and most would employ them only for unskilled positions. Government vocational-training programs usually discriminated against nonwhites. Moreover, the Army Air Corps and the Marine Corps were lily-white, the navy used blacks only as messmen, and the army had few places open within its four small Negro units.

Blacks were unwilling to accept this situation, unlike their fathers during World War I, who had closed ranks with whites against foreign enemies. Negroes in 1940 used with increasing intensity their customary weapons of the 1920s and 1930s. By lobbying in federal agencies, they elicited orders to defense industries to stop discrimination in hiring, but these directives were rarely taken literally. Blacks pressed members of Congress for assistance, but they usually found little sympathy. With somewhat greater effectiveness, Negroes exerted pressure on executive agencies to increase the number of positions open to them in the civil and armed services.

It was clear that traditional means were not enough. War-borne prosperity still eluded great numbers of blacks. The next step, taken in late 1940, was to hold mass protest meetings in various cities, but these were scantly more successful. Then in January 1941 A. Philip Randolph, the head of the Brotherhood of Sleeping Car Porters, unveiled a more potent weapon. Writing in the Negro press, he called for a march of ten thousand blacks on Washington. Randolph added muscle to his plea by leading the formation of the March on Washington Movement, the first national, all-black mass organization concerned with economic affairs. The response was heartening to Randolph, for it was apparent that many Negroes were ready for militant action. The date for the march was set for July 1, and the number of blacks called for was increased from ten thousand to fifty thousand.

The March on Washington Movement demanded, among other things, that President Roosevelt issue executive orders abolishing discrimination under defense contracts and in job-training programs, as well as eliminating segregation in the civil and armed services. The few concessions that the government made to avert the embarrassment of a mass Negro demonstration in Washington were to no avail. Finally on June 25, 1941, Roosevelt issued Executive Order 8802, and Randolph responded by calling off the march.

The order provided less than had been sought, but it was a large step forward. Defense vocational-training programs were commanded to halt discrimination, and all new defense contracts were to include a provision "obligating the contractor not to discriminate against any worker because of race, creed, color, or national origin." A Committee on Fair Employment Practices was to be established to deal with the overall problem of job discrimination by defense contractors and government agencies. Although tangible results came slowly, Executive Order 8802 represented a great advance, not only because for the first time the government had used its authority to combat job discrimination, but also because the tactic of mass militancy had been employed to spur government action. Clearly, precedents had been set.

Regarding civilian employment, the work of the Fair Employment Practices Committee and other federal agencies was fairly effective. Not only did the proportion of blacks in the civil service increase, but the types of positions open to them improved. Between 1938 and 1944 the number of Negro federal civil servants increased from 82,000 to 274,000, and the percentage of those in custodial jobs decreased from as high as 90 to about 40. Segregation within government service decreased markedly, and almost all government cafeterias operated on a nonsegregated basis. There were similar trends in many private businesses, most prominently among firms holding government contracts. From 1940 to 1944 the number of black civilian workers rose from 4,400,000 to 5,300,000. Black membership in labor unions increased from 600,000 in 1940 to 1,250,000 by the end of the war. Wages mounted significantly. In 1939 black males as a whole received only 41.4 percent of the average amount paid to white males, while by 1947 they averaged 54.3 percent of the income of white males.[10]

Black leaders were also concerned with expanding opportunities for Negroes in the armed forces. In 1940 the army responded with a gesture in the promotion of Benjamin O. Davis, Sr., to brigadier general—the first Negro on active service to attain that rank. More substantial were the appointments of William H. Hastie as civilian aide to the secretary of war and Campbell Johnson as assistant to the Selective Service director. Thanks to the efforts of these and other Negro government advisers and to pressure from the Negro press and Negro organizations, the army by 1943 was taking 10 percent of its selectees from among black citizens. The Air Corps and the Marine Corps were opened to Negroes, and the navy increased the number of blacks in its ranks.

To the dismay of Negro leaders and soldiers, the army remained almost completely segregated throughout the war and indeed, more often than not, offered blacks service only in unskilled or semiskilled noncombatant units. Yet, even with these restrictions, almost eight thousand Negroes received army commissions, and considerable numbers of others acquired training in various skills. Eighty-six thousand black inductees passed successfully through army literacy training schools. The navy and the marines were far slower in accepting black officers and in fact commissioned only a handful. The Marine Corps, however, assigned Negroes to a variety of duties, often on an unsegregated basis. In 1944 the navy began to assign Negroes to general shore service and even to selected ships, and it began some integration of blacks and whites.[11] Even so, a great change in the military's racial policies had to wait for another president and another war.

There was progress in other areas, too. The NAACP made headway in its series of lawsuits for equalization between the salaries of Negro and white teachers, which had been started in the late 1930s. In 1941 the Supreme Court held in *Mitchell* v. *U.S.* that a black could not be denied Pullman accommodations when they were available to whites. In 1944, in *Smith* v. *Allwright*, the Court found that the Democratic party of Texas could not, under the Fifteenth Amendment, bar Negroes from voting, a ruling that helped to expand black suffrage in the South during the following decade. These and other favorable court decisions were only chinks in the wall of discrimination, but the structure began to show signs of stress.[12]

The intellectual assault on racist ideas was also important during the 1930s and especially during the war. Responding to the liberal atmosphere of the Roosevelt years, the rise in black militancy, and the ugliness of Nazi racism, intellectuals increasingly focused on the problems posed by intolerance. This was illustrated by the mounting publication of scholarly books on race and racism by such authors as Jacques Barzun, E. Franklin Frazier, Claude McKay, and Gunnar Myrdal. Related to this concern were the increasing success and impact of black novelists and poets such as Richard Wright and Gwendolyn Brooks. The growing flow of fiction and nonfiction on racial themes helped to prepare the way for advances in racial understanding, as did the rise of Negro artists such as Paul Robeson, Canada Lee, Katherine Dunham, Duke Ellington, and Lena Horne on the American stage, screen, and radio.

The geographical movement of blacks and other minorities during World War II was heavy—and significant. Some 2,729,000, or about 20 percent, of the nonwhite population migrated. Of these, 964,000 moved within one state, 578,000 between contiguous states, and 1,187,000 between noncontiguous states. Urban nonwhite population increased by two-and-one-half million. The proportion of the nation's nonwhites living in the South declined from 75 to 63 percent, while the nonwhite population of the Northeast, Middle West, and Far West rose substantially. The significance of these population shifts was to become increasingly clear after the war, in terms of political strength, black aspirations, and intergroup alliances.[13]

In short, World War II brought dramatic changes in the position of racial minorities. Almost all benefited from the increased employment necessitated by war production, and service in the armed forces was a boon to many of the more than one million nonwhite soldiers and sailors. But these benefits had not occurred automatically. Black Americans had to launch an intense and continuing crusade to share in the job boom and, along with Japanese-Americans, had to struggle for the right to wear the nation's uniform, even on a segregated basis. And the setbacks during the war were painful. In being packed off to concentration camps, Japanese-Americans suffered severe losses in property, income, and social acceptance. Jews felt sorely afflicted by a wartime rise in anti-Semitism at home, and reservation Indians suffered somewhat because of restrictions in federal aid programs. The war's overall domestic effect on minorities, however, was beneficial. By 1945 employment and income for them stood at record levels, more opportunities for advancement had appeared, and they had acquired additional skills. Moreover, the membership of the NAACP had increased from 50,556 to 351,131 between 1940 and 1945, giving the association the base to emerge as a major force in postwar politics.[14]

Blacks, overwhelmingly the largest of the nation's minorities, particularly profited from wartime developments. Large-scale migration, military service, and the expansion in jobs, income, skills, political influence, and organization strengthened their resolve not to return to their prewar condition of semiservitude. They also believed that for their participation in the war effort the United States owed them the right to share equally the rights and opportunities of other Americans. And many other Americans viewed the situation in the same light. Educated by the egalitarian generalizations of New Deal spokesmen during the 1930s and the war, and becoming increasingly aware of racial tensions, large numbers of white citizens were agreeable to advancement for minorities; indeed some were willing to help. This was evident in the hundreds of new interracial and human-relations groups that had been formed, especially after the widespread race riots of 1943. Assistance also came from other victims of discrimination. Jews had mobilized to meet the growth of anti-Semitism, and Japanese-Americans were battling to throw off the scapegoat role assigned to them during the war. Some Mexican-Americans and Indians were striving for improved positions for their peoples, and they would soon be joined by some Puerto Ricans as that group bulked larger in America as a consequence of heightened migration to the mainland. A civil-rights coalition was being formed, composed largely of Negroes and Jews, but with support from other minorities and sympathetic whites.

The priorities of the various civil-rights groups varied, but the shape of their overall program was plain. They wanted legislation fostering fair employment practices, outlawing discrimination in education and in the use of public facilities and accommodations, prohibiting racial and religious restrictions on property sale, increasing protection against violence, creating equality of treatment in the use of public funds, and improving educational opportunities. Increasingly, they were to fight against segregation as the greatest barrier to progress. Above all, they wanted respect for human dignity. Minorities, in short, sought not only to keep what they had gained during the war but to obtain what most Americans already enjoyed. And by 1945 minorities were much stronger in resolve, economic status, organization, and skills than ever before, and therefore better prepared than ever before to quest for equal rights.

2 A NEW MAN IN THE WHITE HOUSE

Franklin Delano Roosevelt died suddenly, victim of a cerebral hemorrhage, on the afternoon of April 12, 1945. Almost unanimously Americans hailed the dead president for his high ideals and his contributions to the cause of racial justice. As the NAACP's *Crisis* said, "The struggling masses of common folk over the globe of every race, color, and religion, have lost a champion and friend."[1]

Harry S. Truman was now the president. Minority-group Americans knew little about him, as was clear from the speculations of most of the black newspapers. The *Afro-American* (Baltimore) showed its concern for the southern influences of Truman's Missouri homeland. The *Call-Post* (Cleveland) wrote that his record showed nothing "to indicate that he conceives in any way the crusade of tolerance to be any part of public leadership." The *Chicago Defender* worried because South Carolina's James Byrnes was a close adviser to the new president, but it hoped that Truman would "prove himself another Justice Hugo Black."[2]

Yet there were exceptions. The *Crisis* wrote that Truman "has a good record on matters affecting Negro citizens. He is entitled to a chance to add to that record as president and in our judgment of him, pressing as our problems may seem to us, we must remember that we are but a part of the great problem facing America and the world." Surprisingly the *Amsterdam News* (New York), one of his antagonists during the 1944 election campaign, was optimistic about the new president. It liked his honesty and his record on economic issues, investigation of war expenditures, FEPC, and poll-tax repeal. "We view," it said, "with distaste those self-named liberals and experts who see every issue as a reason to 'abandon hope.' "[3]

13

What was Truman's background on civil rights? He had not been a crusader for minority-group rights, which was understandable in view of the southern tint of Missouri politics. There was, however, another reality in Missouri—the 20,000 Negro voters in Kansas City, Truman's base of power, and another 110,000 elsewhere in the state. In running for office, first for Jackson County judge and later for United States senator, Harry Truman did not overlook that. He may have flirted with the Klan in the 1920's, but he did not join it. More important was Truman's identification with Tom Pendergast's Jackson County machine, which, despite its corruptions, had been the protector of Negroes in its domain. The organization had looked to Harry Truman, as one of its liege men, to serve its purposes in relaxing racial tensions. It also, as Alonzo Hamby pointed out, "brought him into contact with city minority groups and urban politics, giving him a breadth of view and necessitating a tolerance which many politicians with his rural background never achieved."[4]

Truman reflected the Pendergast policy toward Negroes as presiding county judge, in which position he gained recognition for able administration of county homes for Negro boys and girls and the Negro aged. This was apparent from the support he received from black voters in his first campaign for senator in 1934. Once in the Senate, Truman continued to enlist the backing of Missouri's Negroes. He had a hand in removing Lincoln University from politics. He was a supporter, albeit reluctant, of the Costigan-Wagner antilynching bill of 1935 and of similar legislation in 1938. In that latter year and in 1940 he battled successfully to keep intact the functions of the office of recorder of deeds in the District of Columbia. That office, headed by Dr. William J. Thompkins, was a leading source of Negro jobs in the federal government.[5] Truman was to be repaid by Thompkins's active support in his successful campaign for reelection to the Senate in 1940. And the senator needed that support, for the Pendergasts had lost power in Kansas City and he was now on his own.

Thompkins, who was president of the National Colored Democratic Association, traveled in Truman's behalf and helped write his opening campaign speeches. These talks, given at Sedalia, Missouri, on June 15, contained a strong appeal to Negroes. At ground-breaking ceremonies for a new Negro hospital, the senator deplored poor housing and job opportunities for blacks and exploitation of them by emporian pirates. He championed the right of Negroes to be educated and "to exercise their privileges as free men." Later that day, speaking at the Pettis County courthouse, he asserted that "the stronger group should not impose upon the weaker obnoxious conditions or situations. In all matters of progress and welfare, of economic opportunity and equal rights before the law, Negroes deserve our every aid and protection." He was careful to say, however, that "their social life will naturally remain their own." Truman expressed similar sentiments in a speech before the National Colored Democratic Association in Chicago a month later. Then he warned that "a crisis will develop" if the Negro continued to be ladened with indignities and antagonisms. The solution was clear: "We should recognize his inalienable rights as specified in our Constitution."[6]

Mild as these statements would seem a few years later, they were bold in much of America in 1940. Truman accepted the fact that segregation was still the norm and that progress had to be worked for from within that framework. That was realistic when given the sentiments of most Americans, even many Negroes. Yet overlooked in his Chicago talk had been any awareness on his part that there could be racial mixing in federal housing when he said, "Whenever it is possible, Negro managers will be employed in the housing projects tenanted mainly by colored people."[7]

Truman was active in other respects. He supported the anti-discrimination amendment to the 1940 Selective Service Act. In 1941 he worked to reduce discriminatory employment practices, and he introduced legislation to continue General Davis on active duty. Although in 1944 Truman voted in subcommittee for the Russell amendment, which forbade the executive transfer of funds to the FEPC, he worked to appropriate funds for the committee's continuance. He usually supported anti-poll-tax legislation and twice voted for cloture against filibustering on the bill. In short, Truman's record on civil-rights matters was good, especially for a border-state senator. It enabled him to declare when he was under attack during his 1944 vice-presidential election campaign:

I am a liberal, as proved time and again by my record in the
    Senate, and I dare anyone to challenge these facts.
I am for a permanent FEPC.
I am for a federal law abolishing the poll tax.
I am for a federal anti-lynching law.[8]

His record was strengthened by his longstanding friendship with Jews and his appointment of a rabbi as lodge chaplain when he was grand master of the Missouri Masons. Moreover, in Truman's first speech after becoming vice-president, he observed that the United States was extremely vulnerable to intolerance because of the diversity of its peoples and creeds. Then he proceeded to lambaste "evil doctrines of discrimination" and of "racial and religious intolerance."[9]

This was Harry S. Truman's record. What it meant for his presidency was difficult to predict, for his was an ambiguous legacy, the legacy of an astute Missouri politician seeking the confidence of his constituents. No one can say precisely what had motivated him or what would. It is too pat to say that he was cadging votes, or that he was influenced by his rural stars-and-bars background, urban bossism, or New Deal idealism. Truman was a complex of ideas and impulses, prejudices and principles. Most important was that he was an honest man who was proud of his record and intended to do the best he could constitutionally by all men. He recognized trends and pressures and adjusted to them, sensing the need to maintain a rough equilibrium between shifting powers. He also had a keen sense of loyalty and justice. He was loyal to those who helped him, although he did not shut out those who criticized him, and he abhorred having anyone get kicked around. He was no snob: he talked to anyone regardless of background, unless they were insulting. Truman was the kind of man who might accommodate the rising tide of black strength and aspirations.

Toward the close of the war, Negroes and most other minorities were better off than ever before. Greater optimism and leadership and a much-improved financial and political condition came out of the war years, thus making it possible for minorities to sustain the drive for equal rights. Also of great value was their substantial contribution to America's war effort. Blacks, reds, and yellows believed that the nation owed them something. It owed them the right to walk freely into the sunlight of society, to enjoy the rights and opportunities of other Americans.

That feeling was fortified by logical deductions from America's rationale for fighting the war. The United States could not crusade abroad against Nazi racism and brutality and Imperial Japanese oppression and still condone racism, brutality, and oppression at home. The nation could not offer more to oppressed peoples abroad than it was willing to grant disadvantaged peoples at home. America was now the earth's leading military and economic power, and thought of itself as the greatest moral power. Furthermore, the nation in 1945 had made formal commitments to human rights by ratifying the Act of Chapultepec and the United Nations Charter. It could not afford the embarrassment of inconsistency, most minority-group leaders thought, between its preaching and practices in a world that riveted much of its attention on events in the United States.

Other currents swirled in the mid 1940s. Sociologist Louis Wirth pointed out that with the "intermingling in the armed forces, in industry, and in day-to-day living, there took place an extensive commingling of mores and attitudes" that made all Americans more aware of the facts of prejudice and discrimination. This was augmented by the growing interest in racial themes in the films and press and on the radio. Columnist Earl Conrad saw as three great elements of change the creation of a large Negro voting bloc in the North resulting from the "Great Migration," labor's increased interest in black workers, and the glaring contradiction, during the war, between domestic racism and America's avowed democratic goals. Writing later, other observers also saw the war as a turning point. Charles Silberman asserted that the war destroyed black "fear of white authority." He added, "What Negroes discovered during the war . . . was their power to intimidate—not by violence, but by their very presence." Wilson Record associated the rising aspirations of Negroes with their geographical mobility. Thanks to their wartime experiences, many came quickly to know the advantages of regular cash income, better schooling, indoor plumbing, telephones, radios, supermarkets, and what not. "In other words, they got a close-up look at some of the more attractive features of American life, and they wanted 'in'—not merely for their great-grandchildren but for themselves, too."[10]

Equally important was the fact that Negroes were organized as never before. The Urban League and especially the NAACP had grown markedly during the war. The association had become really national and was representing the black community to a greater extent than ever before. It had gained prestige by not having faltered during wartime in seeking Negro rights, despite the risk of being charged with jeopardizing national security. The Negro press had also been unstinting in its quest for black equality and opportunity. Because of these developments, Walter White, the executive secretary of the NAACP, could write in 1945 that "Negro militancy and implacable determination to wipe out segregation grew more proportionately during the years 1940 to 1945 than during any other period of the Negro's history in America."[11]

Also noteworthy was the slowly growing replacement of Snow White by black beauty in the Negro press. True, advertisements continued to be overwhelmingly of products designed to straighten and dye ladies' hair—such as Lady Lennox Hair Dye and Gordon's Positive-Action Straightening Comb—or to achieve lighter skin—such as Nevoline or Dr. Fred Palmer's Skin Whitener. During the war, however, appeared Jay Jackson's *Chicago Defender* comic strip "Speed Jaxon," which pictured the exploits in the discriminatory army of a brilliant, courageous, and handsome young Negro. Toward the end of the war there were advertisements of "Sun Tan Dolls," touted as "The World's Prettiest Negro Dolls," and of baby food featuring a Negro child. Also important was the launching in 1945 of *Ebony*, a picture magazine that would play up colored beauty. These and other examples of black self-awareness were, S. I. Hayakawa pointed out in his newspaper column, "deeply significant, though beginning steps, towards trying to change the content of our ideals."[12]

Yet minorities drank at the fountain of fear with the approach of peace. Resettlement for Japanese-Americans meant facing new as well as old antagonists and trying to regain what they had achieved before the war. For all, remained the questions: What would happen to their jobs as wartime needs evaporated? What would happen to the gains made in seeking first-class citizenship? Erosion of economic advances was threat enough, but there was also, as the Urban League's Lester Granger commented, "enough organized anti-Negro and anti-Jewish sentiment already existing in this country to provide the nucleus of a formidable Fascist party in the postwar period."[13]

Some hope was seen in the development of interest among many whites. This optimism was based not only on the growth of human-relations and interracial groups, but also in the rising attention given to minority-group questions in the white press. This had begun about 1942 with concern about anti-Semitism, which later shifted to encompass bias against Negroes and Japanese-Americans. In 1945, minority-group matters ranked among the leading subjects covered on front pages or in editorials during thirty-three weeks, as contrasted with twenty weeks during 1944.[14] Apparently large numbers of whites, intellectually strengthened by the growing egalitarianism of the New Deal period and encouraged by minority-group spokesmen and concerned writers, were agreeable to minority-group advancement. Indeed some of them were willing to lend a hand.

Another wellspring of aid was found within the religious minorities. Some Catholics, despite their general absorption into traditional American society, were sensitive to the plight of other minorities. *America*, the Jesuit weekly magazine, early in 1945 stood up staunchly for a permanent FEPC. Students at twenty Catholic institutions in the

East called for the admission of qualified blacks to Catholic schools. In 1945 the American Jewish Committee formulated a plan to fight prejudice in labor, business, and industry, based on the philosophy that discrimination could not be eliminated against Jews unless it was eliminated against all minorities in America.[15] This did not mean that the various minorities lived in harmony. Discord was evident in anti-Semitism among blacks, the reluctance of Oriental-Americans to associate with Negroes, and racism among Catholics. But it was plain that there was a gradual coming together of minorities, or at least of their leaders, to fight for common goals.

It was at the crest of this high tide of minority-group strength, apprehension, and aspiration that Harry S. Truman became president. In his first message to Congress and the people, on April 16, he pledged to follow in Roosevelt's footsteps in seeking "peace and progress" and the improvement of "the lot of the common people." Although he made no reference to racial problems, twice he alluded to race, creed, and color. Truman held his first press conference the next day, and Harry McAlpin, the only Negro reporter present, asked him where he stood on "fair employment practice, the right to vote without being hampered by poll taxes, and all that?" The president answered, "I will give you some advice. All you need to do is to read the Senate record of one Harry S. Truman." As the conference ended, he shook hands with McAlpin.[16] It was a shrewd performance.

During his first month in the White House, Truman took care to meet with a couple of Negro leaders. On April 27 he received a visit from J. E. Mitchell, the managing editor of the *St. Louis Argus* and a 1944 presidential elector. Truman met on May 5 with the NAACP's Walter White, who protested that the United States was siding with Great Britain and France in obstructing the eventual independence of colonial peoples under the proposed United Nations Charter. White urged him to tell the UN founding conference at San Francisco that he would call for an international meeting to deal with the questions of dependent peoples, territorial trusteeships, and human rights.[17]

NAACP and other Negro leaders were aware, more than was the government, that the issues of human rights and colonialism were among the factors that would probably shape the world's future. White, along with W. E. B. DuBois and Mary McLeod Bethune, went to San Francisco to serve as NAACP observers at the UN conference. There they worked with other observers to influence the American delegation to support arrangements for colonial trusteeships and a human-rights commission. The chairman of the delegation, Edward

R. Stettinius, Jr., conceded to White that the pressure forced the American delegates to be more flexible on such questions.[18]

The United Nations Charter, fashioned during the summer of 1945, provided for trusteeships for many dependent peoples and fostered the founding of some independent nations within a generation. The Charter also, under Article 55 (c), obligated the UN and member states to work for "universal respect for, and observance of, human rights and fundamental freedoms for all without distinction as to race, sex, language, or religion." President Truman in his closing message, June 26, to the San Francisco UN conference did not comment on the colonial and trusteeship questions as Walter White had asked him to do, but he did champion an international bill of rights. He asserted that unless fundamental human freedoms were achieved "for all men and women everywhere—without regard to race, language, or religion—we cannot have permanent peace and security." The only disturbing note was his indication that such a bill of rights had to be "acceptable to all the nations involved."[19] Nonetheless, his statement was a strong endorsement of the idea of framing an international declaration of human rights.

All this was well and good, but it did not deal with the problems nearest to America's minorities. Before long, Negro leaders were pressing Truman to meet with them to consider interests at home as well as abroad. To allay criticism, David K. Niles, the president's white adviser on minority affairs, recommended that Truman see the executive committee of the black National Newspaper Publishers Association during its meeting in Washington the end of May. Truman received the group cordially and listened to them with interest. The publishers urged him to make an enforceable fair employment practices bill and an anti-poll-tax bill administration measures. They also asked that the attorney general work to give full effect to the *Smith* v. *Allwright* decision on opening primary elections to all voters and that a Negro be appointed assistant veterans administrator to guarantee all veterans their benefits under the law. The president made no direct commitments in response to these requests. This and Walter White's complaint, a few days earlier, about discrimination against Negroes who applied for federal housing insurance constituted the beginning of black pressures on domestic matters.[20]

Truman was ready to support creation of a permanent FEPC. Minorities had been disappointed by the enactment of the Russell amendment in 1944, which subjected FEPC appropriations to congressional approval, and by Congress's failure to establish a permanent committee. For some time public support had been building for a statutory committee, starting with the formation of the National Council for a Permanent FEPC, under A. Philip Randolph's leadership, in 1943. The movement had enlisted the backing of a wide range of labor, racial, religious, civil-liberties, and civic groups. The Socialist and Communist parties and the 1944 Republican platform also favored some kind of permanent FEPC. However, bills to make the committee a statutory agency had perished in the legislative labyrinth from 1942 through 1944.[21]

The movement continued its efforts in 1945. Only $500,000 had been appropriated for the FEPC in 1944, and there was strong congressional opposition to appropriating additional funds to the committee. Moreover, Roosevelt had not supported the movement for a permanent FEPC, and the Republican bill provided for a toothless committee. These disadvantages were somewhat offset by the passage of the New York State Law Against Discrimination in March 1945, the first such state statute, which the Negro press brandished in the face of the Democratic administration as an example of what could be done.[22]

Thirteen bills to establish a permanent FEPC were introduced in the House of Representatives and two in the Senate at the beginning of the Seventy-ninth Congress. A House bill sponsored by Chairman Mary T. Norton of the House Labor Committee was favorably reported on February 20, 1945. Mrs. Norton asked the Rules Committee for a special rule scheduling a vote on her bill, but the committee procrastinated. When a Senate bill was reported on May 24, pressure for action began to build up. President Truman had indicated to the Negro publishers and to Walter White that the House was the main stumbling block. White urged him to seek action from the Rules Committee. Another problem was that proposed funds for the current FEPC were bottled up in the Appropriations Committee. Roosevelt had asked that $599,000 be appropriated for the FEPC beginning July 1, but the House committee had failed to report the budgetary item on the grounds that legislation was pending to make the FEPC a permanent agency. Truman was on the spot, however, caught between the fire of minorities and their allies and that of southerners and conservatives.[23]

Truman decided to work for both a permanent FEPC and funds for the existing agency. On June 5 he wrote Chairman Adolph J. Sabath of the House Rules Committee that it was "unthinkable" that the FEPC should be abandoned while wartime needs demanded "the participation of all available workers." The president added, "Even if the war were over," the fair employment issue "would be of paramount importance." Employment discrimination would lead to "industrial strife and unrest. It has a tendency to create substandard conditions of living for a large part of our population. The principle and policy of fair employment practice should be established permanently as a part of our national law." He urged that the members of the House have the opportunity to vote on both the funding and the statutory FEPC measures. Truman sent a copy of this letter to Dennis Chavez, the chief sponsor of Senate FEPC legislation, writing, "As soon as it becomes appropriate in the Senate, let me know and I shall send a similar letter." Truman had spoken boldly, thereby giving new life to the FEPC issue. The contrast with Roosevelt was clear, as Negro leaders knew.[24]

Truman persisted, repeating in a June 13 news conference his wish that the House be given the opportunity to vote. A "Save the FEPC" rally was held in New York City on June 19, and the president, in a telegram to that group, reiterated his support of permanent FEPC legislation. He again expressed his support of the FEPC in messages to the Negro Freedom Rally and to black leaders in Kansas City in late June. As fall approached, he did not abandon the issue, asserting in his Labor Day statement that "the bigotries of race and class and creed shall not be permitted to warp the souls of men."[25]

Regardless of presidential messages and mass meetings, the House and Senate bills for a statutory FEPC were dead. Sabath tried to get the Norton bill out of the Rules Committee, but all he could produce was a six-to-six tie vote, which kept the bill off the House floor. Mrs. Norton's parliamentary maneuvers also failed. In the Senate, Chavez and the other sponsors of the bill for a permanent FEPC decided that it was inadvisable to bring it up for a vote in 1945.[26]

Meanwhile action began on appropriations for the existing FEPC. A subcommittee of the House Appropriations Committee had recommended in May an appropriation of $250,000 for the agency, but the full committee shelved that recommendation. When the pertinent money measure, the war agencies appropriations bill, came up on June 7, Vito Marcantonio insisted that the questions of a permanent FEPC and funds for the existing agency were separate and that the House should act on the funding question. Marcantonio took the issue to the Rules Committee and gained the support of Chairman Sabath, who used Truman's letter and the revelation that President Roosevelt, on the day of his death, had asked him to work for continuance of the FEPC. Marcantonio also moved to amend the bill to provide $599,000 for the FEPC's work. The two congressmen were unsuccessful, as the House refused to consider the appropriation.[27]

In June a similar situation developed in the Senate, as its Appropriations Committee failed to report FEPC funding in the war agencies bill. The committee did, however, authorize Senator Chavez to ask the full Senate to add an FEPC appropriation to the bill. When the bill came up for debate, Senator Theodore Bilbo of Mississippi seized the floor and for several days conducted a one-man filibuster against the FEPC. Majority Leader Alben Barkley enlisted both sides in a compromise that would provide $250,000 for the agency. It was suggested at the time that the FEPC supporters in the Senate were strong enough to close debate and adopt Chavez's amendment, but that Barkley acted to forestall the Republicans from claiming credit for such a result.[28] Be this as it may, the end of the fiscal year was drawing near, and many senators probably would have shrunk from delaying war-agency funds by seeking a cloture petition.

FEPC backers in the House felt no compunction about holding up the war-agencies bill there. The new fiscal year dawned without Senate and House having reached an agreement. The upper house had a bill that contained at least a mutilated FEPC appropriation, and the lower-house bill, thanks to the parliamentary tactics of Representatives Marcantonio, Norton, and Emanuel Celler, went forward without appropriations for over half of the sixteen agencies involved. The Senate stood firm, and the House thrashed about in its misery. Finally, on July 11, the House Appropriations Committee reported out the same war-agencies bill that had been approved by the upper chamber, except for a proviso that the FEPC would be considered in the process of being liquidated. That compromise was agreed to by the full membership of the House and the Senate. The compromise gave no cause for jubilation among the proponents of the FEPC.[29]

The White House played no significant role in the battle aside from Truman's letter to Sabath and his several public statements. There is no evidence that Truman cracked the whip over Congress, but neither is there evidence that he had a whip to crack or that on this particular issue Roosevelt would have done so. If anything, by putting himself publicly on record for a permanent FEPC and for funds for the existing agency, the new president had gone well beyond his predecessor. As would be frequently the case on controversial issues during Truman's administration, the White House had neither enough public or congressional support nor other weapons at hand to win. It is doubtful that Roosevelt, with his charm and cunning, could have advanced further against the strong tide of congressional opposition than did Truman by relying on forthrightness. One has only to recall President Roosevelt's many failures after 1938 to put Harry Truman's difficulties with Congress into perspective. All the huffing and puffing and arm-twisting in the world would probably not have availed on civil-rights legislation at the end of the war. As Walter White commented in 1945 on Truman and the permanent FEPC bill, "It was not his fault a tie vote prevented action."[30]

There were, of course, other Negro pressures and fears that swirled about Truman. Blacks were much concerned about the new president's appointments. Many people, leery of Truman's Missouri background, feared that he would appoint southerners to office and feared what that might mean for Negroes. With the early appointments of Commodore James K. Vardaman as a White House assistant and Tom Clark as attorney general, alarums were sounded in some quarters. What really hurt was the nomination in June of James Byrnes to be secretary of state. Not only was that the most prestigious cabinet position, but under the law at that time, if Truman had died, Byrnes would have succeeded him as president. The South Carolinian, on the basis of his record, was plainly hostile to black men, and Negro reaction to his appointment was severe. The *Pittsburgh Courier* labeled him "a white supremacist of the first rank"; and the *Afro-American* charged, "It is plainly the policy of Mr. Truman to make the executive department as full of southern ideas as is Congress."[31] The appointment of Byrnes, combined with the fact that no Negroes had been given appointments, was hard to swallow; it offset the favorable impression that Truman had made by his support of the FEPC.

By September the pattern of appointments began to change, with the nominations of Senator Harold Burton to the Supreme Court and Robert Patterson as secretary of war. Burton had been active in the NAACP and supported the FEPC, and Patterson had won a reputation for not being unfriendly to the Negro in the army. The appointment of a Chicago attorney, Irvin C. Mollison, to the Customs Court in October came as a pleasant surprise, not only in itself, but also because for the first time a black had been appointed to a federal judgeship higher than that of the Washington Municipal Court within the continental United States. Some of the edge of the sharp Negro reactions to many of Truman's appointees was further dulled by the appointment of Dr. Ralph Bunche to the Anglo-American Caribbean Commission.[32]

Negroes had other complaints, including ones about discrimination and segregation in the Veterans Administration and in some government cafeterias. Moreover, civil-rights groups had been seeking legislation to outlaw lynching, poll taxes, segregated travel accommodations, and assaults on soldiers and sailors. Little was done to meet Negro requests. The only legislative success, apart from the FEPC appropriation, was the House passage of the anti-poll-tax bill in June. It was expected, though, that a filibuster would prevent the Senate from acting on the measure, as had been the case in previous years. Two presidential actions were encouraging. In November Truman decided that government cafeteria workers, most of whom were Negroes, should receive the same pay for five days of work as they had for the wartime six-day work week. On December 22 he vetoed a bill that would have returned the Employment Service to state operation, which black leaders thought would heighten employment discrimination in many states.[33]

Nevertheless, in 1945 all these were secondary issues. The focus was on the FEPC; and it was to remain there throughout that year and well into the next, for minorities knew the importance of having an established agency to help them get and keep jobs. There were some, however, who saw the economic issue in a broader scope. On August 27 the Urban League sent a long memorandum to Truman, apparently to assist in the preparation of his September 6 economic message to Congress. The memorandum not only urged continuance of the FEPC, but also expressed support for a full-employment act, increased benefits for social security and unemployment compensation, improvement of the Employment Service's effort on behalf of Negroes, low- and middle-income housing, elimination of restrictive covenants in realty agreements, better educational and medical opportunities and facilities, equal and unsegregated administration of veterans' programs, desegregation of the armed forces, and a general attack on "fear, hate and conflict within the American population."[34]

The administration, of course, had its own goals to emphasize: winning the war and then the peace, and smoothing the path to economic reconversion. Everything else in 1945 was secondary. The president was willing to help out on other pressing issues, partly out of duty and partly out of the hope of keeping the confidence of liberals and minorities. He could not, however, make racial issues into primary causes without jeopardizing the nation's goals with regard to the military, foreign affairs, and reconversion. These Truman had to move rapidly on, for they would admit of no delay. Abroad there were too many commitments to be kept or reviewed. Literally there was a world to be won or lost. At home the coming of peace meant the unraveling of the wartime economy, with its attendant problems of shifting from wartime to peacetime production, of inflation, of shifts in employment, of absorbing veterans into the labor force. Here there was a nation to be won or lost in trying to navigate between the Scylla of inflation and the Charybdis of depression.

Working in minority concerns where it could, the administration's program paralleled much of that of the Urban League. The president supported appropriations for the existing FEPC and the establishment of a permanent committee, and temporary continuance of and increased funds for the federal Employment Service. He requested additional public housing, more unemployment compensation, and legislation to allow the government to pursue full employment. He also asked for a comprehensive program to expand "health security for all, regardless of residence, station, or race—everywhere in the United States."[35] Nevertheless, glowing words and glittering proposals were unlikely to dissolve the hostile coalition of Republican and southern conservatives in Congress. Truman would have his hands full striving to preserve what existed.

This was nowhere more evident than with the FEPC. The huge slice in the committee's funds meant that its operations would be cut sharply. By December its staff had been reduced from 128 to 31, and it had shut down all but three of its field offices. Even had it continued at full force, the agency's jurisdiction was rapidly being pared as war contracts were canceled. Toward the end of summer 1945, the FEPC, the Urban League, and the National Council for a Permanent FEPC pressed Truman to help. The FEPC emphasized that up to two million minority-group workers would be handicapped in getting new jobs unless discriminatory employment practices were abandoned. The committee contended that in the probable postwar contests between labor and management, "elements in both will exploit racial antagonisms for selfish ends." The president's response was to make a permanent FEPC "must" legislation in his economic message of September 6.[36]

This demand for a permanent FEPC elicited even less reaction from Congress than his earlier letter to Sabath. For one thing, whites, sensitive to the possibility of another depression, felt the job market tightening. For another, "must" legislation under Truman was clearly less imperative than under Roosevelt. The Missourian had neither the strength nor the aura of his predecessor, and conditions were not ripe for development of them. Yet Truman received credit for trying. The *Crisis* gave recognition to the president for his support of FEPC when the rest of the government "seems to have turned a cold shoulder to legislation for a permanent FEPC."[37]

This did not mean that the pressure was off—far from it. In December the *Crisis* demanded that "the greatest of pressure" be exerted on leaders of both parties on the FEPC issue. Indeed, pressure since summer had been steaming out of the black press. Since August a group headed by A. Philip Randolph had been seeking "to discuss with the president the question of his action in behalf of FEPC." Truman was not eager for advice on the question, and the White House went to great pains to avoid scheduling a meeting. Of course, there was no great purpose in such a meeting, but it was impolitic to be evasive with Randolph's group. It led to a bad reaction among some Negroes, who wondered how Truman could be too busy to discuss matters so vitally important to so many Americans.[38]

Before 1945 ended, Truman was confronted by a more important matter in connection with the FEPC. One of his greatest problems had been work stoppages arising from tension between labor, which was seeking to keep wartime gains, and management, which was striving for postwar retrenchment. When, for the second time within a month, a wildcat strike shut down the services of Washington's Capital Transit Company, the president, on November 21, directed the Office of Defense Transportation to seize and operate the company.[39] The FEPC, which had for years been seeking to have Capital Transit employ Negroes, decided to take advantage of the situation. On November 23 the committee decided to direct the company to desist from discriminatory employment practices. The next day the White House ordered that the FEPC directive should not be issued. On November 25 Charles H. Houston wrote Truman on behalf of the committee that the FEPC had received no direct orders from him. Houston asked for such orders and for a conference between the president and the committee. Truman inscribed on Houston's letter: "Hold it up!"[40]

A week passed without the letter being acknowledged, and in disgust Houston resigned from the FEPC, charging that "the failure of the government to enforce democratic practices and to protect minorities in its own capital makes its expressed concern for national minorities abroad somewhat specious, and its interference in the domestic affairs of other countries very premature." Truman replied on December 7, contending that the powers assigned him for seizing property in a labor dispute required that the facility be operated under the employment conditions in effect at the time of seizure. He added, "As anxious as I am for Congress to pass legislation for a permanent FEPC,

I cannot contravene an act of Congress in order to carry out the present committee's aims." Administration spokesmen also said that the committee had been derelict in not delivering a directive to Capital Transit after findings of fact the preceding April about the company's discriminatory hiring practices.[41]

The NAACP snapped up the issue and telegraphed the president on November 23, urging him to back the FEPC's proposed action. Three days later David Niles telephoned Walter White to say that Judge Samuel I. Rosenman had counseled Truman that he could not legally change the labor policies of a seized corporation. The NAACP pressed Truman on the matter. Its Board of Directors sent him a resolution which charged the administration with giving "nothing more than lip service" to the legislative struggle against discrimination in hiring. Regarding the Capital Transit case, the directors criticized the president not only for prohibiting the FEPC to issue its directive, but for giving neither due notice nor "an opportunity for the committee to present its views." The resolution closed: "We believe it is time for the administration to demonstrate whether it proposes to take any effective action toward insuring fair employment practices for all."[42]

The FEPC admonished the president that its necessarily limited activities were no "substitute for effective enforcement of national policy." It gave notice that because of staff reductions, it would concentrate on dealing with discrimination in civil-service hiring and studying employment problems of minorities in general. Even on this basis, its work could go on for only a few more months.[43] In response to NAACP and FEPC pressure, Truman indicated that he would continue pressing for a permanent FEPC and that he would take action to support the existing agency during its waning months. Then on December 18 the president wrote to all heads of government agencies, stressing that refusal to reemploy wartime federal workers from other offices on the basis of race or creed violated existing law and regulations. He asked the agencies to analyze their personnel policies and practices in order to facilitate fair consideration of these government servants for new appointments. He also requested "full cooperation with FEPC in all matters affecting the employment of minorities in government." The same day Truman ordered the FEPC to "investigate, make findings and recommendations, and report to the president, with respect to discrimination in industries engaged in work contributing to the production of military supplies or to the effective transition to a peacetime economy."[44]

The FEPC faded away before the end of the fiscal year. Its final report to the president indicated that "the wartime gains of Negro, Mexican-American, and Jewish workers are being dissipated through an unchecked revival of discriminatory practices." It strongly recommended federal legislation in regard to fair employment practices and the compilation of complete statistics on employment and unemployment by race and sex. The report added, regarding the government's policy against discrimination in civil-service and contract work, that the executive "take steps not only to promulgate its policy more widely, but to enforce it as well." Truman replied that "the degree of effectiveness which the Fair Employment Practice Committee was able to attain has shown once and for all that it is possible to equalize job opportunity by governmental action, and thus eventually to eliminate the influence of prejudice in the field of employment."[45] This was the FEPC's promise, but it was also its epitaph.

Harry Truman had had a trying year on civil-rights questions during 1945. He had spoken out for continuing the FEPC, but little had been accomplished on that or on other issues of interest to minorities. Perhaps the president did no more because he wanted to muster as much conservative Republican and southern support as possible for his foreign and domestic programs. The fact was, however, that his foreign program was not jeopardized by Congress and that he was getting little cooperation on most of his domestic proposals. The fact was also that regardless of what he did, the FEPC stood scant chance of success. Indeed, by his outspoken support he increased the hope of FEPC advocates, and with its fading, the hope-maker—Truman—became the scapegoat.

Another factor was the collapse of the assumption that Truman, the veteran senator, would have at least as much influence with Congress as Roosevelt had had. He did not, nor had he the skills as president that his predecessor had developed during his long tenure of office. Truman was further hampered by the lack of public adulation that Roosevelt commanded and by the fact that seasoned officials were flocking from their jobs. The former he would never attract; the latter retarded the organization of a distinctively Trumanesque administration, filled with men upon whom he could rely. Another point cannot be overlooked. Civil-rights issues, despite the ardor of minority-group leaders, were not paramount while the nation was involved in ending the war and in securing peace and reconstruction. Because of that and the complicated nature of the presidency, Harry Truman could not have given, unless he had been unusually sensitive, great amounts of his time and high priority to minority problems. He was no zealot on civil rights. It would take a crisis and mounting pressure to raise minority rights on the scale of priorities.

3 TENSION AND STRIFE

The year 1946 was to be a crucial one for civil-rights advocates. Minority-group workers not only experienced cutbacks in jobs, but had to compete in the labor market with millions of demobilized soldiers and sailors. Returning nonwhite servicemen were to be "put in their place," as reports of assaults on Negro, Japanese-American, Indian, and Mexican-American veterans and soldiers indicated. Urban housing, which was already cramped, worsened as demobilization progressed.

The Truman administration from the beginning viewed the situation as national in scope. In formulating its domestic program, it acted on the premise that a national solution to economic, veterans', health, and housing problems would contribute substantially to relieving problems of minorities. The government was also cognizant, at least in its demands for a continued FEPC, that minorities had special problems. On January 3, while the second session of the Seventy-ninth Congress prepared to meet, President Truman took to the radio networks to reiterate his proposals to meet "the goal of full production and full employment." He complimented Congress for its cooperation on foreign affairs, but he criticized it for its failures in providing answers to domestic questions. He made a special point of denouncing the "small handful of Congressmen" in the House Rules Committee who prevented a vote on a permanent FEPC.[1]

Truman's radio appeal was greeted by the Negro press with approval, although the question was raised whether his going over the heads of Congress to the people would lead to success. Truman's personal image was also aided by his appointment, early in January, of William H. Hastie as governor of the Virgin Islands. As the *Afro-American* pointed out, it was, along with Irvin Mollison's earlier ap-

31

pointment to the Customs Court, a "break with precedent." The president was also praised for his veto of legislation to return the Employment Service to the states, where Negroes felt they would receive less help than was currently the case.[2]

The FEPC remained the leading issue among minorities. In 1945 most of the action for a permanent FEPC had taken place in the House of Representatives, where Mary Norton fought repeatedly, but unsuccessfully, for her bill. In 1946 action was to shift to the Senate. The Chavez bill for a statutory FEPC had been reported favorably by the Senate Education and Labor Committee, but had not been brought up for debate. Chavez, on January 17, took the FEPC opponents by surprise and began debate on his bill. The next day, however, in a parliamentary maneuver, Chavez's foes seized the floor and started a filibuster.[3]

On January 21 Truman again entered the picture, sending up to Congress his State of the Union message. In it he championed a number of issues that were of interest to minorities. He stressed the need for passage of legislation regarding full employment, increase in unemployment pay, a higher minimum wage, medical care, continued federal operation of the Employment Service, increased self-government for citizens of the District of Columbia, and, of course, the FEPC. He described the establishment of fair employment practices along with fair wages as minimum standards for the conduct of the nation's business affairs. The question was, however, as the *Amsterdam News* wrote, "Can President Harry S. Truman deliver?"[4]

The Senate filibuster continued, despite the efforts of Democratic and Republican friends of the FEPC to break it up. In his news conference of January 24, Truman said that the filibuster was "a matter that the Senate itself must settle without outside interference, especially from the president." But he did add that he had "always" been for cloture to allow a vote. On February 6 he wrote to A. Philip Randolph, "I regard the Fair Employment Practice legislation as an integral part of my reconversion program and shall continue my efforts to give the Congress a chance to vote on it."[5]

The fight for the FEPC in the Senate continued. On February 4 Majority Leader Alben Barkley filed a cloture petition signed by half of the Senate's members. The FEPC opponents deferred a vote on cloture by debating Barkley's appeal that the Chavez bill was the unfinished business before the Senate. By February 7 the senators had tired themselves. The leaders of the opposing groups agreed to put the cloture petition to a vote two days later, with the understanding that if it was not favored by two-thirds of those voting, the fight for the Chavez bill would be abandoned. When the vote was taken, twenty-five Republicans and one Progressive joined with twenty-two Democrats to support cloture, while twenty-eight Democrats and eight Republicans voted against. Cloture had failed to receive the necessary two-thirds support. Accordingly, the Senate voted to consider other legislation. Thus the upper chamber had at least gone through the motions of political warfare on the issue.

It had been a relatively friendly war, conducted on the basis of a five-day week with normal overnight recesses. Good-fellowship was generally the rule among the senators, despite hot exchanges in speeches on the floor. Nevertheless, the Senate's business had been brought to a standstill, and the nation's attention had been riveted on the question of a permanent FEPC. Half of the senators and the president had taken their stand clearly, if not always vigorously, for the legislation. If they did not do more, and if other senators did not join them in the cloture test, it was partly because American public opinion was flaccid on the question. It had had three weeks to make itself felt, and it had come forth like a pussy cat.[6]

The chances for federal fair employment legislation were dead for 1946 and, as it turned out, for good. There were still body jerks as rigor mortis set in. A. Philip Randolph went over the land protesting the Senate's action. Mass protest meetings were held, including one at Madison Square Garden which seventeen thousand people attended and to which Truman sent a message of support. There was even consideration of a march on Washington, but nothing happened. It was suggested that Truman could act by executive order; but that overlooked the Russell Amendment, which stipulated that the FEPC could be funded only with legislative approval, which had already been refused. The president did about all he could do in 1946 when he reaffirmed the policy of nondiscrimination in civil-service and government-contract hiring. In July he directed his civil-rights adviser, David K. Niles, "to have the appropriate agencies of the government investigate and take the necessary steps where complaints are made and discrimination is alleged."[7]

There were, however, other issues. In February Congress responded to Truman's request for full-employment legislation. The Employment Act of 1946 declared that the government would use all its resources to maximize employment opportunities and authorized the president to formulate programs to reach this objective.[8] This was one of Truman's few noteworthy legislative successes in 1946. Congress, however, returned the Employment Service to the states, where discriminatory orders for workers could be accepted. Price control came to a halt; housing programs were slighted; self-government in the District of Columbia and an increase in the minimum wage were refused.

As the year progressed, Negroes gave more attention to the renewal of the longstanding battles for anti-poll-tax and antilynching legislation. The fight against lynching had been stymied, but a bill outlawing poll taxes had passed the House in 1945. This was of importance in the development of the political power of minorities, because seven states still required payment of a special tax before citizens could qualify to vote, an effective barrier to the polls for millions of poor Negroes, Mexican-Americans, and whites.[9]

Truman had not made the anti-poll-tax bill an administration measure, although he was personally on record as favoring its enactment. By March the National Anti-Poll-Tax Committee, seeking Senate passage of the bill, felt that David Niles was not handling the matter satisfactorily. The group's leaders wanted to see Matthew Connelly or "any other secretary—in fact anyone except Mr. Niles—re this issue." Connelly's answer was, "Tell them sorry." This reflected the fact that President Truman, as he wrote to Irving Brant on March 29, was "not looking for another filibuster. The program has been almost ruined by one filibuster and I think that is enough for a season."[10]

He could not evade the issue, however. While in Chicago, on April 6, Truman held a news conference with the Keen Teen Club. During the conference, one shy, nervous girl asked, "Do you see any immediate solution to the poll tax in the South?" He replied that he did not. It was a question of education and "a matter that they will have to work out for themselves, and they are gradually working it out." The president had blundered. Negroes, seeing no evidence that the poll tax was being worked out, were incensed. As the *Afro-American* editorialized, "If he's going to welch on the poll tax now, there is nothing to stop him from welching on the antilynching bill and on the measure for a permanent FEPC." The newspaper added pointedly, "Maybe Mr. Truman doesn't plan to run again."[11]

The administration worked feverishly to repair the damage. Lowell Mellett, a staunch journalistic defender of the administration and a former White House aide, explained in his column that Truman "meant only to imply that the United States Senate never would succeed in enacting anti-poll-tax legislation. That he believes in federal legislation on the subject he demonstrated more than once while a member of the Senate." Philleo Nash, David Niles's assistant, compiled Truman's record on the issue in preparation for a presidential counter-offensive. Niles in turn briefed the chief executive for his regular press conference, scheduled for April 11.[12]

The question was raised at that conference, and Truman read a statement that Niles had written for him. The president asserted that he favored both federal and state action, and he suggested that "the possibility of federal action has stimulated state action." He thought this may have been the case on fair employment practices, too, where a number of cities and states had acted. Then he departed from his text to say, "And you must have the support of the people for any law. The prohibition law proved that."[13]

Truman's statement helped, although its value was weakened by his remark that a law needed popular backing. When Senator John Bankhead of Alabama wrote to congratulate him for his comment to the Chicago high-school journalists, the president told him that his later press conference statement covered the topic "completely and thoroughly." Whatever Truman personally believed, he remained on record for anti-poll-tax legislation, although plainly he intended not to make a major issue of it. Like the FEPC bill, the poll-tax measure encountered a filibuster. It finally went down to defeat in July.[14]

Of course, not all federal civil-rights matters were legislative. Many concerned executive action. Looming large was the question of the role that minorities would play in the peacetime armed services: would the momentum of wartime progress continue, or would it be braked or even reversed? Lester Granger, the Negro consultant to Navy Secretary James Forrestal, stressed in his reports that despite improvement in the service conditions of black sailors and marines, many commanders tenaciously clung to their prejudices. In following up Granger's reports, Forrestal in December 1945 disapproved the Bureau of Naval Personnel's recommendation that "officers can handle Negro personnel 'without any special indoctrination'." The secretary directed that "special screening and indoctrination procedures" be established for officers who were to command Negro sailors. He also asked for progress reports on the use by Negroes of Red Cross facilities on Guam, Negro shore patrols in the Pacific area, instructional programs for promotions qualifications, and the assignment of ratings to appropriate billets. Furthermore, the Marine Corps announced in December that Nisei would—at last—be accepted for enlistment.[15]

Forrestal took another action, in December 1945, that bespoke progress. The aircraft carrier *Croatan* had refused to take 123 returning Negro soldiers on board because segregated arrangements could not be made. That led to a wave of indignation; and Forrestal asserted that this would not happen again, saying that the navy's nondiscriminatory policy applied to "authorized personnel of all the armed services of this country aboard Navy ships or at Navy stations and activities." Another sign of progress was the Bureau of Naval Personnel's statement early in 1946 that Negroes would "be eligible for all types of assignments in all ratings in all activities and all ships of the naval service." Moreover, no separate provisions would be made for the use by Negroes of housing, eating, and other types of facilities; and no naval unit would have more than 10 percent black personnel by October—with the obvious exception of the Steward's Branch.[16]

All this was to the good, but it applied to fewer and fewer Negroes as postwar demobilization progressed. By 1947 there was only one black officer left in the navy, and the proportion of Negro sailors dropped from 5.32 percent in 1945 to 4.82 by 1947 and to 3.7 by early 1950. The rollback was more drastic in the Marine Corps, where a quota of 2,880 was set, but was never met by 1949. As late as that year no new Negro recruits were accepted for general service. In 1947 ranking officers of the Coast Guard opposed legislation to end segregation in the armed forces, which indicated that all was not well in that service.[17]

The chief complaint of minorities about the army was that it practiced segregation, a policy upon which the service had basically not budged. In July 1945 Secretary of War Henry L. Stimson opposed a bill to desegregate the armed services because it was a matter "not susceptible to treatment by legislation" and one that would require radical changes in the army's basic organization. In any event, he wrote, "Whether such a change would operate in the interest of producing an efficient military establishment is questionable at this time."

Yet the subject of segregation in the army was undergoing study. Reports from all army forces and commands were being compiled. Chief of Staff George C. Marshall wrote, apparently as a result of a survey of special mixed platoons, that he thought "the practicability of integrating Negro elements into white units should be followed up." Truman K. Gibson, Jr., before leaving his post as civilian aide early in the fall, recommended the creation of a board to study and suggest the changes necessary "to effect the most efficient utilization of Negroes in the army." Under Secretary Robert Patterson promptly approved of the recommendation, which led to the establishment, October 4, of the

Gillem Board, a group of three general officers headed by Lieutenant General Alvan C. Gillem.[18]

The generals worked quickly. By November 17 their preliminary report was circulating within the War Department for comment and was somewhat revised as a consequence. Meanwhile Negro opinion expected the final report to recommend termination of segregation in the army. The report, however, did not bear out that optimism, for the Gillem Board strove to meet objections to liberalization.[19]

The final report was issued on February 26, 1946. It stated that the Negro "should be given every opportunity and aid to prepare himself for effective military service in company with every other citizen who is called." The report also conceded that the army had made insufficient plans for the use of and leadership by Negro soldiers during the war. To overcome this, it recommended that Negroes be used in a variety of tasks, with emphasis on the development of leaders and specialists; that the ratio of blacks to whites in the nation's population determine the racial composition of the army; that all officers be given "equal rights and opportunities for advancement and professional improvement"; that "groupings of Negro units with white units" be continued; that "qualified individuals be utilized in appropriate special and overhead units"; that black units be stationed in areas where local attitudes are not hostile; that recreational facilities continue to be segregated; and that no Negro unit be larger than a regiment.[20]

Little in the Gillem Report was new. It was more a picture of current army practices than a blueprint for new policies. The board gave black troops a pat on the back by indicating that their service problems had been largely environmental, not congenital. It did not consider segregation to be an ironclad requisite for the use of Negroes in the army, and indeed it did suggest some blending of blacks and whites in special and overhead units. Most Negroes, however, did not view the report as emancipation, gradual or otherwise, from segregation in the military. As the *Amsterdam News* wrote, "All it did was to slice jim crow a little thinner and spread it around more so it wouldn't make such a stinkin' heap in the middle of the national floor."[21]

Despite criticism, the army employed the Gillem Report as the basis for its official policy for using black soldiers, as embodied in War Department Circular No. 124 of April 27, 1946. A barely perceptible oblique face had been taken on the question. It did not satisfy Negro and white opponents of segregation in the army, who continued to press for dismantling its paperwork walls.

The chill currents of disappointment with the army's racial policies ran swifter with the drastically reduced calls for Negro inductees in April, the suspension in July of black enlistments except in a few specialties, and the September decision not to allow volunteer draft inductions. To the army, the reasons for these actions were justifiable: it had agreed that only about 10 percent of its strength would be Negro, but by summer 1946 black troops constituted 16 percent of the total. To Negroes, it was discriminatory not to take everyone qualified for service. Although black enlistments were later reopened, another problem rose in the army's reluctance to assign Negroes to Europe and the fact that few black men were accepted as regular officers—only 36 in contrast to almost 12,000 whites by early 1947—and few men were assigned to specialized units.[22]

In viewing the army's immediate postwar activities, one can agree with Marcus H. Ray, the secretary of war's Negro civilian aide, that the service had "established a very poor public relations." One can also agree with Colonel Ray that the army was limited by budgetary restrictions and a paucity of trained personnel in handling Negro soldiers.[23] Yet these circumstances did not justify trying to enforce an artificial quota system. A uniform screening procedure and progressive desegregation would have been more acceptable and fair. But the army, partly out of unimaginative leadership and partly out of fear of the consequences of change, clung to the old ways of quota and segregation. It could not expect, therefore, but to be an inviting target for civil-rights sharpshooters.

Another target was the administration of veterans' benefits. Veterans were eligible for unemployment benefits of twenty dollars a week for a year, employment counseling, preference in civil-service hiring, housing and business loans, educational allowances, and medical care for service-connected disabilities. There were, however, difficulties involved in minority-group veterans taking advantage of these. A frequently lower level of education, combined with the tendency of officials to give short shrift to minorities, meant less effective counseling about benefits. The unemployment pay proved a boon during the difficult period of readjustment, but proportionately fewer minority veterans took advantage of educational provisions. In April 1947 it was reported that although about 13 percent of all veterans were enrolled in educational programs for veterans, only an estimated 5 percent of Negro veterans were.[24]

The NAACP as early as 1944 had pressed for desegregation of veterans' hospitals and full use of qualified black personnel. The association reiterated that position to General Omar Bradley, the new veterans administrator, in September 1945. Bradley agreed with the idea of maximizing use of Negro personnel, but could not see desegregating facilities in the segregated South. It was reported in December that seventeen of the ninety-seven veterans' hospitals did not admit black veterans, and twenty-four others housed them in separate units. The matter was complicated by the fact that many Negroes favored developing all-Negro hospitals in the South patterned after the one at Tuskegee. In response to pressure from the NAACP, the National Newspaper Publishers Association, and the Negro National Medical Association, the Veterans Administration suspended plans in 1945 to construct another all-black hospital in the South. Nevertheless, the policy was, according to General Bradley: "Wherever the local customs are such that integration might easily interfere with the proper operation of the hospital, we have followed local custom."[25]

The pressure continued. In a March 1946 meeting with the executive committee of the National Newspaper Publishers Association, President Truman was urged to abolish segregation in the veterans' hospitals. His politic reply was, "It fits in with what I have been talking about for twelve years." Nevertheless, the day before, Bradley had indicated that the VA would build an all-Negro hospital in Mississippi. Although Negro organizations and the American Veterans Committee protested the move, black public opinion was divided. A *Negro Digest* poll showed that 34 percent of those asked accepted the idea of all-Negro veterans' hospitals and only 28 percent opposed it, with the rest undecided. Yet the plans were suspended, although White House aide David Niles wrote Congressman Powell that announcement of a Negro VA hospital had not been "authorized, made, or contemplated."[26] Niles may have believed that, but it was the kind of statement that earned him the sobriquet of "Devious Dave" in some circles.

Time ran out in March 1947, when Truman approved the building of a Negro veterans' hospital in Mound Bayou, Mississippi. The action led to spirited protest, at least from northern Negroes. The *Afro-American* wrote that the approval was "a gratuitous insult, not only to veterans but to some twenty-odd national groups who have consistently opposed it since the first hint that it was being considered." Whether because of the force of disapproval or the problems of finding qualified personnel to staff Negro veterans' hospitals, the one at Mound Bayou was the last one established. Nonetheless, the Truman administration made few inroads on existing segregation in veterans' hospitals, although it strove to improve other services to minority-group veterans.[27]

The picture was not as unpleasant in 1946 in all areas of federal action. One demand was met with the appointment of Joseph C. Albright as special assistant for minority affairs to the veterans administrator. There was William Hastie's appointment as governor of the Virgin Islands, and that of Morris de Castro as secretary—the first Virgin Islander to serve in the administration of the area. The nomination in July 1946 of Jesús Piñero to be governor of Puerto Rico marked the first selection of a native for that position. Other significant minority appointments during Truman's first two years in the White House included Raphael O'Hara Lanier as minister to Liberia, Truman K. Gibson to the President's Committee on Universal Training, and advisers and policy makers in the War Department, Housing Administration, Employment Service, Office of Price Administration, Retraining and Reemployment Administration, Justice Department, and Post Office Department. There was the renewal of annual Department of Commerce conferences on the Negro in business in 1946, with Secretary W. Averell Harriman in attendance. Also in 1946 the Federal Reserve System opened its eating and lavatory facilities to all employees.[28]

During 1946 housing pressures mounted, largely because living areas for minorities in cities were becoming increasingly crowded with continued migration to urban areas and with the return of veterans. The NAACP had already decided to make a major court issue of restrictive land-purchase covenants. Housing Administrator Wilson Wyatt and his staff were keenly aware of the need for low-cost housing for Negroes and worked for passage of the Wagner-Ellender-Taft bill and emergency veterans' housing as ways to meet the need. This sensitivity was mirrored in the president's concern with housing in his messages to Congress during the postwar period. Furthermore, in August 1946, the Justice Department announced antitrust action against thirty-eight New York City mortgage firms for manipulation of rents and financing conditions for Negro and Puerto Rican families. The case ended in June 1948 when thirty-three of the firms were enjoined from discriminatory practices in regard to investment in and management of real estate.[29]

The year 1946 saw an important court decision in *Morgan* v. *Virginia*. In 1944 the driver of a Richmond Greyhound Lines bus had ordered Irene Morgan to move to the rear of the vehicle to make room for a white passenger. She refused and was arrested and convicted of violating the Virginia segregation statute. The case was taken to the United States Supreme Court, which ruled that because state laws varied so much on transportation segregation, they were a burden to interstate commerce. Therefore, the Virginia law was declared unconstitutional in order to promote uniformity and to protect the comfort of passengers in interstate travel.[30]

The government was also active in trying to regularize claims against it by Japanese-Americans and Indians. The Interior Department sponsored a bill to repay the losses of Japanese and Japanese-American wartime evacuees up to $2,500 per claim. Secretary Julius A. Krug urged enactment "as a matter of fairness and good conscience, and because these particular American citizens and law-abiding aliens have borne with patience and undefeated loyalty the unique burdens which this government has thrown upon them." Although the bill was approved in the Senate, it failed to pass the House.[31]

The proposal for settlement of Indian claims had a long history. The Interior Department had sponsored legislation during the 1930s to establish a commission to settle Indian claims against the government. In 1937 such a bill passed the Senate, but was lost in the House. In 1939 and 1941 President Roosevelt refused to support similar legislation because of the prospective cost and because it seemed that such a commission would not dispose of Indian claims, as Roosevelt put it, "with finality." The question was held in abeyance during World War II, but was introduced soon afterward. Indian tribes had many claims against the United States, but the process of settlement was cumbersome, expensive, and by no means just. Before a claim could be adjudicated, Congress had to pass a special act, the provisions of which might severely limit the scope of the trial. The case could then be taken to the Court of Claims, which was restricted in the law that it could apply in hearing such specialized claims. The result was lengthy litigation, with small chance of success. In fact, of the 118 claims presented to the court between 1881 and 1950, only 34 were successful.[32]

In 1946 the Interior Department again sponsored legislation to establish an Indian-claims commission. This time the president, Truman, approved it, noting, however, that "we should be exceedingly careful not to allow claims which are already settled to be opened and considered again." Truman wanted to "be sure that we are not unloosening a Frankenstein." The bill was enacted by Congress, and the president signed it in August. The three-man commission was given broad authority to consider Indian claims once and for all over a ten-year period, subject to review by the Court of Claims. The Interior Department intended not only that the commission would settle the claims justly and finally, but that in the long run its work would lead to reduced expenditures for Indian affairs. Hopefully, the latter would be accomplished by a lightening of the departmental load in rehashing old claims and by the possibility that the funds awarded might put many tribes on a self-sustaining basis. Secretary Krug also believed that the law would strengthen the moral authority of the United States at home and abroad "in the eyes of many other minority peoples."[33]

The Indian Claims Commission did not live up to expectations. It was unable to dispose of the claims in ten years, and in 1956 its life was extended for another six years. Some 852 claims were filed. By 1956, 102 claims had been adjudicated and 21 had been allowed recovery to a total of $13,283,477. Indians were not happy with the small number of favorable decisions and the paucity of the awards, but the procedure was fairer and less frustrating than what had previously existed by way of adjudication.[34]

If the administration's accomplishments were less than satisfactory to minorities, its civil-rights pronouncements were laudable. Its statements were important, for they gave a yardstick against which actions could be measured, and they served the cause of education by enlightening some whites and by encouraging minority people to seek justice. Harry Truman was setting new presidential standards in speaking out for civil rights. He had put in his word for fair employment practices and even equal voting rights, but there were other presidential statements, growing increasingly tough, in behalf of advancing human rights.

In talking with the executive committee of the National Newspaper Publishers Association in March, the president mentioned the need "to give us the Bill of Rights as it was written. . . . We want to see equal opportunity for everybody, regardless of race, creed or color." A few days later he vented his frustration with Congress, before a conference of the Federal Council of Churches, when he sought "an Isaiah or a Saint Paul to reawaken this sick world to its moral responsibilities." He emphasized that "if we really believed in the Brotherhood of Man, it would not be necessary to pass a Fair Employment Practices Act."[35]

He sent a message in June to the annual NAACP convention, demanding jobs for veterans "at fair wages without discrimination by employers or unions because of race, color, religion, or ancestry." He also called for protection against terrorism and of the right to vote. A month later Truman said to the 442d Combat Team, in awarding the Nisei unit its seventh presidential citation: "You fought not only the enemy, but you fought prejudice—and you have won. Keep up that fight, and we will continue to win—to make this great republic stand for just what the Constitution says it stands for: the welfare of all the people all the time."[36]

In July the president appointed the National Commission on Higher Education to inquire into how the functions of American colleges and universities could best be performed. Charles G. Bolte, the chairman of the American Veterans Committee, wrote to compliment Truman on establishing the commission and to urge that the group examine the practice of admitting minority-group students to colleges on a quota basis. Bolte also urged the president to give his "wise counsel and firm guidance" to the development of equal justice and opportunity for all Americans. Officials in the War Mobilization and Reconversion Office recommended that Truman answer Bolte at length in order to counteract increasing racial tensions and minority-group disappointment. The president accepted the WMRO's suggested reply almost *in toto*.[37]

On August 28, in a public letter, he wrote Bolte that the commission was concerned with eliminating "barriers of discrimination" in colleges. Truman took the occasion to assert that despite the war America had just fought against hatred, "in this country today there exists disturbing evidence of intolerance and prejudice. . . . Discrimination, like a disease, must be attacked wherever it appears. This applies to the opportunity to vote, to hold and retain a job, and to secure adequate shelter and medical care no less than to gain an education compatible with the needs and ability of the individual."[38] That was a strong statement, and the Truman who sent it was different from the man who in March had wanted to avoid another filibuster and had commended the fight to another Isaiah, another Paul.

What created this different Truman? It was violence—unwarranted attacks on black Americans—that moved him and his administration. Late in 1945 many Negro leaders had predicted that tension and violence would rise during the coming year. They did not foresee that it would be as bad as it was. The activities of the Ku Klux Klan and similar-minded groups and individuals had intensified. Assaults on Negroes and Japanese-Americans had been common in 1945, but the first major outbreak came early in 1946 in Columbia, Tennessee. There, on February 25, after an altercation between a white radio repairman and a black customer and her son, the son was arrested. A white mob soon formed and rushed the county jail, but was warded off by the sheriff. Meanwhile Negro residents gathered in the black business section and prepared to defend themselves in case a mob struck out in that direction. At night some city police entered the section to investigate reports of gunfire. Shooting broke out, and four policemen were wounded. The Highway Patrol and the State Guard were called in and arrested some seventy Negroes. Others were later arrested. The black district was victimized by vandalism and looting during a systematic search for weapons. No action was taken to disarm white civilians in Columbia, and only four were arrested. While military law in effect reigned in the small city, two Negro prisoners were killed in the jail.[39]

The Columbia incident touched off widespread protests from Negroes and liberals, and the federal government quickly responded. David Niles, for the White House, wrote Attorney General Tom Clark that satisfaction had to be given "that the federal government is doing all it can in order to protect civil rights." People and groups seeking to discuss the matter with the president were referred to the attorney general and his assistants, who endeavored to talk with all interested parties. Agents of the Federal Bureau of Investigation were ordered to Columbia, and Clark directed United States District Attorney Horace Frierson to convene a grand jury to investigate whether there were violations of federal law. The attorney general also promised to dispatch Justice Department representatives to work with the grand jury.[40]

The federal intervention into activities at Columbia had little effect, though, for the government had no real weapon to wield in the applicable law, the Enforcement Act of 1870. The grand jury found that vandalism had been committed while the area was under the control of the Tennessee Highway Patrol and State Guard, but no remedy was offered. The grand jury found that the arrests, killings, and searches of homes were justifiable under the circumstances, although it did issue a strong warning against the "dissemination of half-truths and falsehoods" that could lead to racial violence. There was one happy conclusion, thanks probably to federal intervention and the great publicity given the case. Most of the Negroes arrested were released, and a change of venue in the state courts was granted to the remaining twenty-five defendants. Of those only two were found guilty of assault, and even they were subsequently freed by a retrial.[41]

The outbreak of other incidents fired civil-rights organizations in maintaining pressure on the federal government to counteract racial terrorism. There was heated reaction to Senator Theodore Bilbo's statements which virtually sanctioned the use of violence to keep Negroes from voting in Mississippi. A vivid illustration of racial violence came in the report of the punching out of the eyes of Sergeant

Isaac Woodard by an Aiken, South Carolina, policeman, only three hours after Woodard was separated from the army. The attack was forcefully brought to President Truman's attention by R. R. Wright, a Spanish-American War veteran and probably the nation's most prominent black banker, who wrote: "To 'gouge out the eyesight' of a man who had used his eyes to safeguard the freedom of our country is surely a disgrace unheard of in any other country in the world." Much of the press joined Major Wright in being appalled at this example of violence, and the NAACP offered a $1,000 reward for the apprehension and conviction of the man who blinded Woodard.[42]

As summer came there was also news of a lynching in Georgia, which had just nominated a leading racist, Eugene Talmadge, for governor. Macio Snipes, the only Negro to vote in his district, was killed in his front yard by four white men. More shocking was the lynching on July 25 outside Monroe, Georgia, of Roger Malcolm, who had just been released from jail on bond for stabbing his employer. Two Negro women and another black man, who happened to be with Malcolm, were also shot and killed.[43] That set off a tidal wave of protest which was not soon to subside.

The directors of the black National Newspaper Publishers Association met to ask President Truman to demand that Congress enact an antilynching law. The American Council on Race Relations called upon mayors' and governors' human-relations groups to do all they could to end mob violence. The Civil Rights Congress offered a $1,000 reward for the Monroe lynchers. The *Amsterdam News* wrote that "the struggle against Talmadge-Bilboism lynch terror calls for an all-out effort. All forces that want Americanism must join together to demand: 'BRING THE GEORGIA LYNCHERS TO JUSTICE!'" The NAACP and the American Council on Race Relations joined together to "call a conference of groups against mob violence." The amount of rewards for information leading to the conviction of the lynchers rose to $30,000, as the NAACP threw in $10,000 and the state of Georgia, through the efforts of Governor Ellis Arnall, raised almost an equal amount. Nearly four hundred members of the National Association of Colored Women marched to the White House to demand an end to lynching, and they set up a picket line that was to continue for over a week. Dr. Max Yergan, the president of the National Negro Congress, led a march of more than one thousand persons from Washington Union Terminal to the White House, after which he assailed Truman for not condemning those involved in racial violence. Other mass demonstrations were held, and thousands of letters of protest were sent to the president and to the attorney general.[44]

The government had already begun to act. Attorney General Clark, on July 26, ordered an investigation of the Monroe lynching and soon announced that the Justice Department was probing the Ku Klux Klan in seven states. Four days later Truman released a statement through Clark expressing his "horror at the crime." He said that he had directed the attorney general to use all of his department's resources to investigate "this and any other crimes of oppression."[45]

The rumble of discontent grew louder as additional reports of racial violence came. On August 6, in response to the call of the NAACP and the American Council on Race Relations, black and white representatives of forty civil-rights, religious, labor, professional, and veterans organizations met in emergency session as the National Emergency Committee Against Mob Violence. The new committee's goal was to press the president and the attorney general "to throw the full force of the federal government behind our actions and sentiments in bringing before the bar of justice and convicting the lynchers." Even leading white newspapers were giving considerable attention to racial violence. In August in New York City fifteen thousand people held a mass protest meeting, and in Washington another fifteen thousand paraded to the Lincoln Memorial to demand action against the Monroe "murderers," passage of antilynching legislation, and outlawing by executive power of the Ku Klux Klan and similar organizations.[46]

There was little effective action that Truman and the executive branch could legally take. They could not outlaw anything by fiat. As they were doing, they could investigate and could urge citizens and state and local authorities to act. The margin of federal law upon which the executive branch could act was narrow and slippery. The two pertinent provisions, sections 51 and 52 of the 1870 Enforcement Act, applied only to conspiracies and to willful action by public officials, both crimes being exasperatingly difficult to prove, and the civil rights involved had been slenderly defined by the courts. Moreover, the chances for conviction were further narrowed considering that even if indictments were procured, the trials would be held in communities that were hostile or at best indifferent.[47]

Truman could have called Congress into special session to enact appropriate legislation, as some protestors urged, but he was undoubtedly restrained by the well-founded conviction that the legislators would not have acted. For the time being, he contented himself by indicating, on August 1, that he favored an antilynching law. A more forceful endorsement came in mid August from Attorney General Clark, who vowed that he would urge Congress to pass antilynching legislation. He also called upon all citizens and law-enforcement officials to do all they could to deal with the situation.[48]

At the urging of David Niles, Postmaster General Robert E. Hannegan, and Navy Secretary James V. Forrestal, Truman in September sent more than the usual ceremonial greetings to the annual conference of the Urban League. He declared, "If the civil rights of even one citizen are abused, government has failed to discharge one of its primary responsibilities. We, as a people, must not, and I say to you we shall not, remain indifferent in the face of acts of intimidation and violence in our American communities. We must, however, go beyond the mere checking of such intimidation and violence, and work actively for an enduring understanding and cooperation among citizens of all religious and racial backgrounds." Truman's message was bitingly clear, but words were not enough. Most Negroes believed with Walter White that "a dread epidemic is sweeping across our country."[49] They wanted a remedy stronger than presidential prose.

Meanwhile the National Emergency Committee Against Mob Violence and its affiliated organizations, now grown to forty-seven, were striving to mobilize public opinion. They enlisted churches, business associations, and unions in a crusade to urge people to combat hate groups and to press congressmen, state and local officials, law-enforcement officers, editors, and radio and motion-picture executives to meet the problem of mob violence. The committee also voted to send a delegation to meet with President Truman, and a meeting was arranged for September 19.[50]

Walter White came to the White House with Channing Tobias, CIO Secretary James Carey, Boris Shiskin of the AFL, Frederick E. Reissig of the Federal Council of Churches, and Leslie Perry of the NAACP's Washington office. Several others, including Eleanor Roosevelt, Bishop Bernard Sheil, and Governor Ellis Arnall of Georgia, could not come but sent telegrams expressing their grave concern. White served as the spokesman for the delegation. A statement was presented to Truman which conveyed the group's dismay with the growth of mob violence against Negroes and the lack of remedial action. He was petitioned to step up the work of federal agencies in dealing with lynchers, to arouse the people "to oppose actively every form of mob violence," and to reconvene Congress to enact antilynching legislation. White detailed acts of violence for the president. Truman sat with clenched hands through the recounting, his face mirroring shock at the story of Isaac Woodard's blinding. When White had concluded, the president got up from his chair and said, "My God! I had no idea that it was as terrible as that! We've got to do something!"[51]

Truman knew that there was little he could do under the existing law, but he promised to confer with Attorney General Clark the next day. At that point, David Niles, who had been sitting in on the meeting, suggested that Congress be asked to establish an investigatory commission on mob violence and civil liberties. The president agreed that that was a good idea. It is possible that White, as he wrote in his autobiography, then pointed out that such a commission would not be approved by Congress, and that Truman replied that he would establish it by executive order. More probable is the account in White's October report to the NAACP Board of Directors. According to the report, White wrote to Truman the day after the White House meeting, warning him that Congress would envelop the proposed commission in the deadly embrace of a filibuster. A few days later the White House responded, by telephone, saying that the commission would be established by executive order.[52]

Truman was also scheduled to see a delegation from Paul Robeson's American Crusade to End Lynching, including representatives from Negro publishers, Negro churches, the National Negro Congress, the Southern Conference for Human Welfare, and the National Council of Negro Women. The group saw Truman on the morning of September 23; the result was mutual antagonism. When one of the delegates suggested that there was little difference between lynchings in America and the Nuremberg war-crimes trials, the president shot back that the United States could handle its affairs without concern for happenings abroad. Then Robeson and Truman disagreed sharply on America's moral position in world affairs, and Robeson asserted that unless mob violence was soon stopped, foreign intervention would be in order. Ruffled, Truman responded that he would deal with the situation in the most expeditious fashion. David Niles had thought of using this meeting to explore further the establishment of a civil-rights study committee, but as bitterness pervaded the atmosphere, the president's aide dropped the idea.[53]

Black reaction to the American Crusade's meeting with the president was caustic. The *Journal and Guide* (Norfolk, Virginia) saw Truman as retreating from his position with Walter White's group. The *Amsterdam News* linked this "boner" with Truman's dismissal of Henry Wallace from the cabinet. The newspaper added, "We condemn Truman as a fraud." Yet matters were percolating. Even before the meetings with White and Robeson, the president had written and made public his strong letter against prejudice to Charles Bolte and had sent vigorous civil-rights messages to the sesquicentennial convention of the African Methodist Episcopal Zion Church and the Urban League.[54] In effect, Truman had already spoken out against mob violence, as Robeson's group demanded.

As for another of the American Crusade's demands, the Justice Department had done as much as it legally could to deal with mob action and lynching. Tom Clark had come to the attorney generalship in 1945 with a good record on civil-rights matters, having served energetically as head of the department's Criminal Division. In 1946 he had been prompt and vigorous in dealing with the Columbia and Monroe cases. Moreover, when in September Director J. Edgar Hoover complained that the Federal Bureau of Investigation was spending too much time probing civil-rights incidents in which the probability of federal jurisdiction was small, Clark answered forthrightly, writing: "In each case the complaint made is indicative of the possibility of a violation, and if we do not investigate we are placed in the position . . . of having failed to satisfy ourselves that it is or is not such a violation." The attorney general agreed with Hoover that frustration would largely be the fruit of such work, but he said, "As you know it is my purpose to report these matters to Congress in the hopes of securing a broader and more substantial basis for federal action."[55]

The administration's chief immediate hope, however, in furthering the protection of human rights lay with a federal civil-rights committee, which had been discussed with Walter White's delegation. The committee's roots were tangled. The idea had been pondered by a number of people after a series of race riots in 1943. Saul K. Padover, who was Interior Secretary Harold L. Ickes's adviser on minority problems, had proposed a national committee on race relations. A similar committee had been discussed by sociologist Howard W. Odum and Presidential Assistant Jonathan Daniels, but President Roosevelt, Daniels reported, did "not think well of the idea." Probably the seed of Truman's civil-rights committee was contained in a 1943 proposal of David K. Niles, then one of Roosevelt's assistants. Niles suggested the formation of a national citizens' committee that would develop, in conjunction with local committees, programs to alleviate racial tensions and, in case of violent outbreaks, to arrange for dealing with them.[56]

Niles was an amiable man. Of Truman's senior assistants, however, he was probably the least involved in White House affairs. As

Jonathan Daniels said, "He liked to be a man of mystery." And he was a mystery to many other White House denizens and to a large number of minority-group leaders. This stemmed largely from the fact that his interests centered on labor, Jewish, and urban matters, in which he was highly effective. Other pertinent problems were usually left to Niles's assistant, Philleo Nash, an able man with a Ph.D. in anthropology, who, however, lacked the rank to have great influence.[57] This situation helps to explain the disconnected civil-rights approaches of the early Truman days and, later, the involvement of a number of White House staff members, including Clark Clifford, Stephen Spingarn, and George Elsey, in human-rights matters. Nevertheless, during the summer of 1946 Niles could not avoid the menace of mob violence and the swelling pressure to counteract it. Then, if at no other time, he played a major role in Negro affairs.

Many other people were credited with the idea of a civil-rights committee, including President Truman, Walter White, and Tom Clark. It was Niles, however, who proposed a civil-rights commission during the White House meeting with the National Emergency Committee group. Columnist Louis Lautier later wrote that he had asked at the White House whose idea it was and had been informed that it was Niles's.[58] Taken as a whole, Niles's 1943 proposal, his suggestion at the meeting between Truman and White's delegation, and Lautier's report, it would seem that he was most likely the father of the civil-rights committee.

The important thing is that the idea of a civil-rights committee was launched at the September 19 White House meeting and that steps were soon taken to develop it. As has been indicated, within a few days it was decided that the president would create the committee, because it was unlikely that Congress would do so. It was anticipated that the committee would contain between ten and fifteen members, and Walter White was asked to suggest names. The NAACP secretary consulted with several of the association's directors and staff members, and nominated twenty-three people. It was also promised, according to White, that the committee would be authorized by October 10.[59]

News of the proposed civil-rights committee soon leaked out to the press. Drew Pearson, in his September 26 column, reported that the White House was considering forming a commission to investigate lynching, and in early October Negro newspapers carried a similar story. As to what the committee presaged, speculation was withheld, with the *Chicago Defender* writing, "Effectiveness of the agency will be determined of course by the people who compose it."[60]

Pressure on the White House had not ceased as a result of press rumors. In fact, a black voting backlash was developing against the Democrats in the forthcoming congressional elections. Negroes had been disappointed by lack of legislative success in 1946, the apparent ineptitude of the executive branch, and the rising levels of violence. In February Charles Houston had written in the press, "The president may do this and he may do that as leader, but if he cannot produce, well, there is no such thing as gratitude in politics." One action taken by Truman during the summer did temporarily strike a favorable note. That was his public opposition to Kansas City Congressman Roger Slaughter's renomination. Slaughter had opposed much of Truman's program, including the FEPC, and the president was not going to tolerate a foe in his own political backyard. Truman's choice, Enos Axtell, won over Slaughter by almost three thousand votes, with heavy support from black Democrats. The victory was greeted joyously by many Negroes, but it turned to ashes as highly publicized, though largely unsupported, charges of voting irregularities were used to smear the president. Axtell's loss to his Republican opponent in November made the whole undertaking seem quixotic.[61]

Election or no election, the administration was not to be rushed in its preparations for a civil-rights committee. Certainly, the committee was going to be concerned with more than mob violence. On October 11 Tom Clark submitted to Truman a draft of an executive order to establish "the President's Committee on Civil Rights" to consider the broad goal of "preserving and implementing our civil rights." Clark recommended, more warmly than was usual in such communications, promulgation of the executive order. The *Chicago Defender* on October 26 reported that the president was going to announce the "appointment of a 'Federal Commission on Lynching'" the week before election. That, of course, did not happen. Time was needed to smooth out the order and to line up a group of worthies for service on the committee.[62] It can also be hypothesized that if Truman believed that a Republican Congress would be elected, he also thought that it would be politically wiser to save the announcement of the committee until after the election, because by itself the committee's establishment was unlikely to change the election results.

A Republican Congress was returned on November 5. The new Eightieth Congress would have fifty-seven more Republicans than Democrats in the House and six more in the Senate. Negroes still largely voted for Democrats, but the Republicans were pressed to justify whatever inroads they had made, and hoped to make later, among black voters. Truman, too, was on the spot. He had sought action and had, however good the reasons, come up short. But a civil-rights committee might remove the pressure from him temporarily and also be the vehicle to reach his twin goals of solving the nation's civil-rights problems and reenlisting minority-group support. Certainly, it would allow him to salve his own conscience. The violence of 1946 had shaken him. In the future he would often refer to the perturbation that he had felt as the result of assaults on the persons of minority groups. Standing out in his mind even after leaving office was the case of Isaac Woodard, "a Negro veteran, still wearing this country's uniform, [who] was arrested and beaten and blinded."[63]

On December 5, 1946, President Truman issued Executive Order 9808, which established the President's Committee on Civil Rights "to inquire into and to determine whether and in what respect current law-enforcement measures and the authority and means possessed by federal, state, and local governments may be strengthened and improved to safeguard the civil rights of the people." All executive agencies were directed to cooperate fully with the committee, and the executive order was prefaced with a strong statement condemning "the action of individuals who take the law into their own hands and inflict summary punishment and wreak personal vengeance." In the order, Truman named Charles E. Wilson, the president of General Electric, as committee chairman. Other members were Mrs. Sadie T. Alexander, an outstanding Negro lawyer; James B. Carey, secretary-treasurer of the CIO; John S. Dickey, president of Dartmouth; attorney Morris L. Ernst; Rabbi Roland B. Gittelsohn; Frank P. Graham, president of the University of North Carolina; Francis J. Haas, a Catholic bishop; Charles Luckman, president of Lever Brothers; attorney Francis P. Matthews; Franklin D. Roosevelt, Jr.; Henry Knox Sherrill, the presiding Episcopal bishop; AFL economist Boris Shiskin; Methodist churchwoman Dorothy Tilly; and Dr. Channing Tobias, a director of the Phelps-Stokes Fund. It was an outstanding group. All of the committee members were prominent either nationally or in their areas of endeavor. Most of them had been active in civil-rights affairs, and the others had been experienced in social-welfare work. The committee was also well balanced, if not geographically, at least in terms of occupations, religion, and, with Mrs. Alexander and Dr. Tobias, race.[64]

Equally important was that the committee was charged with studying the whole spectrum of civil rights, not just mob violence. Attorney General Clark was at least partly responsible for that, because of his concern with the overall problem of protecting civil rights and with the forging of tools to deal with it. The announcement of the committee was backed up by Clark's "I Am an American Day" address, in which he asserted that all the law at his disposal now and in the future would be used to protect civil rights. Credence was given his statement by the launching of the Justice Department's income-tax prosecution of the Ku Klux Klan.[65]

Black newspaper reaction to appointment of the committee was somewhat mixed. Most attention was given by the *Chicago Defender*, which editorialized, "If the committee is not hampered in its inquiry and if its recommendations are not circumvented by a welter of administrative procedures, the results should be far more consequential to us than anything that has happened in the United States since the abolition of slavery." The *Afro-American* and the *Call* (Kansas City) also played up the story, but the *Courier* (Pittsburgh) and the *Amsterdam News* indicated that they were not impressed, because the problems were already well known.[66] Generally, however, the Negro press was mildly pleased with Executive Order 9808, although it was obvious that it was reserving judgment until the committee actually did something.

The year 1946 was a mixture of horror and promise for minorities. The victories at the polls of Senator Bilbo and Eugene Talmadge; attempts to curb Negro voting in the South; the blocking of proposed FEPC, poll-tax, and antilynching legislation; and, most of all, racial violence were discouraging examples of reaction. Moreover, Japanese-Americans had received only slight encouragement in their quest for compensation of wartime losses resulting from evacuation; and American Indians, although heartened by the passage of the Indian Claims Commission Act, were discouraged because of deteriorating conditions on some of their reservations. Yet, not all was bleak; for there were, among other things, Governor Ellis Arnall's work to effect understanding between the white and black races, the appointment of the President's Committee on Civil Rights, the Supreme Court's *Morgan* decision, Hastie's appointment as governor of the Virgin Islands, and the increased activity of interracial and human-relations groups throughout the nation.

Probably most encouraging from a long-range standpoint was Harry Truman's outspoken interest in civil rights. Franklin Roosevelt had acted to establish the Fair Employment Practices Committee in 1941 only under extreme pressure at a delicate time. Moreover, in the face of intense, widespread racial violence in 1943, he had said nothing and done little. Truman, confronted by less intense racial crises and subjected to less pressure, often spoke out not only to favor tolerance and equal rights but also to condemn those who opposed them. As the *Call* wrote, "Since the Missourian has been in the White House, there has been no occasion for Negroes to sigh, 'If only the president would speak out!' "[67]

4 WHERE THEY STOOD

By 1947 the racial tensions of the postwar period had been relaxed. Violence, in particular, had declined, partly because federal investigation and prosecution had harassed the assault forces of racism. The job situation had stabilized for minority people, who found that they generally had not reverted to their prewar positions. Many minority-group veterans were enjoying the government benefits to which they were entitled. Moreover, rapport with the White House and other federal offices was improving. In short, 1947 was stable enough to allow time for consolidation of goals and forces, for stocktaking.

The wartime breakup of Little Tokyos scattered Japanese-Americans across the land and gave them a feeling of unsettledness. But they rose to the challenge by taking maximum advantage of educational and economic opportunities. As William Caudill observed in his study of the twenty thousand Japanese-American newcomers in Chicago, by 1947 "white employers and fellow employees accepted the Nisei and were enthusiastic in their praise of them." Japanese-Americans also won acceptance in white lower-middle-class neighborhoods, largely because the Chicago middle class had "projected their own values into the neat, well-dressed, and efficient Nisei in whom they saw mirrored many of their own ideals." What happened in Chicago occurred to a greater or lesser degree in other communities. Furthermore, the Japanese-American Citizens League, captained by the indefatigable Mike Masaoka, forged ahead in relieving the artificial burdens placed on its people. In 1946 the Senate passed an evacuation claims bill, and prospects for House and Senate approval in the new Eightieth Congress were good. Also a dent was made on laws restricting land ownership by alien Japanese when in 1947 Utah repealed its alien-land law.[1]

Chinese-Americans benefited, too. The favor extended to them during World War II continued into the postwar period. Job barriers remained low, and good will was the usual standard in relations between them and white America. In fact, by 1950 their median incomes were to exceed those of poor whites and all other racial minorities except Japanese-Americans. A 1946 amendment to the Immigration Act of 1924 allowed alien wives of citizens to be admitted to the United States on a nonquota basis and gave preference in the quotas to the alien wives and children of resident aliens. The War Brides Act of 1947 permitted the entry of Oriental wives of American servicemen, a victory for both the Chinese- and Japanese-Americans.[2]

Indians were preparing to take advantage of the Indian Claims Act of 1946, and they were pressing for elimination of barriers to voting and to allocation of state funds for social-security benefits in Arizona and New Mexico. Indeed some hope could be gained from the fact that since 1938 five states had removed restrictions on voting by reservation Indians. Most critical was the situation of the Navajos, who were threatened with starvation with the onset of the winter of 1947. In early December President Truman reported that in addition to regularly appropriated relief funds, the government was making available to the Navajos surplus food, clothing, and equipment. Later that month Congress appropriated additional relief funds for the Navajos, and for the Hopis, who lived in their midst.[3]

During the 1940s another minority group, the Puerto Ricans, emerged in force. As American nationals, they had the right of free entry into the continental United States. Almost 70,000 had settled on the mainland by 1940. Between 1942 and 1945 there was a net migration of 25,000 more. The exodus, however, occurred thereafter, thanks to cheap airline passage and high hopes. By the middle 1950s about 490,000 had settled in the continental United States, and approximately 80 percent of them were in New York City. Most of the Puerto Ricans had few marketable skills and little knowledge of English. They were ripe for attack by loan sharks and landlords, and usually ran last in the race for jobs. They had not been on the mainland long enough by the time of the Truman administration to be well organized. Consequently, they had few defenders, politically and otherwise. As Earl Brown wrote in 1947 of the Puerto Ricans coming to New York, their arrival "is not unlike the migration of southern Negroes to it after World War I. The only difference is that the Puerto Ricans who come here are worse off than the Negroes were. And that's hard to believe."[4] The Puerto Ricans not only faced problems traditionally encountered by newcomers to the United States, but many of them carried the additional cross of color. Little was done to help them. Indeed it was only in the late 1940s that they slowly came to be recognized as an element in the nation's spectrum of minority problems.

Some advances had taken place among the more than two million Mexican-Americans. The broader outlook of the some quarter-of-a-million Mexican-Americans who saw wartime military service contributed somewhat, as did increases in urbanization, unionization, and job opportunities. Yet these were only beginnings. Most Mexican-Americans were at the bottom of the labor market. Their language and the pattern of employment in gangs isolated them from contacts with the general community, and the formation of leadership was a slow process. Additional handicaps were that many of them had questionable claims to citizenship and that there was a continual and sizable infusion of fresh migrants, legal and illegal, from Mexico to meet the calls for farm labor in the Southwest. In brief, Mexican-Americans generally were second-class citizens and often in a position in the Southwest below that of Negroes.[5]

Religious minorities were in a different situation. Catholics still smarted from minor discriminations—occasional college admissions quotas, for example. Moreover, in the postwar period, there were spectacular attacks against them as agents of the supposedly monolithic structure of the Vatican. Surprisingly, much of this came from such men as Paul Blanshard and Harold E. Fey, who were veteran battlers for civil rights. Yet, these attacks were prime examples of the fact that anti-Catholicism was often the anti-Semitism of the intellectuals.[6] American Catholics did not constitute a monolith, but a large minority that was itself made up of many smaller minorities, some better off than others. Only a few, such as Latin-American and Negro Catholics, were greatly disadvantaged, but most of the subminorities were no worse off than most Protestant groups in America.

The situation for Jews was somewhat different. Discrimination was more widely practiced against them in education, employment, housing, resorts, and clubs. Their problem was not that of getting a stake in society, but of being as free as the majority of Americans to do what they wanted to with that stake. Theirs was not a struggle for basic political, economic, and educational rights, but for good will, freedom to develop further, and respect for their merits as individuals. In these respects, 1947 was an encouraging year for Jews. The Anti-

Defamation League, in its report on anti-Semitism during 1947, acknowledged "the substantial and heartening advances toward good will, understanding and cooperation among racial and religious groups in the United States. Important sections of the pulpit, press, radio, motion pictures and other opinion-molding media gave increased attention to the problems of prejudice and bigotry and stressed the ethical and practical need for democratic unity." The League could also exult about President Truman's Committee on Civil Rights, his Commission on Higher Education, and the "successful operation" of fair employment practices commissions in Connecticut, New Jersey, and New York.[7]

American culture was responding somewhat to the cry for justice for minorities. Gordon Allport noted that universities, schools, churches, government agencies, and even some industries were giving attention to cultural conflicts. He wrote that since the 1930s "there has been more solid and enlightening study in this area than in all the previous centuries combined." For example, the number of master's and doctoral theses dealing with the Negro had greatly increased, from 76 in 1932 to 182 in 1939, to 330 in 1947, to 571 by 1950. The pronouncements of Protestant church organizations reached flood stage between 1945 and 1947, when at least seventy statements against prejudice and discrimination were issued. The landmark was the declaration of the Federal Council of Churches in March 1946, which renounced "the pattern of segregation in race relations as unnecessary and undesirable and a violation of the Gospel of love and human brotherhood." Yet, Frank S. Loescher pointed out in 1948, "There is little evidence yet that the convictions of the rank-and-file membership of Protestant denominations are greatly influenced by these official actions."[8]

The number and variety of books on human rights rolling off the presses in 1946 were impressive. They included Buell G. Gallagher's *Color and Conscience*, which was a plea for Christian deeds to reduce racial tensions; Margaret Halsey's *Color Blind*; Fisk University's series of Social Science Source Documents; the volumes in the *Annals* of the American Academy of Political and Social Science entitled *Essential Human Rights* and *Controlling Group Prejudice*; J. Howell Atwood's *The Racial Factor in YMCAs*; and the *Police Training Bulletin: A Guide to Race Relations for Police Officers*, sponsored by the American Council on Race Relations and the California Department of Justice. The years 1947 and 1948 saw more of the same, most notably Charles S. Johnson's *Into the Main Stream*; Robin W. Williams, Jr.'s *The Reduc-*

tion of Intergroup Tensions; Malcolm Ross's powerful plea to end segregation in *All Manner of Men*; John Hope Franklin's *From Slavery to Freedom*; and Robert C. Weaver's *The Negro Ghetto*. Also significant were the inexpensive Freedom Pamphlets published by the Anti-Defamation League, including by 1948 Arnold M. Rose's *The Negro in Postwar America*, W. Henry Cooke's *Peoples of the Southwest*, and Gordon Allport's *A B Cs of Scapegoating*. The dam had burst. The trickle of studies, essays, and manuals that had started during the late 1930s was now a steady stream, and it would grow—with the addition of such classics as Lillian Smith's *Killers of the Dream*, Morton Grodzins's *Americans Betrayed*, and Carl Rowan's *South of Freedom*—into a river of data, concepts, and protests. This river would not wash away prejudice and inequality, but it would erode them.

Such writings were supplemented in other cultural areas. Novelists found race relations an increasingly intriguing theme, as testified to by such best-selling books as Sinclair Lewis's *Kingsblood Royal*, William L. White's *Lost Boundaries*, and Ann Petry's *The Street*. Appearances by Negroes on the New York stage continued to rise, with twenty shows employing 219 black actors in 1945 and twenty-eight using 279 in 1946. The NAACP and Jewish organizations worked to gain decent portrayals of minorities in motion pictures. Their endeavors were partly responsible for the production of a number of films during the late 1940s that attacked prejudice and discrimination. The NAACP also labored to improve the Negro's image in public media generally, enlisting the help of prominent people in radio, theater, publishing, and advertising.[9]

Other advances came. In athletics, Jackie Robinson signed to play for Montreal, becoming the first Negro to enter modern big-time baseball. Trackmen Herb McKinley and Buddy Young covered themselves with sports glory at Illinois. Young was also one of college football's first black stars in a generation. In 1946 Negro nurses were admitted to the American Nurses Association in fourteen hold-out states. By the same year a number of newspapers, including the *New York Times*, *Detroit News*, *Dallas Morning Sun*, *Christian Science Monitor*, *Providence Journal*, *Des Moines Register*, and *Fresno Bee*, had dropped the practice of identifying people by race unless it was essential to a story. Negroes broke into the larger press world, so that by 1947 eighteen of them worked as full-time newsmen on newspapers of general circulation. By then, thanks to pressure from the National Newspaper Publishers Association and individual reporters, black newsmen were accredited to the State Department. Similar developments took place in white-collar, scientific, technical, and professional jobs. A 1948 Urban League survey of twenty-five cities found 7,734 Negroes in such positions, almost all in jobs closed to them but a few years before and in communities covered by strong fair employment practice laws. There was a new look to advertisements in black newspapers by 1948. National business firms not only increased their advertising but adorned it with pictures of attractive or prominent Negroes. The new code of the Association of Comic Magazine Publishers stated that "ridicule of or attack on any religious or racial group is never permissible." Negro membership in labor unions continued to be high, and, in fact, even increased from 1,250,000 during the war to 1,500,000 by the 1950s.[10]

Important gains were made in education. The number of Negroes enrolled in high schools in seventeen southern and border states and the District of Columbia rose from 254,580 in 1939–1940 to 338,032 in 1949–1950, while the black population remained relatively stable. The number graduating from high school increased from 30,009 to 45,291 in the same years, and the elementary- and secondary-school year lengthened from 156 to 173 days. The amount of funds allocated to Negro education in ten southern states on a classroom-unit basis between 1939–1940 and 1949–1950 skyrocketed from $441 to $2,197, or some 400 percent. That rise looks less dramatic, however, when compared to increases in funds for white classroom units over the same period, which grew from $1,096 to $3,291. That meant a dollar increase of $2,195 per white unit compared to one of only $1,756 per Negro unit. Black colleges bulged during the postwar era, with 79,391 students enrolled and 8,504 degrees awarded in 1949–1950. The problem was that there was insufficient room for prospective black enrollees in either Negro or white colleges. Only some twenty thousand of about one hundred thousand Negro veterans eligible for college under the GI Bill were able to find an institution that would accept them, and some 70 percent of those were enrolled in segregated institutions. Another fifteen thousand applied but were turned away for lack of space.[11]

There were other school developments. In 1947 Archbishop Joseph Ritter desegregated the Catholic schools of St. Louis, and the following year Archbishop Patrick O'Boyle began integrating the Washington, D.C., parochial schools, a process that spread gradually to other dioceses. Illinois passed legislation in 1945 and 1949 to force complete desegregation of its public schools; and in 1947 New Jersey ratified a constitutional provision declaring that no person shall "be discriminated against in the exercise of any civil or military right, nor be segregated in the militia or in the public schools, because of religious principles, race, color, ancestry, or national origin." The New Jersey constitution was unique in that in effect it equated segregation with discrimination, thereby denying that separate racial establishments could be equal.[12] Such legal provisions, however, had little impact on de facto school segregation, which continued to victimize most racial minorities.

Clearly, the formal barriers to mixing the races in educational institutions were starting to crumble, as white colleges and schools began to accept Negro students and to offer courses dealing with race problems. Even a nucleus of black teachers at white colleges had developed. By 1947 some sixty of the three thousand Negro college professors in the United States taught at white institutions. In 1948 Allison Davis was promoted to professor of education in the University of Chicago, the first of his race to hold that rank on a permanent basis in a great American university.[13] It all was a modest beginning, but one that lent hope for better educational opportunities for minorities. Moreover, it was part of an overall movement that made the nation's colleges and universities more cosmopolitan, as sprinklings of Indian, Oriental, Spanish-speaking, and especially Negro students were found on campus, along with large numbers of Jews, foreigners, and Catholics. At the same time there was an infusion of Jewish and Catholic professors at public and nonsectarian private institutions. It must be said that liberal attitudes had opened the gates, but the GI Bill had pushed a greater diversity of students and teachers onto campus.

Housing was another area of development. Federal statistics showed that between 1940 and 1947 overcrowding (where an average of more than one-and-a-half persons lived per room) in nonfarm housing decreased from 6 to 4 percent for whites and from 18 to 15 percent for nonwhites. The percentage of dwellings that required major repairs or lacked private baths and flush toilets declined from 34 to 22 for whites and from 75 to 61 for nonwhites. The percentage without electric lighting decreased from 40 to 20 for nonwhites, while for whites it stood at about 2. The percentage of nonwhites who owned their homes grew from 23.8 in 1940 to 33.6 in 1947, although white homeowners rose from 42.7 to 54.5. There were also slight advances in combating discrimination and segregation in assigning public housing under the new laws of several states in the period 1945–1947, notably in Illinois, Indiana, Minnesota, New Jersey, New York, and Pennsylvania. The federal government, however, took the path of least resistance on segregation by following local law and policy in granting aid to housing projects.[14]

Although fair employment practices legislation was stymied in Congress, there was much activity in the statehouses during the middle 1940s. From 1944 through 1949, fair employment bills were introduced fifty-nine times in twenty-seven states and enacted in ten. Both Democratic and Republican legislators were responsible for such legislation, although they were generally spurred by coalitions of Negro, Jewish, and interracial organizations as well as by some Protestant and Catholic groups. Support from labor, civic, and veterans' organizations came at best sporadically, which perhaps accounted in part for the fact that several of the laws had no teeth.[15]

Employment patterns and income held up well compared with those of 1940. The percentage of jobless nonwhites ran 5.4, as compared with 3.3 for whites in 1947. The percentage of employed nonwhite males in various occupations rose between 1940 and 1948: in government work, from 1.7 to 4.2; professional services, 2.9 to 4.2; manufacturing, 16.1 to 24; construction, 4.8 to 6.7; mining, 1.8 to 5.1; trade and finance, 11.7 to 13.6; transportation, communication, and public utilities, 6.7 to 9.6. The percentages declined from 43.3 to 22.4 in agriculture and from 8.3 to 7.6 in domestic and personal services, indicating a considerable improvement in the types of work found by nonwhites. Median wage and salary income of the individual nonwhite grew from $364 in 1939 to $863 in 1947 and to $1,210 in 1948, and of whites during these same years from $956 to $1,980 to $2,323. The median nonwhite income increased from 38.1 percent of median white income in 1939 to 43.6 in 1947 and to 52.1 in 1948, although the dollar gap widened. Moreover, probably because of higher nonwhite unemployment, the median nonwhite family income dipped from 56.6 percent of white median family income in 1945 to 51.1 in 1947.[16]

Apparently there was a rise in the volume of Negro businesses. Although the assets of banks owned and operated by blacks only grew from $28,584,815 in 1945 to $31,307,345 in 1947, assets of Negro insurance companies jumped from $72,787,542 in 191 firms in 1945 to $118,705,607 in 216 companies in 1948. The number of policies increased from 3,789,989 to 4,944,464. In 1943 Negro savings and loan institutions reported their worth as $3,131,399, while in 1947 they counted assets of $8,864,342.[17]

During the 1940s, based in part on the rising prosperity of minorities, a civil-rights coalition was formed. The coalition was composed largely of Negroes and Jews, supported by other minorities and by sympathetic whites among Catholics, Protestants, and the unchurched. The coalition's work was best seen in the struggles in Congress and state legislatures for fair employment laws, although after 1945 it was active on other fronts too. It reached its high point about 1949–1950, after which, distracted by the effects of the Korean War and the country's loyalty-security psychosis, the coalition lost momentum.

During the 1940s the coalition was somewhat sustained by the nation's slowly changing attitudes. Competing with the belief that America had a Negro, or Indian, or Mexican-American, or Oriental, or Jewish, problem was the idea, as Lillian Smith said in 1946, that there was a "white problem." Even more significant was the developing concept in many areas that there had to be cooperative approaches to the problem, whatever it was called. In St. Louis in 1946, for example, this idea took the practical form of thirty-six community organizations holding a week-long institute to seek techniques to encourage better race relations. Over the following three years this seed fruited both in the desegregation of the governing boards, staffs, memberships, and clients of numerous organizations and social agencies in the city, and in a mounting number of interracial and interfaith conferences.[18]

This is not to say that understanding was achieved among men of good will, even among such men in minority groups. There were antagonisms, for example, between Negroes and Jews because of a residue of mutually unfavorable views and occasionally unpleasant contacts. Even when they gathered together to discuss civil-rights questions, as Kenneth Clark observed, condescension often marked the attitudes of Jews. Yet earnest efforts were made to overcome these problems for the common good. The fact that in its first issue *Commentary*, sponsored by the American Jewish Committee, published Clark's straightforward article on Negro-Jewish relations was one example. Black writers and leaders such as Gordon Hancock and A. Philip Randolph pointed out the sufferings of Jews because of prejudice.[19] Most significant was the joining of forces to lash out against discrimination. Not only were Negro and Jewish groups actively cooperating in seeking fair employment legislation, but the Anti-Defamation League struck out at prejudice wherever it found it. The pattern of mutual cooperation was set early in the postwar period and would be repeated in case after case.

Cooperation was not limited to Negroes and Jews, for leaders in many minorities believed that what affected one group could affect all. In New York City, as early as 1945, the Japanese-American Citizens League (JACL) sponsored a rally for a permanent FEPC, which used two Negroes and two Japanese-Americans as speakers. A Mexican American challenge to school segregation in California was supported by amicus curiae briefs filed by the NAACP, the National Lawyers Guild, the American Jewish Congress, the American Civil Liberties Union, and the JACL. At a Memorial Day dinner of Japanese-American veterans in Chicago in 1946, segregation was condemned, in general, and Senator Bilbo and Representative John Rankin, in particular, as high priests of Jim Crowism. In Los Angeles and San Francisco, Negroes during the war had moved into the Little Tokyo sections; and when the Japanese-Americans returned from detention camps, the two groups lived together in amity. The American Jewish Congress joined the JACL and the ACLU in contesting California's alien-land law before the Supreme Court. And Negro newspapers spoke their piece for Japanese-Americans, with the *Afro-American*, for example, writing that "American prejudice and hatred of Japanese-Americans is one of the blackest pages in our history."[20]

Among Negroes, a change of emphasis was developing. The postwar period saw an increasing demand for racial integration as well as equality. Early in 1946 the *Courier*, in discussing school segregation, championed the mixing of races in the schools. NAACP Secretary Walter White inveighed against de facto segregation of public facilities. Writing Fiorello H. LaGuardia about a proposed new hospital in a black area of New York City, White wrote that "segregation can never be the answer to racial discrimination, whether it be imposed from without or established from within." Even a southern Negro moderate like Charles S. Johnson in 1947 wrote, "For the Negro to accept segregation and all of its implications as an ultimate solution would be to accept for all time a definition of himself as something less than his fellow man."[21]

For years the NAACP had battled for equal educational facilities, and since the middle 1930s it had worked for admission of black students to public white professional schools when separate-but-equal facilities were not available. By 1947 the association's lawyers began an all-out assault on school segregation, "on the ground," as Charles H. Houston wrote, that "there is no such thing as 'separate but equal,' that the only reason colored people are segregated is to prevent them from receiving equality." In taking this line of attack, the NAACP had the backing of counsel for the American Jewish Congress. Negroes were further encouraged by a federal court decision against segregating Mexican-Americans in California's schools. As Lawrence Scott wrote, the ruling "opens the way to an attack on the whole expensive, segregated school system of the South and Middle West. It shows the possibility of a favorable ruling by the Supreme Court."[22]

Other groups sought to break down racial barriers. The Catholic Interracial Council of Los Angeles challenged a state law prohibiting interracial marriages. In the test, which involved a Negro and white Catholic couple, the California Supreme Court in 1948 invalidated the law. Coalition was also evidenced in politics. Blacks and Mexican-Americans in San Antonio joined together to elect a Negro to the junior college's board of trustees and a Mexican-American to the school board.[23]

In 1947 Walter White, in his role as Pontifex Maximus of interracial forces, complained that there was insufficient coordination in the holy war against prejudice. He proposed establishment of a Supreme Headquarters Against All Bigotry. Such a headquarters was never established, but White, as much as any man, must have been aware of the increase in cooperative efforts to combat intolerance and discrimination. Not only was there considerable cooperation among Jewish and Negro groups, but also a certain amount with Japanese, Catholic, and Mexican-American elements as well as with general organizations like the Marxist Civil Rights Congress (formerly the International Labor Defense), the ACLU, the American Veterans Committee, and the CIO. Indeed, the high point was reached during the late 1940s, thanks to the economic resources available to the groups involved, their many common goals, and the increasing receptivity of the nation and the Truman administration to civil-rights pressures. This intensity of concern was seen on the local as well as the national level. Carey McWilliams wrote in 1948 that there were some seven hundred organizations interested in civil rights. In 1949 there were official human-rights agencies in twenty-one states and fifty-one cities. The American Council on Race Relations later conducted a census which revealed that 1,350 groups around the nation were concerned with improving intergroup relations.[24]

The international situation was another factor that stimulated action by those who quested for civil rights. The concepts of the interrelatedness of peoples and the need for international cooperation reached a peak in the 1940s partly because of the wartime alliance against the Axis powers and partly because of the later search for a way to avoid another, an atomic, world war. Many people were also aware that happenings in the United States, the greatest of the superpowers, would be observed with keen interest abroad. St. Clair Drake and Horace R. Cayton had stated it well when they wrote in 1945,

"What happens to one affects all. A blow struck for freedom in Bronzeville finds its echo in Chungking and Moscow, in Paris and Senegal. A victory for fascism in Midwest Metropolis will sound the knell of doom for the Common Man everywhere."[25]

This became all the more important as America cast about for allies to stave off what it considered to be the postwar threat of international communism. American government pronouncements on behalf of principles of democracy, freedom, and human rights in the East-West struggle for the allegiance of men all over the world were somewhat heartening, partly because they paralleled the goals of the nation's minorities and partly because of growing official awareness that violation of them at home was an embarrassment abroad for the United States. The work of the United Nations was also encouraging, and the attempts to establish the UN Commission on Human Rights and an international bill of rights were of particular interest. As Edward Stettinius, America's representative on the UN Preparatory Commission, reported, through the efforts of a human-rights commission "the United Nations will be able to focus world attention continuously upon the promotion of human rights and freedoms and upon violations of these rights and freedoms whenever and wherever they occur." To minorities in America, this promised that their problems would draw additional interest at home and abroad. Certainly, there was a paradox involved in America's concern for democracy on the world scene and its treatment of minorities at home. It was high irony, for example, that the United States was more concerned with democratic elections in Poland than in the American South.[26]

The government was not unaware of the paradox. In April 1946 Under Secretary of State Dean Acheson, in response to a request by FEPC Chairman Malcolm Ross, wrote "The existence of discrimination against minority groups in this country has an adverse effect on our relations with other countries. We are reminded over and over by some foreign newspapers and spokesmen, that our treatment of various minorities leaves much to be desired. . . . Frequently we find it next to impossible to formulate a satisfactory answer to our critics in other countries." President Truman stated the problem more succinctly in February 1948 when he told Congress, "There is a serious gap between our ideals and some of our practices. This gap must be closed."[27]

The problem was not only one of the distance between principle and practice for America's minorities. Nonwhite diplomats in Washington often encountered the barriers of the segregated city when they left their chancelleries, which left them unfavorably impressed with

America's ideals and manners. At least one case cost the United States the prestige and economic advantage of securing an arm of the UN. The University of Maryland offered a site and buildings for the establishment of the headquarters of the Food and Agricultural Organization, but the existence of segregation in the vicinity of the nation's capital was an important factor in the decision to locate the FAO in Rome.[28]

The UN Human Rights Commission was formed in 1946, and work was begun on formulating an international declaration of human rights. The commission itself became a forum for grievances from minorities in various countries, including India's untouchables, South Africa's Indians, and the Palestinian Jews. America's National Negro Congress also approached the UN with complaints from blacks. W. E. B. DuBois recommended during the summer of 1946 that the NAACP petition regarding the problems of America's Negroes, a tactic approved by the association. DuBois was joined by Rayford W. Logan, Milton R. Konvitz, Earl B. Dickerson, William R. Ming, Jr., and Leslie S. Perry in preparing the long petition, which documented the injustices and proscriptions suffered by Negroes in the United States. The document, entitled *An Appeal to the World*, was filed with the UN's Human Rights Commission October 23, 1947. It was not formally acted upon because of official American opposition and the reluctance of the powers to establish the UN's authority in domestic affairs. Nevertheless, the petition created an international stir as the foreign press and foreign governments gave it great attention.[29]

The document also had an impact at home. Some people were angered at the NAACP's boldness, others were encouraged, and still others surprised. Attorney General Tom Clark told the National Association of Attorneys General, "I was humiliated, as I know you must have been, to realize that in our America there could be the slightest foundation for such a petition. And that the association could conclude that amongst all of our honorable institutions there was no tribunal to which such a petition could be presented with hope of redress." Clark may have felt some pangs of humiliation, but the grievances of black men could have come as no surprise to him. Indeed, it is apparent that he was using the petition to support the federal government's quest for solutions to civil-rights problems, when he announced that he was going to strive to enlarge and strengthen the Justice Department's Civil Rights Section.[30]

Although the State Department and Eleanor Roosevelt, the American delegate to the Human Rights Commission, had not welcomed the

NAACP petition, the association was in 1948 invited to designate a consultant to the United States delegation to the UN General Assembly. Walter White was designated, and served in that capacity, becoming the first of many Negroes to serve with the delegation. Meanwhile, the Human Rights Commission drafted the Universal Declaration of Human Rights, which enumerated rights to such things as life, liberty, security of person, equal protection under law, equality of rights within a nation, fair trial, and free choice of employment, among others. The Declaration was overwhelmingly adopted by the General Assembly in Paris in 1948. It immediately affected the civil-rights struggle in America in that it added more international opinion and legal and moral arguments to the minorities' arsenal of weapons.[31]

There can be no doubt that since 1940 the position and importance of minorities in America, particularly of their upper and middle classes, had considerably improved. There also can be no doubt that the change had been fought for every step of the way. True, a small and increasing number of whites agreed that change should come, and still others were willing to yield under moderate pressure. The struggle would continue bitterly, however, because most whites would seldom grant even minor concessions graciously—and sometimes not at all.

5 A YEAR OF RELAXATION, OF PREPARATION

During 1947 the Republican-controlled Eightieth Congress took up its duties. Negroes and other minorities waited to see if the change in party control would lead to action on civil-rights measures. Few black leaders expected much, but they did challenge the Republicans to live up to their past promises. As the *Afro-American* wrote, "The Republican party for years has been saying that it would gladly pass a federal anti-poll-tax bill, FEPC, and antilynching legislation comparable to the federal antikidnapping law but didn't because it didn't have the votes. Well, it has the votes now. . . . If the GOP means business, . . . it now has its best opportunity in years to prove it."[1]

The NAACP and other minority organizations approached the new Congress with a sizable legislative program, asking for action on the FEPC, lynchings, poll taxes, filibusters, aid to education, jim-crow travel, housing, rent control, school lunches, farm aid, various changes in the District of Columbia, and for the ouster of Theodore Bilbo from the Senate. Japanese-Americans sought passage of their claims bill and liberalized citizenship and immigration provisions, and Indians wanted increased appropriations.

President Truman abetted this drive. In his State of the Union address of January 6, he pointed out "numerous attacks upon the constitutional rights of individual citizens as a result of racial and religious bigotry" and said that he was "not convinced that the present legislation reached the limit of federal power to protect the civil rights of its citizens." Two days later Truman sent his Economic Report up to Capitol Hill and asked for a number of general measures of interest to many Americans and particularly to minorities, including rent control, increasing the minimum wage, extending the Fair Labor Standards

Act to a larger number of workers, and raising and expanding the coverage of social-security benefits. He added, "We must end discrimination in employment or wages against certain classes of workers. . . . Discrimination against certain racial and religious groups, against workers in late middle age, and against women, not only is repugnant to the principles of our democracy, but often creates artificial 'labor shortages' in the midst of labor surplus."[2]

Congress responded but slightly to minority-group demands. Although Bilbo was not drummed out of the Senate, he was not allowed to take his seat. The question became academic, however, for Bilbo soon died. In March the Senate Rules Committee ordered the admission of Negro correspondents to the press gallery, and the House of Representatives soon followed suit. The Senate Rules Committee, also in March, took action against discrimination in the operation of Capitol and Senate Office Building restaurants used by Senate employees.[3]

Action on legislative proposals moved slowly, however. No hearings were scheduled on the fifteen FEPC bills in the House. Senate hearings were held on S. 984 in June and July, but the Labor and Welfare Committee failed to report this FEPC bill until the following year. Little prodding came from the executive branch, and Truman only alluded again to fair employment practices in a June speech. Moreover, the White House decided to dispose of A. Philip Randolph's pleas for presidential support by not answering them. Labor Secretary Lewis B. Schwellenbach did not testify before the Senate Labor Committee, although in August, after the first session of Congress adjourned, he did send a long and strong endorsement of S. 984 for inclusion in the record.[4]

No action was taken on antilynching proposals or on Adam Clayton Powell's bill to forbid segregaton in interstate transportation. Only a minor victory was achieved in the effort to limit filibusters, and that was to extend the cloture rule to Senate motions not considered to be pending business. Only three measures in which civil-rights advocates were interested met with some success: the House passed the anti-poll-tax and Japanese-American-claims bills, and the Senate and the House enacted legislation providing for the people of Puerto Rico to elect their own governor. Some pleasure was taken in Truman's vetoes of the restrictive Taft-Hartley labor bill and the measure excluding newspaper and magazine vendors, a group which included many Negroes, from social-security coverage.[5]

Nevertheless, these actions gave scant cause for joy. Negroes knew that the poll-tax bill would be filibustered to death in the Senate.

Moreover, regarding the FEPC, who could forget House Speaker Joseph Martin's blunt statement in January that "we are not going to pass the FEPC bill" because of opposition from industrialists who were the Republican party's chief financial supporters. The general reaction of the Negro press and Negro leaders was that the first session of the Eightieth Congress was a failure. The *Defender*, using a phrase that Harry Truman would make famous a year later, called the Republican Congress a "do-nothing Congress."[6] There was plenty of evidence, certainly, that it would be "business as usual" throughout the Eightieth Congress unless something remarkable happened.

Harry S. Truman had his ups and downs with minorities in 1947, and deservedly so. Although his January State of the Union message and Economic Report dealt favorably with many issues of concern to minority groups, he did little to press specific civil-rights questions. Furthermore, on January 23, he crossed a CORE picket line that was protesting the refusal of Washington's National Theater to admit black people to performances. His blunder was widely taken as an insult to Negroes.[7] Several interpretations of the president's apparently relaxed position early in 1947 can be suggested. One is that he was hoping to ride out civil-rights problems without doing much of anything. Another is that he was not yet fully aware of the situation and therefore drifted, now that the pressures of 1946 had lessened. Still another is that Truman and his government were in the process of transition, of adjusting to the new powers in Congress and a new set of emerging postwar problems. The fourth is that he knew what was happening and was biding his time for the right moment to strike. Cases can be made for all four of these views, but the evidence favors the third one, that Truman was caught up in a transitional tide.

A considerable number of weighty problems had roosted on the president's shoulders. Among them were the attenuation of relations with the Soviet Union and its satellites, recruitment of allies, development of the United Nations, reconstruction of war-torn Europe, and, at home, treatment of the problems of civil rights, inflation, labor-management relations, and welfare services. These had to be dealt with in the face of Republican control of Congress, opposition from the Left and the Right within the Democratic party, and shifts of power within executive circles; and they had to be done by an overworked chief executive who was far from popular within his nation. In view of all this, it can be conjectured that Harry Truman, before taking action on civil rights, decided to wait upon the report of his civil-rights committee, which was longer in coming than expected, and to see what the Republicans did.

Some Democratic strategists, however, were busy. Liberals were forming in ranks that would support and push the president toward a more advanced civil-rights policy. After the Democratic defeat in the congressional elections of 1946, a group of these liberals, led by Federal Security Administrator Oscar R. Ewing, came together to discuss how Truman was to recoup the party's losses. Liberalism had to be the road, and the president, according to Ewing, would have to emerge as "the champion of various groups." A band of administration liberals, beginning late in 1946, met at Ewing's apartment every Monday evening to talk about how to influence Truman on policy. In on these discussions and in developing influence on presidential policy were, among others, Ewing, White House Special Counsel Clark Clifford, Leon Keyserling of the Council of Economic Advisers, Assistant Interior Secretary C. Girard Davidson, Assistant Labor Secretary David A. Morse, and Presidential Administrative Assistant Charles S. Murphy. Interior Under Secretary Oscar Chapman was an important ally, for he, more than anyone else who held Truman's confidence, had wide connections with minority groups, including Negroes, Indians, Japanese-Americans, and territorial peoples.[8]

These men were concerned with many things, and in general, as Cabell Phillips has written, with "a liberalism focused on the creation and equitable distribution of abundance."[9] Minority problems were subsumed under this approach. The administration liberals, however, were just forming in 1947. Their effect was to be gradual, for they represented a transition from earlier, less coordinated influences on Truman. They also represented the elements that would help the president structure his Fair Deal program. This development was not just one of stimulus and response. Truman's decision to listen increasingly to the administration liberals made it clear that he welcomed their advice.

At least an equally important development was the formation of the Americans for Democratic Action (ADA) and the Progressive Citizens of America (PCA). The ADA, headed by Leon Henderson, Chester Bowles, Wilson Wyatt, and other militant New Dealers, was pitted against the PCA, which rallied around Henry Wallace. Both groups appealed to liberals in the Democratic party and sought to pick up what they thought was the shattered leadership of the party.[10] Both placed pressure on Truman from the Left. He responded, with the assistance of the Ewing group, by joining in the fight for liberal and minority-group support, finally gaining the reluctant backing of the ADA, while the PCA dissipated its strength in Wallace's quixotic candidacy for the presidency in 1948.

These struggles and influences left their mark on Truman's statements and actions in 1947. His State of the Union message and his Economic Report showed this, as did his decision to present the annual Wendell Willkie awards to Negro journalists in February, when he lauded the black press for its "courageous and constructive manner" in dealing with race relations. He also carried the message of human rights abroad. In addressing the Inter-American Conference in Rio de Janeiro in September, the president referred to "the belief of our people in the principle that there are basic human rights which all men everywhere should enjoy." A president as forthright as Truman would have been prepared to make such a statement only if he was also prepared to seek those rights for his own people. Moreover, although he did not make an issue out of civil-rights legislation in 1947, he did fight for other legislation of interest to minorities—for the adjustment of income to prices, extension of wages-and-hours and social-security laws, public housing, rent control, and price ceilings.[11]

The most publicized of Truman's civil-rights statements was his June 29 address to the annual meeting of the NAACP. Walter White invited him to speak to the association's closing session at the Lincoln Memorial. The president accepted and told White to send "a memorandum of the points you think I ought to emphasize in my speech."[12] Plainly, Truman wanted to demonstrate his earnestness on civil rights. Furthermore, his speech could serve as a holding action until the civil-rights committee made its report.

This was to be no quiet statement to Negroes, but a major address. In preparing the message, Truman rejected David Niles's suggestion to devote only the last paragraph to civil rights. Instead, the speech was devoted solely to that subject. Not only was Truman's appearance to be staged at the Lincoln Memorial, with the probability of a large audience, but he was to share the speaking with Eleanor Roosevelt and Republican Senator Wayne Morse, no small crowd drawers themselves. Truman's talk was to be precedent-breaking in that no president had previously addressed the NAACP. The four major radio networks broadcast his speech, as did most independent radio stations; and the State Department arranged to transmit the message by shortwave all over the world.[13]

In the address, Truman solemnly declared, "We must make the federal government a friendly, vigilant defender of the rights and equalities of all Americans. And . . . I mean all Americans." After he said, "There is no justifiable reason for discrimination because of ancestry, or religion, or race, or color," Truman enumerated the fundamental rights that each citizen should have. These were "the right to a decent home, the right to an education, the right to adequate medical care, the right to a worthwhile job, the right to an equal share in making public decisions through the ballot, and the right to a fair trial in a fair court." He added that the evils of insult, intimidation, physical injury, and mob violence had to be dealt with. "We cannot wait another decade or another generation to remedy these evils . . . we can no longer afford the luxury of a leisurely attack upon prejudice and discrimination . . . we cannot, any longer, await the growth of a will to action in the slowest state or the most backward community. Our national government must show the way." After Truman sat down, he said to Walter White, "I said what I did because I mean every word of it—and I am going to prove that I do mean it."[14]

Truman's address left him open to criticism from some whites, and indeed to the charge that any sign of friendship for Negroes was a form of being a Communist fellow traveler. Yet a great deal of attention was given the speech abroad, and there were reports that many whites took it well at home. Black response was enthusiastic. Walter White summed it up when he told Truman that the speech "was the most forthright pronouncement any American president has yet made on this issue." Of course, understandably, there were those, such as the *Chicago Defender* and the *Amsterdam News*, that pointed out that although the words were great, there was no substitute for deeds.[15] And this was not to take anything away from the president. His words had been electrifying. But the question was sincerely meant, what was the government going to do?

The answer, until the President's Committee on Civil Rights reported, was, not much. One thing in the works was the Freedom Train. Sponsored by the American Heritage Foundation, with the cooperation of the White House and the attorney general, its goal was to exhibit across the nation such documents of American freedom as the Bill of Rights and the Emancipation Proclamation. Thanks to a resolution by Charles E. Wilson, the foundation's board of directors voted to withdraw the train from cities that tried to segregate visitors to the exhibit. Not only was the Freedom Train a public-relations effort in behalf of basic concepts of freedom, but it was an object lesson in civil rights, however small, in that the train's stops were canceled in

Memphis and Birmingham, which had insisted upon segregation of those who wanted to see the documents.[16]

More significant were governmental action and inaction on matters of concern to minorities. Federal employment constituted one area of interest. That fair practices in government employment had not been achieved was strongly suggested by data gathered from various federal agencies on the employment of blacks in their Washington offices as of August 1947. The figures showed that employment patterns varied greatly among the agencies that supplied useful information. The National Labor Relations Board employed 69 Negroes and 280 whites in the capital, and the Civil Service Commission, 422 and 1479; while the Bureau of the Budget had 25 Negroes to 545 whites, and the Tariff Commission, 10 to 219. More than 10 percent of the employees were black in the Federal Security Agency, the Public Housing Authority, the Federal Housing Administration, the Housing and Home Finance Agency, and in the Commerce, Navy, and State departments. The Interior and Agriculture departments and the Interstate Commerce Commission had less than 10 percent. Although the employment percentages varied considerably among these fourteen agencies, the types of positions given to Negroes were almost unvarying. Only in two agencies—Federal Security, and Housing and Home Finance—was the proportion of Negroes to whites in professional positions more than one in ten. The black-to-white ratio in professional jobs averaged under one in a hundred in the other twelve agencies, with indeed none reaching as much as three in one hundred. In all agencies except the Commerce Department, Negroes outnumbered whites in the lowest category, the CPC (Custodial, Protective, and Crafts) level.[17] Blacks were plainly the victims of the low level of education afforded them and of discriminatory patterns of employment in the civil service.

Another area of concern was the appointment of Negroes to executive positions. The black press contended that the number of Negroes in high-level government jobs had declined markedly, and it was said that the caliber of some of those who remained was lower. The usual example of this was Marcus H. Ray, the civilian aide to the secretary of war, who was considered weaker than his two predecessors, William H. Hastie and Truman K. Gibson. A few battles were won, for example in the Department of Labor, which appointed a black to the Women's Bureau and another one to increase integration of black youths in the apprenticeship training program. One prestige appointment was that of President Charles S. Johnson of Fisk University to be an American delegate to the United Nations Educational, Scientific and Cultural Organization.[18]

Negroes were also keenly interested in the whites who occupied the highest government positions. The appointment of General Omar Bradley as army chief of staff was widely approved. Commenting on his work as veterans administrator, the *Afro-American* said that he had "under the most trying conditions demonstrated his ability and courage to do a job." More predictable were the compliments given to Tom Clark. The *Chicago Defender*, for example, named the attorney general to its Honor Roll of Democracy for 1947, citing him for conceiving the Freedom Train idea, pressing to upgrade the Justice Department's civil-rights unit, and interceding in litigation involving racially restrictive covenants and the union rights of black railway firemen.[19]

The NAACP was disturbed about appointments to several agencies. The association's labor secretary, Clarence Mitchell, appeared before the Senate Civil Service Committee to challenge confirmation of Jesse M. Donaldson as postmaster general because of evidences of racial discrimination while he had been first assistant postmaster general. Although Donaldson was confirmed, a subcommittee was appointed to investigate Mitchell's charges. Walter White took this matter up with the president, along with that of Carl Gray, who had been named to head the Veterans Administration. White contended that Donaldson and Gray possessed undesirable racial attitudes, and he urged Truman "that particular attention be devoted to examination in the future of the racial and religious attitudes of all others who may be considered for federal government posts." Truman responded cordially, but in effect indicated that he did not need White's advice. "When I make administrative appointments, I try to make them on the basis of the ability of the man to do the job, and I think that has been followed in almost every instance."[20]

Negroes were also concerned with developments in the defense establishment. The appointment of Kenneth C. Royall as secretary of war met with opposition. Columnist Louis Lautier said that Royall was less liberal on race relations than his predecessor, Robert Patterson, and was thought to be "responsible for reactionary moves of the department." Black leaders were pleased with the appointment of James V. Forrestal as the first secretary of defense. Some were, however, unhappy that in the new, unified defense establishment, only the army had a Negro adviser.[21]

Negroes were interested in more than appointments in the reconstruction of the military services. The Supreme Court's decision in the

Morgan case against segregation of passengers on interstate busses led the army to rule: "It is not the function of military police to compel military personnel to obey state laws." Military police could intervene only to protect soldiers involved in a dispute or when the soldiers conducted themselves in a discreditable manner. The army custom of burying soldiers and veterans in national cemeteries on a racially segregated basis yielded in 1947 to the pressure of black protest.[22]

The segregation of national guardsmen was another and more important pressure point. Citizens' committees had been formed in six states to urge racial integration of their Guard and Reserve components. In response to NAACP pressure on the army, Civilian Aide Marcus Ray recommended in April that each locality be permitted to decide whether to integrate its Guard and Reserve units; but the recommendation was "nonconcurred in" by Lieutenant General C. P. Hall, the director of organization and training, and Major General W. S. Paul, the director of personnel and administration. They suggested instead that the Reserve be governed by Circular No. 124, and that integration of the National Guard be left up to the states, with the proviso that troops would in no case be mixed racially within companies. Hall's reasoning was that "individual integration will not be accepted on a nation-wide basis in time of emergency" because it would lead to discontent. This statement was accepted by Chief of Staff Dwight D. Eisenhower and Assistant Secretary of War Howard C. Peterson. Ray swallowed the policy recommendation, but he cautioned that it might lead to well-founded court cases which "would endanger the orderly and progressive movement toward a full utilization of our manpower as outlined and envisioned by Circular 124." He also indicated that black and liberal-white elements would "line up against ·the army and this may well be felt in Universal Military Training."[23]

Adoption of the Hall-Paul recommendation would have been a step forward, although a short one. It might even have averted the crisis in the army in 1948 over official state pressures to desegregate the Guard. Secretary of War Patterson, however, decided to make no change in policy. The letter that went out in response to the NAACP's communication, after being mulled over for two-and-a-half months, was a model of evasion. Colonel Edward J. Geesen, the acting chief of the National Guard Bureau, conceded the importance of questions relating to racial integration of guardsmen and said that the War Department had "studied them earnestly and in detail." The crux of his answer was, "You, of course, will realize the impossibility of making a decision of such consequence based on an abstract or hypothetical presentation. A question of this kind will be determined, if presented in regular course, on inquiry from official sources."[24] In other words, there would be no change. Patterson had evidently decided that the army had more to lose from southern reaction to change than from the antagonism of Negroes and white liberals. The test of his wisdom would come in 1948, forcefully, "on inquiry from official sources" in northern states.

As indicated by these National Guard, burial, and military-police matters, the army brass, although slow, was not unmovable. Intransigence in 1947 was provided mainly by the secretary of war. More evidence that some top uniformed leaders of the army were willing to consider change was supplied by an experiment in Europe. Lieutenant General Clarence R. Huebner, chief of staff for the European command, believed that black soldiers could benefit greatly from improved training and indoctrination. This he personally sponsored in Europe from 1947 on, with General Paul's encouragement. His program also included greater use of Negro officers with black units and a genuine effort to qualify more Negroes for use in specialties. Huebner's program was to lead to considerable advancement of black troops in terms of pride and skills.[25]

Conscription had lapsed early in 1947. With the emergence, however, of the cold war between Russia and the United States, debate began about the need for a peacetime draft, either along wartime lines or in the form of universal military training for all qualified young men. Negroes decided to exert pressure for nondiscriminatory and unsegregated conscription procedures. Therefore, during the fall of 1947, A. Philip Randolph and Grant Reynolds organized the Committee against Jim Crow in Military Service and Training, which was widely supported by Negro newspapers and leaders.[26] Thus the stage was set for a battle royal in 1948 on several fronts concerning blacks and the armed services. Negroes wanted to be consulted; they wanted an end to discrimination and segregation in the services; they wanted fair treatment and equal opportunities in an area of life that affected so many of them so much; and they were willing to make a major political fight for achievement of these goals.

President Truman had chosen to meet America's future manpower needs through a program of universal military training. Under this plan, all young Americans would spend a period of their lives in military training, so that there would always be a considerable number of men in service and, after a while, a large body of trained men that could be drawn upon in case of emergency. Late in 1946 the president appointed a commission of prominent citizens to study the question of universal training and how best to achieve it. Truman K. Gibson, Jr., was named to it, as was Charles E. Wilson, the chairman of the President's Committee on Civil Rights, which militated against the commission taking a segregationist line.

In May 1947 the President's Advisory Commission on Universal Training made its report, strongly opposing segregation in a citizen's army. That did not settle the question, however, for Truman did no more than to present the report to Congress with his endorsement. Additionally, an experimental unit established at Fort Knox, to show how universal training would work, contained no Negroes, in order to avoid raising the question of race in the eyes of southerners.[27] What it did, of course, was to raise the issue of military segregation all the more forcefully in the minds of blacks and liberals.

Another group that added to the official pressures for civil rights was the President's Commission on Higher Education, which had been appointed during the summer of 1946. Its report, made public beginning in December 1947, urged, "The time has come to make public education at all levels equally accessible to all, without regard to race, creed, sex or national origin." The commission's report confirmed, as the *Chicago Defender* wrote, that Jim Crowism was "officially under fire." The reaction among Negroes was a happy one, perhaps all the more because of the consternation and bitterness created in the South by the commission's recommendations.[28] The report reinforced sentiment among minorities to challenge discrimination in education, but it also stiffened the determination of southern whites to meet the challenge either by outright resistance or by trying to improve educational opportunities for minorities within the framework of separate-but-equal schools.

The most eagerly awaited official civil-rights activity of 1947 was, of course, the work of the President's Committee on Civil Rights. The committee met for the first time on January 15 at the White House, where President Truman gave it a big send-off. He told the committee that he wanted to stop a recurrence of the Ku Klux Klan terrorism of the 1920s. "I don't want to see any race discrimination. I don't want to see any religious bigotry break out in this country as it did then." Yet he charged the committee with more than meeting current problems. As he said, "I want our Bill of Rights implemented in fact. We have been trying to do this for 150 years. We are making progress, but we are not making progress fast enough." The president found it difficult to state in detail what he wanted, but it was something that would work a change in people's hearts, "accomplish the purposes which we have been trying to accomplish for 150 years," and clarify the powers of the federal government in protecting citizens' rights. "It's [a] big job," he told the committee. "Go to it!"[29]

The committee got down to work that same day. It established three subcommittees which were to investigate existing federal laws and to suggest new legislation to remedy inadequacies; to consider the social, economic, and public relations aspects of civil rights; and to study elements that contributed to the derogation of minority rights. The question of securing an executive secretary for the committee was discussed, and it was decided that "it would be better to get a younger person who would put in a lot of time" and "who in no way was connected with any group or organization." Chairman Charles E. Wilson told his colleagues that no fiscal ceiling had been placed on the committee in doing its work. As to how much time the committee had for its work and to whom it should report, he said that the president would receive the report and that recommendations along legislative lines were expected within sixty days, so that they could be acted upon by Congress during the current session. As to how Congress should be approached, the committee concluded that its report "ought to go as a 'massive approach.' "[30]

The President's Committee on Civil Rights (PCCR) met again on February 5 and 6. Wilson announced that President John S. Dickey of Dartmouth College and Franklin D. Roosevelt, Jr., would be vice-chairmen and would serve with him as the members of the executive committee. Assignments were made to the three subcommittees, which were expected to become active immediately. In addition, the committee met with representatives of the Justice Department to discuss its civil-rights activities. The appointment of Robert K. Carr as executive secretary was announced.[31] Carr's appointment was fortunate. He was a professor of government and chairman of the department at Dartmouth. For the preceding two years he had been part of the Cornell University research project on civil liberties, with particular concern for the operations of the Civil Rights Section of the Department of Justice. Carr was to prove an able, energetic, and well-informed executive secretary.

The members of the PCCR varied in their backgrounds and interests, so that keeping track of such a large group, fifteen, was no small problem for Wilson and Carr. Absenteeism occasionally became a problem because of illness and conflicting engagements; and at least once—on April 17—not enough members turned up to constitute a quorum at a meeting. Yet, most committee members showed zest for their work and indeed a keen sense of mission. That sense was best shown in their singular action in taking a special oath of office: "I do solemnly swear that I will well and faithfully discharge my duties as a member of the President's Committee on Civil Rights and that I will bear true faith and allegiance to the ideals to which this committee is dedicated. So help me God."[32]

President Truman, in his January 15 talk, had said that his office and the attorney general would aid the committee. The White House did assist considerably in making administrative and fiscal arrangements for the PCCR and its staff. Philleo Nash and David K. Niles kept in close touch with the committee and its work. The White House was well aware of the group's potential value. Of course, the committee was meant to draw up a blueprint for dealing with the overall problem of civil rights. It was further hoped that the PCCR would serve the purpose of educating the people to the need for action. But the committee also had the function of removing Truman from immediate civil-rights pressures until a program could be formulated. This was seen in the fact that the PCCR, during its existence, became the chief vessel to contain pressure, protests, and ideas. The best illustration of this was in the case of Willie Earle's lynching on February 17. Walter White urged the committee to investigate the lynching. Charles Wilson replied immediately, "Appreciate your wire. Federal investigations under way. This crime will command our closest attention. Urge that you forward President's Committee additional information and advice. Deeply concerned." Niles exulted in a memorandum of February 19 to Matthew Connelly: "The president may be interested to see how his Civil Rights Committee is taking him off the hot seat. Day before yesterday there was this brutal lynching in South Carolina. They immediately moved in on it."[33]

The Justice Department also helped the PCCR, probably viewing it as a public-relations and pressure-group adjunct to its own operations. The department prepared drafts of possible civil-rights legislation for the committee's inspection. Although the department was not pressing specific bills onto the committee, it did make plain its concern for adequate legislative sanctions against violations of civil rights. As Turner Smith, chief of the Civil Rights Section, told the committee on February 6, "My trouble is not personnel. Our real difficulty is legal trouble." At the committee's suggestion, Smith promptly submitted a paper outlining the problems that appeared "to be of principal public concern." These included lynchings; the Ku Klux Klan; discrimination in primary elections; discrimination in transportation and public accommodations; police brutality; and issues peculiar to Japanese-Americans, Mexicans and Mexican-Americans, and Jehovah's Witnesses. Progress had been made in dealing with some of these problems, but Smith made it clear that the legal bases for action left much to be desired.[34]

Attorney General Tom Clark appeared before the committee on April 3. He stressed that prosecutions in civil-rights cases had steadily increased over the past five years, indeed that more than half of all such prosecutions in the nation's history had taken place during that period. Clark urged the PCCR to take seriously its educative potential in preventing lynchings and mob violence. "Law enforcement," he said, "largely depends upon the communities. You can't legislate morals in the people; you have to educate morals into people. We have to cause communities to become more interested and more public-spirited in this regard." Yet legislation had its place. What he recommended was enlargement of "the present Sections 51 and 52 of the Civil Rights Statutes so that those who engage in mob activity or lynching activity, as it is commonly known, might be found guilty of a federal offense."[35]

While materials from the Justice Department were piling up, the committee elicited recommendations from other parties. Late in February Executive Secretary Carr sent letters to 194 groups and 112 individuals asking for recommendations and information. Responses came from 82 people and 141 organizations, including those as diverse in interest as the American Bar Association, the Red Cross, the National Education Association, *Time* magazine, and the United Automobile Workers, as well as such obvious respondents as the NAACP, the American Jewish Committee, and the American Civil Liberties Union. The PCCR corresponded with many other groups and individuals, and had extended exchanges with some of the original correspondents, on civil-rights questions. Some twenty-five federal agencies and many state and local units of government also assisted the committee.[36]

The members met in full committee ten times and even more often in their subcommittees. Additionally, they exchanged with Carr and each other a considerable volume of letters, recommendations, memoranda, and reports. At their meetings they sometimes heard witnesses —about forty—in open or closed sessions. The PCCR's staff churned up a large number of studies that shed light on a broad range of minority-group problems. This activity showed how true was Presi-

dent Truman's comment that "it's a big job." By February it was clear
that the committee could not study the problem thoroughly enough to
make well-supported legislative recommendations by the middle of
March. The target date for the final report was moved to June 30.
That soon proved unrealistic too, so on March 19 the committee voted
to set October 1 as the date for its report.[37]

By late April the PCCR had made substantial progress. It was
hoped that the committee and its subcommittees could complete their
remaining investigations by late May or June, so that the committee
could determine its final recommendations and the writing of the report
could begin. This was, however, a case of too much optimism. It had
taken much time to develop the positions of the various committee
members and of the subcommittees; these positions had yet to be reconciled. Moreover, since the members were busy people, the problem of
scheduling committee meetings intruded on the progress of the PCCR
and its staff. And then there was the necessity of moving the staff
offices into a different building in May. Other delays hampered progress. For example, on May 23 Carr wrote the attorney general asking
for the Justice Department's advice on four points; but Tom Clark did
not send a reply for almost two months.[38] In any event, not enough
members of the committee could find time to come together in late
May or early June to make the decisions on what should be included
in the report. Carr was able to schedule a session for June 30 and July
1 in Hanover, New Hampshire, and it was there that the PCCR made
most of its decisions.

There were, of course, disagreements among the committee members at Hanover, as there had been at most of their meetings. But, as
Channing Tobias later related, little struggle was involved in bringing
the committee to essential agreement. The PCCR invested much time
in deciding what not to recommend. They discarded suggestions for
antilynching legislation directed against whole communities; invoking
of the congressional-representation penalty clause of the Fourteenth
Amendment against states where minorities were denied voting rights;
self-government for dependent areas; joining of a permanent Civil
Rights Commission with the Justice Department's civil-rights program;
grants-in-aid for health, education, and housing; criticizing the Housing Authority on restrictive covenants; abolishing the Un-American
Activities Committee; and repeal of sedition laws. These were dropped
for a variety of reasons, probably because they were out of the committee's purview or were impolitic, or because other approaches to the
problems were thought to be more satisfactory. Disagreement, when it

cropped up, was confined mainly to discrimination in schools, proposed nonsegregation stipulations on federal grants-in-aid, the role of the Federal Bureau of Investigation in civil-rights cases, and the administration of federal loyalty programs.[39] Lest it appear that the committee was drastically shaving its responsibilities, it must be said that it decided to be bold in the many areas that it decided to tackle. It would make recommendations for state and local as well as federal action. It would attack segregation as well as discrimination in American life. This is plainly seen in the PCCR's final report.

The committee's recommendations were largely settled at the Hanover meeting, and it was left up to the staff to tie up loose ends in consultation with committee members and to translate the recommendations into acceptable language. The PCCR agreed to keep the final report within 100 to 250 pages in length.[40]

Now came the task of writing. Robert Carr believed that the Hanover session had gone well, although he wrote to Morris Ernst, "We are not entirely out of the woods yet, and I suppose we won't be until the finished report is finally submitted to the president." Carr wanted to spend the first two weeks of July reviewing what had happened at Hanover and then to enter a "period of intensive activity" of composing the draft report. He believed that the report could be drafted and circulated among the committee members by September 1, when he wanted the committee to meet again in final session. Charles Wilson thought that date too optimistic and suggested postponing the meeting until September 12–13.[41]

There were other affairs to attend to. The PCCR had pressed for government action on civil-rights violations on several occasions. One had been the Willie Earle lynching. Another came up in July, when one committee member, Mrs. Tilly, wrote with alarm about a series of violent incidents in Georgia and urged the attorney general to intervene. Carr indicated that he was in touch with the Justice Department on the "veritable reign of terror" in Georgia. In fact, he added that the committee staff "has brought pressure on the department with respect to a variety of matters and I think our influence is being felt."[42]

The draft report was circulated early in September, and responses came from committee members within the week. Mrs. Alexander made twenty-five comments, especially in the areas of violations of rights and strengthening of laws, and she did it in a forceful and convincing manner. Bishop Sherrill's comments were minor and aimed chiefly at pointing up that the problem of civil rights was not just a southern one. Mrs. Tilly believed that the draft put "too much hope on legislation as a cure all." All would not be well even if legislation were procured. She also felt that the report was too belligerent toward the South, not because the accusations were unjust but because they might "undo the social progress the South has made in the last twenty-five years." Particularly she opposed an attack on segregation, because she doubted that Truman would accept the report, because of its political implications among southerners, and because "the South will stay ignorant before it will be forced to having non-segregated schools."[43]

Apparently the Justice Department was the only government agency given the opportunity of commenting on the draft report. Reaction came in the form of a pained letter of protest from J. Edgar Hoover to Chairman Wilson. The Federal Bureau of Investigation had been criticized in the draft for the laxity of its standards in a couple of cases, and Hoover complained that the PCCR had not inquired of him so that he could make available all the facts in those cases. The committee allowed the bureau to submit data that led to a change in the report. Specifically, allegations that the FBI was reluctant to handle civil-rights investigations and that it disagreed with the Civil Rights Section over investigatory standards were toned down, although not eliminated.[44] Hoover had not swept the rug clean; he did not, and would not in the future, convince anyone that he was dedicated to the cause of civil rights.

The committee met as scheduled September 12–13 and disposed of all but two of its remaining disagreements—nonsegregation stipulations on federal grants-in-aid and school discrimination. Under Wilson's and Carr's smooth direction and with White House assistance, the report was quickly guided through the final editorial and printing stages, and a date for presentation of the document to the president was set for October 29, almost a month later than scheduled.

While the PCCR was doing its work, there had been much speculation among Negroes as to the results. At the end of May, James E. Boyack, writing in the *Courier*, indicated that "sweeping changes in the nation's civil rights law will be recommended by the President's Committee." Charles H. Houston was pessimistic that the committee would be tough enough to try to "challenge the conscience of this country to the stark necessity of establishing true democracy at home." Louis Lautier wrote that the committee had "been laboring ever since it was appointed last December and is about to bring forth a mouse." The *Chicago Defender* believed, however, that the committee's report would meet "squarely the issues which disturb us," but asserted that its work, in order to mean anything, had to be followed up by President

Truman and Congress. The conflicting speculation resulted from the fact that the PCCR had kept its work confidential. Perhaps secrecy was advisable, as Negro columnist Lem Graves, Jr., suggested, so that the committee could work outside "the glare of the public spotlight," even though this had led to mediocre press relations.[45] Certainly the fact that the committee kept out of the limelight enabled its report to receive considerable publicity when it was released, because it was not stale news.

The PCCR gathered at the White House on the morning of October 29 and submitted its report to the president. When Truman received the document, he told the committee: "I have stolen a march on you. I have already read the report and I want you to know that not only have you done a good job but you have done what I wanted you to." Truman made the report public the same day. He urged all Americans to read it and suggested that it might be "an American charter of human freedom in our time," one that would be at home "a guide for action" and abroad "a declaration of our renewed faith in . . . the integrity of the individual human being . . . protected by a government based on equal freedom under just laws."[46]

The PCCR's report, which was called *To Secure These Rights*, was divided into four main parts. The first part reviewed the American heritage, asserting that it was based on the premise that "all men are created equal as well as free." This was a postulate that the committee believed had been recognized by the people in making their state and national constitutions. The committee further contended that there were four basic rights for Americans—those of "safety and security of the person," "citizenship and its privileges," "freedom of conscience and expression," and "equality of opportunity." These were the rights that the nation had to labor to perfect. The second section of *To Secure These Rights* was the largest and dealt with the state of basic rights in America. It summarized the disparities between the promises of freedom and equality and their achievement—a roll call of the grievances of American minorities, particularly those of the Negro. The third part concerned the federal government's responsibilities in securing people's rights. As the PCCR saw it, the need for federal action stemmed from the inability of states to eliminate outrages, the prestige of the national government in showing the way for local communities, the necessity to offset the unpleasant international implications of America's failure to achieve equal human rights at home, the tendency of people to look to Washington for protection of their rights, and the federal government's direct responsibility for the rights of its employees, clients, and the people in its territories. The constitutional powers of the national government to act were extensive, the committee emphasized; but to be effective they required specific legislative and executive action.

The committee's recommendations, which made up the fourth and last part of the report, constituted the most eagerly awaited section. The reasons given for the recommendations were moral, economic, and international. The gap between America's civil-rights aims and accomplishments, the PCCR said, created "a kind of moral dry rot which eats away at the emotional and rational bases of democratic beliefs." It was also costly, for it drained off much of the nation's "human wealth, its national competence." Moreover, the country "is not so strong, the final triumph of the democratic ideal is not so inevitable, that we can ignore what the world thinks of us or our record." The committee made thirty-five recommendations. In short, federal, state, and local governments, as well as private citizens, were called upon to enlist in a crusade for the elimination in America of discrimination and segregation, of intimidation and mob violence, and of violations of rights.

The PCCR's specific recommendations were so significant that they will be reproduced here, although without their lengthy explanations.

I. To strengthen the machinery for the protection of civil rights, the President's Committee recommends:

1. The reorganization of the Civil Rights Section of the Department of Justice to provide for: The establishment of regional offices; a substantial increase in its appropriation and staff to enable it to engage in more extensive research and to act more effectively to prevent civil rights violations; an increase in investigative action in the absence of complaints; the greater use of civil sanctions; its elevation to the status of a full division in the Department of Justice.

2. The establishment within the FBI of a special unit of investigators trained in civil rights work.

3. The establishment by the state governments of law enforcement agencies comparable to the federal Civil Rights Section.

4. The establishment of a permanent Commission on Civil Rights in the Executive Office of the President, preferably by Act of Congress; and the simultaneous creation of a Joint Standing Committee on Civil Rights in Congress.

5. The establishment by the states of permanent commis-

sions on civil rights to parallel the work of the federal Commission at the state level.

6. The increased professionalization of state and local police forces.

II. To strengthen the right to safety and security of the person, the President's Committee recommends:

1. The enactment by Congress of new legislation to supplement Section 51 of Title 18 of the United States Code which would impose the same liability on one person as is now imposed by that statute on two or more conspirators.

2. The amendment of Section 51 to remove the penalty provision which disqualifies persons convicted under the Act from holding public office.

3. The amendment of Section 52 to increase the maximum penalties that may be imposed under it from a $1,000 fine and a one-year prison term to a $5,000 fine and a ten-year prison term, thus bringing its penalty provisions into line with those in Section 51.

4. The enactment by Congress of a new statute, to supplement Section 52, specifically directed against police brutality and related crimes.

5. The enactment by Congress of an antilynching act.

6. The enactment by Congress of a new criminal statute on involuntary servitude, supplementing Sections 443 and 444 of Title 18 of the United States Code.

7. A review of our wartime evacuation and detention experience looking toward the development of a policy which will prevent the abridgment of civil rights of any person or groups because of race or ancestry.

8. Enactment by Congress of legislation establishing a procedure by which claims of evacuees for specific property and business losses resulting from the wartime evacuation can be promptly considered and settled.

III. To strengthen the right to citizenship and its privileges, the President's Committee recommends:

1. Action by the states or Congress to end poll taxes as a voting prerequisite.

2. The enactment by Congress of a statute protecting the right of qualified persons to participate in federal primaries

and elections against interference by public officers and private persons.

3. The enactment by Congress of a statute protecting the right to qualify for, or participate in, federal or state primaries or elections against discriminatory action by state officers based on race or color, or depending on any other unreasonable classification of persons for voting purposes.

4. The enactment by Congress of legislation establishing local self-government for the District of Columbia; and the amendment of the Constitution to extend suffrage in presidential elections, and representation in Congress to District residents.

5. The granting of suffrage by the States of New Mexico and Arizona to their Indian citizens.

6. The modification of the federal naturalization laws to permit the granting of citizenship without regard to the race, color, or national origin of applicants.

7. The repeal by the states of laws discriminating against aliens who are ineligible for citizenship because of race, color, or national origin.

8. The enactment by Congress of legislation granting citizenship to the people of Guam and American Samoa.

9. The enactment by Congress of legislation, followed by appropriate administrative action, to end immediately all discrimination and segregation based on race, color, creed, or national origin, in the organization and activities of all branches of the Armed Services.

10. The enactment by Congress of legislation providing that no member of the armed forces shall be subject to discrimination of any kind by any public authority or place of public accommodation, recreation, transportation, or other service or business.

IV. To strengthen the right to freedom of conscience and expression, the President's Committee recommends:

1. The enactment by Congress and the state legislatures of legislation requiring all groups, which attempt to influence public opinion, to disclose the pertinent facts about themselves through systematic registration procedures.

2. Action by Congress and the executive branch clarifying the loyalty obligations of federal employees, and estab-

lishing standards and procedures by which the civil rights of public workers may be scrupulously maintained.

V. *To strengthen the right to equality of opportunity, the President's Committee recommends:*

1. In general: The elimination of segregation, based on race, color, creed, or national origin, from American life. The conditioning by Congress of all federal grants-in-aid and other forms of federal assistance to public or private agencies for any purpose on the absence of discrimination and segregation based on race, color, creed, or national origin.

2. For employment: The enactment of a federal Fair Employment Practice Act prohibiting all forms of discrimination in private employment, based on race, color, creed, or national origin. The enactment by the states of similar laws; the issuance by the President of a mandate against discrimination in government employment and the creation of adequate machinery to enforce this mandate.

3. For education: Enactment by the state legislatures of fair educational practice laws for public and private educational institutions, prohibiting discrimination in the admission and treatment of students based on race, color, creed, or national origin.

4. For housing: The enactment by the states of laws outlawing restrictive covenants; renewed court attack, with intervention by the Department of Justice, upon restrictive covenants.

5. For health services: The enactment by the states of fair health practice statutes forbidding discrimination and segregation based on race, creed, color, or national origin, in the operation of public or private health facilities.

6. For public services: The enactment by Congress of a law stating that discrimination and segregation, based on race, color, creed, or national origin, in the rendering of all public services by the national government is contrary to public policy; the enactment by the states of similar laws; the establishment by act of Congress or executive order of a unit in the federal Bureau of the Budget to review the execution of all government programs, and the expenditures of all government funds, for compliance with the policy of nondiscrimination; the enactment by Congress of a law prohibiting discrimina-

tion or segregation, based on race, color, creed, or national origin, in interstate transportation and all the facilities thereof, to apply against both public officers and the employees of private transportation companies; the enactment by the states of laws guaranteeing equal access to places of public accommodation, broadly defined, for persons of all races, colors, creeds, and national origins.

7. For the District of Columbia: The enactment by Congress of legislation to accomplish the following purposes in the District; prohibition of discrimination and segregation, based on race, color, creed, or national origin, in all public or publicly-supported hospitals, parks, recreational facilities, housing projects, welfare agencies, penal institutions, and concessions on public property; the prohibition of segregation in the public school system of the District of Columbia; the establishment of a fair educational practice program directed against discrimination, based on race, color, creed, or national origin, in the admission of students to private educational institutions; the establishment of a fair health practice program forbidding discrimination and segregation by public or private agencies, based on race, color, creed, or national origin, with respect to the training of doctors and nurses, the admission of patients to hospitals, clinics, and similar institutions, and the right of doctors and nurses to practice in hospitals; the outlawing of restrictive covenants; guaranteeing equal access to places of public accommodation, broadly defined, to persons of all races, colors, creeds, and national origins.

8. The enactment by Congress of legislation ending the system of segregation in the Panama Canal Zone.

VI. To rally the American people to the support of a continuing program to strengthen civil rights, the President's Committee recommends:

A long term campaign of public education to inform the people of the civil rights to which they are entitled and which they owe to one another.[47]

These were the PCCR's recommendations. They were unanimously agreed upon by the committee except that a minority, at least Mrs. Tilly and Dr. Graham, believed that abolition of segregation should not be required to establish eligibility for federal grants-in-aid.

Another minority disagreed on the idea that states should pass laws to prohibit discrimination in the admission and treatment of students in public and private nondenominational educational institutions.[48]

The report was news—big news—and press commentary was widespread. Although many white southern newspapers condemned the report, others felt that there was much in it that was worth considering. Elsewhere, the *Chicago Sun Times* thought that *To Secure These Rights* would "be the book of the year." The *Washington Post* called the report "monumental," and the liberal New York newspaper *PM* hailed it as "unprecedented in the nation's history." The *Washington Star* believed that it was a "fine statement," but grumbled because the PCCR placed too much "dependence on compulsion under law."[49]

Negro commentaries usually recognized that the report would not satisfy all civil-rights advocates and that its words had yet to be implemented, but they hailed it generally and generously. Walter White, writing in the *New York Herald Tribune,* said the report was "the most uncompromising and specific pronouncement by a governmental agency on the explosive issue of racial and religious bigotry which has ever been issued." He was pleased that Wilson and Luckman were among the authors of the report, because it meant that "for the first time, distinguished representatives of industry have spoken out on the subject." The *Afro-American* called *To Secure These Rights* "one of the most significant documents of all time." The *Journal and Guide* complimented the committee for a fine report and President Truman for his "moral courage." The *People's Voice* (New York) considered the report "of extreme historical importance," because finally the government had admitted that "segregation and discrimination were cancerous sores sapping the strength of democracy and making it a mockery before the world."[50]

The PCCR did not rely just on the press to give publicity to its report. With White House support, it kicked off its own campaign to educate the public. The committee ordered 25,000 copies of *To Secure These Rights* for distribution to the press; various federal and state officials; public libraries; diplomats; and farm, business, professional, civic, fraternal, labor, consumer, Negro, religious, international-relations, social-welfare, veterans, and women's organizations. Other elements took up the educational task, too. The *Courier* and the *Afro-American* ran the report in serial form, with a maximum circulation of 500,000. By the middle of February 1948, 37,700 copies of the government edition of *To Secure These Rights* and 36,000 copies of Simon and Schuster's one-dollar edition had been distributed. *PM* had circulated 160,000 copies with its Sunday magazine and had sold another 230,000 reprints at ten cents apiece. The American Jewish Congress prepared and distributed 200,000 copies of a summary of *To Secure These Rights*. This group also assisted in the writing of the Public Affairs Committee pamphlet on the report, and went to great lengths to publicize the document through newspapers, publicists, the radio, and various organizations. The American Council on Race Relations published a fifty-nine-page pamphlet on how to achieve the rights referred to in the report. The *Pacific Citizen*, the organ of the Japanese-American Citizens League, gave much of its space to the report. On radio, CBS's Peoples Platform, ABC's Town Meeting of the Air, and Mutual's American Forum of the Air devoted sessions to discussion of *To Secure These Rights*, as did the intellectual's radio paradise, the University of Chicago Round Table. The Methodist Woman's Society of Christian Service made the document part of its 1948 study program. Other organizations that helped publicize the report included the National Association for the Advancement of Colored People, the American Civil Liberties Union, the Illinois Inter-Racial Commission, the CIO Committee to Abolish Discrimination, the Columbus (Ohio) Council for Democracy, the American Friends Service Committee, the Anti-Defamation League, the National Conference of Christians and Jews, and the Council Against Intolerance in America. The Advertising Council issued one-minute spots on radio emphasizing racial and religious tolerance and understanding.[51] In short, a great educational campaign had been set in motion by the PCCR's report.

But there were other results. State civil-rights committees were established in Massachusetts and Michigan, chaired respectively by Charles Luckman and Bishop Haas. Civil-rights audits were begun in Montclair and Plainfield, New Jersey, and Minneapolis, Minnesota; and the American Association of University Women encouraged its local units to develop such projects for the measurement of the state of civil rights in their own communities. *Collier's* published Charles Luckman's article "Civil Rights Means Good Business" in its January 17, 1948, issue. Articles on civil rights appeared in other leading magazines. In December 1948 the Federal Council of Churches in America called racial segregation "unnecessary and undesirable" and declared that "as proof of their sincerity, the churches must work for a nonsegregated church and nonsegregated society." These were only some examples of the positive reaction that the President's Committee on Civil Rights could claim to have set off or encouraged.[52]

There can be no doubt that *To Secure These Rights*, as William L.

White wrote, "stirred America's conscience." It was widely distributed and publicized, discussed and debated. In that regard, it secured expanded recognition both of the dimensions of the problem of securing human rights and also of the potential solutions to that problem. As President Truman wrote, in 1949, it became "a charter of human rights for our time."[53] As such, it has been drawn upon directly and indirectly for manifesto after manifesto over the years. Indeed, *To Secure These Rights* served for a generation as the basic statement of most of the goals of civil-rights advocates.

But the PCCR's report had more immediate effects. It galvanized civil-rights movements into greater activity in efforts to implement its recommendations. Not only did the report consolidate goals for these movements, but it gave them a yardstick by which to measure their success.[54] The document also gave President Truman and other members of his administration a blueprint to work with. Truman, in his press conference of November 6, equivocated on the report, indicating that he had not yet read it carefully. When asked if the report would be used as part of his 1948 State of the Union message, he replied, "It could be used as a foundation for part of the message—some of it, maybe." As far as public appearances were concerned, the president was wise in going slowly. He would have an abundance of public reaction to bear once his intentions were fully revealed. He certainly knew, as Mrs. Tilly had written earlier, that "the political implications of the report could be terrific," that "the South knows how to *REBEL*."[55] For the time being, he was not above muddying Suwannee's waters.

Yet Truman was about to launch an unprecedented civil-rights venture. Not only was the need to act strong, but the pressure was intense. Within a matter of days in the fall of 1947 had come the NAACP petition to the United Nations, the report of the PCCR, Henry Wallace's opening appeal for Negro votes, and Attorney General Tom Clark's warning in dedicating the Freedom Train that "all over the world, now, people are watching us Americans. . . . They want to know whether we practice what we preach."[56] Soon, too, would come the antisegregation recommendations of the President's Commission on Higher Education.

Truman and the White House staff were making plans. Clark Clifford has said that as soon as the president received the PCCR's report, he had wanted to send a message to Congress, which was shortly to meet in special session. Truman was counseled against haste, so it was planned to bring up civil-rights questions early in the next regular session of Congress. During November and early December, Truman discussed with various administration officials what he should do, and, of course, he received a variety of advice. The die was cast when, on December 9, he asked Special Counsel Clifford to consult with Attorney General Clark in drawing up a recommendation. The president's spokesman on civil rights in the Senate, J. Howard McGrath, even earlier had begun to be briefed by Assistant Interior Secretary C. Girard Davidson on civil-rights matters.[57] Truman, by putting himself in the hands of three civil-rights liberals—Clark, Davidson, and Clifford— made it plain that he did not intend to be stopped by threats of southern white opposition. He would risk their alienation in order to seek the national interest and the political support of civil-rights elements. A civil-rights program for action in both the legislative and executive branches was in the offing. The year 1947 had been one of relative relaxation, of preparation; 1948 would unleash a new offensive, the president's civil-rights program.

6 OF PROMISES MADE AND DELAYED

On January 7, 1948, speaking to Congress in person and to the nation by radio, President Truman delivered his State of the Union address. His message was a request for vital legislation as well as a reaffirmation of the progressive tradition in America. But it was more. "Our first goal," the president noted slowly and deliberately, "is to secure fully the essential human rights of our citizens," for "any denial of human rights is a denial of the basic beliefs of democracy and of our regard for the worth of each individual." After briefly indicting the various forms of discrimination in America, Truman referred to the report of his Committee on Civil Rights, which "points the way to corrective action by the federal government and by state and local governments." He would take the lead, he promised, and soon send a special message to Congress dealing with the problem of civil rights in America. In the following days and weeks, the president virtually deluged Congress with special messages, including his budget message of January 12, in which he requested a one-million-dollar appropriation for a National Commission Against Discrimination in Employment.[1]

Civil-rights leaders and the Negro press were pleased. Referring to the president's request for a permanent FEPC, Elmer Henderson noted that "the president has pointed the way" and that Congress must "follow his lead." There were, of course, denunciations from those who viewed the State of the Union message as a plea for votes in November, which prompted the *Chicago Defender* to regret only "that more of the other aspirants to the presidency do not follow his example."[2] Actually, only the politically innocent could suppose that politics was

96

not involved, for in fact Truman's annual message of January 7 was the opening gun of his campaign for nomination and election in 1948.

There was nothing precipitant about the decision to launch the campaign with the State of the Union address. In September 1947, for example, a White House assistant spelled out the importance of the message in the campaign politics of 1948. The memorandum noted that its principles would "inevitably become the basis for the Democratic party platform in June 1948" and should set the party's campaign course.[3] Nor was there anything precipitant about other campaign strategy. Although Truman's stock had risen considerably by the summer of 1947, according to public-opinion polls, Democratic campaign strategists were keeping their optimism subdued. As early as the summer of 1947, various members of the administration, the Democratic National Committee, and the White House staff had begun sifting and exchanging ideas for the politics of 1948. One memorandum, unsigned and undated but apparently written in August 1947, dealt with the problem of the president's image, suggesting in particular that until the Democratic convention, the president speak *"not as a candidate for election,* but as the representative of the whole people."[4]

These materials apparently provided some of the background and ideas for a forty-three-page confidential memorandum of November 19, 1947, over Clark Clifford's name, which outlined the campaign strategy for 1948. Predicting that the Republicans would nominate Thomas E. Dewey and that Henry A. Wallace would be the Progressive candidate, the memo pointed to six "major points of conflict" in 1948, including civil rights. It assured the president, however, that the South was safely Democratic and that civil rights could be pursued without fear of a Dixie rebellion. The political dividend was that Negro and Jewish voters in heavily populated northern states might provide the margin of victory in the fall of 1948.[5]

How much influence the Clifford memorandum exercised on Truman and subsequent campaign strategy remains undocumentable at this point. What seems clear, however—given the rhetoric of the cold war, the president's own personal commitment, the continuing militancy of black leaders, and the political circumstances of a campaign year—was that civil rights would be an important issue in 1948, with or without the Clifford memorandum. For years, Negro politicians and leaders had argued that the black vote provided the balance of power in heavily populated states of the North, particularly in close presidential elections; it was a fulcrum that could be used to pry performance as well as promises from the two major parties. Walter White was to remind the president of this power in May 1948, when he sent him a copy of Henry Lee Moon's recently published *Balance of Power: The Negro Vote*, accompanied with the unsubtle hint: "You will enjoy and profit from reading it."[6] And there could be no assurance that the Negro vote would go Democratic in 1948 as it had in every presidential election since 1936. It was never clear how much of the Negro vote was for FDR personally instead of the Democratic party generally, and southern domination of the congressional wing of the party for the previous ten years had been both irritating and embarrassing to civil-rights advocates within the party.

Moreover, the defection of some Negroes from Democratic candidates in the elections of 1946 was cause for alarm, particularly in New York, the home state of the leading contender for the Republican nomination, Governor Dewey. His appointments of Negroes to important state positions, his endorsement of New York's FEPC legislation of 1945, and his statements in favor of justice for American minorities made him a force to fear. Indeed, to many black Republicans, he seemed the logical successor to Wendell Willkie. To a considerable extent, however, Truman had offset Dewey's appeal as a result of his speech to the NAACP in June 1947, his requests for civil-rights legislation, and his vocal endorsement of the report of his Committee on Civil Rights. And the reluctance of many congressional Republicans to vote for civil-rights legislation was not lost upon Negro leaders. In January 1948 the *Call* saw the Negro vote as "fluid" and observed that Truman had halted the trend toward the Republican party, in part because of the report of his civil-rights committee, which prompted Negro voters to "Stop, Look and Listen!"[7]

The Democrats, however, had other fears. On December 29, 1947, Henry A. Wallace announced for the presidency as a third-party candidate sponsored by the Progressive Citizens of America, an announcement that carried with it a sense of political urgency. Since late November, Wallace's aides had sought to persuade him to announce his candidacy, so that he would "get the credit for forcing any progressive gestures which Mr. Truman makes."[8] The former vice-president had appeal for a broad range of liberals who wanted more democracy at home and less belligerency abroad. Since his abrupt departure from the administration in 1946, he had been a consistent critic of Truman's foreign policy, arguing that the policy of containment was plunging the nation down the road to a third world war. Wallace's domestic program likewise had its attractions. In addition to his espousal of advanced social-welfare legislation, he had repeatedly condemned prejudice in all of its forms. In May 1946, according to a poll of the *Negro Digest*, 91 percent of the black voters favored Wallace for the Democratic presidential nomination in 1948. Thus, it came as a great shock to many civil-rights leaders when he resigned under fire as commerce secretary in September 1946. Many Negroes expressed dismay, including Walter White, Henry Lee Moon, and Bishop W. J. Walls; and one columnist noted that, except for Tom Clark and Julius Krug, the administration was "bereft of heads of departments who have a fair and impartial attitude toward colored people."[9]

In November 1947 Wallace toured the South under the sponsorship of the Southern Conference for Human Welfare, defying southern tradition by speaking to integrated audiences and advocating equal justice. His appeal to many Negroes was obvious, and the presence of Paul Robeson and Canada Lee on some of his speaking tours added credibility to his rhetoric. To those Negroes who had come to believe that neither major party would do anything to bring about justice in American life, Wallace was especially appealing. "Voting for a Democrat or Republican is like voting for different ends of the same egg," Charles H. Houston asserted in February 1948. "Wallace offers the American people something different."[10]

At the beginning of 1948, then, the Wallace threat seemed real; for he might drain away enough Democratic votes, including those of the Negro, to deny Truman his bid for election in his own right. The administration responded accordingly. The report of the President's Committee on Civil Rights offered a foundation for action, and his special message of February 2, 1948, would build on it. To the administration, the report and the message were part of the same package, and the one called for the other.[11] But Wallace's third-party candidacy strengthened the sense of urgency within the White House and probably contributed to the timing as well as the substance of Truman's message on civil rights. The vagaries of politics thus meshed with the president's personal commitment to justice and fair play; and in his message he sought to appropriate the civil-rights issue as his personal property in the campaign of 1948, much as Henry Wallace was attempting to do.

The February 2 message was historic, if only because it represented the first occasion upon which an American president had dispatched a civil-rights message to Congress. It was also eloquent and forceful. Pointing out that the founding fathers had contended that all men were created equal, the president indicted the "flagrant examples" of discrimination spelled out in the report of his civil-rights committee. Although there had been racial progress, *To Secure These Rights* also illuminated "a serious gap between our ideals and some of our practices," which, he said, "must be closed." The president then developed the particulars of his program, including ten recommendations for congressional action. Specifically, he requested abolition of the poll tax; establishment of a fair employment practices committee as well as a permanent commission on civil rights; federal protection against lynching; creation of a civil-rights division in the Department of Justice; home rule for the District of Columbia and suffrage for its residents in presidential elections; strengthening of existing civil-rights statutes; statehood for Hawaii and Alaska and a greater measure of self-government for the territories; prohibition of segregated facilities in interstate transportation; removal of the inequities in naturalization laws; and settlement of the evacuation claims of Japanese-Americans. All this, the president concluded, represented a "minimum program" for Congress.

Truman also promised executive action, particularly an executive order to prevent discrimination in federal employment, one with the necessary authority to ensure compliance. Moreover, he had already directed the secretary of defense to eliminate, as quickly as possible, "the remaining instances of discrimination in the armed services." He carefully avoided the word "segregation"; that would come later. In conclusion, he placed his campaign for civil rights in the context of the cold war, contending that "the peoples of the world are faced with the choice of freedom or enslavement." To set the proper example, "we must correct the remaining imperfections in our practice of democracy."[12]

The message was not a carbon copy of *To Secure These Rights*, primarily because of certain omissions. The president, for example, carefully refrained from attacking segregation directly, except in interstate transportation, where the Supreme Court had already pointed the way. Moreover, the executive branch itself was not doing its utmost to eliminate discrimination in civil-service employment, in the armed forces, or in the rendering of public services. On the other hand, the message clearly outlined and anticipated the course of the struggle for equal rights over the next two decades. Given the racist circumstances of 1948 and the muted but sometimes resentful disagreement within the administration over civil rights, the message represented a clear-cut victory for advocates of racial justice in America.[13]

And with few exceptions, the northern press and civil-rights organizations accepted it as such. Some wondered, however, if Truman had not requested too much. The *New York Herald Tribune*, for one, accused the president of throwing the book at Congress and suggested that he set aside "the more bitterly controverted items." Others indicated that he was simply playing politics, particularly to offset Wallace. Negroes, however, were on the whole delighted. The *Journal and Guide* compared Truman with Roosevelt at the latter's expense, though it did comment on the absence of any generous proposal in the presidential message to aid American Indians, "who are perhaps more oppressed, cheated, disfranchised, and sinned against than even the Negro, if that is possible." The Negro weekly also observed that the president would not profit politically, if only because he had "alienated the vast majority of the white South" in doing "a great and selfless thing." The *Call*, with considerable prescience, argued that the message had made the Negro a permanent political issue until justice was a reality. Even the *Amsterdam News*, already committed irrevocably to Governor Dewey for the presidency, found praise possible.[14]

It was the white South that found the message unpalatable. Having studiously ignored the State of the Union address, southerners now released their pent-up anger and frustration. Letters poured into the White House; southern politicians denounced the program on the floor of Congress; and southern governors threatened secession from the party. In a classic understatement, Senator Tom Connally of Texas informed a constituent: "We are deeply distressed in the utterances of the president and the position in which he has placed our party."[15]

These opinions were neither isolated nor scattered. It was clear that significant numbers of southern leaders were mobilizing against Truman, as indicated by the attempt of a committee of the Conference of Southern Governors to force the administration to capitulate. On February 23, 1948, five southern governors, led by J. Strom Thurmond of South Carolina, conferred at some length with J. Howard McGrath, chairman of the Democratic National Committee. Actually, it was more of a grilling. Tight-lipped and with the pose of a prosecutor, Governor Thurmond fired question after question at Senator McGrath, who, though sorely tested, not only maintained his composure but staunchly resisted any compromise that would be meaningful to the South. Responding to Thurmond, McGrath indicated his support of Truman's civil-rights message of February 2, opposed restoration of the two-thirds rule in the nomination of presidential candidates (by which the South could have denied Truman the nomination), agreed with the presidential request for the abolition of segregation in interstate transportation facilities, refused to exercise any influence to withdraw civil-rights bills then under consideration in Congress, and endorsed the move to establish a civil-rights division in the Department of Justice. McGrath offered to compromise only when he suggested that the party's plank on civil rights in 1944 might be adequate for 1948, but at this point the governors were clearly more interested in the president and his program than in the Democratic platform. The governors departed with the warning shot that "the South was no longer in the bag."[16]

In mid March the Southern Governors Conference received the report of its committee that had met with McGrath. With all but four southern states represented, the Conference recommended that delegates to the Democratic National Convention oppose Truman's nomination and that presidential electors refuse to vote for any candidate in the general election who favored civil rights. At a news conference early in April, Governor Fielding Wright of Mississippi declared that the people of his state meant business and that the South would hold its own convention should Truman win the Democratic nomination. A meeting in May of "volunteer citizens" in Jackson, Mississippi, summarized the thinking of militant southern segregationists: they would oppose Truman's nomination and the adoption of a plank on civil rights at the Democratic convention in July; if unsuccessful, they promised to meet in Birmingham, Alabama, on July 17 to take action appropriate under the circumstances.[17]

Yet it was plain from the outset that the South was not solid in its hostility to Truman or in the strategy that it should follow. Politicians, for instance, feared the effect that secession from the party might inflict on their careers. Moreover, there were voices of moderation and instances of courage, even in the deep South, where secession from the party seemed most likely to occur. One such example took place in Atlanta, where white and black advocates of civil rights, representing eleven southern states, gathered to draft resolutions in favor of equal justice and federal civil-rights legislation. Others were also taking a strong and positive stand. Monsignor T. James McNamara, pastor of a Catholic church in Savannah, speaking to a local business organization, defended the president's civil-rights program and labeled the South's reaction an "ostrich-like attitude." The clamor of white supremacists, unfortunately, not only muffled these voices of reason but also intimidated others into remaining silent.[18]

The militancy of the white South surprised the administration. Truman had anticipated a cold congressional reception, similar to that given to his State of the Union message, not a fiery southern response.

In retrospect, it is difficult to understand the administration's miscalculation. It is true that southerners had repeatedly threatened secession from the party of Franklin and Eleanor Roosevelt, but it is equally clear that Roosevelt had taken some of this talk seriously, studiously skirting those racial issues that might offend the South and sometimes regretting his wife's civil-rights activities. It is also true that white racists, perhaps for political purposes, deliberately misrepresented the president's position and the contents of his special message, particularly when they contended that he favored "mongrelization" of the white race. Yet Congressman Oren Harris of Arkansas spoke for many white southerners when he informed the president in a letter of February 9 that compromise was impossible. "We cannot agree to relinquish our violent opposition to proposals for Anti-lynch, Anti-poll tax laws and the establishment of FEPC," he wrote, and any "concession" from the administration would only be considered as adding "insult to injury."[19] One cannot avoid the conclusion that many white southerners clearly understood the long-range implications of the president's civil-rights programs. Although the message did not directly attack the citadel of segregation, its rhetoric and its opposition to segregation in interstate transportation facilities and in the nation's capital clearly foreshadowed an assault on segregation everywhere in America. Moreover, Truman had implied that discrimination and segregation were one and the same thing—as Negroes had argued for years and as the administration would soon contend vigorously in various amicus curiae briefs before the Supreme Court.

The extent and volume of the southern reaction persuaded the administration to shift to low gear in its drive for civil rights, particularly in matters that would command public scrutiny. Truman had yet to win the nomination of his own party, hopefully with some southern support and without making his position on the issues untenable in the fall campaign against Wallace and the Republican presidential nominee. It was a delicate political situation, and the administration consequently held certain matters in abeyance until after the Democratic convention. This included the White House staff's omnibus civil-rights bills, which had been drafted concurrently with the president's special message and which incorporated several of its legislative suggestions.[20]

Shortly after the president's message of February 2, the White House had sent the bill to Senate Minority Leader Alben Barkley, with the request that he submit it to Congress. The vehemence of the southern protest, however, coupled with the fear that a southern fili-

buster on the bill might jeopardize the passage of other vital legislation, apparently prompted the administration and Barkley to put the
bill under wraps. The president's comment during his news conference
on March 11 made it abundantly clear that a civil-rights bill would
not be forthcoming from the administration during the current congressional session.[21]

The administration also stalled on the presidential promise to
issue an executive order to ensure equal employment opportunities in
federal civil service. In his news conference of May 13, when pointedly
asked about it, Truman stated that the administration was not preparing the order "at the present time." In rebuttal, the *Afro-American*
contended that drafts of such an order already existed but that administrative disagreement over its political effects had delayed issuance.
Actually the Civil Service Commission had submitted a draft, but
members of the White House staff found it too weak, one that "would
incur as much wrath as a stronger order and yet would not gain any
favor." In a letter in April to the president, Walter White sought to
minimize the importance of the southern rebellion, while "eagerly
awaiting the issuance of your promised executive order." The president, however, decided that the order could wait until after the Democratic convention.[22]

If the administration procrastinated on some of its promises, it
had also made it clear to the white South that the civil-rights message
itself was not negotiable. And if the president had initially misjudged
the reaction of many southerners to the message, they too had misjudged the president. It was out of character for Truman to cave in to
pressure of any kind. He might temporize, but capitulation was out
of the question; and the suggestion of Congressman Frank W. Boykin
of Alabama, shortly after the special message, that the president reassure the South by announcing his firm belief in states' rights and his
opposition to federal civil-rights legislation could stem only from a
gross misreading of Truman's nature as well as of the political climate
of 1948.[23]

Nonetheless, throughout the winter and spring of 1948, rumors
circulated that Truman would modify his civil-rights requests of Congress, rumors that the White House repeatedly denied. Within days of
the special message, a "highly placed Senate source" suggested Truman's willingness to accommodate the South, which Press Secretary
Charles G. Ross quickly scotched during one of his regular morning
press conferences. "There will be absolutely no retreat on any point,"
said Ross, raising the matter himself; "the whole story is without foun-

dation and fact." On March 8, when Senator McGrath announced to the press that Truman would accept the presidential nomination, he brought up the issue of civil rights, asserting, "The president's position remains unchanged since he delivered that message." On March 12 Truman attended a luncheon with members of the cabinet and the Democratic National Committee at which he informed everyone, including southern committee members, that he retracted nothing: "I stand on what I said; I have no changes to make."[24]

It was the same in April and May. Although some civil-rights advocates grumbled when Truman delivered an address in May at Philadelphia's Girard College, which denied admission to Negroes, the president could point to his speech in April at the College of William and Mary, where he referred twice to civil liberties and the Bill of Rights in the presence of Virginia's segregationist governor, William Tuck. A few days after this speech, Senator Allen J. Ellender of Louisiana conferred amicably with the president on various matters, including civil rights. "The president said he considers it a good program," Ellender announced afterwards, "and that he wouldn't change it." Through it all, Truman refused to comment on reported southern defections, except to jest during a news conference in April, when asked if he had heard anything about a back-to-Truman movement on the part of southern Democrats, that "there were a great many who never left Truman."[25]

Even if Truman had been personally disposed to grant various concessions to the white South, the militancy of the black North would have made it politically difficult, if not impossible, particularly in view of the Wallace candidacy. The president was walking a tightrope. Negroes, of course, had applauded his special message of February 2 and had taken special delight in the consternation of the white South. Actually, the South's reaction paid an extra dividend with northern black leaders. One Negro columnist noted that although Truman was "a better New Dealer to Negroes" than Roosevelt, "he so far has not been able to convince Negroes that he is not a backwoods Missourian at heart. But the present abuse of Mr. Truman by certain southern gentlemen is lifting the president to a new level in the estimation of Negroes and other liberals."[26]

The administration sought to perpetuate this advantage even in little things, such as inviting Mrs. Thomasina W. Johnson, the Labor Department's adviser on minorities, to the White House for tea. There were also more substantial activities. When the president toured the Caribbean late in February, he invited three representatives of the black press, the first time that Negroes had received press accreditation on a presidential tour. In the Virgin Islands, he publicly paid tribute to the abilities of his "friend" Governor William H. Hastie. His short address, studded with references to freedom, celebrated the centennial of the emancipation of slaves in the Virgin Islands. Numerous pictures showed the president in the receiving line with the black governor and his wife, which of course did nothing to soothe southern anxieties. When critics dismissed it all as politics, the *Afro-American* countered with praise for Truman's ability to win the hearts of oppressed peoples and expressed its appreciation for politicians who "in paying attention to the farm vote, the labor vote and the big business vote also pay attention to our vote."[27]

But this activity was not enough to assuage the feelings of some Negro leaders who wanted tangible accomplishments. Black militancy was on the rise in 1948, not only because it was an election year, but also because of the international situation. The cold war had begun in earnest in 1947, and the Communists throughout the world delighted in exposing the hypocrisies of an America that preached democracy and practiced discrimination. Negroes at home became increasingly determined to use the rhetoric of the cold war to their advantage; and that rhetoric became even more pronounced in 1948, particularly when President Truman addressed a joint session of Congress on March 17. In a speech replete with references to freedom, democracy, and justice, the president indicted the "ruthless" policies of the Soviet Union. To combat them, he pleaded for speedy congressional approval of the Marshall Plan for western Europe, universal military training, and temporary enactment of selective service.[28] The Berlin blockade beginning in June 1948, and the American airlift response, added yet another dimension to the cold war and another problem for the Truman administration.

The situation late in 1947 and early in 1948 seemed ready-made for A. Philip Randolph, who was shrewdly attempting to exploit a deteriorating international condition as he had in the spring of 1941 when Roosevelt finally succumbed and created a fair employment practices committee. In the fall of 1947 Randolph and Grant Reynolds organized the Committee against Jim Crow in Military Service and Training and quickly launched a campaign of propaganda and pressure. The time seemed propitious, and not only because of the cold war. After all, there had been the report of the President's Committee on Civil Rights, which condemned "the injustice of calling men to fight for freedom while subjecting them to humiliating discrimination,"[29] and Truman's announcement in his message of February 2 that he had directed the secretary of defense to eliminate discrimination in the military. Both indicated a commitment on the part of the president to democratize the military.

On February 5, 1948, Randolph met with officials of the Democratic party in order to ask National Chairman McGrath, who was absent, to issue a strong statement denouncing segregation in the military and to attempt to influence Congress in its action on the bill for universal military training. Upon advice from William Dawson, Chicago's black congressman, the party spokesman responded with caution and without promises, while quoting portions of Truman's message on civil rights. Then on March 22, five days after Truman's address to the joint session of Congress, Randolph and Reynolds conferred with the president. Once again they pleaded their case, requesting in particular that the president issue an executive order to abolish segregation in the military and to inform state governors that the federal government would no longer dictate racial policy in the National Guard. Moreover, Negroes were of the "mind and temper," Randolph warned, "of not wanting to shoulder a gun to fight for the protection of democracy abroad until they have democracy at home." Visibly disturbed, Truman replied that he was doing his best under difficult circumstances; he also apparently considered the statement a threat, although Randolph insisted that he was simply reporting a "deep emotional feeling" throughout black America.[30]

At the end of March, Randolph came up with his most dramatic ploy. Testifying before the Senate Armed Services Committee, then holding hearings on universal military training, he stated flatly that he would counsel American youth, black and white alike, to boycott the military, to refuse to register and to serve unless segregation was abolished. When Randolph argued that he would urge civil disobedience even in time of war, Senator Wayne Morse of Oregon cautioned him about the possibility of treason; but Randolph reminded the senator of the existence of a higher law. Truman K. Gibson, black member of the President's Advisory Commission on Universal Training, sought to offset Randolph in his testimony, labeling the threat "shocking"; and White House aides believed that he had succeeded to some extent.[31]

The reactions of the Negro community to Randolph's threat represented a fairly accurate barometer of black opinion in 1948. No one disputed his goals, but some questioned the method of civil disobedience. The *Journal and Guide* more or less summed up press reaction in its editorial caption: "Protest, Yes; Treason, No!" Few, however, were disposed to accuse Randolph of treason; and one, the *Afro-American*, annointed him "the John the Baptist of a new emancipation."[32]

On the other hand, an NAACP poll of Negroes eligible for the draft reported that 71 percent were sympathetic with the position of civil disobedience. Congressman Adam Clayton Powell endorsed civil disobedience and excoriated Truman Gibson as "the rubber stamp Uncle Tom who was used during the war by the War Department to cast aspersions on Negro troops in Italy, while these same Negroes were shedding their blood and dying." George S. Schuyler, the acidulous columnist of the *Courier*, gloated about the administration's embarrassment over the threat of civil disobedience "at a time when our government is beaming to all countries, especially Russia, loud self-serving praise of the freedom and justice enjoyed under the Stars and Stripes." Although Schuyler seemed to endorse Randolph's position, he later became less enamored of the idea, perhaps because he was then traveling the road to reaction.[33]

A similar ambivalence prevailed throughout civil-rights organizations. The reaction of the NAACP was typical, as well as revealing of the political questions involved. Shortly after Randolph had testified, Walter White wired Senator Morse of the Armed Services Committee that "our association is not advising Negroes to refuse to defend their country if it is in danger"; but he pointedly did not repudiate the tactic. Morse, however, was unhappy with the association's equivocation. Faced with the prospect of incurring the wrath of a strong civil-rights advocate in the Senate, White wrote a conciliatory letter to Morse in which he clearly disavowed civil disobedience. Randolph himself was not as easily dissuaded and continued his protest, which included picketing the White House in May against the "Jim Crow Army."[34]

In the meantime, other Negro leaders were applying pressure elsewhere, particularly on Secretary of Defense James Forrestal, in an attempt to persuade him to implement the president's instruction to eliminate discrimination in the military. Forrestal's position in the winter and spring of 1948 was not enviable. He was then attempting to win congressional approval of military appropriations and of selective service, while struggling to establish his primacy over the secretaries of the army, the navy, and the air force; at the same time, he sought to follow the president by liberalizing the racial policies of the three services, particularly those of the army. In short, Forrestal was caught in a squeeze between the White House, Congress, the service secretaries, and professional military men. Although sympathetic with the goal of racial integration, Forrestal preferred a gradual approach to the problem, much like the one that the navy had pursued during and after the Second World War. On March 18, 1948, he met with eleven Negro editors and publishers, seven of whom were scheduled to begin a two-week inspection of army installations in Europe. Their report upon their return surprised no one, including Forrestal, and consisted largely of a ringing indictment of the debilitating and costly effects of segregation.[35]

The meeting of March 18 was but a prelude to a much larger and more significant gathering on April 26, a "National Defense Conference on Negro Affairs" sponsored by Forrestal and Lester Granger, who served as chairman. Fifteen of America's most prominent Negroes, representing a virtual who's who of black America, were in attendance; but Randolph was pointedly not invited. Representing the military were Forrestal, the service secretaries or their representatives, and military and civilian aides. The meeting was not a happy one. Although encouraged with the progress of the navy, the black conferees found much room for improvement. They were less sanguine about the air force, which admittedly still followed the general guidelines of the Gillem report even though it was now a separate service. And they were altogether unhappy about the army, particularly the attitude, both personal and official, of Secretary Kenneth Royall, who contended vigorously that segregation could exist without discrimination. As a result, the Negro conferees pledged not to serve in any advisory capacity to the Department of Defense as long as such attitudes were tolerated, which indicated a significant turning point in the tactics of "moderate" blacks.[36]

Another result was that Royall and the army were severely criticized in the Negro press. The *Crisis*, the official organ of the NAACP, summed up its attitude in the editorial title "Stonewall against America." The *Chicago Defender* declared that it was time "to build an American Army and not a Confederate Army." Royall, for his part, was also displeased. On April 30, in a memorandum to Forrestal, he contended that neither the air force nor the navy had been completely candid during the conference and that the absence of the other two secretaries had resulted in his being placed in the spotlight.[37]

Actually, the limelight was on the White House, and its occupants were beginning to feel the heat. On May 12 Clark Clifford and other staff members met with Forrestal to devise what could be done immediately without incurring the wrath of everyone concerned. At that point, the White House was considering the appointment of a committee within the Department of Defense to deal with the accusations of discrimination. The situation was extremely sensitive, for it was feared that any action concerning segregation in the military beyond the president's directive of February 2 would endanger passage of the selective-service bill. The proposed committee was thus held in abeyance, although by late June the White House had apparently decided to issue an executive order to establish a presidential committee on July 26—after the Democratic convention and after Congress had adjourned.[38]

Amidst the furor of the winter and spring of 1948, there was some progress in one area of military segregation—that involving the National Guard units of various northern states. The struggle epitomized in microcosm the complex problems facing the administration—including pressure from northern governors and Negro leaders, opposition from southerners, and the recalcitrance of the army—all in the context of campaign-year politics, growing apprehension over Communist successes abroad, and frustration with Congress's painfully slow deliberations. The concern in 1947 with democratization of northern National Guard units developed into a squabble early in 1948 as a result of the request of Governor Alfred E. Driscoll of New Jersey to permit integration of the state's National Guard in conformance with a provision in the new state constitution. Other governors, with the vocal support of civil-rights advocates but without Driscoll's constitutional mandate, made similar requests. Army Secretary Royall was not disposed to grant concessions. Prodding from Forrestal, however, persuaded him to inform Driscoll on February 7 that, "for the present, Army militia units of New Jersey, if otherwise qualified, will not be denied Federal recognition on the ground of nonsegregation." Royall indicated, however, that he acceded to the request only because the people of New Jersey, "by direct majority vote," had lodged desegregation in the state constitution. He would recognize nothing other than a constitutional proviso.[39]

Presidential Assistant Philleo Nash, however, had other ideas. Responding to pleas that Royall's position contradicted both the report of the president's civil-rights committee and the president's special message of February 2, Nash suggested in April that the president press the army to permit the individual states to determine the racial policies of National Guard units not on active federal duty. The army should recognize any state action in this regard, be it a constitutional provision, legislative enactment, or gubernatorial order. In endorsing Marcus Ray's position of 1947, Nash considered a states' rights approach as the most progressive and only immediate, although partial, solution. But for the moment, David Niles had the upper hand and persuaded the White House staff to do nothing and let Forrestal worry about it.[40]

Clark Clifford, however, was becoming increasingly sensitive to the political consequences of inaction. Working closely with Forrestal and his special assistant, Marx Leva, Clifford forced a concession from Secretary Royall. Although Royall still refused to recognize a gubernatorial order, at least until he received a report from the army's Committee on National Guard and Reserve Policy, which was then considering the problem, he indicated in May that he "would be inclined" to accept state legislative action as well as a constitutional provision. This represented a partial victory for the White House over Royall. Clifford reluctantly and temporarily approved Royall's position, perhaps in deference to the political and international situation of the moment. Moreover, it was also clear that Royall's position was more progressive than that of parts of the professional military. The Committee on National Guard and Reserve Policy, for example, subsequently reported against integration of any Guard unit by any means.[41]

Royall probably conceived of his policy as a compromise between the White House and the National Guard committee. His timing in implementing it, however, was politically inexpedient to say the least. On July 8, only hours before the Democratic convention opened, he drafted letters to Governors James C. Shannon of Connecticut and Luther W. Youngdahl of Minnesota, denying requests for integration of Guard units by gubernatorial order. The White House, understandably enough, held up the letters and delayed any decision until after the convention and after the creation of the President's Committee on Equality of Treatment and Opportunity in the Armed Services on July 26. Royall was then informed that the new committee would consider the problem, and the secretary dutifully informed the governors to that effect.[42]

The concessions of 1948 permitted progress. In 1949 several states abolished segregation in Guard units by legislative action. And after the Minnesota legislature memorialized Congress to abolish segregation in the Guard, the army accepted Governor Youngdahl's executive order as a legitimate expression of the will of the state's people. From there, it was but a short step to acceptance of a gubernatorial order without any legislative mandate whatever. In 1950 the General Staff made the recommendation that the army recognize the authority of the governors, which the army eventually accepted. There the matter stood, to continue as standard policy through the Eisenhower and

Kennedy administrations, with several states, not all of them southern, still clinging to segregation in the National Guard.[43]

Despite the militancy of black leaders in the early months of 1948 and despite the administration's limited response to their demands, Henry Wallace had difficulty in attracting black leaders to the Progressive standard. After barnstorming across the country for several months, he could count only a handful of prominent Negroes behind his candidacy, although the backing of such people as Paul Robeson, Canada Lee, William E. B. DuBois, Benjamin J. Davis, and Bishop Walls gave the illusion of considerable support, perhaps in part because of the vigor with which they denounced the major parties. Davis, for example, contended in the pages of the *Daily Worker* that Truman "speaks Negro rights, but he acts white supremacy."[44]

It was soon apparent, however, that the black press, most leaders of civil-rights organizations, and Negro politicians and labor leaders would not support Wallace. For this there were many reasons, both ideological and practical. Even before Wallace announced his candidacy, Lester Granger of the Urban League attacked his record of accomplishment as a member of the Roosevelt and Truman administrations. Wallace's glittering promises in 1947 and 1948 far exceeded his plodding performances on racial matters as secretary of agriculture and as secretary of commerce. As early as 1940, when he ran as the Democratic vice-presidential nominee, a Negro columnist had pointed to the "prejudice-ridden branches" in the Agriculture Department, with "the worst record" in the federal government. When Will Alexander left the Department of Agriculture in 1940, the last thing that Wallace allegedly said to him was: "Will, don't you think the New Deal is undertaking to do too much for Negroes?" Wallace himself almost admitted as much in 1948, when he conceded in an interview that he had not become concerned about segregation until 1944.[45] Wallace's past record, however, probably had little effect in determining the attitudes of 1948. Negro leaders were hard-boiled traders, willing to overlook the indiscretions of the past in favor of the promise of the present; and the politics of the present worked to Wallace's disadvantage.

To a considerable extent, Truman's strong position on civil rights, coupled with the prospect of Governor Dewey as the Republican nominee, neutralized Wallace's appeal.[46] But a major handicap facing Wallace in 1948 was the persuasive charge that he could not win, a fear echoed repeatedly in the Negro press and in the speeches of various black leaders. Though conceding the need for a new party, "because both of the major parties are afflicted with dry rot," Walter White nonetheless contended that a third party in 1948 was "dangerously perhaps even tragically ill-advised." His reasoning was not difficult to comprehend. "If the Negro vote swings in a bloc of decisive proportions to Wallace," argued the *Journal and Guide*, "neither of the major parties will have any sense of obligation to fight for a better deal for us." Congressman Adam Clayton Powell saw Wallace's candidacy as "extremely unwise at this time," for it might persuade Republicans to nominate a more conservative candidate rather than "a great American like Eisenhower whom I am ready to support 100 percent." Other black leaders, including A. Philip Randolph, disavowed "the extreme Left" in order not to jeopardize civil-rights legislation in Congress. Long accustomed to the nuances of politics, Negro leaders were not about to jettison their greatest opportunity in an election year for a ride with rhetoric, which was all Wallace could produce.[47]

There were also ideological considerations. By 1948 few black leaders viewed the Soviet Union as a haven for oppressed minorities, and few shared Wallace's views about the cold war. Indeed, although some still hesitated, most Negro leaders were then shifting from a non-Communist to an anti-Soviet position, a process accelerated by Truman's message to Congress on March 17, 1948, outlining the international situation. Although more excited than most, the *Afro-American* struck a responsive chord when it editorialized, "If Russia really believed it could whip the U.S. today, it would declare war before sunset."[48]

Although black leaders did not give Wallace the endorsements he sought from them, the administration did not assume that the Negro voter was reacting similarly, for it was not clear that the voter would play follow-the-leader in 1948. It was disturbing, for example, when Leo Isacson, a congressional candidate of the pro-Wallace American Labor party, trounced all other candidates in a by-election in a New York district composed mainly of Jews and Negroes on February 17. Some polls reported that Wallace would receive from 20 to 30 percent of the black vote. William L. Batt, Jr., head of the Research Division of the Democratic National Committee, was shocked when political leaders in Harlem and Brooklyn predicted that Wallace would receive 75 percent of the black vote in their wards. Having already established a "very informal advisory group . . . on the Negro situation," the committee now made plans to organize a formal, functioning operation. It would also help, Batt noted in April, if the administration would issue its executive orders on fair employment in civil service and discrimination in the military; and he wondered if the administration had accurately gauged southern sentiment. Unlike the White House, Batt apparently had yet to realize the full import of the southern rebellion, particularly its possible effect on the president's nomination in July.[49]

Unfortunately for Democratic strategists, Wallace was not the only candidate suffering from the "no-win" syndrome. The president was also afflicted. As his popularity plummeted early in 1948, various elements of the Democratic party sought nervously, then frantically, to dump Truman in favor of General Eisenhower, whose only apparent qualification for the presidency was his unrivaled popularity. No one knew either his party preference or his political position on the divisive issues of the day, although he had made one thing clear when he had repeatedly disavowed any political ambitions. Nonetheless, in the most unusual development of a bizarre campaign year, an unabashed alliance of big city bosses, labor leaders, New Deal ideologues, liberals of the Americans for Democratic Action, and southern white supremacists strove to impose the ultimate indignity on the man in the White House. The absurdity of the campaign was nowhere better exemplified than in the joining together of Hubert Humphrey of Minnesota and J. Strom Thurmond of South Carolina to make common cause against Truman and for Eisenhower.[50]

What made the alliance of opposition Democrats particularly unholy was the issue of civil rights, which the ADA had consistently championed and which the South had steadfastly resisted. Eisenhower may have been a political enigma, which permitted diverse groups to coalesce around his candidacy, but there was at least one crack in the facade as a result of his appearance early in April before the Senate Armed Services Committee. At that time he had testified generally in favor of the policies of the Gillem report, advocating the continuation of segregation in the military, at least for the present. To northern liberals, however, election victory was apparently more important than principle; so they continued to champion his candidacy, while preparing simultaneously, and incongruently, for a civil-rights confrontation at the Democratic convention. Negro leaders, however, would have none of it. After Eisenhower had testified, Walter White apologized to readers of his weekly column for his previous praise of the general. Though some Negro papers withheld comment, there was considerable disenchantment; the *Chicago Defender*, for example, saw the general as "just another brass hat with a glib tongue and a ready smile."[51]

Through it all, the president preserved a stony silence; he really had little choice. Moreover, he could take only cold comfort from the fact that no convention in the twentieth century—Democratic or Republican—had denied the nomination to its incumbent president, for his predicament was without parallel. Yet if Truman was ever threatened by the draft-Eisenhower movement, the general came to his rescue, only days prior to the convention, when he emphatically disavowed any interest in the presidency. It was then too late for the opposition to close ranks behind any other possibly successful candidate.[52]

The final challenge to the president came from the Republican-controlled Eightieth Congress. From January to July 1948, Truman was confronted not only with the politician's task of winning his party's nomination but also with the presidential duty of persuading a reluctant Congress to pass legislation in the national interest. Shortly after his address on March 17, Congress responded to his request for approval of the Marshall Plan, but his bid for selective-service legislation ran into several snags. Randolph was not the only one playing politics with the issue. Southern Democrats threatened its passage when they backed an amendment, introduced by Senator Richard Russell of Georgia, to permit a draftee the choice of serving in a unit of his race, a thinly disguised attempt to offset the president's directive to end discrimination in the armed services. Both Forrestal and Royall paraded to the Hill to testify against the amendment. The Senate Armed Services Committee subsequently rejected it, and the Senate later concurred by voice vote. The other threat came from Senator William L. Langer of North Dakota, who, opposed to the draft altogether, sought to defeat it by proposing several civil-rights amendments, including an outright ban on segregation in the military.[53]

The Senate, however, overwhelmingly defeated all of the Langer amendments, except one exempting soldiers from payment of a poll tax in federal elections. The final bill also incorporated an innocuous provision prohibiting discrimination "in the selection of persons for training and service." But at least the administration had its bill. Although Senate Democrats had united with Republicans to defeat the Langer proposals, Republicans received much of the criticism in the Negro press. Columnist Louis Lautier, although distressed with Senate Democrats, was furious with Republicans; while the *Afro-American* saw Langer's "greatest service" in "laying bare, for all to see, the hypocrisy of the Republican party's 1944 platform which called for specific civil rights legislation."[54]

Negroes were also angry over the fate of other civil-rights legislation. It was bad enough when Republicans refused to bring antilynching, anti-poll-tax, and FEPC legislation to a vote; but the party's determination of priorities made matters even worse. Since the war, FEPC had replaced antilynching legislation as the foremost demand of black Americans; and A. Philip Randolph, also serving as cochairman of the National Council for a Permanent FEPC, reminded Republicans of this fact in a speech early in 1948. He suspected that the Republican leadership would push an antilynching bill instead of legislation for an FEPC, "which is opposed by the N.A.M., the Chamber of Commerce, and other forces." The black leader had exposed a raw nerve, for many businessmen with influence within the Republican party viewed an FEPC as an infringement on their rights, both personal and property. Some also considered it Communist-inspired, and Randolph was quite conscious of the need to deal with the "red bogey."[55]

Randolph's suspicions were confirmed in April when Senate Republicans voted top priority to antilynching legislation, with the explanation from Senator Taft that "it's the easiest to get through." Randolph, however, considered it "shocking" for the Republican majority to give preference "to the least needed of the three major civil-rights bills." But that was only part of the priority. According to a report in May, the Republican Policy Committee had devised two priority lists, with antilynching legislation at the bottom of the second list and with no other civil-rights measures scheduled for consideration. Roy Wilkins wondered about the party "of bad faith and broken promises."[56]

Both parties in Congress, however, were guilty of ignoring many of the requests made by the President in his civil-rights message of February 2. A bill providing home rule for the District of Columbia reached the floor of the House, but the rush for adjournment allegedly prevented a vote on it. Statehood for Alaska was never considered; and the Senate refused to approve a House bill, passed during the first session, providing statehood for Hawaii. Moreover, at least two measures not included in the president's message came up for consideration. One was an attempt to incorporate antisegregation and antidiscrimination amendments into the Taft-Ellender-Wagner housing bill; it was beaten down. When the housing bill finally passed during the special session, Negroes were displeased not only because it lacked any antidiscrimination provisions but also because of the limited nature of the bill itself.[57]

The other measure involved an attempt by a House subcommittee to deny federal grants-in-aid to states practicing school discrimination, which had been recommended by the Committee on Civil Rights but not by the president. The provision, of course, had no chance of passage, which the NAACP recognized when it endorsed the education bill without the denial clause. Black leaders were aware that if Congress denied federal funds to southern states on the grounds of discrimination, Negro school children would suffer even more. But even without the restriction, the bill failed. The defeat of another bill concerned with segregation in southern schools, however, represented a victory of sorts for the foes of discrimination. In February 1948 the Conference of Southern Governors had proposed that fourteen states form a regional educational compact to pool resources and, ostensibly, to provide better facilities in higher education. Though race was not mentioned, the compact was actually a device to circumvent the Supreme Court's ruling for equal educational opportunities. Formulated in a bill, the proposal passed the House, but by a close vote the Senate sent it back to committee, where the bill died.[58]

Negroes were understandably unhappy with the Eightieth Congress, but they were not the only minority group with a grievance. Jews were furious over the final provisions of the displaced persons bill, which, although providing for the admission of over two hundred thousand displaced persons in Europe for the next two years, discriminated against Jews. Leaders of various Jewish organizations inundated the president with appeals for a veto. American Catholics, on the other hand, were generally pleased with the provisions affecting members of their faith. "Since I cannot discern or admit alleged anti-Catholic aspects of displaced persons bill passed by Congress," Francis Cardinal Spellman wired the president, "I respectfully urge you in the name of charity and national honor to sign it." Caught between religious minorities but convinced that something had to be done, the president "with very great reluctance" signed the bill on June 25. He denounced it, however, as a bill that mocked the "American tradition of fair play" in its "callous" discrimination against Jews and "many displaced persons of the Catholic faith who deserve admission." The issue had ominous political overtones; for the Jewish vote, like that of Negroes, could well be a decisive factor in determining the electoral votes of large states in November. Yet Truman's recognition of Israel on May 14, after weeks of vacillation and contradiction, considerably offset any lingering anger over his acceptance, however reluctant, of the displaced persons bill.[59]

There was yet another bill that might have precipitated a clash between American minorities. Early in the year Congressman Walter H. Judd of Minnesota introduced a bill, drafted by the State Department and the Immigration and Naturalization Service, which provided for a token increase in Oriental immigration. Of more importance, it repealed the prohibition against naturalization of Orientals—one of the president's recommendations in his civil-rights message. The bill, however, was not only discriminatory because of the token number of immigrants that it would have admitted but also because it favored Japanese over Chinese immigrants.[60] But the bill had no chance of passage, and a possible confrontation between Chinese- and Japanese-Americans was thus avoided. Japanese-Americans, however, were mollified with the passage of the Japanese Evacuations Claims Act, which the president had also recommended and which constituted a belated but only partial apology for the property losses they had suffered during the Second World War.

The Japanese Evacuation Claims Act was the only civil-rights recommendation of the president to survive the Congress; and as adjournment neared late in June, the impatience and irritation of black leaders mounted. The party of Lincoln had not produced; the *Crisis* summed it up in the editorial title "From the GOP Congress: Nothing."[61] It was that record of "nothing" that Truman chose to exploit, beginning with his "nonpolitical" tour of the West in June 1948. Yet, up to this point in the year, Truman and the Democrats generally had also produced little in the way of concrete results; for the early months of 1948 had been primarily a record of promises made and delayed as the parties prepared for the fall campaign and as the presidential candidates jockeyed for position in the conventions and on the issues.

7 VINDICATION
OF A COMMITMENT

During the winter and spring of 1948 Truman followed the high road of presidential politics and spoke as the representative of all the people rather than as a candidate for election. If he was tempted to descend into the political arena then, the rumbles of southern white revolt, the militancy of northern black leaders, the ponderous deliberations of Congress, the Democratic draft-Eisenhower movement, Wallace's third-party candidacy, and the deterioration of the international situation persuaded him to remain above the clamor as much as possible. It was good politics to appear calm in the face of tribulations at home and provocation abroad. But the time arrived when Truman had to take the offensive in order to ensure his nomination at the Democratic convention and to bolster his sagging popularity. The vehicle for his first attack was a "nonpolitical" tour of the West from June 4 to June 18, 1948. The ostensible purpose of his transcontinental journey was to accept an honorary degree and to deliver the commencement address at the University of California at Berkeley.

There was nothing new, of course, about a presidential "nonpolitical" tour; but it did offer a convenient, if transparent, excuse to leave Washington before the adjournment of Congress and to sound out the sentiment of the country. Various people, including Truman himself, have taken credit for the idea. One of the first suggestions appeared in a memorandum from Gael Sullivan of the Democratic National Committee in August 1947. The memo urged the president, prior to the Democratic convention, to "show himself to the nation via the back platform of a cross-country train." It also advocated a change in presidential style. Noting that the president's "easy manner of speaking ... informally" was often "lost in translation to the people via radio and speaking tours," it suggested that "the entire approach to the president's speeches be changed. It would be well to gain more natural delivery, even if some rhetorical effects are lost."[1] Whether by accident or design, Sullivan's recommendations became part of the campaign strategy of 1948. Indeed, although Truman had spoken informally with notes on various occasions in the spring of 1948, the "Give 'em hell, Harry" approach was born during the "nonpolitical" tour of June.

Whistle-stopping across the country, the president repeatedly labeled the Republican-controlled Congress as one of "special interests" designed to frustrate the needs of the people. His was a well-balanced attack. In large cities, he indicted Congress for its inadequate record of legislation on labor, social security, housing, and price control. In agricultural areas, he pleaded for stronger legislation to guarantee farm profit. And in various small towns, he emphasized issues peculiar to them. His autumn appeal to workers, farmers, and consumers was already taking shape. He was careful, however, to restrict his indictment of Congress to domestic matters, for he desperately needed its cooperation in foreign and military affairs.[2]

Nor did Truman completely neglect the issue of civil rights. In his first major speech, in Chicago, the president stood firm on his commitment. There, in addressing the Swedish Pioneer Centennial Association on June 4, he emphasized the courage of American pioneers, the injustice of the displaced persons bill pending in Congress, and the need to provide democracy at home in order to offset the appeal of American Communists. In particular, he promised that the federal government would be "a friendly, vigilant protector" of the ideals of freedom and equality and contended that the "menace" of communism within the United States "lies primarily in those areas of American life where the promise of democracy remains unfulfilled." When people "are arbitrarily denied the right to vote or deprived of other basic rights, and nothing is done about it," he continued, "that is an invitation to communism."[3]

The speech was not lost upon American minorities. Negroes were especially appreciative. Traveling with the presidential special, Stanley Roberts, a columnist for the *Courier*, was elated. "If apprehensive Negroes feared, or southern revolt Democrats hoped, that the man would backtrack from civil rights advocacy as an integral part of the program," he wrote, "the fears of the former were needless, and the hopes of the latter have gone with the wind." Republicans, however, were outraged with the "nonpolitical" tour: it was as "nonpolitical as the Pendergast machine," said Carroll Reece, chairman of the Republican National Committee. And Senator Robert A. Taft was incensed with Truman's "blackguarding Congress at every whistle station in the West."[4] It was in that mood and with the expectation of nominating the next president that the Republicans opened their national convention in Philadelphia on June 21.

Black leaders, too, had high expectations concerning both the Republican platform and the candidate. Before the convention opened, various Negroes, including Walter White and Channing Tobias, testified in favor of a strong civil-rights plank before the resolutions committee. White frankly expressed his disappointment over the failure of the Eightieth Congress to enact legislation on the civil-rights provisions of the 1944 Republican platform. Tobias warned that both parties "face a long, strong line of Negro voters never before seen in the history of this country," which prompted a southern member of the committee to inquire if that was "a considered statement or a threat." Tobias straddled nicely, placing it in the category of a "considered statement," though "it may be interpreted as a threat."[5]

As the platform emerged from committee, however, it was more liberal than the Eightieth Congress was on civil rights, although it represented no improvement over the 1944 version. The plank hedged in calling for the abolition of the poll tax without specifically endorsing federal legislation. More important to black leaders, the plank failed to mention the FEPC by name and was content to "favor the enactment and just enforcement of such federal legislation as may be necessary" to ensure the "right of equal opportunity to work and to advance in life."[6]

In view of the fact that fair employment practices had become the foremost legislative demand of black Americans, this fuzzy endorsement was unacceptable to many. Louis Lautier pronounced it a "platitude" and viewed the civil-rights plank as "weak, to say the least. It is vague and indefinite and promises little." A. Philip Randolph's comments were predictably more colorful. "This is lousy," he concluded, contending that the Republican party had descended "to its lowest depths of opportunism and has become more 'Dixiecrat' than Mississippi and South Carolina." But the plank's equivocation on the FEPC was probably not designed to appeal primarily to the South. The initials had become inexorably associated with Franklin D. Roosevelt, whom Republicans longed to forget, and, more recently, with the charge that it was not only an infringement on the rights of employers but was also Communist-inspired. In view of the plank's statement of opposition "to the idea of racial segregation in the Armed Services of the United States"—a position repugnant to the white South—it is probable that the absence of the famous initials stemmed from a desire to appeal to businessmen and to Democratic as well as Republican patriots rather than to southern whites in particular.[7]

Although disappointed with the plank, some Negro leaders were able to console themselves with the expectation that Thomas E. Dewey would be nominated. There was great concern, however, that Senator Taft might win. Although Taft had the support of old-guard Negro Republicans, the more militant blacks within the party were lining up with Governor Dewey. They feared Taft's conservatism on social-welfare legislation at a time when it appeared that the Republican nominee would also be the next president.[8]

Not all Negro leaders, however, were enamored with the New York governor. Some supported his nomination only because of the mediocrity of his competitors among Republicans. Others, like Walter White and the *Chicago Defender*, believed that the Democratic party was the most promising vehicle for civil-rights progress, if only because the party's presidential wing seemed more receptive to the pleas of black Americans. As early as July 1947, the *Defender* had launched a campaign against Dewey and his position on states' rights. In March 1948 Walter White devoted one of his newspaper columns to Dewey, "whose record is best described as spotty" and whose ambivalence justified the widespread wisecrack that he "would rather be president than right." In June, White argued in particular that the New York governor had refused to support fair employment legislation in his state in 1944 until after he had secured the presidential nomination. But others were edging toward an endorsement of Dewey for president in November even before his nomination in June. In May, for example, the *Amsterdam News* declared outright for Dewey. "In the White House," the editor wrote, "this great American and friend of the Negro and human decency would have greater influence to advance the cause of democracy throughout the nation."[9]

Certainly the Republican party came up with an attractive ticket when it nominated Governor Dewey on the third ballot and chose Governor Earl Warren of California as his running mate, even though earlier in the year the latter's record on civil rights had been a matter of some dispute. In April, in a biting editorial entitled "Warren? Are You Kidding?", the *Afro-American* had listed many grievances against the California governor. "Mention the name of . . . Warren as a potential compromise candidate for the Republican presidential nomination," contended the editor, "and colored voters in Los Angeles will laugh in your face." Three weeks later, the paper abruptly reversed itself, suggesting that there was nothing wrong with Warren's heart, only with his tactics in failing to win civil-rights measures from the state legislature.[10]

Actually, as far as black Americans were concerned, the ticket of Dewey and Warren was the best they could expect from the Republicans. In fact, there was considerable jubilation, although Ralph Matthews, columnist for the *Afro-American*, reminded his readers that they were "still only the front men for a motley collection of mediocre performers whose actions in Congress have been something less than lousy," which was an inelegant way of saying that Dewey had to run on Taft's record. Even the *Chicago Defender*, which would endorse Truman in the general election, applauded this "notable victory" of the liberal wing of the Republican party. It also issued a warning: "Those Democrats who are determined to repudiate President Truman and his civil rights program are courting disaster for the Democratic party. Should they win control in Philadelphia, they will drive Negroes . . . into the Republican camp."[11]

Black leaders were understandably nervous about the Democratic convention, set to open on July 12, and their concern embraced both the platform and the prospective candidates. The collapse of the Eisenhower boom shortly before the convention, however, ensured Truman's nomination and permitted Negroes and northern liberals, led by members of the ADA, to concentrate attention on the party's platform. Rumors about the civil-rights plank were disquieting. On June 22, 1948, Congressman John Rankin of Mississippi emerged from the White House to deliver a prepared statement in which he implied that the South would adhere to a plank along the lines of the generalized version in the 1944 platform, a plank unacceptable, as it turned out, in the heated politics of 1948.[12]

As usual, Walter White appeared before the platform committee to deliver an impassioned plea for a strong plank. "The day of reckoning has come," the NAACP leader warned, "when the Democratic party must decide whether it is going to permit bigots to dictate its philosophy and policy or whether the party can rise to the heights of Americanism which alone can justify its continued existence." During his testimony, as well as that of Channing Tobias, according to a report in the *Afro-American*, "a strange silence" greeted their sharply worded demands, and southern members of the committee "merely sat back and smiled." This prompted the paper to conclude that "it looks like a deal has already been made."[13]

The *Afro-American's* suspicions were partially correct, although the situation was a good deal more complicated than the newspaper's commentary implied. Having virtually bagged the nomination, Truman sought to prevent a massive southern walkout over the civil-rights plank by seeking the middle ground between the demands of white southerners and those of northern liberals, although, apparently, there was disagreement within the Truman ranks over what the middle ground should be. The evidence suggests that administration stalwarts in Congress, particularly Senators Francis J. Myers, Scott Lucas, and Howard McGrath, were willing to settle for a paraphrase of the 1944 plank, as McGrath had suggested in his meeting with southern governors in February and to reporters during a news conference on July 10.[14] The White House staff, led by Clark Clifford, apparently wanted something stronger and more specific, while stopping short of a plank that would provoke widespread southern rebellion during and after the convention.

In the days prior to the convention the White House staff was in constant communication with William Batt, director of the Research Division of the Democratic National Committee, exchanging ideas as well as specific drafts of the platform. On July 9 Batt congratulated Clifford on the "superb stuff" in the fourth draft of the platform, particularly the "powerful Civil Rights plank." The statement on civil rights, though written mostly in general terms, specifically endorsed legislation "recommended by President Truman," which obviously would offend southern sensibilities. On July 11 Clifford discussed the administration's platform proposals in Philadelphia with Senator Myers, chairman of the platform committee, devoting considerable time to civil rights. Clifford also indicated to Myers that the president "was convinced that he could not run on a weak civil-rights plank."[15]

Nonetheless, what emerged from a platform subcommittee over the weekend was only a thinly disguised rewrite of the weak 1944 statement, one that was unacceptable to the militants of the Americans for Democratic Action as well as to southern conservatives, who had found a similar plank distasteful but not unpalatable in 1944. Caught in the middle, the Truman forces united and eventually agreed upon a plank more specific than the subcommittee's version and stronger than southerners wanted, although weaker than the White House draft. ADA leaders, led by Andrew Biemiller and Hubert Humphrey, were still dissatisfied; and in a final committee session marked by discourtesy and rage on both sides, the northern rebels lost their fight to commit the party to the specific civil-rights proposals outlined by the president in his message of February 2. Senator Lucas epitomized the temper of the session when he asked about Humphrey, then mayor of Minneapolis and a candidate for the Senate: "Who is this pipsqueak who wants to redo Franklin D. Roosevelt's work and deny the wishes of the present president of the United States?"[16] Although the ADA forces were soundly defeated in the committee, Biemiller promised to carry the fight to the convention floor.

The administration's forces could not take Biemiller's threat lightly, not only because of the damage that a floor fight might inflict on the public image of a party already rent with dissension but also because the ADA's strength was greater than the number of its delegates—120—might indicate. This pregnant fact emerged in a floor fight on July 13, when a Negro delegate challenged the credentials of the Mississippi delegation because of its pledge not to support the party if the convention nominated Truman and adopted a civil-rights program. Pandemonium broke loose; and when order was finally restored, the motion was defeated. It was clear, however, that many northern delegates were in an angry mood; and this encouraged the Biemiller forces to strive to amend the civil-rights plank on the floor of the convention. They were also encouraged when some of the northern big-city bosses, desperately hoping to win on the local level even if Truman went down nationally, promised support for the minority plank. One of them concluded, "This is the only way we can win the election, by stirring up the minorities and capturing the cities," adding, "and besides, I'd also like to kick those southern bastards in the teeth for what they did to Al Smith in 1928." And the ADA delegates were elated when Hubert Humphrey agreed to present the minority plank to the convention, although only after the addition of a statement commending the president for "his courageous stand on the issue of civil rights," which permitted the young politician to maintain a bridge with the administration.[17]

The floor fight erupted on July 14, when four amendments to the civil-rights plank were introduced before the convention. Three were southern proposals with a states' rights flavor and the fourth was the ADA plank, which differed mainly from the majority version in its demand for congressional action on fair employment practices, mob violence, and equality in political participation and military service. In presenting their amendments, southern spokesmen were modest and restrained; and it was Humphrey, speaking last for the liberal plank, who infused the lackluster session with enthusiasm. "There are those who say to you—we are rushing this issue of civil rights. I say we are a hundred and seventy-two years late," the young mayor exclaimed. Then he said, "There are those who say—this issue of civil rights is an infringement on states' rights. The time has arrived for the Democratic party to get out of the shadow of states' rights and walk forthrightly into the bright sunshine of human rights." With that, northern delegates erupted into a ten-minute demonstration. The convention then moved to a vote, and the three southern amendments went down quickly at the hands of a coalition of northern liberals and administration forces. The alliance then split. Although most of the administration's congressional leaders, in collaboration with the South, voted against the Humphrey-Biemiller amendment, the northern liberals carried the day by a close vote. Incredibly enough in the face of the South's obstinance and the administration's reluctance, a strong civil-rights plank had become part of the platform.[18]

Through it all, the president preserved a discreet silence. The final plank was probably stronger than he would have liked as a presidential candidate confronted with the possibility of losing most of the South in November, despite his later statement that the plank was his own.[19] But all he had to do was accept it. After all, the final civil-rights plank still fell short of some of the recommendations in his message of February 2. It did not include, for example, any mention of home rule for the District of Columbia, though it did endorse suffrage for its residents. Nor did it identify the FEPC by name; instead, much like the Republican platform, it called for "the right to equal opportunity of employment." Moreover, although generally stronger than its Republican counterpart, the plank promised only "the right of equal treatment in the service and defense of our nation," while the Republicans had specifically declared their opposition to segregation itself. The platform also embraced other civil-rights recommendations of the president, thus appealing to minorities other than black Americans. It urged immediate statehood for Hawaii and Alaska and increased self-government for the Virgin Islands, Guam, Samoa, and Puerto Rico, and condemned the "inadequate and bigoted" displaced persons bill passed by the Eightieth Congress.[20]

Southern reaction to the platform and to Truman's nomination was predictable. Some delegates walked out shortly after the adoption of the minority civil-rights plank, while others remained to cast their presidential ballots for Senator Richard Russell. Truman, however, won on the first ballot, though he was denied the traditional unanimity;

and Senator Barkley, a southern moderate on the race issue, was selected as his running mate. The president's acceptance address delighted the delegates. Reflecting his new oratorical approach, Truman spoke from an outline in terse, biting phrases. He promised victory in November—which his audience found difficult to believe in, despite the euphoria of the moment—boasted of the many Democratic achievements, and displayed contempt for the Eightieth Congress of "special privilege." He also dealt skillfully with the civil-rights issue. Referring to his recommendations to Congress on civil rights, he noted that "some of the members of my own party disagree with me violently on this matter. But they stand up and do it openly! People can tell where they stand." He continued by saying that the Republicans "all professed to be for these measures. But Congress failed to act." In concluding, he surprised the delegates and angered Republicans when he revealed his intention of calling Congress into special session, on July 26, so that the conservative Republican Congress would have the opportunity to translate their party's liberal platform into law.[21]

Never before had black Americans been so jubilant, and their enthusiasm often embraced the candidates and platforms of both parties. Columnist Louis Lautier spoke for many when he noted: "Colored voters find themselves fortunately situated. Both President Truman and Governor Dewey are excellent candidates . . . both parties are committed to a civil-rights program." Walter White declared that the strong civil-rights plank in the Democratic platform marked "the greatest turning point for the South and for America since the Civil War"; and he argued that both parties were now committed to the recommendations of the President's Committee on Civil Rights.[22]

Meanwhile southern dissidents were busy transforming talk into action. Faithful to their pledge of May 10 at Jackson, Mississippi, to hold a rump convention if the Democrats nominated Truman and adopted a civil-rights plank, various southern Democrats assembled in Birmingham, Alabama, on July 17 to launch the States' Rights party. It was clear from the beginning that only a part of the South would secede from the party of Harry S. Truman. But what the convention lacked in wide southern support, it more than made up for in enthusiasm. Waving Confederate flags, while rebel yells pierced the convention hall, the delegates unanimously nominated South Carolina's Governor J. Strom Thurmond for president and Mississippi's Governor Fielding Wright for vice-president on a platform denouncing "totalitarian government" and advocating "segregation of the races." Although the so-called Dixiecrats could not realistically expect victory in November, they could vengefully hope to deprive Truman of victory.[23]

Those backing Henry Wallace's third-party candidacy were equally displeased with the results of the Democratic convention, particularly the adoption of the strong civil-rights statement. They feared, with good reason, that Truman and the platform would limit their inroads into the minority vote. Indeed, shortly after the Democratic convention, some Negro commentators called for Wallace to withdraw as a candidate. C. B. Baldwin, Wallace's campaign manager, tried to head off such suggestions when he noted sarcastically that the Democrats had nominated "the man nobody wanted and adopted a program nobody meant." There was further cause for alarm in the fact that Wallace's popularity had not increased. From January to July 1948 Wallace had been running downhill, as both foreign and domestic events seemed to conspire against him. He had also compounded his problems with a number of political blunders, the most monumental of which was his refusal to disavow Communist support at a time when genuine fear of the Soviet Union was on the rise.[24]

None of this seemed to faze the delegates of the "new party" as they trooped enthusiastically into Philadelphia for the opening of their convention on July 23. Consistent with the party's bid for minority votes, blacks played conspicuous roles throughout the convention. Charles P. Howard, a black lawyer and a former Republican, delivered the keynote address after W. E. B. DuBois, although he was in attendance, had declined; Shirley Graham, the biographer of Frederick Douglass, spoke about the tyranny of America; Larkin Marshall, the first black senatorial candidate from Georgia since Reconstruction, nominated Senator Glen Taylor of Idaho for the vice-presidency; Paul Robeson spoke and sang; and Dean Joseph Johnson of Howard University's medical school occasionally presided over the platform committee and served on the drafting committee with Mrs. Paul Robeson.[25]

The delegates of the "new party" opted for the name Progressive party and nominated Wallace and Taylor on a platform that condemned Truman's foreign and domestic policies. The civil-rights plank, as might be expected, not only indicted the record of the old parties but specifically condemned "segregation and discrimination in all of its forms and in all places."[26] The whole was an attractive package to minorities; but Communist influence on the deliberations of the convention, although it has been exaggerated, largely offset the platform's appeal at this stage of the campaign.

The actions of the Truman administration in the weeks following the Democratic convention also contributed to the increasing isolation of the Progressive party. After his nomination had been secured and Congress had approved the Marshall Plan, selective service, and military appropriations, Truman could respond to his own promises and to the increasing pressures of the civil-rights movement. He also had the advantage that an incumbent president has of being able to campaign while appearing to be engaged in his official duties. On July 20, for example, he paid public tribute in a special White House ceremony to Brigadier General B. O. Davis, Sr., upon the Negro soldier's retirement from the army after a half-century of service.[27]

On July 26 Truman delivered his surprise packages, Executive Orders 9980 and 9981. Fulfilling a long-delayed promise made in his special message of February 2, Executive Order 9980 proclaimed the policy of "fair employment throughout the federal establishment, without discrimination because of race, color, religion, or national origin," and directed each department of the executive branch to appoint a fair employment officer to supervise operating procedures, to receive complaints, and to take "necessary corrective or disciplinary action" in consultation with his department head. The order also established a Fair Employment Board in the Civil Service Commission to review cases and to report to the president when necessary to maintain the fair employment program. Obviously, the program would take time to implement; and there would be variances in departmental operating procedures, although at least eighteen agencies had established such procedures by the end of the year. There were also outright refusals to obey the presidential order. On September 17, for example, Mortimer Jordan, Collector of Internal Revenue in Alabama, informed Secretary of the Treasury John Snyder that he had no intention of following the directive. Jordan was subsequently removed.[28]

The other order, 9981, was more significant, not only for its political import at the moment but also in terms of its impact. The order paraphrased the Democratic platform in calling for "equality of treatment and opportunity for all persons in the armed services without regard to race, color, religion, or national origin," and it promised implementation "as rapidly as possible." To assist or prod the military toward achieving this goal, the president created the Committee on Equality of Treatment and Opportunity in the Armed Services.[29]

Although the administration had apparently decided late in June to issue such an executive order, the statements of both major party platforms concerning discrimination in the military and the pressure of civil-rights advocates made it imperative to release the order directly after the conventions. A. Philip Randolph, for example, had repeatedly threatened that Negro youths would fail to register for the new draft, scheduled to begin on August 16, unless the president issued an executive order abolishing segregation. Behind this threat he had a new organization entitled the League for Non-Violent Civil Disobedience Against Military Segregation. On July 15 he and Grant Reynolds had written to the president, contending that the statements of both platforms had presented him with a "bipartisan mandate to end military segregation forthwith by the issuance of an executive order." They also pointed out that "the date for registration under the draft is only a month away and it is the hope of all Negro youth that there will be an alternative beyond submission to a discriminatory law and imprisonment for following the dictates of self-respect." The ADA's Leon Henderson had also reminded Truman of the platform promises of both parties and had urged an executive order abolishing segregation "so that the armed forces of the world's greatest democracy may become in truth the world's most democratic armed forces."[30]

Public reaction to the president's order on military discrimination was divided. Henry Wallace denounced it as an "empty gesture," and southerners came up with the usual strictures. Surprisingly, Negroes were far from unanimous. The *Chicago Defender*, already committed to Truman, contended that the executive orders were "unprecedented since the time of Lincoln" and argued that American citizens would not "permit Mr. Truman to be crucified on a cross of racial bigotry." Others, however, observed that the word "segregation" did not appear in the presidential order and wondered if black Americans were about to be given another example of white obfuscation.[31] The situation was complicated further when the press picked up Chief of Staff Omar Bradley's statement that the army was not a social laboratory and would change its racial policies when the nation as a whole had changed. Although General Bradley's statement carried the connotation of insubordination, he had not read the president's order, was unaware that reporters were in the audience, and had inadvertently mixed up his words.[32]

As it turned out, Bradley's bobble worked to the advantage of black Americans and, ultimately, to the administration itself. The matter inevitably came up in the president's news conference of July 29. Truman denied that Bradley had favored "segregation in the lower echelons of the army," but more important was his response to a reporter who wondered if his order envisioned "eventually the end of segregation." "Yes," replied the president flatly; and that was that.[33]

For the first time, Harry Truman had publicly committed himself to the end of segregation in the armed forces, although he had implied earlier that segregation was discriminatory, particularly in his special message of February 2.

The rest was anticlimactic. When A. Philip Randolph wondered if Truman would fulfill his public commitment, Senator McGrath met with his group on August 2 and assured them that the president's committee would follow the directives of the president. On August 18 Randolph announced the end of his civil-disobedience campaign on the basis of "assurance that segregation in the armed services is unequivocally banned under the executive order of July 26," an expression more of hope than of fact. But the executive orders deflated the pressure from black leaders for the remainder of the election campaign. Although the NAACP did not endorse a presidential candidate, because of its nonpartisan status, most of its members were happy with Truman. "His new orders," editorialized the *Crisis*, "represent a spirit and a courage on these issues as refreshing as they are rare. A standard has been set for government administrators of the present and the future."[34]

Truman had been making political capital elsewhere. His announcement of a special session had allowed him a momentary political advantage, of which the opposition was clearly aware. The *New York Times* observed that the president's purpose was to "attempt to put the Republicans on the spot for their failure to enact legislation—principally in the matter of low-cost housing and price-control." Truman admitted this later in his *Memoirs*. "Of course," he recalled, "I knew that the special session would produce no results in the way of legislation. But I felt justified in calling the Congress back to Washington to prove to the people whether the Republican platform really meant anything or not."[35]

To dramatize the special session, Truman appeared in person before a joint session of Congress on July 27, where he presented his legislative requests. Speaking in careful, restrained language, in striking contrast with the strident tone of his acceptance address, the president identified two critical areas—housing and inflation—for congressional action. He also hoped for "other important legislative measures on which delay would injure us at home and impair our world relations." Among other things, he urged the enactment of those measures that he had "recommended last February to protect and extend basic civil rights of citizenship and human liberty." Noting that Congress had enacted legislation only with respect to Japanese-Americans, he pleaded for those other measures "necessary to carry out our American ideals of liberty and justice for all."[36]

Truman apparently hoped for congressional action on housing and inflation, despite the confession in his *Memoirs* that he was playing politics. No one seriously expected Congress to pass a civil-rights bill, least of all the president, and he carefully played down the issue. But it was hoped that some action would be taken on other matters, and careful planning on the part of the administration preceded delivery of the message to Congress. In particular, the White House consulted with members of the cabinet and with Democratic leaders in Congress. Democratic strategists also sought to mobilize outside forces in support of the president's requests and at least to create the illusion of administrative efforts for civil rights. Consulting with representatives of the NAACP, the ACLU, and other civil-rights organizations, members of the Democratic National Committee's Research Division urged them to press for continuation of the session until the president's civil-rights program had been enacted, but warned, "Under no circumstances must it be a political football and used to becloud the pressing problems of inflation, housing, education."[37] This is to a large extent what happened. Few liberal Democrats, in the White House or in Congress, were willing to put civil rights first, which lessened their credibility among racial minorities and weakened the civil-rights movement of the time.

Faced with the prospect of easy victory in November and having a presidential candidate who was reluctant to become entangled in the politics of the special session, Republicans planned less carefully. Herbert Brownell, Dewey's campaign manager, sought to offset any criticism of congressional inaction by arguing that before the Republicans could enact their platform, it was first necessary to elect a Republican president to lead a Republican Congress. The *Afro-American*, however, rejected this logic, contending that "the opportunity is certainly theirs. What they do with it will be a fair test of the party's leadership."[38]

But Republicans were not bereft of inspiration. If the president could play politics, so could they, and Senate Republicans came up with the tactic of placing an anti-poll-tax bill first on the agenda. Such a bill had passed the House in 1947 and now awaited consideration in the Senate. To prevent a vote on it, Republicans reasoned, southern Democrats would launch a filibuster, thereby embarrassing the president. Thus, on July 29, Senator Kenneth S. Wherry moved to consider the anti-poll-tax bill, and the inevitable occurred when southern Democrats objected strenuously on the grounds of unconstitutionality. On August 2 Wherry sought to invoke cloture on the measure, but the chair ruled that under existing rules cloture could not be applied, and the debate continued. Seeking to offset southern arguments concerning constitutionality, Senator Morse reminded his colleagues that Congress had legislated specifically against the poll tax in the soldier vote bill of 1942. He also recalled that Truman and Barkley had voted then against the anti-poll-tax amendment to that bill, though both had supported the final soldier vote bill which included this provision.[39] The subsequent debate and maneuvers on the 1948 anti-poll-tax bill consumed half of the two-week special session. Finally, on August 4, the Senate voted sixty-nine to sixteen in favor of a motion by Wherry that automatically removed the anti-poll-tax bill from the agenda. That action effectively terminated consideration of civil-rights legislation in the special session.

Civil-rights organizations had been painfully reminded of the power of southern Democrats to prevent action on civil-rights measures. But they were also keenly aware of the fact that Senate Republicans had voted unanimously for Wherry's motion, while liberal Democrats and the Democratic leadership had supplied all sixteen votes in opposition. Even before the end of the session, Walter White unleashed a torrent of invective at the Republican leadership and southern Democrats, identifying the latter as those "morons of the Senate who fear with a mortal terror that any interference with the Dixie sport of lynching, disfranchisement or second class citizenship for Negroes would instantaneously mean that their wives and daughters would flee in ecstasy to the Harlems of the South." Republicans were delighted with the Dixiecrat filibuster, he maintained, and "sat back and chortled, believing that the voters are so dumb that they could not see through the transparent dishonesty of the *opera bouffe* which was being staged."[40]

Republicans were scarcely more responsive to other presidential requests. Although Congress did provide for bank and consumer credit controls as well as for additional public housing, these provisions fell short of Truman's recommendations. The administration's political ploy therefore had been a success. On August 12, shortly after the adjournment of the special session, the White House released a scorecard contrasting the president's requests with Congress's inadequate action. This also prompted comparisons between the performance of the Republican Congress with the promises of the Republican platform. Moreover, during his news conference on the same day, Truman was asked if he would label it a "do-nothing" session. Quickly exploiting the situation, he replied that indeed the term "do-nothing" applied to the deliberations of the entire Eightieth Congress.[41]

The administration had taken the offensive, and the customary August lull during a campaign year was not allowed to destroy the advantage. Throughout the month, while other candidates prepared for the fall campaign, the president skillfully exploited the advantages of his office, issuing various statements denouncing the "feeble" efforts of the Eightieth Congress. At the urging of David Niles, he also met with Negro leaders of Harlem, including the "unofficial" mayor, who pledged their support.[42] And behind the scenes, Democratic strategists prepared for the greatest effort in the history of the party to attract the black vote.

Organized Negro pressure on the administration had evaporated, but no one assumed that the black voter was a captive of the Democratic party, particularly because of the threat of Wallace's candidacy. The Research Division of the Democratic National Committee, created earlier in the year, contributed many tactical suggestions as well as detailed data, including a twenty-three-page "fact sheet" outlining the administration's accomplishments in the area of civil rights. It was a comprehensive brief, which, aside from the obvious, included such things as the Justice Department's amicus curiae briefs in the restrictive covenant cases of *Shelley* v. *Kraemer* and *Hurd* v. *Hodge,* a report of the administration's intervention in court cases in New Mexico and Arizona to permit Indians in those states to vote, and the Justice Department's argument in the Supreme Court case of *Takahashi* v. *Fish and Game Commission of California,* which contended successfully that the state law prohibiting Japanese-Americans from commercial fishing violated the Constitution.[43]

In August, William Batt of the Research Division also forwarded to Clark Clifford a six-page memorandum outling strategy for the president's campaign, which Clifford in turn, after slight revision, sent to the president. The document stressed three main objectives—to win the majority of political independents by identifying Dewey with the "failures" of the Eightieth Congress; to solidify the Democratic appeal to workers, veterans, and Negroes without overlooking farmers and small businessmen; and to cut into normal Republican areas by highlighting the president's program for "peace." The president should "speak out fully" on his civil-rights contributions. "His record proves that he *acts* as well as *talks* Civil Rights," the memo argued; "the Negro votes in the crucial states will more than cancel out any votes the president may lose in the South." Geographically, the president should tour the Midwest and Far West and then finish in the East, where he should emphasize the housing shortage, inflation, labor, and civil rights. And in New York he "should appear for a major speech at a mass meeting in Harlem, a center of Negro population. His appearance there would have a powerful effect on Negro voters throughout the United States." Finally, the memorandum implied that the South should be ignored, except for a brief trip where the president could remind southerners of the economic benefits of the New Deal.[44]

It was a well-reasoned document and, with some variations, accurately described the campaign that Truman would wage. On his transcontinental tour, beginning on September 17, he launched a well-balanced attack, indicting the "do-nothing" Congress everywhere, while exploiting issues of local concern. As he swept across the country, he ignored civil rights, an issue that had never electrified the farmers and small-town people of the West. California, where Wallace was considered strong and where Warren had much home-state appeal, was another matter. In a major address in Los Angeles, Truman opened fire on Wallace, contending that Communists controlled his party, that a vote for him was wasted, and that the Democratic party was truly liberal in seeking, among other things, to "extend civil rights."[45]

On his return journey through Texas and Oklahoma, he studiously avoided any mention of civil rights, or of Strom Thurmond, for that matter, which prompted some newspaper comment. In Dallas, Truman reportedly spoke to a desegregated audience in Rebel Stadium; and it did him no harm, with black or white voters, when he said in response to Tom Clark's introduction of him as the man who stopped Joe Louis: "It wasn't Joe Louis I stopped—it was John. I haven't quite that much muscle." Moving north into Oklahoma and then to southern Illinois, the "Little Egypt" area of agriculture and coal mining, Truman evoked the memory of William Jennings Bryan, as he warned his audiences that "big-business Republicans have begun to nail the American consumer to the wall with spikes of greed." In southern Illinois he also informed his audiences that his administration had "continued the fight to expand our civil liberties by new measures against discrimination." He did not go beyond that for the time being. On October 2 the president was back in Washington, satisfied with his performance and with his reception.[46]

The administration's strategy was clear. By avoiding a confrontation over civil rights and by refusing to admit Thurmond's existence, Truman hoped to restrict Dixiecrat strength to the deep South. Indeed, for the remainder of the campaign, he ignored the South, except for speaking in Miami to the American Legion Convention, where he stressed the issues of peace and war, and in Raleigh, North Carolina, where he spoke at the dedication of a monument to Presidents Jackson, Polk, and Johnson. Truman's Raleigh speech was a thoughtful and skillful performance, designed to appeal to southern moderate opinion and yet to reaffirm his commitment to fulfill his constitutional duty. Identifying himself with the three presidents, each of whom had fought "the forces of pressure and persuasion which sought to make him act as a representative of a part of the nation only," Truman formulated a single message from this lesson of the past: "Do your duty, and history will do you justice."[47]

From the moment that Thurmond had opened his campaign at a watermelon festival in Cherryville, North Carolina, he had tried desperately to provoke Truman into a debate, or at least to force him to respond to his accusations. And Thurmond was a clever performer. He concentrated on equating the civil-rights program with communism, an association that was becoming increasingly popular in right-wing circles. On August 21, for example, he alleged that the administration was "honeycombed" with Communists who were dictating policy, particularly on civil rights. His running mate, Governor Wright, declared that the FEPC was "hatched in the brains of Communists."[48]

On September 25 Thurmond wired Truman in El Paso, noting "the amazing parallel between the ideology and administrative provisions of the proposed FEPC bill, which you support, and Communistic Russian all races law promulgated by Stalin." He hoped that Truman would "not duck any of these issues while in the South." There were also naked appeals to the racist vote. A form postcard sent to southern workingmen urged labor unions to fight Truman, the man seeking to "force you to work with Negroes and other undesirables." Through it all, Truman remained imperturbable, and the strategy paid political dividends. By mid October, it was clear that the States' Rights party was becoming increasingly isolated. Prestigious southern newspapers shunned the party; politicians feared the loss of patronage or remembered past favors; and nearly everyone realized the hopelessness of the cause.[49]

Although a few black critics carped at the president for his reluctance to speak out boldly on civil rights during the first part of his campaign,[50] most of the major Negro newspapers maintained a discreet silence—and for a somewhat embarrassing reason. Many were now in the process of endorsing Governor Dewey,[51] who was actually saying no more about civil rights than the president and a good deal less about social-welfare legislation. Indeed, both Dewey and Warren, who had initially won political reputations as relentless prosecutors, were resting their case on a mountain of platitudes, content with the expectation of a landslide victory in November. Such an approach was a serious miscalculation as far as the Negro vote was concerned. Although Dewey's record on race relations was impressive, it was also unknown to the average black voter outside the state of New York. Truman, however, had reaped the benefits of vast publicity since the report of his Committee on Civil Rights. The Republican National Committee did seek to publicize Dewey's record through the activities of its Negro Division and lavish advertisements in the Negro press.[52]

The New York governor, however, made no serious effort to entice black voters; and Negroes in his audiences responded accordingly. Negro columnists traveling with the "Dewey Victory Special" as it clicked across the country commented on the lack of enthusiasm for the governor and on the small number of Negroes in his average-sized crowds. And in Oakland, California, where one-third of the audience was black, he said nothing about civil rights, although in Santa Fe he did refer to the existence of an FEPC in New York state. Black citizens were also distressed when Dewey advocated that the African colonies be returned to Italy; this prompted the National Council of Negro Women, meeting in its thirteenth annual convention, to criticize the governor.[53]

Although Dewey took a firm stand on civil rights in New Castle, Pennsylvania, his speech in New York City on October 21 best illustrated his low-keyed campaign approach to the issue of equal justice. Then Dewey declared:

> Government . . . must guide its way by one single standard of equal justice and equal treatment for all.
>
> By a faithful adherence to this standard we can meet even our most difficult problems of discrimination against minority groups, of prejudice, of bigotry, of denial of certain human rights.
>
> From my own experience in this state with the largest minority groups in the nation, I have found it possible to find peaceful, honest solutions to problems which fester when they are ignored or explode if they are mishandled.
>
> By a simple re-discovery of our devotion to human rights and the protection of others from the abuse of those rights, we

can draw a line through every conflict and draw it straight and true. It can be drawn so that both civil liberty and social responsibility complement and fortify each other.

We should deal with the problem of social injustice wherever it is to be found in America and solve that problem in American terms.[54]

Nor were the Republican leaders that were speaking for Dewey going overboard in their enthusiasm for civil rights. In Charlotte, North Carolina, Harold Stassen promised southern voters that Dewey, if elected, would find "an intelligent compromise between states' rights and human rights which would satisfy Dixie." Although Senator Taft contended to a northern audience that a Republican Congress would enact something in the way of civil-rights legislation, he dropped the subject in the South, where he took a states' rights approach and indicted the "planned economy and totalitarian regulation of the Truman New Deal." Plainly, neither major party was inclined to discuss the issue in the South, although both were interested in the region's votes.[55]

Henry Wallace was not as reluctant, and during the fall he invaded the South, where several untoward incidents occurred. His campaign again took him to all parts of the country, but the enthusiasm shown earlier in the year was no longer apparent, except in New York City. The Progressive convention may have inspired some of the faithful, but the allegations of Communist influence on its proceedings and within the party increasingly isolated Wallace from the mainstream of America, particularly as the cold war promised to warm up. And the leadership of the Americans for Democratic Action, now in the Truman camp, was not about to allow anyone to forget the charges. In October the ADA released a forty-two-page indictment of Wallace, the burden of which was to pin the Communist tag on the Progressive party.[56]

Although Negroes generally had been reluctant to indulge in such accusations, perhaps because they, too, had been the object of suspicion, an increasing number of blacks began to perceive a reddish hue to the party. Columnist Earl Brown, who had attended the Progressive convention, reported that he "saw Communists and their allies and stooges running the Third Party convention as ruthlessly as any dictator ever ran a political show." Although appreciative of Wallace's courage, the *Chicago Defender* noted that "in order to love him, you must also love his motley crew of Communist stooges, for he has refused to repudiate the Commies." A. Philip Randolph, too, joined the chorus of condemnation, although he restricted his praise to Norman Thomas, then campaigning for the sixth and last time as the Socialist party's presidential nominee.[57]

The Wallace candidacy also ignited long-smoldering differences within the NAACP, particularly between Walter White and W. E. B. DuBois, its research director. An avid supporter of Henry Wallace, DuBois found White's thinly disguised admiration for Truman unbearable, particularly when White excoriated Wallace in his syndicated column for his notoriously "bad" performance on racial matters while secretary of agriculture and of commerce. In subsequent columns, White evaluated Dewey's record on human and civil rights as "that of a man who coolly appraises political advantage and acts accordingly," while "it must be recognized that no president in American history has made as frontal an attack on racial and religious discrimination as Truman." The bitter disagreement between the two NAACP executives led to DuBois's ouster as research director.[58]

The affair had portentous consequences for the NAACP. White's public expressions in favor of Truman challenged the credibility of the organization's claim to nonpartisanship, and White found himself the subject of increasing criticism in the Negro press, particularly from those newspapers championing Dewey. In his own inimitable way, George Schuyler undoubtedly spoke for many when he concluded: "While I do not usually agree with Darkwater (W. E. B. DuBois), the Leftwing octogenarian who has long and futilely aspired to the leadership of U.S. Senegambians for the benefit of Stalin, I must admit that he 'has something' when he charges that Blondie (Walter White) is riding the Truman New (?) Deal bandwagon. Of course, Walter replies that the NAACP is non-partisan, but the people who believe that should have their heads examined."[59]

Democratic strategists did not permit White's virtual endorsement of Truman to delude them into assuming that he, or any Negro for that matter, could deliver the black vote in November.[60] Although Wallace's overall appeal had fallen from its crest, it appeared that he still retained impressive support from black citizens, at least judging by the crowds of them in his audiences and by the number of Negroes running on the Progressive ticket for local offices. As a consequence, the Democratic National Committee was engaged in its greatest effort to woo black Americans. The 1948 Democratic campaign was far more than a one-man affair. Early in August, National Chairman McGrath publicly announced that the committee's Negro Division had been disbanded and its black members distributed throughout the staff; segregation and discrimination, he announced, were inconsistent with the president's policy with regard to federal employment and the armed forces.[61]

Under the supervision of John P. Davis, a Negro who was Assistant Director of Publicity, the committee also published a four-page newspaper entitled the *Truman Record*, which contained articles by William L. Dawson, Channing Tobias, and others, emphasizing Truman's contributions to civil rights. A million copies were distributed, with special concentration on the key states of New York, Pennsylvania, and Illinois. In addition to other pamphlets and brochures, the committee published three million copies of a pictorial history of *The Story of Harry S. Truman*, which the opposition labeled a comic book. The booklet pictured the president repeating phrases from his State of the Union address of January 7, 1948, including his statement that "our first goal is to secure fully the essential human rights of our citizens," while someone in the background observed that "the right to vote must be shared by all!" The Political Action Committee of the CIO also issued a leaflet entitled "A Look at Truman's Record on Civil Rights."[62]

But the most significant tactic was the summoning of Governor William Hastie of the Virgin Islands, whose activities were designed almost entirely to undermine Wallace. On October 13, speaking at the headquarters of the Democratic National Committee, Hastie promised to visit nineteen cities on behalf of the president. He focused his criticisms on the Progressive party, "a political puppet securely tied to the Communist party line." A memorandum of White House Assistant Stephen Spingarn summarized Hastie's approach and contribution: "Throughout the campaign Hastie was the Democratic party's primary weapon against the Wallace move to suck in the uninformed Negro vote."[63]

Moreover, the Truman forces had the untiring efforts of Congressman William L. Dawson, who headed the all-black National Citizens Committee for the Reelection of President Truman. The committee pledged itself to raise $500,000; and it issued various pieces of propaganda, including a four-page statement on the "Truman Policy on Negro Health." The occasion for the statement was the publication of Federal Security Administrator Oscar R. Ewing's *The Nation's Health: A Report to the President*, a 186-page report in support of the president's national health-insurance program. Among other things, the document promised medical services to everyone "without regard to his race or religion, the color of his skin, his place of national origin or the place he lives in our land," and urged the abolition of discrimination in the training and employment of medical personnel.[64]

The Ewing report received considerable coverage. Dawson stressed its significance in his article in the *Truman Record*, and Walter White gave it a paragraph in his statement praising the president. Although the timing of the book coincided nicely with the needs of the campaign, it was not primarily a tract for the moment, for it would become the basis for the administration's proposed health program. Moreover, Ewing took his work seriously and was primarily responsible for the agreement earlier in the year to permit Negro medical personnel to practice in Gallinger Hospital in Washington, D.C. Ewing was also an active compaigner for the president. Speaking in Richmond, Virginia, to three hundred delegates of the National Urban League on September 9, he lauded Truman for his controversial and courageous stand on civil rights, insisting that every Negro who "loves his race" should support him.[65]

Finally, there remained the president, who had played down civil rights for over a month, apparently ignoring the advice of Clifford and Batt in August to speak out boldly on the subject. True, early in October he had toured Philadelphia's South Street—a black ghetto—and the *Defender* happily highlighted the fact that he was the first president to do so. But in speeches elsewhere throughout most of the month, he had avoided the issue of civil rights, except where it might be raised obliquely in connection with displaced persons legislation. Although there were indications that he already had impressive support from the black rank and file, he decided to take no chances. In the last week of the campaign, he launched an overt, almost blatant, appeal for the votes of American minorities, particularly those of Negroes, Catholics, and Jews. In arriving at the decision to do this, Truman was taking a calculated risk. Although he apparently considered most of the South safely Democratic, he also had to take into account the existence of antiminority prejudice elsewhere, for a Roper poll in September indicated the possibility of a white Protestant backlash.[66]

The new offensive was quite apparent in his speech in Chicago on October 25, where his campaign invective degenerated into demagoguery. Speaking from a prepared text, Truman ignored the "contemptible Communist minority" in order to concentrate on the "crackpot forces of the extreme right wing"—all located in the Republican party. Indeed, he more than implied that the forces behind Hitler, Mussolini, and Tojo paralleled those in influential positions in the Republican party—those who were "stirring up racial and religious prejudice against some of our fellow Americans." Nor was it simply a solitary reference. He returned to the subject, asserting that "dangerous men, who are trying to win followers for their war on democracy, are attacking Catholics, and Jews, and Negroes, and other minority races and religions"; and he particularly indicted the voices of religious prejudice for passage of the displaced persons bill. Although more subdued in Cleveland the following evening, he pointed out that the special session had not responded to his plea to enact legislation "to protect the basic rights of citizenship and human liberty."[67]

In the remaining days of the campaign, he devoted speeches to each of America's three most prominent minorities. Speaking in Boston on October 27, he concentrated on the Catholic vote, though he did note almost parenthetically that Massachusetts had abolished slavery during the Revolutionary War because "the people held that liberty was not for any one race or creed." In the course of his address, he denounced religious bigotry, particularly in the "shameful" campaign of 1928 in which "the Republican appeal was based on religious prejudice because of Al Smith's Catholic faith."[68]

Truman then moved on to New York, where he delivered a major address in Madison Square Garden. There, he appealed to Jewish members of the audience by discussing the administration's policy toward Israel, which at that moment was involved in fighting with Arab nations. The president warned his audience that he would not allow domestic politics to influence that policy, which must have provoked little applause. He then declared, however, "I have never changed my position on Palestine or Israel," which would have been news to the Zionists in the crowd, because of his earlier equivocation on the recognition of Israel.[69]

Despite the importance of the Jewish vote, particularly in New York, it should be emphasized that Truman had sought religiously to keep the Palestine issue out of the campaign. Until late October he had restricted his appeal for Jewish votes to an indictment of the Displaced Persons Act. On October 22, however, Dewey released a statement reaffirming his support of a Jewish homeland. Only then did Truman mention his own attitudes and actions in this regard, first in a public statement on October 24, then in his speech on October 28 in Madison Square Garden.[70]

His speech in Harlem the next day, however, was the highlight of the New York tour. It was a significant occasion, not only because he was the first president to speak in Harlem but also because he was to receive the Franklin D. Roosevelt Memorial Brotherhood Medal. It was, moreover, the first anniversary of the report of his Committee on Civil Rights. Consequently, Philleo Nash of the White House staff prepared carefully, and it required at least six drafts to get a message that would strike the proper tone, one without invective and virtually devoid of partisanship.[71] Speaking thoughtfully and carefully from his prepared text before an audience estimated at sixty-five thousand, the president emphasized the contribution of his Committee on Civil Rights in preparing the way for the achievement of equality and justice in America. He pointed out that over one million copies of the committee's report had been printed, and he stressed its educational value to all Americans. Governmental agencies, both state and federal, could and would act, he reminded his audience, but private action was also necessary, "for in the last analysis, freedom resides in the actions of each individual." After briefly mentioning his executive orders of July and the Department of Justice's contributions before the Supreme Court, he closed with the promise to work for the attainment of equal rights "with every ounce of strength and determination that I have." The speech was an impressive performance, but at that late date in the campaign it probably influenced few votes. In fact, some Negro papers that had endorsed Dewey failed to report it. Some southerners were aware of it, however, and at least one white editor accused the president of having advocated the abolition of southern segregation in his address.[72]

A few speeches remained, then Truman returned to Independence to vote and to await the election results. The polls showed Dewey in front, though Truman had narrowed the gap in the final weeks of the campaign. Still no one, except Truman apparently, really expected his stunning upset victory. In popular votes, Truman received 24,179,345 to Dewey's 21,991,291, Thurmond's 1,176,125, and Wallace's 1,157,326. In electoral votes, Truman won 303, with Dewey and Thurmond receiving 189 and 39, respectively. Careful strategy had paid off. Thurmond's electoral votes were confined to Alabama, Louisiana, Mississippi, and South Carolina, except for one from a Tennessee elector. The administration had been able to isolate the States' Rights party and to cut into the Wallace vote in the North at the same time. Truman also received approximately 69 percent of the black vote, and in many areas—Harlem, for example—he ran well ahead of Roosevelt's margin in 1944.[73]

Although Truman had a sizable plurality, the electoral count of 303 to 189 was misleading, for he had carried California, Illinois, and

Ohio by a total of only 58,584 votes. Had the voters shifted slightly in all three states, Dewey would have won the electoral vote and the White House. Here, the black vote played its role, for the concentration of that vote in the cities of heavily populated states contributed mightily to Truman's margin of victory in the electoral college. For example, Truman won California by 17,865, yet Negro voters in Los Angeles gave him a 25,028 margin over Dewey. Truman carried Illinois by 33,612, while Chicago's Negroes alone gave him a 128,541 plurality. In Ohio, Truman squeezed through by a mere 7,107 votes, but Negroes in Cleveland provided him with a margin of 14,713. And so it went.[74]

The substantial black vote for Truman was no mystery. Aside from the obvious propaganda value of his Committee on Civil Rights, his special message of February 2, the civil-rights plank in the Democratic platform, and the issuance of executive orders 9980 and 9981, Truman had other things working for him, including the memory of Franklin D. Roosevelt. Wallace was fatally handicapped. The increasing tension of the cold war and the accusations concerning Communist influence within his party, which Hastie effectively exploited, alienated Wallace from a growing number of black Americans. And over it all hung the indisputable fact that Wallace simply could not win. Although Dewey had a respectable record on civil rights as governor of New York, that record was largely unknown to many black voters, and Dewey chose not to enlighten them in his campaign speeches in 1948. Moreover, when white southerners rebelled out of fear that the president really "meant it," some Negroes were finally persuaded to take the Missourian at his word.

There were other reasons, economic as well as racial. The depression of the 1930s was still a vivid and painful memory to those black Americans who had lived through it. The widespread fear of a postwar depression had not materialized, and Truman reaped the benefit. Moreover, black Americans, like other low-income groups, favored social-welfare legislation, and Truman's espousal of such measures and his hard-hitting indictment of the "do-nothing" Eightieth Congress was effective in convincing many Negro workers that he was a fitting representative of the New Deal tradition. In voting for Truman, these people were motivated as much by class as by race.

Nor did Truman's veto of the Taft-Hartley Act and his exploitation of the fact during the campaign do him any harm with most black voters. Indeed, the act had been a divisive, though minor, issue within the black community since its passage in 1947. Although blacks were still blocked from entering into many unions, particularly the skilled crafts unions of the AFL, many now belonged to the CIO as a result of recruiting drives during the 1930s and of the labor shortage and the actions of Roosevelt's FEPC during the Second World War. Furthermore, leaders of the CIO, black and white alike, did their homework in educating workers to the political realities of the time.[75]

Negro workers were thus part of the CIO's bitter campaign against revision of the Wagner Act. When the Republican Congress passed the Taft-Hartley Act in 1947, prominent black leaders chose sides. Those who opposed substantial revision of the Wagner Act and supported Truman's veto included Walter White and the NAACP, A. Philip Randolph and other labor leaders, several columnists, and the *Chicago Defender* and several minor Negro newspapers.[76] Most of the major Negro papers, however, lined up in favor of Taft-Hartley, in part because of its abolition of the closed shop (which appealed to them as employers) and because it contained a clause aimed at discrimination in labor unions.[77] Thus, when the Taft-Hartley Act became a significant issue in the campaign of 1948, blacks were involved. While several Negro newspapers urged the election of Dewey in part because of the Republican-enacted Taft-Hartley Act, black as well as white CIO workers prepared to troop to the polls to vote for Truman, which in the last analysis probably hurt Wallace more than Dewey.[78]

If black workers could vote along class as well as racial lines, so, too, could black employers—which offers some explanation for the fact that all of the major Negro papers, except the *Chicago Defender*, endorsed Dewey for the presidency. Historically Republican until the New Deal, some Negro publishers were eager to return to the Republican fold; and the nominations of Willkie in 1940 and Dewey in 1944, rather than someone like Robert Taft, persuaded them to drop Roosevelt after 1936. The *Call*, in fact, had never endorsed Roosevelt, so that its support of Dewey in 1948 was completely consistent with its past editorial policy. In 1948 Dewey's strong record on civil rights persuaded some black publishers to see a standoff on that issue, and this permitted them to endorse the governor for economic reasons. Thus some favored Taft-Hartley; others wanted lower taxes; one endorsed "free enterprise"; still others were not convinced of the sincerity of the man from Missouri. The Dixiecrat rebellion persuaded some that the Democratic party was a hopeless vehicle for progress on civil rights if the rebels should return. And several reasoned that at that moment in history civil-rights legislation stood a better chance of enactment with a Republican president and a Republican Congress. With a Republican in the White House, Republicans in Congress would be under pressure to support his program, while most northern Democrats would go along because of their personal commitment and their black constituents.[79]

Truman, of course, was not without support from the black press. In addition to the *Chicago Defender*, several smaller papers across the country, including some in the South, endorsed his candidacy. Moreover, he had the support of many black columnists, who endorsed him at the same time that their editors were eulogizing Dewey. Finally, the majority of black political reporters supported the president. On the eve of the election, they polled themselves: there were fourteen in favor of Truman, three for Dewey, two for Wallace, and, unbelievably enough, one for Thurmond.[80] Thus, in some ways, black journalism in 1948 paralleled its white counterpart.

Truman's upset victory of 1948 has become part of American folklore, but the entire campaign was much more than that. For years, black Americans had anticipated the day when their votes would become numerous enough to affect presidential elections. As early as 1924 Professor Kelly Miller of Howard University had argued that as a result of the migration of southern Negroes to northern cities during the First World War, "the solid Negro vote constitutes the balance of power in the closely contested states of the North and West which usually determine the issue between the two parties."[81] The announcement was premature, but the election of 1948 made the wish a reality. It demonstrated that in a close contest the weight of America's most numerous racial minority could determine the electoral votes of large states and hence the election, assuming, of course, that the black vote was fluid enough to shift according to the interests of the moment rather than to the dictates of memory.

Moreover, throughout the year, civil rights had occupied a position of importance, evidenced by the strong statements in both party platforms and the unprecedented activities of both national committees; the president's message of February and his executive orders of July 26; the Dixiecrat defection and Wallace's courageous campaigning. This position represented the fruition of a movement that had begun at least ten years before to increase public awareness of civil-rights problems. No longer could the issue of civil rights be ignored, and in the future both parties would vie for the black vote. "From that time on," Roy Wilkins has written, "the civil-rights issue has been squarely in the national political picture of both major parties (not around the fringes as in the old days), and the non-southern Negro voting power is now balanced (in the Democratic party) against the Deep South white vote."[82]

There were other significant results. In voting for Truman in 1948, Negroes demonstrated a loyalty to the party as well as to the president. During the 1930s black Americans had abandoned their historic allegiance to the Republican party, and from 1936 on, they had voted for Roosevelt, primarily for economic and emotional reasons. The New Deal convinced most blacks that the Democratic party was preferable on "bread and butter" issues, although many still looked to the party of Lincoln for progress on civil rights. Truman's contribution was not only to confirm the Democratic party's commitment to social-welfare legislation and to invoke the memory of the economic appeal of the New Deal but, of equal importance, to champion civil rights as no Democratic president had ever done, thus neutralizing the traditional appeal of Republicans on this issue. This was quite an achievement, particularly in view of the presence and power of southern Democrats in the party, and it made it increasingly difficult for Republicans to cut into the black vote.

The election of 1948 contained other hints of the future, particularly with regard to alterations in customary voting habits and the increasing complexity of campaign strategy. In 1948, while Truman was solidifying the allegiance of Negroes to the Democratic party, he was also persuading some racist white voters to look elsewhere: the States' Rights party was the first significant manifestation of white backlash in the twentieth century—a fact that both major parties had to keep in mind when bidding for black votes in subsequent elections. In 1948 the issue of civil rights provoked conflicts only between the North and the South and within the Democratic party, although beneath the surface in northern ghettos of various white ethnic minorities lay unasked questions and unresolved answers concerning Truman's egalitarian policies. In the future, the white backlash would emerge and be present, in varying degrees, in every part of the country. Moreover, the revolt of the white South also encouraged the party of Lincoln to look South for votes in the future. But for the moment, the events of 1948 brought hope to minorities that progress would continue.

8 A NEW DAY DAWNS?

Truman's victory in November stirred hope throughout black America, for civil-rights advocates chose to interpret his election as an endorsement of his stand for equal rights. Walter White lost no time in cabling the president. "Your triumph, achieved over both the extreme Right and extreme Left," he maintained, "is a mandate under which you and the new Congress can proceed to carry out the program you outlined so clearly and courageously to the people." "The people have spoken!" exclaimed Mrs. Sadie Alexander to Francis Matthews, a fellow member of the president's civil-rights committee. "They have approved President Truman's appointment of a Committee on Civil Rights, the report of that committee and the president's determination to make the recommendations of that report a reality." Matthews agreed. Writing to the president on November 12, he rejoiced "in the vindication of your championship of our committee's report and recommendations." Truman's response was more than *pro forma*; after the customary pleasantries of thanking Matthews for his "generous words of congratulations and commendation," he penned at the bottom: "We shall win that civil rights battle just as we won the election, I am sure."[1]

Although some did not share Truman's certainty about victory on the field of civil rights, few doubted his personal commitment, and the pages of the black press were replete with glowing tributes to the president. "The future for civil rights looks brighter than it has in the history of this country," concluded a reporter for the *Courier*. "Democracy Reborn with Truman Victory," went the headline of a front-page article in the *Call*, erstwhile supporter of Governor Dewey. "No candidate for the presidency ever faced a greater combination of hostile power," editorialized the *Chicago Defender*. "In the face of such opposition Harry Truman never wavered once. He discussed every issue from civil rights to foreign policy and he took his stand without qualification or compromise."[2]

But if there was little doubt in the black press about the president, there was considerable apprehension about the new Congress, for the election had also resulted in Democratic majorities in both houses. Here, black opinion was divided. The *Chicago Defender* was convinced that Democratic control of Congress would ensure enactment of the president's program and that Truman possessed enough patronage power to keep southern politicians in line. At the very least, several newspapers expected the new Congress to legislate against lynching and the poll tax. But the *Journal and Guide* was deeply distressed. Pointing out that Sam Rayburn of Texas would serve as speaker of the House, that Vice-President Barkley of Kentucky would preside over the Senate, and that southerners would chair important committees, the paper concluded on the wry note that these facts "should give Negro leaders who had advocated Mr. Truman's election very little to be happy about."[3]

Nevertheless, for the moment Truman had the advantage, which he was determined not to lose, either with black America or with the new Congress. On November 16, in his first news conference after the election, he promised a civil-rights statement in his State of the Union message. This prompted Jonathan Daniels to write in the *Raleigh News and Observer*: "There is nothing strange about that. Indeed, one certain thing is that Harry Truman means what he says." In another news conference on December 2, Truman delighted black America with his response to a question concerning how Dixiecrat electors ought to cast their votes. "I don't want the Dixiecrat vote," the president retorted. "We won without New York and without the solid South, and I am proud of that."[4]

All this helped, of course, when Congressman Frank W. Boykin of Alabama declared in a postelection speech in Mobile that Truman, prior to the election, had confided: "Frank, I don't believe in this civil-rights program any more than you do, but we've got to have it to win." The Associated Negro Press picked up the story and also reported that Truman had "no comment" on the matter. The ANP predicted, "The statement will continue to plague and haunt him until he makes some definite statement on the congressman's speech." The alleged statement actually haunted no one. The White House subsequently denied it in private correspondence, and most Negro papers did not even bother to report it. The *Call* refused to accept it at the outset, denouncing Boykin as a southern politician habituated to "skullduggery."[5]

In his resolution not to waver on civil rights, Truman had solid support from several Democratic spokesmen and senators. When Senator Sparkman of Alabama sought to prevent a showdown in Congress by proposing the appointment of a congressional committee to investigate the problems of minorities in America, Senator Pepper of Florida rejected the idea, stating that the administration was determined to move quickly on civil rights. Vice-President-elect Barkley also chose to let people know where he stood. In a speech in New York in mid December, he made an exceptionally strong and vigorous statement in favor of civil-rights legislation, noting that "the controversial aspects of it cannot minimize our obligation to deal with it." And when Senator Sparkman promised a fight if the president refused to compromise, Senator McGrath reported that he saw "no change in the president's attitude. He is still determined to press for his program as he outlined it before the 80th Congress and during the campaign."[6]

Truman also had the same message for Walter White when he called at the White House on November 29 to present the statistics of the black vote. White later emerged to announce the president's determination to pursue his civil-rights program. "I saw no sign of any compromise," he reported. The NAACP leader was unusually optimistic. Speaking to the tenth constitutional convention of the CIO, he proclaimed that "the outlook is infinitely brighter for the stopping of reaction, for the repeal of anti-labor legislation and the enactment into law of civil-rights and social welfare legislation than any time in recent history." Yet his critical faculties had not escaped him. In his column in the *Chicago Defender*, he noted that the old guard might die but would never surrender, which "makes it imperative that liberals, and especially Negroes, waste no time jubilating over the election of a somewhat more enlightened Congress . . . or the defeat of those who attempted to lynch Harry Truman because of his civil rights program."[7]

Truman also conferred with other civil-rights advocates. On December 10 he met with four members of the National Committee on Segregation in the Nation's Capital, who presented him with the published, and abbreviated, version of the committee's comprehensive investigation of discrimination in the District of Columbia. With financial support from the Julius Rosenwald Fund, the committee had been privately organized in the fall of 1946, at the same time that Truman had created his own Committee on Civil Rights. In fact, the two committees had worked closely together. Four members of the president's

committee—Sadie Alexander, James Carey, Dorothy Tilly, and Channing Tobias—had also served on the National Committee on Segregation in the Nation's Capital, and the latter committee had supplied
the president's committee with the source material for its brief indictment of discrimination in the District.[8] Truman thus had good reason
to accept the report in an "extremely warm and cordial" manner, as
George N. Shuster, chairman of the committee on segregation in
Washington, later revealed to the press.[9]

The committee's published report, entitled *Segregation in Washington*, had been prepared by Kenesaw M. Landis, who had ruthlessly
cut the original manuscript to a brief, hard-hitting, and well-illustrated
ninety-one pages, hoping thus to achieve the maximum impact. He
succeeded. In casting a bright light on the dark side of racism, *Segregation in Washington* did for the District what *To Secure These Rights*
had done for the nation.[10] By word and picture, *Segregation in Washington* illustrated the plight of blacks living in the shadow of the
Capitol, who were suffering the degrading effects of discrimination in
employment, recreational facilities, education, restaurants, theaters,
and housing. By inference, it revealed that on racial matters the nation's capital combined the worst features of discrimination, northern
as well as southern. As a showplace of American democracy, the capital was a disgrace.

The discrimination in the District was apparent the moment a
visitor deplaned at Washington's National Airport, located on the Virginia side of the Potomac, because of its rigidly segregated restaurant
facilities. Discrimination at the airport had a long and complicated
history. Almost from the moment it opened in June 1941, Negroes had
lodged complaints. When Edgar G. Brown, then president of the
United Government Employees, was denied service and referred to
the basement to dine with the help, he staged a one-man sit-down
strike; the Southernaires, a prominent black radio group, also protested. And everyone was confused by premature reports that discrimination would not be tolerated because the airport was supervised
directly by the Civil Aeronautics Administration, which was located
within the Department of Commerce.[11]

In 1945 the situation was clarified, or so it seemed, with the settlement of a longstanding boundary dispute between the state of Virginia
and the District of Columbia. The federal government was given
exclusive jurisdiction over the National Airport, constructed on re-
claimed land on the Virginia side of the Potomac; but the law contained a joker. It stipulated that certain sections of the federal criminal

code applied to the airport, including Section 289, which provided that when the federal government assumed control of state land, the criminal laws of the state would nonetheless remain in effect; and Virginia law required segregation in "public halls." To complicate matters further, a private corporation, Air Services Terminal, Inc., was the concessionaire; and it opposed integration of its restaurant facilities.[12]

On the surface, it seemed a hopeless situation for advocates of desegregation, although some obviously were unaware of the finer points of the law. In 1945 and 1946 criticism of the Civil Aeronautics Administration mounted, and Henry Wallace, then secretary of commerce, came in for much abuse. Apparently Wallace's solicitor had informed him that he lacked authority to integrate the airport in view of the Virginia law, although a White House assistant later recalled that Wallace had never responded to White House referrals on the subject.[13] The NAACP then protested to his successor, W. Averell Harriman, who received similar advice from departmental lawyers. But unlike Wallace, Harriman pursued the matter and personally urged Congress to adopt legislation requiring integration of facilities at the National Airport. As a result, the *Chicago Defender* placed Harriman on its honor roll in 1947 "for his role in ending discrimination in the Washington airport restaurant." The announcement was premature. Congress failed to respond to Harriman's request and rejected Congressman Everett Dirksen's bill to eliminate segregation at the airport.[14]

There the matter stood while politics were being played, although the airport situation threatened to become an issue. It cropped up occasionally in criticisms of Henry Wallace, and a court case instigated by the NAACP posed a special problem for the administration. After several postponements, the case was scheduled to be heard by Judge Albert Bryan in federal district court on October 28, 1948; and the administration was thus faced with the possibility of embarrassment in the closing days of the campaign. The matter was referred to John R. Steelman, assistant to the president, who consulted with the Department of Commerce as well as with the president. Apparently, the solicitor for the Commerce Department concluded that the department lacked authority to issue a desegregation order.[15]

The Department of Justice, however, had already decided otherwise. In an unsolicited opinion, Acting Attorney General Philip B. Perlman informed Commerce Secretary Charles Sawyer on October 27 that he had the necessary authority. Pointing out that the Justice Department had been in contact with Judge Bryan, which evidently led to a further postponement of the case, Perlman requested action by the Commerce Department "at an early date." The Justice Department had thoroughly studied the problem, Perlman contended, and believed that the Civil Aeronautics Administrator could issue regulations for the airport. Presumably, the Department of Justice was insisting that a restaurant was not a "public hall," as stipulated in the Virginia segregation statute. Secretary Sawyer, however, chose not to issue an order at that time.[16]

With the matter apparently at a standstill, Truman decided to intervene. The immediate occasion for his action stemmed from a letter of November 10, written by Sadie Alexander. Upon deplaning at Washington National Airport on August 9, she informed the president, the soda fountain offered to serve her a glass of milk only if she would carry it "to the ladies room or drink it in the lobby." She refused to suffer the indignity and promised to take the case to court, which she did in October. Mrs. Alexander, however, preferred executive action. Therefore, she asked the president to request an opinion from the attorney general, who, she was convinced, must "advise you that the defendant cannot deny the same service . . . solely because of color." Francis P. Matthews also promised Mrs. Alexander that he, too, would urge presidential action. The White House responded. David Niles requested an opinion from the Department of Justice, which of course was favorable to executive action, and Clark Clifford participated in writing the order.[17]

On December 27, 1948, after seven years of agitation, black Americans had a small amount of satisfaction when D. W. Rentzel, CAA administrator, announced that the government, on the advice of the Justice Department, had ordered the end of racial segregation at Washington National Airport. Mrs. Alexander, writing to the president, saw the action as "further evidence of your conviction that democracy can and must be made a living force in America." She also dropped her court case immediately.[18]

The problem of segregation at Washington National Airport revealed in microcosm all of the difficulties involved in razing the wall of segregation in America. In removing only a stone, the cause of justice had to combat legal technicalities, ignorance, bureaucratic inertia, departmental opposition, political calculations, and general indifference, both within the government and without. Nor was the case closed. Air Terminal Services, Inc., the concessionaire, refused to serve six Negroes within twenty-four hours after the CAA order, and it appealed to the federal district court for an injunction. On January 3,

1949, Judge Albert Bryan denied the injunction, holding that the Civil Aeronautics Administration had ample authority to erase the color line at the airport; and Virginia authorities indicated that they would not contest the order. It was only fitting that Edgar G. Brown, who had launched the first sit-in protest in 1941, was the first to be offered service on January 4, although during the three-hour wait while the waitress ignored him, he lost his appetite and "couldn't even drink their water." His black companions, however, dutifully consumed ham and eggs.[19]

There were to be other gratifying moments for black America. On January 3, the House of Representatives stripped the Rules Committee, which had a strong Dixiecrat-Republican flavor, of its almost absolute power to bottle up bills. Previously, it had required a petition signed by 218 members of the House to force a bill out of the Rules Committee; now, any committee chairman could request a vote of the House to place any bill on the calendar that had been in the committee over twenty-four days. It was a decisive victory for the administration and promised to facilitate consideration of various progressive measures, including civil-rights bills.[20] Indeed, some members of the White House staff later saw the move as one of great significance, for in 1949 the threat of action by committee chairmen persuaded the Rules Committee to report bills dealing with housing and social security, which Congress subsequently passed. In addition to this reform, black Americans also took pride in the appointment of Congressman William Dawson as chairman of the Committee on Expenditures in Executive Departments—the first Negro "to head a major congressional committee in modern times."[21]

Then there was Truman's State of the Union address on January 5. In his news conference the week before, he had indicated that the message would "cover the waterfront." It did. Speaking to a joint session of Congress, the president offered a bold program to provide every American with the opportunity "to obtain his fair share of our increasing abundance." In requesting low-cost housing, an increase in the minimum wage, repeal of the Taft-Hartley Act, extension of Social Security, federal aid to education, and various controls over the economy, Truman revealed clearly the contribution of the New Deal to his own Fair Deal. The address included more, however, for he also called for national medical insurance and enactment of civil-rights legislation. Speaking with deliberation, he referred to the requests in his special message of the previous February 2. "The civil rights proposals I made to the 80th Congress, I now repeat to the 81st Congress. They should be enacted in order that the federal government may assume the leadership and discharge the obligations clearly placed upon it by the Constitution." To dispel any doubt about his commitment, he closed with the statement, "I stand squarely behind those proposals," which he emphasized with voice inflection and hand gesture. And in news conferences after the address, he reaffirmed the commitment.[22]

Yet, in requesting civil-rights legislation from Congress, Truman was determined not to go beyond his message of February 2, 1948, which had aroused so much controversy. At that time, for example, he had requested home rule for the District of Columbia and nothing more, unless "local corrective action" failed in the "near future," in which case he said that he would ask for a "model civil rights law for the Nation's Capital." Thus, despite the recommendations of *To Secure These Rights* and the stinging indictment of racism in *Segregation in Washington*, the president, for reasons known only to himself and his advisers, chose not to fight for such legislation in 1949. Perhaps he feared that a congressional battle over liberalization of racial policies in the District might jeopardize the passage of legislation, civil rights and otherwise, that would benefit Negroes everywhere in the country, although one correspondent pointed out that southerners could not employ the argument of states' rights in debates over civil-rights legislation for the District.[23] Perhaps, too, the administration feared vigorous opposition from white residents of the District. An editorial in the *Washington Post* in December 1948, for example, had conspicuously omitted any mention of corrective legislation for the District, while calling for a cautious approach on civil-rights legislation generally.[24] Whatever the reason, from 1949 on, the administration would attack discrimination in the District obliquely and piecemeal through the actions of various executive agencies, particularly the Interior and Justice departments. The president would also make a telling point about segregation in Washington during inaugural week.

The State of the Union message was anything but bland, and it set off a discordant chorus. While liberal Democrats sang hosannahs, many Republicans decried his proposals for "state socialism" in concert with the wails of southern politicians. Congressman E. E. Cox of Georgia, for example, gloomily predicted that approval of the civil-rights program would create "the greatest social disturbance the country has ever known," although Hugh Scott, chairman of the Republican National Committee, maintained that Truman was "as bold in urging socialized medicine as he is now timid in hastily skimming over the explosive civil rights issue."[25]

Few black leaders agreed with Scott. Walter White, as usual, immediately wired the president, praising him for the "unequivocal reaffirmation" of his stand on civil rights as well as for his espousal of various social-welfare measures. "We are more hopeful today than at any time in recent history," editorialized the *Chicago Defender*. "The president has strengthened the faith of all of us and struck another blow for freedom." Black Americans were also pleased with the request in his budget message of January 10, 1949, for a hefty increase in the appropriation for Howard University. Moreover, two days later Truman met with a delegation representing the National Citizens Council on Civil Rights, whose spokesman declared afterwards that the president had promised action "right away" and that his staff was already in the process of drafting various civil-rights bills.[26]

The highlight of the new year, however, was yet to come, for Harry S. Truman's inauguration was destined to be an historic occasion for black America. Negroes had eagerly anticipated the ceremonies since December 25, when the *Afro-American* had headlined a second-page story: "TRUMAN'S TO BE FIRST INAUGURATION WITHOUT COLOR LINE." The story noted that "for the first time since the administration of William Howard Taft . . . the foes of segregation have gained a foothold, and plan a completely integrated program on a city-wide basis." To facilitate integration of the festivities, the inaugural committee named William L. Houston, a Negro lawyer, to serve as a committee chairman. One of the first public indications of this change in policy occurred at the Truman-Barkley Club Dinner on January 18, where the president made his first speech of inaugural week. In the audience were four blacks, guests of Welborn Mayock, general counsel of the Democratic National Committee and treasurer of the Truman-Barkley Clubs.[27]

The parade, too, was a revelation, although the army predictably stymied complete integration by separating the races by platoons. The crews of light tanks, however, were integrated, while the men of the Coast Guard were completely scrambled. Moreover, the Women's Army Corps "showed a dark face in a sea of white ones." Blacks also sat in the president's reviewing stand and were delighted with the president's apparent snub of Governor Thurmond as he passed before the president. Negroes attended the President's Reception and danced at the President's Ball. There were, of course, some incidents in the privately owned hotels and restaurants which maintained a fairly rigid color line; but the threats of several delegations to cancel reservations unless Negro guests were accepted sometimes resulted in their admission.[28]

In describing inaugural week, the highly partisan *Chicago Defender*, for once, reflected the feelings of most Negro newspapers when it concluded: "For the first time in history Negro citizens were fully integrated in the inaugural celebration and it was obvious to everyone that the lily-white era of Washington's official social life had come to an abrupt end. It was made clear that when President Truman talks about the American people, he is talking about all the people."[29] The reports of the inauguration in the Negro press also revealed a subtle, though significant, change in the vocabulary of black America. For years, Negroes, like whites, had generally used the words "desegregation" or "unsegregated" to describe the erasure or the absence of the color line; but the reports in the press of January 1949 indicated that black America, or at least part of its leadership, was well on the way to general usage of the word "integration," which was not only a stronger and more positive expression of their desires but was also inflammatory to some whites who interpreted it to mean "social equality" and the "mixing" of the races. It was also an indication of greater determination and hope on the part of black America and a hint of the progress then taking place under the Truman administration.

There were, in addition, many tangible accomplishments in race relations across the country, in state and local governments as well as in the private sector. In many instances the exhortations and actions of the Truman administration, coupled with the pressure applied by various civil-rights organizations, resulted in dramatic breakthroughs on the color front. Some of these gains resulted from court decisions, both state and federal, and affected minorities other than black Americans. For example, *To Secure These Rights* had indicted the states of Arizona and New Mexico for their disenfranchisement of reservation Indians. In July 1948, encouraged by an amicus curiae brief filed by the Departments of Justice and Interior, the Arizona Supreme Court ruled that those Indians who met the state's educational requirements must be permitted the right to vote. The following month, a special federal court, after listening to another brief from the two departments, ruled similarly for New Mexico. Both cases were historic, if only because they "removed, once and for all," wrote the *Afro-American*, "the remaining abridgements of suffrage which have plagued the nation's Indians." The federal court decision did not sit well with the New Mexico legislature, however, and in 1949 only the governor's pocket veto prevented enactment of a bill designed to contravene the court and to disenfranchise the Indians again.[30]

The courts were also upholding the right of Negroes to vote in the South. Since 1944, when the Supreme Court case of *Smith* v. *Allwright* had outlawed the white primary, various southern states had adopted ingenious devices to keep Negroes from the polls; but federal judges, particularly South Carolina's courageous J. Waties Waring (who was eventually hounded out of the South), repeatedly ruled them unconstitutional.[31]

Mexican-Americans, too, were profiting from the postwar awareness of minority grievances. For years, their children had been segregated in various schools in the Southwest, often without legislative sanction. In California, for example, the state law called for segregation only with respect to Indians and certain Orientals; but Mexican-Americans were in fact also segregated, ostensibly because of a language problem. As a result, a few parents joined with LULAC—the League of United Latin American Citizens—to bring a successful court case against the segregation policies of four school districts in Orange County, California. A federal circuit court upheld the decision. In the so-called *Delgado* case in Texas in 1948, a similar ruling was reached, except that separation might be permitted in the first grade if language problems existed.[32]

Although there were few serious attempts, at least immediately, to implement the court decisions, the California case apparently had some connection with the legislature's decision to drop all mention of segregation from the educational code. Moreover, because of the organized activities of LULAC and the increased voting power of Mexican-Americans, some politicians were becoming sensitive to their grievances. In 1949, for example, when small-town authorities in Texas denied the right of chapel services and interment for the body of Felix Longoria, a Mexican-American killed in combat during the Second World War, Senator Lyndon B. Johnson intervened and arranged for burial in Arlington National Cemetery.[33]

While Congress continued to frustrate creation of a federal FEPC in the postwar years, by 1949 nine states had followed the pioneering efforts of New York and established their own commissions; and in Kansas and Nebraska, state commissions were investigating employment discrimination. Although their laws varied widely in scope and in effectiveness, eighteen of the more populous states had enacted laws banning discrimination in amusement facilities and places of public accommodations, such as hotels, restaurants, libraries, parks, public conveyances, and educational institutions. Seven states had expressly abolished segregation in their National Guard units, while two others —New York and Pennsylvania—had paraphrased the Democratic platform in calling for equality of treatment. Only a few states, however, had taken steps to outlaw discrimination in public or semipublic housing. Oregon and Utah had both repealed their alien-land laws, by which they had traditionally prevented certain Oriental groups from owning real property.[34] By the standards of the late 1940s, a time when the old verities and prejudices still imprisoned the minds of most whites, such state action represented advances in the attempt to establish equality in America, particularly because the most populous states were generally those involved in attempting to implement a new order.

That progress resulted not only from the Truman administration's leadership by word and deed but also from the irrepressible activities of civil-rights organizations and from the ever-increasing number of Negroes elected to state legislatures and city administrations—people who could speak with some authority concerning the needs of the black community. It would be misleading, however, to suggest that Negroes, or any underprivileged minority, for that matter, held the semblance of a balance of power in any state or local government unit, for the rate of progress was agonizingly slow.[35] The fact that most state legislatures were gerrymandered in favor of rural America while most American minority groups were concentrated in large cities only indicated that proportionate representation was far in the future, even on the city level, where similar gerrymandering was a frequent practice. It was indeed a sad commentary on American democracy when Mexican-Americans in Los Angeles, the city's largest minority, went without representation on the city council from 1881 to 1949. Even New York, with its large Jewish population, did not send a Jew to the United States Senate until 1949, when former Governor Herbert H. Lehman replaced the ailing Robert F. Wagner; in fact, Lehman was the first Jew to be popularly elected to the Senate from any state.[36]

Although American minorities generally lacked the muscle at the polls to elect their own people, they could and did unite with concerned white American Christians to elect sympathetic whites to various local offices. Furthermore, some major cities did respond with their own fair employment practices ordinances, notably Chicago, Cincinnati, Cleveland, Milwaukee, Minneapolis, and Philadelphia. Attempts to enact local housing ordinances, however, almost invariably failed, despite the combined efforts of various Jewish, Negro, and church organizations. Yet, thirty-three cities had established commissions on human relations since 1943—when the first was created—to investigate, to give advice on, and to seek solutions to the problems of racial tension and discrimination.[37]

If only because there was so much room for improvement there, some of the most dramatic progress occurred in the South. And there were good reasons for the improvement. Concerned southern whites hoped that correction of the most blatant examples of racism might forestall action on the part of the federal government and the federal courts; sympathetic whites were encouraged and emboldened by the commitment of the Truman administration and by the report of the Committee on Civil Rights; and black Americans were registering to vote in record numbers. In 1948 alone—the year of the Dixiecrats—forty-seven meetings were held throughout the South to discuss civil rights, according to reports of the Southern Regional Council.[38]

Moreover, as a result of the abolition of the white primary in 1944 and the increasing determination of the federal courts to strike down the newly created barriers to Negro participation in the southern electoral process, the number of Negroes qualified to vote jumped in the postwar period. From an estimated 250,000 black voters in 1940, the number increased to 750,000 in 1948 and 1,008,614 in 1952. Although the 1952 figure represented only 20 percent of the potential black vote in the South, it was an impressive increase over the 5 percent of 1940 and compared well with the 28 percent of 1960. Further, by the end of the 1940s, only five southern states—Alabama, Arkansas, Mississippi, Texas, and Virginia—retained the poll tax as a prerequisite for voting; and at this point its existence was as much an irritating symbol of discrimination as an effective deterrent to registration.[39]

This liberalization, coupled with the continuing migration of blacks from the country to urban areas, increased somewhat their political awareness and effectiveness in contests for local offices in the South. On the statewide level, however, rural control of the legislature completely negated their growing influence within southern cities. Nonetheless, there were encouraging signs on the local level. Negroes were elected to city councils in Richmond, Virginia, and in Winston-Salem, Fayetteville, and Greensboro, North Carolina. Others were appointed to positions as precinct officials. In 1949 Governor Kerr Scott of North Carolina named a black educator to serve on the state board of education; this represented progress, if only because such tokenism had been politically unnecessary a decade earlier.[40]

Moreover, as a result of the Supreme Court's insistence, Negroes began serving on southern juries with increasing frequency, even in areas where a black juror had not been visible since the turn of the century. Black policemen, too, were becoming more common, if not commonplace; and the annual report of the Southern Regional Council in 1948 revealed that only Mississippi and Louisiana contained all-white police departments. Between 1947 and 1952, the number of Negro police tripled, while the number of southern cities with such personnel doubled. In 1951, 443 black officers were on duty in eighty-two cities of thirteen southern states, although, predictably, their authority almost invariably extended only to black people in all-black areas and was usually enforced without benefit of sidearms.[41]

Although none of these advances immediately threatened the white southern way of life—in fact, some were designed to perpetuate that way of life—there had to be a beginning somewhere at some point; and the faint signs of increasing tolerance gave hope where none had existed before. The wall of segregation, however, remained virtually impassable for Negroes, except when traveling on interstate transportation facilities or when entering the hallowed halls of a few professional and graduate schools in the upper South. To be sure, there were sometimes diligent efforts to equalize health, educational, and recreational facilities, but only within a segregated pattern and usually for the purpose of undermining the rationale for federal action. The Supreme Court, in particular, was becoming a frightful specter to many white southerners in the late 1940s.

In some other parts of the country, however, there were concerted efforts to remove the barriers of segregation, particularly on the part of private and professional organizations and in the entertainment world. "Americans of every faith, race and ancestry," noted the National Council of Civil Rights in its report near the end of the decade, "are proving their convictions that freedom is indivisible—and that the surest way to safeguard their own precious liberties is to protect the rights of their neighbors." Although the statement was as much an expression of hope as of fact, it did focus attention on those activities that promised to reshape the nation's racial practices. Moreover, in publicizing racial progress, civil-rights organizations had the ever-increasing support of numerous popular magazines—*Collier's, Woman's Home Companion, Parent's Magazine, Seventeen, Ladies' Home Journal, Reader's Digest, Newsweek,* and *Time*—which published occasional pieces on the plight of America's minorities.[42]

Religious periodicals, too, were involved in propagating the new faith. And although eleven o'clock Sunday morning continued to be the most rigidly segregated hour of the week, various churches were at least making verbal commitments to equal rights and to an integrated society. Although individual churches had generally ignored the 1946 plea of the Federal Council of the Churches of Christ in America to renounce "segregation in race relations," the council reaffirmed its position in even stronger language in subsequent years and pledged a specific course of action. In 1949, for example, it promised full support to the equal-education cases in Texas and Oklahoma when they appeared before the Supreme Court.[43]

The United Council of Church Women, representing ten million members of eighty-four Protestant denominations, also adopted a series of resolutions in 1948 calling for a program of persuasion to accompany a package of legislation. That same year Archbishop Robert Cushing publicly pointed to the actions of a "staggering" number of religious and racial bigots, contending that "no true Christian could support or participate in any such activity."[44] The growing realization of many Catholic and Protestant leaders of an apparent contradiction between scriptural injunction and church practice, and the increasing cooperation between them and various Jewish organizations that had long been committed to the fight against intolerance, provided further evidence of a new and viable civil-rights coalition in the country.

Many professional organizations, too, decided to pay at least lip service to democracy and to the cause of equal rights. In 1949, for the first time in its history, the American Medical Association accepted a Negro physician into its House of Delegates; and there were even more impressive signs of change in the actions of its constituent societies. For example, in 1948 the Baltimore County Medical Society unanimously approved admission of Negro physicians; in 1949 the Missouri State Medical Association dropped the word "white" from its constitution, and, later in the year, the St. Louis chapter began accepting black membership applications; and in 1950 the Florida State Medical Association altered its bylaws to remove the white label. Moreover, in June 1950, during its annual convention, the AMA passed a resolution that urged local societies with racial restrictions to review them in light of present developments. Apparently, those developments included not only a growing conviction in favor of integration in American society but also increasing public support for Truman's national health-insurance program, which the AMA vigorously denounced as "socialized" medicine. Many Negro physicians suspected that the recent, and belated, "democracy" of the AMA was a crude overture for the support of the black National Medical Association, which had endorsed such legislation as early as 1946.[45]

The American Nurses Association, with no ideological or self-interest issue to champion, proved more progressive than the AMA. In 1948 the association not only provided for direct memberships in the national organization to nullify the racial restrictions of district chapters, but also elected a Negro to its board of directors. By the end of 1949, only chapters in Georgia, Louisiana, Texas, Virginia, South Carolina, and Washington, D.C., continued to refuse the applications of black nurses.[46]

The American Bar Association lagged behind both the AMA and the ANA. Although its constitution nowhere mentioned race as a qualification for membership, the association had long practiced a lily-white policy. The National Lawyers Guild, however, had accepted both blacks and whites since its organization in 1936; but its effectiveness was limited because of its small membership and the growing number of accusations by superpatriots of its alleged subversiveness. By the late 1940s, the Federal Bar Association, which was composed primarily of the federal bench and bar, contained at least four black members, while the ABA had relented enough to extend membership to some half-dozen Negro lawyers, perhaps because it was under considerable pressure from various state associations. In 1949, for example, the New Jersey State Bar Association recommended that application blanks eliminate references to race, creed, and color.[47]

Other organizations were more in tune with the times. In 1949 the American Association of University Women amended its bylaws so that local chapters could not discriminate against otherwise qualified applicants. The Red Cross finally began distributing blood without indicating the race of the donor. Records were kept, however, should a physician request such information. And the National Interfraternity Conference recommended that college and university fraternities drop their restrictive membership provisions, although the real battle on the campuses was more than a decade away. The Congress of Racial Equality also reported some progress in integrating public accommodations across the country.[48]

The most dramatic and visible penetrations of the color barrier came in the entertainment world, particularly in athletics and motion pictures. Until 1947 major-league baseball was a white man's sport, although usually with a speckled audience. But the rhetoric of the times and the appeal of the box office combined to produce the first modern major-league contract for a black player, Jackie Robinson, who became the storybook hero of the decade. His phenomenal success with the Brooklyn Dodgers in 1947 persuaded other teams to follow suit. By 1951 eighteen Negroes were playing on six teams, and the number would accelerate rapidly in the 1950s.[49] Integration quickly became a fact, and complete acceptance was not far behind.

In football, the story was much the same. Although it was national news when the Yale University team selected Levi Jackson as its captain for the 1949 football season, professional football—particularly the maverick and short-lived American Conference—was already exploiting the talents of black players. The National Football League had originally excluded Negroes, but in the late 1940s it, too, met the spirit of the times. By 1951 eighteen Negroes were playing on six of the league's twelve teams, and each year thereafter saw a substantial increase. On both the college and professional levels, however, integrated basketball lagged behind. Occasionally various college teams paraded a Negro or two, but the solid evidence of black talent emerged most clearly in the colorful and skillful performances of the Harlem Globetrotters, who delighted audiences and intrigued coaches across the country. In 1950 the New York Knickerbockers of the National Basketball Association had seen enough and signed Nathaniel "Sweetwater" Clifton of the Globetrotters. The precedent was set, and within two decades black players would dominate the sport at the professional level.[50]

The story was different, however, in those sports that had limited box-office appeal and those that required leisure time and a degree of affluence. In tennis, some of the private courts maintained a color line, though the United States Lawn Tennis Association did not. The first Negro to play at Forest Hills, for example, was Althea Gibson, in 1950, who went on to become one of the greatest women players in the history of the game. But black men were conspicuously absent from most courts until the 1960s. Golf was even more difficult for blacks to penetrate, largely because it required financial resources beyond the means of most of them. Nearly all private clubs, and some public courses as well, drew a color line when it came to playing the game. Moreover, only Joe Louis's threat of a law suit persuaded the Professional Golfers Association to drop its ban on "non-whites." The story was similar in professional bowling and wrestling. By the end of the decade, however, black and white alike—outside of the South—were beginning to accept integration as the new way of life in the nation's athletics.[51]

Equally significant for the present and the future was Hollywood's changing of the images of American minorities, a process that began during the Second World War and accelerated in the postwar period. In 1945, however, it was not at all clear that Hollywood would continue the trend, and there were repeated criticisms of the industry for its perpetuation of stereotyped casting and token representation. There were also fears that the new psychic mysteries would include the eye-rolling, knee-quaking, "skaird-of-haints" Negro in the tradition of Stepin Fetchit. Decades of futile protest had prepared blacks to expect the worst and to recognize that progress was neither linear nor permanent.[52]

The fear was genuine but misplaced, for a number of postwar factors and events persuaded Hollywood to make the greatest effort in the industry's history to remove stereotypes, to expand opportunities for black performers, and to propagate better understanding of all minority groups. The grotesque revelations of the Nazi concentration camps, the increasingly shrill rhetoric of the cold war, the preachments of the Truman administration, the pressures from various civil-rights organizations, the threats of blacks to boycott the box office, the competition of television, and the occasional compassion of white actors, directors, and producers combined to produce a new epoch in the history of Hollywood and to persuade the industry to exchange some of its white southern audience for an equally large northern audience. Hollywood's commitment, of course, was neither unanimous nor complete; and movies sometimes worked at cross-purposes, while they almost always stopped short of advocating equality between black and white.

Perhaps predictably, Hollywood launched its first postwar attack against religious bigotry, thus continuing a trend developed during the war and at the same time attacking a subject that was less inflammatory than white mistreatment of blacks. Indeed, as a result of *Going My Way* (1944) and *The Bells of St. Mary's* (1945), Bing Crosby, Barry Fitzgerald, and Ingrid Bergman made Catholicism a respectable and entertaining theme, while simultaneously humanizing the clergy. Treatment of anti-Semitism, however, was a more delicate matter. During the war, a number of pictures had excoriated Nazism for its anti-Semitism; but its existence at home was ignored, except in *Pride of the Marines* and in several other movies that made oblique references to it. But the appearance of Edward Dmytryk's *Till the End of Time* in 1946 signaled the beginning of a direct assault on American anti-Semitism, although Walt Disney's *Abie's Irish Rose*, denounced by the Negro press and the National Conference of Christians and Jews, provoked momentary bewilderment concerning the direction in which Hollywood was heading.[53]

Two pictures in 1947, however, dissipated nearly all doubt. Dmytryk's *Crossfire* centered directly on anti-Semitism in America, and the picture's financial success sparked hope in the black community. "If the producers continue to make intelligent films and make money on these films," Walter White noted, in praising *Crossfire*, "perhaps in time Hollywood will have the courage to attack anti-Negroism." And when *Gentleman's Agreement* appeared later in the year, *Ebony*—the black counterpart of *Life* magazine—labeled it "undoubtedly the most daring picture ever made in Hollywood."[54] The trend was evident, and Negroes hoped to profit from it.

But the impact of such films was less evident than the purpose, and some commentators feared that audiences might react adversely to the message. In particular, some contended that these movies worked at cross-purposes, that their visual messages differed from their verbal ones. One critic, for example, observed that the persecuted Jew in *Crossfire* had all the characteristics of the stereotype—"soft-handed, flashily dressed, suave, artistic"—which might "reinforce rather than abate" the emotions that feed anti-Semitism. Although studies were taken of audience reaction to *Crossfire*, which indicated a decrease of racial prejudice among those who saw it, others were quick to note that Hollywood generally produced pictures with only a vague idea of audience reception and without any systematic research into their effects. Throughout the late 1940s and early 1950s, experts continued to plead for such studies, including an examination of the unconscious impact versus the "message" in the antibias film.[55]

The box-office appeal of the pictures of 1946 and 1947 exploring anti-Semitism did not persuade directors and producers to plunge immediately into a similar examination of racial prejudice. In fact, Walt Disney's *Song of the South* in 1946 set off a chorus of criticism. Although recognizing the film's artistic merit, the NAACP regretted its glorification of slavery. *Ebony* could find no merit anywhere. Denouncing James Baskett, who played Uncle Remus, as an "Uncle Tom–Aunt Jemima caricature complete with all the fawning standard equipment thereof—the toothy smile, battered hat, grey beard, and a profusion of 'dis' and 'dat' talk," the critic lamented the appearance of another one "of those Mammy-minded, plantation-prejudiced movies that . . . has done more to . . . set back Negro progress than a fistful of Bilbo speeches in Congress."[56]

The years 1947 and 1948 were more promising. *Body and Soul* co-starred Canada Lee as a black boxer on a first-name basis with his white friend, John Garfield; and *The Burning Cross* cast a bright light on the white-sheeted bigots of the Ku Klux Klan. There were also little things, such as the absence of the "yas, sah, boss" convention in *The Long Night*, the unobtrusive presence of black people in crowd sequences of *The Best Years of Our Lives*, and the use of the title "Mrs." to address a black maid in *Cass Timberlane*. In 1948 *The Boy with Green Hair* circuitously attacked color prejudice; pro-football-star Kenny Washington lobbed hand grenades at the Vietnamese as a member of the French Foreign Legion in *Rouges' Regiment* (a touching irony which escaped the critics); and Jackie Robinson played himself in *The Jackie Robinson Story*. Many of the stereotypes continued, of course, and *Ebony* magazine complained about "perennial Hattie McDaniel donning an apron for the 83rd time since she first went before the cameras in 1931."[57]

The big breakthrough came in 1949, when a few directors decided to deal with themes that were traditionally *verboten*. *Lost Boundaries*, for example, dealt with the subject of "passing." So did *Pinky*, which also raised the explosive issue of intermarriage but, predictably, without its consummation and with Jeanne Crain posing as a Negro in order to "pass" as white. (The candid, though strained and somewhat unimaginative, approach of *Guess Who's Coming to Dinner* was still far in the future.) *Intruder in the Dust* starred Juano Hernandez in a powerful indictment of lynching, and *Home of the Brave* and *Battleground* recaptured some of the courage and bigotry of the Second World War.[58]

For the first time in its history, Hollywood was systematically exploring the roots of racism in America, although the message almost invariably fell short of black expectations. Critics, for example, denounced the selection of Jeanne Crain for the lead role in *Pinky*. Nonetheless, there was rejoicing throughout the black community. "Hollywood Comes of Age," editorialized the *Courier*; "The handkerchief was snatched off," concluded a film critic; "Hollywood can never go back to its old portrayal of colored people as witless menials or idiotic buffoons," exulted Walter White.[59]

Nor was the trend only momentary. As a result of box-office success, between 1950 and 1953 several films continued to exploit black-white relationships. In 1950 *No Way Out* featured Sidney Poitier in a sensitive role as a black intern in a white hospital, which *Ebony*, usually hard to please, saw as "the most outspoken, hardest-hitting picture ever filmed on racial hatred." In 1951 other themes were developed in *Bright Victory, The Breaking Point, The Well*, and *Steel Helmet* (which reflected the recent integration of troops in Korea).[60]

The Red Ball Express, starring Jeff Chandler, Alex Nicol, and Sidney Poitier, was the big story in 1952. The picture dramatized the actions of truck drivers, black and white alike, in a completely integrated unit, who rushed supplies to the rapidly advancing forces of General George Patton during the Second World War. A black private performed the most heroic act when he voluntarily drove his truck through a minefield (and was killed in the process), and the film presented a "first" when Poitier slugged a white soldier. But if the film was good propaganda, it was poor history, for the real Red Ball Express was a segregated outfit. In fact, the ironies of the film were intriguing. While the picture was being produced, black actors and actual black soldiers lived under semisegregated conditions at Fort Eustus while filming the story of an integrated company that was actually segregated.[61]

By 1953 the Negro trend was subsiding. Some themes were exhausted at the box office; others were considered too explosive for white sensibilities; blacks who customarily performed stereotyped roles were at loggerheads with the NAACP; and the pall of McCarthyism hung over every production. But there was no turning back. Although stereotypes continued, such as those in *Uncle Tom's Cabana*, the degrading Stepin Fetchit role was a thing of the past, which the actor himself discovered when he came out of retirement in 1951. The revolution in the industry between 1943 and 1953 had also broadened the traditional roles for black actors and paved the way for the candid productions of the 1960s, particularly after 1953, when Hollywood revised its production code and struck miscegenation from the list of forbidden topics.[62]

Nor were Catholics, Negroes, and Jews the only minorities to profit from Hollywood's concern. The American Indian, too, was stereotyped but in a manner quite different from the Negro. Although he generally lost the war, the Indian often won a battle or two in which he displayed savage ferocity. His bravery, his essential manhood, was seldom questioned, while the Negro generally appeared as a docile, dumb, sometimes demented creature, who evoked laughter, derision, and occasional pity. In the postwar period the Indian demanded justice, not manhood, from the hands of Hollywood. As three Oklahoma Indians, all members of the state legislature, noted in a resolution: "It's a battle if the white man wins, a massacre if the Indian is victorious." In 1950 *Broken Arrow* sought to correct matters. James

Stewart married the leading Indian lady; and Jeff Chandler played a creditable Chief Cochise, although the substitution of a sun-tanned white for a natural red was somewhat irritating to the few Indian actors in Hollywood. In congratulating Twentieth Century–Fox, Walter White praised the studio for "smashing all of the old cliches about Indian treachery and barbarity." In 1951 Burt Lancaster starred in *Jim Thorpe—All American*, and in 1953 an Indian played a visible, though minor, part in *Take the High Ground*.[63]

In shattering a stereotype, there was always the danger of creating or perpetuating another. In *The Oxbow Incident*, for instance, Leigh Whipper's sympathetic role as a black preacher was offset by the portrayal of a greasy villain with a Mexican accent, a continuation of a usually unfavorable Mexican-American stereotype. Yet during the postwar period the portrayal of the Mexican was ambivalent, as in *The Treasure of the Sierra Madre*. In 1950, however, Paramount decided to depart momentarily from the Bing Crosby–Bob Hope tradition and produced *The Lawless*, a gripping drama about discrimination against, and hatred of, Mexicans in the American Southwest. In the same year, Metro-Goldwyn-Mayer released *Right Cross*, featuring Ricardo Montalban as Johnny Monterez, a Mexican-American boxing champion who feared that Anglos would treat him as a social leper once he lost the crown. The plot was strained, but *Right Cross* did give off "sparks of social conscience."[64]

There was also concern for Orientals. Though Chinese-Americans were often portrayed as grinning, menial laborers, they could take some consolation in the exploits of Charlie Chan, who invariably solved crimes after white detectives had failed. And Japanese-Americans won belated recognition in 1951 in *Go for Broke*, which not only exposed the bigotry of white officers but also extolled the courage of the Nisei 442d Regimental Combat team during the Second World War. The film, however, was small compensation for the bucktoothed, inhuman villains of Hollywood's wartime productions.[65]

Although the competition of television spurred Hollywood to new heights of tolerance, television itself threatened to compromise this progress. For years, the radio show of "Amos and Andy" had burlesqued and stereotyped black America, perhaps unintentionally, and repeated protests about it had no effect. Television premiered the program in 1951, despite vigorous objections. The "Beulah" show—"the ridiculous and nauseating Beulah"—was also offensive. Moreover, the industry generally continued to boycott black performers on other programs.[66] Nor was that all. In 1952 the Japanese-American Citizens

League lodged a protest against the old Hollywood productions then appearing on television, some of which depicted Japan as monstrous and Japanese-Americans as spies and saboteurs. Negroes, too, remonstrated against the release of pictures with prejudiced themes, those that portrayed blacks "as goofs, simpletons, dumbbells and half-savage buffoons"; but television would remain generally unresponsive until the 1960s.[67]

The gains nearly everywhere, however, were appreciable. Some of the progress smacked of condescension, of tokenism, of lip service. Occasionally, one form of discrimination replaced another. Yet progress was unmistakable at all levels of government and within the private sector of the nation. America was still a long way from President Truman's hope to fulfill the promises of the Declaration of Independence and the Constitution of the United States. As he expressed it in his special message on civil rights in February 1948, "We know the way. We need only the will."[68] At the end of the decade, the will was present as never before, and the question was not simply if the country would continue to move ahead on racial matters but more if it would be able to maintain the same rate of progress.

9 DEADLOCK IN CONGRESS

The country's change in mood regarding racial and religious tolerance encouraged civil-rights advocates to hope for a similar alteration in the attitude of Congress, which had been consistently unresponsive to pleas for equal-justice legislation, at least for black Americans. The facility with which the House of Representatives restricted the arbitrary power of the Rules Committee on January 4, 1949, was a comfort, although everyone recognized that the Senate, in which southerners held grimly to the power of the filibuster, was the key to legislative progress. Everyone was also aware that the Senate would have to tighten the cloture rule before civil-rights measures could be brought to a vote.

Traditionally reluctant to limit debate, the Senate had adopted Rule XXII in 1917, which provided that debate on a "pending measure" could be terminated by a two-thirds vote. While presiding one day during the special session of 1948, Senator Vandenberg chose to interpret the rule in a narrow, legalistic fashion and sustained Senator Russell's point of order that cloture could not be applied to debate on a "motion," only on the measure itself. In view of the obvious fact that a motion to consider a bill had to precede a vote on the measure, the effect of Vanderberg's ruling was to nullify Rule XXII and to grant southerners the opportunity to debate endlessly on motions to consider civil-rights bills.[1]

Two courses of action were available. The Senate could amend Rule XXII to apply to a motion as well as to the measure itself, or it could seek another ruling from the new presiding officer, Vice-President Barkley. The Republican leadership chose the former method and backed the Hayden-Wherry Resolution, reported from committee on February 17, 1949, which provided for the application of cloture at any point by a two-thirds vote of those present. Senate Democrats, led by Majority Leader Scott Lucas, held back, seeking to determine the best course of action, although Lucas himself personally favored a stronger "gag" rule, one that would terminate debate by a majority of the entire membership.[2]

The paucity of Democratic support for the Hayden-Wherry Resolution—indeed, the absence of any concerted Democratic effort to amend the rules—worried and irritated civil-rights advocates. Seeking to apply pressure, Walter White denounced the "pattern of evasion" of certain members of the Senate; and the NAACP sent telegrams to its sixteen hundred branches, urging a grass-roots movement to press senators to vote in favor of a rule that would allow cloture by majority vote. White also wired the president, complaining, "Not one Democrat has as yet fought for or even spoken out to end filibusters. We are perturbed. We trust our perturbation is premature, despite evidence to the contrary."[3]

Despite this protest and a similar one from A. Philip Randolph, the White House did not respond. As Philleo Nash noted in an interoffice memorandum: "I know of nothing we could say at this point, except that the matter is entirely congressional. This would be so unsatisfactory that I am sure it is better to say nothing."[4] Since the election, the president had carefully stressed congressional prerogatives in several news conferences, while expressing hope for enactment of his proposed legislation. At the opening of the new Congress, the administration obviously did not want to jeopardize its relationship, and thereby its program, by publicly interfering with the determination of Senate rules.

Moreover, Senate Democratic leaders were faced with a delicate situation. In the process of organizing the Senate and in determining legislative priorities, they had to consider the possibility that a protracted debate over civil-rights legislation might imperil the president's entire Fair Deal program. They were also caught in a triangular squeeze between the Republican attempt to seize, or at least to share, credit for facilitating passage of civil-rights legislation, the refusal of southerners to consider any genuine compromise of the cloture rule, and the demands of many civil-rights organizations to change Rule XXII so that a simple majority could invoke cloture.

Indeed, on February 5, representatives of twenty-one organizations met in New York, where they adopted a resolution calling for bipartisan support of an amendment to Rule XXII to permit cloture by a majority of senators present. And the demand could not be dismissed as the ravings of a few impotents, for the participants included representatives from the CIO, the AFL, the NAACP, the ACLU, ADA, the National Catholic Welfare Conference, the American Jewish Congress, the American Council on Human Rights, the American Jewish Committee, the National Newspaper Publishers Association, the National Council for a Permanent FEPC, the National Baptist Convention, and the AME Church and the AME Zion Church.[5] It was an impressive demonstration of interracial and interreligious solidarity and a pregnant reminder of the political potential of such a coalition. In short, the Democratic leadership in the Senate was on the spot.

While Lucas equivocated and while the Hayden-Wherry Resolution languished in committee, Senator William F. Knowland of California sought to perpetuate the initial Republican advantage by moving to bring to a vote his own bill to limit cloture. In a rare display of unanimity, every Democratic senator voted against the motion, which was defeated by a vote of fifty-six to thirty-one. Senator Lucas was furious and accused Republicans of attempting to determine the calendar of a Democratic-organized Senate. Although Lucas promised to take up the issue of cloture in "due time," Senator Wayne Morse caustically retorted that the Democrats were seeking "to keep civil rights in the background, because they know it will split their party wide open."[6]

Whatever was passing through the mind of the new majority leader, he was obviously off to a poor start. Finally, on February 16, with the Hayden-Wherry Resolution about to emerge from committee, the report went out that Democrats and Republicans would unite to support the amendment but that it would not be brought to the floor until February 28. Lucas indicated, however, that he would set aside the resolution whenever priority legislation was ready for action. He had botched it again. To civil-rights advocates, nothing was more important than equal-justice legislation.[7]

At this point, the president intervened. Meeting with Lucas and other Democratic leaders on February 28, Truman directed his congressional lieutenants to meet the issue "head-on," even if it meant delaying consideration of other legislation. That afternoon, Lucas moved to consider the Hayden-Wherry Resolution, and the anticipated southern filibuster began. For nearly two weeks, southern wails echoed throughout the Senate chamber. Senator John L. McClellan raised the Red bogey in labeling cloture a compromise with communism, and J. William Fulbright somehow found passages from the encyclopedia pertinent to the issue at hand.[8] In his maiden effort in the Senate, Lyndon Johnson rose to denounce cloture as "the deadliest weapon in the arsenal of parliamentary procedures," against which "a minority has no defense." When the NAACP urged Senator Lucas to hold round-the-clock sessions in an effort to break the filibuster, the majority leader demurred on the grounds that the tactic might kill older members.[9]

While the filibuster was in progress, Truman ventured his own views on cloture in a news conference on March 3. In response to questions, the president stated flatly that he would reduce the requirement for cloture to a majority of those present, if he "had anything to do with it." Of course, he had nothing to do with it at this point, but his endorsement of the position taken by the twenty-one civil-rights organizations a month earlier set off a cacophony in the Senate. Senator Wherry charged that Truman had "tossed a monkey wrench" into efforts for a workable cloture rule, while Russell of Georgia now claimed proof for his accusations of a conspiracy on the part of the administration. Even Senator Lucas felt compelled to disagree with the president and reaffirmed his position in favor of requiring only a majority of the membership for cloture. At the same time, to soothe southern sensibilities, if only because important legislation other than civil rights was at stake, he offered the guarantee that a majority of the Senate's Democrats would support cloture by a two-thirds majority if southerners would permit a vote on the issue. Predictably, the southern senators rejected the overture.[10]

But northern Democrats still held a trump, or so they thought. As early as March 1, Lucas had indicated that he would circulate a petition proposing another ruling on cloture by the new presiding officer, Vice-President Barkley. But the petition was momentarily delayed when several senators argued that southerners had not been "sufficiently provocative," although Senators Knowland and Lucas subsequently collected the signatures of seventeen Democrats and sixteen Republicans, which they presented to Barkley on March 10.[11]

Although Truman was taking the sun in Key West, Florida, he followed events closely through contact with White House assistants. On March 8, for example, Charles Murphy dispatched a long message to the president in which he pointed out the necessity for senatorial action on cloture in the near future. Important legislation was piling up, Murphy noted, such as bills on housing, repeal of Taft-Hartley, extension of rent controls, deficiency appropriations, and extension of the European Recovery Program; and the only hope appeared to be a favorable ruling by the vice-president. This was the key vote, he reasoned, and the president agreed. Responding to Murphy, Truman urged the Democratic leadership to "carry our fight to a successful conclusion. We shouldn't show any weakness and if Barkley's ruling can be sustained we will be in pretty fair shape." Senator Lucas, however, was less optimistic and informed the White House on March 8 that he did not have the votes to uphold a favorable ruling.[12]

Lucas was correct. On March 10 Vice-President Barkley ruled favorably on the petition, which permitted the application of cloture to a motion as well as to the measure itself and in effect reversed Vandenberg's decision in 1948. But Senator Russell quickly appealed the ruling of the chair, and on the following day, by a vote of forty-six to forty-one, the Senate overruled Barkley's decision. It was a crushing blow for the administration and for civil-rights advocates everywhere. Twenty-three Republicans had united with twenty southern and three western Democrats to keep the South in the saddle.[13]

In the numerous post-mortem analyses, there were spastic criticisms of nearly everyone. In a refrain that would become increasingly familiar, some critics rebuked Lucas for his "timid strategy and fumbling leadership." One member of the NAACP board of directors singled out Walter White for special criticism: his "inept leadership" in not mobilizing the support of other organizations, said Alfred Baker Lewis, led directly to the defeat of Barkley's ruling. In his column in the *Chicago Defender*, White admitted that organized pressure on individual senators was lacking, so much so that "senator after senator told me that he had seen no great interest in the civil rights program"; but White was not about to criticize himself.[14]

Nor was President Truman immune. The *Afro-American* contended that a "smarter" president would have made civil rights a bipartisan matter, and there were grumblings about his absence from Washington. The most outspoken criticism came from the *New York Times*, which declared it "scarcely disputable" that the president's "impromptu" endorsement of cloture by a mere majority "came at the least fortunate moment in the whole discussion, alarmed the moderates, stiffened the die-hards." Perhaps, but civil-rights advocates did not think so. Except for the *Courier*, nearly all Negro newspapers, black columnists, and civil-rights organizations had praised Truman for his position on cloture. Moreover, despite the certainty of the *New York Times*, what impact Truman's statement had was disputable, for no hard evidence indicates that it changed a single senatorial mind or lost a vote.[15]

Despite such scattershot criticism, there was virtual unanimity concerning the responsibility of Senate Republicans. In a careful analysis of the vote, Robert K. Carr demonstrated that a coalition of midwestern Republicans and southern Democrats was largely to blame. Of the eighteen Republicans from the Midwest, fourteen voted to overrule Barkley, whereas eight of the nine New England Republicans voted to sustain the ruling. Condemnation was bitter and generally unrestrained. Walter White denounced the "GOP reactionaries" and wondered if "the famous initials of Abe Lincoln's party should henceforth read 'Gone Old Party?'" The *Afro-American* confessed its error in supporting Republicans during the campaign of 1948, and a columnist for the *Chicago Defender* tersely concluded that "the Elephant has embraced the Skunk."[16] The memory of the vote of March 11 would linger long in the minds of black Americans.

Nor were the roles of individual Republicans ignored in the criticism. Although Knowland and Taft voted to sustain Barkley's ruling, Wherry and Vandenberg did not, and Vandenberg may have been the key figure in the entire affair. On March 2 he had released his fellow Republicans from any obligations of personal or party loyalty to his ruling of August 1948. However, in an impassioned address on March 11, only hours prior to the final vote, Vandenberg struck hard at Barkley's "ingenious thesis," which he considered an affront to legislative due process. It was also a personal affront, and Vandenberg's pride was obviously involved. His speech may not have changed a single vote, but it was impressive. "We are lost," groaned several Democrats following his address, while Walter White contended that Vandenberg "cost us from five to seven votes. He has given an aura of respectability to those who wanted an excuse to vote to upset Mr. Barkley."[17]

The vote on the Barkley ruling was fraught with meaning. The debacle highlighted the reluctance of most Republicans to support civil-rights legislation because of the party's more conservative position on social and economic matters and illustrated the power of a Republican–southern-Democratic coalition. The geographical distribution of the vote was also a painful reminder to Negro leaders of the limitations of black power at the polls. Although the Negro vote might constitute the balance of power in a close presidential contest, it did not exercise the same political muscle with respect to the Senate, where only a handful of senators had to fret about a large black constituency. Thus, western Democratic senators, such as McCarran of Nevada and McFarland and Hayden of Arizona, could vote against the Barkley ruling with the assurance of impunity, and there was nothing that civil-rights advocates could do about it. Finally, the ruling itself was vital for the future of civil-rights legislation. From the vantage point of 1952, Roy Wilkins considered it the most "crucial vote on civil rights in the past ten years," not only because it "would have paved the way for shutting off the filibuster on the motion to take up FEPC" but, more important, because it would "have forestalled the adoption of the infamous Wherry-Hayden Rule 22 on filibusters which stands as a permanent roadblock to civil-rights legislation."[18]

Wilkins was referring to the so-called compromise that followed in the wake of the defeat of the Barkley ruling, when Senators Wherry and Hayden sponsored a substitute amendment for their original cloture resolution. Although the substitute sanctioned the application of cloture to a motion, it was obviously designed to appeal to the South, for it required a "constitutional" two-thirds majority—that is, two-thirds of the entire membership rather than the current requirement of two-thirds of those present—to invoke cloture. Moreover, the amendment prohibited the application of cloture to a motion to amend Rule XXII in the future.[19]

In short, Vandenberg's ruling in 1948 and the Senate's defeat of Barkley's ruling in 1949 led to the adoption of a new rule that increased the power of the South to frustrate enactment of civil-rights legislation. Although thirty Democrats and twenty-two Republicans had signed the petition endorsing the Wherry-Hayden amendment, which all but guaranteed its passage, administration Democrats led by Senator Lucas sought to delay the inevitable. But Lucas had lost control of the Senate. Tempers flared, even among friends of civil rights. Walter White frantically wired senators that "a vote for the Wherry substitute resolution means that the Senate will never pass any civil-rights legislation or ever amend Rule 22 again." It was of no use. On March 17, 1949, the Senate voted sixty-three to twenty-three to approve the substitute resolution, and the fight was over. Only fifteen Democrats, led by the hapless Lucas, and eight Republicans had held out to the bitter end.[20]

It was a subdued Harry Truman who greeted reporters at his news conference on March 18 in Key West. Asked if he still hoped to win senatorial approval of civil-rights legislation, he refused to comment "because the matter hasn't reached the conclusion." Asked about the rumor that the Senate had agreed to pass only a poll-tax bill, he offered no comment, except to point out that he only advised the Congress and that the United States had three "independent prongs" of government.

Faced with the expiration of rent control on March 31 and with a growing backlog of bills, particularly appropriations for the Marshall Plan, Truman was obviously shoring up his political fences. Yet the following week, during a news conference in the White House, he expressed hope that "we will get that program through."[21]

But the NAACP was no longer thinking in terms of winning the total program. At its April meeting, following the cloture debacle, the Board of Directors departed from precedent and voted to "establish priority of FEPC over all other legislation on civil rights." Previously, the organization had insisted that all parts of the civil-rights package were of equal importance, although ever since the war it had been clear that civil-rights supporters considered the FEPC first among equals.[22]

Regardless of the adoption and the feared effects of the new cloture rule, the Truman administration proceeded with its plans to push civil rights. Even while the filibuster was in progress, members of the White House staff were drafting legislative proposals, which they circulated to various executive agencies for recommendations and approval. In the meantime, Representative Mary Norton introduced the administration's anti-poll-tax bill in the House on March 3, and by the end of the month the administration's complete program was ready for introduction.[23]

For the moment, however, the White House stalled. In response to an inquiry from Mrs. Norton, the president advised her on April 5 that he would "rather not discuss it publicly until we are sure exactly where we stand."[24] The statement was deliberately nebulous, perhaps because the 1948 appropriations for the European Recovery Program had expired on April 3 and authorization for new funds would not clear both houses until April 13. Whatever the case, on April 28, Senator McGrath introduced the administration's civil-rights program in the Senate, an ambitious package obviously meant to encompass most of the president's recommendations in his special message of February 2, 1948.

Aside from the bills concerning lynching, the poll tax, and a compulsory FEPC, the program included a surprise omnibus bill, which proposed some legislative novelties. The bill called for the establishment of an executive commission on civil rights, creation of a joint congressional committee on civil rights, elevation of the Civil Rights Section of the Department of Justice to a full division headed by an assistant attorney general, amendment of existing civil-rights statutes to close loopholes, additional guarantees to protect the right to vote, and prohibition of discrimination and segregation in interstate commerce. In the House, Emanuel Celler sponsored the omnibus and anti-lynching bills, and Adam Clayton Powell, erstwhile Truman critic, introduced the administration's FEPC proposal.[25]

For ten days in May, a parade of witnesses, mostly favorable to the bill, passed before Powell's subcommittee. The white South, of course, had its day; and Congressman Laurie C. Battle of Alabama appeared to denounce the FEPC as "unconstitutional, unenforceable, and unwise." Congressman Charles E. Bennett of Florida suggested that Communists and "a lot of pretty wild people, with pretty long hair" in the North were behind the scheme to destroy the South's "traditional democracy," which prompted Chairman Powell to retort that it was the president's bill, not the Communist party's. Clare E. Hoffman, a Republican congressman from Michigan, saw it as "another step toward dictatorship." He was also certain that one objective of the FEPC was to encourage "social intermingling" and intermarriage among the races. Nor was he alone in having this obsession. The candid and offhand testimony of one southern congressman clearly exposed a man hung up on the fear of interracial sex.[26]

The testimony in favor of the bill was more impressive and more to the point. Secretary of Labor Maurice Tobin vigorously supported the administration's bill, particularly because of its strong enforcement provisions, but assured his audience that its authority would not be invoked precipitantly or arbitrarily. Felix S. Cohen, representing the Association on American Indian Affairs, eloquently argued that the Indian's problem was more economic than social, for "Indians are the last to be hired and the first to be fired." Herman Edelsberg of the Anti-Defamation League, in reply to the argument that Congress could not legislate love or legislate prejudice out of existence, pointed out, "The bill is not aimed at prejudice, the bill is aimed at discrimination, at overt acts which you might call the bitter fruits of prejudice."[27]

In further testimony, Mike Masaoka of the Japanese-American Citizens League, though conceding "tremendous improvement" in employment practices since prewar days, presented an impressive array of statistics documenting the degrees of employment discrimination against Japanese-Americans as one moved from the West Coast, where prejudice was still rampant, to New York, where the situation was "heartwarming." Masaoka attributed the bright prospects in New York to the state's fair employment practices law. He also made it clear that his plea for a federal FEPC embraced the cause of all minorities in America. Clarence Mitchell of the NAACP argued that the bill would strike at discrimination in employment in both North and South; and he reported on an investigation of fifty-one firms in eighteen states, which revealed that only eleven employed blacks in skilled positions and that only five of twenty-nine with apprentice-training programs would admit Negroes.[28]

Finally, the Department of State reintroduced Dean Acheson's statement of 1946 concerning the adverse effects of discrimination on America's international relations. Indeed, on May 20, Congressman Powell observed that all witnesses favorable to the bill had stressed the international implications of white America's prejudice against darker minorities. This contrasted with the absence of such testimony and such observations during hearings in 1945 and 1946.[29] The cold war was obviously exercising an impact on domestic affairs in more ways than one. Opponents of fair employment practices legislation alleged that the proposal was a Communist conspiracy from within; proponents argued more plausibly that the cold war from without demanded that America put its house in order.

One of those who appeared before Powell's subcommittee to speak against a compulsory FEPC was Congressman Brooks Hays of Arkansas, who had been designated as the spokesman for several moderate southerners. By this time, Hays was widely known for his so-called Arkansas plan for compromise on civil rights, which he had presented in a speech to the House in February 1949. His program called for a constitutional amendment to outlaw the poll tax, a modified antilynching law that would permit federal intervention only when local authorities failed to act, abandonment of attempts to deal legislatively with segregation in interstate transportation, and establishment of a counseling service in the Labor Department in lieu of a compulsory FEPC.[30]

On February 5, when a member of the White House staff apprised Truman of Hays's interest in seeking compromise, the president ignored the overture; and in July he personally informed Senator Russell that the Arkansas plan was unacceptable. Aside from his own personal feelings, Truman had to consider the political implications of any move on his part to dilute his program, which he had already described as the minimum in order to achieve equal justice in America. Most civil-rights advocates considered Hays's program a surrender to the South rather than a step in the right direction. As Thomas L. Stokes put it in commending Hays for his courage, the so-called compromise begged "the essential issue involved. This is that there are basic rights guaranteed in the Constitution which hardly can be compromised in justice. They have been compromised since the Civil War, which seems too long. The weakness of the southern position is the assumption that there is anything to compromise in the first instance."[31]

Obviously, Truman already had enough troubles with Congress without inviting the bitter opposition of the civil-rights coalition, tenuous and temporary as that coalition might be. The entire Fair Deal program, however, was in jeopardy, along with other priority items of the administration. Thus, on May 24, following a meeting with the president, congressional leaders announced their hope to adjourn by July 31, unless Congress failed to act on the three "top must" measures —consent to the North Atlantic Pact, extension of the Reciprocal Trade Agreement program, and repeal of Taft-Hartley.[32]

The determination of priorities distressed the critics. The ADA, noting the absence of civil-rights and social-welfare measures, accused Democrats of hoisting the "flag of surrender." Despite the president's attempt to temper the announcement of his congressional leaders, and despite his comment on May 25 that he would continue to press for enactment of his program, the criticism came thick and fast. The NAACP released a statement that spared the president but lashed at the leadership of both parties and the "faint-heartedness" of some liberal Democrats. The June issue of the *Crisis* was even less generous. Expressing its shock at the "runout" on the party's pledges, the NAACP organ warned that if "Mr. Truman and his congressional leaders fail at this point to apprehend the extent of the growing doubts and disillusionment they may understand them more clearly after the 1950 election."[33]

The administration moved quickly to heal the breach. After meeting with the president and with the members of the Senate Democratic Policy Committee on May 31, Senator Lucas distributed a prepared statement that promised to extend the congressional session beyond July 31 to enact "the most urgent proposals" of the president. Although he did not specifically identify the "urgent proposals," Lucas pledged "every effort" to enact civil-rights legislation in spite of the Wherry-Hayden rule on cloture.[34]

The statement only partially accomplished its intent to mitigate black criticism. On June 20 Roy Wilkins reminded White House Assistant David Niles that Negro hopes for "a stout effort" to change the Senate rules had been "dashed" since January 1. Now Congress was "fiddling around" with a weak antilynching bill and with the "wholly unsatisfactory attack on the poll tax through constitutional amendment." Wilkins's distress with administration leaders in Congress was clear, and his letter was apparently an appeal for Truman to intervene more directly in the question of congressional priorities. Others were equally critical of the leadership of both parties in Congress. Robert R. Church, perennial Republican and chairman of the black Republican American Committee, fumed that the "illegitimate intimacy between a majority of Republican senators with southern poll tax Dixiecrats is a national scandal and a disgrace to the party of Abraham Lincoln."[35]

Faced with the penchant of some Republican congressmen to look south for political comfort and with the tendency of some northern and western Democrats to wander far from the party's program, the president was confronted with the necessity of an urgent search for votes. There were, of course, many gratuitous suggestions from well-intentioned sources, such as that a bipartisan approach to civil rights was needed or that additional pressure should be applied on recalcitrant senators. But no one could present a precise formula, except to emphasize the president's power of patronage. And that, as Truman well knew from his own senatorial experience, was a slender reed. Some also suggested that he punish Dixiecrat congressmen following his victory in 1948 by denying them key chairmanships and by withdrawing patronage. Truman, however, quickly and wisely dissociated himself from this route. In his news conference of December 2, 1948, he pointed out that the designations of committee assignments was a matter for Congress; and it was soon apparent that he would not distribute patronage on the basis of party loyalty during the 1948 campaign.[36] In submitting an ambitious program to a new Congress, Truman needed all the good will and support that he could muster from members of his own party; and to urge reprisals in congressional assignments might cost him the allegiance of several Democrats who otherwise had little sympathy, either personally or ideologically, with their southern colleagues. Having served in the Senate himself, Truman was intimately familiar with Congress's jealousy of its prerogatives.

Of course, there were some actions that could not be tolerated, particularly the defection of southern members of the Democratic National Committee during the 1948 campaign. With the president's blessing, the new chairman of the committee, William M. Boyle, Jr., announced in August 1949 the expulsion of six southern members representing the states of South Carolina, Mississippi, Alabama, and Georgia. J. Strom Thurmond was one of the casualties.[37]

Moreover, although the president would not seek revenge for past congressional defections, he made it clear in his news conference of April 28, 1949, that he expected support of his present program. Appropriately enough, Truman's statement coincided with Senator McGrath's presentation of the administration's civil-rights program to Congress. To reporters, Truman stated flatly that the voting records of Democrats in Congress on the Fair Deal would determine the allocation of patronage, which might or might not affect Dixiecrats, depending on their future votes. Senator McGrath preferred to apply it to past records as well, though he accepted the presidential statement with the acknowledgement that "he makes the appointments."[38]

Truman's announcement immediately set off a flurry of speculation and heated rhetoric. The *Chicago Defender* reported that Congressman John H. Rankin of Mississippi had already "felt the lash of the president's patronage whip in the appointment of two Mississippi postmasters on whom he was not consulted by the White House." When a Mississippi physician accused the president of denying patronage to the entire delegation of his state, Truman replied that he "hadn't heard about it." Yet there was some substance to the charge, for it was repeated by Congressman John Bell Williams of Mississippi, who complained that the White House had yet to approve any postmaster appointments for his state. Moreover, the office of L. Mendel Rivers, congressman from South Carolina, reported that the Census Bureau director had advised Rivers that his name did not appear on a White House list for recommendations for appointments to that agency.[39]

Actually, the White House staff had been keeping close tabs on congressional voting for some time and had devised a scorecard of "Hold" and "Clear" lists concerning appointments. The strategy was simple. Some appointments were held up indefinitely, so much so that after the congressional elections of 1950 narrowed the Democratic majorities in both houses, thereby increasing southern power within the party, Congressman E. C. Gathings of Arkansas expressed the hope that "maybe some southern postmasters will finally be appointed."[40]

Important vacancies had to be filled as soon as possible, but the president simply ignored the recommendations of some who fought his program. And here he ran into trouble. In the fall of 1949, for example, Truman appointed Neil Andrews as an interim federal judge in the northern district of Georgia without consulting Senators Russell and George. In August of 1950 the senators had their revenge when the Senate refused to confirm Andrews in a voice vote. No one questioned the judge's qualifications, but the president had violated the hoary tradition of "senatorial courtesy." At the same time the Senate rejected his appointment of Carroll O. Switzer as judge for the southern district of Iowa, after Democratic Senator Guy M. Gillette termed the nomination a "direct affront."[41] The Senate also rejected the nomination of Martin A. Hutchinson to the Federal Trade Commission, after Senators Harry F. Byrd and A. Willis Robertson of Virginia had declared Hutchinson unfit for the position.

Truman could not win. While the Senate rejected some of his nominations on the grounds of "senatorial courtesy," others criticized him for allowing some southerners to retain their customary patronage. Moreover, it was always clear that some southern congressmen preferred the loss of patronage to the accusation that they supported parts of the president's program, which could be more damaging when election time rolled around.[42]

Another problem that plagued the president during the Eighty-first Congress was the inclination of certain senators to use civil rights as a political football. The game began in the first session over the administration's housing bill, when Republican Senators John Bricker of Ohio and Harry Cain of Washington, who led the opposition to public housing, proposed an amendment prohibiting discrimination in all units authorized by the bill. It was a shrewd maneuver. Aware that support for public housing came mainly from northern liberal and southern senators, Bricker and Cain sought to drive a wedge between the two traditionally inharmonious groups, thus destroying any chance for passage of the bill.[43]

It was a nasty situation and led to a split in the civil-rights coalition, both within and without the Senate. The NAACP, the American Council on Human Relations, and the National Negro Congress were willing to take a chance that the bill with the amendment would not be defeated, while the National Council of Negro Women and other organizations were not. In the House, the two black congressmen went opposite ways, with Adam Clayton Powell favoring such an amendment, while William Dawson, reflecting the strategy of the administration, concluded that addition of antidiscriminatory provisions would insure the defeat of the housing bill. A similar breach occurred in the Senate when Wayne Morse and Paul Douglas, although civil-rights champions, vigorously spoke against adoption of the Bricker-Cain amendment, which they considered tantamount to a vote against public housing itself. It was again the old question of priorities.[44]

On April 21 the Senate rejected the Bricker-Cain proposal, 49 to 31, and the House buried a similar amendment on June 29 by a vote of 168 to 130. This led to passage of the housing bill shortly thereafter. The Housing Act of 1949, which called for the construction of 810,000 public housing units over the next six years, was the greatest domestic triumph of the Eighty-first Congress. Neither Congress nor subsequent administrations fulfilled the commitment, however, so that by 1964 only 356,203 units had been constructed.[45]

A similar donnybrook developed with respect to federal aid for education, although injection of the issue of separation of church and state meant that a religious complication was added to that of a conflict over race. The Senate bill, which the president privately preferred,[46] would have allowed the states, if they so chose, to allocate federal funds to parochial schools for textbooks and for school bus service; it would also have required states with segregated schools to provide "just and equitable apportionment" of federal funds between white and black systems. The NAACP drafted an amendment to the bill that would have denied federal aid to those states with segregated schools, and Senator Henry Cabot Lodge was persuaded to sponsor it in the Senate. In contrast to Bricker, Lodge was sincere, though he was also naive if he entertained any hope of its adoption. The opposition was strong and included Hubert Humphrey, who contended that the issue of civil rights should be fought on civil-rights bills alone. "As much as I detest segregation," he noted, "I love education more." On May 3 the Senate overwhelmingly rejected the amendment by a vote of sixty-five to sixteen, and on May 5 a bipartisan coalition voted fifty-eight to fifteen to pass the bill itself.[47]

The NAACP, however, refused to concede defeat, and on May 9 its board of directors passed a resolution to continue the fight. In a letter to the branches, Acting Secretary Roy Wilkins outlined the new strategy of seeking to amend the House bill on federal aid to education. In view of the developments in the House, that hope was tragically misplaced. Graham A. Barden of North Carolina chaired the hearings and reported a bill to the full Committee on Education and Labor that differed markedly from the Senate bill in at least two respects. It eliminated completely the guarantee for equal allotment of funds to black and to white school systems and prohibited the use of any federal money for parochial schools on the grounds that such procedure violated the constitutional guarantee of separation of church and state.[48]

The situation quickly became hopeless. John Lesinski, chairman of the full committee, accused Barden of drafting an anti-Negro, anti-Catholic bill that dripped "with bigotry and racial prejudice" and promised that the bill would never emerge from his committee. House Majority Leader John McCormack, also a Catholic, chimed in with similar accusations. Francis Cardinal Spellman also found the issue irresistible and attacked Barden as a "new apostle of bigotry." This led to Cardinal Spellman's celebrated dispute with Eleanor Roosevelt, who defended Barden because of the religious issue involved. As Lesinski had promised, the bill never emerged from committee.[49]

Straight civil-rights bills fared little better, although the House did pass Mary Norton's anti-poll-tax bill on July 26 by a strong bipartisan vote of 273 to 116, the fifth time in seven years that the lower house had approved such a bill. But no one was excited about its prospects in the Senate, and the bill died in the Senate Rules and Administration Subcommittee, chaired by John Stennis of Mississippi. The House Judiciary Committee failed to report an antilynching bill, while the Senate Judiciary Committee approved Republican Homer Ferguson's bill on June 6 rather than those offered by Humphrey and McGrath, which provided for much stiffer penalties. But the Senate bill went nowhere, despite the propaganda and agitation that accompanied the lynching of a young black in Georgia. The NAACP opposed the Ferguson bill anyway—as ineffective and much too weak. There was even less action on the administration's omnibus bills, which failed to reach the full committee of either house.[50]

Truman's elevation of Senator McGrath to attorney general also added a serious complication, for Senator Pat McCarran, head of the Senate Judiciary Committee, appointed James Eastland of Mississippi to succeed McGrath as chairman of the subcommittee responsible for all civil-rights bills in the Senate, except for those involving the FEPC and the poll tax. "We are mighty sorry about this," editorialized the *Call.* "President Truman has made a gallant fight for civil rights," although he could not dictate to the Senate. "But what else can we do but hold the Democrats responsible?" Nor was Truman happy about it. In his news conference of September 15, when asked for his reaction to the appointment of Eastland, he snapped a "No Comment," with exclamation point.[51]

Finally, as expected, Congress failed to pass an FEPC bill, although civil-rights pressure here was intense. On June 2, 1949, spokesmen for the NAACP, the AFL, the CIO, ADA, and various Jewish organizations met with a White House adviser to urge first priority for FEPC legislation; and on July 7 they delivered the same opinion to Senator Lucas. In a conference on September 9, Democratic leaders in the Senate agreed to place the FEPC first on the civil-rights agenda. The president was already committed. In a meeting on August 30 with Adolph Sabath, chairman of the House Rules Committee, Truman requested that the FEPC be considered as "must" legislation when the House resumed full sessions on September 21. Although the Committee on Education and Labor had reported the bill in August, Sabath promised nothing except to see "what can be done." The corresponding committee in the Senate, however, did not report the bill until October, and then without any recommendation.[52]

Nonetheless, something had been accomplished, if only that the path had been cleared for prompt consideration of the FEPC in the second session. Official confirmation of postponement came on October 3, following the president's regular conference with legislative leaders, when Senator Lucas promised early action on the FEPC in the second session. He also noted that the decision to postpone civil-rights legislation until 1950 was made after consultation with the "principal minority groups of the country," although there had been some grumbling from the ADA, the American Council on Human Rights, and the *Courier*.[53]

It had not been a satisfying legislative year for black Americans. There were a few benefits, though one had to strain to find them. For one thing, the appropriations for Howard University were the largest in the history of that institution. A black columnist was pleased that Congress had refused appropriations to the District of Columbia Redevelopment Land Agency for the purchase or condemnation of homes in the Marshall Heights area, for the result would have been the displacement of blacks by whites. The *Afro-American* was happy about the passage of the Housing Act and the increase in the minimum wage from forty to seventy-five cents an hour but complained that civil-rights bills, "those hardy perennials," again had "withered on the vine."[54]

The refusal of Congress to enact the administration's national health-insurance program was also a matter of concern. The *Chicago Defender* viewed the program as one of the largest potential benefits "for Negroes and low income groups . . . since the passage of social security and minimum wage legislation under the Roosevelt New Deal," and most black leaders agreed. Yet the National Medical Association (NMA), reflecting some of the conservatism of the American Medical Association and perhaps influenced by its intense campaign of opposition, adjourned its annual meeting without taking a position on the plan. This prompted the NMA's new president to declare that "if you support the stand against Truman, you will receive a pat on the back from the AMA, but condemnation from ten million Negroes and the NAACP."[55]

The legislative successes of 1949 were all too few, and civil-rights supporters were largely impartial in criticizing both parties in Congress while remaining generally favorable to the president. The *Amsterdam News* described the situation and the dilemma. The Republican party, declared the editor, "is pictured as—and frequently is—the party of archconservatism, opposed to social changes that are needed by underpaid and handicapped groups such as Negroes. The Democratic party claims to be—and sometimes is—the party of liberal reform. But the Democratic party is also the party of the reactionary South." The editor concluded that President Truman, although well-meaning and sincere, "knows perfectly well that he is a prisoner of his party."[56]

Perhaps—but Truman did not think so, and in the fall of 1949 he fired a concentrated barrage of statements in favor of human rights that had not been equaled by any earlier president. Some of the rhetoric, of course, had an obvious connection with the cold war. In accepting the honorary chairmanship of National Brotherhood Week, he contended that "America is dedicated to the conviction that all people are entitled by the gift of God to equal rights and freedoms even though they may differ in religious persuasion, in social and political views or in racial origin." The following day, October 6, he reaffirmed his commitment to eventual integration of the armed forces. On October 24, when laying the cornerstone for the United Nations building in New York City, he paid tribute to the UN for its devotion to "fostering respect for human rights." In taking part in a program on "Religion in American Life" on October 30, he asserted that America's strength was its spiritual faith, a faith that "makes us determined that every citizen in our own land shall have an equal right and an equal opportunity to grow in wisdom and in stature, and to play his part in the affairs of our nation." Speaking in St. Paul on November 3, as part of Minnesota's Truman Day celebration, he minced no words in holding that "all Americans are entitled to equal rights and equal opportunities under the law, and to equal participation in our national life, free from fear and discrimination." The pronouncements were coming in such rapid fire that the *Call* predicted that when the record of the Truman era was fully written, "among the surprising things about it will be the way in which the Democratic president . . . stood firm in the pledge to make Negroes equal before the law."[57]

The high points of November, however, were speeches before two prominent human-rights organizations. Speaking at a luncheon of the National Conference of Christians and Jews, Truman eulogized the members of his audience for their "fight against the forces of intolerance, to bring light to the dark by-ways of prejudice, and to spread the spirit of tolerance and brotherhood which unites our country." He also referred to his recommendations for legislation, contending that "in

view of the fundamental faith of this country and the clear language
of our Constitution, I do not see how we can do otherwise than adopt
such legislation."[58]

In his address to the annual meeting of the National Council of
Negro Women, he devoted most of his remarks to the United Nations,
which the NCNW was honoring as part of its convention. But he did
not overlook the opportunity to discuss "the extension of freedom and
opportunity to all our citizens without racial or religious discrimination," noting that "we are awakened as never before to the true meaning
of equality—equality in the economic world. We are going to continue
to advance in our program of bringing equal rights and equal opportunities to all citizens. In that great cause," he concluded, "there is no
retreat and no retirement."[59]

The statement was pure Truman in content if not in form, and for
more reasons than one. In particular, his plea for economic equality
was neither a verbal slip nor a speechwriter's inspiration of the moment. Truman had never accepted the idea of intermarriage or of
intense socialization, which he called "social equality" and which he
would continue to oppose long after leaving the presidency. But economic equality was another matter; and if segregation interfered with
that right, then it had to go. On December 6, 1949, the first anniversary of the UN's Universal Declaration of Human Rights, he climaxed
his appeal for justice and tolerance with a proclamation declaring
December 10, 1949—and that day in each succeeding year—as United
Nations Human Rights Day.[60]

Meanwhile the White House staff was quietly working in other
directions. In November, Elmer Staats of the Budget Bureau informed
Stephen J. Spingarn, a White House assistant, of the inadequate budget
request of the Justice Department for its Civil Rights Section. In
particular, the section had only seven lawyers in contrast with eight
in 1948, and of the thousands of complaints received annually, only a
few were investigated and even fewer prosecuted. In view of congressional inaction on the presidential request to elevate the section
to a division, Spingarn suggested to Clark Clifford that the administration ought to increase the present size of the section to fifteen. Moreover, Spingarn asserted that such action "would be further assurance
that the administration meant business in the civil rights field and
would offset the legislative defeats in this field which we are likely to
receive in 1950." When Clifford postponed decision, then left with the
president for Key West, Spingarn approached Charles Murphy, Clifford's assistant, who in turn talked with Attorney General McGrath.

The new attorney general was more than agreeable and responded with a request for fifteen additional lawyers in the Civil Rights Section, which both Staats and Spingarn considered excessive and cut to a total of fifteen.[61]

The upshot of the matter was that Truman's budget message for fiscal year 1951, delivered to Congress on January 9, 1950, included a request for an additional $110,000 for the Justice Department's Criminal Division, primarily for "a substantial expansion" in the civil-rights program. The president's budget message also contained the usual pleas for appropriations to finance the proposed creation of a Fair Employment Practices Commission, a permanent Commission on Civil Rights, and the appointment of an assistant attorney general to supervise a civil-rights division in the Department of Justice.[62]

Civil-rights champions were pleased not only with the budget statement but also with the president's State of the Union message of January 4, 1950, in which he gave no hint of retreat or compromise on civil rights. In some ways, the statement of 1950 was stronger than that of 1949, or at least it was more specific. In addition to his request for enactment of legislation to guarantee "democratic rights" and "economic opportunity," he specifically urged statehood for Hawaii and Alaska, home rule for the District of Columbia, and more self-government for the island possessions. He also expressed his disenchantment with some of the actions of Congress. "Some of those proposals have been before the Congress for a long time," he concluded. "Those who oppose them, as well as those who favor them, should recognize that it is the duty of the elected representatives of the people to let these proposals come to a vote."[63]

Cloture was the problem, as both the president and civil-rights advocates realized. Although the NAACP had been caught napping during the fight over the Barkley ruling in March 1949, it had no intention of nodding again. In mid October 1949, representatives of various NAACP branches met in New York to map strategy for pressure activities in the second session and to call an organizational meeting on November 10 to establish the National Emergency Civil Rights Mobilization. At that meeting, various church, labor, civic, and trade associations began formulating detailed plans for a meeting of delegates from sixty organizations in Washington on January 15–17, 1950, for the purpose of lobbying for civil-rights legislation. The group, however, was cautious about its invitations and fended off attempts of the Civil Rights Congress to infiltrate the movement.[64] Given the growing hysteria concerning communism, it was difficult enough to preserve the legitimacy of civil rights without the additional burden of a suspect organization.

With Walter White on leave, secretly honeymooning on a world tour as a member of the "Round the World Town Meeting," Roy Wilkins had become the acting secretary of the NAACP, which led to his appointment as chairman of the mobilization. Although Wilkins lacked White's contacts at the White House, he quickly sought to persuade the president to address the mobilization's convention. David Niles vetoed the idea, but did agree with Spingarn's suggestion that Truman receive a delegation from the conference. Spingarn was particularly concerned that Truman "set at rest the rumors inspired by Negro Wallaceites and Republican sources that the president gives lip service only to the civil-rights program. Since the likelihood of enactment of any consequential civil-rights legislation in 1950 seems remote, it would appear to be particularly desirable that the president . . . demonstrate (as we know to be the case) that he means what he has said about civil-rights legislation."[65]

The mobilization was more successful than anticipated, at least in its propaganda value and in demonstrating interorganizational, interracial, and interreligious unity. Although representatives of the NAACP constituted a majority of the more than 4,000 delegates, the attendance figures of other organizations were impressive, with 383 from the CIO, 350 from the Anti-Defamation League, 185 from the American Jewish Congress, and 119 from the AFL, as well as many delegates from other concerned organizations. Of equal importance, the delegates came from thirty-three states, "a spread," according to Roy Wilkins, "never before achieved by any other delegation to Washington."[66]

The most significant result of the conference was the agreement on legislative priorities. Organized labor subordinated its opposition to Taft-Hartley, as did the various Jewish organizations to the Displaced Persons Act, to vote top priority to the enactment of FEPC legislation in the second session of the Eighty-first Congress. It was a long way from the bleak, lonely days of 1939 and 1940, and the NAACP was ecstatic with the "ever-expanding support for legislation to extend equal economic, social and political rights to all American citizens."[67]

Armed with the unanimity of the conferees, Roy Wilkins led a delegation to the White House for an audience with the president. As Wilkins began reading a prepared statement that appealed for support in pushing FEPC legislation through Congress, Truman interrupted to point out, "You don't need to make that speech to me, it needs to be made to senators and congressmen." He informed the delegates that congressional leaders had assured him that they would bring civil rights to a vote, even "if it takes all summer," and noted also that his program was necessary "if we are going to maintain our leadership in the world." In the course of his remarks, Truman pointed to the recent passage of a resolution in the Rules Committee, which he termed "a blow that is serious and backward-looking. I am doing everything possible to have that motion beaten when it comes up for consideration on the floor of the House."[68]

The president was referring to the action of the Rules Committee on January 13, 1950, when members voted nine to two to repeal the "twenty-one day rule" adopted the year before. The administration was alarmed, for the rule had permitted chairmen of standing committees to by-pass the Rules Committee during the first session. Moreover, of immediate concern was the fate of the House FEPC bill, which the Rules Committee had refused to report—an action that prompted John Lesinski of the House Education and Labor Committee to announce his intention of bringing up the bill under the twenty-one-day rule on January 23. Should the House sustain the resolution of the Rules Committee, that opportunity would be lost.[69]

The administration quickly mobilized its forces, suggesting to minority groups that a vote for the resolution was a vote against civil rights; and the president himself enlisted the aid of Speaker Rayburn and House Majority Leader McCormack. At the same time, members of the National Emergency Civil Rights Mobilization buttonholed and pressured congressmen to defeat what they termed "the Dixiecrat effort to restore the old power of the Rules Committee to bottle up civil rights and social welfare legislation." On January 20, after Speaker Rayburn insisted that the entire Fair Deal program was at stake, the House rejected the resolution of the Rules Committee by a healthy margin of 236 to 183. Upholding the administration were 171 Democrats, 64 Republicans, and Marcantonio of the American Labor party. Those opposed included 98 Republicans and 85 Democrats, with nearly all of the latter from below the Mason-Dixon line, which clearly revealed the central position of civil rights in the effort to restore the power of the Rules Committee.[70]

The way now seemed clear for Lesinski to move for House consideration of FEPC under the twenty-one-day rule. Yet there might be trouble, for Speaker Rayburn, who did not enjoy a reputation as a civil-rights enthusiast, had consistently refused to indicate if he would recognize Lesinski for that purpose. Adam Clayton Powell, for one,

suspected the worst and wired the president, demanding that he in-
struct Rayburn to recognize Lesinski or all was lost. He also reminded
Truman that he had personally instructed congressional leaders in the
past concerning such bills as those on social security and the minimum
wage. In view of past differences between the congressman and the
president, the tone of the telegram was impolitic, and it failed to have
its intended effect. On January 22 Rayburn announced his intention
to ignore Lesinski on the grounds that the "atmosphere" of the House
was not "right" for consideration of the FEPC.[71]

Obviously, there was something wrong with the atmosphere somewhere, and Congressman Marcantonio of the American Labor party
quickly located it within both parties as well as in the White House.
The question arose early in the president's news conference of February 2, and Truman was forced to admit that he had not requested
Rayburn to recognize Lesinski. "I didn't ask him to recognize any-
body," he stated. "That's the business of the speaker. He has been in
charge of that, and nobody can tell him whom to recognize."[72] Perhaps—although in this instance Truman seemed to be genuflecting too
much in the direction of the Hill. As Powell had pointed out in his
telegram, the president did not always refrain from urging the "Big
Four"—the Democratic leaders in Congress—to move on other priority
items of the administration.

Actually, Truman was probably influenced by a combination of
the old question of priorities and a sense of futility over Rayburn's
attitude, for there was no good reason to question Truman's sincerity
concerning the enactment of effective civil-rights legislation. On January 12, 1950, for example, he had agreed with an assistant's suggestion
that Charles Murphy approach Attorney General McGrath to persuade
him to use whatever influence he possessed with his former colleagues
on the Senate Judiciary Committee to bring the omnibus bill to the
Senate floor. Despite rumors of a harmony meeting between northern
and southern Democrats, Truman made it abundantly clear that he
would not accede to Dixie overtures. In a meeting with Congressman
Brooks Hays, he listened courteously but indicated that his own FEPC
proposal was not negotiable. Given the unwillingness of civil-rights
organizations to accept diluted proposals, he probably had no choice
anyway. In his news conference of January 27 Truman indicated his
refusal to accept a voluntary FEPC, and when queried about an organized southern attempt to present a negotiable civil-rights package,
he responded tersely: "My compromise is in my civil-rights message."[73]

Clearly, the president had made up his mind. On February 9,

when a reporter asked if he cared to comment on the bill recently introduced in the Virginia House of Delegates to abolish segregation in the state, he said, "No. That is Virginia's business," but then volunteered that he was "glad to hear it, however." Obviously, the pressure of civil-rights stalwarts did not require this type of comment. Nor was it necessary, for political reasons, for him to extemporize on civil rights on February 15 to the Attorney Generals Conference on Law Enforcement Problems, meeting in the capital, where he expressed his desire "to emphasize particularly equality of opportunity. I think every child in the nation, regardless of his race, creed or color, should have the right to a proper education," he contended. "And when he has finished that education, he ought to have the right in industry to fair treatment in employment."[74]

In the meantime, Congress again became embroiled in civil-rights matters. There was great alarm over the new statement of policy adopted by House and Senate Republicans and released to the press on February 7, 1950. It was sad enough when the statement declared that "the major domestic issue today is liberty against socialism," which was precisely the argument of many who opposed enactment of FEPC legislation. But it was altogether tragic that it made only a passing, general reference to civil rights. The statement read: "The right of equal opportunity to work, to vote, to advance in life and to be protected under the law should never be limited in any individual because of race, religion, color, or country of origin. Therefore, we shall continue to sponsor legislation to protect the rights of minorities."[75]

Such a position was virtually meaningless, and some of the strongest criticism came from Republicans. In view of the fact that the party had selected a Lincoln Day rally as the occasion for issuing the manifesto, Congressman Jacob Javits regretted that it "did not declare unequivocally for FEPC, antilynching and anti-poll-tax legislation in the best Lincoln tradition," while Senator Lodge deplored the absence of any commitment to break the southern filibuster. Unable to suppress his disappointment, Senator Irving Ives argued that the statement fell far short of the Republican platform of 1948, "particularly on civil rights, labor-management relations and social responsibility." The *Afro-American* was bitter. "Instead of a strong, aggressive document," wrote the editor, "the 2,000-word GOP statement turns out to be another anti-Democratic pronouncement with a measly 49 words addressed to civil rights."[76]

The policy announcement had immediate relevance, for northern House Democrats were searching desperately for ways to bring the

FEPC bill to the floor. Confronted with Rayburn's opposition and with the apparent lack of any real commitment on the part of most House Republicans, they wondered if it was worth the effort. Nonetheless, the House had to act if an FEPC bill were ever to reach the statute books, for Senate Democrats had decided to await the action of the lower chamber, where admittedly the chances of passage were much greater because of the absence of the filibuster.[77]

The "House-first" strategy on FEPC legislation was a new wrinkle and put administration Democrats to the test. After repeated failures to force it out of the Rules Committee, and after both Powell and Franklin D. Roosevelt, Jr., were unable to obtain the required 218 signatures on a discharge petition, which most House Republicans boycotted, civil-rights Democrats seized upon the device known as "Calendar Wednesday." Under this procedure, Speaker Rayburn was required to recognize chairmen of standing committees on successive Wednesdays, at which time they could introduce legislation. Chairman Lesinski's turn came on February 22, 1950, and FEPC was finally on the floor. But the customary bickering and parliamentary maneuvering permitted Republican Samuel K. McConnell of Pennsylvania to introduce a substitute FEPC bill, which expressed opposition to discrimination and proposed a commission to investigate and to recommend, but which did not provide for effective powers of enforcement.[78]

On February 23 a coalition of southern Democrats and conservative Republicans carried the day and adopted the McConnell amendment by a vote of 222 to 178. As the NAACP put it, "The friends of FEPC are the 178 Congressmen who voted against the McConnell amendment," which included 128 Democrats, 49 Republicans, and Marcantonio; the "enemies" were the 104 Republicans and 118 Democrats who supported it. On a motion to recommit the bill to committee for further study, the "friends" of FEPC shifted tactics and voted against the bill on the grounds that referral to committee would kill FEPC in the House for the remainder of the session and that the presence of even a weak bill would force the Senate to act.[79]

The decision to oppose recommittal belonged to Roy Wilkins and Congressman Dawson, which prompted a few criticisms in the Negro press. One columnist contended that "Roy used poor judgment" and suggested the recall of Walter White to "active duty." But if there was disagreement over a tactical situation, there was unanimity concerning the McConnell bill's lack of merit. Although Truman ducked a question during his news conference of February 23, his answer was clear enough to indicate his opposition. Faced with a southern filibuster in the Senate no matter what type of FEPC was under consideration, Senator Lucas promised to take up the Senate's much stronger bill and to ignore McConnell's proposal.[80]

It was now up to the Senate, and no one was particularly sanguine, for coupled with the southern resort to the filibuster was Senator Lucas's tendency to procrastinate. Indeed, much of the growing disenchantment with the administration stemmed from the majority leader's refusal to abide by his promise in October 1949 to place FEPC first on the agenda in the second session. In this, Lucas was not alone, for the White House was generally a willing ally as well as an occasional promoter of decisions to postpone a showdown on FEPC. Thus, when Truman departed for Key West in March 1950, a White House assistant, remembering the criticism showered on the president because of his absence during the Barkley ruling in March 1949, wondered if it would not be advisable to avoid Senate action on FEPC until his return around April 10. More to the point, on April 11 Truman urged Senator Lucas to give priority to foreign-aid measures, particularly appropriations for the third year of the Marshall Plan, which he considered "more important at this time" than controversial domestic items; and the Senate Democratic Policy Committee quickly agreed.[81]

The decision sparked the usual complaints. Roy Wilkins, for one, wired the White House, expressing his shock and dismay for the "continued delay and evasion on the part of the Democratic leadership in the Senate." White House Assistant David Niles responded, explaining the president's position and assuring the NAACP leader of his determination to bring FEPC legislation to a vote. Truman himself sought to soften the criticism during his news conference of April 13, when he explained the necessity for immediate action on Marshall Plan appropriations. He also promised that "FEPC will be carried to the logical conclusion, and every effort will be made to pass FEPC promptly without starting a filibuster against an international matter that is of vital importance to the whole world." In response to another question, the president implied that he regarded all forms of segregation as discriminatory.[82]

It was not enough for some of the critics. In an editorial entitled "The Sad and Gloomy Truth," the *Courier* accused Truman of continuing "to kid Negroes," for everyone knew that civil-rights legislation was "completely dead." And as the president prepared to depart on a short speaking tour, ministers of the African Methodist Episcopal

Church requested members of their congregations to stand quietly during his addresses and refuse to applaud.[83]

The Senate showdown took place on May 19, although not before Lucas had permitted southerners to filibuster the FEPC bill in an easy, lackadaisical manner, with plenty of time for everyone to prepare for dinner. On that day, a motion for cloture on the bill, which now required two-thirds of the entire Senate, went down by a vote of thirty-two to fifty-two, twelve short of the required number. As usual, the NAACP subjected the vote to intense scrutiny. Of the fifty-two votes in favor of cloture, the Democrats produced only nineteen as against thirty-three Republicans, while twenty-six Democrats (five from outside the South) and six Republicans were opposed. Moreover, there were twelve absentees, ten of whom were not southerners. On the basis of these figures, the *Crisis* concluded: "So neither the Republicans nor the northern Democrats can blame the Dixiecrats. Cloture on FEPC was blocked by northern and western senators of both parties, nine Republicans and twelve Democrats." Actually, the magazine was a bit too impartial, although others were also disposed to equalize the responsibility. Given the fact that it was an administration-backed bill, the Democrats gave a sorry performance, which Walter White subsequently admitted in pointing to the "very bad" record of Senate Democrats.[84]

Although Truman himself escaped most of the criticism, the administration moved quickly to repair the political damage. When the Fahy Committee on Equality of Treatment and Opportunity in the Armed Services, which had been created by executive order in 1948, prepared to submit its report to the president on May 22, 1950, the White House staff drafted a statement relating the report to the Senate's actions on FEPC. On May 22 the president released the statement, in which he praised the Fahy Committee for its diligence in preparing the way, "within the reasonably near future," for equality within the military. In concluding, he referred to the commotion in the Senate over the fair employment practices bill, contending that the accomplishments of the Fahy Committee illustrated the value of a commission in the "admittedly difficult field" of civil rights. "I hope the Senate will take this report into consideration as it debates the merits of FEPC," he continued, "and that, as I urged in my State of the Union Message in January, it will permit this important measure to come to a vote." He was referring, of course, to a vote on FEPC itself rather than on a motion to consider the bill, which was what the vote of May 19 was about. Nor did he have a watered-down compromise in mind. During his news conference of May 25, he stated flatly that he would not accept the McConnell version of FEPC.[85]

White southerners were naturally unhappy with the accomplishments of the Fahy Committee in moving toward integration of the armed forces and attempted to destroy legislatively what the president was accomplishing administratively. In deference to the wishes of Senator Russell, the Senate Armed Services Committee amended the administration's selective-service bill to permit draftees and volunteers the option of selecting a segregated unit, which, according to Russell, both white and black southerners preferred. When the bill appeared on the floor, Senator Lucas and Senator Leverett Saltonstall, Republican of Massachusetts, introduced identical amendments to eliminate the provision; and the Senate adopted the Lucas version on June 21, 1950, by a bipartisan vote of forty-two to twenty-nine. But Russell refused to surrender and sponsored another amendment that called for a poll of the entire military, stipulating that if a majority of men from thirty-six states preferred segregation, they would be assigned to segregated units; if they favored integration instead, the amendment would be voided. But the same coalition beat it down by a vote of forty-five to twenty-seven.[86]

In the meantime, Senate Democrats and the White House were girding for a final battle over FEPC, with another vote on the motion to consider the bill scheduled for July 12. The White House staff prepared carefully, and divided senators into four categories according to their past votes on FEPC. It was plain that pressure had to be applied. "We should not go to the polls in November with only the poor showing we made on May 19," one assistant warned; and he called for "every possible effort . . . to have the 30 potential civil rights Democrats present and voting on July 12." To achieve this purpose, Murphy and Spingarn urged the president to wage "an all-out campaign," although realistically they noted: "It looks as though cloture will be unsuccessful in any case, but it seems desirable to get as high a Democratic vote as possible."[87] Truman gave them the green light, and the staff quickly contacted Senator Lucas and William Boyle, chairman of the Democratic National Committee. Lucas was already buttonholing senators and sending out telegrams, and Boyle quickly telegraphed Democratic party officials throughout the country, requesting their assistance in securing full attendance in the Senate in support of the president and the party platform.[88]

The vote on July 12, however, confirmed the suspicions of everyone, when the Senate failed to invoke cloture on the motion to consider FEPC by a vote of thirty-three to fifty-five, nine short of a two-thirds majority. Although the Democratic vote for cloture was an improvement over that of May 19, it was not enough to offset six Republican votes against cloture. If the administration hoped that the second effort would neutralize some of the criticism, it was disappointed, for the Negro press was replete with commentary on the divided nature of the Democratic party. Nor were Republicans spared. The *Afro-American*, for one, maintained that Taft's leadership "prevented the Senate from passing even a watered-down FEPC bill." Some also blamed the Wherry-Hayden resolution, under which cloture required a two-thirds vote of the entire membership, although the fifty-five of eighty-eight votes of July 12 would still have fallen short of cloture under the old rule.[89]

The failure to achieve cloture on July 12, 1950, spelled the end of efforts to pass an FEPC bill in the Eighty-first Congress. Indeed, events seemed to work against its enactment. The bill had long been suspect, and southerners were not alone in accusing it of being Communist-inspired, particularly after Senator Joseph R. McCarthy began his fear campaign in February 1950. Moreover, the outbreak of the Korean War in June necessitated a drastic reshifting of administrative priorities, both at the moment and in the future, although one NAACP leader argued that the war made it imperative to enact FEPC legislation, "not only because our country can no longer enjoy the luxury of wasted industrial manpower but also because our men in Korea need to know in their hearts and minds that they are not fighting in vain." The war did seem to offer a lever, which A. Philip Randolph was quick to grasp. Taking a page from his own past—in particular, the pressure that the March on Washington Movement had exerted on President Roosevelt to create an executive FEPC—the black labor leader urged another executive order to cope with the problems of another war. As the months passed, others took up the cry.[90]

It was a sad year legislatively for civil rights. Although the president appealed twice in 1950 for home rule for the District of Columbia, the House District Committee refused to act on a Senate bill, passed during the first session, which provided for a modicum of self-government. Congress also ignored the president's request for appropriations to expand the Civil Rights Section of the Department of Justice. In fact, the hearings on the matter were a farce. Six of the eight Democratic members of the Senate subcommittee of the Committee on Appropriations were from the South, and Chairman Pat McCarran was no civil-rights advocate. In the course of the testimony, some even questioned the legitimacy of the Civil Rights Section itself, which had functioned since 1939. Federal aid to education went nowhere, for it was still hung up on the knotty religious question of public assistance to parochial schools.[91]

Yet three of the president's recommendations in his special message of February 1948 were able to survive the congressional obstacle course. In July, Congress authorized Puerto Ricans to vote on reorganizing their government as a commonwealth in association with the United States. Under this plan, which was implemented in 1952, Puerto Rico became free, as long as it was consonant with the federal constitution, to decide its internal affairs, including taxes. Also in July 1950, Congress granted to the people of Guam citizenship, a bill of rights, local self-government, and an independent court system. Another of Truman's 1948 recommendations cleared Congress, on August 28, but not without grievous injury to its purpose. This was an amendment to the Nationality Act of 1940. The White House was of two minds about the bill, and its staff prepared both acceptance and veto messages, with the Justice Department and Budget Bureau in favor of the veto. The first section of the amendment contained what the president wanted, granting the right of naturalization to those Asians, mostly Japanese, who still lacked that privilege. Section two was something else. It denied naturalization to those who had belonged to a totalitarian party within ten years prior to the initiation of proceedings and provided for cancellation of citizenship for membership in such an organization within five years after naturalization.[92]

Truman chose to checkmate the spread of what would soon be called McCarthyism. In his veto message of September 9, 1950, he praised section one, but said that section two was "so vague and ill-defined that no one can tell what it may mean or how it may be applied." Moreover, he maintained that the act would create "a twilight species of second-class citizens, persons who could be deprived of citizenship on technical grounds, through their ignorance or lack of judgment." He then urged Congress to reconsider the amendment, preserving section one and removing "those ill-advised provisions" in section two. "At a time when the United Nations' Forces are fighting gallantly to uphold the principles of freedom and democracy in Korea," he concluded, "it would be unworthy of our tradition if we continue now to deny the right of citizenship to American residents of Asiatic origin."[93] Had Truman known then what he learned later, that on September 23 Congress would vote to override his veto of the Internal Security Act, which contained some of the same provisions as section two, he might have signed the amendment to the Nationality Act. As it turned out, he lost on both counts. Having urged and received congressional cooperation in legislating against communism abroad, the president was finding it difficult to cool congressional fever over communism at home.

The Truman administration's concern for the American Indian was also apparent during the Eighty-first Congress. Part of the government's awareness stemmed from the increasing activities of Indians themselves, who were demonstrating a disposition to organize and to propagandize in the postwar period. Prior to the war, most of the organizations devoted to the welfare of Indians were composed of and led by concerned whites. In 1944, however, Indians from all over the country met to establish the National Congress of Americans Indians, which strove to become the red man's counterpart to the NAACP. By 1950 the organization claimed a membership of one hundred thousand and operated from an office in Washington, D.C.[94]

Nonetheless, red men had little political strength. Although the Indian population was rapidly approaching the half-million mark by 1950, Indian leaders and white compatriots were acutely aware of the limitations of red power on election day. In a speech to a black audience in 1949, Charles Eagle Plume of the Montana Blackfeet placed part of the responsibility for their tragic economic situation—"The Georgia Negro eats better than the American Indian"—on the political fact that Indians could not "carry a single county in the nation" on election day. And it was the Indian's economic plight, not his power at the polls, that prompted the Truman administration to propose a program of relief and rehabilitation, particularly for the long-suffering Navajos and Hopis of the American Southwest.[95]

On December 2, 1947, the president reported publicly on the dismal situation facing the tribes of New Mexico and Arizona, outlining executive action to alleviate hunger and requesting stopgap appropriations for the winter, which Congress quickly approved. He also promised to submit to Congress a long-range program to help solve Indian problems. Privately, he directed Secretary of the Interior Julius L. Krug to draft the proposed legislation, which Krug submitted to the White House in February 1948 and, with presidential approval, to Congress shortly thereafter.[96]

The bill, dubbed the Navajo-Hopi rehabilitation bill, proposed a ten-year program, with an initial appropriation of nearly ninety million dollars for agricultural, commercial, and industrial development and for improved health, educational, and housing facilities. Although the proposal failed to pass the Eightieth Congress, it got an unexpected boost when opponents of the Marshall Plan decided that something should be done first to relieve economic distress at home; thus the Navajo soon became part of the crusade against communism. Not to be outstripped, opponents of the administration's Navajo program also invoked the specter of communism in labeling the bill an attempt to "sovietize" the American Indian.[97]

During the legislative deliberations of 1949, passage of the bill seemed certain until it became ensnarled in the problem of discrimination by the states of New Mexico and Arizona in distributing benefits to the Indians. In this particular case, Arizona and New Mexico denied all social-security benefits to the Indians, pleading an inability to match federal payments because of their large Indian population. Critics pointed out that the remaining forty-six states somehow found the financial means to carry their end of the program, though in all fairness it should be noted that the other states did not have as many large reservations exempt from state taxation.[98]

In July 1948, Oscar Chapman, Under Secretary of Interior, urged the president to press the Social Security Board to enforce the law and to withhold all social-security funds from the two states until they abandoned their discriminatory policy. "The spectacle of Indian dependent children and old people starving in Arizona and New Mexico because they are excluded from Social Security benefits," Chapman warned, "would besmirch the record of this administration for faithfully executing the humane requirements of the Social Security Law." The administration was in a quandary, for it was not that simple. If the states of New Mexico and Arizona continued to deny payments to their Indians, starvation and disease would result; if the Social Security Board withheld all federal funds, white and red alike would suffer. Under pressure from the Social Security Administration, New Mexico and Arizona agreed to permit Indians to apply for social security, which had the effect of buying time but only until it became painfully apparent that no applications would be approved.[99]

In 1949 senators from the two states introduced a bill that would have required the federal government to pay up to 80 or 90 percent of the social-security benefits to reservation Indians of New Mexico and Arizona. As one critic put it, "They now ask Congress to discriminate *in favor* of Indians to overcome the effect of their own discrimination *against* members of that race." Although Congress did not approve this particular proposal, it did incorporate its provisions into section nine of the administration's Navajo-Hopi rehabilitation bill, increasing the federal share of social-security payments from 60 to 92 percent. Section nine also proposed to transfer jurisdiction over inheritance and water rights from tribal authority and federal courts to the state courts of New Mexico and Arizona, which was enough to make any Indian advocate shudder.[100]

Despite the bill's overall merit, protests poured into the White House, including one from the Navajo Tribal Council, urging a presidential veto. In nearly every case, the protests embraced both parts of section nine, although the Navajo Tribal Council, for obvious reasons, did not object to the social-security provision. Others did. For example, Oliver La Farge contended that federal assumption of 90 percent of social-security payments was "a vital breach in the non-discrimination provisions of the Social Security Law. It segregates the Navajo and Hopi peoples . . . for special treatment under that law. By so doing it establishes a dangerous precedent, and jeopardizes the rights under the Social Security Law of all other Indian groups and of other minorities."[101]

Although members of the White House staff and cabinet officials were less than enthusiastic about the social-security provision in the bill, they realized that it was one solution to the government's dilemma. Oscar Chapman was reconciled to its inclusion, recognizing that it permitted a better solution in the future and also constituted "the sugar which spurred this bill along." The proposal to transfer authority to the state courts, however, was another matter, and on October 17, 1949, the president vetoed the bill on these grounds. He deliberately said nothing about the social-security proposal and promised to approve the bill if Congress deleted the "objectionable provisions" of section nine. Congress quickly responded, and on April 19, 1950, Truman signed the bill.[102] A solution, however temporary and unsatisfactory, had been found to the problem of social-security benefits for the Indians of New Mexico and Arizona.

The Indians of New Mexico, and opponents of segregation everywhere, received another boost when the president signed a bill in October 1949 appropriating matching federal funds for the construction and continued support of a nonprofit general hospital in Albuquerque. According to Truman, the bill would "encourage the integration of hospital facilities for the care of Indians and non-Indians in the same community." Although he regretted that Congress had deleted "the meritorious provisions which would have guaranteed complete protection for Indian patients against possible future discriminatory practices," he was satisfied with the assurance of the Interior Department that it could insure nondiscriminatory practices through a judicious administration of future funds. Moreover, county officials had promised "that no forms of discrimination or segregated services were ever intended, nor will they be permitted, in the operation or maintenance of the hospital." Accordingly, Truman approved the bill, confident that "fair and equal treatment will be accorded all patients of the hospital." The future sustained the president's faith, for the hospital in Albuquerque, financed jointly by federal and state appropriations, subsequently became the model for construction of hospital facilities elsewhere in Indian country.[103]

Indians and their allies had good reason for optimism in 1950. By his actions in 1949 and 1950, Truman had indicated his continuing desire to include the "forgotten American" in his civil-rights program, a commitment that began with the Indian Claims Act of 1946. The government's amicus curiae briefs in the Indian voting cases in Arizona and New Mexico in 1948, the economic-rehabilitation program for the Navajo and Hopi tribes in 1950, and the president's public opposition to the traditionally segregated facilities for Indians in much of the West gave promise of more to come. So, too, did the president's appointment of Oscar Chapman as Secretary of the Interior in 1949, a move that brought universal applause from Indian organizations everywhere and that represented one of the best appointments during the Truman administration. Chapman's nomination encouraged the belief that some order might be established in the Bureau of Indian Affairs, which had seemed to function haphazardly since John Collier's resignation in 1945. Moreover, in March 1950, the president appointed Dillon S. Myer, renowned for his achievements as head of the War Relocation Authority, as commissioner of Indian Affairs. That action also suggested that justice and order would replace what too often in the past had appeared to be indifference or vacillation. The future promised great hope but would deliver disappointment, in part because of Myer.

The future would also deliver additional disappointment to those who advocated civil-rights legislation, but the record of Congress in 1949–1950 was poor. For the Negro specifically, Congress had passed nothing substantial, although the House had approved an anti-poll-tax bill in 1949 and a toothless FEPC bill in 1950. Neither measure had had a chance in the Senate. The president's determination of priorities, the ineffectiveness of patronage in securing loyalty to the administration's program, the midwestern-southern Democratic coalition, and the senatorial rule on cloture had combined to produce defeat on civil rights. The responsibility was broad, and both parties had to share it.

10 OF PATRONAGE, HOUSING, AND LAW

While Congress debated and procrastinated on civil-rights legislation, the executive and judicial branches took steps of their own to serve the cause of justice and equality. Three of the key issues were patronage, housing, and equality before the courts.

Patronage was of particular importance to black Americans. Of the racial minorities, only they had developed enough interest and political power to gain serious consideration on appointments. Consequently, the pressure on President Truman to name Negroes to federal office mounted after the civil-rights battles of 1948. Louis Lautier pointed out in January 1949 that the report of the President's Committee on Civil Rights was "comprehensive," except for its silence on the subject of the virtual exclusion of blacks from important federal jobs. Indeed at the beginning of 1949 only six black men held presidential appointments that required Senate confirmation.[1]

Although Truman was apparently not eager to nominate Negroes for important federal positions, neither was he necessarily opposed to doing so. Moreover, he was often willing to appoint some whites who were considered sympathetic to Negroes. These included the designations of Tom Clark to the Supreme Court; Charles Fahy to the Circuit Court of Appeals for the District of Columbia; James P. McGranery—a former Pennsylvania congressman who had represented a largely black area—to a district judgeship; and Howard McGrath—the sponsor of the administration's civil-rights program in the Senate—to replace Clark as attorney general. Yet appointments of sympathetic whites would not allay Negro interest in black appointments.

The testing ground for Truman's sincerity in 1949 came in the area of a judicial appointment. Pressure here grew strong in 1949 be-

205

cause of the creation of twenty-seven new federal judgeships and the increasing demonstration of the talents of Negro lawyers in civil-rights cases. As early as May 1949, NAACP President Arthur B. Spingarn urged the appointment of the association's chief counsel, Thurgood Marshall, to a district judgeship, a recommendation strongly endorsed by Spingarn's nephew, White House aide Stephen J. Spingarn. Marshall would have to wait a dozen years for a seat on the federal bench, but the rumor grew, as the summer passed, that President Truman was willing to consider a black for the regular federal judiciary.[2]

Negroes in Philadelphia were particularly active in pressing for a federal court appointment. An important element in the politics of a pivotal state, Philadelphia's Negroes—who were endowed with a number of able lawyers and represented by one of liberalism's leading apostles, Senator Francis J. Myers—held that such an appointment would be a test of the senator's and the president's sincerity with regard to civil rights. Although several names were mentioned, the strongest support from Philadelphia rallied behind Raymond Pace Alexander— a nationally prominent black attorney—for nomination to the District Court for Eastern Pennsylvania.[3]

The Negro most often thought of for judicial appointment by Truman, however, was not Marshall nor Alexander, but William H. Hastie. Hastie had a record of government service unmatched by any other American Negro. During the Roosevelt years he had been assistant solicitor of the Interior Department, district judge for the Virgin Islands, and civilian aide in the War Department. He had also been dean of Howard University's Law School, and had served the president ably as governor of the Virgin Islands and as a campaigner in the 1948 election. Truman, in fact, had been so pleased with Hastie's role in the campaign that he spontaneously wrote him, "We won a great victory because we defined the issues and carried them to the people. Your part in that victory was no small one and I really do appreciate it."[4] Truman would soon have occasion to express his appreciation tangibly.

Hastie had been mentioned for a judicial appointment in 1945, and the question had been raised again in 1949, when a number of people recommended him for the Supreme Court. The White House had also received endorsements of him for other judicial posts. Hastie had considerable support for appointment to the Third Circuit Court of Appeals, including endorsements from the presidents of the Trenton, New Jersey, and Wilmington, Delaware, branches of the NAACP and from a Philadelphia luminary, former Attorney General Francis

Biddle. This plainly put Hastie on a collision course with Philadelphia's Negroes, who were disturbed by the rumors that Hastie might receive an appointment in their vicinity, partly because he had no connection by birth, training, or residence with the area. The Philadelphia Negroes were also displeased because they believed that a Negro district judge could do more for race relations than an appellate judge. And there were other problems. The New Jersey Bar Association thought that an appointment from its state was in order, and Delaware made a campaign for the appointment of Daniel F. Wolcott.[5] Apparently the White House did not seriously consider these bids.

Pennsylvania's Democratic leaders were under fire. They wanted a Negro appointment to satisfy the state's black voters and to lend credibility to the liberalism of the nation's Democrats. Senator Myers requested and received an appointment with Truman for himself and National Committeeman David L. Lawrence for September 28 to discuss the circuit and district court nominations. He also asked that the president "postpone any action he may contemplate until after our visit." What they discussed was not revealed, but about this time Myers hinted to Philadelphia's Negro attorneys that Hastie would receive one of the two judgeships. Moreover, on October 5 the president wrote Francis Biddle of his high opinion of Hastie, who was "under serious consideration" for the third circuit bench.[6]

Also interesting are the nomination papers for Hastie that were prepared for Truman by Attorney General McGrath. An unsigned note dated October 13 and attached to the summary of Hastie's qualifications shows the words "McGranery" and "Alexander for Dist Ct" crossed out and, below them, left standing, "Clear Sen Meyers [*sic*] before sending up."[7] This suggests that Myers had proposed McGranery's promotion and Alexander's nomination, since that move would have been politically helpful to the senator in Philadelphia. If so, it is probable that the White House convinced Myers that it was important to appoint Hastie—that a national figure in a post more prestigious than district judge would in the long run mean more to Negroes, the party, and the nation. Whatever happened, local interests had lost out to national concerns.

On October 15 Hastie was appointed to the Third Circuit Court of Appeals on an ad interim basis and was nominated for Senate confirmation for permanent appointment. Negroes were generally pleased with Hastie's appointment to the highest judicial position ever held by a black American. As the *Chicago Defender* wrote, "The long cherished dream of Negro representation on the United States Supreme Court came nearer realization [with Hastie's designation] than at any time in our history. . . . The new appointment bears out the fact that President Truman is mindful of his pledges to the American people."[8]

The Hastie matter was not yet finished. He had to win Senate confirmation, and there he encountered trouble. A number of senators were opposed to any Negro appointment, but additionally, Chairman Pat McCarran of the Senate Judiciary Committee held up approval until July 1950 because of charges that the judge had been a member of several Communist-front groups. The White House fully backed Hastie. Neither in terms of prestige nor politics could it afford to lose this struggle. President Truman asked Vice-President Barkley to deal with one of the objectors—a fellow Kentuckian, Senator Garrett L. Withers. Barkley reported that Withers had satisfied himself that Hastie was acceptable. The White House also sent to the vice-president eight pages of material received from the Americans for Democratic Action, emphasizing Hastie's anti-Communist views and his loyalty to the Democratic party.[9] The judge was finally confirmed, and Negroes received their most prestigious appointment to that date from a president.

Hastie's was only one of a number of significant Negro appointments made or considered during Truman's second term. One appointment soon after the second term commenced was that of Mrs. Anna Hedgeman to be a general assistant to Federal Security Administrator Oscar Ewing. In the spring of 1949 Dr. Ralph Bunche, the head of the UN's Trusteeship Division, was offered a position as assistant secretary of state, but refused it because of financial considerations and the racial discrimination prevalent in the nation's capital. As Bunche put it, "There's too much jim crow in Washington for me—I wouldn't take my kids back there." Toward the end of the year Interior Secretary Oscar Chapman offered to recommend his old friend Walter White for nomination as governor of the Virgin Islands, which the NAACP secretary declined because he wanted to work in broader areas of responsibility.[10]

During 1950 pressure developed to fill some of the new District of Columbia judgeships with Negroes. National Bar Association President Thurman L. Dodson pointed out that only one of the thirty-eight judges in Washington was black. Now that three more judgeships had been authorized for the city, he hoped that "at least two of the proposed appointments will be colored." Dodson specifically suggested consideration of Assistant United States Attorney Andrew J. Howard, Jr. In March 1950 the White House received John Sengstacke's protest about "what appeared to be a by-passing of the Negro in the administration's program." The letter arrived while Truman was in Key West, but David K. Niles wrote to the prominent Negro publisher "that the passage of time will make clear that there is no intentional or unintentional by-passing of Negroes in the administration's program." Niles also pointed to the appointment of Congressman William L. Dawson as vice-chairman of the Democratic National Committee and Sengstacke's own membership on the President's Committee on Equality of Treatment and Opportunity in the Armed Services.[11]

By summer Truman decided to add another Negro to the District of Columbia bench. In August he nominated Emory B. Smith to be a judge of the Municipal Court. Judge Smith died, however, after thirteen days in office, so Truman named Andrew J. Howard, Jr., to fill his place. Similar appointments were made periodically, so that they were becoming less of a curiosity. Dr. Ambrose Caliver was named assistant commissioner of the Office of Education, and Mrs. Edith Sampson as an alternate delegate to the UN General Assembly during the summer of 1950. In September came the appointment of Daniel W. Ambrose, Jr., as government secretary for the Virgin Islands, and in November Professor Robert P. Barnes of Howard University was named to the board of the National Science Foundation. Indeed, even before these 1950 appointments, the White House could point to seventy Negroes in policy-making, executive, or racial-relations positions in federal agencies and to five foreign-service officers, including three in Europe. In addition, there were eleven holding presidential appointments, including five judges, one ambassador, a collector of internal revenue, and four members of boards or committees.[12]

By the end of the Truman administration the Democrats claimed to have placed Negroes in ninety-four key positions. There was substance to Louis Lautier's statement in 1950 that "President Truman had the courage to go beyond the traditional political plums which went to colored persons during the Harding, Coolidge, Hoover and Roosevelt administrations." It is true that Truman did not go far beyond, but it required gumption and political astuteness to take a couple of steps beyond his predecessors—gumption to get out of the mold and to run athwart racism in Congress, astuteness in terms of Negro votes and America's world image. Moreover, it marked an upturn in the types of appointments given to Negroes that was to continue over the years, with the Eisenhower administration setting additional precedents in the appointments of J. Ernest Wilkins as assistant secretary of labor in 1954, E. Frederic Morrow as special assistant to the president in 1955, and Archibald J. Carey as chairman of the Committee on Government Employment in 1956.[13] By 1967 there would be Negroes in the cabinet and on the Supreme Court. If these were gestures, they were substantial ones, not only in themselves, but also in giving the lie to old ideas about Negro capabilities and in increasing legitimate demands for more blacks in government and for their acceptance by whites. The door was opening slowly, but it was opening.

Another door opened during the Truman administration, and that concerned legal restrictions on the ownership and use of property by minority people. Minorities keenly felt the effects of segregated housing, not only because it was a blow to their pride, but also because it stifled opportunities for decent housing, schooling, and employment. Local laws had enforced housing segregation before 1917, but in that year, in *Buchanan* v. *Warley*, the Supreme Court declared such laws to be in violation of the Fourteenth Amendment. Segregationists circumvented that decision by inserting covenants into property deeds that bound the owners not to rent or sell their property to members of minority groups. The courts usually sustained these covenants as valid limits on property use. The employment of restrictive covenants became so widespread by the 1940s that racial minorities and many Jews found themselves restricted not only to living in ghettos but to living in ghettos that had little chance of expanding. The restrictive covenant was complemented by the general practice among realtors of refusing to show property in white, so-called Christian neighborhoods to members of minority groups. This in turn was reinforced by the *Underwriting Manual* of the Federal Housing Administration, which thoroughly discouraged integrated housing.[14]

By 1945 the foundations of a massive legal challenge to restrictive covenants were laid. Not only had the tensions of ghetto living become aggravated during the war, but the intention of minorities to escape the prison of the ghetto and their ability to finance their intention had grown. Four cases—two in the District of Columbia and one each from Wayne County, Michigan, and St. Louis, Missouri—were instituted in the courts. The NAACP, along with interested lawyers in the localities involved, decided to carry the cases to the Supreme Court. The association was also interested in using the cases as a testing ground for sociological as well as legal evidence on racial questions. Other groups soon joined in the effort. In 1947 the American Jewish Congress filed a brief that struck out at the covenants, and Indians began testing the restrictions in California. By the end of 1947 a dozen organizations representing blacks, labor, Jews, Japanese-Americans,

Indians, and various churches had filed briefs in the restrictive-covenant cases, and other groups planned to do so.[15]

Developments within the federal government encouraged and assisted this activity. In September, Interior Under Secretary Oscar Chapman wrote to Attorney General Tom Clark, strongly urging that a federal amicus curiae brief be filed in the cases. The report of the President's Committee on Civil Rights (PCCR) called for a "renewed court attack, with intervention by the Department of Justice, upon restrictive covenants." Many racial, religious, and civil-rights organizations also asked the department for action. The day after the PCCR's report was made public, the Justice Department decided to file an amicus curiae brief in the cases. A motion for intervention was filed in November by Attorney General Clark and Solicitor General Philip B. Perlman.[16]

By the time the cases came before the Supreme Court in oral argument in January 1948, eighteen amicus curiae briefs had been filed. They contained a wide range of arguments against restrictive covenants: the denial of adequate living space; the indignity of segregation; the artificially high prices; the breeding of delinquency, disease, and vice; incompatibility with the Bill of Rights and the doctrines of Christianity, democracy, and brotherhood; and the adverse impact on foreign affairs.[17]

Most striking was the government brief entered by Clark and Perlman. Their basic legal argument was that "judicial enforcement of racial restrictive covenants constitutes governmental action in violation of rights protected by the Constitution and laws of the United States from discrimination on the basis of race or color." It was further contended that enforcement contravened the common-law principles "governing the validity of restraints in alienation." The legal points were supported by statements of the attorney general, the solicitor general, and other government officials that restrictive covenants were prejudicial to the implementation of government policy as expressed in legislation, executive pronouncements, and international agreements, and to the operation of government programs. This in turn was buttressed by a strong sociological argument as to the social, economic, health, and psychological effects of the covenants, based on government reports and on such works as Gunnar Myrdal's *An American Dilemma*, Charles S. Johnson's *Patterns of Negro Segregation*, and St. Clair Drake and H. R. Cayton's *Black Metropolis*. The government's sociological view bears repeating not only for itself, but because the argument would often be repeated in future cases in one form or another.

> Poverty is, of course, a major cause for the dilapidated, over-crowded, unsanitary, and inadequate homes in which the mass of colored people now live, but it is residential segregation in severely limited areas which accentuates these conditions and bars their alleviation. . . .
>
> It is perhaps almost superfluous to add that . . . the combination of inadequate housing with racial segregation has most unfortunate economic, social, and psychological effects. Colored people are forced to pay higher rents and housing costs by the semi-monopoly which segregation fosters. The incidence of crime and juvenile delinquency is much greater and the occurrence of death and disease among Negroes is substantially increased. And to the corrosion which such congestion and inadequate living conditions work upon any poorly housed individual's mental health, as a citizen and human being, there must be added the peculiarly disintegrating acid which enforced segregation distills to harm not only the victim alone, but the whole fabric of American life.[18]

The Supreme Court's opinions were rendered May 3, 1948, when all four of the cases were decided in favor of the appellants. Chief Justice Fred Vinson, speaking for a unanimous court, said that no court may use its power to enforce racially restrictive covenants designed to achieve housing segregation. Restrictive covenants in themselves were not illegal if voluntarily entered into and enforced. The rub in these cases was that "but for the active intervention of the state courts, supported by the full panoply of state power, the petitioners would have been free to occupy the properties in question without restraint." This was a clear violation of the Fourteenth Amendment.[19]

The victory seemed sweet to America's minorities. The *Afro-American* gave the *Shelley* v. *Kraemer* decision, as it was commonly known, the newspaper's boldest headlines in years and gloried in the fact that the Supreme Court had affirmed "the right of each man to live anywhere in this country he wishes." The *Defender* wrote that the court "has made, perhaps, the greatest contribution to American democracy that is within its power to make." In recounting the many people supporting the test cases, the black press gave high praise to Truman, Clark, and Perlman. As the *Afro-American* put it, "It's mighty comforting to know that we have friends."[20]

Yet the *Shelley* v. *Kraemer* decision was only the beginning of the fight. Many state officials still enforced restrictive covenants, and the courts had to reiterate the new rule on covenants and expand it to cover all minorities. Segregationists sought other ways to restrict the use of property by minorities. Violence and intimidation, against both buyers and sellers, to prevent property transfers were not uncommon. Bittersweet reasoning was also used, as the question was often asked, "Why do Negroes object to living together in one area, when Italians, Irish, Japanese, do not mind?" One attorney retorted, "It's the difference between romance and rape. What you choose willingly is romance—forced on you it's rape!" Other legal avenues to support segregation were sought, most frequently the collection of damages from property owners who broke restrictive covenants. In the District of Columbia and the five states where this approach was used between 1949 and 1952, only Missouri and Oklahoma upheld awards for damages. The question came before the Supreme Court in 1953 in *Barrows* v. *Jackson*. Speaking for the court in a six-to-one decision, Justice Sherman Minton said that damage awards by courts constituted state action in support of restrictive covenants and therefore was in violation of constitutional rights.[21]

Federal policy itself was an important obstacle to the expansion of minority housing. The maze of discouraging federal regulations and practices was a blatant exercise in discrimination, the end result of which was perpetuation of segregation despite court decisions against restrictive covenants. To combat discrimination in housing, civil-rights groups placed much pressure on the Federal Housing Administration. In 1947 the FHA gingerly relaxed its practices by establishing a Racial Relations Service to assist minorities and by eliminating racial terms and recommendations of restrictive covenants from its *Underwriting Manual*. Nevertheless the manual still referred to "incompatible groups" and social factors in discussing neighborhoods and property values. In February 1949 the agency announced that it was altering its rules "to eliminate type of occupancy based on race, creed or color as a determining factor in the approval of mortgages for FHA insurance." The NAACP, however, declared it was "not an effective policy change."[22]

Meanwhile the spotlight shifted to Congress, where public-housing legislation was under consideration. As previously noted, Republican Senators John Bricker and Harry Cain offered an amendment forbidding racial and ethnic discrimination in public housing constructed under the measure. The amendment was lost, largely because liberals feared that the bill with the amendment would be defeated—an argument that sounded the death knell for much antidiscrimination legislation during Truman's second term. Congress passed the bill in June. The Housing Act of 1949 was a victory for the administration in that it authorized additional low-rent housing, but the law was seriously compromised in the eyes of blacks, because it did not forbid discrimination or give the poor people dispossessed by slum clearance priority in moving into new public housing.[23]

Federal Housing and Home Finance Administrator Raymond M. Foley was pressed to implement nonsegregated public housing administratively. He believed, however, that to do so would hurt the program's effectiveness in the South and would create additional opposition to future housing legislation, which already had an abundance of opponents. Foley therefore followed the policy of permitting local housing officials to decide the nature of their programs, which was a slight improvement over earlier policies that encouraged segregation. In response to this policy, and to civil-rights pressures, nine states and a number of cities by 1950 prohibited discrimination in public housing. The total impact, however, was limited by the coming of the Korean War. In response to the need for economy in the use of materials and funds and to pressures from foes of public housing, new construction was considerably restricted.[24]

During the fall of 1949, at the behest of civil-rights groups and apparently the Justice Department, the White House urged housing finance officials to liberalize their rules. Housing and Home Finance Administrator Foley worked out rules to stop his agency from supporting restrictive covenants with federal lending authorizations, but withheld implementation until the Veterans Administration decided to follow the same policy. David Niles suggested to President Truman that he bring Foley and Veterans Administrator Carl Gray, Jr., together on lending policies. Truman acted immediately by telling Gray to try to work out a consistent policy with Foley, and the two officials soon devised mutually acceptable policies. Foley's policy, announced on December 2, was that "no property will be eligible for FHA mortgage insurance if, after a date to be specified [later] and before the FHA insured mortgage is recorded, there has been recorded a covenant racially restricting the use or occupancy of the property." It was announced that the Veterans Administration was taking like action on veterans' mortgages. The agencies also specified that a restrictive covenant could not be inserted as long as the federal insurance continued in force. The effective date was set for February 15, 1950; and in 1951 the policy was extended to repossessed FHA-insured housing.[25] The new mortgage-insurance policy was a step in the right direction; but, like the elimination of judicial enforcement of restrictive covenants, it did not solve the problems of minority housing. Minority peoples still were not free to settle where they could afford to, because of zoning laws, intimidation, a variety of self-enforcing or extra-legal contractual devices, and the discouraging tactics and chicanery of many administrators and most realtors. Nevertheless the pressure for open housing and better housing continued, as did the Truman administration's responses. The Racial Relations Service reached out to soften the attitudes and strengthen the programs of several federal agencies and even of some builders. The Housing and Home Finance Administration (HHFA) staffed its Division of Slum Clearance and Urban Redevelopment with several specialists on race relations, and the Public Housing Administration and the Federal Housing Administration also added a large number of minority advisers in Washington and in the field. Another development was the appointment, in 1950, of Col. Campbell C. Johnson to the National Capital Housing Authority, the only Negro on the one-hundred-man body. Johnson set as his prime goal the desegregation of public housing in the District of Columbia. In 1952 his resolution to that effect was passed, and by 1954, 87 percent of Washington's public housing had been desegregated.[26]

Black pressure against segregation in housing was unrelenting. In 1951 the NAACP called upon the government "to cease and desist from aiding the development of housing on a racially discriminatory basis." The *Chicago Defender's* "National Grapevine" column asked pointedly a year later why the government insured the borrowed monies of private builders who excluded blacks from their projects and why segregation was not abolished in public housing that received federal assistance. When FHA Commissioner Franklin D. Richards resigned in 1952, Robert C. Weaver of the National Committee Against Discrimination in Housing and Walter White asked President Truman to take the occasion as an opportunity to change the racial policies of that agency. Philleo Nash, who had succeeded David K. Niles as Truman's adviser on minorities, pointed out that less than 2 percent of FHA projects was available to Negroes, compared with up to 35 percent of public housing projects. He urged his boss to charge the new commissioner with increasing the amount of FHA housing open to Negroes, to have the FHA's position on restrictive covenants reviewed by the Justice Department, and to establish better communication with the HHFA on integration of FHA operations with programs of defense housing and slum clearance. Truman's response was "This looks all right."[27] Of course, the question was, could much be accomplished by the various agencies concerned with housing in the seven months left of Truman's administration?

Some things did happen. The FHA stepped up its interest in redressing the racial imbalance in housing after Commissioner Richards's resignation. It added more racial advisers, prepared detailed surveys of demand for minority housing in larger cities, and directed field offices to set goals for minority housing and financing. In October the VA announced that it would demand fair treatment for all veterans in regard to home insurance and that its local offices would stop using the term "Negro" on home-loan appraisals. Furthermore, Housing Administrator Foley apparently agreed to two other policies recommended by the National Committee against Discrimination in Housing. The first was that all public housing owned and operated by the federal government would be open on a nondiscriminatory basis, although by January 1953 this policy had been ordered only for defense housing. The second was to guard against displacement of the poor by slum-clearance projects. In that area Foley, in January, issued a statement of procedures designed to assure that urban redevelopment and slum-clearance projects "will not result in decreasing the total living space available in any community to Negro or other racial minority families."[28] The statement was golden; but implementation, depending as it did upon a new, opposition administration, was tinny.

It was clear that federal housing programs and actions during the Truman administration brought little satisfaction to minorities. What then was achieved? The percentage of Negroes who owned their own homes increased from 23 to 34 from the 1940s to the 1950s. In 1940 Negroes occupied 44,754 of 134,056 units of federal public housing, but in 1951 they occupied 181,431 of 656,693 units. In other words, more space was available to blacks, but proportionally less than eleven years earlier. The Supreme Court decisions in *Shelley* v. *Kraemer* and *Barrows* v. *Jackson* allowed, however limited the occurrence, for the development of integrated private housing. The decisions also permitted the expansion of ghettos, which resulted in alleviation of crowding for some minority peoples. It was a pathetic improvement, however; a step from misery to slightly less misery.[29]

The HHFA and the VA reversed their position from one of encouraging segregation in private housing to one of barely tolerating open occupancy. On public housing, President Truman proudly noted that by 1950, 177 projects were unsegregated, an eight-fold increase in eight years. This was part of an upward trend, with 210 open by 1952, 297 by 1954, and 341 by 1955. Moreover, the number of states that had some racially open public housing grew from nineteen in 1952 to twenty-seven by 1955, and the number of communities rose from 70 to 131. Another set of figures indicates that of the 136,043 federal housing units lived in by blacks in June 1953, 102,988 were completely segregated, 26,984 were wholly integrated, and the rest partly integrated—a contrast with total segregation in 1945.[30]

Despite the Truman administration's growing concern, by 1953 the housing problems of minorities were still severe. There was insufficient decent housing available to racial minorities. So little public housing was replacing the units demolished in slum clearance that blacks could justifiably charge that urban renewal was really Negro removal. Resistance from realtors and from potential sellers and neighbors, coupled with vigilante violence, continued to frustrate residential integration. Ghettos remained ghettos, however much they expanded, and the contiguous areas that slum dwellers spilled into were usually slums too. Prices were high as sellers took advantage of an artificially tight market. Federal housing policies, even if turned in a more favorable direction, would take a long time to become even somewhat effective.[31] In short, the Truman administration, except for accomplishing a modicum of desegregation, only arrested the spread of the cancer of inadequate minority housing instead of shrinking it.

More substantial were the results of court action during the Truman years. Many cases in behalf of minority rights had already been won before the president's 1948 civil-rights message to Congress. Most of these, however, were part of the prologue to what was to come. Increasingly, minorities took to the courts to seek their rights, and with growing success. In 1948 the Supreme Court reiterated that systematic exclusion of blacks from juries was unconstitutional. The court also sustained a Michigan law providing for equal accommodations in transportation, held that Oklahoma could not deny access to state-supported institutions for legal education on racial grounds, and undermined the foundations of California's Alien Land Law. In the lower federal courts, it was ordered that the swimming pool in Montgomery, West Virginia, and the public golf courses of Baltimore, Maryland, be opened to Negroes. The California Supreme Court invalidated the state's law against interracial marriages as a violation of the federal Constitution's equal-protection clause.[32]

The year 1949 saw many victories in state and lower federal courts in a broad range of civil-rights cases, but 1950 was a year of resounding legal achievements. That year the Supreme Court decided three of the twentieth century's most important civil-rights cases—*Henderson*, *Sweatt*, and *McLaurin*. The *Henderson* case was of longest standing. In 1942 Elmer W. Henderson had been denied service in a railway dining car, and his complaint had, over the years, wended its way up to the high bench. The Interstate Commerce Commission in 1949 prepared a motion to affirm the position that segregation of Negroes in diners was not discriminatory. The document was sent to Solicitor General Philip Perlman for his signature, but he rejected the motion as being based on unsound law.[33]

Indeed Perlman went a step further and in October 1949 filed an amicus curiae brief in support of Henderson. The solicitor general sought invalidation of an ICC order approving segregated arrangements in dining cars, not only because he thought it was contrary to law but because it worked against the social and personality development of Negroes and weakened the moral values of whites. Perlman also called for reversal of the separate-but-equal doctrine of *Plessy* v. *Ferguson* (1896) in order to dismantle the legal structure that worked "a denial of rights and privileges and immunities antagonistic to the freedoms and liberties on which our institutions and our form of government are founded." He based his brief not only in law but also in the works of leading social scientists, which further buttressed the use of sociological materials in civil-rights cases. In April 1950 Attorney General McGrath joined Perlman in arguing the case before the Supreme Court, thereby making it clear that the Truman administration was in dead earnest in striving to narrow the gap between America's preachings and its practices.[34]

Meanwhile, the Supreme Court had accepted the *Sweatt* and *McLaurin* cases for argument. In Sweatt's case a Texas court had ordered the state to provide racially equal facilities for legal education. The black law school that was subsequently established was rejected by Sweatt as not affording equal training. McLaurin had compelled the University of Oklahoma to admit him to graduate study, but the university's officials had segregated him within classes, the library, and the cafeteria.

These two cases were of great importance, because they represented the redoubled postwar assault of Negroes on segregated education and their refusal to accept devious ways of meeting court orders. The work of minorities had already led to the opening of a number of institutions. In 1948 the University of Arkansas Medical School was opened to Negroes, and the University of Delaware admitted black graduate students to courses not offered at the state's Negro college. That same year, New York became the first state to enact a law barring discrimination on grounds of race, religion, or national origins in the admission of students to nondenominational educational institutions.[35]

Minority groups hoped that the *Sweatt* and *McLaurin* cases might lead to overturning the separate-but-equal rule, thereby giving a more solid basis to future legal challenges. The issue was sharpened early in 1950 when Solicitor General Perlman filed an amicus curiae brief in behalf of Sweatt and McLaurin, contending that equality could not be reached under the separateness of the Plessy doctrine. The massive 1950 legal challenge to segregation by Negroes and the government indicated that, as Louis Lautier wrote in his syndicated column, "not since the Dred Scott decision in 1857, has the United States Supreme Court been faced with a more far-reaching question."[36]

In the quiet of its cavernous chamber the court rendered decisions in the *Henderson, Sweatt,* and *McLaurin* cases on June 5, 1950. Justice Harold Burton, speaking for the high bench in an eight-to-zero decision, held that segregation in dining cars ran contrary to the Interstate Commerce Act and was therefore illegal. Chief Justice Fred Vinson also spoke for a unanimous court in his opinions on the other two cases. Regarding Sweatt, he ruled that the law school established by Texas for Negroes did not afford equality of legal instruction. "We hold that the equal protection clause of the Fourteenth Amendment requires that petitioner be admitted to the University of Texas Law School." That clause was also applied to the *McLaurin* case, where the court judged that physical separation of a Negro within the University of Oklahoma impaired and inhibited the student's ability "to study, to engage in discussions and exchange views with other students, and, in general, to learn his profession." The cases had been won, but without the court's having grappled with the challenge to the Plessy doctrine. The available law was so clear, as Justice Burton indicated in his *Henderson* opinion, that "we do not reach the constitutional or other issues suggested." Yet it was obvious to many observers that the court could not stall forever on the separate-but-equal issue. As the NAACP's chief counsel, Thurgood Marshall, asserted, "The complete destruction of all enforced segregation is now in sight."[37]

Minorities had taken great strides forward during the postwar period in their resort to the courts. Yet, with or without government support and despite favorable court decisions, the results were less tangible than they seemed to be. For example, some railroads still sought to segregate patrons in dining cars, although with less success; and segregation continued unimpaired in aspects of interstate transportation such as station facilities. The ICC did not show itself to be interested in rooting out passenger segregation until 1955, and even then compliance was not thoroughgoing and its rules did not apply to intra-state modes of transportation.[38] Nevertheless Elmer Henderson's crusade helped to reduce racial separation in interstate transportation and laid the foundation for the assault waves that by the middle 1960s eradicated segregation from almost all aspects of public transportation in America.

As for black optimism in 1950 on the elimination of segregation in schools, it seemed realistic at the time, considering the trend of judicial decisions. Court orders had jarred the foundations of school segregation and cut holes in its roof. Further jarring and cutting followed the *Sweatt* and *McLaurin* decisions, as in 1950 nine southern and border states loosened some of their restrictions on the enrollment of Negroes in publicly supported colleges and universities. Hope for additional gains was high, especially for the biggest triumph of all—the reversal of the separate-but-equal doctrine and achievement of integrated schooling on all educational levels.[39] And progress was made suit by suit, court order by court order, until finally, in 1954, the Supreme Court reversed *Plessy* v. *Ferguson*. It was to be after that, however, that the hard-core problem—implementation of integration in the face of massive resistance and de facto segregation—was to become obvious.

11 INTEGRATING THE MILITARY

Solicitor General Perlman's amicus curiae briefs in the Supreme Court cases of 1950 were eloquent testimony to the administration's commitment as well as being legal landmarks in furthering integration in America. But the most stunning achievement of the Truman era in the field of civil rights involved desegregation of the armed forces, which could not have been accomplished if the president had not appointed and unwaveringly supported his Committee on Equality of Treatment and Opportunity in the Armed Services, which was established as a result of Executive Order 9981 on July 26, 1948.

The committee, popularly known as the Fahy Committee, was a distinguished group by the standards of any time or place. As chairman, the president appointed former Solicitor General Charles H. Fahy, a Georgia-born Catholic who, in the words of David Niles, was "totally reconstructed on the subject of race." Other members included William E. Stevenson, president of Oberlin College; Dwight R. G. Palmer, president of General Cable Corporation; business executives Alphonsus Donahue and Charles Luckman, neither of whom played a major role in the committee's activities; John H. Sengstacke, publisher of the *Chicago Defender*; and Lester Granger, head of the National Urban League. E. W. Kenworthy, a newspaperman and free-lance writer, was subsequently named as executive secretary.[1]

There were some objections to the composition of the committee. Granger was appointed over the protests of Secretary of the Army Royall, who was irritated because of Granger's "unjust criticism" of himself and of the army. Royall believed that the army's treatment of the Negro was "equal to that of the air force and superior to that of the navy," which was true only if segregation was considered nondiscriminatory. One black scholar also objected subsequently to the ratio of two blacks to three whites on the actual working committee, a ratio that was nothing short of revolutionary in the 1940s.[2]

Although Fahy's presence in Europe during the fall of 1948 prevented the committee from getting under way officially until January 1949, the groundwork for cooperation between the military and the committee was established in October 1948. Upon his return, Fahy also conferred with the president concerning the *modus operandi* of the committee, suggesting that it should adopt a persuasive rather than a coercive attitude toward the military in seeking implementation of the president's order. Truman agreed, assuring Fahy of his own active support. The committee already knew its ultimate goal; for although the presidential order had called, somewhat vaguely, for the establishment of equality, the president had flatly stated in his news conference of July 29, 1948, that the order meant the eventual end of segregation. Truman meant business and did not consider his creation a political gimmick. In his remarks to the opening session of the committee on January 12, 1949, and in the presence of James Forrestal and the three service secretaries, the president demanded "concrete results—that's what I'm after—not publicity on it" and promised, if necessary, "to knock somebody's ears down" to get the job done.[3]

The committee also had the support of Forrestal and of his successor, Louis Johnson, who replaced the ailing secretary of defense in March 1949. Indeed, on April 6, Johnson issued a directive to the service secretaries in which he proclaimed as general policy the equality of treatment and opportunity in the armed forces, noting in particular that "individual merit and ability" would determine enlistments, retentions, promotions, assignments, and attendance at schools. Moreover, although some all-black units might be retained, Johnson continued, "qualified Negro personnel shall be assigned to fill any type of position ... without regard to race"—a statement clearly at variance with existing army policy. In conclusion, Johnson directed the three services to submit, not later than May 1, 1949, a report of their "detailed implementation" of this policy.[4]

The Fahy Committee was delighted. "It is much better to have the military do these things on their own hook," Kenworthy noted, "rather than to have a presidential directive which will raise all kinds of hob on the Hill." Moreover, in testimony before the committee, the military had "revealed itself somewhat tepid" about the president's policy, but Johnson's statement "means man-to-man integration way beyond the limitations" of existing army policy.[5]

The committee was already optimistic about progress in the air force and the navy. As early as November 1948 the air force had devised a new personnel policy that prepared the way for eventual integration of nearly all units. Although some high-ranking air-force officers, like many in the navy and army, opposed integration, Air Force Secretary Stuart Symington did not. Symington, whose attitude on racial matters was enlightened, even if his language was not, informed both the president and the committee in the opening session in January 1949 that "our plan is to completely eliminate segregation in the air force," promising to take his "fine group of colored boys" and integrate them 100 percent throughout all subdivisions.[6]

The air force presented its new program in testimony to the Fahy Committee in January 1949, a program that fell short of complete integration but one that the committee considered a "great advance" over existing policy. The group, however, had two objections to the program—the discretionary authority of local commanders to determine which Negroes should be assigned to racial units and the stipulation that no integrated unit should be more than 10 percent black. The air force subsequently deleted the two limitations, then submitted its new personnel policy to the secretary of defense in response to his directive of April 6. The Fahy Committee had scored its first victory.[7]

The air-force program, announced publicly on May 11, 1949, was promising. It pledged equality of treatment and opportunity and specifically prohibited "strength quotas of minority groups in the air force troop basis." Paraphrasing Johnson's order of April 6, it also stated that all matters affecting personnel would be determined on the basis of individual merit, although some all-black units might be continued. Secretary of Defense Johnson accepted the policy and announced, as an indication of good faith, that the first step in the air-force program of integration would be deactivation of the 332d Fighter Wing, an all-black tactical group, and distribution of its personnel throughout the air force.[8]

With its objections met, the Fahy Committee decided to postpone further recommendations to the air force until it could investigate the results. The committee was not disappointed. By January 31, 1950, the number of integrated units was 1,301, leaving only 59 predominately black, which contrasted strikingly with 106 all-black and 167 integrated units in June 1949, when the policy had gone into effect. The air force had accomplished what many had deemed impossible, for the program was working without any serious racial incidents, thus disposing of one of the army's big bugaboos.

In an investigation of air-force installations in the latter part of January 1950, committee members saw blacks and whites working, eating, and living together in relative harmony.[9] Moreover, black officers were commanding white as well as black enlisted men without any apparent animosity on either side, thus disproving another favorite army bogey. Such command, however, was only token in the air force, primarily because of the small number of black officers—only 351, a pathetic 0.6 percent of the officer corps.[10]

The navy was equally cooperative with the committee, although there was some opposition to any liberalization of policy. One navy captain, for example, found it impossible to accept the navy's current program of integration, arguing that "the armed forces should fight it step by step, and accept only the degree of non-segregation which is forced upon them—and that the heads of the armed forces should propose no plan which enhances its principles." He concluded his memorandum with a warning: should desegregation in the navy continue, "I predict wholesale resignations and retirements from the navy, if not open mutiny. Command of white officers and men by Negroes would have equally dire results."[11]

Fortunately, the captain's attitude did not reflect that of the high command, particularly the civilian leadership, which had moved gradually toward integration since 1944. In fact, the navy was so satisfied with its racial policies that it responded to Johnson's directive of April 6 by insisting that an examination of navy practices and procedures revealed no inconsistencies with Johnson's prescribed policies. The secretary of defense, however, disagreed and rejected the navy's statement, recommending that the Fahy Committee indicate "informally" to the army and navy those steps necessary "to bring their policies into line" with those of the president and himself.[12]

The committee quickly recommended that the navy (1) inaugurate a program aimed at recruitment of Negroes for general ratings, to dispel the widespread belief that blacks were assigned only to the Stewards Branch; (2) recall several Negro officers to active duty; (3) grant chief stewards the grade of chief petty officer; and (4) launch an educational program to persuade talented Negroes to enroll in the naval ROTC program. The navy's revised program, submitted to the secretary of defense on May 23, included all of the committee's recommendations as well as the additional promise to integrate the training facilities of the Marine Corps. The committee, with the backing of the president and the secretary of defense, had scored again.[13]

The navy wasted little time in launching its new program. In his report of December 22, 1949, Under Secretary of the Navy Dan Kimball revealed that all black Marine Corps recruits were going through training on an integrated basis, although some still went into all-black units after basic training. The navy had vastly expanded its recruitment program. Five black officers had been recalled to active duty, and the *U.S. Navy Occupational Handbook* contained pictures of blacks and whites working together, as would the new edition of *Life in the Peacetime Navy.* Moreover, to attract more Negroes into the ROTC program, the navy had enlisted the aid of the Urban League. The navy had also changed the status of chief steward to chief petty officer, as requested by the committee, as well as having elevated stewards first, second, and third class to the status of petty officers. Kimball was quite sanguine about it all. "The results attained during a comparatively brief period," he noted in conclusion, "indicate forcibly that racial tolerance is spreading and it is only a question of time until it will no longer present a problem within the navy."[14]

The Fahy Committee was inclined to agree, though it was disappointed that few Negroes were qualifying for the ROTC program. It was also disappointed that by March 1950 there were only seventeen black officers on active duty. But there had been unmistakable progress elsewhere. At the close of the war, almost 95 percent of the Negroes in the navy were in the Stewards Branch; by 1950, that percentage was reduced to 57.4, with the rest scattered throughout general service. Moreover, Kenworthy reported in 1950 that "in schools and in general service, Negroes work, eat and sleep under integrated conditions, ashore and afloat." The committee's investigation of naval facilities also revealed the absence of racial friction, which added another weapon to the committee's arsenal in its running battle with the army.[15]

And it was the army that almost brought the Fahy Committee to the point of despair. Army Secretary Royall's initial reaction to the presidential order of July 26, 1948, was to suggest an experimental integrated unit in each of the three services, which both the air force and navy rejected as meaningless in view of their own existing integrated programs. His reaction to Louis Johnson's directive of April 6, 1949, was similarly evasive, and self-satisfied. On April 21 he informed Johnson of the army's opinion that its practices and procedures were "sound in the light of actual experience" and also met the intentions of the president's executive order. Royall declared that all Negro personnel had equal opportunity to obtain promotions and to attend service schools; but this, as the Fahy Committee put it, "did not accurately reflect the existing situation." For example, as of August 1949, there were no authorizations for Negroes in 198 of a total of 490 active occupational specialties. Even more revealing, again as a result of the army's segregation policy, there were black quotas only for 21 of 106 service courses offered in the spring of 1949. Royall's report and the army's racial policy, which even fell short of the Gillem report, were patently unacceptable; and the secretary of defense directed the army to try again. He also requested the Fahy Committee to forward its recommendations to the army for consideration.[16]

The Fahy Committee was well prepared after months of investigation, and it quickly forwarded a package proposal to the army. Although the recommendations deliberately avoided calling for the immediate end of segregated units, because of the administrative problems involved and the obstinacy of army staff officers, they established the principle of equality and, ultimately, of integration. In particular, the committee proposed that the army open all positions and all service schools to all of its personnel, regardless of race; that it rescind the Gillem Board policy of limiting Negroes to black units and overhead installations, and assign all personnel on the basis of individual ability; and that it abolish the Negro quota of 10 percent. If accepted and faithfully executed, the proposals obviously meant the establishment of widespread integration, which the army at this juncture refused to accept.[17]

On May 26, 1949, Royall dispatched his second reply to Secretary Johnson. In essence, the report ignored the recommendations of the Fahy Committee and countered with misleading information and a reaffirmation of the status quo. By this time, Louis Johnson's patience was wearing thin. On June 7 he returned the army's second proposal to Secretary Royall, expressing his sympathy with the "grave problem" confronting the army but remaining convinced that it had yet to meet the basic intent of his and the president's directives. Johnson asked for a third statement of policy, advising the army to "consider very carefully the informal suggestions of the Fahy Committee, which, I understand, have been made available to you."[18]

A series of long, wearisome meetings with representatives of the army followed. The Fahy Committee now had the army on the run; and though its ultimate success depended upon the continued support of Johnson and the president, for the moment the committee had the backing of both. It also received a more sympathetic hearing when Gordon Gray replaced Royall as secretary of the army in June 1949. As a result of its extensive investigation of army records as well as the information provided in testimony, the committee was prepared to hoist the army on its own petard in the discussions that followed. For years, the army had insisted that it was neither a social laboratory nor an institution of prejudice. Segregation was necessary, ran the time-worn argument, to achieve maximum utilization of manpower and to maintain morale. But the committee had carefully examined the army's own evidence and had concluded otherwise.

At this point it was clear, even to the myopic army, that segregation was administratively inefficient and did not achieve maximum utilization of talented blacks, which the committee's proposal of assignment to any unit on the basis of ability would permit. When the army contended that Negro units had performed poorly in combat, thereby implying that blacks were inherently cowards, the committee countered with the army's evidence that segregated units, primarily because of educational disadvantages in civilian life, contained far too many men in the lowest intelligence classification. White men with similar classification also fell short of expectations, and it naturally followed that integration would solve part of the problem. The committee had bested the army on its own ground, and for the first time the army had its back to the wall. Moreover, the success of integration in the navy and the air force testified eloquently against the army's argument that desegregation would cripple service morale and create severe racial friction. Stripped of its traditional defenses, the army resorted to the argument of morality, contending that segregation protected black officers and enlisted men from competition with superior whites—which spoke volumes about the army's interest in achieving maximum efficiency. The committee could not resist the temptation to point out that the president desired equal opportunity, not preferential treatment, for Negro soldiers.[19]

Discussions with the army continued from June through September 1949, with Army Secretary Gray seeking to arrive at some compromise with the committee. In a meeting with members of the committee on September 16, Gray and Vice Chief of Staff Wade H. Haislip agreed in substance with the committee's first three recommendations; the fourth, the 10 percent quota on black soldiers, would be held in abeyance for further consideration. In essence, the army appeared to agree to open all positions and all service schools, without regard to race, and to assign graduates of army schools to any unit that required their skills. This represented a major breakthrough. Fahy was pleased with such "great progress," as he expressed it to the president, although he made it clear that the committee wanted to review the army's new proposals before they were forwarded to Secretary of Defense Johnson for approval.[20]

But the army now tried to outmaneuver the committee. On September 30 Johnson announced his acceptance of the army's third set of recommendations. Although Fahy and his associates had not seen or approved the army's final draft, Gray's report to Johnson left the impression that they had. As a further irritation, the army was evasive on the committee's third suggestion, to the point that it seemed merely a reaffirmation of the Gillem Board recommendation that qualified blacks could be assigned to overhead units at largely white installations. Fahy found this unacceptable. In a memorandum to Truman on October 11, he noted that the effect of the army's qualification of the committee's third recommendation would largely nullify the other two. Simply put, if the army continued to restrict blacks to segregated units and to a few overhead assignments, the opening of all occupational specialties and training schools meant practically nothing. Fahy promised the president that he would continue discussions with the army to solve this problem as well as that of the quota.[21]

The army's attempt to circumvent the committee surprised no one, but Johnson's acceptance of the army's proposal did. In view of his staunch position up to this point, it seemed inexplicable, although his commitment was never as firm as that of the Fahy Committee.[22] Perhaps Johnson was simply tired of it all. Perhaps he was beginning to share the army's fear that desegregation would lower combat efficiency at a time of severe cold-war tensions. Or perhaps he accepted the report in good faith without questioning Secretary Gray's implication that it had the committee's approval, for liaison between Fahy and Johnson had never been close during these trying months. Perhaps it was a question of alternatives. Johnson's decision to accept the army's third proposal concerning equalization of opportunity should be considered in the context of the equally difficult problem of successfully unifying the armed services. The grumbling over unification in 1947 and 1948 had turned into a vocal, bitter issue in 1949. Secretary of the Navy John L. Sullivan had resigned in April, when Johnson abruptly canceled construction of a new aircraft carrier—an action that led to the celebrated "revolt of the admirals." The navy was also opposed to the largesse granted to the air force, which even exceeded the president's requests. Although the army was generally satisfied with its position in the new defense arrangement, it was most unhappy about the pressure for integration; and Johnson wanted the army's support in the interservice battle.[23]

Whatever the case, Johnson now had a third problem, for his acceptance of the army's racial policy triggered a storm of protest from civil-rights advocates, who had generally exhibited patience during the summer as the army fought off the Fahy Committee. Moreover, the announcement came at that moment when it became apparent that the first session of the Eighty-first Congress was not going to do anything about the administration's civil-rights program. Roy Wilkins, A. Philip Randolph, and Grant Reynolds sent telegrams of protest to the White House, while the Americans for Democratic Action publicly denounced Secretary Johnson's "sellout on jim crow in the army." The *Amsterdam News* viewed the order as "an act of insult and insubordination"—an insult to fifteen million black Americans and insubordination to the president.[24]

When Secretary Johnson spoke in New York City in December, the Committee Against Jim Crow in Military Service and Training picketed the building, protesting Johnson's "wholesale faking." The *Chicago Defender* thought enough of the story to give it a screaming front-page headline. The *Call* (Kansas City) demanded a showdown. Truman "has indulged the army, his stubborn child, long enough," cried the editor. "We call upon him now to order the secretary of the army either to comply in letter, spirit and completeness with his executive order . . . or to find himself another job. If the navy and the air force can abolish segregation, so can the army."[25]

Truman had no intention of firing Secretaries Johnson and Gray, for he was having enough difficulties because of interservice rivalry. He also had no intention of compromising at this point. He had promised to support the Fahy Committee, and support it he did. In his news conference of October 6, 1949, he sought to blunt some of the sharp criticism by labeling the announcement of September 30 as only a "progress report," pointing out that the committee would continue to make recommendations to achieve "what we contemplated in the beginning"—eventual integration of the army. In the same month Truman rewarded Charles Fahy with an appointment to the District of Columbia Court of Appeals, which Fahy accepted on the provision that he be allowed to complete the work of the committee. "Whatever arrangements you choose to make on your taking office as judge will be entirely satisfactory to me," Truman responded, and then added in longhand: "You've done a grand job on the Civil Rights Board."[26]

Fahy had indeed done well; but the committee's job continued to be a thorny one, for the army was not through with its opposition. The army's Division of Personnel and Administration subsequently defied the president, the Fahy Committee, and Secretary Gray on October 27, when it issued a "clarifying" statement regarding the order of September 30 that effectively precluded the assignment of black personnel to a white unit. When Secretary Gray learned of the clarification, he was furious and quickly declared it a violation of his recently announced policy; he also explained that black specialists "would be assigned to some white units," which did not mean, however, "that existing Negro units will be broken up or that Negro personnel of these units will be scattered throughout the army."[27]

The Fahy Committee, however, was satisfied neither with the order of September 30 nor with Gray's explanation of the clarification; so an impasse developed. Representatives of the army now became even more intransigent. On November 8 Fahy had to remind Secretary Gray that the assigned liaison officers had refused to consult with the committee for several weeks concerning the assignment of qualified blacks to white units and the removal of the quota. Gray's reply was conciliatory, though he pointed out that the committee had yet to devise a formula that, in the absence of the 10 percent quota, would afford assurance against a disproportionate number of blacks in the Army.[28]

In short, the army feared that removal of the quota would result in a dramatic increase in black enlistments and upset the racial balance that it worshiped. At this point, the army was in the process of rewriting Circular 124, its official statement on racial policy, to bring it into line with the order announced on September 30. On November 21 two high-ranking officers delivered it by hand to the White House for approval. There, David Niles bluntly informed the "messengers" that White House acceptance hinged upon the Fahy Committee's approval; another circumvention would not be possible. The committee itself threatened to issue a public denunciation if the army released its revision of Circular 124 without the committee's approval.[29]

The army had met its match. The breakthrough came on December 27, following a long conference between Gray and Fahy, when the secretary of the army agreed essentially with the committee's position on assignment of qualified black personnel to white units. Fahy was pleased. "I feel we are much closer to agreement than at any time in the past," he informed his associates, "and I am very hopeful . . . we can reach entire agreement."[30]

Fahy's optimism was well placed. On January 14, 1950, the committee approved the army's second revision of Circular 124, which involved some compromise in language to permit "gradual" integration but stipulated that black manpower would be utilized in accordance with its skills and qualifications and would be "assigned to any . . . unit without regard to race or color." On January 16, 1950, the committee informed the president that it was in agreement with the army's new racial policy; and the army released the new Circular 124 to all commands the same day. Unfortunately, for public consumption as well as for the committee's own sense of satisfaction, the victory was soured slightly when Lt. Gen. E. H. Brooks, the army's director of personnel and administration, volunteered the gratuitous opinion that army Jim Crow might go "in two years or fifty years," a statement that accounted in part for the mixed reactions of civil-rights advocates to the new policy.[31]

If some were dubious about the army's latest policy, Secretary of Defense Johnson was not; and he quickly proposed to the president that he abolish the Fahy Committee. Clark Clifford and David Niles, however, pointed out to the president that the committee and the army had yet to agree on the matter of the quota. The White House then urged Fahy to reach an agreement with the army as soon as possible; and on January 30 Fahy conferred with Gray, advising him of the committee's intention to resubmit its recommendations and supporting evidence in favor of abolishing the quota.[32]

But Fahy was unaware of the latest dilemma facing Secretary Gray, who was caught between the demands of a newly created army board, an organization of which the army seemed fond, and those of the Fahy Committee. In the fall of 1949 a board of general officers, headed by Lt. Gen. S. J. Chamberlin, began investigating the army's racial policy. Early in February 1950 the Chamberlin Board presented its report, which consisted mainly of the old saw concerning the limited value of black personnel. In essence, the report paraphrased that of the Gillem Board, recommending retention of segregation and the 10 percent quota.[33]

This latest development was most delicate for Gray, and he chose to take his problem directly to the president. An understanding was soon reached. Gray agreed to drop the 10 percent quota on black enlistments on a test basis. "If, as a result of a fair trial of this new system," he subsequently wrote the president, "there ensues a disproportionate balance of racial strengths in the army, it is my understanding that I have your authority to return to a system which will, in effect, control enlistments by race." Truman jotted "approved" on the bottom of the memo, and the Fahy Committee seemed to have its victory.[34]

Apparently, the Fahy Committee never knew of this agreement, but it made little difference anyway. Fahy was satisfied, and he went along with the army's decision to announce its new instructions in routine fashion without fanfare. The order went out on March 27, 1950, and the battle of the quota was over. On May 22 the Fahy Committee submitted to the president its formal report, entitled *Freedom to Serve*, which expressed the hope that there would be, "within the reasonably near future, equality of treatment and opportunity for all persons in the armed forces with a consequent improvement in military efficiency."[35]

The president was also satisfied. In accepting the report, he praised the members of the committee for the time, energy, and commitment they had devoted to the "mission." "Every American who believes sincerely in the language of the Constitution and the Declaration of Independence," he noted, "owes them a debt of gratitude." *Freedom to Serve* was indeed a landmark document, and the White House saw to it that over seventy-five hundred copies were distributed across the country. At the request of the secretary of defense, who felt "rather strongly about having a watch-dog committee set over him," the president relieved the Fahy Committee of further responsibilities on July 6, 1950, but kept in effect Executive Order 9981 in the event that the future might require an investigation of military conformance with the committee's recommendations.[36]

The Fahy Committee's contribution requires no lengthy summation or spirited defense. The group had prodded the navy and the air force into going beyond their limited programs of integration and into adopting policies that would rapidly integrate existing units. As for the army, it would not have dropped a policy of fairly rigid segregation in favor of proposals for eventual integration without the committee's existence and insistence. The president's firm backing was vital, of course. In the last analysis, the triumph of the Fahy Committee represented a victory of civilian leadership over the military, although it was not yet clear how decisive or how permanent that victory would be. Lester Granger, for example, was not overly optimistic. In his column in the *Amsterdam News* he indicted the army brass for its stubborn resistance but praised Secretary Gray for his "conversion" to the committee's point of view. Granger labored under no delusions, however. On September 28 he wrote Truman that the committee's proposals "constituted a minimum rather than a maximum plan of action" and urged the White House to exercise "constant vigilance" over the army.[37]

E. W. Kenworthy was even more apprehensive. The committee had expected the army to move with more deliberation than speed, but after six months there seemed scarcely any movement at all. In his final memorandum to Judge Fahy on July 25, Kenworthy could "only conclude from the little progress . . . over the six months since the army adopted the committee's proposals on January 16 that the army intends to do as little as possible towards implementing the policy which it adopted and published."[38]

In view of the army's tortoise pace, Kenworthy's gloom was understandable, but even at that moment the Korean War was forcing the military to democratize its racial practices. And it was here that the Fahy Committee's insistence upon the provisions for assignment of black personnel to white units and for removal of the 10 percent quota paid its highest dividends. Following the army's removal of the quota in April, black enlistments rose sharply and continued to do so after the outbreak of war in June 1950; by August, blacks constituted 11.4 percent of the army's total strength. Flooded with black recruits, some local base commanders opted to integrate basic-training facilities, which was permissible under Secretary Gray's order of January 1950.[39]

But the most visible change took place in Korea itself. From the very beginning, personnel in the navy and air force were integrated. In July an air-force spokesman reported the presence of black pilots in mixed squadrons over Korea. Ensign Jesse L. Brown, the first black pilot in the nation's history to fly naval combat missions, chalked up an impressive record before being shot down. And it was sociologically significant when a white pilot was awarded the Medal of Honor for his courageous, but futile, attempt to save Brown's life, for it had usually been the other way around. Nor did the marines hesitate long. Having integrated basic-training facilities before the outbreak of the war, the Marine Corps decided to integrate the fighting front as well.[40]

The greatest integration, however, occurred in the army, primarily because segregation was still the rule in July 1950 when American troops first arrived on the Korean peninsula. But combat losses, accidental assignments, and the desire of some commanders to implement Secretary Gray's order of January 1950 led to dramatic changes in the first year of the war. The logic of the situation often required integration in order to maintain combat efficiency. Faced with the decimation of several white units and lacking sufficient replacements, field commanders took the necessary step of assigning blacks to white combat units. Such was the case with the Ninth Infantry Regiment, which consisted of one overstrength black and two undermanned white battalions; the "force of circumstances" persuaded the commanding colonel to assign the surplus blacks to white contingents.[41]

Similarly, when Maj. Gen. Clark L. Ruffner assumed command of the Second Infantry Division, he discovered Negroes sprinkled throughout his combat regiments, a situation which he considered not only logical but successful. But his corps commander, Lt. Gen. Edward M. Almond, perhaps recalling his unhappy experiences with the all-Negro Ninety-second Division in Italy during the Second World War, ordered a return to segregation, which compelled Ruffner to resort to ingenuity in order to maintain top combat performance. Obviously, the situation demanded the development of a coherent policy; but high army brass, as usual, was moving much too cautiously.[42]

Although whites at home were generally unaware of the ad hoc integration under way in Korea, which was proceeding without any publicity from the army, readers of the black press were better informed. As early as July 29, 1950, the *Amsterdam News* editorialized about the extent of integration in the first weeks of the war, although the editor was premature in announcing that "Negro GIs are now distributed throughout the service as soldiers and men and not as Negroes."[43] Many of the initial reports were confused, because the fighting front itself was confused and because white correspondents were concentrating on the American retreat toward the Pusan perimeter. More reliable evidence arrived, however, after Negro correspondents roamed across the front, ferreting out stories of integration and black heroism.

One of the best was James L. Hicks, who seldom missed an integrated unit. "In short," he concluded one lengthy dispatch, "name a fighting unit over here and I'll show you a colored soldier fighting in it." Black reporters focused particularly on the activities of the Twenty-fourth Infantry Regiment, one of the few all-black combat units in Korea. In September 1950 Hicks reported widespread sentiment on the part of general officers of the Twenty-fifth Infantry Division, of which the Twenty-fourth Regiment was a part, in favor of mixing the colors of the three combat regiments. Actually, some mixing had been under way for some time; and the commanding officer, Maj. Gen. William B. Kean, was in favor of complete integration in order to increase the fighting effectiveness of his division.[44]

One of the reasons for the growing support for complete integration of the army was its reported success on the battlefield. The biggest boost came from Col. S. L. A. Marshall, the army's roving "efficiency expert" on infantry operations, who closely examined the performance of mixed units during the headlong retreat of UN forces from the Yalu River in November and December 1950. It was his first experience with integrated units, and he was both surprised and pleased. At the request of Gen. Walton Walker, commanding officer of the Eighth Army, Marshall released his findings to the press. He had nothing but praise for the combat performance of integrated units of the Second Infantry Division, particularly of one company with a black officer as second in command. "That company's stand was perhaps unequalled in American military history," Marshall concluded. "It entered action with 125 men and withdrew only on regimental orders with its tail up fighting like hell 24 hours later with only 34 men not wounded."[45]

In short, integration was a success—or at least what Marshall saw of it. Unfortunately, Marshall quickly received word from the headquarters of Gen. Douglas MacArthur in Tokyo that it frowned on racial mixing. Distressed, the colonel flew to Tokyo, where he discovered a "completely negative" attitude on the part of high-ranking officers on the staff, who informed him, among other things, that the army was not a "guinea pig" for those who desired social change. Although Marshall was unable to gain an audience with MacArthur, subsequent developments suggested that the attitude of MacArthur's staff reflected the general's attitude as well. MacArthur later admitted that he had done nothing about integration in the Far East because Washington had sent him segregated units, which he assumed represented army policy.[46] Actually, had he been concerned, he could have directed his field commanders in Korea to use their own discretion, as they had done anyway. Secretary Gray's order of January 1950 provided MacArthur with all the authority he needed, particularly in the emergency situation that existed in Korea during the first year of the war. Moreover, it should be noted that MacArthur was not always as scrupulous in following other hoary traditions of the army—or in obeying presidential orders, for that matter.

The ad hoc integration in Korea was heady stuff for those Negro leaders who had fought military segregation for over a decade, although they continued to insist on nothing less than complete integration. Equally exhilarating were the first press reports of the fighting capabilities of the all-black Twenty-fourth Infantry Regiment. On July 29, 1950, the *Afro-American* ran banner headlines—"Colored Troops Win First Victory For U.S. in Korea"—in reporting the regiment's capture of Yechon after a sixteen-hour battle. Other papers gave it similar play, and a Massachusetts congressman took the floor of the House to announce: "Communist propaganda took it on the chin at Yechon when the Korean Reds were blasted by American Negro troops who believed—not only in the United States as it is, but in the better nation that it will become when intolerance is also defeated." The *Call* was ecstatic. Headlines in August proclaimed, "Negro GI's Hold Their Ground In Korea," "Negro Troops Capture Key Mountain Peak," "24th Infantrymen Seize 'Little Cassino' In Three-Day Battle."[47]

But the euphoria was only of the moment. At the same time that black America reveled in the heroism of the Twenty-fourth, disquieting reports of discrimination and white racism appeared in the Negro press. As early as August 1950 the white commander of the black Twenty-fourth was reported to have announced: "During the last two wars your race has not done so well. I am going to make this the fighting Twenty-fourth, not the frightened Twenty-fourth." And that was only the beginning. In September, James Hicks reported the existence of racial conflict between white and black officers in the Twenty-fourth and quoted the commanding colonel as having declared that "colored people are yellow and they just won't fight."[48]

Black morale sagged, both at home and in Korea, when correspondents revealed that a captain from division headquarters was interrogating officers and men of the Twenty-fourth, ostensibly to determine the feasibility of integration. Negro reporters, however, were not far off the mark when they interpreted the captain's presence as an attempt to discredit the Twenty-fourth in particular and black soldiers in general, as well as to collect evidence for court-martial proceedings. The growing doubt about the fighting effectiveness of the Twenty-fourth received popular confirmation in an article in the *Saturday Evening Post* in June 1951, where Harold H. Martin contended that its record was indeed a poor one, but primarily because of black resentment of segregation; though lopsided, the article was in essence an argument in favor of integration.[49]

Meanwhile, the NAACP had become involved in a matter that literally involved life and death, for accusations of cowardice in 1950 were only a prelude to the initiation of widespread court-martial proceedings against black officers and men. One of the first reported cases concerned Lt. Leon Gilbert, a company commander in the Twenty-fourth, who was convicted of cowardice and refusal to obey orders in the face of the enemy. President Truman, however, intervened early in this particular case and commuted the sentence from death to twenty years. As the number of convicted blacks rose in the fall of 1950, the NAACP became alarmed. Thurgood Marshall, the organization's head counsel, announced that the association would defend anyone who requested aid; and letters came in, eventually reaching a total of thirty-nine.[50]

Marshall was also concerned because of what appeared to be gross discrimination, for not only did some sentences appear excessive, but during the same period only two whites were convicted for violations of army regulations. To find out for himself, he decided to visit Japan and Korea to interview those involved. But MacArthur's headquarters denied his first request, and it took a direct appeal from Walter White to General MacArthur to obtain approval of the mission. Incredibly enough, MacArthur later admitted his ignorance of the number of sentencings in the summer and fall of 1950 and conceded that it might have been excessive. On January 11, 1951, Thurgood Marshall left for the Far East, where he spent the next five weeks investigating the circumstances surrounding the convictions. From Tokyo, he cabled that the "suspicions of racial discrimination in most of these cases is well grounded."[51]

While Marshall was investigating in Japan and Korea, his associate, Jack Greenberg, represented convicted GI's before the judge advocate general in Washington, and Walter White appealed directly to the president. In particular, White argued that both white and black troops had broken under fire, but "after the colored soldiers won their first major battle at Hill 303, there seemed to be a determined effort to offset favorable publicity and try to discredit the colored soldiers." In all probability, more than discrimination was involved in the charges; but the upshot was that the NAACP was successful in winning a few suspended sentences in addition to reductions of prison terms for the rest. Obviously, the penalties were excessive if nothing else.[52]

Another result was that Thurgood Marshall became completely disillusioned with the MacArthur myth, although the general had never been a favorite of blacks anyway. Upon his return from the Far East, Marshall indulged in several choice criticisms of the general, which may have had some connection with the decision of Congressmen Dawson and Powell to boycott MacArthur's "farewell address" to Congress in April 1951. Finally, it should be noted that blacks were not the only minority to suffer mass injustice during the Korean War. According to the *Amsterdam News*, ninety-four Puerto Ricans were convicted for disobeying an order to attack in November 1952.[53]

While the NAACP fought for the rights and reputations of court-martialed Negroes, black leadership continued to agitate for complete integration in the armed forces. In January 1951 Walter White wired all of the service secretaries, urging them to take "immediate steps to eliminate segregation and discrimination from all phases of military life." On February 28 White and A. Philip Randolph led a delegation of Negro leaders to the White House, where they presented the president with a list of six "requests," which included additional black appointments to government positions, establishment of an executive FEPC, elimination of segregation in the nation's capital, and abolition "once and for all" of racial segregation in the army. The Negro press agreed with the strategy of exploiting the exigencies of another war to create a better America, and it contributed its share of criticism and pressure.[54]

Other civil-rights advocates were active. Senator Hubert Humphrey, distressed with the army's segregation of the recently activated —and integrated—Minnesota National Guard, informed army brass, "You've got to decide who you want trouble with, the southerners or us." On June 25, 1951, Senators Humphrey and Lehman also wrote a joint letter to Secretary of Defense George C. Marshall, asking for specific evidence concerning the extent of integration. Actually, by May 1951, the statistics were impressive—at least in comparison with those of the previous year—for now 61 percent of the infantry combat companies in the Eighth Army were operating on an integrated basis. Moreover, in March 1951 the army had announced that it had achieved complete integration of training facilities in the United States; and the navy reported the absence of segregation in all units, including those of the Marine Corps, although one navy spokesman concluded, "We haven't hit the millennium yet."[55]

In March the army spokesman had given the impression of a harmonious, coherent, and progressive policy of integration; but the army actually had a confused program, at best, throughout the winter and spring of 1951. To army brass, the absence of the quota was the big problem. By February 1951 the percentage of Negroes in the army stood at 12 percent, as compared with 4 percent and 6 percent, respectively, in the navy and the air force. And by May the percentage of Negro troops in Korea had reached 13.5, although less than one-half were actually serving in combat units. The problem was that the number of Negroes in the army exceeded the available "Negro spaces," and the only solution was to restore the quota or to integrate further. Nor were Negroes the only concern during the war. From July 1, 1950, through March 31, 1952, the army inducted some twenty-seven thousand Puerto Ricans, about twice as many as were necessary to maintain Puerto Rican army units. Here, the fear of racial friction was subordinate to the obvious language problem, for most of the recruits spoke only Spanish. The army eventually came up with a partial solution when Selective Service cut the Puerto Rican quota and when the army itself established language schools.[56]

Some army officers were already prepared to accept the logic of the situation. In December 1950 the inspector general, noting that integration had created no racial friction, contended that the army must ultimately accept full integration. Predictably, others were apprehensive. The fundamental barrier to integration, noted one high-ranking officer to the chief of staff, was the "social problem." "Solution of this must be one of evolution within the communities of the United States, and is not a problem that can be dissolved or solved by army effort alone." Nonetheless, he recommended that the Chamberlin Board reconvene in February 1951 to study the army's racial policy in light of recent developments on the battlefields of Korea.[57]

The Chamberlin Board, however, found the tug of tradition too powerful. Although the three general officers concluded that integrated units had fought well in Korea, with a corresponding decrease in racial friction, they resisted both logic and military efficiency in recommending reimposition of the 10 percent quota and retention of the segregated system. For the moment, the army suspended the report. The army also polled a group of high-ranking officers with personal knowledge of integration in Korea. The majority supported integration, although only if the percentage of blacks in combat units was rigidly regulated.[58] Still, the army marked time.

Clearly, there were those who were desperate, for the spontaneous integration during the Korean War had unhinged the plans of those officers who were determined to perpetuate segregation. The politics of procrastination could not endure indefinitely. The assistant secretary of the army, Earl Johnson, was then in the process of recommending that all surplus Negro personnel be assigned to white units, which, in the words of the acting chief of staff, would "in effect eliminate racial units and would require complete integration within the army."[59]

Confronted with external pressure and an internal dilemma, the army, in March 1951, dispatched "an urgent requirement for information concerning the most effective utilization of Negro manpower"—or as one person inelegantly explained, "The Army wants to know what to do with all their niggers"—to a government-sponsored research team of civilians under the auspices of the Operations Research Office of Johns Hopkins University.[60] Operating under the code name of "Project Clear," the team of social scientists conducted extensive interviews in Japan and Korea, and eventually in the United States as well. Although unable to meet the army's urgent deadline of July 1, 1951, the investigators did come in with a preliminary report on July 13 and a final report on November 1.

Project Clear all but destroyed any lingering, organized opposition within the army to integration. It concluded that all-Negro combat units were less effective than their white counterparts because of low morale and because of the concentration of less-skilled and educationally disadvantaged personnel. When integrated, however, black soldiers performed on a par with whites in the same units, without any decrease in white morale. The conclusion was inescapable: "Integration enhances the effectiveness of the army," the social scientists contended; and its extension throughout the army was "feasible" without reimposition of a racial quota.[61]

Military integration had also become more palatable on the home front. Some southern politicians were already resigned to it, while others were willing to accept the word of high military and civilian leaders concerning the inefficiency of segregation, a system that could hardly be justified during time of war. Some white southerners, of course, were never reconciled. Early in 1951 Congressman Arthur Winstead of Mississippi proposed an amendment to the current selective-service bill to permit draftees the choice of refusing to serve in an integrated unit, but the House easily throttled this last gasp of southern opposition.[62]

The preliminary report of Project Clear to the vice chief of staff on July 13, and to the chief of staff and the secretary of defense on July 23, came none too soon, for Gen. Matthew B. Ridgway, who had succeeded MacArthur as commander of all UN forces in the Far East in April 1951, was impatiently awaiting action on his request to integrate all forces under his command. On July 20 Defense Secretary Marshall confidentially advised Senators Humphrey and Lehman, who had been pressing him for an official announcement in favor of integration, of the army's intention to order integration of all units in Japan and Korea and of deactivation of the Twenty-fourth Infantry Regiment. Only the Fortieth and Forty-fifth Infantry divisions, then training in Japan, would remain segregated, to be integrated later through the normal flow of replacements. On July 26, 1951, the army announced its new Far Eastern policy, which was accompanied by General Ridgway's own sweeping order. It was anticipated that within six months every unit in the Far East would be thoroughly integrated.[63]

Although Negro leaders felt a twinge of nostalgia as the colors of the Twenty-fourth were permanently retired, they were jubilant over the new policy of the Far Eastern Command. Integration, of course, did not come overnight to all units. A few local commanders continued to resist it. Moreover, military efficiency demanded that much of the integration occur gradually through the flow of replacements. According to the Department of Defense, the process was completed by May 1952, although even at that late date an all-black service unit cropped up occasionally. "By Armistice time in Korea," Gen. Mark Clark later observed, "our basic infantry squads were a hodgepodge of tongues and people." As he pointed out, the average squad was composed of "four white Americans, one Negro American, two and a half Koreans and the remainder Puerto Ricans, Mexicans, Hawaiians, and American Indians."[64]

The army's order of July 1951 to desegregate units of the Far Eastern Command did not affect its racial policies elsewhere, and for the next few months the army continued to limp along without a consistent policy. When black correspondent James L. Hicks investigated army posts throughout the United States in the summer and fall of 1951, he found no uniformity on racial matters. True, all basic-training facilities were integrated, as the army had announced in March, but on regular army posts he found both complete integration and "open defiance" of the president. At Fort Belvoir, Virginia, for example, he reported that both military and civilian personnel were "disgracefully segregated" and that Fort Jackson, South Carolina, represented "one of the best examples of large scale integration this writer has ever seen." On the other hand, he discovered that the navy and the air force had done well, although occasionally he stumbled across segregated facilities.[65]

Clearly, the exigencies of war had led to integration of army forces in Japan and Korea, but there was less urgency for similar action at home, which permitted the brass in Washington to stall. Yet pressure was present even here, both externally from civil-rights advocates and internally as a result of too many black soldiers for the available "Negro spaces." Once again, the Fahy Committee's insistence on abolition of the quota was paying off. In September 1951, for example, the all-black units were thirty-four thousand men over strength—"a costly and needless waste of manpower," according to a high-ranking officer in Washington. Still the chief of staff and others were not prepared "to rush integration" throughout the United States; and the commander of army forces on the Pacific Coast, who had requested permission to integrate, was informed that the army would not consider its next step until it received the final report of Project Clear in November. By

December 1951, confronted with increasing ad hoc integration and with the evidence in the final report of Project Clear, the army could delay no longer. Without publicity, the Department of the Army ordered integration of all units, with considerable discretion as to time and place left to base and regional commanders.[66]

In the meantime, the same rate of integration, pragmatic or otherwise, had not occurred within units of the American command in Europe. The presence of segregated units in Europe was an American gift to the Soviet Union in the cold-war propaganda battle, for it was painfully evident that black American soldiers were ostensibly preserving a freedom for others that they did not enjoy themselves. During the summer of 1951 Army Secretary Frank D. Pace, Jr., visited the Austrian command of Lt. Gen. Stafford L. Irwin, who was finding the Soviet propaganda all too true and much too embarrassing. "I want to integrate," Irwin informed Pace; and the secretary soon gave his approval. Irwin integrated his command so quietly that some high Pentagon officials learned of it only after its completion.[67]

Matters were quite different elsewhere in Europe, primarily because of the opposition of Gen. Thomas C. Handy, who commanded American forces in France and Germany. Despite the dramatic changes in the army's racial practices as a result of the Korean War, General Handy was dragging his feet, barely meeting the requirements of Secretary Gray's order in January of 1950 concerning the assignment of qualified blacks to overhead positions. In the summer of 1951 Army Assistant Secretary Earl Johnson dispatched Professor Eli Ginzberg to Europe to inform Handy of the army's desire to integrate all forces. Ginzberg met considerable resistance and even disbelief, and he reported to Washington that a majority of Handy's officers believed that integration would not come in "less than a hundred years."[68]

This would not do, and pressure had to be applied. Secretary Pace and Chief of Staff J. Lawton Collins requested General Handy to submit his plan for integration to Washington for approval, well aware that Handy had no plan. Finally, in December 1951, General Handy came up with a policy that fell short of the Pentagon's expectations, for the general was prepared only to integrate combat units. Most Negroes were in service units, and Handy's policy would therefore perpetuate segregation indefinitely.[69]

While these negotiations continued behind the scenes, the existence of widespread segregation in the European command became a matter of public knowledge as a result of the revelations of Claude A. Barnett, director of the Associated Negro Press. Following a short tour of Europe in January and February of 1952, Barnett returned to denounce the army's integration policy in Europe as a "farce." The Negro press was concerned. "Our brass hats in Europe," fulminated the *Chicago Defender,* "are either unaware of the new orders for integration in the Defense Department or they are stubbornly defying these orders. Something is wrong, radically wrong." Something was wrong, as Barnett's subsequent articles indicated. In one column, for example, he quoted extensively from General Handy's letter of February 7, which was a response to Barnett's earlier query concerning the general's racial policies. Handy revealed that all detachments of women in Europe were integrated, but that only about two thousand out of a total of thirty thousand Negro soldiers were then serving in integrated units. In order to desegregate units designated as all-black, Handy contended that he needed orders from Washington.[70]

At best, his argument was a circumvention in view of what had already transpired. In any event, he soon had his orders, which called for integration of combat units within a year and of service units within one to two years. On April 1, 1952, General Handy announced his new policy, carefully noting that "the Department of the Army has directed this command to initiate a . . . program of racial integration." There were no complications. By September, the Seventh Army reported visible progress, particularly in its combat units, with blacks composing 9 to 12 percent of the rifle companies—a percentage that most commanders sought to maintain. Though progress was slower in the service companies, the army in Europe hoped to complete its integration program within another year. And everyone expressed pleasure, at least publicly, with the results. "They are fine soldiers now," asserted one general officer in describing the performance of black soldiers previously part of a segregated and ineffective battalion, "working harder and more efficiently than they did when they were all together in one group."[71]

The movement to integrate the military also had several tangential effects. One involved segregation of dependent children in schools on military bases. A Negro correspondent in June 1951 called attention to the rigid segregation at Fort Bragg, North Carolina, where white children were educated on the post and black children were bussed to jim-crow schools in surrounding communities. Others quickly queried Defense Department officials, who sought to avoid the issue by explaining that local communities operated most of the schools in question, and in the South, of course, segregation was the law. It came as a surprise, then, when the elementary school at Fort Bragg opened in the fall of 1951 on an integrated basis and with one black face among the faculty.[72]

It was a complicated situation. Local authorities operated and staffed most of the schools for military dependents, with the military itself controlling the remainder. Actually, in October 1951 the military operated only six schools in southern states, of which four, including the one of Fort Bragg, were now desegregated. Those operated by local authorities in the South, however, constituted the majority—and the dilemma. State law required segregation; and if the military itself assumed control and ordered integration, it might result in the withdrawal of teachers, loss of accreditation from state agencies, and additional expense.[73]

There were also political considerations. Southern politicians were already unhappy with the integration of the four army schools and struck quickly in September and October of 1951 to restore the purity of the South's sacred system. At that point, Congress was considering a bill to provide federal aid to schools in critical defense-housing areas. When the bill moved from committee to the floor of the Senate, however, it contained a stipulation that the commissioner of education should operate these schools in conformance with the laws of the state in which the federal property was located. In brief, the bill would turn back the clock and require resegregation of the four schools.[74]

Incredibly, the bill rolled through both houses of Congress without any organized opposition and was presented to Truman on October 20. The "buck" stopped at the White House. Although both the Department of Defense and the Federal Security Agency, despite certain misgivings, urged the president to sign the bill, and although liberals in the Senate had permitted its passage by a simple voice vote, Truman refused to accept it.[75] In his veto message of November 2 the president observed that the bill would restore segregation of schools on military bases then operating successfully with integrated programs, which "would constitute a backward step in the efforts of the federal government to extend equal rights and opportunities to all our people." After noting the progress in the achievement of equality of opportunity in the federal civil service and the armed forces, he explained that not all schools on federal property were integrated, for the government always considered "pertinent local factors"; nonetheless, the government must move forward. In concluding, he placed the issue in the context of the cold war. "We have assumed a role of world leadership in seeking to unite people of great cultural and racial diversity for the purpose of resisting aggression, protecting their mutual security and advancing their own economic and political development," he contended.[76]

The president had held the line, but the problem of school segregation on most military bases in the South persisted throughout the campaign year of 1952. Finally, as a result of pressure from Senator Humphrey and Clarence Mitchell, director of the NAACP's Washington bureau, Assistant Defense Secretary Anna Rosenberg decided to force the issue. In a letter of January 10, 1953, to Commissioner of Education Earl J. McGrath, she pointed out that such segregation violated the policies both of the Department of Defense and of the president. The authority to integrate, she continued, rested not with the Defense Department but with McGrath's agency. McGrath's reply was all that integrationists could want. If the department ordered integration of school facilities, he responded, the Office of Education would comply and provide "other arrangements" to teach the children if local authorities in the South found it impossible to circumvent segregation laws.[77] McGrath's letter not only hinted at the difficulties involved but also revealed the reluctance of the Defense Department to issue such a directive.

That reluctance continued into the Eisenhower administration. Shortly after taking office, the new president promised to look into the matter; and within a week the White House disclosed that it had directed that segregation cease at all schools operated by the military. The order was almost meaningless, for it affected only Fort Benning, Georgia; local authorities operated the remaining twenty-one school systems for dependents in the South.[78] No matter what the degree of its commitment to civil rights may have been, the Eisenhower administration was confronted with the same thorny problems as the Truman administration had been.

In a lengthy memorandum to Eisenhower of May 1953, Secretary of Defense Charles E. Wilson carefully explained the situation. Local educational agencies in the South could not desegregate the twenty-one schools without changing state laws, and the federal government could not assume control without jeopardizing the entire school program. In conclusion, after a paragraph of equivocation, Wilson recommended a target date of September 1955 for inauguration of integration, hoping that the procedures could somehow be worked out. Perhaps he and others also hoped for a favorable decision from the Supreme Court on the school desegregation cases then pending before the tribunal. In any event, the court's decision in May 1954 to strike down segregation as unconstitutional removed all complications and permitted integration of schools located on military bases, although black children who lived in off-base housing in the South continued to attend segregated schools.[79]

The Eisenhower administration also inherited another tangential problem of integration. Since 1949, when the Fahy Committee had accepted the navy's program of integration, criticism of that service was minimal. In October 1951, however, Clarence Mitchell of the NAACP protested the segregation of restrooms, water fountains, cafeterias, and other facilities for civilian employees at southern naval stations. The navy's reply was totally unsatisfactory, and the matter continued to simmer as the 1952 election campaign approached.[80] Finally, in May 1952, Lester Granger wrote to Secretary of the Navy Kimball, expressing his shock at the navy's departure from "its recently fine record of equal opportunity" and labeling its policy for civilian employees as a "backward step." Although conciliatory in tone, Kimball's response exposed the navy's opposition to integration of civilian facilities. "[We] cannot permit, direct or enforce any course of action which might jeopardize the fulfillment of the mission of the shore establishment," he explained. "The navy must, therefore, in a very realistic way recognize the customs and usages prevailing in certain geographical areas of our country. In these areas to which I refer, the navy . . . must conform with these usages and customs, some of which, incidentally, are backed up by law."[81]

Although official policy allowed local commanding officers to use their own discretion, Kimball's explanation clearly indicated that the navy expected them to retain segregation of civilian facilities at southern naval stations. Dissatisfied, Granger mailed all correspondence to Donald Dawson, a White House assistant, who forwarded it to minority expert Philleo Nash, who in turn shuffled it to the president's naval aide and requested an early conference with the admiral. There the matter rested, despite a strongly worded telegram to President Truman from the NAACP during its annual convention in June, which argued that Kimball's refusal to integrate civilian facilities was "an incredible assault upon the magnificent stand you have taken against racial bigotry."[82] Apparently, the president was never informed of the issue, and the administration completed its tenure in office without taking any action.

The NAACP, however, had not forgotten. During the early months of the Eisenhower administration, Walter White and Congressman Powell applied pressure, which Navy Secretary Robert B. Anderson resisted by repeating the myth that to defy local custom would "inevitably lead to disruptive employee relations, poor community relations, and an ultimate breakdown of efficiency accompanied by lower production." But Eisenhower had pledged to end segregation in federal facilities, and Anderson soon got the message. On August 20, 1953, he announced the administration's program for "complete elimination" of racial segregation of civilian employees on the twenty-three out of forty-three southern naval stations that were still practicing the policy. In November, Eisenhower announced the integration of all naval stations, except for those at Newport News and Charleston, where gradual desegregation was scheduled for completion in January 1954. Walter White was pleased, although he disliked the gradualism. "All that needs to be done," he complained, "is to remove the jim-crow signs which should be a matter of minutes."[83]

The navy's poor showing on this issue prompted black critics to peer closely at other navy practices, for up to this point the army had virtually monopolized their attention. They grimaced at what they found. Between 1950 and 1953, during the Korean War, the percentage of black seamen in the Stewards Branch had remained constant at about 50 percent, while the total percentage of Negroes in the navy had declined. Moreover, the Stewards Branch was actually a segregated outfit, with 98 percent of its personnel either Negro or Filipino.[84]

Navy Secretary Anderson, however, was no longer insensitive to black complaints, and in September 1953 Lester Granger was brought in to an advisory position. As it turned out, the appointment was practically meaningless, for the navy rejected his suggestions, particularly those concerning the Stewards Branch. In March 1954, however, the navy did abandon its practice of recruiting blacks specifically as messmen and inaugurated the policy of putting all personnel through the same basic-training program. But this would affect only the future; and on June 25, 1954, Granger resigned in disgust, protesting that "the only way to end segregation is to break up the whole branch, consolidate it with the commissary group, and then gradually parcel out the men on a greater extent of integration." Thereafter, the navy's pace was painfully slow; and as late as 1963, 23 percent of all black personnel in the navy was still concentrated in the food-service field, despite a substantial increase in black enlistments.[85]

On the other hand, the army, which had fought integration so tenaciously, began to look better and better; and its civilian leadership took pride in the results. On January 19, 1953, the day before he left office, Army Secretary Frank Pace wrote to Walter White, expressing the opinion that "one of the outstanding accomplishments of this period has been the army's marked success in the integration of Negro personnel." In conclusion, he thanked White and his associates for their "understanding and constructive assistance to the Department of the Army during this period." At this point, it was only a matter of time. In August of 1953, as the Korean War dragged to a close, the army reported that it was 90 percent integrated, with only ninety-six all-black units remaining, which would be phased out in the usual manner. In July 1954 the percentage of integrated units stood at 98, with only fifteen all-black complements, each of less than company size. On October 30, 1954, the army closed the book, reporting that all units were integrated except for an occasional small detachment, which represented a "transient" condition.[86] Henceforth, blacks would be roughly in the same category as other American minorities—a category in which discrimination was unofficial and often individual—but at least they no longer suffered the special indignity of segregation.

Once the army had abolished segregation, it became the most egalitarian branch of the service, if only because of the number of its black officers and men. In 1962, for example, the Commission on Civil Rights found that blacks composed over 11 percent of army personnel, 8 and 7 percent respectively of the air force and marines, but less than 5 percent of the navy.[87]

Perhaps integration of the armed forces was not "the greatest thing that ever happened to America," as Truman viewed it in 1953 in a private conversation; but few events in the twentieth century surpassed it in importance for white as well as black America. Truman's pride was justifiable, for he could point to some impressive statistics in addition to integration itself. For example, during his administration, the number of Negro graduates of West Point increased dramatically and compared favorably with the number in subsequent classes as late as 1969. Actually, the five black cadets who emerged from West Point in 1951 represented only a beginning, but in the next fifteen years that number was equaled only in 1955, a class that matriculated during the Truman administration, and was not exceeded until after 1965.[88]

Moreover, when James C. Evans released the Defense Department's progress report on integration in 1954, he observed that equal opportunity for civilian employees in the department lagged behind that in the military. Fifteen years later the situation was apparently no better. In 1969 Carl T. Rowan indicted all three presidents of the 1960s for permitting the department to become "the biggest racial discriminator in employment." Rowan contended that of 523 top level positions in the department, Negroes held only 3, of which 2 were really "civil rights" jobs, comparable in some ways to the race-relations advisers of the Roosevelt era.[89]

Black leaders during the 1960s could legitimately wonder what had happened to the bright new world of 1954. The Eisenhower administration, after completing what remained of Truman's integration program, allowed the issue of equal opportunity in the military to drift, although, incredibly enough, Eisenhower later took credit for integrating the armed services. Black leadership itself contributed to the drift by easing the pressure. Not until 1962, when President John F. Kennedy appointed his Committee on Equal Opportunity in the Armed Forces, did another administration undertake a serious examination of America's racial policies in the military. In the same year the Commission on Civil Rights conducted a parallel survey. The commission found discrimination in occupational assignments, particularly in the navy, and in recruitment and promotion procedures. Discrimination in off-base housing continued to be a serious problem, while segregation still remained in a few NCO clubs and in many social activities. Even more distressing, segregation still existed for children of black military personnel in many off-base schools in the South.[90]

When the Defense Department reported the end of segregation in 1954, it also pointed to certain remaining "problem areas," including the lack of opportunity and the presence of discrimination in college ROTC programs, reserve forces, and National Guard units. Here again, practice lagged behind promises. As late as 1968, for example, not one predominantly Negro college had a naval ROTC program, which explained in large part why the navy had only 330 black officers that year.[91]

The National Guard, however, continued to be the big offender. When the head of the National Guard Bureau reported in December 1964 that "token integration had been achieved in all National Guard units," it was certainly no more than that. In February 1964, for example, five states had no black guardsmen whatever, while seventeen states reported fewer than ten. Actually, only 1.5 percent of all National Guard units in the country was Negro, partly because blacks themselves expressed little interest and partly because of discrimination and "token integration." In short, little was accomplished in the ten years following the Truman administration.[92]

Finally, a statistical comparison documents another part of the story. In 1945 blacks represented only 0.7 percent of all officers in the army; the percentage rose to 1.7 in 1949 and to 2.9 at the end of the Korean War. But in 1962, it stood only at 3.2 percent. In other words, the percentage of black officers in the army increased by more than 2 percent during the Truman administration but only by 0.3 percent in the next eight years. Similarly, in 1954 the percentage of Negro officers in the air force was 1.1, up 0.5 percent from 1949, but eight years later the percentage stood only at 1.2, an increase of 0.1 percent. During the same period, the percentage in the navy went from 0.1 to 0.3, and in the marines from 0.1 to 0.2 percent.[93] In short, the military was only marking time.

The war in Vietnam did bring improvement, along with suffering and dying. In March 1966, for example, the three major service academies combined had only 52 black students. In 1968 there were 116, although 47 had just entered. The war also undoubtedly contributed to the promotion of Col. F. E. Davison to brigadier general; but as only the third black American to reach the rank of general, after B. O. Davis, Sr., in 1940 and B. O. Davis, Jr., in 1954, the promotion seemed to prove little. More encouraging were the promotion of Daniel James to brigadier general in the air force in 1970 and the promotions in 1971 of Samuel L. Gravely, Jr., to rear admiral and of Oliver W. Dillard, James F. Hamlet, and Roscoe C. Cartwright to the rank of brigadier general in the army.[94]

In 1968 Secretary of Defense Clark Clifford released additional evidence of black gains in the military. Contrasting the situation in 1948, when President Truman issued his executive order, with that in 1968, Clifford revealed that the number of officers in all branches of the service had more than quadrupled. The army went from 1,306 black officers in 1948 to 5,637 in 1968, the navy from 4 to 330, the Marine Corps from 1 to 180, and the air force from 310 to 2,417.[95] The statistics did represent improvement, but they were also misleading, for they failed to include percentages for the number of black officers in comparison with the total. Moreover, if compared with the percentages immediately after the Korean War, those of 1968 would not have appeared out of the ordinary.

If anything, Clifford's report unintentionally illustrated the need for greater improvement on the part of the military, particularly the navy and Marine Corps. Moreover, although the military was still the most integrated aspect of American society and probably the most harmonious as well, the war in Vietnam resurrected grave charges of discrimination on the part of whites and revealed the disruptive presence of racism, black and white alike. The military thus threatened to become a reflection of the tension and torment of American society in general, whereas in 1953 it had stood as a beacon that illuminated the road to progress in domestic affairs.

12 EQUAL EMPLOYMENT OPPORTUNITY

President Truman's Executive Order 9981 of July 26, 1948, which called for the establishment of equality of treatment and opportunity in the armed forces, had resulted in the most dramatic civil-rights victory of his administration. Its companion order, 9980, designed to achieve the same results in federal civilian employment, was less spectacular and less successful. The order reaffirmed the federal policy of employment without discrimination because of race, color, creed, or national origin and called for the appointment of a fair employment officer in each executive agency, who would receive complaints, establish operating procedures, and redress legitimate grievances in consultation with the agency head. The order also established a Fair Employment Board in the Civil Service Commission, whose functions were to synchronize the program, to serve as a watchdog, and to provide a court of last resort. Although the FEB lacked enforcement powers, which distressed civil-rights advocates, it could appeal directly to the president when an agency refused to reverse or to alter a policy of obvious discrimination. Primary responsibility for the operation and success of the program, however, rested with each department or agency, while the FEB's main function was appellate.[1]

From the beginning of its operations, the FEB contained congenital weaknesses, as a comparison with the Fahy Committee reveals. Although both were largely advisory in nature and had to rely primarily upon persuasion, the similarities ended there. For one thing, discrimination in government agencies, except for certain segregated facilities and agencies in the South, was hard to uncover, much less to prove. As the FEB pointed out, "Actual discrimination may be so subtly disguised under ostensibly correct procedure that it is difficult to identify or clearly establish."[2] On the other hand, the military's policy of discrimination—particularly segregation of troops, limited specialty training, and observance of a racial quota—was there for everyone to see. In short, the Fahy Committee's task, though admittedly difficult, was clear-cut, while the FEB had to establish procedures to eliminate discrimination that supposedly did not exist.

Moreover, the Fahy Committee had to negotiate only with representatives of the three services, while the FEB had to contend with scores of departments and agencies. The very size of the federal bureaucracy, with its amorphous character, complicated the board's task in suggesting procedures for the hearing and disposition of grievances. Yet the FEB may have compounded the problem. For example, the board rightly concluded that the diversity of the federal establishment required some flexibility, but its suggested operating procedures were unduly complicated. The board recommended that an employee initiate his complaint with his supervisor. If dissatisfied, he should present his case in writing to the deputy fair employment officer in his organization and, if still unhappy, then to the fair employment officer of the department, thence to the head of the department, and finally to the Fair Employment Board itself. Such a procedure was not only cumbersome but one that would tax the patience of Job. The board, however, did permit departments to reduce the number of appeal steps.[3]

Although this procedure carefully preserved the chain of command, the FEB might have adopted the less tidy but more effective approach of the 1960s, which permitted a complainant to appeal directly to the board. The FEB eventually realized the complicated nature of the process of appeal, and in May 1951 it simplified the procedure. At the same time, it established procedures for disposition of complaints filed by civil-rights organizations representing numerous employees and applicants.[4]

In contrast with the Fahy Committee, the FEB also labored under almost complete ignorance about the number of Negroes and other minorities employed in federal civilian agencies. As a result of military studies involving the most efficient utilization of manpower, the Fahy Committee had no dearth of statistical evidence. But there were no corresponding figures or studies relating to civilian employment for the period since the end of Roosevelt's FEPC in 1946, a gap which the FEB considered one of its "greatest obstacles."[5]

There were still other differences between the Fahy Committee and the FEB. The former, for example, was determined from the outset to do something about segregation in the military, while the latter never declared its outright opposition to segregation in civilian agencies, unless it adversely affected the "equality of economic opportunity of such segregated employees." Admittedly, segregation in federal employment in the South was a more difficult problem than segregation in the army, for no single board could possibly scrutinize all government agencies nor could it hope to secure compliance in the South of the late 1940s and early 1950s. Yet the report of the board in December 1951 conspicuously failed to mention or discuss segregation in any way. And when the report used the word "integration," it meant only the integration of minority personnel into new job classifications. In November 1951 the board sought to determine the presence and extent of segregation in sixty-two federal agencies. Forty-five reported no segregation whatever, although these reports were not necessarily reliable. The remaining seventeen revealed a checkered pattern of segregation, ranging from one to several segregated units consisting primarily of messengers, mailmen, and chauffeurs. There was progress, but segregation in federal civilian employment existed as late as 1965.[6]

The Fair Employment Board also differed both in its *modus operandi* and its type of personnel from the Fahy Committee. The members of the latter had been appointed by the president and reported directly to him, which insured the continual involvement of the White House staff in the Fahy Committee's running battle with the army. The Civil Service Commission, however, appointed the members of the FEB, which meant that the White House received reports from the board only after they had cleared the Civil Service Commission.

Moreover, the personnel differed in degree of commitment. Men with a mission composed the Fahy Committee, while the FEB appointees, although prominent, seemed less certain of where they wanted to go. Guy Moffett, a government personnel expert, was the first chairman of the board. The other members included Fred C. Croxton, a former conciliator in the Labor Department; Daniel W. Tracy, former assistant secretary of labor and president of the AFL Brotherhood of Electricians; Dr. Ethel C. Dunham, former medical research director of the Children's Bureau; Judge Annabel Matthews, formerly a member of the Board of Tax Appeals; Eugene Kinckle Jones, general secretary of the Urban League; and Jesse H. Mitchell, president of the Industrial Bank of Washington.[7] Although both Jones and Mitchell were Negroes, their counterparts on the Fahy Committee —John Sengstacke and Lester Granger—were much more involved in the civil-rights struggle in the postwar years.

Certain members of the White House staff were never happy with the FEB's performance. For example, in December 1950 the Fair Employment Board came up with a self-satisfied report, contending that the civil-service record on fair employment was "extremely good" and that "considerable progress has been made and that continuing progress may be expected." David Niles could not have disagreed more. "Last year we had a similarly mild and ineffectual report," he complained to fellow White House assistant Donald Dawson. "Could we let the board know that next year we will be wanting a report with enough substance to become a public document?" Niles further suggested that the board ought "to plan some more affirmative steps of its own." Philleo Nash and Martin L. Friedman concurred with Niles's evaluation of the report and urged Dawson not to make it public.[8]

Inexplicably, however, Dawson misinformed the president in a memorandum of December 28. In describing the report, he neglected to mention the distress of Niles, Nash, and Friedman and raved about the "considerable progress" and the "extremely good" record of the federal civil service. Indeed, Dawson's memorandum was more enthusiastic than the FEB report itself, and the president could be forgiven when he subsequently praised the board's performance in several public addresses. The following year the FEB did prepare and publish a report on *Fair Employment in the Federal Service*, which was superior to past reports, though Martin Friedman still maintained that "they don't have much to brag about in my opinion."[9]

The FEB seemed to approach its task both gingerly and leisurely. In March 1949, for example, the board issued comprehensive instructions to federal departments and agencies concerning regulations and operating procedures. But when it reported to the Civil Service Commission in September, the board noted, without expressing dismay, that some agencies were still involved in revising their procedures in response to the directive of March.[10] At that pace, some agencies would accomplish nothing.

The FEB's policies seemed to compound endemic difficulties. In February 1950, for example, a Denver field representative of the Budget Bureau reported that the performance of the civil service, which had made "no headway under the stimulus of Executive Order 9980," contrasted sharply with the advancement of civil rights in the armed services. Part of the problem was procedural, he contended, and he suggested that the Civil Service Commission appoint regional fair employment officers to scrutinize the policies of area agencies and to receive complaints directly from applicants for or employees in federal employment.[11]

Although this proposal had some virtue, the FEB was apparently more concerned with the niceties of the organizational chart than with a full-scale assault on discrimination. The board replied that any interposition of authority on its part would "dangerously" weaken the "chain of direct responsibility." The FEB did concede, however, that the use of the same person as fair employment officer and chief personnel officer in an agency created "embarrassing problems of split objectives and responsibilities" and recommended that the fair employment officer be relieved of all other duties.[12]

There were also problems over which the FEB had no control. The board had to contend with the "rule of three," a civil-service regulation that permitted the appointing officer to select one of the top three applicants from the Civil Service register. In the application of this rule, the board warned, "lies a vast potentiality of discrimination unless it is used with sole regard to merit and fitness"; and in one case involving several Negroes, the board found a clear-cut example of racial discrimination. But such examples were difficult to prove.[13]

Perhaps the most critical limitation on the board's ability to function properly was its meager budget, which had to be sliced from the operating funds of the Civil Service Commission. The budget restricted the board in the number of days that it might meet, so that by the end of 1951 it had met formally only 121 times since its organization in October 1948. Its expenditures were even more revealing. In four years of operation, the FEB spent slightly over $100,000, a figure that included all salaries and expenses not only for regular members but also for an executive secretary, an examiner, and a clerk-stenographer. Confronted with this financial straitjacket, the FEB was never able to establish effectively a "constructive" or "preventive" program. Therefore its major contribution was "corrective" in hearing the appeals that survived the arduous climb up the chain of command.[14]

Despite these limitations and weaknesses, the board and various agencies functioned effectively in many instances. In December 1951, the FEB reported that 488 complaints had been filed in the twenty-seven agencies that employed 97 percent of the total personnel in federal service. In nearly 60 percent of the cases, no discrimination was found to exist. The FEB itself heard sixty-two appeal cases, finding discrimination in thirteen. The board and the fair employment program continued to function in the Eisenhower administration, and by July 30, 1954, the number of formal complaints had reached 865, of which 12.6

percent required corrective action.[15] Thus, Truman's executive order provided some machinery—however inadequate—for a fair employment policy and insured its continuity into another administration.

The statistics of the Truman administration tell only part of the story, for the very existence of the presidential order and the Fair Employment Board prompted some agencies to comply. Some agencies responded to the spirit of the order and diligently worked for a nondiscriminatory policy, while others responded when civil-rights organizations, armed with the presidential statement demanding a fair employment program, applied pressure. The Post Office Department was a case in point. Early in 1948 Senator William Langer and the NAACP demanded a Senate investigation of discriminatory practices in southern postal facilities, and an investigator subsequently found several instances where eligible Negroes were passed over for appointment and promotion. The FEB quickly issued a directive to correct the situation. Following its own hearings, the FEB also advised post offices in New Orleans, San Antonio, and Memphis to employ Negroes as clerks.[16]

The presidential order also precipitated the end of segregation in the cafeteria of the Government Printing Office, the last federal agency in Washington to integrate such facilities. Although the cafeteria committee of the Printing Office balked and voted against integration, the public printer, observing that segregation conflicted with the announced policies of the administration, took the matter in hand and ordered the integration of cafeteria facilities effective July 25, 1949. Thus ended a bitter struggle that had begun during the administrations of William Howard Taft and Woodrow Wilson.[17]

There were less happy results elsewhere. The commissioners of the District of Columbia ignored the presidential directive, apparently with the acquiescence of the FEB, which interpreted 9980 as inapplicable to the District. The Department of Agriculture remained generally unreceptive to pleas for the employment of blacks in positions with higher ratings in its Washington office, thereby preserving its poor record in regard to race relations. Field officers of the Department of the Interior in Alaska apparently refused to hire Negroes except when other labor was unavailable, although the department's overall record was often praiseworthy.[18]

In 1950 the *Afro-American* indicted the Census Bureau on six counts of racial discrimination, which included not only its discriminatory hiring policies and its overall operations in the South but also the terminology the bureau employed in taking the census and its definition of what constituted a Negro. On the other hand, both the FEB and the Bureau of the Budget insisted upon the elimination of photographs and other identifying devices (unless necessary for statistical purposes) on employment forms, and the Bureau of Immigration and Naturalization also abolished the practice of stamping "black" on the passports of Negro Americans.[19]

One of the toughest problems concerned the Treasury's Bureau of Engraving and Printing, which had traditionally discriminated against minority groups. Although the bureau employed some twenty-five hundred Negroes in 1949—which represented 50 percent of its total work force—fewer than twelve worked in clerical, supervisory, or administrative capacities. But that was only part of the picture. From 1938 to 1950 the bureau recruited seventy-five apprentice plate printers. Although Negroes competed in the examinations, they received no appointments, despite having higher scores than some whites who were subsequently appointed. In fact, in the entire history of the bureau, no Negro had ever served either as an apprentice plate printer or as a journeyman, and the future promised more of the same.[20]

Yet, the shortage of plate printers was as obvious as the discrimination, and in 1949 civil-rights advocates turned a spotlight on the darker side of the bureau's operations. As a consequence, the Fair Employment Board held hearings in January and February 1950 to investigate the growing pyramid of complaints. Reporting on February 23, the FEB held that discrimination did exist and recommended that the Bureau of Engraving and Printing should not only hold its competitive examination, which it had recently scheduled for March 15, but should also inaugurate a continuous in-service training program.[21]

At this point, the Bureau of Engraving and Printing was prepared to agree with the FEB, but Congress now complicated the picture. In February 1950 bills were introduced in both houses to limit competitive apprenticeship examinations to veterans and to permit any veteran in the country to participate, whereas the Treasury Department had restricted the examination to those already employed in the Bureau of Engraving and Printing. Although the congressional bills seemed innocuous enough, being ostensibly designed to favor veterans and to checkmate the closed-shop approach of the bureau, the real purpose seemed to be an attempt to preserve the lily-white complexion of the journeymen and the printer's union, which, incidentally, supported the legislation. Congressional advocates even made the bill retroactive to March 1 in order to nullify the results of the bureau's March 15 examination, which, given the number of eligible Negroes, would almost surely have resulted in black appointments. The House Committee on Post Office and Civil Service moved with indecent haste to gain passage of the bill, which Congressmen Dawson and Marcantonio denounced on the floor. Amid charges of discrimination and bigotry, the bill passed the House on May 1 but died later in the Senate.[22]

In the meantime the White House and the Treasury Department had agreed upon a policy of delay. The department held the exam on March 15, then sat tight, waiting for Congress to adjourn before announcing the results and the new appointments.[23] The strategy worked, and in January 1951 seventeen Negro veterans began apprenticeship training in the Bureau of Engraving and Printing. It was a victory definitely worth boasting about, but apparently the results were not permanent. In November 1953 the *Pittsburgh Courier* devoted a scathing editorial to the bureau—which still "resolutely sets its face toward the fading sun of Kluxism"—for terminating the apprenticeship program in May 1953, thus restoring the all-white complexion of the printing crew.[24]

There was, however, steady and permanent progress in the Department of State, again as a result of Executive Order 9980 and black pressure. Throughout the postwar period, civil-rights advocates had repeatedly agitated for more prestigious appointments, for the chronic complaint centered around the low ratings of most Negroes in federal service. And if one sought prestige, the Department of State was the place to serve. The pressure campaign on the Department of State began in earnest in 1950, when Professor Rayford W. Logan of Howard University published a series of articles in the *Courier*. Logan made one thing very clear. The department's policy was one of near exclusion, particularly in the Foreign Service, where there were only thirty-three Negroes serving in any capacity.[25]

Since the onset of the cold war, the department had been extremely sensitive to the charge of discrimination, particularly where neutral and underdeveloped nations were concerned; and the Korean War increased the department's sensitivity. Black leaders decided to exploit this vulnerability. On February 28, 1951, twelve prominent Negroes, headed by Walter White and A. Philip Randolph, presented the president with six "requests," two of which called for additional black appointments to policy-making positions at home and to diplomatic posts abroad.[26]

On April 13 a smaller Negro delegation met with Secretary of State Dean Acheson and found him somewhat responsive to the group's requests. During the conference he outlined the department's employment policy at great length and balked only at the committee's request for the appointment of a black assistant secretary of state, explaining that the earlier offer to Ralph Bunche had been based entirely on his ability, not on the color of his skin. He also invited the group to discuss the department's employment policies in greater detail with the director of the Office of Personnel.[27]

The last suggestion may have been a political improvisation, but it turned out to be one of lasting benefit. The group met with Haywood P. Martin, director of personnel, on April 19, 1951; and the discussion led to regular conferences thereafter with Martin and his successor, E. N. Montague, which continued into the Eisenhower administration. In March 1952 A. Philip Randolph wrote to Acheson, thanking the secretary and his subordinates for their "splendid attitude" and "cooperative efforts" during the conferences and for the promises of additional appointments. Randolph was usually hard to please, as the president had discovered long before.[28]

Perhaps the most significant appointment was that of John A. Davis in May 1952 as consultant to the State Department's personnel office. Other appointments, however, signified the department's intention to brighten its image both at home and abroad. By June 1952 thirty-four American blacks were working abroad in the Point Four program, although twenty-six were concentrated in Liberia, the traditional "home" for Negroes on foreign service. The department's personnel director, however, continued to labor diligently to overcome resistance both from within the State Department and from other countries to the appointment of skilled black personnel. "We are on a spot," Montague confessed at one point to Joseph C. Green, the American ambassador to Jordan, in stating his desire to appoint more Negroes to Arab nations.[29]

In a progress report of March 1953, Montague summed up the results of the department's efforts over the past two years to attract more Negroes. Nearly sixty Negroes were employed in prestige positions in the Foreign Service, seventeen of whom were serving in traditionally noncolored posts. One held the rank of ambassador, predictably to Liberia. There were also seven Orientals in the service. Moreover, the department had at least fifteen blacks in positions of high rank in the Washington office. It was not nearly enough. Indeed, it was only a beginning, and Montague indicated that he would keep pushing ahead. "The cold war and the present Korean war," he contended, "both make it incumbent upon the department to make sure that racial issues are not allowed to confuse the basic issues of *totalitarianism vs. democracy*."[30]

Other government agencies, under less pressure from Negro leaders, were less responsive to the spirit of the president's order. Some indulged in tokenism. In August 1951, for example, the Justice Department added a third black lawyer to its staff of thousands. Others seemed more concerned. In the fall of 1951 Secretary of Labor Maurice Tobin reminded the annual convention of the National Council of Negro Women that the number of black federal employees was approximately 300 percent greater than in 1940. That statistic, however, might have been less impressive if it had been computed on the basis of 1945, the end of the war.[31]

The president, too, sent in some distinguished nominees, including a few white liberals, to sensitive positions. Although the NAACP had petitioned the president to name a Negro to the vacancy on the three-man Board of Commissioners for the District of Columbia, Negroes were nonetheless pleasantly surprised with the civil-rights performance of his white appointee, F. Joseph Donohue, who took a forthright stand against segregation in the District. They applauded, too, when Truman named Governor Luther W. Youngdahl of Minnesota as a judge of the District Court for the District of Columbia. They had not forgotten the governor's staunch fight to integrate the Minnesota National Guard and to enact FEPC legislation in his home state.[32]

The president also chipped in a few black appointments in 1951. In September he named Dr. Channing Tobias as an alternate delegate to the United Nations and Earl W. Beck, former head of the Jackson County, Missouri, home for Negro children, as recorder of deeds—the traditional slot for Negroes in the District of Columbia. Truman had worked with Beck when he was an administrator in Jackson County, and the appointment of his old colleague seemed to present no problem. The nomination, however, hit a snag when the Senate hearings revived old charges of Beck's mismanagement of the children's home; and Beck's feeble testimony only aggravated the problem. Under fire, Truman refused to withdraw the nomination, and the upshot was a stinging defeat for the president. Not only did the Senate refuse to confirm Beck's appointment but, more important, Congress subsequently passed a bill that invested the District commissioners, rather than the president, with the power to appoint the recorder of deeds.[33]

Truman also came under fire for other appointments in 1951. When he named Robert Ramspeck as chairman of the Civil Service Commission in March 1951, civil-rights advocates were dismayed. As a former congressman from Georgia, now to be responsible for supervising the operations of the Fair Employment Board, Ramspeck was suspect, to say the least. Apparently, most critics failed to examine his credentials. As chairman of the House Civil Service Committee, Ramspeck had fashioned a reputation for concern with the merit system in federal employment. Indeed, the act of 1940, which provided for extensive reform of the civil service, not only bore his name but also included a provision prohibiting discrimination in federal employment. As it turned out, Ramspeck was one of the administration's happier appointments.[34]

Ramspeck might not have become an object of public controversy had it not been for the appointment of another southerner, Millard F. Caldwell, Jr., to head another key operation—the administration's civil-defense program. Lumped together, the appointments suggested that Truman was pursuing a policy of southern appeasement. As a former governor of Florida, Caldwell had gone beyond the usual requirements of southern politics in matters of race relations. He had consistently championed segregation, to the point of disagreeing emphatically with the Supreme Court's decision outlawing the white primary and of masterminding the southern regional-schooling concept to circumvent the Supreme Court ruling on jim-crow colleges.[35]

At the very least, the appointment of Caldwell was politically inept, for it sparked the heaviest concentration of fire from civil-rights advocates of any appointment during the Truman administration. Nearly every major Negro paper in the country devoted blistering editorials to the subject. In a manner reminiscent of the early 1960s, it also prompted worried queries concerning the priorities governing various bomb shelters. Some wondered if Caldwell would insist upon segregation, and the *Defender* warned that "any racial nonsense in a life and death crisis could create far more trouble than an atomic bomb dropped by those mad Russians." One critic pointedly noted the absence of any centrally located bomb shelter in Harlem and the ineffectiveness of the warning sirens in the area.[36]

Caldwell's appointment also aroused the ire of the NAACP, which had been in Truman's camp since 1947. On February 21, 1951, the association dispatched a public letter to the president, in which it conveyed the unanimous vote of the board of directors in favor of dismissing Caldwell. And on February 28, when Walter White and other black leaders met with the president, White used the occasion to indicate their displeasure over the appointment. In his letter inviting civil-rights organizations to a meeting in May, White confessed his distress over the administration's apparent desire to appease "discredited Dixiecrats and other reactionaries." Furthermore, one member of the NAACP's board of directors resigned from the New York Advisory Council of Civil Defense to protest the appointment of the "white supremacy" advocate.[37]

Partly because of his appointments and partly because of his refusal to create a Korean War FEPC by executive order, the president was in the most serious trouble with the disciples of civil rights that he had been in since 1946, when he had responded with the appointment of his Committee on Civil Rights. The response in 1951 was less dramatic and less successful, although it eventually stilled some of the criticism. In March, Caldwell spoke in Philadelphia, where he assured his audience of the impossibility of constructing "an effective civil defense on the basis of race, creed, or color. . . . We must get down to brass tacks with the folks next door, whoever they are. An A-bomb does not discriminate." In April he invited the NAACP and the National Urban League to participate in a conference on civil defense. The NAACP rejected the offer, however, to the dismay of some Negroes, whose fears about Caldwell were slowly dissipating. President Truman also sought to reassure the black community when he appointed Mary McLeod Bethune to the civilian-defense council that advised Caldwell.[38]

The storm eventually blew over, but it left in its wake a readiness, almost an eagerness, to castigate the president on other matters. Black leaders, for example, contended that the president himself was violating the spirit of 9980 when he neglected to appoint more Negroes to important positions. When David Niles resigned as the president's minority adviser in May 1951, the *Chicago Defender*, "at the risk of sticking our nose into this situation again," demanded a black appointment. Truman picked Philleo Nash, a white, but an excellent choice. When Truman appointed a white ambassador to Haiti, blacks complained that no Negro had represented the United States in Haiti since the administration of William Howard Taft.[39]

But the most consistent criticism centered on Truman's failure to appoint more Negroes to prestigious judicial positions, particularly to vacancies in New York and the District of Columbia. In his column in the *Chicago Defender* in June 1951, Walter White summed up all his grievances concerning various appointments and wondered, in conclusion, "if Mr. Truman has completely forgotten his gratitude in 1948 and if he is going to continue to reward those who fought him and ignore those who supported him." Others felt similarly betrayed, although most critics were generally careful not to forget William Hastie's appointment to the Court of Appeals.[40]

In fact, the appointments of Hastie and others in 1949 and 1950 provided a partial explanation of the president's problem in 1951. A revolution of rising expectations, prompted in part by Truman's response to the needs of American minorities, was threatening to engulf the administration. Blacks were demanding more of Truman than they had of any previous president. Their complaints, of course, were legitimate, for there were enough qualified Negro lawyers to fill several judicial posts. At this point, however, Truman had no credit in his bank account with the Senate, which had already bounced some of his white nominees for federal judgeships.

Perhaps the most serious threat, however, to the effectiveness of 9980 and the government's fair employment program stemmed from another presidential executive order issued in March 1947. As a result of a rash of charges concerning Communist activity within the federal government and of the growing estrangement of the United States and the Soviet Union, Truman had issued Executive Order 9835 on March 21, 1947, which directed the Civil Service Commission to investigate the loyalty of all employees in the federal establishment. Although the president and the commission attempted to provide procedures to protect the innocent, the investigations that followed inevitably infringed upon the civil liberties of countless employees.[41]

From the beginning of the loyalty program, black leaders also feared that it would threaten the civil rights of minority employees of the government. The president sought to allay these fears, insisting that the order "was most carefully drawn with the idea in view that the civil rights of no one would be infringed upon and its administration will be carried out in that spirit." But Walter White believed otherwise. In a telegram to the president in November 1947, he expressed the NAACP's regret and surprise over the absence of a Negro lawyer or scholar on the Civil Service Commission's twenty-man loyalty board. Quoting from his telegram to Commission Chairman Harry B. Mitchell, White gave a hint of what was to come when he argued that "prejudiced officials could utilize false charges of disloyalty against minorities to eliminate them from government employment. This is particularly true of the Negro minority since some officials regard as 'subversive' any insistence by a Negro that he be given same rights and opportunities as other citizens."[42]

Some members of the White House staff were also concerned. "In connection with civil rights," John L. Thurston observed in 1947, "the attitude is widespread within the government that it is dangerous to have a 'liberal' thought." By April 1949, Stephen J. Spingarn had decided that "the consuming fear of communism has led many sincere persons into the belief that . . . change (be it civil rights or a compulsory national health program) is subversive and those who urge it are either Communists or fellow travellers."[43]

The issue remained submerged during most of the 1948 campaign, but surfaced on the front page of the *Courier* shortly before election day. The *Courier* revealed that as a result of the loyalty order, numerous Negro postal employees were under investigation, generally because of past and present activities in the field of civil rights. In particular, one postman in Santa Monica had been suspended because of his association with some suspect organizations while picketing a local store that refused to employ Negroes. The NAACP quickly came to his aid and secured his reinstatement in short order. Others were less fortunate, and Negroes feared a wholesale purge in the Post Office Department. And the chairman of the loyalty board, Seth W. Richardson, was less than reassuring when he admitted that prejudiced persons could institute charges without permitting the accused the protection of regular court procedures.[44]

A pattern of discrimination was soon obvious. Some government investigators considered that an employee was suspect if he possessed recordings by Paul Robeson. One interrogator even had the audacity to ask an employee who was under investigation if she had written a letter to the Red Cross protesting the segregation of blood. In protesting to the president in November 1948, Walter White expressed his dismay with the "increasing tendency on the part of government agencies to associate activity on interracial matters with disloyalty." In particular, he noted that investigators were asking government employees if they associated socially with other races. Moreover, some Negroes were currently under investigation "because they have actively opposed segregation and discrimination in their places of employment or in their communities." White urged the president to appoint a special committee to restudy the whole loyalty program.[45]

Another correspondent put his finger directly on the problem. "If the F.E.P.C. order for the federal government is to be enforced it will be necessary for either individual federal employees or their organizations to bring instances of discrimination before the F.E.P.C. Board for review," he pointed out to the president. "In light of the record established by the loyalty probers, I am afraid that government employees who will have the temerity of bringing such cases of discrimination

. . . will run the risk of losing their jobs under a 'disloyalty' brand." In short, if an employee utilized Executive Order 9980 to report evidence of discrimination, he might automatically become suspect under 9835. This was particularly possible in the postal department where the personnel chief also served as fair employment officer and chairman of the department's loyalty board.[46] It was a tragicomedy. While the president preached the cause of civil rights in America, the gnomes of some loyalty boards scurried throughout the bureaucracy equating the issue with communism.

The evidence of discrimination in the Post Office Department continued to mount in 1949. In January an officer of the all-Negro National Alliance of Postal Employees reported that of the 120 to 135 employees facing disloyalty charges, 66 were Negroes and 43 were Jews. Congressman Andrew Jacobs had similar figures, and he wrote to the president in March, asking why 128 of 139 persons suspected of disloyalty were Negroes or Jews. The president's secretary replied, quoting extensively from an explanatory memorandum from the head of the Civil Service Commission, which denied the insinuation of discrimination but did not dispute the figures. There could be no discrimination, the memo maintained, because employee records contained no mention of race. The answer missed the point, for many Negroes and Jews had once belonged to civil-rights organizations that were ensconced on the attorney general's list of subversive groups. Moreover, some names and addresses made it possible to identify people as to their race or religion.[47]

No one in the administration seemed to be particularly concerned. In 1950 Carl Murphy of the *Afro-American* complained in a letter to the president that no Negro served on any of the 150 government loyalty boards, and he requested some black appointments to insure fair procedure and proper questioning. The White House forwarded the request to the Civil Service Commission for a response. The chairman of the Loyalty Review Board, Seth Richardson, could see no reason why a "proper" Negro should not serve on the board, but neither could he visualize any "particular purpose" in such a move, for "any element relating to race which creeps into any loyalty hearing is purely accidental and entirely out of harmony with our procedures and would stand no chance of survival as the program proceeded." The White House's response to Murphy, nearly two months after his protest, was clearly a brush-off and emphasized that the commission, not the president, was responsible for appointments to the loyalty boards.[48]

Although Truman subsequently became concerned about possible excesses in the loyalty program and about the deteriorating morale of federal employees, the onslaught of McCarthyism forced the administration into a defensive position. Moreover, no evidence exists of any presidential concern for the fact that Executive Orders 9835 and 9980 sometimes worked at cross purposes. Indeed, Truman may never have realized it. During his news conference of March 2, 1950, his response to a reporter's question concerning a possible conflict revealed his failure to understand the import of the query.[49]

During the Truman years the number of employees actually fired because of "excessive" zeal on civil rights or because of past or present membership in suspect civil-rights organizations was miniscule. But no one will ever know how many resigned under pressure or out of fear, how many applicants were rejected because of past or present affiliations, or how many employees refused to report examples of discrimination for fear of a counterinvestigation of their own loyalty. These intangibles, these fugitive statistics, suggest a much larger and even less wholesome story.

Although minority-group leaders appreciated the president's appointment of a Fair Employment Board in civil service and although they found large portions of the loyalty program distasteful, they never allowed their appreciation or their concern to divert them from the main goal of securing an FEPC to scrutinize and enforce fair employment practices outside the governmental bureaucracy. A. Philip Randolph, in particular, continued to agitate for what he considered the black man's most important goal—economic equality and opportunity in America. With the refusal of Congress to pass FEPC legislation, Randolph, Walter White, and others shifted their attention to the White House. Although the mass militancy that Randolph had exploited so effectively in 1940 and 1941 was absent in 1950 and 1951, the Korean War seemed to provide the necessary leverage. On July 26, 1950, Randolph wired the president, urging that he "issue an Executive Order similar to President Roosevelt's 8802 . . . as an integral factor in the mobilization of manpower against North Korean Communist aggression." As the military situation in Korea deteriorated throughout the summer of 1950, Randolph, White, and Lester Granger sought to persuade government officials of the necessity for maximum utilization of human resources—which meant the fair employment of minorities in defense industries.[50]

On August 10, 1950, as UN forces fought a desperate holding action in southeastern Korea, black leaders representing a dozen organizations met with Stuart Symington, head of the National Security

Resources Board, and Secretary of Labor Maurice Tobin to urge a five-point defense program, with a presidentially created FEPC at the top of the list. On August 15 Symington also conferred with Urban League officials, who advocated similar action. Although Symington agreed with the necessity for some sort of manpower policy, nothing happened for over two months, despite Walter White's concerned inquiries. By mid October, White could only assume that the Korean War and the approaching congressional elections had something to do with the delay.[51]

Actually, from mid August to mid October 1950, the proposal was stalled in the Department of Labor. Suddenly, the department came off dead center, and the last two weeks of October saw a flurry of activity and a series of meetings with Negro leaders. The result was a draft of an executive order that took a manpower rather than an FEPC approach to the problem. The draft was quickly forwarded to the White House, which was reportedly scheduled to issue or say something on October 30.[52] Again, nothing happened. Perhaps the forthcoming congressional elections had something to do with the White House decision not to act. It is more plausible that the delay was connected with the continuing war in Korea. For at that moment UN forces were streaming across North Korea, following their dramatic break-out of the Pusan perimeter and their amphibious landing at Inchon in September; and General MacArthur was soon publicly to predict an early end to the war. Indeed, he had already privately assured the president of victory during a conference at Wake Island. And the end of the war would obviate a manpower policy, at least in the administration's eyes.

Meanwhile officials of the Department of Labor held a conference on November 29 with Negro leaders, who "rejected" a proposed executive order because it failed to include any centralized administration or any provision for enforcement. Unhappy with the Labor Department, they planned next to seek an appointment with the president, although they could not have been overly optimistic at that point. Once again, however, the misfortunes of war abroad promised to aid minorities at home, for UN forces in Korea had suffered a drastic reversal as a result of MacArthur's ill-advised rush to the Yalu River in late November 1950. Chinese troops were now flooding into North Korea, threatening to drive UN forces completely from the peninsula. On December 14, as Truman prepared to declare a national emergency, Randolph appealed to him to include an executive order establishing an FEPC in his proclamation. The following day, Truman informed the American people of the "great danger" to the United States as a result of the grave turn of events in Korea and announced the appointment of Charles E. Wilson to head the new Office of Defense Mobilization. And on December 16 he declared a national emergency, without, however, mentioning the FEPC.[53]

Yet Negroes were hopeful at this point. On December 27, 1950, faced with the prospect of a longer war and with the incessant pressure of civil-rights organizations, the Department of Labor forwarded to the White House a proposed executive order that called for the establishment of a fair employment practices committee with adequate powers of enforcement. In his covering letter, Secretary of Labor Tobin observed that "for some time to come the federal government will be spending billions of dollars for defense purposes. It is unthinkable that the federal government should permit these funds to be expended without imposing on those favored with government business the obligation to refrain from unsocial discriminatory employment practices and without providing effective means of enforcing such an obligation." The National Security Resources Board also submitted its own version of a "Manpower Resources Board," and predictions of early White House action quickly appeared in the Negro press.[54]

Although encouraged, Walter White, Randolph, and others were also wary, for they were old hands at dealing with the government and its various devices of delay. Moreover, they knew that the White House had referred the Labor proposal, as was customary, to the Bureau of the Budget for approval and that persistent pressure had to be continued. Thus, on January 4, 1951, they met with Stuart Symington and Charles Wilson and received the enthusiastic support of both. Wilson in particular indicated that he would strongly urge issuance of the executive order immediately.[55] The next stop was the president. On January 9 White, Randolph, Tobias, and Granger—indeed, the major Negro leaders of the day—requested an audience to discuss "certain policies for our government to adopt in this war crisis which we consider of vast and vital importance to the unity and strength of our country." But the White House was not receptive and urged a conference with Mobilization Director Wilson, which Randolph rejected. The White House was developing a case of nerves, however, and briefly considered a presidential statement to the people explaining that the Budget Bureau was studying several FEPC proposals and comparing them with existing statutes to determine their legality.[56]

Instead, on January 17, 1951, Truman issued a National Manpower Mobilization Policy, which called for "the maximum development and use of our human resources." Among other things, the policy urged all executive agencies to provide assistance to private industry in "promoting maximum utilization of the labor force including women, physically handicapped, older workers, and minority groups" and promised to invoke government manpower controls to assure success of the program. But the program was largely voluntary and was even less satisfactory than an FEPC without enforcement power, for it left to the discretion of various government agencies how and to what extent they would encourage employment of minorities. The policy prompted a question during the president's news conference the following day. Asked if he intended to create an FEPC for war industries, Truman ducked the question with a piece of irrelevancy; then he dispatched a follow-up query with a quip, to the delight of the reporters present.[57]

But Negroes were neither amused with the attempt at humor nor mollified with the manpower policy. Several editorials appeared in the black press, crisply demanding the establishment of an executive FEPC; and the National Newspaper Publishers Association, meeting in executive session in Atlanta, made the sentiment unanimous. Moreover, Randolph and other Negro leaders kept insisting upon an audience with the president, but the White House staff kept referring them elsewhere.[58]

The next step in the administration's campaign of conciliation and circumvention was a series of seven executive orders, issued between February and October 1951. The first order, appearing on February 2, authorized the Departments of Defense and Commerce to exercise their wartime powers in the handling of defense contracts. It also specified: "There shall be no discrimination in any act performed hereunder against any person on the ground of race, creed, color or national origin, and all contracts hereunder shall contain a provision that the contractor and any subcontractors thereunder shall not so discriminate." Six subsequent orders extended these provisions to an additional nine executive departments and agencies.[59]

The orders, however, provided neither for adequate enforcement nor for a committee to oversee the contracts; and thus they were inadequate as means to eliminate discrimination in defense employment. Moreover, although Roosevelt's FEPC had expired in 1946 as a result of the Russell amendment, the requirement in his executive order of 1943 that all government contracts contain a nondiscrimination clause remained in effect throughout the Truman period.[60] At best, Truman's inclusion of a nondiscrimination provision in his executive orders simply reaffirmed and revitalized the stipulation of 1943 and served as a gentle reminder to executive agencies to do what had been required of them since the Second World War. Politically, it seemed to represent a concession to the politics of civil rights and an attempt to divert pressure and criticism elsewhere.

Predictably, the order of February 2 did not pacify Negro leaders. Following a conference early in February with Charles Wilson, who agreed to issue a public statement in favor of a strong FEPC but only after presidential approval, they renewed their request for an appointment with the president. Reportedly, the buck-passing stopped at the White House; and by this time, the Negro group was weary from riding the bureaucratic merry-go-round. The White House finally relented and scheduled the meeting for February 28. Truman's staff prepared carefully for the confrontation, briefing the president on the six points that they expected the group to present. In response to the request for an executive order creating an FEPC, the president would reply that although everyone was demanding such action, only he seemed aware of the problems with regard to authority and budget. When the Bureau of the Budget found the answer to various statutory restrictions, the president would act. As expected, the twelve Negro leaders submitted the six requests to Truman on February 28, and the president presumably responded according to plan.[61]

Although pressure for an FEPC continued to mount, the White House remained silent and unresponsive. It was painfully clear that the administration was deliberately stalling. For example, when a rumor circulated outside the government that Charles Wilson intended to act shortly on an FEPC, the Bureau of the Budget, which had been "studying" the executive order for at least a month, inquired of the White House if the story was authentic. In particular, the people in the bureau wanted to know if they should "change their signals" or "continue to study" the Department of Labor's proposed executive order. The White House quickly phoned the Budget Bureau reporting "no change of signals."[62]

The "signals" clearly called for indefinite delay, but the reasons for the administration's procrastination were much less obvious. The ostensible reason was the Russell amendment of 1944, which prevented the president from expending any funds for an agency that had been created by executive order and had been in existence for more than one year, unless Congress specifically authorized or appropriated such expenditures. The amendment was aimed directly at Roosevelt's FEPC and had contributed to the committee's demise in 1946. There was, of course, no direct prohibition against the establishment of such a committee. The critical problem was how to finance it, and this constituted one of the administration's greatest concerns.[63]

Civil-rights advocates, who had also studied the amendment, argued that even a strict interpretation of the amendment did not preclude the establishment of a committee for one year, which the president could finance from his emergency fund. Congress, however, kept a tight rein on the emergency fund and repeatedly slashed presidential requests, even during the Korean War. More important, the Russell amendment also stipulated that the one-year provision applied to any newly created committee that performed a function "substantially the same or similar" to that of a previously established committee; and the Department of Labor's proposed executive order would presumably fall into this category. In other words, the proposed committee apparently had already had its year. Civil-rights advocates also argued that Congress had not challenged the Fair Employment Board's right to function or to expend funds, but they had overlooked the fact that the limited budget of the FEB, financed from the regular operating funds of the Civil Service Commission, had hobbled the board from the beginning.[64] The administration could also have retorted that Congress was much less sensitive to the establishment of fair employment practices in federal civil service than to coercive measures applied to private employers with government contracts.

Certainly there were problems. When Labor Department representatives met with Negro leaders on November 29, 1950, they carefully explained the restrictions to the delegation; but the recital of difficulties failed to convince the black attorneys present, who offered convincing arguments in opposition. Apparently the Negro group converted the Department of Labor, for its proposed executive order sent to the White House on December 27, 1950, provided for a strong FEPC, to be financed either from the president's emergency fund or from appropriations under the Defense Production Act of 1950. But a presidential assistant, in his analysis of the order—which seemed to contain a tone of irritation with the Labor Department, perhaps because the heat was now on the White House—professed to see statutory as well as financial problems.[65]

The analysis, apparently written by David Niles, was not encouraging, and Negroes soon blamed "Devious Dave" for the "snail's pace" of the proposed order. They were convinced that an FEPC was legally and financially possible because of legislation supplemental to the Russell amendment of 1944. This was their best argument, for the

Independent Offices Appropriation Acts of 1945 and 1946 permitted the establishment of interagency committees without congressional authorization or approval if they were engaged "in authorized activities of common interest" that required no additional compensation or appropriation. And it was under the authority of this supplemental legislation that Truman eventually created his Committee on Government Contract Compliance in December 1951.[66]

So there was a road around the Russell amendment, but the administration chose not to travel it for almost a year after the Labor Department had proposed an executive order. Civil-rights advocates wanted to know why, although they had their own ideas. They were convinced that the administration was deliberately appeasing Dixiecrats in order to unify the party in preparation for the election of 1952. The appointments of Ramspeck and Caldwell seemed part of this pattern, as did the president's subordination of the civil-rights issue in his State of the Union message in 1951. So, too, did restoration of patronage to the congressional delegation from Mississippi.[67]

Yet the "unity" argument as applied to the campaign of 1952 is not convincing, because Truman subsequently took an even stronger stance on civil rights in 1952 than he had in 1948. True, the administration sought unity in 1951, but primarily because of the Korean War. On December 9, 1950, as UN forces were retreating pell-mell down the peninsula, Under Secretary of State James E. Webb urged the president to alter his tactics in his civil-rights battles with the South. Noting the necessity for "national unity in these perilous times," Webb observed that many southern Democrats expended much of their time and energy in "defensive operations" against the administration's civil-rights program. To enlist southern support during the emergency, he then suggested that the president adopt a "rattlesnake formula"—which meant that in matters disagreeable to the South, the president would not "strike" without warning, thus leaving southern legislators free to consider other matters of vital national interest.[68]

The unity theme was most obvious in the president's annual message to Congress on January 8, 1951. Speaking at a moment when it was debatable if UN forces in Korea would be able to stem the Red tide, the president devoted the bulk of his message to the war and the alleged Soviet threat elsewhere in the world, and his major legislative requests revolved around the international situation. He closed with a ringing peroration for unity, requesting everyone to "put our country ahead of our party, and ahead of our own personal interests." Presumably as part of his own contribution to national unity, he did not specifically request the enactment of civil-rights legislation—the first time he had failed to do so since 1948. Yet in issuing a clarion call to freedom-loving people everywhere, he could not completely ignore those who were deprived of it at home. Tucked in near the end of his address was the entreaty that "we must assure equal rights and equal opportunities to all our citizens."[69]

Truman was keenly aware of the problems that he faced in the winter and spring of 1951, if others were not. In an off-the-record meeting on May 21 with several members of the Americans for Democratic Action—including Francis Biddle, Joseph L. Rauh, James B. Carey, Hubert Humphrey, Arthur Schlesinger, Jr., Reinhold Niebuhr, and Col. Campbell C. Johnson—the president carefully explained the reasons for the delay in creating an FEPC and promised action at the earliest possible date. He emphasized that the civil-rights issue was only part of the liberal program, and that the total program had to survive the campaign of 1952. It also had to survive 1951, as did those measures necessary for the war effort; the president was particularly worried about the pending appropriations and manpower bills. Those in attendance went away convinced of Truman's continuing commitment to the liberal cause and sympathetic with his political difficulties. "He has his head in the lion's mouth," Campbell Johnson noted later, "and this is no time to tickle the lion."[70]

Truman's fears were not imaginary, for by May 1951 his program was in deep trouble with Congress. For one thing, he had requested authority for temporary reorganization of federal agencies concerned with the national emergency; but when the bill appeared on the floor of the House, southerners professed to see an administrative maneuver to establish an FEPC by executive order. On March 13 Truman suffered his first outstanding legislative defeat of 1951 when the House rejected the bill. The coalition of southern Democrats with Republicans was at work. Of the 169 votes for the bill, 161 were Democratic, while 181 Republicans and 46 Democrats, mostly from the South, voted against it. The same coalition also reduced his request for low-rental housing from fifty thousand to five thousand units and cut other requests severely.[71] Congress was in a vengeful as well as a tight-fisted mood.

In view of the House vote on executive reorganization, the conservative coalition obviously suspected the president of not operating according to Webb's "rattlesnake formula"; and some evidence suggests that the administration did plan to strike without warning on an FEPC. In his 1951 budget message Truman requested an appropriation of $25 million for his emergency fund to use at his discretion "for emergencies affecting the national interest, security, or defense which may arise at home or abroad." The request was a dramatic increase over the usual $1 million appropriation for the fund, and southerners suspected that Truman had an executive FEPC in mind.[72]

They may have been right. Truman's request for the unusually large appropriation also included the provision that none of the funds could be used to finance a function or project for which the administration had submitted a budget request that Congress had subsequently denied. Interestingly enough, Truman's budget message included an appeal for congressional establishment of an FEPC, but the budget itself contained no request for appropriations for such a committee, although such requests had been included in past budget messages. Thus, by omitting any request for appropriations for an FEPC, which Congress would inevitably reject, the president could use his emergency fund to finance the committee. If this was White House strategy, the House on the Hill thwarted it. On May 4 the conservative coalition shattered any hope of financing a fair employment committee created by executive order when it slashed the president's request from $25 million to $1 million.[73]

If the administration harbored a secret strategy, it had to be kept from everyone, including civil-rights advocates. Truman was in a dilemma, for Negro leaders refused to accept the "unity" argument as a satisfactory explanation for inaction on an executive FEPC. Throughout the spring and early summer of 1951, the drumfire of criticism and the application of pressure continued. Telegrams and letters poured into the White House. Civil-rights organizations pleaded for executive action, and the Negro press denounced the president in stinging editorials.[74]

Through it all, Truman remained publicly imperturbable. In his news conference on June 21, for example, he simply refused to comment on the matter. The campaign for an executive order peaked on June 25, 1951, the tenth anniversary of Roosevelt's issuance of 8802 and the first anniversary of the Korean War. Truman was reminded of both when sixteen national civil-rights, labor, and liberal organizations wired the White House, urging a new FEPC "to assure to every American, regardless of race, religion, or national origin, an equal opportunity to contribute his utmost skills and talents to the production of the tools and weapons so urgently needed by our armed forces, and to demonstrate to the peoples of the world that the United States is the exemplar as well as the exponent of democracy." Governors of seven states and mayors of eight cities also proclaimed June 25 as Fair Employment Practices Day.[75]

It was an impressive outburst of sentiment and unity, but the president refused to respond. Moreover, the volume and tone of the protests dropped off in the fall, particularly after Truman vetoed the bill that would have required segregation of schools for military dependents in southern states. Nonetheless, the administration came off dead center near the end of October when Truman told Charles Murphy to draft an order "along the World War II line" so that he could "issue it as soon as possible." And on December 3, 1951, after Congress had adjourned and after the Korean War had shown decided improvement, the president issued Executive Order 10308 from his vacation home in Key West, Florida.[76]

In his covering statement, the president explained that the order was designed to correct a deficiency in the government's program of nondiscrimination in defense contracts. Although a clause to that effect was included in each contract, the system lacked uniform regulation and inspection. The order thus invested in each contracting agency of the federal government the primary authority to secure compliance from the contractors in the private sector. To oversee the operation, the president created the Committee on Government Contract Compliance, which would "examine and study the compliance procedures now in use and . . . recommend to the department and agency heads changes that will strengthen them." Truman also explained that "as part of its functions, the committee may confer with interested persons"—a euphemism which meant that the committee could hold hearings but lacked the power of the subpoena.[77] By investing his new committee with the cumbersome and inelegant title of "Committee on Government Contract Compliance," Truman was seeking to avoid not only the political onus of the letters "FEPC" but also any comparisons with Roosevelt's committee because of the statutory restrictions of the Russell amendment.

It took only a glance to reveal the inadequacies of Executive Order 10308. For one thing, it placed primary responsibility on the contracting agency, which meant not only a dispersal of responsibility and authority but also left enforcement to the discretion of federal officials who may have been less than enthusiastic about the program. In this respect, the order paralleled 9980 and the operating procedures of the Fair Employment Board. Similarly, the Committee on Government Contract Compliance (CGCC) had only advisory and recommendatory functions. Without the power to issue cease-and-desist orders, its major contribution would be hortatory and educational.

The scope of the CGCC was also much more restricted than that of Roosevelt's FEPC. Truman's committee was authorized to deal only with government contractors and subcontractors, whereas the FEPC had had powers to examine discrimination in transportation, labor unions, and other economic activities. Of course, this was not simply an oversight, for in drafting the new order the administration was extremely careful to avoid anything that might conflict with the Russell amendment.[78] Caution was clearly necessary, for the CGCC could not afford to become ensnarled in a legal hassle or placed in political limbo. From the moment of its creation, the committee was suspect— to some because it seemed to promise so little, to others because it lacked congressional approval and seemed to threaten the sanctity of private enterprise.

Finally, the CGCC was financially hampered. Its expenses came from the regular budgets of the five government agencies represented on the committee, and the public appointees on the CGCC served without pay. Furthermore, its staff was too small to engage in effective investigation of complaints. To illustrate the problem, the personnel of Roosevelt's second FEPC included fifty-six professional people and sixty-three clerks, in contrast with only six professionals and four clerks attached to Truman's committee.[79]

Yet the CGCC was not completely impotent. It could publicize instances of discrimination through hearings and press releases. It could recommend action to Charles Wilson, director of defense mobilization, and, through him, to the president. The committee could also urge the federal contracting agencies, who held such power, to cancel contracts with private employers who continued to discriminate against minority groups on government projects. Unfortunately, no government contracting agency during the Truman administration ever canceled a contract because of failure to observe the nondiscrimination clause, despite abundant evidence in some cases. In fact, in 1969 the *Courier* reported that the government had never revoked a contract solely on the grounds of racial discrimination.[80]

The White House, however, did not conceive of the CGCC as an idle gesture or as a political pacifier. Impressed with the success of the Fahy Committee in persuading the military to establish procedures to end segregation in the armed forces, the administration hoped to achieve the same result with the CGCC through cooperation and consultation with private employers who held government contracts. This expectation, though misplaced, pervaded the White House staff. When press secretary Joseph Short explained the order to reporters in Key West, he noted that it should be compared with the executive order establishing the Fahy Committee, which had "pointed the way toward ending discrimination in our fighting forces." The hope of similar success in employment was also symbolized in the appointment as chairman of the CGCC of Dwight R. G. Palmer, who had served as a member of the Fahy Committee. In his letter of appointment to Palmer, the president recalled his "significant contribution" to the Fahy Committee and expressed confidence that "the techniques of close cooperation with the departments that you and your associates worked out in that earlier committee will provide a sound basis for the new program."[81]

Given the obvious weaknesses, both internal and external, of the CGCC, no one could expect unanimous applause from the black community. Actually, the reaction of civil-rights organizations was mixed, while white southern opinion was uniformly critical. To J. William Fulbright of Arkansas, the presidential order appeared as a "diversionary movement" to take the public spotlight off the tax-collection scandals, and to Senator Walter F. George, as the opening gun in Truman's campaign for reelection in 1952. On the other side of the racial spectrum, the strongest criticism came from leaders of the NAACP. Clarence Mitchell of the association's Washington bureau was depressed because of the order's lack of enforcement power, and Walter White contended that the administration could have issued a more effective order. Elmer Henderson of the American Council for Human Rights was similarly disappointed.[82]

Yet there was also impressive support in black editorials, for Truman had surprised many editors who no longer expected or demanded executive action. The *Courier*, for example, saw it only as "half-a-loaf FEPC" but the best Truman "could do under the circumstances." The *Afro-American*, although it also desired a stronger committee, argued that Truman had "again demonstrated the courage and steadfastness of purpose which will characterize his place in history." Even Lester Granger, who seldom overlooked an opportunity to criticize the president, found much to applaud in the CGCC. Undismayed by the committee's lack of enforcement power, he contended that the "negotiative and consultative process . . . can often yield more important results than . . . legislative or judicial fiats."[83] Perhaps he, too, was speaking with the authority of his experience on the Fahy Committee.

Even those who were most disappointed with the order, however, were willing to concede the possibility of accomplishment if the president appointed the right people to the CGCC. Here, the administration indicated its seriousness of purpose. The committee consisted of ten members, four of whom were ex officio representatives of the Departments of Defense and Labor, the Atomic Energy Commission, the General Services Administration, and the Defense Materials Procurement Agency. In addition to Palmer as chairman, the president also appointed James B. Carey of the CIO; Irving M. Engel of the American Jewish Committee; George Meany of the AFL, who soon resigned because of the pressure of time and was succeeded by Boris Shishkin; Oliver W. Hill, a Negro attorney and former member of the Richmond City Council; and Dowdal H. Davis, general manager of the Kansas City *Call*.[84] Thus, the six working members of the committee included two Negroes and two Jews, though, typically, an Anglo-Saxon chaired the committee.

Despite the caliber of its membership, no one was inspired with the first six months of the committee's operation. In June 1952 Clarence Mitchell accused the CGCC of taking no "concrete action on discrimination in employment" and submitted various recommendations to expedite matters. And in fact, the committee seemed to be moving with glacial speed. It did not hold its first meeting until February 19, 1952, at which time Palmer emphasized the advisability of not issuing any press releases and of avoiding all publicity until the committee had gathered extensive data. That decision meant that the CGCC would not use the power of public exposure to prompt conformance with the nondiscrimination clause. Although the committee examined a few complaints of discrimination in the spring, it was not until April that an executive secretary was appointed. And not until November did the committee finally decide upon what size contracts should be to contain nondiscrimination clauses.[85] This seemingly leisurely pace inevitably created the impression of indifference and inactivity.

Actually, the committee clearly understood its function and what it could hope to achieve. Restricted both in authority and by time as to what it could accomplish during the last year of the Truman administration, the CGCC concentrated on the future, attempting to ensure a stronger program through a number of recommendations based on a thorough study of the entire contract process. As far as private contractors were concerned, the CGCC "found the nondiscrimination provision almost forgotten, dead and buried under thousands of words of standard legal and technical language in government procurement contracts." Although the committee reported that some employers had attempted to fulfill the spirit of the nondiscrimination clause, most saw it "as just another contractual clause of relatively minor importance and have made little, if any, attempt to adhere to its standards."[86]

Nor did the government contracting agencies have anything to boast about, for they were partly responsible for the indifference of private contractors. In the course of its year in operation, the CGCC studied the contract and compliance procedures of twenty-eight government agencies and found only two that had made any real effort to determine the extent of compliance. Admittedly, the problem in part was one of inadequate staffing and financing. It was also one of indifference and opposition, for the committee discovered three federal agencies that failed to include nondiscrimination clauses in their contracts, which was in direct violation of all executive orders. That "neglect" was quickly corrected. Moreover, after consultation with representatives of the Office of Defense Mobilization, the Bureau of Employment Security, the Bureau of Apprenticeship, the Maritime Administration, the Office of Education, and the Veterans Administraton, the committee confessed only "a meager degree of success in its attempts to persuade these key agencies to establish the principle of equal employment opportunity as one of the basic operating criteria of their programs." The Office of Defense Mobilization, however, finally promised to include a strong statement against discrimination in its regular policy directives. But the District of Columbia balked, refusing even to include the nondiscrimination clause in contracts, because it claimed to operate under the legislative branch of the government where presidential executive orders had no authority.[87]

Throughout the year the committee also held discussions with official representatives of the twelve states and several cities that had fair employment commissions, discussions that again illuminated the fact that discrimination respected no geographical, industrial, or ideological boundaries. Various members made spot checks across the country, including a visit to Texas to assess the extent of discrimination against Mexican-Americans. Yet the CGCC, as was true of other agencies and organizations involved in attempts to establish equal employment opportunities, concentrated primarily on discrimination against Negroes, for that was where most of the pressure, the numbers, and the problems existed. Seeking advice and information, CGCC members also contacted experts in various universities and municipal commissions and took testimony from several civil-rights organizations.[88]

Discrimination was everywhere, particularly against black Americans, and the statistics told only a small part of the story. From February to December 1952, the CGCC received only 318 complaints, but that was considerably more than the total of 40 received by the government contracting agencies. The committee could only conclude that most workers knew nothing of the nondiscrimination clause or of the procedures for registering grievances and that most contracting federal agencies lacked uniform machinery for handling complaints. The CGCC could not doubt the existence of widespread discrimination after a few of its own investigations. A survey of three industrial plants in West Virginia, for example, revealed only 130 Negroes employed in a work force of 12,000, and most of the 130 were custodial workers.[89]

The Committee on Government Contract Compliance was active, it was concerned, and it did persuade and press some employers to adopt more enlightened hiring policies. The very existence of the committee automatically prompted some compliance. And there were impressive gains in minority employment during this period, which stemmed, however, from influences in addition to the administration's fair employment policies. Certainly the increased need for civilian and military manpower during the Korean War and the incessant pressure of civil-rights organizations played prominent roles in dropping the unemployment rate of black Americans in 1951 and 1952. In fact, not until 1969—during another war—would the rate again be as low.[90] Yet the major contribution of Truman's Committee on Government Contract Compliance rested primarily on whatever influence it might exert on the future. This the committee realized from the beginning of its operations, and it designed its final recommendations for the benefit of the next administration.

In its report to the president on January 16, 1953, the CGCC presented twenty-two recommendations for action on the part of federal executive agencies, Congress, local governmental units, private employers, and labor unions. Although the Eisenhower administration implemented some of the committee's suggestions, others seemed consigned permanently to limbo. Of greater significance was the simple fact that Truman's establishment of the CGCC made it impossible for subsequent administrations to ignore the necessity for similar programs. In August 1953 Eisenhower created the President's Committee on Government Contracts, which the Kennedy administration in turn replaced with the President's Committee on Equal Employment Opportunity.[91]

Truman's CGCC thus ensured the continuation of a government fair employment program, but it could guarantee nothing else, least of all any improvement. In 1961 the U.S. Commission on Civil Rights reported that employment patterns of government and nongovernment contractors alike generally reflected the racial mores of the local community or region.[92] Thus, while minority groups benefited from fair employment in federal civil service and from increased opportunity in the armed services, they continued to suffer from discrimination in the private sector of the economy. In 1969, for example, the Department of Defense awarded contracts to several southern firms, despite evidence that they practiced discrimination and despite reservations on the part of the government's Office of Federal Contract Compliance.[93]

The persistence of discrimination on the part of employers and labor unions and the continued indifference of some government agencies throughout the 1950s and 1960s thus provide the perspective by which to judge the actions of the Truman administration. As a result of Truman's Fair Employment Board and the Committee on Government Contract Compliance, fair employment policy became a permanent part of the federal system. Unfortunately, the government has yet to translate that policy into consistent and meaningful fair employment practices.

13 DEFEAT IN CONGRESS

"Vote Republican, Nov. 7, and End Truman Double-Talk" went the punch line of a Republican campaign tract in October 1950. Prepared by Val Washington, Negro assistant to the chairman of the Republican National Committee, the pamphlet represented the party's major effort to capture Negro votes in the congressional elections of November 1950. Entitled *Civil Rights Double-Talk—The Egg That Truman Laid*, the leaflet made a few telling points as well as the usual campaign distortions in indicting the president and the Democratic Congress for inaction on racial discrimination in America.[1]

Although Val Washington may have believed that he had scored significantly by recounting certain select senatorial votes, particularly those on cloture, Walter White was nearer the mark in his column in the *Chicago Defender*. White argued that the key vote on civil rights in the Eighty-first Congress concerned the Barkley ruling, which would have permitted the application of cloture to a motion as well as to the measure itself. Moreover, the defeat of the Barkley ruling led directly to the adoption of the Wherry-Hayden "compromise," which made cloture even more difficult. On these votes, the Republican record was shaky at best. Although White endorsed neither party, his resurrection of the Barkley vote was primarily a criticism of the Republican-Dixiecrat coalition that had stymied so much progressive legislation.[2]

In truth, the Republican party was hard pressed to find strong black support anywhere in the country. For the first time in memory, the *Call* endorsed Democratic candidates so as to provide President Truman with a working majority in both houses of Congress. The *Chicago Defender* indicted the "coalition of tory Republicans and Dixiecrats," who "succeeded in gagging and diverting every serious attempt to match the promises with performances." It seemed to the *Defender* that "President Truman has been unyielding in his demand for action on civil rights and we should elect a Congress that will support his program." And the president gave indications that he would continue the fight. Although Truman followed the customary presidential practice of not compaigning for Democratic candidates in an off-year election, he did deliver one highly partisan speech in St. Louis in which he pledged his party to renewed efforts for better education and health "for all our citizens, without discrimination on account of race, creed, or color."[3] It was that kind of commitment that prompted many black Americans to remain with Truman throughout 1950.

On the eve of election day, an Associated Negro Press (ANP) poll predicted widespread black support for Democratic candidates.[4] There were good reasons, both historical and contemporary, for such loyalty to the Democratic party. Senator Joseph R. McCarthy's campaign against communism in the government may have persuaded some independent white voters to support Republican candidates; but Negroes were more concerned with "bread and butter" legislation, which the Democratic party had championed since 1933. Moreover, although Congress had not enacted any of the major presidential requests for civil-rights legislation, Truman himself had come through with several significant appointments and with two key executive orders, one of which at that moment was leading to integration of the military in Korea. His appointees in the Department of Justice had also filed amicus curiae briefs in several significant court cases between 1948 and 1950.

The congressional elections of 1950 fulfilled the ANP forecast, if not the hopes of civil-rights organizations for additional friends in Congress. An analysis of the black vote in ten northern cities revealed continued support for all Democratic candidates, except in Baltimore, where Senator Millard Tydings won only 23 percent of the Negro vote in contrast with Truman's 54 percent in 1948. The combination of the Maryland senator's poor record on civil rights and Senator McCarthy's vicious campaign against him all but made Tydings's reelection impossible.[5]

To most black Americans, however, Senator Tydings's defeat was one of the few happy results of the congressional elections. In a record turnout for an off-year election, the American voters increased GOP membership by twenty-seven in the House and by five in the Senate. Although the Democratic party still held a paper majority in both houses, the senatorial margin of two members was the smallest since the period 1931–1933. In the House, the voters whittled Democratic strength to 235. Of equal importance, the elections also resulted in defeats for some who had usually supported civil rights. In the Senate, the Democrats lost both of their leaders when Congressman Everett Dirksen defeated Majority Leader Scott Lucas, and James H. Duff retired Majority Whip Francis Myers.[6]

The postmortems were painful. Although Lucas had never inspired the black community, the *Afro-American* feared that his defeat would result in the selection of Georgia's Richard Russell as the new majority leader; the editor also growled about the increased strength of the conservative coalition. The *Journal and Guide* was even more depressed, noting that "Republicans, siding with southern Democrats, can keep civil rights legislation from leaving committee or defeating it unmercifully on the floor." The *Chicago Defender*, however, professed to see light amidst the gloom of the election returns. "Some of the stalwarts of the Truman administration bit the dust but the Democrats still control both houses of the Congress," the editor rationalized. He also took a close look at local elections around the country and noted happily that "there were more Negroes elected to public offices throughout the nation than at any time in our memory."[7]

The pessimism following the November elections was justified, for the Eighty-second Congress got off to a poor start on January 3, 1951, the opening day of the first session. In the House of Representatives, the Republican-Dixiecrat coalition succeeded in repealing the "twenty-one-day rule" and in restoring the power of the Rules Committee to control the flow of proposed legislation. By a final vote of 244 to 179, the coalition rebuffed the administration's forces and demonstrated beyond doubt where power resided in the new House. Of the 244 votes in favor of the Rules Committee, 152 were by Republicans and 92 by Democrats, mostly from the South. The government could muster only 136 Democrats, 42 Republicans, and one Independent. Although the administration could still utilize the petition method or the "Calendar Wednesday" approach to by-pass the Rules Committee, the loss of the twenty-one-day rule was critical. Since its adoption in 1949, the rule was invoked eight times to circumvent the Rules Committee and get bills on the floor, most of which were "must" measures of the administration. The proposals for Hawaiian and Alaskan statehood and the bill to outlaw the poll tax, which passed the House during the Eighty-first Congress, were in this category. As the *New York Times* editorialized, it was "A Bad Beginning."[8]

Matters were no better in the Senate on opening day, when Democrats were scheduled to elect a majority leader and a whip to replace Lucas and Myers. Earlier, when asked if he had any preferences, Truman said no; that was the Senate's decision. Truman's refusal to become involved was the only realistic course open to him. Given the conservative coloration of the Senate, the choice of a majority leader was probably not vital. Nonetheless, it was a bitter moment when Senate Democrats named Ernest W. McFarland of Arizona and Lyndon B. Johnson of Texas as majority leader and whip, respectively. Both had consistently opposed civil-rights legislation, and both had bolted in 1949 and voted against the Barkley ruling.[9]

Civil-rights advocates were never enamored with Lucas and Myers, but the combination of McFarland and Johnson was altogether distasteful. The NAACP reacted quickly and denounced both as foes of civil-rights legislation. The *Afro-American* saw them as part of the "unholy alliance" in control of both houses of Congress. The *Chicago Defender* had explained away the results of the congressional elections of 1950, but it could not ignore the action of the Republican-Dixiecrat coalition in the House in restoring the power of the Rules Committee and the action of Senate Democrats in the selection of McFarland and Johnson. These two developments, the editor now confessed, "may very well destroy the fair deal program of the administration and particularly the civil rights measures." It was Congressman Powell, however, who expressed publicly what most muttered about privately. "There will be no civil rights in this session of Congress," he announced flatly in an article in the *Amsterdam News*. "They will not even be considered. There will be no progressive nor liberal legislation enacted. As far as homefront democracy is concerned, the 82nd Congress is not even interested."[10]

The developments in both houses inevitably came up in the president's news conference the following day. With reference to the restored power of the Rules Committee, Truman could say only that Congress made its own rules and that the administration would proceed in the normal manner with its legislative requests. In response to a question concerning his opinion of McFarland and Johnson, he replied that he was "very fond" of McFarland, to whom he had already sent a congratulatory letter, and that Johnson was also a friend.[11] Even had he preferred other leadership, he had no choice but to sound pleased with the results.

Faced with a more conservative Congress, with a perilous situation in Korea, and with the need for war appropriations, Truman chose not to indulge in a mock battle over civil-rights legislation. In his State of the Union message on January 8, 1951, he stressed the theme of unity and mentioned civil rights only in passing, without specifically urging the enactment of any legislation. In his news conference of January 11, a reporter observed, "Some people are assuming that civil rights has been put aside for a while?" Given the phraseology of the question and the expectations of civil-rights organizations, Truman had no alternative but to answer no, though, significantly, he did not elaborate on his answer.[12]

He had more to say in his budget message on January 15. The Korean situation demanded wise utilization of all available manpower resources, he argued, and the nation could not afford to discriminate against minority groups. "Following the federal experience with a Committee on Fair Employment Practice in World War II," he continued, "eight states and a number of cities have established successful regulatory commissions to deal with employment practices. I again recommend that the Congress enact legislation to establish a Federal Fair Employment Practice Commission to prevent discrimination in interstate industries."[13]

That was the extent of it, and Negroes were not overjoyed. The *Journal and Guide*, for example, called attention to the presidential statement giving priority to defense measures and to his omission of any demand for civil-rights legislation. But the paper understood some of the realities facing the president and the country. "More than any other president," the editor maintained, Truman had "courageously" demanded action on equal-justice legislation, "but he is a good enough politician and ex-soldier to know when to 'retire to previously prepared positions.' That is exactly what has been done. He has retired from the conflict over citizenship equality." The editor concluded that Truman might be an adroit politician, "but in the eyes of true believers in freedom, he has circumscribed his stature as a statesman by abandoning a program he once gave top priority to himself."[14]

Although everything in 1951 seemed to conspire against enactment of equal-justice legislation, civil-rights organizations went through the traditional motions of raising a ruckus. Once again, they gave top priority to revision of the Senate's cloture rule and passage of an FEPC. As the *Afro-American* explained, the fear of economic lynching had replaced the old terror of physical lynching as the "real enemy" of black Americans. Indeed, the editor gave the FEPC priority over everything else, including the current contests in courts across the country to break segregation in education, primarily "because education will serve of little purpose if all the doors of opportunity to use that training remain closed."[15]

The legislative priorities of civil-rights organizations accurately reflected the emerging economic and social patterns of American Negroes. Physical lynching of blacks was primarily a rural, southern preoccupation and had dropped significantly in the postwar years. Moreover, as a result of black migration to northern and western cities, economic opportunity in industry was now the foremost need. By 1951 only a handful of northern Negro leaders believed that an FEPC was not the most pressing issue, although some argued that for political reasons it should be used primarily as a club to force other—less controversial—civil-rights measures through Congress. Congressman William Dawson was in the latter category, and this probably explained why the NAACP began looking to Adam Clayton Powell to lead the fight in the House.[16]

Congress went through the motions of considering civil-rights legislation in 1951, but so desultorily as to irritate nearly everyone. Although the usual bills were dropped in the hopper, including two Senate and seven House bills for an FEPC, nothing reached the floor of Congress during the first session. In fact, Senator Humphrey and eight of his liberal colleagues did not introduce their FEPC proposal until June 25, which testified eloquently to their own lack of optimism. The leisurely pace of Congress and the priorities of the president prompted the *Defender* to print a scorching editorial warning Democrats that the Negro vote was the captive of neither party. "The civil rights program of the administration has been hidden so well in Washington that Sherlock Holmes couldn't find it," the editorial continued. "The emergency has been used as a smokescreen to evade the issue." After a few choice criticisms of Congress and the president, the editor concluded that "the record of the Democrats is not inspiring although we must confess that the current Republican leadership gives us the creeps." Some papers did not bother to comment, concentrating instead on the need to increase integration of public and private facilities across the country.[17]

Of course, passage of an FEPC required revision of the senatorial rule on cloture, and the Senate did take a half-step in this direction. During the first session, four proposals for revision were introduced, and the Senate Rules Committee agreed to hold hearings. Although Senator Wherry believed that the Wherry-Hayden compromise of 1949 was workable if Democrats would get out their votes, he was willing to consider revision to permit a working majority to invoke cloture.

But the leaders of both parties were unwilling to make an issue of it. In October the Senate Rules Committee heard the testimony of representatives of the usual organizations—including the NAACP, the ACLU, the CIO, ADA, the American Council on Human Rights, the American Jewish Committee, the American Jewish Congress, and others—but the committee failed to report any of the proposals to the floor. Moreover, Senator McFarland flatly refused to hold the Senate in session until it had considered civil rights.[18] The best Congress could do positively for black Americans in 1951 was to pass a bill in September authorizing the coinage of fifty-cent pieces "to commemorate the lives and perpetuate the ideals and teachings of Booker T. Washington and George Washington Carver." Given the pressing needs of black America, the bill was only an insult.[19]

Confronted with an unresponsive Congress, the civil-rights coalition began to crumble in 1951. In April, Walter White had issued a call to fifty national church, fraternal, labor, civic, and minority-group organizations to participate in a civil-rights conference in Washington on May 22 and 23. As a build-up to the conference, White issued several statements critical of the president and Congress, arguing that the president was stalling on administrative action and that Congress was engaged in "a wilful sit-down strike against civil-rights."[20]

Yet when the conference convened on May 22, only sixty-seven delegates representing thirty-one organizations were present. It was a far cry from the conference of January 1950. In his opening remarks, Walter White tried to make up in spirit for what the meeting lacked in numbers, and his criticisms of the president were the sharpest of his career. The conference concentrated primarily on the enactment of legislation, and its three "demands" included revision of the Senate's cloture rule, passage of an FEPC, and legislation to protect servicemen from assault by civilians. Yet most politicians cast only a passing glance at the conference; no one seemed intimidated.[21]

Part of the problem stemmed from past success. For example, as Japanese-Americans readjusted successfully to American society, aided by the government's payments of wartime claims, they began to inch away from their earlier commitment to the coalition. As overt anti-Semitism decreased and as the problems of the new state of Israel increasingly attracted Jewish attention in America, the traditional Jewish organizations seemed less militant about civil-rights legislation. Moreover, the restoration of the power of the House Rules Committee in January 1951 had a discouraging influence on the American Jewish

Committee, whose report of legislative inaction in 1951 sounded almost like an epitaph.[22]

Finally, there was no mass militancy anywhere, and without it, intimidation was virtually impossible. In 1941 A. Philip Randolph could point to spontaneous, grass-roots uprisings in the black community everywhere outside the South as evidence that Negroes would no longer tolerate discrimination in defense industries. Although some feared that the masses had grown soft and complacent, others observed that the employment situation in 1951 represented a dramatic improvement over that of 1941, not only because of the Korean War but also because of the fair employment laws and ordinances in several states and cities and because of a more tolerant attitude generally. The fact that no Negro leader seriously considered a mass march or demonstration in 1951 was persuasive evidence that such strategy would probably have backfired. The only threat that seemed to carry any political weight was the Negro vote of 1952; but the growing evidence that Senator Taft, never a favorite of minority groups, would be the Republican nominee in 1952 allowed many Democratic politicians to ignore it. Thus, neither the president nor the Eighty-second Congress had much to worry about in the way of reprisals.[23]

Yet any verdict on the first session would be incomplete without mentioning what it prevented, for the session consisted primarily of a holding action on civil rights. For example, as the military became increasingly integrated in Korea in 1950 and 1951, southerners in the House backed the Winstead amendment to permit draftees the choice of refusing to serve in integrated units. The House, however, rejected Winstead's contention that integration would lead to race riots and knocked his proposal out of the selective-service bill by a vote of 178 to 126.[24]

Southerners also feared integration of Veterans Administration hospitals in the South, and Congressmen John D. Rankin of Mississippi sought to head it off when he sponsored legislation to construct an all-Negro hospital in honor of Booker T. Washington in Franklin County, Virginia. Opposed on the floor by Congressmen Dawson and Powell and by messages from the NAACP and the Veterans Administration, the bill lost by the comfortable margin of 223 to 117. The defeat was all the more noteworthy because of the fact that identical bills had passed the House during the Eightieth and Eighty-first Congresses, only to die in the Senate.[25]

But Congress missed on one count. On November 2, 1951, Truman vetoed a bill that would have required the federal government to operate schools for military dependents in conformance with the laws of the state in which the facilities were located. The intent of the bill was clear, for it would have meant resegregation of four military schools in the South and no possibility of integrating such institutions in the future. "Step by step we are discarding old discriminations; we must not adopt new ones," the president explained in his veto message. Inexplicably, congressional liberals had raised no serious, concerted objections to the measure; and the *Chicago Defender*, for one, wanted to know the whereabouts of Humphrey, Lehman, Douglas, Aiken, Taft, Morse, and Ives when the bill went through the senatorial committee on which they served.[26]

The bill itself was only of passing importance; but Truman's veto had a much larger meaning, which was evident in the unrestrained chorus of Negro approval. The demand for an executive FEPC and for equal-justice legislation had diminished appreciably in the fall of 1951; and the civil-rights coalition, then in the process of coming apart, was apparently about to concede defeat. Truman's veto revived hope everywhere and symbolized everything that had been sought and achieved over the past decade. The *1952 Negro Year Book* put it in a capsule: "President Truman's veto message is unprecedented in this generation."[27]

On October 20, 1951, the last day of the first session, Truman did something that was unprecedented in American history when he announced the appointment of Gen. Mark W. Clark as the first United States ambassador to the Vatican. Roosevelt had taken the initial step in 1939 when he appointed Myron C. Taylor, without Senate approval, as his personal representative to the Pope. Despite protests from several Protestant churches and clergymen, Taylor had remained on until January 1950, when he submitted his resignation to Truman. The Vatican let it be known that it would be delighted with the appointment of an ambassador but would frown upon another personal representative. Most major Protestant organizations, however, were opposed to either course and deluged the White House with appeals not to replace Taylor. Even a Sunday-school class of the First Baptist Church of Washington, D.C., which Truman attended, submitted a petition to the president. Pastor Edward H. Pruden was embarrassed about it, but Truman urged him not to worry, for "it is simply a part of the duty of the presidential office to listen to everybody's viewpoint."[28]

But Pruden was also opposed to any representation at the Vatican, and he urged Truman to meet with a large Protestant delegation to hear their point of view. Noting the strong opposition from American

Protestants, black and white, liberal and conservative, Pruden declared that he knew "of no matter on which there has been such unanimity of feeling among Protestants of every shade and variety . . . and . . . a large section of the Jewish community has also expressed itself . . . as being strongly opposed to Vatican representation."[29]

The prospect of an ambassadorial successor to Taylor thus brought to the surface the fears of many Protestants and Jews about the political nature of the Vatican and the principle of separation of church and state in America. It also provided bigots with another issue that they could use in berating the Truman administration, which had been subjected for some time to irrational accusations of selling out to the Pope.[30]

Truman waited until the storm subsided, then announced Clark's appointment as ambassador on October 20, 1951. Presumably to lessen opposition, Press Secretary Joseph Short released a statement explaining the appointment on the grounds of "diplomacy and humanitarianism." "It is well known that the Vatican is vigorously engaged in the struggle against communism," the statement expounded. "Direct diplomatic relations will assist in coordinating the effort to combat the Communist menace." If that was the president's purpose, he might well have heeded an idea of members of the White House staff, who had suggested a roving ambassador to represent the president at the seats of all major religions around the Soviet periphery. During his news conference on October 25, Truman testily noted that the proposed nomination in no way conflicted with the principle of separation of church and state. Although he stated that the appointment had not created as much "hullabaloo" as he had expected, protests poured into the White House and the State Department. Within ten days of the announcement, the former had received five thousand letters and telegrams and the latter around ten thousand, most of them opposed.[31] No appointment during the Truman years aroused as much general opposition.

The affair also threatened to damage his already deteriorating relations with Congress. Senator Tom Connally, who would handle the appointment as chairman of the Foreign Relations Committee, announced his personal opposition to Clark because of his strategy in the Italian campaign during the Second World War; the Texas senator was particularly distressed about the high rate of casualties suffered by a Texas division in that campaign, which to him revealed Clark's unfitness for high office. Connally promised to pigeonhole the nomination permanently, if and when the president submitted it to the Senate.

Truman did not offer Clark a recess appointment, because that would have required the general to retire from the army, so the appointment was held over for the second session in January. But the continued protests, including the threat of a Protestant march on Washington, prompted Clark to withdraw his name on January 13, 1952, and prompted Truman to back off during the remainder of his administration.[32]

Opposition to an ambassador to the Vatican was not the only backlash of 1951 and 1952. More serious as far as racial and religious tolerance were concerned, for the present as well as the future, was the fresh outbreak of white "Christian" violence against Negroes and Jews. In October 1951 the Anti-Defamation League reported the results of several polls that showed a significant decline in racial and religious bias. From a wartime peak of prejudice in 1945, the League reported a "dramatic" drop of 40 percent by 1950 and 1951. Moreover, despite the tense situation internationally, "scapegoating of the minority groups seems to have considerably lessened."[33] The report may have been valid for the country as a whole, but the steady pressure for integration in the postwar period and Truman's insistence on equal justice for everyone was difficult for many whites to accept. In 1951 their inability to adjust to the alterations in traditional racial patterns emerged, sometimes in childish behavior, at other times in ugly manifestations of racism. Some luxuriated in the symbols of a bygone era, while others seized upon extralegal means to preserve the status quo.

The most widely used symbol of protest by 1951 was the Confederate flag. An owner of a flag company in Virginia reported that there were more Confederate flags in that state in 1951 than during the Civil War. In September the largest flag company in the world, located in New York City, revealed that it was unable to meet the demand for Confederate flags, which exceeded that for Old Glory. From the nation's capital came a similar report. In Fordyce, Arkansas, high-school students donned Confederate hats, flew rebel flags, and marched to "Dixie," while using Confederate money as legal tender at the school store. The *New Yorker* magazine carried one advertisement that urged its readers to purchase the Stars and Bars to "show where you stand." The annual convention of the Veterans of Foreign Wars became acrimonious when southern delegates insisted upon placing the Confederate emblem over the American flag.[34]

Although initially disposed to attribute such behavior to retarded adolescents, Negro leadership began to take it seriously, especially when the rebel flag cropped up consistently on military vehicles. In

September the *Courier* reported that in one army convoy that was returning from "Exercise Southern Pine" over half of the vehicles were
flying the flag. Again, according to "reliable sources," the paper revealed that Negro paratroopers stationed in North Carolina refused to
jump from a plane with a rebel flag painted on its nose. Apparently,
the stories contained more than a grain of truth, for in October the
Defender commented on an air-force warning to all commands that
display of the Confederate flag was a violation of military regulations.
Walter White, too, pointed out that there was widespread display of
the flag in military units in Germany, Japan, and Korea.[35]

Although the flag fetish was physically innocuous, it had serious
psychological and political implications, which the Negro press sought
to comprehend. The *Defender* saw the flag fad generally as "rebel
nonsense," but the paper feared that it might lead to racial violence.
The *Courier* asked: "Is the revival of the Confederate flag a harmless
'mystical fad,' a reaffirmation of the dogma of the old and defeated
South, or is it symbolic of a growing resentment of Trumanism? That's
a top question today."[36] Undoubtedly, various factors were involved,
and "Trumanism" was clearly one of them. In the late summer and fall
of 1951 a flood of newspaper articles commented on the political storm
brewing in the South. Truman was the issue, partly because of his
stand on civil rights and partly because of the supposed socialistic
trend of his administration; and southerners were threatening to secede
from the Democratic party unless the president stepped down in 1952.[37]

The flag fad was at least a peaceful protest, but other manifestations of a white backlash were not. The thrust of the Truman administration since the *Shelley* case of 1948 toward further integration in
public and private housing brought to the surface all of the economic
fears and social prejudices of lower-class whites. In July 1951, as a
Negro couple prepared to occupy an apartment in all-white Cicero,
Illinois, a mob of four thousand to six thousand whites broke through
a National Guard barricade and set the building afire. Called out by
Governor Adlai Stevenson in anticipation of trouble, the guardsmen
eventually restored order, but not before twenty-three soldiers, policemen, and rioting whites had been injured. No Negroes were involved,
and not until the 1960s would they respond in kind.[38]

The riot in Cicero received worldwide attention. Visiting in Singapore, Governor Dewey was irritated to discover that "an incident of
racial prejudice involving a few hundred people . . . is front page news
in Singapore and elsewhere, and is considered worthy of a four-column
photograph on the front page." But Cicero was more than an isolated

incident or a passing phenomenon. After the riot, the Associated Negro Press noted that the population of Cicero was generally first- and second-generation Bohemian, of whom about 80 percent were Catholic. The ANP also observed that some of the recent violence in and about Chicago had occurred in Catholic areas, much to the distress of the local Catholic clergy and leading Catholic laymen.[39] Cicero thus became the prototype of an increasingly familiar story of a minority group whose time had arrived pitted against another whose time was yet to come. The oppressed of the past had become the oppressor of the present.

A Cook County grand jury subsequently indicted those who had aided the black couple in renting the apartment, accusing them, among other things, of "conspiracy to injure property . . . by causing a depreciation in the real estate market by renting to Negroes." The day after the indictment, the Department of Justice intervened and impaneled a federal grand jury, which eventually indicted and convicted three policemen, including Cicero's chief of police, for violating the civil rights of the couple. The chief had threatened the couple when they attempted to occupy the apartment, and then had denied them police protection when whites had threatened to riot. Truman later publicly praised his officials for preventing "a gross miscarriage of justice."[40]

Although undoubtedly the most flagrant illustration of white violence in 1951, Cicero was also a harbinger of other extralegal action, particularly the use of bombs to intimidate various minorities. In Dallas, a series of bombings of Negro homes prompted the president of the city's Council of Negro Organizations to announce that the city faced its most crucial moment. In Miami, minorities suffered a "reign of terror" as bigots bombed Jewish synagogues and a Negro housing project. In California, simultaneous time bombs destroyed the three homes of a Negro, a Jew, and a Mexican-American.[41]

Tragedy had to happen. On Christmas Day 1951 the bombing of a Negro home in Mims, Florida, took the lives of Harry T. Moore and his wife. A school principal in Brevard County, Moore had long been on the firing line of civil rights, which made him a "marked man," as the NAACP later put it. In the postwar years Tuskegee Institute had sighed with relief as the annual lynching rate continued to drop, but the single lynching reported in 1951 failed to tell the story of racial violence. Lynching "has gone out of style," Tuskegee noted, to be replaced by other forms of intimidation. Walter White put it more tersely: "The bomb has replaced the lynchers' rope."[42]

The death of the Moores became the rallying point in 1951 and

1952, as had the blinding of Isaac Woodard in 1946. Walter White quickly wired Attorney General McGrath, requesting an appointment to discuss cooperative efforts to curb terrorism in Florida and to solve the Moore murders. On January 8, 1952, representatives of eighteen organizations met with McGrath to urge a full-fledged federal investigation. The Department of Justice was active, examining the series of racial crimes in Florida and eventually winning a federal grand jury indictment of those allegedly involved in the bombings of a Negro housing development in Miami. But those who murdered the Moores were never apprehended.[43]

The white backlash thus added another dimension to the problems facing Truman in 1951. The best he could do—given the war, the need for unity, the composition of Congress, and the backlash—was to maintain a holding action and to keep the issue of civil rights before the American public. Thus, as on previous occasions, he attempted to exploit the educational possibilities of the presidency through a series of low-keyed public addresses and formal messages. For example, on March 1, 1951, he sent a message to the fourth annual Conference on Civil Liberties, in which he expressed the hope that the Eighty-second Congress would not adjourn without enacting his civil-rights program. He also pointed with pride to the "tremendous gains" in civil rights since the report of his committee in 1947, particularly in education, housing, employment, and use of public accommodations.[44]

In dedicating the Carter Barron Amphitheater in Washington, in May, Truman discussed the faith of the country's founders, a faith expressed in the Declaration of Independence and the Constitution. "We must believe in the faith of our fathers," he said. "We must believe in human rights and civil rights for every man, be he yellow, red, black, or white." On July 4, in a radio broadcast commemorating the 175th anniversary of the Declaration of Independence, he opened by stressing that the United States was based on a new idea, the idea that all men were created equal. He noted, "We have made great strides in broadening freedom here at home. We have made real progress in eliminating oppression and injustice and in creating security and opportunities for all." In conclusion, he urged greater effort to achieve liberty for everyone.[45]

But Truman did more than orate; he took action that symbolized what he expected of America. In August 1951 the Sioux City, Iowa, Memorial Park Cemetery denied burial to Sfc. John R. Rice, a Winnebago Indian killed in Korea. Mrs. Rice, a non-Indian, had purchased the lot, unaware of a restrictive clause limiting burial to Caucasians.

Officials of the cemetery therefore halted the ceremony after the conclusion of military rites, and the casket remained in front of the open
grave. The story was front-page news the next morning, and Harry H.
Vaughan, the president's military aide, called it to Truman's attention.
Truman's reaction was decisive and irate. In an angry telegram to the
mayor of Sioux City, the president pointed out that "national appreciation of patriotic service should not be limited by race, color or creed."
A similar telegram went to officials of the cemetery, who quickly apologized and offered a free lot for Rice's burial. Through Harry Vaughan,
however, the president had already arranged for burial in Arlington
National Cemetery, and Mrs. Rice accepted the "greater honor."[46] Rice
thus became the second serviceman of a minority group to be buried
under similar circumstances in Arlington National Cemetery, following
Felix Longoria, the Mexican-American from Texas, who had won such
burial honors as a result of Lyndon Johnson's intervention in 1949.
The White House mail ran heavily in favor of Truman's action. In
January 1952 General Vaughan telephoned the mayor of Phoenix when
he learned of a private cemetery's refusal to bury a Negro killed in
Korea, and the mayor took action to resolve the matter locally after a
dispute of nearly six weeks.[47]

During these trying months of congressional inaction, the president also initiated a conference and established a commission, both of
which helped to keep alive the issue of discrimination, to involve additional people in the civil-rights struggle, and to emphasize those areas
in need of correction and improvement. In August 1949 Truman had
called for a Midcentury White House Conference on Children and
Youth, and after several preliminary meetings on the local and national
level, he scheduled the main event for December 1950. Sponsored by
personnel of the Children's Bureau and chaired by Oscar Ewing of the
Federal Security Administration, the conference attracted over five
thousand delegates and guests from home and abroad. In addition to
several technical addresses, there were thirty-five working groups and
thirty-one panels at the conference, in which Protestants, Catholics,
Jews, and Negroes participated.

The delegates were concerned about discrimination, particularly
the effect of racial segregation on the "healthy personality development" of school children. The platform endorsed the "full program" of
the President's Committee on Civil Rights and urged that prompt steps
be taken "to eliminate all types of racial and religious segregation, and
that this conference through its most appropriate channels appeal
immediately to the federal government to abolish segregation in the

nation's capital, making Washington an example to the world of a truly working democracy without discriminatory practice on the basis of race, creed, color, or national origin."[48]

The president took more important steps in late 1951. In addition to creating the Committee on Government Contract Compliance, he also issued an executive order on December 29 establishing the President's Commission on the Health Needs of the Nation. Consisting of a chairman—Dr. Paul B. Magnuson, formerly of the Northwestern University Medical School—and fourteen members, the commission was directed to investigate comprehensively every aspect of the nation's health problems. Although the president admitted that he hoped the commission's findings would dissipate some of the "bitter attacks" on his proposals "to bring adequate health care to all our people," he emphasized the total freedom of its members to come in with any conclusion or recommendation. He also brushed aside the American Medical Association, whose president had publicly denounced creation of the commission.[49]

The commission's investigation was impressive by any standard, and its final report of five published volumes constituted a mine of information. Indeed, volume three contained nearly three hundred pages of statistics, including many white-nonwhite comparisons. In 1949, for example, the death rate for nonwhite children under one year of age was nearly double that of whites, as was the death rate for adults between the ages of forty-five and sixty-four.[50]

Of equal importance was the commission's propaganda value as a result of public hearings involving nearly four hundred witnesses in eight major cities. The commission later expressed its belief in the "tremendous educational value" of the hearings and its gratitude to the press for "the full and impartial manner in which it covered these sessions." Much of the testimony was revealing. In St. Louis, for example, only sixteen of twenty-nine general hospitals admitted Negroes, and of the sixteen only seven were integrated. In Los Angeles County, of the 6,920 licensed physicians, there were only 74 Negroes, 11 Mexican-Americans, 42 Japanese-Americans, and 7 Chinese-Americans. For Indians everywhere, the death rate from tuberculosis was more than ten times greater than for whites, and in Texas the disease took seven Mexican-Americans for every Anglo.[51]

In its final report to the president, the commission made several recommendations involving minority groups. In personal health service, the commission argued for "services to all persons who are declared eligible, with no discrimination as to age, race, citizenship, or place or duration of residence, and with no means test at the time care is needed." Concerned about the shortage of hospital beds for American minorities, the commission unequivocally advocated integration of all hospital facilities, since segregation "detracts from the efficiency and quality of care." For migratory labor, which generally involved Mexican-Americans, it recommended that Congress allocate additional funds and develop a cooperative plan with state and local agencies to provide better health facilities. Perhaps most significant of all, "to meet the need for additional Negroes in the health professions," the commission urged the establishment of special programs to improve preprofessional and professional opportunities. In particular, "the dual system of education in some parts of this country has made it impossible for many Negroes to receive the high quality secondary and college education needed to qualify them for professional training. The discriminatory bars which start at the secondary school level and run all the way through post-graduate training, internship, and hospital affiliation must be removed wherever they exist."[52]

President Truman accepted the commission's report on December 18, 1952, grateful for its "fresh and constructive approach" and hopeful that it would be adopted during the next administration. On January 9, 1953, as he prepared to leave office, he sent a special message to Congress transmitting the commission's recommendations and urging their enactment, stressing especially the proposal for federal grants-in-aid for state and local action in developing comprehensive personal health services.[53]

Truman's oratory and actions in 1951 did not persuade the second session of the Eighty-second Congress that there was an urgent need to enact civil-rights legislation. And the administration was therefore not about to indulge in a sham performance and put it on the "must" list for 1952. In suggestions for the president's State of the Union message on January 9, 1952, only the Departments of Justice and Commerce included recommendations for such legislation. Secretary of Commerce Charles Sawyer was particularly worried about the Soviet Union's "powerful propaganda appeals to the non-white population of all continents, citing discrimination against minority groups in the United States. The most effective answer we can give to this propaganda is to continue to improve the position of minority groups in this country."[54]

Although fully aware that Congress would balk, Truman went through the ritualistic motions in his State of the Union address of calling for action "toward the wider enjoyment of civil rights." After reciting the progress of the executive branch in providing equal treatment and opportunity in the armed services, in the civil service, and in private firms with government contracts, he again called upon Congress to permit civil-rights legislation to be brought to a vote. He was pleased that the Senate had scheduled early action on home rule for the District of Columbia, and he hoped for prompt adoption of legislation granting statehood to Hawaii and Alaska. In his budget message, delivered to Congress on January 21, he renewed his request for appropriations to finance a fair employment practices commission. He noted that with the establishment of his Committee on Government Contract Compliance, the executive branch had acted, "within the limits of its present powers, to see that discrimination . . . does not prevent workers from getting jobs which use their highest skills. Further progress toward this objective will require action by Congress."[55]

Although the State of the Union message was stronger than its counterpart of 1951, it fell short of black expectations. In probably its most critical editorial of the president since the campaign of 1948, the *Afro-American* counted only 104 of 5,300 words devoted to "the burning issue of civil rights. He sadly missed an excellent opportunity to come out slugging." Walter White had also expected more and warned both parties of the political hazards in soft-pedaling the issue in the election year of 1952. The *Chicago Defender* never got over the president's "weak statement." In a biting editorial, the *Defender* saw it "as a disappointing shock to those who had expected an outspoken declaration in face of the reign of terror in Florida which has claimed the lives of three citizens, the wounding of a fourth and the bombings and attempted bombings of Jewish synagogues, a Negro housing project and a Catholic church."[56]

But civil-rights organizations were not prepared to surrender. They had known defeat before—indeed, they lived with it—and the approaching presidential campaign of 1952 provided a psychological boost. Upon the invitation of the NAACP, nine hundred delegates from thirty-five states who represented fifty-two national organizations met for the 1952 Leadership Conference on Civil Rights on February 17 and 18 in Washington. In one of the major addresses, Walter White praised Truman for his courageous actions in the past but expressed concern about recent presidential backsliding. The conference, however, concentrated mostly on Congress and the campaign politics of 1952. Once again, the delegates insisted upon passage of civil-rights legislation and revision of the senatorial rule regarding cloture. "The failure of Congress to restrain the bigots among us through enactment of civil rights measures," the conferees declared, "has brought about a wave of mob violence, bombing, shootings and 'legal lynchings' and has already proved costly to our nation in world prestige and in human life." In conclusion, the delegates drew the only weapon left in the civil-rights arsenal, threatening to "carry this vital fight into the precincts where the people of America live and vote. We shall not rest as long as any American is daily forced to face the humiliation of racial discrimination and segregation."[57]

Yet neither party in Congress made even a half-hearted effort in 1952. In January the Senate Rules Committee approved a resolution to revise the cloture rule to permit two-thirds of those present, rather than two-thirds of the total membership, to invoke cloture; but the Senate took no action after the measure was reported on March 6. FEPC shared the same fate, although Truman gave it an occasional plug. The Senate Labor and Public Welfare Committee, with Senators Taft and Nixon dissenting, did approve an FEPC with strong enforcement powers. The measure would have created an Equality of Opportunity in Employment Commission, a euphemism to avoid the hostility engendered by the symbols FEPC, but the Senate ignored the bill.[58]

The Senate did heed the president's request for home rule for the District of Columbia, when it passed a bill on January 22, 1952, that provided considerable autonomy to residents of the District. The bill then went to the District of Columbia Committee in the House, the graveyard of previous proposals because of southern domination of the committee. Truman did his best to marshal public opinion behind the measure. In a special message to Congress on May 1 transmitting a reorganization plan, he went out of his way to urge home rule. "Local self-government is both the right and the responsibility of free men," he contended. "The denial of self-government does not befit the national capital of the world's largest and most powerful democracy." Again, when Truman signed the bill on June 9 that transferred the power to appoint the Recorder of Deeds from the president to the District commissioners, he explained that he approved it only because it advanced the "even more important principle" of home rule. But the House committee lived up to its reputation and refused to report the bill on home rule. Indeed, despite the entreaties of Presidents Eisenhower, Kennedy, and Johnson and despite subsequent Senate bills for home rule, the House District of Columbia Committee was consistently able to prevent final action.[59]

The Eighty-second Congress did enact legislation on one of the recommendations included in the president's special civil-rights message of February 1948, but it was almost an afterthought in a bill whose primary purpose was to discriminate. In June 1952 Congress passed the Immigration and Nationality Act, or the McCarran-Walter Immigration Act as it was popularly called. The act revised and codified all laws relating to immigration and naturalization, but its main thrust was to continue most of the discriminatory provisions of the National Origins Act of 1924 as well as to introduce a few new ones. In March, for example, the NAACP had protested one provision that restricted immigration from the British West Indies to one hundred per year. In the past, immigrants from the islands had simply been admitted under the regular British quota, and the fact that most were black was enough to convince practically everyone of the racial intent of the new provision.[60]

The president vigorously protested the bill. In a sharply worded veto message on June 25, Truman expressed praise for only a few of its provisions. Noting that the bill completely eliminated race as a barrier to naturalization and permitted at least a minimum quota to all nations of Asia, he reminded Congress and the nation that he had "long urged that racial or national barriers to naturalization be abolished. This was one of the recommendations in my civil rights message to the Congress on February 2, 1948." Then he continued, "But now this . . . provision comes before me embedded in a mass of legislation which would perpetuate injustices of long standing against many other nations of the world, hamper the efforts we are making to rally the men of East and West alike to the cause of freedom, and intensify the repressive and inhumane aspects of our immigration procedures. The price is too high, and in good conscience I cannot agree to pay it." Although he agreed with the necessity of a quota, he objected first to the overall limitation of immigrants; more ought to be admitted. To the president, however, the "greatest vice" of the immigration quota system, which was perpetuated in the bill of 1952, was that it discriminated, "deliberately and intentionally, against many of the peoples of the world." Such a practice violated America's traditions and ideals, the pronouncement of the Declaration of Independence that all men are created equal, and "repudiates our basic religious concepts, our belief in the brotherhood of man." Further, in the bill's regulations for entry, deportation, and administration, the president found provisions "worse than the infamous Alien Act of 1798."[61]

Civil-rights exponents were pleased with the president's veto. "Against the advice of several frightened associates," editorialized the *Amsterdam News*, President Truman "courageously" vetoed the "infamous" bill. To the *Afro-American*, "all the credit goes to the president. The measure . . . was designed with racial discrimination as its clear intent and purpose," for it represented the "Hitlerian master-race doctrine" and "must not be allowed to stand unchallenged on federal statute books."[62]

The plaudits were deserved, but the sighs of relief were premature. Within two days, the president suffered a stinging defeat, and the nation a major embarrassment, when Congress in an ugly, reactionary mood voted to override the veto. In the Senate, twenty-five Democrats and thirty-two Republicans voted to override, while only eighteen Democrats and eight Republicans stood by the president. The Senate vote barely exceeded the required two-thirds, and a switch of two votes would have made the difference. It was therefore infuriating that Majority Leader McFarland and Majority Whip Johnson voted against the president, and it was altogether simple justice that President Lyndon Johnson should later carry through President Kennedy's campaign to revise the law.[63]

In one area of concern, the American Indian, President Truman and Congress did cooperate occasionally on legislation. But most of the controversy in 1951 and 1952 revolved around the policies of the new Commissioner of Indian Affairs, Dillon S. Myer. When Myer took office in 1950, he announced his intention of withdrawing the Bureau of Indian Affairs (BIA) from the management of Indian affairs, as much and as soon as possible. This was not the first time that a proposal had been made or a hope expressed about winding up the affairs of the bureau, which had become a miniature federal government and an ever-expanding bureaucracy, indulging in such diverse activities as health, education, welfare, forestry, general construction, land management, banking, road maintenance, grazing, electric power, irrigation, tribal organization, and so forth.

Myer's first point of business was to bring some order to the BIA's operations, which had suffered from a parade of commissioners and acting commissioners since the resignation of John Collier in 1945. Although a well intentioned, efficient administrator, Myer quickly ran into trouble with Indian organizations, tribes, and advocates. Lacking the human touch and outwardly indifferent to Indian sensibilities as well as to some of their rights, he proposed policy without consulting the tribes involved and sometimes without sufficient thought in regard to normal due process. Thus, in 1952 he sponsored legislation that would have permitted employees of the bureau to carry firearms and to make arrests, without benefit of a warrant, for violations of regulations. The Association on American Indian Affairs denounced the proposal as a declaration of cold war, one that would "probably set Indian relations back at least half a century." Although Myer subsequently explained that the bill would only give bureau employees the same authority as federal marshals and would simply restore power that had inadvertently been withdrawn from bureau agents in an act of 1948, Congress would have none of it and backed away from the proposal. Myer further invited suspicion when his accession to office in 1950 resulted in several resignations, both voluntary and forced, of some influential, dedicated, and highly respected members of the BIA.[64]

He got into trouble in 1951 with the appropriation bill for the Interior Department, which contained a restriction prohibiting the use of federal appropriations or tribal funds for the acquisition of land or water rights in four western states. Oliver La Farge, president of the Association on American Indian Affairs, pronounced it "discriminatory in the extreme." The president of the National Congress of American Indians agreed, and he informed Truman that "this country has never forbidden any group of people to purchase land, except in some few cases where war hysteria and prejudice has dictated such laws with respect to certain Orientals." Although he recognized that Truman could not veto the entire appropriations bill, he requested that the president publicly express disapproval of this particular provision. Truman chose, however, to sign the bill without comment.[65]

But it was Myer's proposed revision of the federal code of regulations as it applied to Indians that provoked the most concerted opposition. The revision required tribal leaders to pursue grievances through a prescribed chain of command, presumably to cut down on the number of Indian pilgrimages to Washington, and permitted the commissioner to reject an attorney with whom the Indians had made a contract if "reasonable cause" existed to indicate that the attorney had solicited the contract. Myer, of course, was concerned with "ambulance chasing," whereby attorneys had become wealthy through representation of Indian claims; but the new rule clearly infringed upon the right of Indians to choose their own attorneys.

Indian advocates were outraged. Far from seeking the withdrawal of the BIA, they contended, Myer was attempting to establish a dictatorship. The Association on American Indian Affairs saw the new code as tending to "destroy those beginnings of self-expression and self-government that have given the Indian people and their friends some hope for an Indian future of unrestricted, unsupervised, constructive citizenship." A special committee of the American Bar Association opposed most of the proposals. In fact, the *New York*

Times could find no one, except Myer, in favor of the new regulations. In an article in the *New Republic* in May 1951, former Interior Secretary Harold L. Ickes denounced Myer as "a Hitler and a Mussolini rolled into one." And in August he wrote a long letter to Interior Secretary Oscar Chapman, in which he devoted four pages to the proposed revision. Myer was setting himself up as a "little tin Hitler" and as the "Commissar" of Indian affairs, Ickes complained to his friend and protégé, and "he should be scourged from his office as an unfaithful public servant who has been persistently recreant to his trust." The old curmudgeon was in fine form. Chapman was not about to fire his subordinate, but he did the next best thing and countermanded the new regulations over Myer's objections.[66]

The controversy over Myer's inept attempts to streamline the bureaucracy and to prevent injustice to the Indians by indulging in some of it himself tended to obscure his main goal of eventual liquidation of the BIA and the integration of the Indian into the mainstream of American society. Since 1948 the Truman administration had moved consistently in the direction of integration of all minority groups; and the Democratic platform of 1952 not only pledged continued efforts to advance "the health, education, and economic well-being of our American Indian citizens" but also expressed the belief that "the American Indian should be completely integrated into the social, economic and political life of the nation."[67]

For the Indian, the administration's program thus had two prongs —the one was exemplified in the ten-year attempt to rehabilitate the Navajo and Hopi tribes, to help those who could not help themselves, and to make the reservation as self-sufficient as possible; the other involved releasing tribes from federal jurisdiction and seeking to integrate Indians into the American economy. For this task, Myer seemed eminently qualified as a result of his experience with the War Relocation Authority in reintegrating Japanese-Americans into the economic, if not the cultural, life of America. The reservation Indian was not only culturally different but he also lacked the necessary skills for economic advancement in an alien world. Yet something had to be done. The reservations could not support the existing Indian population, and the Indian birth rate was far greater than the national average.

Myer had no master plan, although he could utilize the program developed by William Zimmerman in 1947, which proposed a rough timetable for the release of various tribes over the next twenty-five to fifty years. Myer believed that any master plan would be "one of the worst mistakes we could possibly make" in view of the diversity of Indian wealth, education, and acculturation. Instead, his approach was piecemeal. When Truman signed a bill in August 1951 that provided for the disposition of claims granted to the Ute Indians, he noted that the award "has made it possible for the Indians to put their own affairs in order and to prepare themselves for the fullest participation in the affairs of our nation."[68]

Myer also sponsored and supported legislation that would transfer criminal and civil jurisdiction over Indians from the federal to the state governments. The first was the Bosone bill of 1950, which provoked a storm of protest from Indian advocates who feared exploitation by the states and premature attempts at integration. Although the bill never cleared the Senate, Myer continued his efforts to arrange for transfers of authority and reported in March 1952 that legislation for this purpose was pending. But that bill, and legislation to remove discriminatory policies toward Indians, did not pass until the Eisenhower administration. In 1953 Congress removed the federal prohibition against serving liquor to Indians and transferred criminal and civil authority over several tribes to various state governments. The two houses also agreed to a resolution that expressed the desire for further transfers of authority and directed the secretary of the interior to prepare legislation to accomplish this. The "termination" program appealed to Congress not only because it seemed logical but also because it would result in decreased federal expenditures, which delighted the penny pinchers.[69]

The Indians and their white advocates were understandably distraught, although all too often they seemed to want it all their own way —more federal money, less federal control, and no state supervision or authority whatever. "Termination" became a dirty word on the reservations, and it had adverse effects on the Indian, if not on the federal pocketbook. Between 1953 and 1957, for example, the Indians lost roughly 12 percent of their trust lands through unwise sales to non-Indians. There were other unfortunate results, and eventually the Department of the Interior all but halted the "termination" policy,[70] a decision officially endorsed by President Richard Nixon in 1970.

Nor was the last part of Myer's program to integrate the Indian much more successful. The administration seemed to have only two alternative solutions to the problem of the increasing Indian population—to ask Congress for even larger appropriations to purchase additional land for the reservations or to ask for smaller sums to develop economic skills and to relocate Indians in jobs on and off the reservation. Myer and the Truman administration chose the latter course and initiated a modest program in 1951, which included provisions for transportation to the city and financial support for participants until they received their first paychecks. In his budget message of January 21, 1952, Truman request a $15-million increase for the BIA, of which roughly $7 million was "to conduct a constructive program to provide the Indians with training and off-reservation relocation opportunities and to help them to make satisfactory adjustments in new locations."[71]

But if the program ever had a chance of success, Congress jeopardized it with pitiful appropriations. As late as 1957, Congress had increased the appropriation only to $3.5 million, about half of what Truman had requested in 1952, and the results were mixed at best. In moving to the city, Indians discovered what Negroes had known for decades, that both employers and unions discriminated against minorities. In 1961 the Commission on Civil Rights reported that "employment opportunities for Indians appear to be as restricted as they are for Negroes." Forced to live in slums, Indians aggravated the problems of already overburdened cities, often without any benefit to themselves. Some returned, disheartened, to the reservation; some successfully adjusted to the new life of the city; and a few resorted to crime. The increasing urban population also brought about other complications. When new, activist Indian leaders appeared in the late 1960s, they sometimes found their attempts to formulate unified programs jeopardized and their cries of "red power" muted by the conflicting demands of the reservations and the urban Indian population.[72] In any event, because of discrimination on the part of whites and because of the cultural and educational handicaps of Indians, the relocation policy initiated during the Truman administration might have failed even with generous congressional support. But Truman at least could have said that his administration had attempted to solve a problem that is still very much a part of America and which still defies solution.

The Truman administration also grappled with the grievances of another minority, the Mexican-American, though it came late to the problem and never made a large commitment. The administration's interest was engaged initially because of the farm-labor program, which involved many migratory Mexican-Americans and Negroes as well as contract and illegal labor from Mexico. As a result of a labor shortage during the Second World War, the Roosevelt administration had negotiated a series of agreements with Mexico for the importation of braceros for seasonal work in the United States. The wartime program expired in 1947, but the Truman administration had heeded the pleas of growers and arranged new contracts with Mexico from 1947 to 1949. Employers of farm workers also exploited "wetbacks"—Mexican nationals who crossed the border illegally—and by 1949 a sharp domestic controversy had developed. In 1949 the government apprehended and returned about three hundred thousand illegal entrants, and in 1950 the number reached half a million.[73]

The growers insisted upon the necessity of bracero and wetback labor. American workers were unreliable, they contended, and sometimes deserted the fields at harvest time. Indeed, they might even strike when the crops were ripe, which was tantamount to un-Americanism. They also argued that Americans disliked the stoop labor required in harvesting certain crops, and Mexicans were much more productive anyway. It was a theme that would become monotonous, although it was always persuasive to some. In 1947 growers in Texas complained that resident labor refused to work in the fields and urged an expanded bracero program. An investigator, however, noted that for a ten-hour day, seven-day week, the worker received $17.50. Yet if he happened to be a veteran, he could draw unemployment compensation of $20.00 per week for fifty-two weeks. A choice between the two was not difficult to make. The growers and their representatives in Congress also urged Truman to permit the use of wetbacks and to order immigration agents not to return them to Mexico.[74]

The spearhead of the opposition to the bracero program as well as to the exploitation of wetback labor came from LULAC, the League of United Latin American Citizens. Organized in the late 1920s, the organization peaked in membership in 1940, although it had never had much influence. During the war, in contrast with the phenomenal growth of the NAACP, LULAC dropped dramatically in membership. By 1951, however, it had about regained the membership of 1940, but it still lacked a strong professional core because of the tendency of middle-class Mexican-Americans, particularly those who were light-skinned, to disappear into Anglo society. In the postwar period the organization concentrated on improving educational advantages of Mexican-Americans and in curbing the invasion of workers from Mexico. The latter concern was understandable, for Mexican labor inevitably caused a drop in the wage scale for Negroes and Mexican-Americans engaged in the same work. The president's appointment of his Committee on Civil Rights, which dipped briefly into the problem of migratory labor, convinced some LULAC leaders that they had a friend in the White House. When wetbacks flooded across the border at El Paso in 1948, LULAC leaders deluged the president with appeals to tighten border security.[75]

In its opposition to wetbacks and the bracero program, LULAC had some influential allies. Foremost in the group was the AFL's National Farm Labor Union, headed by H. L. Mitchell, who insisted that the domestic labor supply was ample to meet harvesting needs. He also maintained that Mexican nationals lowered wages for American labor, and he denounced their use as strikebreakers. The CIO agreed. So, too, did the NAACP; and in October 1949 Roy Wilkins fired off a letter to Truman protesting the use of Mexican nationals to break a farm strike in California. The Community Service Organization (CSO) was also establishing chapters in various California cities to organize Mexican-Americans into a power bloc at the polls. One of its voluntary leaders was a young migratory worker named Cesar Chavez, who eventually dropped out of the CSO because of its lack of interest in organizing farm workers.[76]

In the initial stages of the domestic controversy, the growers seemed to have the president's ear. When in 1949 Senator Clinton Anderson of New Mexico complained about the alacrity with which immigration authorities were returning wetbacks to Mexico, Truman seemed persuaded that the growers needed additional labor. H. L. Mitchell informed him of the denial of civil rights to American agricultural labor, but Truman responded: "No information had come to me prior to the receipt of your letter concerning any violation of the civil rights of agricultural workers. I am referring your letter to the attorney general for such action as appears warranted, and I believe he undoubtedly will request further facts concerning the instances you cite."[77]

By the summer of 1949, however, the administration was aware of the increasing complexity of the problem. One government official, noting the growing power of LULAC, warned that Mexican-Americans "have not, as yet, become Balkanized into a minority political bloc as they have been Balkanized in slum areas. They are, however, by the inexorable exigency of circumstances, being driven more and more to such extremity." He urged that Truman either establish a commission to investigate the problems of Mexican-Americans or that he assuage their leadership with some appointments to governmental positions. As early as June 1949 White House assistant David Niles advised the president to formulate a more just and consistent policy. In particular, he stressed the necessity of considering together the questions of illegal migration and the welfare of three million Mexican-Americans. Truman agreed with the suggestion and urged assistants to come up with some answers. In November 1949 Truman revealed that the Department of Labor was considering the advisability of a presidential commission, and the public response to the news was favorable. In addition to domestic pressure, the administration also had to worry about the Mexican government, which had been making noise about not renewing the 1949 agreement (which expired in 1951) unless the United States established additional safeguards to protect Mexican nationals in the bracero program.[78]

Faced with pressure at home and abroad and lacking any clear-cut proposals for solving the problem of migratory labor, the president established a five-member Commission on Migratory Labor on June 3, 1950. Maurice T. Van Hecke, professor of law at the University of North Carolina, was named as chairman. Although no Mexican-American was included on the commission, an omission that undoubtedly reflected their relative lack of political muscle, the appointment of Robert E. Lucey, Catholic Archbishop of San Antonio, was the next best thing, for he possessed knowledge and experience of the problems of Mexican-Americans in Texas. In its covering announcement, the White House explained the commission's tasks, which included the related questions of the "social, economic, health, and educational conditions among migratory workers in the United States," the problems resulting from the bracero program, and the extent of wetback infiltration.[79]

After twelve public hearings and numerous conferences with federal and state officials and with representatives of Mexico and Puerto Rico, the Commission on Migratory Labor reported to the president in April 1951. The commission recommended, above all, the establishment of a Federal Committee on Migratory Farm Labor to coordinate all federal activities concerned with itinerant farm workers. It also urged Congress to strengthen the penalties for use of wetback labor, to enact minimum-wage legislation for farm workers, to extend collective bargaining and unemployment compensation to agriculture, to provide minimum standards for housing for migratory workers and appropriations for federal assistance, to supply school aid to migratory children, to amend the Public Health Service Act to provide matching grants to states for health programs, and to restrict the employment of school-age children.

The commission also recommended that the United States systematically reduce its dependence on foreign labor until it was no longer required. When additional labor was needed, first preference should go to American citizens in Puerto Rico and Hawaii. Finally, although the commission found it difficult to measure accurately the effect of foreign workers on the wages of American workers, it did report some interesting statistics. From 1947 to 1950, for example, employers of farm workers in Texas, "blessed" with an abundance of braceros and wetbacks, reduced wages 11 percent, while in California, where there were fewer of both, wages rose 15 percent.[80]

Farm employers found large portions of the report unpalatable, as did some influential newspapers in the Southwest and on the Pacific Coast. Nor were many congressmen impressed with the commission's entreaties for additional legislation. On June 30, 1951, Congress passed a Mexican labor importation bill, sponsored by Representative W. R. Poage of Texas and Senator Allen J. Ellender of Louisiana, which established procedures to permit the administration to negotiate a renewal of the bracero program that would be agreeable to Mexico. But it included little else; and therefore LULAC, the CIO, and the AFL were all unhappy. William Green urged a presidential veto, noting that the Poage-Ellender bill "discriminates against American workers employed in large scale agriculture and provides no means of setting standards of wages or working conditions for our own citizens." Green also pointed out that the bill contained no provision for penalizing growers who employed wetbacks and that it permitted the employment of braceros in food-processing plants, which would have the effect of destroying AFL unions.[81]

Nor was the White House staff enthusiastic about the bill. In a memorandum to the president, David Stowe saw "no clear cut statement of the advantages of veto versus signature as you requested. However, we are all agreed on the deficiencies of the bill and on measures to correct this situation."[82] Truman finally decided to sign the bill, but only because it contained the conditions necessary for renewal of the bracero program with Mexico and only after the Democratic leaders in Congress promised to take immediate action during the first session to correct its deficiencies.

In his message of approval, Truman pointed out that although the bill permitted a new agreement with Mexico, it represented "very limited progress, which hardly touches our basic farm labor problems." He urged legislation to penalize those who employed illegal entrants, to authorize the Immigration and Naturalization Service to inspect fields without a warrant, and to appropriate funds for an increase in border personnel for purposes of inspection and detention. He also promised to submit a supplemental budget request to enable the Labor

Department's Farm Placement Service to expand labor-market studies and to determine the possibility of reducing American dependence on foreign labor. In conclusion, he observed that various executive departments were also examining other recommendations of his Commission on Migratory Labor, including provisions for improvement of housing, education, health, and social security for migratory workers.[83]

Clearly, the president was no longer thinking primarily of the interests of American farm employers. His shift was evident in his letter to the president of Mexico in which he pointed out that congressional leaders had promised additional legislation, which would result in improved working and living conditions for American and Mexican farm workers alike. Further, he proposed that their new bracero agreement be limited to six months, a time restriction that would force Congress to come through with the promised legislation.[84]

Truman kept his part of the bargain and negotiated the new agreement, which went into effect on August 11, 1951. Not surprisingly, however, Senators McFarland and Johnson failed to guide the promised legislation through the first session of the Eighty-second Congress. But the six-months limitation had part of its intended effect. Faced with the expiration of the bracero program on February 11, 1952, mindful of Truman's threat not to renew it again unless Congress acted, and worried about what growers in Arizona and Texas would think, Senator McFarland urged quick action and presented Truman with a bill early in March 1952, which he signed.

The so-called wetback bill made it a felony to employ or harbor illegal immigrants, and it authorized immigration agents to search factories and fields without a warrant—both of which were provisions that the president had requested. The House, however, cut the requested appropriations for expanding the operations of the Immigration and Naturalization Service; and Truman briefly considered a special message, until the Senate restored the funds. But neither house acted upon the proposal to establish a Federal Committee on Migratory Labor, although the Senate Labor Committee reported such a bill. Nor did Congress heed requests for increased appropriations to enable the Justice Department to expand its activities in trying to curb the flow of illegal labor. Yet the wetback bill of 1952, coupled with the Eisenhower administration's "Operation Wetback" in 1953 to strengthen border supervision, did result in a significant decline in the use of wage-depressing illegal Mexican nationals within the United States; but not until the Kennedy-Johnson administrations would the government move to terminate the bracero program.[85]

Congress also took its time in dealing with other recommendations of the President's Commission on Migratory Labor, although Truman also chose not to give them high priority in 1952. An interdepartmental task force comprising various executive administrators elected to defer requests for major legislative action on most of the recommendations until more technical studies were available. But the president did take the first step in his budget message of January 21, 1952, when he requested legislation to prevent "unscrupulous agencies and labor contractors" from exploiting workers in operations that crossed state lines. He also promised that the Department of Labor would step up its efforts to enforce the anti-child-labor provisions of the Fair Labor Standards Act. Concerned about the inadequate education of children of migratory workers, he requested funds to permit the Office of Education to study possible solutions in cooperation with the states. It was not much, but it represented a beginning. The administration also sought to aid Puerto Ricans under the contract programs, and in 1952 some twenty thousand of them were flown to the United States for seasonal farm work. The Labor Department also launched a migration program for industrial workers for the purposes of providing employment for Puerto Ricans in various industrial cities in the United States and, at the same time, dispersing migrants to prevent additional concentrations like that in New York City.[86]

When the Eighty-second Congress adjourned on July 8, 1952, it could boast of few accomplishments in the field of civil rights. In August 1951 it passed a bill that permitted Americans who had voted in Italian elections in 1946 and 1948 to reclaim their citizenship, which affected only a handful. In 1952, five days before adjournment, Congress also approved a bill that granted to federal employees of Japanese ancestry the seniority, grade, and pay that they would have had "except for certain World War II security measures," which affected another handful.[87]

That was it. The record of the Eighty-second Congress on civil rights clearly fell short of the achievements of its two predecessors, although the Eightieth and Eighty-first had little to boast about either. Congress had enacted legislation to settle the claims of American Indians and Japanese-Americans, to remove racial barriers from naturalization, and to provide more self-government for the territories. But the major demands of black America remained unfulfilled. From 1942 to 1952 a total of seventy FEPC bills had been introduced in both houses. Only one, the toothless McConnell bill of 1950, ever got through the House, while the Senate only fought over motions to consider FEPC. Beginning in 1942 the House also passed several anti-poll-tax bills, but Senate filibusters or threats thereof killed them all. The House approved statehood bills for Hawaii and Alaska, but the Senate balked. Neither house passed an antilynching bill during the Truman administration, although the House had approved bills in 1922, 1937, and 1940. It was a sad record; and the big stumbling block was the senatorial rule on cloture, which permitted southern Democrats and a handful of conservative Republicans to dictate what the Senate should consider. Yet congressional and White House liberals would also have to share the responsibility, for they were too often disposed to sacrifice civil rights for welfare, economic, and foreign policy legislation. Time had about run out on the Truman administration. It was also running out on America, although too many congressmen seemed not to know enough to care.

14 A FINAL STAND

On March 29, 1952, speaking to the party faithful at the annual Jefferson-Jackson Day dinner, Harry Truman surprised his audience when he ended his spirited defense of the Democratic party and of his administration with the announcement that he would not seek reelection in 1952.[1] In view of the political liabilities of the administration—the accusations of corruption and communism in government and the growing unpopularity of the stalemated war in Korea—his withdrawal understandably failed to provoke many cries of anguish or pleas to reconsider from the Democrats of the nation.

White southerners were pleased. Ever since 1948, when Truman's candidacy and a strong civil-rights plank had resulted in the Dixiecrat rebellion, Truman had been a constant irritant to the South. The opposition stiffened to the point where, in February 1952, the Alsop brothers predicted that his candidacy would destroy the Democratic party in the South. Early in March a Gallup poll of the region showed Eisenhower receiving 62 percent of the vote, with 30 percent for Truman and 8 percent undecided. With Truman as a candidate, even Senator Taft looked good in magnolia country; Taft was reported to be attracting 46 percent to Truman's 42 percent, with 12 percent undecided. Such vigorous and widespread southern opposition may very well have influenced Truman to remove his divisive presence and permit the party to unify for the campaign of 1952. Above all, Truman was a good party man as well as one who believed that the Democratic party was large enough to envelop diverse views. Predictably, his declaration of withdrawal virtually halted all southern talk of "taking a walk" in 1952.[2]

If Truman's decision to step aside provoked delight from many southerners and relief elsewhere, most Negroes were dismayed. It was one thing to criticize him for not endorsing all of their demands, but it was quite another to imagine him out of the White House. The *Journal and Guide* melodramatically declared that justice, mercy, and a belief in human dignity "died when he decided to yield his right to aspire to another term." The *Call* was certain that the next president would not be as forthright on civil rights as Harry Truman. The *Courier*, although still unreconciled to Truman personally or to a Democratic president generally, reported that no part of the American electorate "was more shocked and befuddled" when Truman withdrew than Negroes, who "rightly or wrongly . . . regarded Mr. Truman as their great white hope."[3]

Negro Democrats were concerned not only because they personally preferred Truman but also because they had fears about who might take his place. Since the first of the year, they had taken the precaution of scrutinizing avowed candidates, pretenders, and sleepers in the event that Truman chose not to run. They were unhappy with what they saw. Early in the year, the only active Democratic candidate was Senator Estes Kefauver, the "crimebuster" from Tennessee whose coonskin cap was a baleful reminder of his southern origins. To Negroes, the key to a candidate's attitude on civil rights was his position on the FEPC, and Kefauver fell short in advocating only a voluntary, persuasive approach. As the *Afro-American* put it, although Kefauver was no Dixiecrat, his progressivism would "not stretch far enough to permit his endorsement of a truly workable federal fair employment practices act." Walter White was also less than elated, but he knew enough to look at the man as well as at his senatorial voting record. In examining the senator's votes, White noted that although he had a "bad" record on civil rights, he had nonetheless voted to sustain the Barkley ruling on cloture in March 1949. Moreover, Kefauver was a symbol of the changing South, a "wise and morally decent" man who realized the political and humanitarian considerations of the day. Yet, although Kefauver subsequently promised to abide by the Democratic plank on civil rights, this was not enough to attract the support of civil-rights organizations.[4]

Kefauver was suspect, but Senator Russell of Georgia was altogether unacceptable, and the latter's victory over Kefauver in the Florida presidential primary in May generated fears in blacks of a potent southern drive to capture a leading spot on the Democratic ticket. In fact, Russell had already been mentioned as a possible running mate with Governor Adlai Stevenson of Illinois. And by the time that Truman announced his decision, most Negro Democrats had concluded that the Illinois governor was the only palatable Democrat, although he had not indicated his availability. As a result of his egalitarian rhetoric, his decisive action in quelling Cicero's white riot in the summer of 1951, and his repeated requests that the Illinois legislature enact an FEPC with enforcement powers, Stevenson seemed eminently qualified. The pages of the Negro press were replete with glowing tributes about his attitude and ability, and Walter White was impressed with his "excellent record" in Illinois. Among the major Negro papers, only the *Courier* was hypercritical, contending that Stevenson was "no worthy opponent for whomever the Republicans nominate, whether it be Taft, Eisenhower or MacArthur."[5]

It soon became apparent, however, that Stevenson might be a weak reed upon which to hang the hopes of black Americans. For one thing, he steadfastly insisted that he was running only for reelection as governor of Illinois, and Negroes could not afford to be caught without a candidate. Further, and more important, he too had become suspect on the critical issue of an enforceable FEPC. In various interviews, he indicated that he supported a strong FEPC for the state of Illinois—which, however, might not be the answer for every state—but that the states should solve the problem. At the same time, he insisted that the problem was so fundamental as to warrant a federal approach in the event that states took no action, and he insisted that the party should not retreat from the Democratic civil-rights plank of 1948. Beneath such obfuscation and evasion rested the indisputable fact of his opposition to a federal FEPC with strong powers of enforcement. Nor were Negroes pleased when he announced that the main domestic issues in the presidential campaign would be inflation, national solvency, and abuses by those in public office.[6]

By May, hints of desperation were cropping up in the statements of Negro leaders. On May 3 Clarence Mitchell of the NAACP observed that most of the avowed candidates were "far below the standards" of Harry Truman on civil-rights legislation; only Senators Humphrey and Brien McMahon of Connecticut had "fully acceptable records," but neither was likely to be the nominee. By this time, however, a new candidate with attractive credentials had entered the race. On April 22 W. Averell Harriman, currently the Mutual Security director, announced his availability and quickly endorsed the president's position on civil rights, advocating a strong federal FEPC and criticizing senatorial filibusters on civil-rights legislation. Campaigning against Kefauver in the presidential primary in the District of Columbia, Harriman also espoused abolition of segregation in Washington's public-school system. On June 17, within a month of the Democratic convention, Harriman crushed Kefauver by a ratio of four to one, and in the Negro wards his victory was even more stunning. This was enough for the leadership of the "nonpartisan" NAACP. Keynoting the annual convention of the association, which was meeting in Oklahoma City, Roy Wilkins declared that Harriman was the only suitable candidate for Negro Americans. In urging enactment of an FEPC with enforcement powers, Wilkins argued, Harriman was supporting the only type "that is worth a hoot." Yet it was a gloomy convention, for everyone realized that Harriman probably lacked the support to win the nomination.[7]

If Negroes were concerned about the Democratic presidential nomination, they were deeply distressed about developments in the Republican party. The spirited opposition to Truman in the South apparently persuaded several influential Republicans, most notably Senator Karl E. Mundt of South Dakota, of the possibility that there would be heavy Republican inroads into the southern vote in 1952. Accordingly, in the spring of 1951 Mundt openly advocated Republican cooperation with southern Democrats to achieve a conservative victory in 1952. In May 1951 a delegation of Negro Republicans urged the Republican National Committee, meeting in Tulsa, to disavow Mundt's "shocking gospel"; but Chairman Guy Gabrielson refused to consider it a committee matter.[8] In February 1952 the *Call* denounced the Republican plan to campaign extensively in southern states, as did the *Afro-American* in March, when Gabrielson promised active solicitation of southern votes, no matter who the Republican candidate might be.[9]

The nominee of the Republican party was the other problem facing black Americans. When Senator Taft announced his candidacy in October 1951, the reaction of most Negro leaders and commentators was predictable. The *Afro-American*, for example, was firmly opposed to Taft, because of his alleged sympathy with the reactionary wing of the party. Noting that Taft's supporters included Mundt, Wherry, General MacArthur, and Senator Joseph McCarthy—"the Wisconsin 'big lie' technician"—the editor also contended that Taft's voting record "clearly indicates that he belongs to that bewildered element in this nation that is desperately afraid of the future." When Taft spoke in Kansas City in November, the *Call* denounced both Taft, for his endorsement of a voluntary FEPC, and the "Uncle Toms" in the audience who applauded him. When the senator seemed to espouse segregation in public schools in a speech to Negro students at North Carolina State College in December, Negro leaders were outraged. Nor was Taft a favorite of the black rank and file. In 1950, when he defeated his undistinguished Democratic opponent for the Senate by a commanding margin of some 430,000 votes, he lost the Negro wards in Ohio by nearly two to one. Taft was clearly unacceptable because of his refusal to endorse an enforceable FEPC and because of a generally conservative record on "bread and butter" issues. In an article in the *Afro-American*, William V. Shannon crisply summed up the black response to Robert Taft: " 'Honest Bob' has led the colored people and others interested in civil rights through a long and wearisome game of Blind Man's Bluff, always coming out at the same place: nowhere."[10]

Nor were civil-rights leaders overcome with gratitude and relief in the next few months when Governor Earl Warren, Harold E. Stassen, and General Eisenhower indicated their availability for the Republican nomination. No one took Stassen seriously, Warren was tagged with a loser's image as a result of 1948, and neither generated any warmth in Negro voters. As the NAACP put it, "Warren has given lip service to civil rights but has failed to deliver in his home state of California." That left General Eisenhower, which to most civil-rights leaders left much too little. It required no taxing of the memory to recall his testimony in 1948 before the Senate Armed Services Committee, when he opposed current demands for integration of the military on the grounds that blacks were ill prepared to compete with whites in integrated units and that legislation could not persuade people to like other people. Since then, he had not publicly disavowed his testimony nor had he revealed his specific beliefs on anything; therefore the *Afro-American* reveled in the wisecrack: "I like Ike, but what does Ike like."[11]

Some Negro Republicans did endorse the general. A black leader among Kansas Republicans made a pilgrimage to Abilene to check Eisenhower's record with Negro residents, who apparently had memories stretching back to Ike's boyhood days. Satisfied with what he heard, the Negro leader launched a campaign through the Midwest to attract convention support for the general. Walter White was unimpressed, though he struggled to find something good to say. He recalled that during World War II Eisenhower had been "genuinely concerned about instances of gross injustice against Negro soldiers" and had "acted swiftly to correct cases of mistreatment when they were called to his attention. Unfortunately, he was reluctant to hit the evil at its roots—the segregated system." White hoped that he had "grown in wisdom and courage." But the general's continued silence was discouraging; and on April 20, 1952, the NAACP found him unacceptable.

The *Afro-American* was impatient. "General, where do you stand on civil rights?" demanded the editor. "Are you for an integrated army? Do you favor compulsory FEPC and federal aid to education? Do you think the federal government should enact legislation against lynching and poll taxes? Speak up, General! Speak up."[12]

Eisenhower spoke up on June 5 from Abilene, Kansas, in his first "political" press conference. In his opening statement, he stressed his philosophical agreement with the Republican declaration of principles of February 6, 1950, in which Republican members of Congress and the national committee had proclaimed the main domestic issue as "liberty against socialism." The endorsement was surprising, for one of his current advisers, Senator Lodge, had opposed the declaration in 1950 because of its extravagance in labeling Truman a socialist and because of its failure to support strong civil-rights measures. In response to a question concerning FEPC, the general emphasized states' rights, vigorously opposed a compulsory federal FEPC, and even refrained from endorsing one with persuasive powers only. Although Eisenhower subsequently indicated that military segregation had to go, the political damage had been done as far as civil-rights advocates were concerned.[13]

Negroes thus had much to fret about as the conventions made ready to meet in July 1952. Four years earlier, as the two parties prepared to nominate Truman and Dewey, both of whom were acceptable to many civil-rights advocates, black leaders were able to concentrate on the platforms. In 1952, however, it was distressingly clear that on civil rights Taft and Eisenhower were not Thomas Dewey, and Stevenson and Kefauver were not Harry Truman. Given the views of Taft and Eisenhower and the inclination of many Republicans to campaign vigorously in the South in 1952, a modest civil-rights plank in the Republican platform was foreordained.

On July 10, after several days of behind-the-scenes bickering over a civil-rights plank, the Republican convention unanimously adopted its platform. On civil rights, the party retreated from its 1944 and 1948 positions. After condemning "bigots who inject class, racial and religious prejudice into public and political matters" and the "duplicity and insincerity of the party in power in racial and religious matters," the plank insisted that states should exercise primary responsibility and timidly promised supplemental federal action on lynching and poll taxes, "appropriate action" on segregation in the District of Columbia, and appointment of qualified persons to federal positions. On FEPC—the nub of controversy in both parties—the Republicans equivocated, advocating legislation "to further just and equitable treatment in the area of discriminatory employment practices," which should not, however, "duplicate state efforts to end such practices; should not set up another huge bureaucracy." Other planks called for home rule for the District of Columbia, statehood for Hawaii and Alaska, eventual statehood for Puerto Rico, and a pledge to aid the American Indian in achieving full citizenship and equal opportunity. Although Negro delegates to the convention had originally threatened a floor fight, they backed off when Eisenhower's supporters pointed out that such a move might increase the conservative strength of Senator Taft. By this time, most Negro delegates were in Eisenhower's corner, and the argument made sense. The Republicans then turned to the nominations, deciding upon Eisenhower after a bitter battle with the Taft forces, and selecting Senator Richard M. Nixon as his running mate.[14]

If the skimpiness of the civil-rights plank was predestined, so was the Negro response. Rarely was there such agreement, as a drumfire of criticism rolled from the Negro press. To the *Call* and various ANP correspondents, it was "weak," "watered down," "diluted," and a "disappointment." The *Journal and Guide* viewed it as a naked appeal for southern votes. The *Courier*, struggling to say something favorable, was forced to conclude that "it must be a considerable disappointment to all who looked for a straightforward espousal of punitive federal fair employment legislation." In a front-page column, the editor of the *Afro-American* charged that "the Republican party appears to have written off as lost forever the traditional support of colored voters."[15] This, of course, was an exaggeration, for neither party could permanently ignore the Negro vote, although the Republican platform of 1952 clearly reflected less concern for the black vote than had its 1944 and 1948 counterparts.

The nominations of Eisenhower and Nixon and the equivocal civil-rights plank placed the Democrats in an advantageous position on the issue. Unfortunately for civil-rights advocates, such developments also played into the hands of those Democrats who had been urging some type of compromise since the beginning of the year. Indeed, following Eisenhower's emphasis on states' rights in his statements at Abilene, Senator Humphrey saw no reason to "harden" the Democratic plank of 1948. Even prior to Eisenhower's statement, Democratic National Committee Chairman Frank McKinney had announced plans to draft a civil-rights plank that would be acceptable to all factions of the party. Some liberal Democrats, however, were not listening to the voices of compromise. Averell Harriman was making a major issue of the president's civil-rights program; and Herbert Lehman was playing the Humphrey role of 1948, insisting upon no retreat whatever.[16]

But it was Harry Truman who headed the fight against any compromise on civil rights. He now had a record to defend, and defend it he did. On May 17, 1952, speaking to one thousand cheering and applauding members of the Americans for Democratic Action, he assailed the "dinosaur wing" of the Republican party and sparked hope for a Democratic victory in 1952. In the course of the address, he emphasized the necessity for firmness on civil rights, hoping that his position would be the basis of the plank in the Democratic platform of 1952. Although pleased with the "good progress" since 1948, he stressed the need for enactment of the civil-rights legislation recommended in his special message of February 1948.[17]

Although the speech was largely a partisan performance, Truman refrained from injecting politics into his discussion of civil rights, except to refer to the forthcoming Democratic platform. And the press chose to emphasize that aspect of the address. The *New York Times* reported that it "threw cold water" on McKinney's hopes for compromise at the Democratic convention. The *Washington Star* believed that it "wrecked" McKinney's plan while launching a determined drive for a vigorous civil-rights plank.[18]

Yet it was Truman's speech on June 13 to the graduating students of Howard University that represented the capstone of his oratorical efforts, an address bereft of partisanship and devoted entirely to civil rights. Using the report of his Committee on Civil Rights as a reference point, the president summed up the progress of the past five years. He was happy that the report and his civil-rights program had given "voice and expression" to the "great change of sentiment" throughout the country. "They are the trumpet blast outside the walls of Jericho—the crumbling walls of prejudice. And their work is not yet done. We still have a long way to go."

He then turned to the record. Noting that only five states retained the poll tax as a prerequisite for voting, he urged abolition. Observing that local, state, and federal authorities had moved vigorously to protect the security of persons, he pressed for a federal antilynching law to complete the program. He was pleased with the court decisions permitting Negro students to attend previously all-white colleges and universities. In housing, the Supreme Court's decision outlawing enforcement of restrictive covenants was a "major step" along the road of progress. So was his public-housing program, under which 177 projects were open in 1950 "to families of all races and creeds." He took special pride in the progress of the federal government, including the work of his Fair Employment Board and his Committee on Government Contract Compliance. He also reminded his audience that eleven states and twenty cities now had fair employment laws on the books. Observing that some of America's "greatest generals" believed in the necessity of military segregation, Truman pronounced it "plain nonsense." He praised Gen. Matthew Ridgway for integrating the Far Eastern command and referred to the recent order calling for integration of American forces in Europe. "From Tokyo to Heidelberg these orders have gone out that will make our fighting forces a more perfect instrument of democratic defense."

Yet, he concluded, the country needed voluntary, local, and state action. It also needed the civil-rights program that he had recommended to Congress in 1948. "I am not one of those who feel that we can leave these matters up to the states alone, or that we can rely solely on the efforts of men of good will," he asserted. The federal government had to fulfill the promises of this country's great historical documents. "The full force and power of the federal government must stand behind the protection of rights guaranteed in the federal Constitution."[19]

It was the most impressive speech on civil rights of his career—or the career of any president for that matter—and black Americans were quick to applaud. The reaction of the Negro press was generally twofold. On the one hand, the editors praised Truman for the most candid presidential statement on civil rights in the country's history. They also interpreted his address as a repudiation of those who were pleading for compromise at the Democratic convention.[20] And Truman intended such an interpretation. Asked during his news conference on June 19 if his speech reflected what he expected in the civil-rights plank, he quickly replied: "Yes, and if you will read the message of 1948, you will find just what it ought to be. There hasn't been any change on my part."[21]

Nor were Truman's efforts only rhetorical. Although he declined to endorse publicly any of the Democratic aspirants for the presidential nomination, he and his staff made a determined effort to influence the language and direction of the platform, particularly the civil-rights plank. For several weeks, his aides had been forwarding various drafts of the proposed platform to John McCormack, chairman of the platform committee. Philip Perlman, Truman's solicitor general, was also working closely with the committee, reputedly as his personal representative.[22]

In the negotiations that followed, Truman and the White House staff decided upon a civil-rights plank calling unequivocally for "enforceable" federal legislation dealing with employment, lynching, and the poll tax. It also included a provision aimed at senatorial filibusters and the arbitrary actions of the House Rules Committee. "In order that the will of the American people may be expressed upon these and other vital legislation proposals," the statement read, "we believe that action should be taken at the beginning of the 83rd Congress to improve congressional procedures so that votes may be had and decisions made after reasonable debate without being blocked by a minority in either House."[23]

As expected, the civil-rights plank was the major bone of contention within the resolutions committee. After days of wrangling, the apostles of compromise—particularly John Sparkman, John McCormack, William Dawson, and Brooks Hays—won some concessions. For his conciliatory efforts, Dawson also won the enmity of his black colleague in the House, Adam Clayton Powell, who denounced Dawson as well as the plank. When the platform reached the convention floor around midnight on July 23, fears that there might be a fight did not materialize. Northern liberals had already agreed not to contest the plank, and southerners lost all opportunity to do so when Sam Rayburn, permanent chairman of the convention, indulged in some fast gavel work. As southerners rose to protest the plank, Rayburn called for a voice vote and quickly declared the platform accepted.[24]

Although the civil-rights plank fell short of Truman's demands, he was willing to accept it. He praised it in a fighting speech to convention delegates on July 26. "They weasel on civil rights," he stated in referring to Republicans. "Read their civil rights paragraph, and then read our paragraph on civil rights, and see which one you want." Later in the address, he also promised to "carry on the fight for the full protection of civil rights to all of our citizens in all parts of the country, without regard to race, religion, or national origin."[25]

Yet lost in most of the news stories heralding the compromise and in the reports of Powell's bitterness was the fact that the civil-rights plank of 1952 represented an advance over that of 1948. Truman had won more than he had lost, and most civil-rights advocates were satisfied with the final product. For example, Walter White called it "a signal victory for the forces of liberalism in the party" and noted that despite some imprecision in language, the plank substantially embodied the demands of the Leadership Conference on Civil Rights. In short, White said that it represented a "distinct advance" over its counterpart of 1948.[26]

Although Truman's demand for a statement calling for "enforceable" federal legislation was sacrificed to the politics of compromise, the plank did favor federal legislation "effectively" to secure equal rights, a statement roughly parallel to that of 1948 "guaranteeing" those rights. Moreover, although the provision urging improvement of procedures to permit majority rule to prevail in both houses was not included in the plank itself, it was included in a separate category immediately preceding the statement on civil rights. To the NAACP, this was the "one item which marks the great advance over 1948," for legislation was impossible without revision of Rule XXII on senatorial cloture. The platform statement also embraced the arbitrary power of the House Rules Committee to bottle up legislation of which it disapproved. The item, concluded the association, was thus "the milk in the coconut."[27]

There were other improvements over the 1948 plank. In 1952 Democrats placed equal employment opportunity first on their list of legislative priorities, whereas in 1948 they had referred first to the right of full political participation, or, in other words, abolition of the poll tax. Nor did the party ignore the advances in civil rights of the past four years, pointing proudly to the progress "made in securing equality of treatment and opportunity in the nation's armed forces and the civil service and all areas under federal jurisdiction." The plank also complimented the Justice Department for "successfully arguing in the courts for the elimination of many illegal discriminations." In a separate category, the party also took pride in the new status of Puerto Rico and pledged continued support for its growth and development.

Finally, the plank of 1952 was broader and embraced minority groups that had previously been ignored. In addition to reiterating earlier pleas for Alaskan and Hawaiian statehood, increased self-government for the territories, and home rule for the District of Columbia, the platform advocated "improvement of employment conditions of migratory workers and increased protection of their safety and health." Another long section promised a fair deal for the American Indian.[28]

Although Congressman Brooks Hays subsequently refused to compare the two Democratic platforms—because "the background was so different"—he did concede that they were similar, noting also that the southern rebels of 1948 would never have accepted the plank of 1952. The latter confession naturally brings up the question of why the South was more agreeable four years later. There is no simple or single answer. Hays suggested a partial explanation when he maintained, perhaps correctly, that the Dixiecrats took a walk in 1948 because the plank specifically commended Truman for his "courageous" position on civil rights.[29] In 1952 neither the White House nor anyone else insisted upon a comparable statement, which represented the major concession to the South in the party platform. In addition, Truman was not a candidate for reelection, and the "traitor" to the South was therefore not a major issue. The Dixiecrats had also suffered the pain of defeat in 1948, thereby learning the virtue of working within the two-party system. Finally, all of the avowed, serious candidates for the Democratic presidential nomination—except Averell Harriman, who had little chance—were either equivocal about or opposed to strong federal civil-rights legislation. The nomination of Adlai Stevenson for the presidency was thus palatable to many southerners, and the choice of John Sparkman of Alabama as his running mate was frosting on the cake.

In contrast with 1948, then, the attitudes of the candidates, and not the civil-rights planks, were probably the major concern of those on the firing line for equal justice. No longer fearful of massive southern defections, Democratic leaders were now worried about losing the votes of northern Negroes and their white allies. Adam Clayton Powell had already promised not to campaign for the national ticket, calling for a boycott of the election unless Stevenson took a stronger position on civil rights. And the Illinois governor was taking his time in catching up with the views of Harry Truman and the Democratic platform. On July 30, when reporters asked if a president should use the authority of his office to influence senatorial revision of Rule XXII, Stevenson equivocated, indicating that he needed further study. Nor would he endorse an enforceable FEPC, as Truman had consistently demanded. On August 4 Stevenson was even more hesitant, when he noted that "it would be a very dangerous thing indeed to limit debate in a parliamentary body in a democracy" and concluded that "perhaps the Senate would be better able to discuss that and adjust it than I would."[30]

The pressure on Stevenson became intense. On August 4, sixteen Eisenhower supporters, including Henry Cabot Lodge, issued a statement declaring that a Republican victory in November would expedite passage of an FEPC with "adequate" enforcement powers. Although the general had not embraced the promise, several Negro Republicans were convinced that eventually he would do so. Truman was also making things uncomfortable for the governor. During a news conference on August 7, when asked his opinion of Stevenson's view on cloture, Truman interrupted to snap, "I am standing on the Democratic platform."[31]

Stevenson soon capitulated. Addressing the New York Democratic convention on August 28, he urged revision of Rule XXII and promised, if elected, to use presidential influence to encourage Congress "to shake off its ancient shackles." He also endorsed an enforceable FEPC. It was enough for Congressman Powell, who declared himself "thoroughly satisfied." So was the NAACP. The association insisted that it was endorsing no one, but its board of directors passed a resolution noting that Stevenson had taken the "most forthright" position on civil rights, particularly because of his views on senatorial cloture and FEPC. Although "impressed" with Eisenhower's sincerity and pleased with his recent pronouncements against segregation in the military and the District of Columbia, the board regretted his failure to support the two key issues that Stevenson had recently endorsed.[32]

The NAACP, however, was unhappy about the "unsatisfactory records" on civil rights of the vice-presidential candidates. The opposition to Sparkman began shortly before his nomination, when Adam Clayton Powell and most Negro delegates, learning of Stevenson's preference for the Alabama senator, stalked from the convention floor. Sparkman's nomination also prompted Walter White to wonder how the party could nominate a candidate who apparently opposed the civil-rights plank of the platform. Yet Sparkman was not about to repudiate what was partly his handiwork, and within hours after the convention, he publicly reaffirmed his support of the plank.[33]

Civil-rights spokesmen and organizations, however, were virtually unanimous in their intial opposition to both candidates. Although Nixon's voting record on civil rights was better than Sparkman's, it was nothing for a nonsoutherner to boast about. Moreover, Sparkman was more progressive on "bread and butter" issues, and impartial observers were declaring a draw between the two. Late in September the Negro press discovered something that both had in common. Both had signed racially restrictive covenants in purchasing homes in Washington, and cries of alarm again appeared in the Negro press. By this time, however, most of the Negro newspapers were in the process of lining up with Stevenson, and a double standard in judging the vice-presidential candidates was soon evident. Because Sparkman was from Alabama, one black editor rationalized that he had "many habits customary for a southerner. . . . He is not riding under false colors. Nixon is a northerner. He should have a far better record than Sparkman, but he hasn't."[34]

Negroes found other palatable things about Sparkman. One editor argued that only on the issue of an enforceable FEPC was the Alabaman "a captive of the region of the country he represents." A columnist saw significance in Sparkman's southern Methodist background, for southern Methodists "have always led in programs of interracial cooperation." And over and over again, blacks were predicting that Sparkman would be another Harry Truman, another Hugo Black, or another Judge Waring.[35]

The predictions of a possible conversion on Sparkman's part were based almost entirely on speculation, although he was surely not the same politician who had declared in Mobile in April 1950 that he was opposed to civil rights—"always have been and always will be." In addition, the mixed reaction of the white South to the Stevenson-Sparkman ticket prompted second thoughts from many Negroes. In September, Governor James Byrnes of South Carolina declared for Eisenhower because of Stevenson's switch on a compulsory FEPC. Apparently, Byrnes had little faith in Sparkman's attitude or influence. Moreover, by October, fifty-six southern papers had endorsed the Eisenhower-Nixon ticket, in contrast with only twenty-nine for Stevenson and Sparkman. "The fact that southerners are turning to Eisenhower," wrote C. A. Franklin, "is evidence enough that John Sparkman is not a bad fellow. If he were a Dixiecrat, he could hold the southern die-hards, but those who voted for Thurmond in 1948 are now supporting Eisenhower and Nixon, not Stevenson and Sparkman."[36]

In the fall campaign both Stevenson and Eisenhower vied for the northern Negro vote, and both emulated Truman by speaking in Harlem. But Eisenhower's unwillingness to endorse an enforceable FEPC or revision of the senatorial rule on cloture, coupled with the southern strategy of the Republican party in 1952, had its price. Negroes were not coming out to hear the general. One black correspondent traveling with the Eisenhower entourage observed that "if there is going to be a wholesale swing of colored voters to the Republican column this year, it will go down as the best kept secret of the century."[37]

Yet the major obstacles to Republican inroads into the black vote were the past accomplishments and the present contentiousness of Harry S. Truman. Republican attacks on his administration for bungling concerning Korea, for corruption, and for communism, as well as Stevenson's frantic attempts to dissociate himself from the administration's liabilities, goaded Truman into another hard-hitting campaign. And it was Truman, not the nominees of either party, who attempted to make civil rights one of the major issues of 1952. He introduced civil rights into the campaign in his Labor Day statement, released on August 28, in which he declared, "We must end the discrimination which has cast shadows on some parts of our great record of freedom." In his Labor Day address in Milwaukee, he also praised Stevenson for his efforts in promoting the cause of civil rights.[38]

Truman launched his major campaign late in September, a whistle-stop performance in which he delivered 211 speeches and traveled 18,500 miles by rail. After a whirlwind tour of the West, he headed north, where he first stressed civil rights in Buffalo on October 9. Thereafter to the end of the campaign, he emphasized civil rights in several addresses and sprinkled references to the issue in others; and his approach of 1948 paled by comparison.[39] On October 11 Truman entered Harlem to receive the Franklin D. Roosevelt Memorial Brotherhood Medal for the second time and to deliver his major civil-rights address. Aside from its partisanship, the speech was largely a paraphrase of his Howard University address in June.[40]

Infuriated because of Eisenhower's endorsement of Senator Joseph McCarthy and others who had vilified Gen. George C. Marshall, Truman struck hard at the Republican presidential candidate. In Brooklyn, he criticized him for opposing the use of federal power for an effective FEPC. Occasionally, he landed some low blows, as when he repeatedly maintained that Eisenhower still favored segregation in the military, despite the general's assertions to the contrary.[41]

Truman also tried to embellish Sparkman's record on civil rights. In Philadelphia, he reminded his listeners that the Alabaman had promised to support the Democratic platform, and added, "John Sparkman is an honorable man and he will honor that pledge." Speaking on Chicago's South Side on October 29, he informed his black audience that Sparkman had had a hand in writing the Democratic platform, which contained "the strongest civil rights stand ever taken by a major political party in this country." He also used the occasion to praise the Fahy Committee for its role in integrating the military.[42]

In fact, Truman's relatively brief message of October 29 was especially noteworthy, if only because of his choice of words. In the early years of his administration, he had consistently denounced discrimination and pleaded for equal justice; but not until after the 1948 campaign had he struck specifically, and then only occasionally, at segregation in his public comments. And when he referred to its absence or to its eradication, he had generally used the words "nonsegregated," "unsegregated," or "desegregation." His speech on Chicago's South

Side, however, was studded with at least a dozen uses of "integration," "integrated," and "integrating." The change in vocabulary was thus symptomatic of the change in the thrust of his administration after 1948.

There were also suggestions of higher priorities. The Republican emphasis on Korea, corruption, and communism was attractive to many Americans who wanted relief from it all. But Harry Truman also had three issues—prosperity, civil rights, and foreign policy—as he contended in a major speech in Detroit on October 30. On civil rights, he declared that his administration had "awakened the conscience of the nation. Instead of falling backward into a period of race hate and prejudice after World War II, we went forward. We are steadily breaking down the barriers of prejudice throughout our economic, cultural, and political life. We still have a very long way to go, but this progress is for me one of the great satisfactions of my whole lifetime."[43]

Never before had he given civil rights such preference. Nor was it simply a passing thought. Speaking over nationwide radio on election eve, he referred again to the three campaign issues. "This election may decide whether we shall go ahead and expand our prosperity here at home or slide back into a depression," he argued in his short address. "It may decide whether we shall preserve and extend our civil rights and liberties, or see them fall before a wave of smear and fear. Above all, it may decide whether we shall finally achieve lasting peace or be led into a third world war."[44]

To most black Americans, Truman had hit the major themes of 1952. As a deprived minority, Negroes were intensely concerned with continued prosperity, progress in civil rights, and world peace. In general, they agreed with Truman that American involvement in Korea was necessary to prevent a third world war. Understandably, as a vulnerable minority, they were never enamored with the wild accusations about subversive elements in government. The charges of corruption, admittedly true in some instances, had never touched the president, and the *Call* denounced as "Pure Bosh" the argument that Ike's election would enthrone honesty in government.[45]

In a reversal of 1948, all of the major Negro papers, except the *Pittsburgh Courier* and the *Daily World* (Atlanta), endorsed the Democratic ticket, as did all of the major Negro magazines.[46] The endorsements demonstrated that the identification of black leadership with the Democratic party had grown stronger during the Truman administration, in considerable part because of Truman himself. Few black editors agreed with the *Courier* when it contended that for all of his fine words, Truman had really done nothing fundamental for Negroes. And they could not see much of an issue in the paper's indictment of both FDR and Truman for appointing white advisers on race relations nor in the *Courier's* statement that "Stevenson will turn this job over to his ghost writer, Arthur Schlesinger Jr., of Harvard, who knows as much about Negroes as the King of Norway."[47]

Three considerations were paramount to most Negro editors in 1952. One was Harry Truman, whose record on civil rights was unequaled by any president and whose campaign for justice and equality in the fall of 1952 was impressive by the standards of any time or place. Stevenson would continue the commitment, some reasoned, if only because of Harry Truman. A second consideration involved the civil-rights planks of both parties and the attitudes of Stevenson and Eisenhower. In 1948, some Negro papers had concluded that both Truman and Dewey were solid on civil rights. Some of the more conservative black editors could thus endorse Dewey for economic reasons without fear of what might happen to civil rights. It was not that easy in 1952, for the two presidential candidates differed significantly on the gut issues of an enforceable FEPC and revision of cloture. Stevenson had embraced both, but reluctantly and only after pressure from Truman and Negro leaders, while Eisenhower refused to commit himself to either.[48] The situation also had its irony; for although the analyses of Negro editors were essentially correct, Eisenhower did speak more vigorously for civil rights in certain northern cities than Dewey had in 1948.

Then, there was also the "I like Ike" sentiment in the South for which Eisenhower was not primarily responsible, even though he was appealing to the region for support. For years, various Republican and southern Democratic leaders had been exchanging wistful glances, and Strom Thurmond's candidacy in 1948 had only momentarily suspended the flirtation. Ike's conservative position on several issues added a fillip to the romance, and as Dixie increasingly embraced the general during the fall of 1952, Negro editors became correspondingly more frigid. To Franklin of the *Call*, Ike was a "changeling," one who simultaneously courted Negroes in the North and James Byrnes in the South. The *Afro-American* pointedly noted that its friends did not include "the Dixiecrats whom Ike loves"; and the *Amsterdam News*, although it endorsed Republicans Irving Ives and Jacob Javits for reelection, could not support the general because of his forays into the South.[49]

This year differed from 1948, in that the opinion of most Negro editors corresponded to that of a majority of black Americans. In a record vote, Negroes flocked to the polls to cast 73 percent of their vote for Stevenson and Sparkman, a 4 percent increase over Truman's percentage of 1948. Stevenson's higher percentage resulted from the return of Wallace voters to the Democratic party as well as from the defection of some Negro Republicans. But the Negro vote as the balance of power was completely ineffective in the face of an Eisenhower landslide. Although Stevenson received twenty-seven million popular votes, Eisenhower won nearly thirty-four million votes and defeated Stevenson decisively in the electoral college by a margin of 442 to 89. In the South, Eisenhower cut heavily into the normal Democratic vote and even carried a few states—the first Republican to do so since 1928. Ironically, the Negro vote as a balance of power did operate in South Carolina, and probably in Louisiana, and Negroes thus had the satisfaction of denying Governor Byrnes the pleasure of delivering South Carolina to Eisenhower. It also increased their awareness of the importance of the southern black vote, and black leadership thereafter placed even higher priority on voter registration in the South.[50]

Although there were predictions that Indians were on the warpath and that 1952 was the first presidential election in which their vote would be noteworthy, they had no effect on the presidential outcome in any state. The newly enfranchised Indians of Arizona, however, did contribute to the defeat of Ernest McFarland by Barry Goldwater; and in Colorado, they provided the margin for Wayne Aspinall's election to the House of Representatives. Indians were also capable of reading the signs of the times, and thereafter they too placed greater emphasis on voter registration. Between 1952 and 1956 the Indians of New Mexico increased their registration from less than 8 percent to more than 24 percent. Elsewhere in the West there were additional increases in the number of Indians registered.[51]

Black Americans took Eisenhower's victory in stride. The *Call* urged everyone to close ranks behind the general, although it expected less progress on civil rights in the ensuing four years. The *Journal and Guide* agreed, seeing no reason for hysteria and subsequently expressing confidence that civil rights would not lose ground under Ike's stewardship. The NAACP observed that Republicans now had to produce, and it expected "Republicans to stop their shadowboxing on civil rights, now that they are in power, and do something about revision of Rule 22 to restore democracy to the Senate."[52]

Stevenson received few accolades from civil-rights leaders, and the bulk of their favorable comments following the election was reserved for Harry Truman as he prepared to leave the White House. In the eyes of most white Americans, Truman may have appeared to be discredited, but black Americans saw him in a different light. Glowing tributes appeared in the Negro press, and personal letters flowed into the White House.[53] On November 14 the National Newspaper Publishers Association (NNPA) presented a plaque to Harry S. Truman, "who has awakened the conscience of America and given new strength to our democracy by his courageous efforts on behalf of freedom and equality for all citizens." And in the weeks that followed, he received similar recognition from the American Council on Human Rights and from the American Jewish Congress, which granted him the Stephen S. Wise Award for 1952.[54]

But Truman was not resting on such laurels. Indeed, during the campaign, he had appointed Clifford R. Moore as a United States commissioner, the first Negro to hold such a position since Reconstruction days. Upon receipt of his award from the NNPA, he promised to continue working for implementation of the report of his Committee on Civil Rights, "for it is part and parcel of the principles for which I have always stood, and for which I will aways stand as long as I live." On November 16, when laying the cornerstone of the new temple of the Washington Hebrew Congregation, he used the occasion to denounce bigotry and to emphasize the importance of religion in the life of the nation. Upon the death of William Green, he publicly praised the AFL leader for his fight against discrimination in employment. When he participated in the dedication of a Presbyterian church in Alexandria, Virginia, he reminded the gathering that the most important function of the church was to "wage a ceaseless war against injustice in our society. The churches in particular are a force which should fight for brotherhood, and decency, and better lives for all our people."[55] Unfortunately, America's churches were lagging far behind the president.

He also kept the faith in his remaining messages to Congress and the country. On January 7, 1953, he sent his last State of the Union message to the Hill. As it was no longer his place or prerogative to present a legislative program, he concentrated on the challenges and achievements of his administration. On civil rights, he expressed satisfaction that the barriers to equality were crumbling "in our armed forces, our civil service, our universities, our railway trains, the residential districts of our cities—in stores and factories all across the nation—in the polling booths as well." The progress was unmistakable at all levels of government and in many private spheres as well. "There has been a great awakening of the American conscience on the issue of civil rights," he concluded. "And all this progress—still far from complete but still continuing—has been our answer, up to now, to those who questioned our intention to live up to the promises of equal freedom for us all." He included the same sentiments, and some of the same phraseology, in his farewell address to the American people on January 15. And in his annual economic report to Congress on January 14 he noted that the elimination of discrimination was a "continuing objective of national policy."[56]

In admitting in his State of the Union address that progress on civil rights was "far from complete," Truman certainly would have conceded that elimination of discrimination in the District of Columbia was one of the remaining tasks. In fact, he confessed as much during the campaign of 1952. The Republican plank on civil rights had pledged "appropriate action to end segregation in the District of Columbia"; and in campaigning on the issue, Eisenhower had accused Truman of procrastination and had promised immediate action of his own. Irritated, Truman replied in a speech in Newark on October 21, 1952, warning the general that more was involved than "waving a wand." He also pointed to the progress in Washington, especially the trend toward integration of theaters, hotels, restaurants, colleges and universities, private elementary and secondary schools, and public parks and playgrounds. He had not done more, he maintained after the election, because he had lacked the authority.[57]

It was indeed a complex situation. Race relations had been the District's most difficult problem in the years after the Second World War, as well as one of the administration's greatest embarrassments in the rhetorical battles of the cold war. As racial barriers began to crack elsewhere in the country during the postwar period, Washington's segregationists strengthened its walls of prejudice, so that by mid 1947 their triumph seemed complete. Thereafter, however, they too fought a delaying—and slowly losing—battle. Although the report of the President's Committee on Civil Rights in 1947 called national attention to the disgraceful discrimination in the capital, breakthroughs began in 1948. As a result of *Shelley* v. *Kraemer* in May 1948, residential segregation showed some signs of erosion. The census of 1950 revealed that housing accommodations for blacks had spread into an additional 459 residential blocks, while those reserved exclusively for whites dropped from 2,041 to 1,956. This indication of progress was compromised by the District's urban renewal program, which generally meant that Negroes were removed even though adequate facilities were not available elsewhere, thus forcing many black families to double up in accommodations that were already inadequate for a single household.[58] In short, too often urban renewal signified Negro removal.

More important than *Shelley* v. *Kraemer* was the report in December 1948 of the National Committee on Segregation in the Nation's Capital, which contained enough statistical material to convince anyone with an open mind of the necessity for drastic improvement. It also gave a shot in the arm to those private organizations, including the NAACP, CORE, the American Friends Service Committee, the Urban League, and the Jewish Community Council, which had long fought the city's racial tyranny. So, too, did integration of the president's inaugural festivities of January 1949. In the years that followed, the struggle to democratize Washington was fought in Congress, the courts, and in the offices of large corporations, the District administrators, the National Capital Park and Planning Commission, the Department of the Interior, and the White House itself.[59]

The District commissioners were initially unsympathetic to the drive for integration and equal treatment, having ignored Truman's 1948 directive calling for nondiscrimination in federal employment. Perhaps their reluctance stemmed from the unpleasant facts that Congress controlled the city's purse strings and that southerners dominated the congressional committees. Whatever the case, the commissioners eventually made concessions under pressure from the Interior Department and the White House.

The main struggle in 1949 and 1950 involved integration of recreational facilites. The matter was unusually complicated because of indistinct lines of authority. Although the Department of the Interior still operated and supervised some of the parks and playgrounds, most of them were under the control of the District Recreation Board, which Congress had created in 1942 with authority to develop a comprehensive recreational program. In carrying out this mandate, the board established a policy of racial segregation for many of the facilities, particularly swimming pools. The Recreation Board did so with the knowledge and apparent support of the National Capital Park and Planning Commission, which functioned as a part of the Department of the Interior. In fact, the board insisted that it had segregated certain areas because the planning commission's map of the District specifically designated them as black or white. Prodded by Under Secretary Oscar Chapman, Secretary Julius Krug in 1949 launched a campaign to integrate all recreational facilities in the District. Krug also applied pressure on the planning commission, which removed the racial designations immediately.[60]

Now the Recreation Board changed its story, insisting that it had full authority under the act of 1942 to determine racial policies. At this point, the president intervened and summoned the three District commissioners to the White House, where he informed them of his desire that all public facilities in the capital be integrated. Although he admitted that the change in policy could not be precipitant, he wanted it pursued "actively and progressively." The commissioners agreed and immediately contacted the chairman of the Recreation Board, who stated that it was only possible to commit the board to the "*progressive* elimination of segregation."[61]

On June 14, 1949, the District Recreation Board rejected the Interior Department's motion to end segregation in playgrounds immediately and adopted another motion which pledged "realistic" efforts toward removal of segregation consistent "with the public interest, public order and effective administration." The board also unanimously agreed to permit the use of public schools and community buildings for interracial meetings. Although Negroes were displeased and agreed with the Negro board member's denunciation of the settlement, the *Washington Post* hailed it as "a discreet but a statesmanlike compromise." The board did seem to be moving in the right direction. It had already opened all tennis courts; and when the Interior Department had offered to transfer jurisdiction of its pools and golf courses, if operated under integrated conditions, the board was agreeable as far as the golf courses were concerned.[62]

But integrating Washington's swimming pools was another matter, for the Recreation Board was clearly opposed to interracial swimming. Civil-rights organizations, however, insisted upon integration, pointing out that whites in the District could utilize forty-one public, private, and commercial pools, while blacks had only four at their disposal. Until 1949, because of white opposition, blacks had not attempted to swim in four of the six integrated pools operated directly by the Interior Department. One day in June, however, fifty Negro youths were refused admittance to the Anacostia pool, and an incident occurred that evening. To avoid bloodshed and to buy time, Secretary Krug closed the pool for the rest of the season.[63]

In the off-season the administration intensified its efforts, although Secretary Krug wavered occasionally, apparently once agreeing to segregate some pools, then denying that he had agreed, which prompted a Washington publisher to call him a "God damn liar."[64] Truman also requested an additional appropriation for construction of an interracial pool approximately a mile from Anacostia, but its location in the heart of the ghetto was obviously intended to produce voluntary segregation. The Interior Department imported Professor Joseph D. Lohman of the University of Chicago to improve the human touch of capital police-men, who were partially responsible for the Anacostia incident. Loh-man subsequently kept in close contact with Philleo Nash of the White House staff. In April 1950 the new secretary of the interior, Oscar Chapman, offered all six pools to the Recreation Board if it would operate them on an integrated basis—an obvious ploy to emphasize the segregation policies of the board and to illustrate his own unwill-ingness to compromise.[65]

Chapman was convinced that blacks and whites could swim to-gether without having riots occur in their wake. In a form letter late in May 1950, as he prepared to open all six pools on an integrated basis, he noted the success of integrated swimming in the military and quoted the Fahy Committee's conclusion that integration decreased racial friction. Nonetheless, the local press predicted riots and bloodshed, and the Recreation Board anticipated catastrophe. But Chapman was right. In September he informed the president that the season had been successful. The department's six pools had accommodated some 90,000 blacks and 146,000 whites without incident. He was also pleased with the disappearance of racial barriers in a number of Washington's privately owned restaurants, hotels, and places of amusement. So was Truman. He found such progress "very heartening" and complimented Chapman for a "wonderful job" and for setting an example "which may clear up situations in other cities."[66]

The experiment was significant, for it undermined the major argu-ment of the bigots and the fainthearted alike. The *Washington Post*, confessing its earlier fear of trouble and its wrong-headedness in op-posing Chapman, now conceded that "nonsegregated swimming is here to stay." Indeed it was, although for the moment the Recreation Board held grimly to segregation of pools under its jurisdiction. The follow-ing year the Interior Department's integrated pools again operated without incident. Chapman was clearly the man of the hour; and Walter White devoted one of his columns in the *Defender* to the secre-tary's persistent efforts to desegregate the District, beginning with his contribution to Marian Anderson's concert at the Lincoln Memorial in 1939.[67]

During the remainder of the Truman administration, Chapman and the Recreation Board were at loggerheads. The board's promise of "gradual" integration seemed farcical. By June 1952, it had integrated only 9 additional playgrounds, all in residential areas in transition from white to black occupancy, while 128 facilities remained segregated. Supported by a Justice Department brief, Chapman filed suit in district court in March 1952, demanding the withdrawal of sixty recreational areas from the jurisdiction of the Recreation Board unless integrated immediately. Although the judge ruled against Chapman, time was running out on the board. Within a year it voluntarily voted to integrate the pool at Rosedale playground, which was a jump over a major psychological hurdle; and desegregation of other facilities soon followed.[68]

By 1951 the trend toward elimination of segregation was faintly visible nearly everywhere in Washington. The District commissioners were evincing increasing sympathy; and in 1950 they appointed a Negro—another "first"—to the three-member boxing commission. Truman's commissioners also broke precedent in naming two blacks to the nine-member Citizens Advisory Council, established to study reorganization of the District government. Moreover, Truman's appointment of Joseph Donohue as a District commissioner undoubtedly strengthened the resolve of his colleagues, for Donohue was as outspoken against segregation as they were silent. In 1951, with the support of the chief of the fire department, the commissioners assigned several black firemen to undermanned white companies. But the chairman of the House District Committee hastened to indicate his displeasure, as did the firemen's union, and the commissioners backed off. The situation was touchy because of the close living conditions of the firefighters. Even when the District commissioners, at Eisenhower's instructions, issued a desegregation order in November 1953, they expressly excluded the fire department.[69]

The halting, painful progress was also evident in the voluntary desegregation of privately owned facilities, although most hotels in the District continued to refuse black guests. But there was noticeable progress in the theaters. In 1952 the National Theater, which had closed in 1948 rather than integrate, reopened under new management on a nondiscriminatory basis. Although several other legitimate theaters were open to all patrons, the downtown motion-picture theaters still excluded blacks, unless they happened to be foreign dignitaries. The restaurant situation, too, was improving, but not without pressure. As a result of extensive picketing over many months, several department stores and dime stores integrated their lunch counters. By 1952, at least sixty-four downtown restaurants and lunch counters were serving black customers.[70]

In the struggle to integrate eating facilities in the city, the federal government had taken the lead, first in government cafeterias and then in Washington's National Airport. But the ultimate victory could not have been won without the persistence of concerned citizens of the District. The legal fight to integrate restaurants began shortly after the National Committee on Segregation in the Nation's Capital discovered the "mysterious" disappearance of the civil-rights acts of 1872 and 1873, which had been passed by the popularly elected District Assembly. The acts made it a misdemeanor for owners of restaurants and certain other public accommodations to refuse service to any well-behaved, respectable person because of his race or color. In 1901 Congress had codified all laws for the city but had omitted the acts of 1872 and 1873 without expressly repealing them. In May 1949 lawyers of the District's chapter of the National Lawyers Guild presented evidence of the validity of these laws to the District commissioners, requesting the board to provide for future enforcement of them.[71]

The commissioners conducted a leisurely investigation of their own, then instructed their lawyers to institute a court case upon receipt of complaints. By this time, civil-rights advocates in the District were well prepared. In September 1949 they organized the interracial Coordinating Committee for the Enforcement of the D.C. Anti-Discrimination Laws to rally the interested and to initiate test cases. The chairman of the committee was the aged and courageous Mary Church Terrell. In company with two other blacks and a white member of the Friends, she sought and was refused service at one of the Thompson restaurants in Washington; and the case of *District of Columbia* v. *John R. Thompson Company* was soon in the courts. In July 1950 a judge of the District Municipal Court ruled that the "lost" laws had been repealed by implication and were therefore unenforceable.[72]

The case then went to the Municipal Court of Appeals. In May 1951, by a vote of two to one, the judges declared the act of 1873 valid. Because the Thompson Company immediately appealed to the Circuit Court of Appeals, the District commissioners announced their intention to ignore the issue until its final disposition in the courts. In the meantime, while the case languished in the higher court, Mary Church Terrell and other members of the committee kept up the pressure on Washington restaurants through sit-ins, pickets, and boycotts.[73]

Mrs. Terrell's committee gained a potent ally in June 1951 when the Department of Justice entered the case. Oscar Chapman, always sensitive to racial events in the District, was apparently the first to notice the Thompson case, and in October 1950 he had called it to the attention of Solicitor General Philip Perlman. The case was then in the

Municipal Court of Appeals; and Perlman promised to participate in the appeal, regardless of the court's decision. He was as good as his word. He first filed a memorandum, and when the Circuit Court accepted the case, he was ready with an amicus curiae brief which had been prepared with the assistance of Philip Elman and T. S. L. Perlman.[74]

Contending that the "lost" laws were valid and still enforceable, Philip Perlman cited three reasons for racial discrimination in the capital being a matter of serious concern to the nation. First, the government had an established policy of nondiscrimination concerning its employees and therefore "particularly deplores discriminations of any kind against its employees because of color, religion, national ancestry, or other irrelevant fact." Second, Washington was the seat of the embassies and legations of foreign countries, and their officials and visiting citizens would receive an "exaggerated" and "misleading" impression of racial discrimination in America as a result of the intolerance of the District. Last, "and perhaps most important," the brief contended, "the existence of racial discrimination in the nation's capital constitutes a serious flaw in our democracy. The need to eliminate this gap between ideals and practices represents a challenge to the sincerity of our profession of the democratic faith."[75]

It was Perlman's fifth and last amicus curiae brief in a civil-rights case, and it encouraged civil-rights leaders to hope for a favorable decision.[76] In January 1953, however, the Circuit Court of Appeals, by a five to four vote, ruled the acts of 1872 and 1873 invalid on the grounds that the District Assembly lacked the authority to enact legislation and that the code of 1901 had implicitly repealed them anyway. It was a tortured decision with which Judge Charles Fahy strongly disagreed. In a dissenting opinion, concurred in by three of his colleagues, the former chairman of Truman's committee for equality in the military struck hard in favor of the legitimacy of the "lost" laws, which he thought were by no means simply "derelicts of the past."[77]

It was now up to the Eisenhower administration and the Supreme Court. In February 1953 the new secretary of the interior, Douglas McKay, urged Attorney General Herbert Brownell to file a petition in the Supreme Court seeking to reverse the decision. Brownell was agreeable. He first "suggested" to the court that it advance the case, then he selected Philip Elman, who had assisted Perlman, to present the administration's amicus curiae brief. In June 1953 the Vinson court unanimously upheld the law of 1873 but left in doubt the legal status of the 1872 act, which had also applied to hotels in the District and which may have been repealed by the law of 1873. Moreover, in deciding in favor of the legality of the 1873 law, the court thereby upheld the right of Congress to delegate its legislative power—as it had done to the District Assembly—and thus gave a big boost to the advocates of home rule.[78]

The *Thompson* case was one of the most significant events in the history of race relations in the District. The head of the Thompson restaurants immediately indicated his willingness to abide by the decision, and others soon followed. By December 1953 every restaurant was reported open, and the police were enforcing the new policy. Because of the ambiguity of the court's opinion about the 1872 act, however, the hotel situation was chaotic; but it, too, would soon change.[79]

The *Thompson* case also spotlighted an embarrassing paradox. While privately owned facilities were becoming increasingly integrated, Washington's public-school system remained rigidly segregated. Moreover, the schools for black children were invariably inferior. In 1947, for example, the District's expenditure per black student was $120.52, compared to $169.21 per white. Classrooms in the ghetto were overcrowded, while space in white schools went unused. Additional appropriations from Congress in 1949 had no meaningful effect on the disparity, which threatened to widen. The first court cases instituted in the city thus concentrated on the glaring inequities and focused on the desperate need for equal facilities. Most organizations backing the protests also avoided a direct attack on segregation itself.[80]

But sentiment in favor of integration was rising. The President's Committee on Civil Rights had vigorously denounced the situation in the District, pointedly noting that "the core of Washington's segregated society is its dual system of public education" and that "reasonable equality" was impossible under segregated conditions. In 1948 *Segregation in Washington* devoted a chapter to the subject, and in 1949 the Catholic hierarchy in Washington was concerned enough to order integration of all parochial schools in the District. Catholic University was already integrated, and American University partially so. By 1952 the public school situation was so chaotic and citizens' groups were so aroused that even the fainthearted now conceded the inevitability of integration "in our time."[81]

In 1952, too, the case of *Bolling* v. *Sharpe*, which dealt with the District's segregation of public schools, was before the Supreme Court, in company with four other cases involving segregated public schools in Kansas, South Carolina, Virginia, and Delaware. For the first time, the court had agreed to hear suits concerning segregation in elementary and secondary schools, and the result would be the historic decision of *Brown* v. *Board of Education of Topeka.* Faced with this threat, some southern states had been moving with indecent haste to try to equalize expenditures and facilities, but the NAACP's staff of lawyers and professional consultants were well prepared for this ploy. Indeed, in the *Sweatt* case of 1950 the NAACP had attacked all forms of segregation on the grounds of its adverse psychological effects. So had Solicitor General Perlman in the *Henderson* case of the same year. Moreover, in 1951, when a federal district court in South Carolina had ruled in favor of segregation, the association had offered expert testimony, much of it first assembled for Truman's Midcentury White House Conference on Children and Youth in 1950, to illustrate the damaging psychological effects of racial segregation.[82]

Not everyone was confident that the Supreme Court would render a favorable decision or that it would expressly reverse the separate-but-equal doctrine. The *Courier* found such a likelihood remote and denounced the NAACP for its frontal assault on *Plessy* v. *Ferguson.* In particular, there was suspicion that in the *Shelley, Sweatt, McLaurin,* and *Henderson* cases, Chief Justice Fred Vinson had gone as far as his intellectual and environmental equipment would permit. Vinson's delay in hearing the cases seemed to add credence to the fear. Even White House Assistant Philleo Nash thought it "unlikely that the court will need to go as far as the constitutional question in order to dispose of the cases," although he added that the government ought to prepare for that possibility.[83]

Nor was the NAACP sanguine at the outset. In fact, the legal staff was initially unhappy with the cases it was representing before the high tribunal. The five cases had resulted by "sheer accident," Thurgood Marshall later recalled, and had developed on the local level with no master plan involved. The cases had upset the association's timetable. After successfully assaulting segregation in professional and graduate schools, the NAACP had planned next to attack its presence in colleges and universities, then finally in secondary and elementary schools. The five cases before the Supreme Court in 1952, however, represented a giant leap to the elementary level, where most of the opposition to integration was concentrated. "We were kind of peeved," Marshall concluded. "We didn't want it, but we had it."[84]

The Supreme Court postponed argument on the cases until December 1952, ostensibly to allow sufficient time for the filing of briefs in all five suits. The delay also conveniently, and probably wisely, removed the cases from the politics of a presidential campaign, which both the court and the Department of Justice may have had in mind. At this point, the Truman administration entered the case. Although it has been suggested that Solicitor General Perlman opposed a government brief in the elementary-schools cases, a statement seemingly at variance with his record, he was no longer involved as a result of his resignation earlier in the year. Instead, Attorney General James P. McGranery, after visiting the White House and receiving Truman's approval,[85] filed an amicus curiae brief on December 2, 1952. He and Philip Elman were its signatories.

In his thirty-two page brief, McGranery struck hard at racial discrimination and its adverse effects both at home and abroad. Observing that Washington was "the window through which the world looks into our house," he placed the argument in the context "of the present world struggle between freedom and tyranny. . . . Racial discrimination provides grist for the Communist propaganda mills, and it raises doubts even among friendly nations as to the intensity of our devotion to the democratic faith." He then quoted Secretary of State Dean Acheson, who had informed him that because of racial discrimination during the past six years, "the damage to our foreign relations attributable to this source has become progressively greater."

The brief granted that the court might not need to reach the question of the validity of the separate-but-equal doctrine, but that if it did, *Plessy* v. *Ferguson* should be reexamined and overruled. For, as the government had already pointed out in the *Henderson*, *Sweatt*, and *McLaurin* cases, the doctrine was "wrong as a matter of constitutional law, history and policy. . . . In sum, the doctrine . . . is an unwarranted departure, based upon dubious assumptions of fact combined with a disregard of the basic purposes of the Fourteenth Amendment, from the fundamental principle that all Americans, whatever their race or color, stand equal and alike before the law."

In conclusion, Attorney General McGranery suggested that if the court overturned the Plessy doctrine, it "should take into account the need, not only for prompt vindication of the constitutional rights violated, but also for orderly and reasonable solution of the vexing problems which may arise in eliminating segregation." In a footnote, however, he called for immediate integration where "the separate schools are also physically unequal and inferior." He also suggested that the court might want to consider a second round of argument to determine a timetable for implementing integration, a recommendation which the court subsequently heeded.[86]

The McGranery brief contained neither psychological evidence about the debilitating effects of segregation nor an insistence that the separate-but-equal doctrine be overturned in these particular cases before the court. The NAACP took care of those arguments in its own brief and its oral presentation. Yet McGranery had vigorously insisted that segregation was unconstitutional and had no place in American life, thus reminding the court that eventually it would have to tangle with the basic question involved. The attorney general also informally requested permission to present an oral argument, but the court apparently rejected the plea on grounds that are as yet unclear.[87]

Not until June 1953 did the Supreme Court speak, and then only with muffled voice. On the same day as the *Thompson* decision, the court asked for more information and evidence from the participants in the *Brown* case, and it rescheduled argument for later in the year. This time, it also requested the new attorney general, Herbert Brownell, to submit both a brief and an oral presentation. Although initially discouraged, the NAACP lawyers soon concluded that a victory of glittering proportions was possible. Moreover, the death of Chief Justice Vinson in September 1953 persuaded some to hope for a more sympathetic replacement, and Thurgood Marshall later contended that Vinson would have caused "trouble."[88] Perhaps, but when Eisenhower quickly offered Earl Warren an interim appointment, they could not have breathed much easier, for Warren's libertarian attitude was a well-kept secret, as Eisenhower himself would shortly discover.

Attorney General Brownell was now on the spot, for he was having difficulty with the requested brief. The Eisenhower breakthrough in the South in the election of 1952 had further encouraged those Republican strategists who were urging a permanent political alliance with Dixie. A strong brief in favor of desegregation would damage that possibility. Yet, some Republican leaders were still committed to the doctrine of equality and were also impressed with the Negro vote in the North. Above all, no one, apparently not even Brownell, knew exactly where Eisenhower stood on the question.[89]

The result was a compromise brief, a cool, dry, 188-page exposition prepared under the direction of Assistant Attorney General J. Lee Rankin and Philip Elman. Its purpose, Brownell explained to curious newsmen, was to present "an objective non-adversary discussion of the questions stated in the court's order of reargument." In short, it equivocated. Although the Brownell brief insisted that the Supreme Court had the authority to pass on the question of segregation and that the "primary and pervasive purpose of the Fourteenth Amendment . . . was to secure for Negroes full and complete equality before the law and to abolish all legal distinctions based on race or color," the brief avoided all discussion of the separate-but-equal doctrine and refused to recommend any action to the court. "Attorney General Brownell's brief was a side-step," wrote columnist Doris Fleeson indignantly. "He told the court it had the power to decide the case. He did not—in contrast to Attorney General McGranery for the Truman administration— tell them they ought to decide it against segregation."[90]

Justice William O. Douglas was also irritated with the brief's evasiveness. When Assistant Attorney General Rankin presented oral argument to the court, Douglas interrupted to ask if it was the department's position "that the court could decide the question either way?" Then, and not before, did the Justice Department indicate its position. "No," Rankin replied, "the court can find only one answer"—which was that the Fourteenth Amendment did not permit segregation on the basis of color. He added that the department associated itself with the views of former Attorney General McGranery, which the Brownell brief had ignored.[91]

On May 17, 1954, Chief Justice Warren, speaking for a unanimous court, announced the epochal decision of *Brown* v. *Board of Education of Topeka*, which broke the back of legalized segregation in America. Because of the inconclusiveness of the historical evidence concerning the intent of the framers of the Fourteenth Amendment, the court had concentrated on the psychological effects of segregation. Citing the intangible but persuasive arguments and evidence introduced in the *Sweatt* and *McLaurin* cases, and referring in footnotes to psychological studies published between 1944 and 1952, Warren announced that segregation "has a detrimental effect upon the colored children. The impact is greater when it has the sanction of the law; for the policy of separating the races is usually interpreted as denoting the inferiority of the Negro groups. A sense of inferiority affects the motivation of a child to learn." Therefore, he noted, "whatever may have been the extent of psychological knowledge at the time of *Plessy* v. *Ferguson*, this finding is amply supported by modern authority. Any language in *Plessy* v. *Ferguson* contrary to this finding is rejected. We conclude that in the field of public education the doctrine of 'separate but equal' has no place. Separate educational facilities are inherently unequal." The *Brown* decision prohibited segregation in all states, and a separate opinion also ruled it unconstitutional in the District of Columbia.[92]

No one will ever know what the decision might have been had Chief Justice Vinson lived. But as Milton R. Konvitz has written, the decisions of the Vinson court in 1950 in the *Sweatt*, *McLaurin*, and

Henderson cases "put the explosives under the Plessy decision" and laid the basis for the *Brown* opinion. And all of the decisions, he contended, were made possible through the activities of the NAACP, numerous other civil-rights organizations, and, "most important of all, the United States, represented by the Solicitor General and the Department of Justice."[93]

The *Brown* decision of 1954 was indeed a fitting climax to the egalitarian thrust of the Truman administration and a worthy tribute to those who assisted, and occasionally prodded, the president and his successor in their attempts to eradicate injustice in America. As a columnist for the *Chicago Defender* noted shortly before the court convened in December 1952: "The high court will not decide the school segregation issue before Mr. Truman says his goodbyes at the White House. But whatever the outcome, it will be remembered as the president's final courageous official blow to strengthen democracy at home and peace in the world."[94]

Yet if the *Brown* decision was an end, it was also a beginning. Although some civil-rights advocates permitted the euphoria of the moment to blind them to the problems of the future, others were acutely aware of what was ahead. In an editorial in February 1953 the *Journal and Guide* correctly predicted the end of legalized segregation in American life. But the editor also reminded his readers of the years of discrimination in which residential lines "have been drawn almost as tightly as precinct or county boundaries. Removing the discriminatory school segregation statutes will not scramble the population. The school populations will remain geographically situated within the boundaries that have been painstakingly established by segregation laws and practices during the past 85 years. The process of change in this area of race relations will be painfully slow."[95] It would also be "painfully slow" in other areas as well, although at this point the Eisenhower administration clearly had the initiative. Unfortunately for America, it rarely chose to pursue it.

15 ASSESSMENT

Although the adaptation of minorities to American life has been varied, by the 1930s most immigrant groups had attained or approached equality of opportunity and rights. It was a different story, however, for those who because of color, geographical origins, or religion differed considerably in their backgrounds from the vast majority of Americans.

The 1930s marked a change in the trends affecting most of the nation's minorities, largely because of the New Deal's efforts to ameliorate their plight. Discrimination and segregation, however, were still standard principles in 1940 in the United States. Only Jews, chiefly because of their European background and advanced skills, were close to the economic and political means of American life. The condition of most Negroes, Indians, Mexican-Americans, and Oriental-Americans was still pitiful.

The Second World War brought substantial changes in the position of the minorities. All except Japanese-Americans profited from the prosperity generated by war production, and military service benefited many of the nonwhites who wore the nation's uniform. By 1945, minority-group employment and income stood at record levels, more opportunities for advancement had appeared, further skills had been acquired, and the National Association for the Advancement of Colored People was emerging as a major political force. Equally important, minority-group leaders resolved not only that their people should keep what they had gained but that they should press harder for equality. In this they sought, with some success, to ally with one another and with sympathetic elements among the majority of Americans.

There were some signs that civil-rights gains would continue in the postwar period. After Franklin Roosevelt's death in 1945, the new president, Harry S. Truman, urged Congress to establish a permanent FEPC and appointed Irvin C. Mollison to the Customs Court, the highest judicial position at that time for an American Negro. Yet, hope soon receded for minorities. They not only experienced cutbacks in jobs but had to compete in the shrinking job market with returning soldiers and sailors. With increasing unemployment and rapid demobilization came mounting racial tensions. Particularly in the South and West, many returning minority-group servicemen faced indignities, intimidation, and even violence. Urban housing, already cramped because of large-scale migration to the cities, worsened as demobilization progressed. Despite strenuous efforts by civil-rights lobbyists, all civil-rights measures before Congress failed, except for the Indian Claims Commission Act of 1946.

It was violence, however, the unwarranted assaults on blacks in 1946, that regenerated civil-rights progress. Outraged, Negro leaders demanded action; and they were supported by a surge of concern among whites. The Department of Justice and the White House sought to curb attacks on nonwhites. Because of the inadequacy of federal laws, however, the government had only a paper sword to wield in the form of investigations and prosecutions, but that at least harassed alleged assailants. Pressure was also brought to bear on southern governors to uphold state laws. Whether these actions, and the nation's shocked reaction to the assaults, were primarily responsible for the calming of tensions remains arguable. Nevertheless, racial violence declined during the latter part of 1946 and remained on a low level for five years.

In effect, 1946 was a turning point, if only because of a conjunction of pressure from indignant civil-rights groups with rising White House determination to forestall a reoccurrence of the racial violence and intolerance that had marred the post–World War I period. And this was set against the willingness of public opinion for some action on civil rights. The immediate result was the scrutinizing of the whole range of minority problems, mainly through the instrumentality of the President's Committee on Civil Rights, which Truman appointed late in 1946.

There is no need here to itemize the actions of the Truman administration or the civil-rights advances in the various sectors of American life. The results can be discussed by categories. The president became the prime educator for the need to secure the rights and dignity of all citizens, and he strove to make opportunity and treatment more nearly equal for minorities in the civil service and the armed forces. He worked, though with little success, for enactment of a cohesive civil-rights program and, with greater success, to block legislation that would jeopardize minority interests. Truman also made occasional appointments of minority-group members to public offices and sought to heighten self-government in America's territories. The federal government became increasingly sensitive to complaints about discrimination in discharging public services. The Justice Department encouraged law officers everywhere to give an even break to minority peoples and intervened, through its amicus curiae briefs, to gain favorable court decisions in civil-rights cases. Like Truman, the department came to accept the argument that segregation and discrimination were inseparable problems, for segregation was a pattern that fostered and perpetuated discrimination. The Supreme Court, building on earlier decisions that had combated the widespread disenfranchisement of nonwhites and segregation in Pullman cars and interstate buses, responded in a series of cases that withdrew the legal bases for restrictive covenants, unequal school facilities, and segregated railway dining cars. Progress also occurred on state and local levels, as an increasing number of laws and ordinances struck at discrimination in hiring, public housing, schooling, and the use of public facilities. Some change came in private areas, as minorities increasingly participated in a wider variety of activities and jobs. Noteworthy was the extent to which civil rights and minorities became acceptable themes in literature and public discussions; and highly significant were Hollywood's changing image of the Negro and the breakthrough of blacks in organized athletics.

These developments, together with advances in social-security benefits, minimum-wage levels, and health programs, constituted a substantial step forward. Minorities, particularly Negroes, occupied a place in government planning and programs as they never had before. They saw heartening responses to their pressures and, from time to time, even tangible results. The pace of change and encouragement had quickened beyond what their leaders had envisaged in 1945.

Progress came about for a number of reasons. Thanks considerably to wartime gains, minority groups—especially Jews and Negroes—now had the money, inspiration, organization, and leaders to fight for advancement. And they had the goals. America's wartime propaganda had held these goals on high; and this reinforced and refined what minority citizens had been telling themselves for years. Moreover, the spate of books and articles on minority problems, beginning in 1940, had well publicized their plight and potential. Migration, especially of blacks to the North, and the growing number of minority-group citizens who could vote honed their sensitivity to the possibility of change and heightened their political power. Minorities were all the stronger because of their informal postwar coalition and because of the greater concern of white liberals and a number of religious and labor leaders, who acted sometimes out of principle and sometimes in search of quid pro quo. In short, minorities had gained a secure foothold in the foothills of American democracy, enabling them to exert pressure that could be felt in the cold high range of the nation's institutions.

Crucial to effective minority pressure was the fact that government was more than ever receptive to it. Harry S. Truman was a man intent upon further securing constitutional guarantees to all Americans—a man who wanted to do, as he often said, "the right thing." Here, too, was a president who increasingly turned to advisers who were not only sympathetic to the quest for equal rights and opportunities, but were also keenly aware of the political advantages, at home and abroad, of assisting that quest. At home, the administration would gain more leverage with congressional liberals, the bedrock of support for the Fair Deal legislative program. The administration's stand on civil rights also strengthened it in vying for liberal and minority-group backing in Truman's bid for nomination and election in 1948. Abroad, America was under serious attack from international communism and from the emerging nonwhite nations because of the gap between its principles and practices in racial matters. As the cold war developed, the Truman administration sought to blunt communism's exploitation of the issue in order to enlist allies from among the new nations, or at least to keep them uncommitted.

The application of nonwhite pressure and the frequently positive response to it during the Truman years were aided by the increasing disposition of some white, Christian Americans to favor progress for minority groups. They were sickened by the brutality of Nazism and had accepted the egalitarian teachings of political liberals and leftists. Many Americans, especially among the young, read of the plight of minorities; some of them came increasingly in contact with Negroes, Jews, Mexican-Americans, Indians, and Oriental-Americans and found that they were in no way diminished or threatened.

The upshot was not a revolution in the lives of America's minority peoples, but by the end of the Truman administration substantial progress had been made. Although Congress had not enacted a fair employment practices law, by 1953 twelve states and thirty cities had adopted such legislation, though it was of varying effectiveness. The general conclusion of studies of fair employment legislation was that where it was enforced, it had an impact in reducing racial and religious discrimination in employment.[1] Of course, the labor requirements of the Korean War, President Truman's wartime National Manpower Mobilization Policy, and especially his Committee on Government Contract Compliance supplemented the work of fair employment agencies and private groups, such as the Urban League.

Generally favorable employment needs and public and private pressures for fair hiring practices created an unusually favorable job situation for minorities. Employment and income rates after World War II remained considerably higher than prewar levels. The coming of the Korean War opened opportunities even wider, and minorities experienced relatively little trouble in finding jobs of some kind. As of 1953, only 4.1 percent of the nonwhite labor force was unemployed, compared to 2.3 percent of whites. Median nonwhite family income rose from $1,614 to $2,338 between 1947 and 1952; and that income grew in its percentage of median white family income from 51 to 57—a record. There was also a great shift in the occupational categories of black Americans, from 19.3 percent in 1940 in professional, white collar, skilled, and semiskilled work to 37.1 by 1950.[2]

Other advances were evident by the end of the Truman administration. Racial minorities benefited from social-welfare measures, such as the 1950 amendments to the Social Security Act, which liberalized payments and covered additional workers, and health and minimum-wage programs. Some progress was made in opening eating places, hotels, parks, and theaters to minorities, although it was uneven and small in terms of the number of people affected. Some unions eliminated or relaxed their discriminatory practices. With little fanfare, the American Medical Association and many medical specialist societies dropped racial bars to membership; and by 1953 twenty-seven medical associations in six southern states and the District of Columbia had black members, whereas none had had any in 1947. Only one state nursing association refused Negro members by 1954. The nonwhite life-expectancy age jumped from 53.1 in 1940 to 61.7 in 1953, compared to 64.2 and 69.6 for whites over the same period. The gap was still monstrous, but it was closing.[3]

There were dramatic changes in schooling, too. The percentage of nonwhites from ages five to nineteen who were enrolled in school rose from 68.4 to 74.8, and of whites from 75.6 to 79.3, between 1940 and 1950. The median of school years completed increased during the decade from 5.7 to 7 for nonwhites and from 8.7 to 9.7 for whites; and the percentage of nonwhites in high school and college rose from 16.7 in 1940 to 20.6 in 1950. Indeed, Woodson and Wesley report that the number of Negroes in institutions of higher education had increased between 1940 and 1950 from 23,000 to 113,735. Partly because of fear that the Supreme Court would force integration in schools, southern states greatly expanded the outlay for Negro education between 1940 and 1952, with the per-pupil expenditure in nine states rising from $21.54 to $115.08, and capital outlay per pupil increasing from $.99 to $29.58, although the dollar increases for white schools were a bit larger. The gap in twelve southern states in the number of years of college training received by white and black teachers narrowed, however, and the dollar increase in average salaries for teachers was slightly larger for Negroes, rising $1,902 compared to $1,846 for whites.[4]

Furthermore, owner-occupied dwellings of nonwhites increased from 23.6 to 34.9 percent between 1940 and 1950, compared to 45.7 and 57 percent for whites. A veritable revolution occurred in the military services, accelerated by President Truman's actions and the Korean War, which was revealed primarily in greater desegregation, integration, and opportunity, but also in racial proportions of manpower strength. In the army the percentage of black officers grew from 1.7 to 2.9, and of enlisted men from 9.6 to 12.3, between 1949 and 1953; airforce figures showed an increase in black officers from 0.6 to 1.1 percent, and of Negro enlisted men from 5.1 to 8.6 percent. The marines and the navy went from virtually no black officers to precious few; and although the percentage of black enlisted men in the navy declined, it rose substantially in the Marine Corps—from 2.1 to 6.5.[5] In short, desegregation of the military was one of the most significant breakthroughs in civil rights in the twentieth century.

That more was not accomplished during the Truman years was disappointing and regrettable in terms of social justice and national welfare. Plainly, not enough whites were willing to go much further in combating discrimination and its effects through private actions or the work of state and local governments, and minorities did not possess sufficient strength to force more progress. The spur of civil-rights advocates was compelling, but the bridle of their opponents was almost proportionately discouraging. As black men struggled to rise economically, politically, and socially in the postwar period, they found themselves increasingly in competition with whites, many of whom felt such confrontation threatening and impossible to accept. Little more could have been expected of Congress, which did little, and of the Supreme Court, which accomplished much. The White House might have dared more—for example, a thoroughgoing attack on discrimination in the civil service and in the rendering of public services, additional appointments of minority-group officeholders and actively sympathetic whites, and the earlier formation of the Committee on Government Contract Compliance (with better financial support). Yet although Harry Truman often moved by fits and starts and left something to be desired, he was the first president to have a civil-rights program, the first to try to come to grips with the basic problems of minorities, and the first to condemn, vigorously and consistently, the presence of discrimination and inequality in America. His endeavors, courage, and accomplishments far surpassed those of his predecessors, and at a time when it would not have been difficult to have treated the civil-rights problem with soft soap alone. The record of the Truman years showed the strength of the American system in that progress was made; but it also revealed society's weakness in its inability, in a whirlpool of conflicting interests and pressures, to move forward either rapidly or wisely enough.

Nevertheless, the position of minorities in 1953 had improved. Jews rarely gave signs of feeling like an aggrieved or besieged minority. Oriental-Americans had moved forward on all fronts, so that today, for example, Japanese-Americans are more middle class than the white majority in terms of education and accomplishment. To be sure, most Indians and Mexican-Americans could complain that matters had not changed markedly for them; and the Puerto Ricans, who had flocked to the mainland to gain their fortunes, had received little. The largest minority by far—black Americans—had gained considerably, however inadequate their advances appear today.

In 1923 had minority leaders been told that the following year their people would possess what they did in 1953, it would have seemed a fantastic achievement. But what black, brown, and red Americans actually enjoyed in 1953 fell far short of fulfilling their aspirations. They too were children of the American heritage. Franklin Roosevelt made the same golden promises to them that he did to whites, and Harry Truman singled out the racial minorities for attention in 1948. The minority peoples knew, as they had witnessed during depression and war, what government could do when it applied its power. They saw the life styles of whites as depicted in motion pictures, advertising, and television. The lessening of discrimination, segregation, and violence was fine as far as it went; so was the increase in opportunities, income, and freedom. But these were not enough, and they were not all that the nation could give. It was clear that America had an obligation to grant more in order to provide the equality under law that it had for generations been promising. Moreover, in view of the cold war, the emergence of nonwhite nations, and the need for domestic stability, the United States could not afford less than full payment of its promises to all citizens—throughout the country, and soon.

Yet, by 1953, the omens were mixed. A new president had made promises, but Congress gave no signs of being less intransigent than in preceding years. Moreover, the civil-rights coalition had been seriously weakened as anti-Semitism diminished and Jews became increasingly caught up in the affairs of Israel and as Japanese-Americans became better integrated into society. During the 1950s, much of the energy of Democratic liberals was spent in combating McCarthyism and, after 1952, in efforts to regain political power. Many civil-rights advocates flagged in their work, stung by repeated charges of communism and even harassment by government agencies.[6] Minorities also were hindered by the repeated declarations that in a prosperous nation, they too *must* be prospering. Blacks found themselves increasingly alone in the civil-rights struggle; and Indians, Mexican-Americans, and Puerto Ricans were seldom in a position to help themselves, much less to help revivify the civil-rights coalition. During the Eisenhower years, some progress was made in education and home ownership. There were also the desegregation decision in *Brown* v. *Board of Education of Topeka*, rudimentary civil-rights legislation in 1957 and 1960, and advances in completing integration in the armed forces. The pace of progress, however, had plainly fallen off.

Had the civil-rights changes brought about during the years from 1945 to 1954 continued at least at the same pace, the adjustment of the races after the *Brown* decision might have been a happier story. But progress slackened. The rate of nonwhite unemployment rose to range between 7.5 and 12.6 percent—more than twice that of whites—between 1954 and 1962. The proportion of nonwhite income to white slid below that of the Korean War average, and the dollar gap in incomes widened alarmingly. The stark fact was that black, brown, and red Americans were not keeping pace economically.[7] Violence and intimidation were still standard commodities in race relations in many areas, and the political rights of most southern blacks were violated. Indeed, massive resistance to civil-rights gains rose in the South after the *Brown* decision.[8] Ghettos and reservations continued to exist with scant improvement. De facto segregation was as oppressive as legal segregation, and plenty of the latter still remained. The government under Dwight Eisenhower after 1954 was less effective, if not less concerned, with meeting minority problems than under Truman; and interest among white citizens declined. Traditional Negro leadership— primarily middle-class oriented—seemed too often during the Eisenhower years to sit back and wait for something to happen, but little did happen for the mass of blacks. Perhaps W. E. B. DuBois's "Talented Tenth" of the race had found satisfaction; but, contrary to expectations, they were not doing enough to raise their less happy brothers with them. Until the mass of Negroes, and indeed of Indians and Spanish-speaking Americans, was better educated and was afforded opportunities for decent work and dignified living, minority problems would remain a cancer in American life.

Yet the gains of the period 1945 to 1954 were not wasted. Not only did they represent some improvement in the conditions of minorities, but, more important, they contributed to consolidation of their goals and to the building of a base of power and skills, at least for blacks. Moreover, every small gain had bolstered hope for the achievement of greater gains. Indeed, by 1954, Negroes had the goals, the pride, and much of the tactics and financing necessary to enable them to press the struggle. Particularly, they had the potential leadership of their young people, a group that had been teethed on the rhetoric of black militancy and equal rights during the preceding fifteen years. Black aspirations had been spurred by what had been achieved by 1954 and by the example of what most whites and the more affluent nonwhites enjoyed. Because these aspirations were not reasonably met, frustration was the accomplishment. And as frustration grew after 1954, blacks drew increasingly on the skills, pride, and potential leadership that they had developed during the years after World War II; and in doing so, they lent support to the later development of similar movements among Indians, Mexican-Americans, and Puerto Ricans. America had let them down, but it had also provided them with the resources and spirit to press forward vigorously, on many fronts, by the 1960s and 1970s.

Notes

CHAPTER 1

1. Materials drawn upon for this chapter include Harold E. Fey and D'Arcy McNickle, *Indians and Other Americans* (New York, 1959); Theodore H. Haas, "The Legal Aspects of Indian Affairs from 1887 to 1957," *Annals*, CCCXI (May 1957); William T. Hagan, *American Indians* (Chicago, 1961); Stuart Levine and Nancy O. Lurie, eds., *The American Indian Today* (rev. ed.; Baltimore, 1970); Charles T. Loram and Thomas F. McIlwraith, eds., *The North American Indian Today* (Toronto, 1943); Alden Stevens, "Whither the American Indian?" *Survey Graphic*, XXIX (Mar. 1940); National Archives and Records Service, Washington, D.C., Record Group 48, Records of the Secretary of the Interior (hereafter cited as RG 48): Felix S. Cohen to M. K. Bennett, Aug. 4, 1944; Roosevelt Papers, Franklin D. Roosevelt Library (hereafter cited as FDRL): John Collier to Roosevelt, Jan. 19, 1945, OF 6C.
2. Oscar Handlin, *The Newcomers: Negroes and Puerto Ricans in a Changing Metropolis* (Cambridge, Mass., 1959), p. 142.
3. See Carey McWilliams, *North from Mexico: The Spanish-speaking People of the United States* (Philadelphia, 1949), especially pp. 187–88; Frank Stokes, "Let the Mexicans Organize!" *Nation*, CXLIII (Dec. 19, 1936); Ruth D. Tuck, "Behind the Zoot Suit Riots," *Survey Graphic*, XXXII (Aug. 1943); Roosevelt Papers, FDRL: E. G. Trimble to L. W. Cramer, June 24, Oct. 25, 1943; Malcolm Ross to Jonathan Daniels, Nov. 4, 1943; Ross et al. to Roosevelt, Jan. 31, 1944; Coordinator of Inter-American Affairs, "Confidential Report of the Conference on the Spanish-speaking Minority Program in the Southwest, July 12–14, 1943," OF 4245G; *Inter-American*, II (Sept. 1943), p. 8.
4. For pertinent information on Japanese-Americans, see Yamato Ichihashi, *Japanese in the United States: A Critical Study of the Problems of the Japanese Immigrants and Their Children* (Stanford, Calif., 1932); Morton Grodzins, *Americans Betrayed: Politics and the Japanese Evacuation* (Chicago, 1949); Jacobus tenBroek et al., *Prejudice, War and the Constitution* (Berkeley, Calif., 1958); Campbell C. Johnson, *Special Groups*, 2 vols. (Washington, 1953), I; Roosevelt Papers, FDRL: draft and copy of Roosevelt to H. L. Stimson, Feb. 1, 1943, OF 197; United States War Relocation Authority, *WRA: A Story of Human Conservation* (Washington, 1946); Leonard Broom and John I. Kitsuse, *The Managed Casualty: The Japanese-American Family in World War II* (Berkeley, Calif., 1956).
5. Regarding Chinese-Americans, see Rose Hum Lee, *The Chinese in the United States of America* (Hong Kong, 1960); Rose Hum Lee, "A Century of Chinese and American Relations," *Phylon*, XI (Third Quarter 1950); Shien-woo Kung, *Chinese in American Life* (Seattle, Wash., 1962); Morton Fried, ed., *Colloquium on Overseas Chinese* (New York, 1958); Fred W. Riggs,

Pressures on Congress: A Study of the Repeal of Chinese Exclusion (New York, 1950).

6. Arnold and Caroline Rose, *America Divided: Minority Group Relations in the United States* (New York, 1948), p. 324.

7. See Donald S. Strong, *Organized Anti-Semitism in America: The Rise of Group Prejudice During the Decade 1930–40* (Washington, 1941); Rose, *America Divided*; Marshall Sklare, ed., *The Jews: Social Patterns of an American Group* (Glencoe, Ill., 1958); Oscar Handlin, *Adventure in Freedom: Three Hundred Years of Jewish Life in America* (New York, 1954); American Jewish Committee, *Annual Report, 1945* (New York, 1946).

8. *Pittsburgh Courier*, Apr. 4, 1942; *Amsterdam News* (New York), Apr. 25, 1942; Adam Clayton Powell, Jr., *Marching Blacks: An Interpretive History of the Rise of the Black Common Man* (New York, 1945), p. 165.

9. For materials on black Americans during the 1930s, see Columbia University, Roy Wilkins oral history transcript; Leslie H. Fishel, Jr., "The Negro in the New Deal Era," *Wisconsin Magazine of History*, XLVIII (Winter 1964–1965); Raymond Wolters, *Negroes and the Great Depression: The Problem of Economic Recovery* (Westport, Conn., 1970); Arthur W. Mitchell, "The New Deal and the Negro," *Congressional Record*, 76th Cong., 3d sess., pp. 3019–26; Allen F. Kifer, "The Negro Under the New Deal, 1933–1941" (Ph.D. diss., University of Wisconsin, 1961); Frank Freidel, *F.D.R. and the South* (Baton Rouge, La., 1965); Powell, *Marching Blacks*; Roi Ottley, *"New World A-Coming": Inside Black America* (Boston, 1943); Constance McLaughlin Green, *The Secret City: A History of Race Relations in the Nation's Capital* (Princeton, N.J., 1967); Charles R. Lawrence, "Negro Organizations in Crisis: Depression, New Deal, World War II" (Ph.D. diss., Columbia University, 1952); Laurence J. W. Hayes, *The Negro Federal Government Worker: A Study of His Classification Status in the District of Columbia, 1883–1938* (Washington, 1941).

10. Regarding Negroes, economics, and World War II, see Herbert Garfinkel, *When Negroes March: The March on Washington Movement in the Organizational Politics for FEPC* (Glencoe, Ill., 1959); Louis C. Kesselman, *The Social Politics of FEPC: A Study in Reform Pressure Movements* (Chapel Hill, N.C., 1948); Louis Ruchames, *Race, Jobs & Politics: The Story of FEPC* (New York, 1953); Robert C. Weaver, *Negro Labor: A National Problem* (New York, 1946); F. Ray Marshall, *The Negro and Organized Labor* (New York, 1965); Columbia University, Benjamin McLaurin oral history transcript; Richard M. Dalfiume, "The 'Forgotten Years' of the Negro Revolution," *Journal of American History*, LV (June 1968); John P. Davis, ed., *The American Negro Reference Book* (Englewood Cliffs, N.J., 1966); Kathryn Blood, *Negro Women War Workers* (Washington, 1945); John A. Davis, "Nondiscrimination in the Federal Services," *Annals*, CCXLIV (Mar. 1946); Jessie P. Guzman, ed., *Negro Year Book: A Review of Events Affecting Negro Life, 1941–1946* (Tuskegee, Ala., 1947).

11. For material on blacks and the armed forces during the war, see Ulysses Lee, *The United States Army in World War II: Special Studies: The Employment of Negro Troops* (Washington, 1966); Richard M. Dalfiume, *Desegregation of the U.S. Armed Forces: Fighting on Two Fronts, 1939–1953* (Columbia, Mo., 1969); Jean Byers, "A Study of the Negro in the Military Service" (mimeographed; Washington, Department of Defense, 1950); Den-

nis D. Nelson, *The Integration of the Negro into the U.S. Navy* (New York, 1951); Richard M. Dalfiume, "Military Segregation and the 1940 Presidential Election," *Phylon*, XXX (Spring 1969); Johnson, *Special Groups*, I; Herbert Aptheker, "Literacy, The Negro and World War II," *Journal of Negro Education*, XV (Fall 1946).

12. Guzman, *Negro Year Book, 1941–46*, pp. 62–64, 297–98; *Mitchell v. U.S.*, 313 U.S. 80; *Smith v. Allwright*, 321 U.S. 649; Donald R. Matthews and James W. Prothro, *Negroes and the New Southern Politics* (New York, 1966) pp. 17–18; V. O. Key, Jr., *Southern Politics in State and Nation* (New York, 1949), pp. 518–22, 578.

13. United States Housing and Home Finance Agency, *Housing of the Nonwhite Population, 1940–1947* (Washington, 1948), p. 4.

14. Lawrence, "Negro Organizations in Crisis," pp. 78, 103.

CHAPTER 2

1. *Crisis*, LII (May 1945), p. 129.

2. *Afro-American* (Baltimore), Apr. 21, 1945; *Journal and Guide* (Norfolk), Apr. 21, 1945; *Chicago Defender*, Apr. 21, 1945.

3. *Crisis*, LII (May 1945), p. 129; *Amsterdam News*, Apr. 28, 1945.

4. Franklin D. Mitchell, *Embattled Democracy: Missouri Democratic Politics, 1919–1932* (Columbia, Mo., 1968), p. 131; *Call* (Kansas City), Aug. 24, Nov. 9, 1934, Jan. 17, 1936, Dec. 1, 1939, Jan. 24, 1941; Lyle W. Dorsett, *The Pendergast Machine* (New York, 1968), pp. 71–72, 75, 82; Alonzo Hamby, "Harry S. Truman and American Liberalism, 1945–1948" (Ph.D. diss., University of Missouri, 1965), pp. 39–40.

5. *Call*, Aug. 3, Sept. 28, 1934, June 5, May 10, 1935, Sept. 3, 1937, July 1, 1938, May 3, 1940; Eugene F. Schmidtlein, "Truman the Senator" (Ph.D. diss., University of Missouri, 1962), p. 98.

6. Schmidtlein, "Truman the Senator," pp. 222, 134; *Call*, June 21, 1940; Jonathan Daniels, *The Man of Independence* (Philadelphia, 1950), p. 338; *Congressional Record*, 76th Cong., 3d sess., App., p. 5368.

7. *Congressional Record*, 76th Cong., 3d sess., App., p. 5368.

8. David S. Horton, ed., *Freedom and Equality: Addresses by Harry S. Truman* (Columbia, Mo., 1960), p. xv; *Courier*, June 28, 1941, Aug. 4, 1944; *Amsterdam News*, Feb. 28, 1944; *Call*, Apr. 20, 1945; *Chicago Defender*, Aug. 5, 1944; Kesselman, *The Social Politics of FEPC*, p. 209.

9. Jewish Telegraphic Agency, *Daily News Bulletin*, Apr. 15, 1945; *Chicago Sun*, Mar. 18, 1945.

10. Louis Wirth, "The Unfinished Business of American Democracy," *Annals*, CCXLIV (Mar. 1946), 4–7; *Chicago Defender*, Apr. 27, 1946; Charles E. Silberman, *Crisis in Black and White* (New York, 1964), pp. 60–62, 64; Wilson Record, *Race and Radicalism: The NAACP and the Communist Party in Conflict* (Ithaca, N.Y., 1964), pp. 186–87.

11. Record, *Race and Radicalism*, pp. 126, 130; *Chicago Defender*, Nov. 17, 1945.

12. *Chicago Defender*, June 2, May 26, Apr. 21, 1945.

13. *Amsterdam News*, Aug. 25, 1945; Earl Spangler, *The Negro in Minnesota* (Minneapolis, Minn., 1961), p. 129; *Call*, Mar. 9, 1945.

14. A. A. Liveright, "The Community and Race Relations," *Annals*, CCXLIV (Mar. 1946), 115–16; James S. Twohey Associates, *Weekly Analysis of News-*

paper Opinion (1944) (Washington, 1944), passim; *Twohey Analysis of Newspaper Opinion* (1945) (Washington, 1945), p. 2 and passim.

15. *Afro-American*, Feb. 24, 1945; *Call*, Mar. 16, 1945; American Jewish Committee, *On Three Fronts: Thirty-ninth Annual Report, 1945* (New York, 1946), pp. 27–30.

16. *Public Papers of the Presidents of the United States, Harry S. Truman, 1945* (Washington, 1961–1966; hereafter cited as *Public Papers* with the date noted), pp. 1–3, 5, 10–11; *Call*, Apr. 27, 1945.

17. Harry S. Truman Papers, Harry S. Truman Library (hereafter cited as HSTL): Presidential Appointments Books, 1945; Walter White, *A Man Called White* (New York, 1948), pp. 299–300; NAACP Papers, Library of Congress: Report of the Secretary (for the June 1945 Meeting of the Board).

18. NAACP Papers: Report of the Secretary (for the June 1945 Meeting of the Board); Arthur B. Spingarn Papers, Library of Congress: Walter White to the NAACP Board, May 9, 1945.

19. *Public Papers, 1945*, p. 142.

20. Truman Papers, HSTL: D. K. Niles to Edwin McKim, May 22, 1945, OF 594; "Statement on Behalf of the Negro Newspaper Publishers Association to the President," filed June 6, 1945, OF 93; White to Truman, May 19, 1945, OF 93; *Call*, June 1, 1945.

21. *Call*, Dec. 22, 1944; Kesselman, *The Social Politics of FEPC*, passim; Ruchames, *Race, Jobs & Politics*, pp. 199–200.

22. *Call*, Jan. 5, 1945; *Amsterdam News*, Jan. 6, 1945; *Chicago Defender*, Mar. 17, 1945; Ruchames, *Race, Jobs & Politics*, p. 202; *Afro-American*, Jan. 13, Mar. 3, 1945.

23. Stanley H. Smith, *Freedom to Work* (New York, 1955), pp. 50–52, 54; *Chicago Defender*, Sept. 15, 1945; Kesselman, *The Social Politics of FEPC*, p. 212, chap. 11; Ruchames, *Race, Jobs & Politics*, p. 122; Truman Papers, HSTL: undated Memorandum re letter of Mary T. Norton to Truman, June 1, 1945, OF 40 Misc.; *Afro-American*, June 2, 1945.

24. *Public Papers, 1945*, pp. 104–5; Truman Papers, HSTL: Truman to Dennis Chavez, June 5, 1945, OF 40; *Courier*, June 16, 1945; *Washington Daily News*, June 6, 1945; *Amsterdam News*, June 16, 1945.

25. Truman Papers, HSTL: Truman to H. A. Atkinson, June 18, 1945, OF 40 Misc.; Kesselman, *The Social Politics of FEPC*, p. 213; *Call*, July 6, 1945; *Public Papers, 1945*, pp. 125, 254.

26. Ruchames, *Race, Jobs & Politics*, pp. 200–203; Smith, *Freedom to Work*, p. 51.

27. Ruchames, *Race, Jobs & Politics*, pp. 122–27.

28. Ibid., pp. 127–30.

29. Ibid., pp. 130–32; *Call*, July 20, 1945.

30. *Chicago Defender*, Sept. 15, 1945.

31. *St. Louis Argus*, May 25, 1945; *Afro-American*, June 2, Aug. 11, 1945; *Call*, May 25, June 15, 1945; *Chicago Defender*, Apr. 21, July 7, 1945; *Courier*, July 7, 14, Aug. 11, 1945.

32. *Call*, Sept. 28, 14, Oct. 12, 26, 1945; *Courier*, Sept. 29, Oct. 10, 1945; *Afro-American*, Sept. 29, Oct. 13, 1945; *Journal and Guide*, Oct. 13, 1945; *Chicago Defender*, Oct. 13, 1945; *Crisis*, LII (Nov. 1945), p. 313.

33. *Courier*, Sept. 29, Oct. 13, 1945; *Amsterdam News*, Aug. 25, 1945; Davis, "Nondiscrimination in the Federal Services," p. 73; A. B. Spingarn Papers:

Washington Bureau NAACP Legislative Action Letter #3, Feb. 24, 1945; *Afro-American*, Dec. 29, 1945; *New York Herald Tribune*, June 13, 1945; Truman Papers, HSTL: P. B. Fleming to Truman, Nov. 9, 1945; Memorandum, Nov. 26, 1945, OF 285D; *Congressional Record*, 79th Cong., 1st sess., pp. 12547–49; *Call*, Nov. 30, 1945.

34. Truman Papers, HSTL: National Urban League, "Racial Aspects of Reconversion—A Report to the President," Aug. 27, 1945, OF 93.
35. *Public Papers, 1945*, pp. 263–309, 475–91.
36. Ruchames, *Race, Jobs & Politics*, p. 132; *Call*, Aug. 31, 1945; Truman Papers, HSTL: Memorandum, Aug. 22, 1945; FEPC, Report to the President, Aug. 27, 1945; A. P. Randolph to C. G. Ross, Aug. 31, 1945; Randolph to Mr. Conley (Matthew Connelly?), Sept. 6, 1945, OF 40; *Afro-American*, Sept. 8, 1945.
37. *Crisis*, LII (Oct. 1945), p. 281.
38. *Crisis*, LII (Dec. 1945), p. 345; Truman Papers, HSTL: A. P. Randolph to C. G. Ross, Aug. 31, 1945; Memorandum, Sept. 4, 1945; Randolph to Mr. Conley (Matthew Connelly?), Sept. 6, 1945; Randolph to Truman, Sept. 29, 1945; M. J. Connelly to Randolph, Oct. 4, 16, 1945; Randolph to Connelly, Oct. 10, 19, 1945, OF 40; *Chicago Defender*, Oct. 13, 1945. David K. Niles apparently directed the strategy of keeping Randolph at arm's length; see Truman Papers, HSTL: M. J. Connelly to Niles, Oct. 2, 13, 1945, OF 40.
39. *Public Papers, 1945*, p. 498.
40. Truman Papers, HSTL: C. H. Houston to Truman, Nov. 25, 1945, OF 40; *Call*, Dec. 7, 1945.
41. Truman Papers, HSTL: C. H. Houston to Truman, Dec. 3, 1945; Truman to Houston, Dec. 7, 1945, OF 40; *Journal and Guide*, Dec. 8, 1945; *Call*, Dec. 7, 1945.
42. NAACP Papers: Report of the Secretary (for the December 1945 Meeting of the Board); Truman Papers, HSTL: Walter White to Truman, Dec. 12, 1945, OF 40 Misc.
43. National Archives and Records Service, Washington, D.C., Record Group 228, Records of the Fair Employment Practices Committee (hereafter cited as RG 228): Malcolm Ross to C. L. Horn, Dec. 14, 1945.
44. RG 228: Malcolm Ross to C. L. Horn, Dec. 17, 1945; Truman to Heads of All Government Departments, Agencies and Independent Establishments, Dec. 18, 1945; Executive Order 9664, Dec. 18, 1945.
45. Fair Employment Practices Committee, *Final Report* (Washington, 1946), pp. v–vii.

CHAPTER 3

1. *Public Papers, 1946*, pp. 1–8.
2. *Call*, Jan. 11, 1946; *Journal and Guide*, Jan. 12, 1946; *Afro-American*, Jan. 12, 19, 1946; Bureau of the Budget, Press Intelligence, "Summaries of Editorials and Column Comment from 9 Negro Weeklies," Jan. 11, 1946.
3. Ruchames, *Race, Jobs & Politics*, pp. 201–3.
4. *Public Papers, 1946*, pp. 52, 66, 40; *Amsterdam News*, Jan. 26, 1946.
5. *Public Papers, 1946*, p. 94; Truman Papers, HSTL: Truman to A. P. Randolph, Feb. 6, 1946, OF 40 Misc.

6. Ruchames, *Race, Jobs & Politics,* pp. 203–6; *Twohey Analysis of Newspaper Opinion,* Feb. 16, 1946.

7. *Chicago Defender,* Feb. 23, Mar. 9, 1946; *Afro-American,* Mar. 2, 29, 1946; Truman Papers, HSTL: M. J. Connelly to A. A. Hedgeman, Feb. 19, 1946, OF 40 Misc.; Truman to D. K. Niles, July 22, 1946, Philleo Nash Files; *Call,* Mar. 8, 29, 1946.

8. Stephen K. Bailey, *Congress Makes a Law: The Story Behind the Employment Act of 1946* (New York, 1950), pp. 227–32.

9. Guzman, *Negro Year Book, 1941–46,* pp. 260–61.

10. Truman Papers, HSTL: R. L. K. to M. J. Connelly, Mar. 25, 1946; Truman to Irving Brant, Mar. 29, 1946, OF 465B.

11. *Public Papers, 1946,* pp. 184–85; *Chicago Defender,* Apr. 13, 20, 1946; *Journal and Guide,* Apr. 27, 1946; *Afro-American,* Apr. 13, 1946.

12. *Washington Star,* Apr. 9, 1946; Truman Papers, HSTL: Philleo Nash to D. K. Niles, Apr. 9, 1946; Niles to Truman, Apr. 11, 1946, Nash Files.

13. *Public Papers, 1946,* pp. 192–93.

14. *Call,* Apr. 19, 1946; *Chicago Defender,* Apr. 20, 1946; *Afro-American,* Apr. 20, 1946; Truman Papers, HSTL: J. H. Bankhead to Truman, Apr. 11, 1946; Truman to Bankhead, Apr. 13, 1946, OF 465B; *New York Times,* Aug. 1, 1946.

15. *Call,* Nov. 16, 1945; Lester B. Granger, "Racial Democracy—The Navy Way," *Common Ground,* VII (Winter 1947); Nelson, *Integration of the Navy,* p. 218; *Afro-American,* Jan. 19, 1946.

16. *Call,* Dec. 21, 1945; RG 80: SECNAV to ALNAV #423, Dec. 12, 1945; Nelson, *Integration of the Navy,* pp. 219–20.

17. Nelson, *Integration of the Navy,* pp. 102, 227; Byers, "The Negro in the Military Service," pp. 260–61; Stephen J. Spingarn Papers, HSTL: S. J. S. to Foley, Feb. 11, 1947; S. J. S. to B. L. Timmons, Feb. 17, 1947.

18. National Archives and Records Service, Washington, D.C., Record Group 107, Records of the Office of the Secretary of War (hereafter cited as RG 107): H. L. Stimson to A. J. May, July 20, 1945; Record Group 319, Records of the Army Staff (hereafter cited as RG 319): G. C. Marshall to J. J. McCloy, Aug. 25, 1945; RG 107: J. J. McC. to R. P. Patterson, Sept. 26, 1945, enclosing Truman K. Gibson, Jr., to J. J. McCloy, Sept. 24, 1945.

19. RG 107: J. J. McC. to R. P. Patterson, Nov. 24, 1945; *Chicago Defender,* Dec. 1, 1945; L. D. Reddick, "The Negro Policy of the American Army since World War II," *Journal of Negro History,* XXXVIII (April 1953), 196; Lawrence J. Paszek, "Negroes and the Air Force, 1939–1949," *Military Affairs,* XXXI (Spring 1967), 8.

20. C. C. Johnson, *Special Groups,* II, 160–69.

21. *Chicago Defender,* Mar. 16, 23, 1946; *Courier,* Mar. 16, 1946; *Crisis,* LIII (Apr. 1946), p. 105; *Amsterdam News,* Apr. 13, 1946.

22. C. C. Johnson, *Special Groups,* I, 175–76, II, 200–201; *Journal and Guide,* Oct. 12, 1946; RG 319: R. P. Patterson to J. O. Dedmon, Jr., Nov. 18, 1946; H. C. Petersen to Mrs. Carl Anthonsen, Mar. 28, 1947; *Afro Magazine,* Feb. 22, 1947, p. M-3; Byers, "The Negro in the Military Service," pp. 262–63.

23. Archibald J. Carey, Jr., Papers, Chicago Historical Society: M. H. Ray to A. J. Carey, Oct. 31, 1946.

24. *Journal and Guide,* May 10, 1947.

25. *Courier,* Sept. 29, 1945; *Call,* Dec. 7, 14, 1945, Jan. 11, 1946.

26. Truman Papers, HSTL: Press Conference #51, Mar. 1, 1946, White House Press File; D. K. Niles to A. C. Powell, Jr., June 19, 1946, OF 8B; *Call,* Mar. 8, 1946; *Journal and Guide,* July 20, 1946; *Courier,* Mar. 16, 1946.

27. *Call,* Mar. 21, 28, 1947; *Chicago Defender,* Mar. 29, 1947; *Afro-American,* Mar. 29, 1947; *Journal and Guide,* Mar. 7, 1953; American Jewish Congress and National Association for the Advancement of Colored People, *Civil Rights in the United States in 1953: A Balance Sheet of Group Relations* (New York, 1954), p. 124 (hereafter cited as AJC and NAACP, *Balance Sheet,* with appropriate date).

28. *Washington Post,* July 26, 1946; *Public Papers, 1946,* p. 358; Truman Papers, HSTL: "Negroes Appointed to Policy-making Positions during President Truman's Administration," Mar. 4, 1947, Nash Files; *Afro-American,* May 4, 1946.

29. Clement E. Vose, *Caucasians Only: The Supreme Court, the NAACP, and the Restrictive Covenant Cases* (Berkeley, Calif., 1959), p. 64; RG 207: B. T. McGraw to W. W. Wyatt, Feb. 19, 1946; L. H. Keyserling to Robert Sevey and David Kadane, Apr. 17, 1946; RG 174: W. W. Wyatt to L. B. Schwellenbach, Aug. 13, 1946; *New York Times,* Aug. 7, 1946, June 17, 1948; *Amsterdam News,* Aug. 10, 1946, July 10, 1948.

30. *Morgan v. Virginia,* 328 U.S. 373.

31. United States War Liquidation Unit, Department of the Interior, *People in Motion: The Postwar Adjustment of the Evacuated Japanese Americans* (Washington, 1947), pp. 53, 55; Dillon S. Myer Papers, HSTL: J. A. Krug to Sam Rayburn, Apr. 24, 1946.

32. Roosevelt Papers, FDRL: H. L. Ickes to Roosevelt, May 14, 1937; Harold Smith to Roosevelt, July 22, 1939; John Blaneford, Jr., to Roosevelt, June 2, 1941; Roosevelt to Ickes, Aug. 18, 1941, OF 2825; Nancy O. Lurie, "The Indian Claims Commission Act," *Annals,* CCCXI (May 1957), 56–57.

33. Truman Papers, HSTL: Truman to director of the budget, Feb. 25, 1946; J. A. Krug to Truman, Aug. 1, 1946, OF 6aa; Public Law 726, 79th Cong., 2d sess.

34. Lurie, "The Indian Claims Commission Act," pp. 56–70; Fey and McNickle, *Indians and Other Americans,* pp. 105–6. The Indian Claims Commission was still in operation in 1970 and by then had approved $359 million in claims. Lawrence, Kans., *Journal-World,* Aug. 24, 1970.

35. Truman Papers, HSTL: Press Conference #51, Mar. 1, 1946, White House Press File; *Public Papers, 1946,* pp. 142–43.

36. Truman Papers, HSTL: Truman to Walter White, June 11, 1946, PPF 393; *Public Papers, 1946,* p. 347.

37. National Archives and Records Service, Washington, D.C., Record Group 250, Records of the Office of War Mobilization and Reconversion (hereafter cited as RG 250): C. G. Bolte to H. S. Truman, Aug. 12, 1946; J. D. Kingsley to J. R. Steelman, Aug. 5, 15, 21, 1946.

38. *Public Papers, 1946,* p. 423.

39. *Afro-American,* Dec. 29, 1945; Guzman, *Negro Year Book, 1941–46,* pp. 217–22, 246–52.

40. Truman Papers, HSTL, Columbia, Tennessee, File: D. K. Niles to Tom Clark, Mar. 6, 1946; Memorandum, Mar. 14, 1946; Clark to Niles, Mar. 22, 1946; Clark to Horace Frierson, Mar. 21, 1946; Niles to C. H. Foreman, Mar. 29, 1946, OF 93C.

41. Guzman, *Negro Year Book, 1941–46*, pp. 252–53.
42. Truman Papers, HSTL: Walter White to Truman, June 15, 1946; Sidney Hillman to Truman, June 24, 1946; R. R. Wright, Sr., to Truman, July 18, 1946, OF 93; *Chicago Defender*, May 4, July 20, 1946; *Afro-American*, July 6, 20, 1946; *Call*, Aug. 2, 1946.
43. *Call*, Aug. 2, 1946.
44. *Journal and Guide*, Aug. 3, 1946; *Amsterdam News*, Aug. 3, 1946; *Call*, Aug. 2, 9, 1946; NAACP Papers: Mary Jane Grunsfeld to Walter White, July 29, 1946; *Washington Star*, July 30, 1946.
45. *Call*, Aug. 2, 9, 1946; *New York Times*, July 31, 1946.
46. *Call*, Aug. 23, 1946; *Chicago Defender*, Aug. 10, 17, 1946; Guzman, *Negro Year Book, 1941–46*, pp. 253–54; NAACP Papers: Walter White et al. to H. S. Truman and Tom Clark, Aug. 6, 1946; Twohey Associates, *Twohey Analysis of Newspaper Opinion* (1946) (Washington, 1946), passim; *Journal and Guide*, Aug. 17, 1946.
47. Robert K. Carr, "Screws v. United States, The Georgia Police Brutality Case," *Cornell Law Quarterly*, XXXIII (Sept. 1948), 48–67.
48. *Public Papers, 1946*, p. 368; *Call*, Aug. 23, 1946; *Journal and Guide*, Aug. 24, 1946.
49. Truman Papers, HSTL: C. G. Ross to D. K. Niles, Sept. 6, 1946; Ross to Truman, Sept. 12, 1946; Truman to L. B. Granger, Sept. 12, 1946, PPF 2685; *Chicago Defender*, Sept. 14, 1946.
50. White, *A Man Called White*, pp. 329–30.
51. Ibid., pp. 330–31; *Call*, Sept. 27, 1946; A. B. Spingarn Papers: NAACP Minutes of the Meeting of the Board of Directors, Nov. 10, 1947; Report of the Secretary for the October 1946 Meeting of the Board; NAACP Papers: "President Truman Sees Delegation Petitioning Action to End Mob Violence," Sept. 19, 1946; *New York Herald Tribune*, Nov. 9, 1947.
52. A. B. Spingarn Papers: NAACP Minutes of the Meeting of the Board of Directors, Nov. 10, 1947; Report of the Secretary for the October 1946 Meeting of the Board; White, *A Man Called White*, p. 331.
53. Truman Papers, HSTL: Paul Robeson to D. K. Niles, Sept. 19, 1946, OF 93A; *Call*, Sept. 27, 1946, Oct. 10, 1952, Nov. 9, 1951.
54. *Journal and Guide*, Sept. 28, 1946; *Chicago Defender*, Sept. 28, 1946; *Amsterdam News*, Sept. 28, 1946.
55. *Amsterdam News*, June 23, 1945; *Courier*, Aug. 6, 1949; *Call*, Apr. 16, 1948; Truman Library, HSTL: J. E. Hoover to Tom Clark, Clark to Hoover, both dated Sept. 24, 1946, President's Committee on Civil Rights Files.
56. Chapman Papers, HSTL: S. K. Padover memorandum, July 3, 1943; Roosevelt Papers, FDRL: H. W. Odum to Jonathan Daniels, Aug. 11, 1943; Daniels to Odum, Sept. 1, 1943; D. K. Niles, "The Minority Situation Today —A Suggested Program" [Aug. 1943], OF 4245G.
57. HSTL, Jonathan Daniels oral history transcript, pp. 24–25, 66; S. J. Spingarn Papers, HSTL: "Notes for My Commentary on Barton Bernstein Paper at Session of American Historical Association Convention on 'Civil Rights in the Truman Administration,'" 1966; S. J. Spingarn to D. R. McCoy, Apr. 4, 1969.
58. *Courier*, Nov. 8, May 31, 1947; Poppy Cannon, *A Gentle Knight: My Husband, Walter White* (New York, 1956), p. 31; *Call*, Oct. 10, 1952; Charles G. Ross Papers, HSTL: "The Washington Merry-Go-Round," Sept. 26, 1946, Pearson folder.

59. A. B. Spingarn Papers: Report of the [NAACP] Secretary for the October 1946 Meeting of the Board.
60. *Courier*, Oct. 5, 1946; *Chicago Defender*, Oct. 5, 1946.
61. *Call*, Feb. 8, July 19, 26, Aug. 9, Sept. 27, 1946; *Crisis*, LIII (Sept. 1946), 265; Alfred Steinberg, *The Man from Missouri: The Life and Times of Harry S. Truman* (New York, 1962), pp. 287–88.
62. Truman Papers, HSTL: Tom Clark to Truman, Oct. 11, 1946, OF 596A; *Chicago Defender*, Oct. 26, 1946; Daniels, *Man of Independence*, p. 340.
63. *Amsterdam News*, Nov. 16, 1946; *Afro-American*, Dec. 7, 1946; Carl T. Rowan, "Harry S. Truman and the Negro," *Ebony*, XV (Nov. 1959), 45; *Chicago Defender*, Oct. 18, 1952; *Courier*, Oct. 18, 1952; Daniels, *Man of Independence*, p. 339; S. J. Spingarn Papers, HSTL: Truman to Spingarn, Oct. 18, 1956.
64. *To Secure These Rights: The Report of the President's Committee on Civil Rights* (New York, 1947), pp. viii–ix.
65. *Washington Post*, Dec. 14, 1946; *Call*, Apr. 16, 1948; *Chicago Defender*, Dec. 7, 1946.
66. *Chicago Defender*, Dec. 14, 21, 1946; *Afro-American*, Dec. 14, 1946; *Call*, Dec. 20, 1946; *Courier*, Dec. 14, 1946, Jan. 18, 1947; *Amsterdam News*, Dec. 14, 1946.
67. *Call*, Dec. 20, 1946.

CHAPTER 4

1. United States War Liquidation Unit, *People in Motion*, p. 1, passim; William Caudill, "Japanese American Personality and Acculturation," *Genetic Psychology Monographs*, XLV (Feb. 1952), 7, 93; Leonard Bloom, "Will Our Nisei Get Justice?," *Christian Century*, LXV (Mar. 3, 1948), 268; *Courier*, Nov. 29, 1947.
2. Lee, *Chinese in the United States*, pp. 410, 17–18.
3. Haas, "Legal Aspects of Indian Affairs," p. 16; Chapman Papers, HSTL: O. L. Chapman to E. A. Badger, Sept. 11, 1947; *Public Papers, 1947*, pp. 503–4.
4. Kingsley Davis and Clarence Senior, "Immigration from the Western Hemisphere," *Annals*, CCLXII (Mar. 1949), 77–78; *Courier*, June 21, 1947; J. Milton Yinger and George E. Simpson, "The Integration of Americans of Mexican, Puerto Rican, and Oriental Descent," *Annals*, CCCIV (Mar. 1956), 127–28; *Amsterdam News*, Aug. 16, 1947; Josefina de Román, "New York's Latin Quarter," *Inter-American*, V (Jan. 1946), 36; Clarence Woodbury, "Our Worst Slum," *American Magazine*, CXLVIII (Sept. 1949), 131.
5. Yinger and Simpson, "The Integration of Americans of Mexican, Puerto Rican, and Oriental Descent," pp. 124–27; McWilliams, *North from Mexico*, pp. 272, 280–83.
6. Carey McWilliams, *A Mask for Privilege: Anti-Semitism in America* (Boston, 1948), pp. 132–41; Harold E. Fey, "Can Catholicism Win America?," *Christian Century*, LXI–LXII (Nov. 29, Dec. 6, 13, 20, 27, 1944, Jan. 3, 10, 17, 1945); Paul Blanshard, *American Freedom and Catholic Power* (Boston, 1949); James M. O'Neill, *Catholicism and American Freedom* (New York, 1952).
7. McWilliams, *Mask for Privilege*, pp. 114–41; Ruth G. Weintraub, *How*

Secure These Rights? (Garden City, N.Y., 1949), passim; Anti-Defamation League of B'nai B'rith, *Anti-Semitism in the United States in 1947* (New York, 1948), pp. 6–10, 28.

8. Gordon W. Allport, *The Nature of Prejudice* (Cambridge, Mass., 1954), p. xiv; Ellis O. Knox, "The Negro as a Subject of University Research in 1950," *Journal of Negro Education*, XXI (Winter 1952), 41; Frank S. Loescher, *The Protestant Church and the Negro: A Pattern of Segregation* (New York, 1948), pp. 41–45, 132–43, 50–63.

9. Nick Aaron Ford, "The Influence of Literature on the Civil Rights Revolution," *Afro Magazine*, Sept. 18, 1948, p. 7; Lovell, "Roundup," pp. 213–15; A. B. Spingarn Papers: Walter White to Spingarn, Sept. 14, 18, 1945; Memorandum to the Committee on Administration [NAACP] from Mr. White, Dec. 17, 1945.

10. *Amsterdam News*, Oct. 5, 1946; *Afro-American*, Aug. 24, Sept. 21, 1946, July 10, 1948; Guzman, *Negro Year Book, 1952*, pp. 42, 46–47, 96; W. Brooke Graves, *Fair Employment Practice Legislation in the United States: Federal—State—Municipal* (Washington, 1951), pp. 87–88; *Journal and Guide*, June 12, 1948; William Z. Foster, *The Negro People in American History* (New York, 1954), p. 498; Marshall, *The Negro and Organized Labor*, p. 49.

11. United States Office of Education, *Biennial Survey of Education in the United States 1952–1954*, chap. one (Washington, 1959), pp. 72–73, *Biennial Survey of Education in the United States 1946–48*, chap. four (Washington, 1951), pp. 7–8; Clayton D. Hutchins and Albert R. Munse, *Supplement—Expenditures for Education at the Midcentury* (Washington, 1954), pp. 38, 34; *Amsterdam News*, Apr. 26, 1947.

12. John Tracy Ellis, *American Catholicism* (Chicago, 1956), p. 146; Robin M. Williams, Jr., and Margaret W. Ryan, eds., *Schools in Transition: Community Experiences in Desegregation* (Chapel Hill, N.C., 1954), pp. 27–29.

13. *Afro-American*, Mar. 17, 1945, July 10, 1948; *Call*, May 2, 1947; *Chicago Defender*, Feb. 8, 1947; *Newsweek*, Sept. 1, 1947.

14. U.S. Housing and Home Finance Agency, *Housing of the Nonwhite Population, 1940–1947*, pp. 6–8, 4; Weintraub, *How Secure These Rights?*, pp. 21–22.

15. University of Chicago Committee on Education, Training and Research in Race Relations, *The Dynamics of State Campaigns for Fair Employment Practices Legislation* (Chicago, 1950), pp. 2–4, 7–8, 12. Not all of the state fair employment practices laws were effective.

16. *Equal Economic Opportunity: A Report by the President's Committee on Government Contract Compliance* (Washington, 1953), pp. 105, 107, 110.

17. Department of Commerce, *5th Annual Report of Banking Institutions Owned and Operated by Negroes* (Washington, 1947), pp. 5, 8; *6th Annual Report of Banking Institutions Owned and Operated by Negroes* (Washington, 1948), p. 7; *3rd Report of Savings and Loan Institutions Operated by Negroes* (Washington, 1948), p. 1; Emmer M. Lancaster, "Insurance Companies Owned and Operated by Negroes," *Business Information Service* (Nov. 1952), pp. 28–29.

18. *Courier*, Mar. 23, 1946; Bonita H. Valien, *The St. Louis Story: A Study of Desegregation* (New York, 1956), pp. 17–20, 23–26.

19. Kenneth B. Clark, "Candor about Negro-Jewish Relations," *Commentary*, I (Feb. 1946), 10; *Call*, May 24, 10, 1946.

20. McWilliams, *North from Mexico*, p. 282; *Afro-American*, Dec. 15, 1945, Aug. 17, May 11, 1946; *Call*, June 7, 1946, Apr. 4, May 3, 1947.
21. *Courier*, Feb. 23, 1946; A. B. Spingarn Papers: Walter White to F. H. LaGuardia, Dec. 22, 1946; Charles S. Johnson et al., *Into the Main Stream: A Survey of Best Practices in Race Relations in the South* (Chapel Hill, N.C., 1947), p. vii.
22. *Afro-American*, Mar. 22, Apr. 12, 1947; *Call*, June 20, 1947.
23. *Afro-American*, May 3, 1947, Oct. 9, 1948; *Call*, Apr. 9, 1948.
24. *Chicago Defender*, Nov. 1, 1947; McWilliams, *Mask for Privilege*, p. 228; AJC and NAACP, *Balance Sheet, 1949*, p. 70; Allport, *Nature of Prejudice*, p. xvii.
25. St. Clair Drake and Horace R. Cayton, *Black Metropolis: A Study of Negro Life in a Northern City* (New York, 1945), p. 767.
26. Edward R. Stettinius, Jr., "Human Rights in the United Nations Charter," *Annals*, CCXLIII (Jan. 1946), 2–3; *Crisis*, LIV (Apr. 1947), 105, (Mar. 1947), 73.
27. RG 228: Malcolm Ross to Dean Acheson, Apr. 3, 1946; FEPC, *Final Report*, p. 6; *Public Papers, 1948*, p. 122.
28. Kenesaw M. Landis, *Segregation in Washington: A Report of the National Committee on Segregation in the Nation's Capital* (Chicago, 1948), passim; *New York Times*, Dec. 17, 1948, Nov. 29, 1949.
29. A. B. Spingarn Papers: W. E. B. Du Bois to NAACP Secretary, Aug. 1, 1946; Du Bois to Mr. White, Nov. 24, 1947; Report of the [NAACP] Secretary for the November Meeting of the Board (1947); J. E. Baxter to Board Members and Spingarn, Jan. 23, 1948; White, *A Man Called White*, p. 358.
30. *People's Voice* (New York), Nov. 8, 1947.
31. A. B. Spingarn Papers: W. E. B. Du Bois to Walter White, Nov. 24, 1947; NAACP Board of Directors Minutes, Sept. 13, 1948; Guzman, *Negro Year Book, 1952*, pp. 329–30.

CHAPTER 5

1. *Afro-American*, Dec. 7, 1946.
2. *Public Papers, 1947*, pp. 9, 29–31, 37.
3. Guzman, *Negro Year Book, 1952*, p. 47; National Association for the Advancement of Colored People, *Annual Report for 1947* (New York, 1948), p. 40; Carey Papers: C. W. Brooks to A. J. Carey, Jr., Mar. 19, 1947.
4. Smith, *Freedom to Work*, pp. 51–52, 55; *Public Papers, 1947*, pp. 311–13; Truman Papers, HSTL: A. P. Randolph to Truman, June 30, 1947, Sept. 24, 1947; M. J. Connelly to D. K. Niles, July 2, Sept. 25, 1947, Nash Files; RG 174: L. B. Schwellenbach to R. A. Taft, Aug. 12, 1947.
5. NAACP, *Annual Report for 1947*, pp. 35–36; *Courier*, July 19, 1947; 61 Stat. 770; United States Senate Library, *Presidential Vetoes* (Washington, 1961), pp. 165, 167; *Call*, Aug. 29, 1947.
6. *Call*, Jan. 10, Sept. 5, 1947; *Afro-American*, Aug. 9, 1947; *Chicago Defender*, Aug. 2, 9, 1947.
7. *Call*, Jan. 31, 1947; *Afro Magazine*, Feb. 1, 1947; *Chicago Defender*, Feb. 1, 1947.
8. Lee Nichols, *Breakthrough on the Color Front* (New York, 1954), p. 84; Cabell Phillips, *The Truman Presidency: The History of a Triumphant*

Succession (New York, 1966), pp. 162–65; Patrick Anderson, *The Presidents' Men* (Garden City, N.Y., 1968), pp. 114–18.

9. Phillips, *The Truman Presidency*, p. 163.

10. Ibid., pp. 202–5, 210–11.

11. *Public Papers, 1947*, pp. 161–62, 429, 348–50, 492–98.

12. White, *A Man Called White*, pp. 347–48.

13. Truman Papers, HSTL: D. K. Niles to M. J. Connelly, June 16, 1947, Clifford Files; George M. Elsey Papers, HSTL: President's NAACP Speech, June 29, 1947, File; White, *A Man Called White*, p. 348; *Public Papers, 1947*, p. 313.

14. *Public Papers, 1947*, pp. 311–13; White, *A Man Called White*, p. 348.

15. Truman Papers, HSTL: e.g., Rufus R. Todd to Truman, July 6, 1947; Catherine J. Moroney to Truman, June 30, 1947; Pleas E. Greenlee to Truman, July 2, 1947; Walter White to Truman, July 9, 1947; C. A. Barnett to Truman, Jan. 17, 1948, PPF 200; *Call*, July 4, 1947; *Courier*, July 12, 1947; *Afro-American*, July 5, 1947; *Chicago Defender*, July 12, 1947; *Amsterdam News*, July 5, 1947.

16. White, *A Man Called White*, pp. 349–52.

17. *Call*, Jan. 17, 1947; Truman Papers, HSTL: Government Departments and Agencies folders, President's Committee on Civil Rights Files (hereafter PCCR Files).

18. *Afro Magazine*, Apr. 5, 1947; *Call*, June 6, Sept. 5, 12, Nov. 7, 1947; NAACP, *Annual Report for 1947*, p. 43; RG 174: W. F. Patterson to secretary of labor, Sept. 3, 1947; *Journal and Guide*, Sept. 27, 1947.

19. *Afro-American*, Nov. 29, 1947; *Chicago Defender*, Jan. 3, 1948.

20. *Courier*, Dec. 20, 1947; Truman Papers, HSTL: Walter White to Truman, Dec. 1, 1947; Truman to White, Dec. 9, 1947, OF 93.

21. *Journal and Guide*, July 26, 1947; *Call*, Aug. 15, Oct. 10, 1947.

22. RG 319: E. F. Witsell to Commanding Generals, Air and Ground Forces, All Armies (ZI), and Military District of Washington, Feb. 11, 1947; *Amsterdam News*, Apr. 19, 1947.

23. RG 107: Digest of memorandum of Marcus Ray to secretary of war, Apr. 2, 1947; W. S. Paul to assistant secretary of war, Apr. 10, 1947; C. P. Hall to assistant secretary of war, Apr. 17, 1947; Ray to H. C. Petersen, May 23, 1947; Petersen to secretary of war, May 24, 1947; Col. McCawley Summary re Integration of Negro Personnel in the Reserve Components, May 16, 1947.

24. RG 107: E. J. Geesen to F. H. Williams, June 12, 1947.

25. Washington National Records Center, Record Group 165, Records of the War Department General and Special Staffs (hereafter cited as RG 165): C. R. Huebner to W. S. Paul, Nov. 1, 1947; Paul to Huebner Dec. 2, 1947.

26. Reddick, "Negro Policy of the American Army since World War II," p. 199.

27. *A Program for National Security: The Report of the President's Advisory Commission on Universal Training* (Washington, 1947); *Public Papers, 1947*, p. 262; Byers, "The Negro in the Military Service," p. 263.

28. President's Commission on Higher Education, *Higher Education for American Democracy* (6 vols.; New York, 1947–1948), I, 38; *Chicago Defender*, Dec. 27, 1947; *Call*, Jan. 2, 9, 16, 1948.

29. *Public Papers, 1947*, pp. 98–99.

30. Truman Papers, HSTL: PCCR Minutes, Jan. 15, 1947, PCCR Files.

31. Truman Papers, HSTL: PCCR Minutes, Feb. 5–6, 1947; release, Feb. 6, 1947, PCCR Files.
32. Truman Papers, HSTL: Special Oath, May 1, 1947, PCCR Files.
33. Truman Papers, HSTL: PCCR folders, Nash Files; Walter White to C. E. Wilson, Feb. 17, 1947; Wilson to White, Feb. 17, 1947, PCCR Files; D. K. Niles to M. J. Connelly, Feb. 19, 1947, OF 596A.
34. Truman Papers, HSTL: PCCR Minutes, Feb. 6, 1947; T. L. Smith to the PCCR, Feb. 21, 1947, PCCR Files.
35. Truman Papers, HSTL: PCCR Proceedings Transcript, Apr. 3, 1947, pp. 3–5, PCCR Files.
36. Truman Papers, HSTL: R. K. Carr letters, Feb. 20, 26, 1947, and responses, PCCR Files; *To Secure These Rights,* pp. xi, 178.
37. *To Secure These Rights,* pp. xi, 178; Truman Papers, HSTL: PCCR Files generally; PCCR Minutes, Mar. 19, 1947, PCCR Files.
38. Truman Papers, HSTL: R. K. Carr to J. B. Carey, Apr. 21, 1947; Carr to Tom Clark, May 23, 1947; Clark to Carr, July 18, 22, 1947, PCCR Files.
39. A. B. Spingarn Papers: NAACP Board of Directors Minutes, Nov. 10, 1947; Truman Papers, HSTL: "Decision Papers in Agenda for Policy Meeting . . . June 30–July 1, 1947," Hanover, N.H., PCCR Files.
40. Truman Papers, HSTL: "Decision Papers," PCCR Files.
41. Truman Papers, HSTL: R. K. Carr to M. L. Ernst, July 9, 1947; Carr to All Members of the staff, July 9, 1947; C. E. Wilson to Carr, July 14, 1947, PCCR Files.
42. Truman Papers, HSTL: M. E. Tilly to R. K. Carr, July 18, 1947; Carr to Tilly, July 25, 1947, PCCR Files.
43. Truman Papers, HSTL: S. T. Alexander to R. K. Carr, Sept. 8, 1947; H. K. Sherrill to Carr, Sept. 9, 1947; M. E. Tilly to Carr, Sept. 8, 1947, PCCR Files.
44. Truman Papers, HSTL: R. K. Carr to T. C. Clark, Sept. 3, 1947; J. E. Hoover to C. E. Wilson, Sept. 9, 1947; Federal Bureau of Investigation folder; cf. Galley Proofs of the PCCR Report (Copy No. 5) paragraph 2 of section 4 with paragraph 2, p. 123, *To Secure These Rights,* PCCR Files.
45. *Courier,* May 31, Nov. 1, 8, 1947; *Afro-American,* Aug. 23, 1947; *Call,* Oct. 3, 1947; *Chicago Defender,* Sept. 27, 1947.
46. A. B. Spingarn Papers: NAACP Board of Directors Minutes, Nov. 10, 1947; *Public Papers, 1947,* pp. 479–80.
47. *To Secure These Rights,* especially pp. 4, 6–9, 139, 146, 148, 151–73.
48. Ibid., pp. 166–68.
49. *Chicago Sun-Times,* Nov. 2, 1947; *Washington Post,* Oct. 30, 1947; *PM,* Oct. 30, 1947; *Washington Star,* Oct. 30, 1947.
50. *New York Herald Tribune,* Nov. 9, 1947; *Afro-American,* Nov. 8, 1947; *Journal and Guide,* Nov. 8, 1947; *People's Voice,* Nov. 8, 1947.
51. Truman Papers, HSTL: Philleo Nash to D. K. Niles, Sept. 29, 1947; Walter White to Niles, Nov. 5, 1947; Niles to C. M. Clifford, Jan. 14, 1948; Niles to Truman, Feb. 16, 1948, Nash Files; Distribution of Report, PCCR Files; American Jewish Committee, *Forty-Second Annual Report, 1948* (New York, 1949), pp. 107–8; Arnold Perl, " 'To Secure These Rights,' " *Hollywood Quarterly,* III (Spring 1948), 267 ff.; James A. and Nancy F. Wechsler, "The Road Ahead for Civil Rights," *Commentary,* VI (Oct. 1948), 298.
52. Truman Papers, HSTL: D. K. Niles to Truman, Feb. 16, 1948, Nash Files; Weintraub, *How Secure These Rights?,* pp. 3–8.

53. William L. White, "The Report That Stirred America's Conscience," *This Week*, Dec. 17, 1950, reprinted in *Negro Digest*, IX (May 1951), 3–5; Truman Papers, HSTL: Truman to Ruby Hurley, Oct. 27, 1949, PPF 393.
54. E.g., Herbert H. Lehman Papers, Columbia University: Lehman to A. W. Rose, Jan. 23, 1952; AJC and NAACP, *Balance Sheet, 1953*, p. 3; American Jewish Committee, *American Jewish Year Book (5709) 1948–1949*, L (Philadelphia, 1949), 202.
55. *Public Papers, 1947*, p. 482; Truman Papers, HSTL: M. E. Tilly to C. E. Wilson and R. K. Carr, Sept. 8, 1947, PCCR Files.
56. *Courier*, Nov. 1, 1947.
57. Nichols, *Breakthrough on the Color Front*, p. 83; William C. Berman, *The Politics of Civil Rights in the Truman Administration* (Columbus, Ohio, 1970), p. 73; J. Howard McGrath Papers, HSTL: C. G. Davidson to McGrath, Dec. 6, 1947.

CHAPTER 6

1. *Public Papers, 1948*, pp. 3, 53–54; Clifford Papers, HSTL: Draft of State of the Union address, 1948.
2. *Amsterdam News*, Jan. 17, 1948; *Chicago Defender*, Jan. 24, 1948; *Afro-American*, Jan. 17, 1948.
3. Clifford Papers, HSTL: G. M. Elsey to Clifford, Sept. 19, 1947.
4. Ibid., Miscellaneous, Political File 1948: C. Wilson to Clifford, July 3, 1947; G. M. Elsey to Clifford, Sept. 23, 1947; Gael Sullivan to Clifford, Aug. 19, 1947; HSTL: William H. Batt, Jr., oral history transcript, p. 1.
5. Clifford Papers, HSTL: Clifford to Truman, Nov. 19, 1947.
6. Truman Papers, HSTL: Walter White to Truman, May 20, 1948, PPF 393.
7. *Afro-American*, Jan. 3, 1948; *Call*, Jan. 9, 1948.
8. Curtis Daniel MacDougall, *Gideon's Army* (3 vols.; New York, 1965), I, 228.
9. *Afro-American*, June 1, Sept. 28, 1946; *Chicago Defender*, Sept. 28, 1946; *Journal and Guide*, Sept. 28, 1946.
10. MacDougall, *Gideon's Army*, I, 201, 220–24; *Afro-American*, Feb. 7, 1948.
11. E.g.. Truman Papers, HSTL: D. K. Niles to Truman, Feb. 16, 1948, Nash Files; Elsey Papers, HSTL: Ewing-Kingsley memorandum to Clark Clifford, Jan. 1948.
12. *Public Papers, 1948*, pp. 121–26.
13. Ibid., p. 124; Steinberg, *The Man From Missouri*, p. 303; Truman Papers, HSTL: Philleo Nash (?) to D. K. Niles, Feb. 27, 1948, Nash Files.
14. Truman Papers, HSTL: D. K. Niles to Truman, Feb. 16, 1948, Nash Files; *New York Herald Tribune*, Feb. 4, 1948; *Journal and Guide*, Feb. 14, 1948; *Call*, Feb. 13, Mar. 19, 1948; *Chicago Defender*, Feb. 14, 1948; *Amsterdam News*, Feb. 7, 1948.
15. Quoted in Susan M. Hartmann, *Truman and the 80th Congress* (Columbia, Mo., 1971), p. 152.
16. McGrath Papers, HSTL: Transcript of Conference of Southern Governors with Senator J. Howard McGrath, Feb. 23, 1948; *New York Times*, Feb. 24, 1948; Irwin Ross, *The Loneliest Campaign: The Truman Victory of 1948* (New York, 1968), pp. 63–64; Key, *Southern Politics*, p. 331.
17. Key, *Southern Politics*, pp. 331, 333–34; *Call*, Apr. 9, May 14, 1948.

18. Matthews Papers, HSTL: M. E. Tilly to Matthews, Mar. 24, 1948; Truman Papers, HSTL: J. W. McCormack, to M. J. Connelly, May 7, 1948, PPF 200.
19. Truman Papers, HSTL: Oren Harris to Truman, Feb. 9, 1948, PPF 200.
20. S. J. Spingarn Papers, HSTL: Spingarn Memorandum for the File, Jan. 21, 1948; Clifford Papers, HSTL: G. M. Elsey to Clifford, Jan. 29, 1948.
21. *New York Times*, Feb. 18, 1948; Ross, *Loneliest Campaign*, p. 64; *Public Papers, 1948*, p. 179.
22. *Public Papers, 1948*, p. 254; *Afro-American*, May 29, 1948; Truman Papers, HSTL: Philleo Nash to C. S. Murphy, Feb. 10, 1948, Nash Files; D. S. Dawson to Clark Clifford, Mar. 8, 1948, OF 596; Walter White to Truman, Apr. 7, 1948, OF 413.
23. McGrath Papers, HSTL: F. W. Boykin to McGrath, Feb. 6, 1948.
24. *New York Times*, Feb. 10, Mar. 9, 13, 1948; *Call*, Mar. 19, 1948.
25. *New York Times*, Apr. 3, 1948; *Baltimore Sun*, Apr. 13, 1948; *Public Papers, 1948*, p. 218.
26. *Call*, Mar. 12, 1948.
27. Ibid., Feb. 20, 27, Mar. 26, 1948; *Public Papers, 1948*, p. 155; Truman Papers, HSTL: Adolf Gereau, "Deny Truman's Virgin Isles Trip 'Political,'" PPF 3737; *Afro-American*, Mar. 6, 1948.
28. *Public Papers, 1948*, pp. 182–86.
29. *To Secure These Rights*, p. 162.
30. McGrath Papers, HSTL: R. M. Moore to McGrath, Feb. 5, 1948; *Call*, Apr. 2, 1948; *Chicago Defender*, Apr. 3, 1948; Reddick, "The Negro Policy of the American Army since World War II," p. 200.
31. *Courier*, Apr. 10, 1948; *Call*, Apr. 9, 1948; Garfinkel, *When Negroes March*, p. 161; Truman Papers, HSTL: D. K. Niles to M. J. Connelly, Apr. 5, 1948, Nash Files.
32. *Journal and Guide*, Apr. 17, 1948; *Afro-American*, Apr. 24, 1948.
33. Garfinkel, *When Negroes March*, p. 161; *Call*, Apr. 9, 1948; *Courier*, Apr. 10, 1948.
34. *Call*, Apr. 9, 23, May 14, 1948.
35. David E. Lilienthal, *The Journals of David E. Lilienthal* (4 vols.; New York, 1964, 1966, 1969), II, 302; Margaret L. Geis, *Negro Personnel in the European Command: 1 January 1946 to 30 June 1950* (Washington, 1952), p. 74; *Chicago Defender*, Apr. 24, 1948; National Archives and Records Service, Washington, D.C., Record Group 330, Records of the Office of the Secretary of Defense (hereafter cited as RG 330): J. C. Evans to Marx Leva, Mar. 5, 1948.
36. RG 300: Marx Leva Memorandum for the secretaries of the army, navy, and air force, Apr. 13, 1948; James V. Forrestal to Channing Tobias, Apr. 10, 1948; Lester Granger to John L. Sullivan, Mar. 15, 1948; President's Committee on Equality of Treatment and Opportunity in the Armed Services Papers (hereafter cited as Fahy Committee Papers), HSTL: Report of the Conference Group of Negro Leaders to Secretary Forrestal, n.d.; RG 330: Transcript of National Defense Conference on Negro Affairs, Apr. 26, 1948.
37. *Crisis*, LV (May 1948), 136; *Afro-American*, May 8, 1948; *Call*, May 7, 1948; *Chicago Defender*, May 8, 1948; National Archives and Records Service, Washington, D.C., Record Group 335, Records of the Office of the Secretary of the Army (hereafter cited as RG 335): K. C. Royall to Forrestal, Apr. 30, 1948.

38. Truman Papers, HSTL: D. K. Niles to Clark Clifford, May 12, 1948; Clifford to Forrestal, May 13, 1948, Nash Files; Clifford Papers, HSTL: G. T. Washington to Clifford, June 29, 1948.

39. *Amsterdam News*, Jan. 17, 1948; Truman Papers, HSTL: J. L. McConaughy to Truman, Feb. 9, 1948; Edward Lopez to Truman, Feb. 10, 1948; Joshua Thompson to Truman, Mar. 14, 1948, OF 155; RG 330: Forrestal to Walter White, Feb. 11, 1948; K. C. Royall to A. E. Driscoll, Feb. 7, 1948.

40. RG 330: Marx Leva to Forrestal, Mar. 8, 1948; Clifford Papers, HSTL: Philleo Nash to Clifford, Apr. 9, 1948; Clifford to Truman, Apr. 9, 1948; Elsey Papers, HSTL: Elsey memorandum, Apr. 10, 1948.

41. RG 330: K. C. Royall to L. W. Youngdahl, May 20, 1948; Marx Leva to Forrestal, May 20, 1948; Clifford Papers, HSTL: K. C. Royall to Clifford, July 8, 1948; K. C. Royall to J. C. Shannon, n.d.

42. Clifford Papers, HSTL: K. C. Royall to Clifford, July 8, 19, 20, 1948; Clifford to Royall, July 19, Aug. 10, 1948; RG 330: K. C. Royall to L. W. Youngdahl, Aug. 10, 1948.

43. Pauli Murray, comp. and ed., *States' Laws on Race and Color* (Cincinnati, Ohio, 1951), pp. 12–13; Truman Papers, HSTL: C. E. Rucker to Truman, Apr. 13, 1949; D. K. Edward to Carl Vinson, May 3, 1951; Philleo Nash to R. L. Neustadt, May 29, 1951, OF 155; RG 319: Gordon Gray to L. W. Youngdahl, Nov. 16, 1949; RG 335: E. R. Bendetsen to the secretary of the army, Apr. 7, 1950; *New York Times*, Dec. 11, 1952.

44. *Daily Worker*, Mar. 14, 1948.

45. MacDougall, *Gideon's Army*, III, 654–55; *Afro-American*, Aug. 24, 1940, Jan. 24, Sept. 18, 1948; Columbia University, Will Alexander oral history transcript, pp. 607–8.

46. *Courier*, Feb. 14, 1948; *Chicago Defender*, Mar. 6, 1948; *Call*, Mar. 26, 1948; *Tribune* (Philadelphia), May 11, 1948.

47. *Chicago Defender*, Jan. 24, Mar. 27, 1948; *Journal and Guide*, Mar. 20, 1948; *Call*, Feb. 2, 1948; *Amsterdam News*, Dec. 27, 1947; *Afro-American*, Jan. 10, 1948; Truman Papers, HSTL: A. P. Randolph to Edgar Kobak, Mar. 12, 1948, Nash Files.

48. *Chicago Defender*, Mar. 13, 1948; *Amsterdam News*, Jan. 10, 31, Mar. 20, 1948; *Journal and Guide*, Jan. 3, Mar. 20, 1948; *Courier*, Feb. 7, 1948; *Afro-American*, Mar. 20, 1948.

49. Ross, *Loneliest Campaign*, pp. 65–66; Clifford Papers, HSTL: W. L. Batt, Jr., to Gael Sullivan, Apr. 20, 1948; Memorandum, Research Division Functions, Apr. 5, 1948.

50. Clifton Brock, *Americans for Democratic Action: Its Role in National Politics* (Washington, 1962), pp. 87–95; Ross, *Loneliest Campaign*, pp. 72–75, 112; *New York Times*, July 6, 1948.

51. *Call*, Apr. 8, 23, May 7, 1948; *Chicago Defender*, Apr. 24, 1948.

52. Brock, *Americans for Democratic Action*, pp. 94–95; Ross, *Loneliest Campaign*, pp. 112–16.

53. James Forrestal, *The Forrestal Diaries: The Inner History of the Cold War*, ed. by Walter Millis (London, 1952), pp. 439–40, 446.

54. 62 Stat. 625; *Call*, June 18, 1948; *Afro-American*, June 19, 1948.

55. *Call*, Feb. 6, 1948; Theodore F. Green Papers, Library of Congress: H. W. Tucker to J. O. Pastore, Jan. 28, 1948; Truman Papers, HSTL: A. P.

Randolph to Edgar Kobak, Mar. 12, 1948; Randolph to Member of the Board, National Council for a Permanent FEPC, Mar. 29, 1948, Nash Files.
56. *Call,* Apr. 16, May 14, 1948; *Afro-American,* May 22, 1948.
57. Congressional Quarterly News Features, *Congressional Quarterly Almanac, 1948* (Washington, 1949), p. 290 (hereafter cited as *C. Q. A.* with appropriate date); *Chicago Defender,* July 10, 17, 1948.
58. *Call,* Apr. 9, May 21, 1948; *Chicago Defender,* May 22, 1948. For strong Negro opposition to the regional compact, see Green Papers, Chronological File, Civil Rights Legislation.
59. Truman Papers, HSTL: Irving Miller to Truman, June 23, 1948; Frank Goldman to Truman, June 24, 1948; David Dubinsky to Truman, June 24, 1948; Francis Cardinal Spellman to Truman, June 21, 1948, OF 127; *Public Papers, 1948,* pp. 382–83.
60. C. S. Murphy Papers, HSTL: S. J. Spingarn to Murphy, Feb. 27, 1948.
61. *Crisis,* LV (June 1948), 167.

CHAPTER 7

1. Harry S. Truman, *Memoirs* (2 vols.; New York, 1965), II, 178; Clifford Papers, HSTL: Gael Sullivan to Clifford, Aug. 19, 1947.
2. Hartmann, *Truman and the 80th Congress,* pp. 187–90.
3. Clifford Papers, HSTL: Swedish Centennial Meeting, Chicago, June 4, 1948; *Public Papers, 1948,* pp. 287–90.
4. *Afro-American,* June 12, 1948; *Courier,* June 12, 1948; Ross, *Loneliest Campaign,* p. 81; Hartmann, *Truman and the 80th Congress,* p. 190.
5. *Call,* June 25, 1948; *New York Times,* June 19, 1948.
6. *New York Post,* June 23, 1948; *New York Times,* June 21, 23, 1948; Guzman, *Negro Year Book, 1952,* p. 300.
7. *Call,* July 2, 1948; *Afro-American,* July 3, 1948; Guzman, *Negro Year Book, 1952,* p. 300.
8. *Inquirer* (Philadelphia), June 27, 1948; *Amsterdam News,* June 19, 1948.
9. *New York Post,* June 23, 1948; *Chicago Defender,* July 26, 1947; *New York Herald Tribune,* Mar. 2, 1948; *New York Times,* June 28, 1948; *Courier,* July 3, 1948; *Amsterdam News,* May 29, 1948. For a defense of Dewey's attitude toward an FEPC for New York in 1944, see *Amsterdam News,* Mar. 24, 1945.
10. *Afro-American,* Apr. 3, 24, 1948.
11. Ibid., July 3, 1948; *Chicago Defender,* July 3, 10, 1948.
12. *New York Times,* June 23, 1948; *New York Herald Tribune,* June 23, 1948; *Call,* June 25, 1948.
13. *Call,* July 16, 1948; *Afro-American,* July 17, 1948.
14. *New York Times,* July 9, 11, 1948.
15. Clifford Papers, HSTL: W. L. Batt to Clifford, June 23, July 9, 1948; S. I. Rosenman Papers, HSTL: Batt to Rosenman, July 2, 1948; J. M. Redding to Rosenman, July 2, 1948; *New York Times,* July 12, 1948. For a copy of the fourth draft of the platform, see Rosenman Papers, HSTL: HST Platform folder.
16. Brooks Hays, *A Southern Moderate Speaks* (Chapel Hill, N.C., 1959), pp. 39–40, 139; Winthrop Griffith, *Humphrey: A Candid Biography* (New York, 1965), pp. 151–52; Ross, *Loneliest Campaign,* pp. 120–21. For the platform

committee's final recommendations, see *New York Times*, July 14, 1948, and copy in Clifford Papers, HSTL: Democratic Platform folder.

17. Griffith, *Humphrey*, pp. 153–55; Ross, *Loneliest Campaign*, p. 122.
18. *New York Times*, July 15, 1948; Griffith, *Humphrey*, p. 158; Ross, *Loneliest Campaign*, pp. 126–27.
19. *Forrestal Diaries*, p. 458; Truman, *Memoirs*, II, 182.
20. *New York Times*, July 15, 1948.
21. *Public Papers, 1948*, pp. 406–10.
22. *Call*, July 30, 1948; *New York Times*, July 16, 1948.
23. Key, *Southern Politics*, pp. 335–42; Ross, *Loneliest Campaign*, pp. 130–32.
24. *Chicago Defender*, July 17, 24, 1948; *New York Times*, July 16, 1948.
25. MacDougall, *Gideon's Army*, II, 510–14, 527, 530, 546–49.
26. Guzman, *Negro Year Book, 1952*, p. 300.
27. *Public Papers, 1948*, p. 411.
28. Guzman, *Negro Year Book, 1952*, p. 53; *Chicago Defender*, Nov. 20, 1948; Executive Order 9980.
29. President's Committee on Equality of Treatment and Opportunity in the Armed Services, *Freedom to Serve* (Washington, 1950), pp. xi–xii.
30. RG 330: Grant Reynolds and A. P. Randolph to Truman, July 15, 1948; Marx Leva to the secretary of defense, July 17, 1948 (and various drafts of letters to Reynolds and Randolph); Truman Papers, HSTL: Leon Henderson to Truman, July 22, 1948, OF 93B.
31. *New York Times*, July 28, 30, 1948; *Chicago Defender*, July 31, 1948; *Amsterdam News*, July 31, 1948; *Call*, July 30, 1948; *Courier*, Aug. 7, 1948.
32. *New York Times*, July 30, 1948; RG 330: K. C. Royall to Truman, July 29, 1948; Truman to Royall, Aug. 4, 1948.
33. *Public Papers, 1948*, p. 422.
34. Grant Reynolds, "A Triumph for Civil Disobedience," *Nation*, CLXVII (Aug. 28, 1948), 228–29; *Call*, Aug. 27, 1948; *Crisis*, LV (Sept. 1948), 264; Columbia University, Roy Wilkins oral history transcript, p. 94.
35. *New York Times*, July 16, 17, 1948; Truman, *Memoirs*, II, 208.
36. *Public Papers, 1948*, pp. 416–21.
37. C. S. Murphy Papers, HSTL: Murphy to Jonathan Daniels, July 30, 1948; W. L. Batt to Clark Clifford, July 28, 1948; Hartmann, *Truman and the 80th Congress*, p. 197.
38. *New York Times*, July 16, 1948; *Afro-American*, July 31, 1948.
39. Hartmann, *Truman and the 80th Congress*, pp. 198–99; *C. Q. A., 1948*, p. 273; *New York Sun*, Aug. 23, 1948.
40. *C. Q. A., 1948*, p. 273; *Chicago Defender*, Aug. 14, 1948.
41. *Public Papers, 1948*, pp. 421–22, 438.
42. Ibid., pp. 436–37, 449–51; Truman Papers, HSTL: Presidential Appointments Books, Aug. 13, 1948, Matthew J. Connelly Files; Lloyd von Blaine to M. J. Connelly, Feb. 9, 1951, PPF 200.
43. Democratic National Committee Papers, HSTL: *"Files of the Facts*, VIII: Civil Liberties."
44. Clifford Papers, HSTL: W. L. Batt to Clifford, Aug. 11, 1948; G. M. Elsey to Clifford, Aug. 13, 1948; Elsey Memorandum, n.d.; Clifford to Truman, Aug. 17, 1948.
45. *Public Papers, 1948*, p. 559.
46. *New York Times*, Sept. 26, 28, Oct. 1, 1948; John M. Redding, *Inside the*

Democratic Party (Indianapolis, 1958), p. 272; *Public Papers, 1948,* pp. 588, 650.

47. *Public Papers, 1948,* pp. 815–22.
48. *New York Times,* Aug. 22, Oct. 14, 1948.
49. Truman Papers, HSTL: J. S. Thurmond to Truman, Sept. 25, 1948, OF 200-2H; Ross, *Loneliest Campaign,* p. 231. The form postcard is in Truman Papers, PPF 200 Support.
50. *Courier,* Oct. 23, 1948; *Journal and Guide,* Oct. 16, 1948.
51. For example, see *Afro-American,* Oct. 2, 1948; *Call,* Oct. 1, 1948; *Journal and Guide,* Oct. 16, 1948; *Amsterdam News,* Oct. 9, 1948.
52. *Amsterdam News,* Oct. 23, 1948; *Call,* Oct. 29, 1948.
53. *Afro-American,* Oct. 9, 23, 30, 1948; *Courier,* Oct. 9, 1948; *Washington Post,* Oct. 14, 1948.
54. *Afro-American,* Oct. 16, 1948; *New York Times,* Oct. 22, 1948.
55. *New York Times,* Oct. 6, 14, Nov. 2, 1948.
56. Ross, *Loneliest Campaign,* pp. 224–30; Chapman Papers, HSTL: Elizabeth Donahue to Chapman, Oct. 11, 1948.
57. *Amsterdam News,* Aug. 7, 1948; *Chicago Defender,* Sept. 25, 1948; *Afro-American,* Aug. 21, 1948.
58. *Call,* Sept. 17, 1948; *New York Herald Tribune,* Sept. 12, 1948; A. B. Spingarn Papers, Library of Congress: Walter White, Graphic Syndicate releases, Sept. 16, 23, 1948.
59. *Courier,* Aug. 21, Oct. 9, 1948; *Afro-American,* Oct. 2, 1948; *Chicago Defender,* Oct. 23, 1948.
60. E.g., HSTL: John E. Barriere oral history transcript, p. 9, and Samuel C. Brightman oral history transcript, p. 37.
61. *Call,* Sept. 17, 1948; *Journal and Guide,* Sept. 4, 1948; *Providence Evening Bulletin,* Aug. 4, 1948.
62. Truman Papers, HSTL: J. P. Davis to D. K. Niles, Sept. 11, 1948; Davis to Philleo Nash, Oct. 21, 1948; CIO Political Action Committee news release, Oct. 12, 1948, Nash Files; John M. Redding Papers, HSTL: Presidential Campaign Material folder; Redding, *Inside the Democratic Party,* pp. 238–39.
63. *New York Sun,* Oct. 13, 1948; *New York Times,* Oct. 14, 1948; *Daily World* (Atlanta), Oct. 23, 1948; S. J. Spingarn Papers, HSTL: Memorandum, "Honorable William H. Hastie," n.d.
64. *St. Louis Post-Dispatch,* Sept. 21, 1948; Truman Papers, HSTL: W. L. Dawson, Memorandum, "Truman Policy on Negro Health," Sept. 21, 1948, Nash Files; Oscar R. Ewing, *The Nation's Health: A Report to the President* (Washington, 1948), pp. 35, 41, 61.
65. *New York Herald Tribune,* Sept. 26, 1948; *Chicago Defender,* Feb. 28, 1948; Truman Papers, HSTL: T. B. Curtis to Truman, Nov. 29, 1948, OF 7-1; *New York Times,* Sept. 10, 1948.
66. *Chicago Defender,* Oct. 16, 1948; *Afro-American,* Oct. 30, 1948; *Amsterdam News,* Oct. 30, 1948; Weintraub, *How Secure These Rights?,* p. 42.
67. *Public Papers, 1948,* pp. 848–53, 868.
68. Ibid., pp. 882–86.
69. *Public Papers, 1948,* p. 913.
70. *Public Papers, 1948,* pp. 843–44; Ian J. Bickerton, "President Truman's Recognition of Israel," *American Jewish Historical Quarterly,* LVIII (Dec. 1968), p. 228.

71. Truman Papers, HSTL: Philleo Nash to G. M. Elsey, Oct. 25, 27, 1948, Nash Files.
72. *Public Papers, 1948,* pp. 923–25; Truman Papers, HSTL: Jonathan Daniels to C. G. Ross, Nov. 23, 1948, OF 93B.
73. *Courier,* Feb. 5, 1949.
74. Chapman Papers, HSTL: Walter White to Chapman, Dec. 15, 1948; Ross, *Loneliest Campaign,* pp. 246–47.
75. *Call,* Jan. 28, 1949.
76. Ibid., June 27, Sept. 12, 1947; *Amsterdam News,* May 10, July 19, 1947; *Chicago Defender,* July 12, 1947.
77. *Journal and Guide,* June 28, 1947; *Courier,* June 28, July 12, 1947; *Call,* June 20, 1947.
78. *Courier,* June 26, 1948; *Journal and Guide,* Oct. 23, 1948.
79. For editorial comments, see *Courier,* Oct. 16, 23, 1948; *Afro-American,* Sept. 18, Oct. 2, 16, 23, 1948; *Amsterdam News,* Oct. 9, 1948; *Journal and Guide,* Oct. 16, 30, 1948; *Call,* Sept. 24, Oct. 1, 15, 29, 1948. See also Cecelia Van Auken, "The Negro Press in the 1948 Presidential Election," *Journalism Quarterly,* XXVI (Dec. 1949), 431–35.
80. Van Auken, "Negro Press in the 1948 Presidential Election," pp. 431–35; *Chicago Defender,* Nov. 13, 1948.
81. Kelly Miller, *The Everlasting Stain* (Washington, 1924), p. 207.
82. Roy Wilkins, "Emancipation and Militant Leadership," *100 Years of Emancipation,* ed. Robert A. Goldwin (Chicago, 1963, 1964), p. 35.

CHAPTER 8

1. A. B. Spingarn Papers: Walter White to Truman, Nov. 4, 1948; Matthews Papers, HSTL: S. T. M. Alexander to F. P. Matthews, Nov. 10, 1948; Matthews to Truman, Nov. 12, 1948; Truman to Matthews, Nov. 29, 1948.
2. *Courier,* Nov. 13, 1948; *Call,* Nov. 12, 1948; *Chicago Defender,* Nov. 13, 1948. See also the excerpts from the Negro press in the *Journal and Guide,* Nov. 13, 1948.
3. *Chicago Defender,* Nov. 13, Dec. 4, 1948, Jan. 15, 1949; *Afro-American,* Jan. 1, 1949; *Journal and Guide,* Nov. 6, 1948.
4. *Public Papers, 1948,* pp. 947, 952, 966; *Raleigh News and Observer,* Nov. 19, 1948.
5. *Call,* Nov. 26, Dec. 3, 1948; Truman Papers, HSTL: J. D. C. Wilson to W. D. Hassett, Nov. 11, 1948; Hassett to Wilson, Nov. 23, 1948; B. F. Seldon to Truman, Nov. 21, 1948; C. G. Ross to Seldon, Dec. 17, 1948, OF 101E.
6. *New York Times,* Nov. 25, Dec. 17, 1948; *Chicago Defender,* Jan. 1, 1949.
7. *New York Times,* Nov. 30, 1948; *Call,* Dec. 10, 1948; *Afro-American,* Dec. 4, 1948; *Chicago Defender,* Nov. 27, 1948.
8. Truman Papers, HSTL: C. H. Tobias to Truman, Nov. 24, 1948, OF 1902; *Call,* Dec. 17, 24, 1948.
9. *Call,* Dec. 17, 1948.
10. Green, *Secret City,* pp. 287–88.
11. *Amsterdam News,* Aug. 16, 1941, Jan. 3, 1942.
12. 59 Stat. 443; *Afro-American,* Dec. 6, 1947.
13. *Journal and Guide,* Aug. 11, 1945; *Call,* June 21, 1946; MacDougall, *Gideon's*

Army, III, 659; Truman Papers, HSTL: Philleo Nash Memorandum for the Files, July 14, 1952, Nash Files.

14. *Journal and Guide,* Dec. 6, 1947; *Afro-American,* Dec. 6, 1947; *Chicago Defender,* Jan. 3, 1948.

15. Truman Papers, HSTL: J. D. Kingsley to M. J. Connelly, Oct. 20, 1948; I. N. P. Stokes to J. R. Steelman, Oct. 22, 1948; Connelly to Steelman, Oct. 25, 1948, OF 93B.

16. Truman Papers, HSTL: P. B. Perlman to secretary of commerce, Oct. 27, 1948, Nash Files; *Courier,* Aug. 6, 1949; *Afro-American,* May 28, 1948. See also Charles Sawyer, *Concerns of A Conservative Democrat* (Carbondale, Ill., 1968), p. 202.

17. *Philadelphia Evening Bulletin,* Oct. 29, 1948; Truman Papers, HSTL: S. T. M. Alexander to Truman, Nov. 10, 1948; D. K. Niles to Tom Clark, Nov. 26, 1948; Philleo Nash Memorandum for the Files, July 14, 1952, Nash Files; Matthews Papers, HSTL: F. P. Matthews to Alexander, Nov. 16, 1948.

18. *New York Times,* Dec. 28, 29, 1948; *Call,* Dec. 31, 1948; *Inquirer,* Dec. 28, 1948; Truman Papers, HSTL: S. T. M. Alexander to Truman, Dec. 28, 1948, Nash Files.

19. *Call,* Jan. 7, 1949; *New York Times,* Jan. 4, 5, 1949.

20. *New York Times,* Jan. 2, 4, 1949; *Washington Post,* Jan. 9, 1949; Murphy Papers, HSTL: C. S. Murphy to H. P. Eberharter, Jan. 6, 1949.

21. Murphy Papers, HSTL: D. E. Bell to C. S. Murphy, Jan. 16, 1950; *New York Times,* Jan. 1, 1949.

22. *Public Papers, 1948,* p. 970; *Public Papers, 1949,* pp. 1–7, 12, 101; Clifford Papers, HSTL: Reading Copy of 1949 State of the Union address.

23. *Public Papers, 1948,* pp. 124–25; Clifford Papers, HSTL: R. K. Carr to C. M. Clifford, Nov. 26, 1948; Clifford to Carr, Dec. 1, 1948.

24. *St. Louis Post-Dispatch,* Dec. 10, 1948.

25. *New York Times,* Jan. 5, 1949.

26. *Call,* Jan. 14, 1949; *Chicago Defender,* Jan. 15, 1949; *Public Papers, 1949,* pp. 77–78; *New York Times,* Jan. 13, 1949.

27. *Afro-American,* Dec. 25, 1948; *Washington Times-Herald,* Dec. 16, 1948; Melvin D. Hildreth Papers, HSTL: C. S. Brown to Hildreth, Nov. 17, 1948; *New York Times,* Jan. 19, 1949; *Call,* Jan. 28, 1949.

28. *Chicago Defender,* Jan. 29, 1949; *Courier,* Jan. 29, 1949; *Journal and Guide,* Jan. 29, 1949; *New York Times,* Jan. 21, 1949.

29. *Chicago Defender,* Jan. 29, 1949.

30. President's Committee on Civil Rights, *To Secure These Rights,* p. 40; *New York Times,* July 16, 1948; Truman Papers, HSTL: Bureau of Indian Affairs Memorandum, "Summary of Navajo Developments, Feb. 1, 1950," Nash Files; *Afro-American,* Aug. 21, 1948; AJC and NAACP, *Balance Sheet, 1949,* p. 19.

31. AJC and NAACP, *Balance Sheet, 1949,* p. 19; *Chicago Defender,* Jan. 1, 1949.

32. Carey McWilliams, "America's Disadvantaged Minorities: Mexican-Americans," *Journal of Negro Education,* XX (Summer 1951), 307; W. Henry Cooke, "The Segregation of Mexican-American School Children in Southern California," *School and Society,* LXVII (June 5, 1948), 417–21.

33. Nellie Ward Kingrea, *History of the First Ten Years of the Texas Good*

Neighbor Commission and Discussion of Its Major Problems (Fort Worth, 1954), pp. 86–87.

34. *Journal and Guide*, Jan. 7, 1950; Weintraub, *How Secure These Rights?*, p. 2; AJC and NAACP, *Balance Sheet, 1949*, pp. 7, 26; Murray, *States' Laws on Race and Color*, pp. 8–19.

35. See Guzman, *Negro Year Book, 1952*, pp. 310–11, for lists of Negro office-holders on the state and local level.

36. AJC and NAACP, *Balance Sheet, 1949*, p. 20; McWilliams, "Mexican-Americans," p. 307.

37. Murray, *States' Laws on Race and Color*, p. 9; Weintraub, *How Secure These Rights?*, p. 2; Carey Papers, "Organizations on Record Supporting the Non-Discrimination in Publicly Aided Housing Ordinance."

38. Weintraub, *How Secure These Rights?*, p. 6.

39. Guzman, *Negro Year Book, 1952*, p. 307; Matthews and Prothro, *Negroes and the New Southern Politics*, p. 18; Harold F. Gosnell, "Politics," *in* E. Franklin Frazier, ed., *The Integration of the Negro into American Society* (Washington, 1951), pp. 154–55.

40. Guzman, *Negro Year Book, 1952*, pp. 313–14; AJC and NAACP, *Balance Sheet, 1949*, pp. 19–20.

41. *Journal and Guide*, Nov. 20, 1948; AJC and NAACP, *Balance Sheet, 1949*, p. 14; Guzman, *Negro Year Book, 1952*, pp. 315, 320–21.

42. *Journal and Guide*, Jan. 7, 1950; Weintraub, *How Secure These Rights?*, pp. 3–4.

43. Frank D. Dorey, "Religion," *in* Frazier, ed., *The Integration of the Negro into American Society*, p. 103; *Chicago Defender*, Dec. 31, 1949.

44. *Chicago Defender*, Jan. 1, 1949; Weintraub, *How Secure These Rights?*, p. 6.

45. W. Montague Cobb, "Medicine," *in* Frazier, ed., *The Integration of the Negro into American Society*, p. 83.

46. *Journal and Guide*, Jan. 7, 1950; AJC and NAACP, *Balance Sheet, 1949*, p. 54.

47. George M. Johnson, "Legal Profession," *in* Frazier, ed., *The Integration of the Negro into American Society*, pp. 97–99; AJC and NAACP, *Balance Sheet, 1949*, p. 54.

48. *Chicago Defender*, Dec. 31, 1949; AJC and NAACP, *Balance Sheet, 1949*, pp. 46, 55.

49. Guzman, *Negro Year Book, 1952*, p. 18.

50. *Chicago Defender*, Jan. 1, 1949; Sterling A. Brown, "Athletics and the Arts," *in* Frazier, ed., *The Integration of the Negro into American Society*, pp. 120–21; Guzman, *Negro Year Book, 1952*, pp. 24, 28.

51. Guzman, *Negro Year Book, 1952*, pp. 30–31; Brown, "Athletics and the Arts," pp. 123–24.

52. William Thomas Smith, "Hollywood Report," *Phylon*, VI (First Quarter 1945), 13–14; *Courier*, Oct. 20, 1945; *Journal and Guide*, Aug. 10, 1946; *Amsterdam News*, Aug. 25, 1945; Leon H. Hardwick, "Screen Stereotypes," *Negro Digest*, IV (May 1946), 58.

53. John T. McManus and Louis Kronenberger, "Motion Pictures, the Theater, and Race Relations," *Annals*, CCXLIV (Mar. 1946), 152–54; Peter Noble, *The Negro in Films* (London, 1948), p. 213; *Courier*, Jan. 4, 1947; "Movie-goers Manual," *Negro Digest*, V (Mar. 1947), 55.

54. *Chicago Defender*, Aug. 23, 1947; *Ebony*, III (Dec. 1947), p. 17.

55. Elliot E. Cohen, "Letter to the Movie-Makers," *Commentary*, IV (Aug. 1947), 113; Leo A. Handel, *Hollywood Looks at Its Audience: A Report of Film Audience Research* (Urbana, Ill., 1950), p. 202, n. 23; Franklin Fearing, "Influence of the Movies on Attitudes and Behavior," *Annals*, CCLIV (Nov. 1947), 71, 78; Fearing, "A Word of Caution for the Intelligent Consumer of Motion Pictures," *Quarterly of Film, Radio, and Television*, VI (Winter 1951), 135–36; Leo A. Handel, "Hollywood Market Research," *Quarterly of Film, Radio, and Television*, VII (Spring 1953), 304–5; Martha Wolfenstein and Nathan Leites, "The Study of Man," *Commentary*, X (Oct. 1950), 388–91.

56. *Courier*, Dec. 7, 1946; *Ebony*, II (Feb. 1947), 36; *Negro Digest*, V (Feb. 1947), 17.

57. *Courier*, June 7, Nov. 1, 1947; *Ebony*, II (Aug. 1947), 17; *Chicago Defender*, Oct. 4, 1947; George Norford, "On Stage . . . ," *Opportunity*, XXV (Summer 1947), 174; *Ebony*, III (Nov. 1947), 23, IV (Dec. 1948), 60, III (Aug. 1948), 56.

58. For various comments, see Dorothy B. Jones, "William Faulkner: Novel into Film," *Quarterly of Film, Radio, and Television*, VIII (Fall 1953), 59; *Courier*, May 14, Aug. 6, 1949; *Amsterdam News*, June 11, 1949; *Ebony*, IV (June 1949), 59; Vinicius De Moraes, "The Making of a Document: 'The Quiet One,' " *Hollywood Quarterly*, IV (Summer 1950), 376.

59. *Ebony*, IV (Sept. 1949), 25; *Courier*, Oct. 8, Dec. 31, 1949, July 1, 1950; *Chicago Defender*, June 25, 1949.

60. *Ebony*, V (Mar. 1950), 31, VI (Mar. 1951), 79.

61. Ibid., VII (June 1952), 51–52.

62. Ibid., VII (Feb. 1952), 65; *Courier*, Sept. 19, 1953.

63. *Afro-American*, Apr. 30, 1949; *Call*, June 30, July 21, 1950; *Courier*, July 1, 1950.

64. Luelyne Doscher, "Notes and Communications: Birth of a Stereotype," *Hollywood Quarterly*, III (Fall 1947), 90–93; Robert Hatch, "Gold Fever," *New Republic*, CXVIII (Jan. 26, 1948), 35; *Ebony*, V (May 1950), 59; *New York Times*, Nov. 16, 1950.

65. *Afro-American*, May 26, 1951.

66. Ibid., Oct. 25, 1947; *Courier*, Apr. 9, 1949; *Chicago Defender*, July 7, 21, 1951; *Call*, Aug. 17, 1951.

67. *Courier*, Apr. 26, 1952, Dec. 5, 1953.

68. *Public Papers, 1948*, p. 126.

CHAPTER 9

1. *C. Q. A., 1948*, p. 273; *New York Times*, Mar. 12, 1949.

2. *New York Times*, Feb. 6, 18, 1949.

3. Ibid., Jan. 23, 26, 1949; *Chicago Defender*, Jan. 29, 1949; Truman Papers, HSTL: Walter White to Truman, Jan. 25, 1949, OF 596A.

4. Truman Papers, HSTL: Philleo Nash to C. S. Murphy, Feb. 8, 1949, OF 596A.

5. *Amsterdam News*, Mar. 12, 1949; Truman Papers, HSTL: NAACP News Release, Feb. 5, 1949, OF 596A Report pro.

6. *New York Times*, Feb. 8, 1949.

7. Ibid., Feb. 16–18, 1949; *Chicago Defender*, Feb. 26, 1949.

8. *New York Times*, Mar. 1, 1949; *C. Q. A., 1949*, pp. 584–85; *Congressional Record*, 81st Cong., 1st sess., p. 1915.

9. *Congressional Record*, 81st Cong., 1st sess., pp. 2043, 2048; *Call*, Mar. 18, 1949; NAACP, *Annual Report, 1949*, p. 12.

10. *Public Papers, 1949*, p. 159; *New York Times*, Mar. 4, 6, 10, 1949.

11. *New York Times*, Mar. 1, 2, 10, 1949.

12. Murphy Papers, HSTL: C. S. Murphy to Truman, Mar. 8, 1949; Truman to Murphy, Mar. 9, 1949.

13. *Congressional Record*, 81st Cong., 1st sess., pp. 2274–75; *C. Q. A., 1949*, p. 585.

14. *Chicago Defender*, Mar. 19, 26, 1949; *Call*, Mar. 25, 1949; *Afro-American*, Jan. 28, 1950; A. B. Spingarn Papers: A. B. Lewis to Spingarn, Mar. 31, 1949.

15. *Afro-American*, Mar. 26, 1949; *Call*, July 15, 1949; A. B. Spingarn Papers: A. B. Spingarn to S. J. Spingarn, Mar. 13, 1950; *New York Times*, Mar. 16, 1949; *Courier*, Mar. 12, 1949.

16. *New York Times*, Mar. 18, 20, 1949; *Chicago Defender*, Mar. 19, Apr. 9, 23, 1949; *Afro-American*, Mar. 19, 1949; *Journal and Guide*, Mar. 19, 1949.

17. *New York Times*, Mar. 3, 12, 1949; *Chicago Defender*, Mar. 26, Apr. 2, 1949.

18. Carey Papers: Roy Wilkins to Carey, Nov. 10, 1952.

19. *C. Q. A., 1949*, p. 586.

20. *Call*, Mar. 25, 1949; NAACP, *Annual Report, 1949*, p. 13; McGrath Papers, HSTL: Walter White to J. H. McGrath, Mar. 15, 1949; McGrath to White, Mar. 15, 1949; T. F. Green Papers, Library of Congress: Walter White to Green, Mar. 17, 1949.

21. *Public Papers, 1949*, pp. 169, 182.

22. NAACP, *Annual Report, 1949*, p. 14.

23. S. J. Spingarn Papers, HSTL: Spingarn to R. W. Jones, Mar. 9, 1949; Jones to Spingarn, Mar. 18, 1949; Truman Papers, HSTL: S. J. Spingarn to Clark Clifford, Mar. 25, 1949, Clifford Files.

24. Truman Papers, HSTL: Truman to M. T. Norton, Apr. 5, 1949, OF 596 Misc.

25. Ibid.: S. J. Spingarn to Clark Clifford, Mar. 24, Mar. 29, 1949, Clifford Files; *C. Q. A., 1949*, p. 589; Truman Papers, HSTL: S. J. Spingarn to Clark Clifford, May 17, 1949, OF 596.

26. U.S. Congress, House, Subcommittee of the Committee on Education and Labor, *Hearings, Federal Fair Employment Practice Act*, 81st Cong., 1st sess., 1949, pp. 18, 20, 28, 45, 48–52.

27. Ibid., pp. 400, 447, 522–29.

28. Ibid., pp. 135–46, 294–95.

29. Ibid., pp. 221, 375.

30. *New York Times*, May 15, 1949; Hays, *A Southern Moderate Speaks*, pp. 43–50.

31. Truman Papers, HSTL: C. G. Ross to Truman, Feb. 5, 1949, OF 596; *Chicago Defender*, July 23, 1949; *Washington Star*, Feb. 18, 1949.

32. *New York Times*, May 25, 1949.

33. Ibid., May 25, 27, 1949; *Public Papers, 1949*, pp. 262, 269; *Afro-American*, June 11, 1949.

34. *New York Times*, June 1, 1949; *Call*, June 17, 1949.

35. Truman Papers, HSTL: Roy Wilkins to D. K. Niles, June 20, 1949, PPF

393; *Afro-American*, June 4, 1949; *Courier*, June 25, 1949; *Journal and Guide*, Aug. 27, 1949; *Chicago Defender*, Aug. 13, 1949.
36. *Washington Star*, Nov. 7, 1948; *Chicago Sun-Times*, Nov. 21, 1948; *Public Papers, 1948*, p. 952; *New York Times*, Jan. 7, 1949.
37. Redding Papers, HSTL: Democratic National Committee News Release, Aug. 26, 1949; *Call*, Sept. 2, 1949; *Chicago Defender*, Sept. 3, 1949.
38. *Public Papers, 1949*, p. 89; *Washington Post*, May 9, 1949.
39. *Chicago Defender*, May 7, 1949; *Public Papers, 1949*, p. 247; *Journal and Guide*, May 21, 1949.
40. C. S. Murphy Papers, HSTL: Murphy to D. S. Dawson, May 5, 1949; *Washington Post*, Nov. 17, 1950.
41. *New York Times*, Mar. 12, 1949, Aug. 1, 10, 1950.
42. Ibid., Aug. 10, 1950; Carey Papers: V. J. Washington to Carey, Apr. 25, 1949; Murphy Papers, HSTL: H. G. Morison to C. S. Murphy, Jan. 5, 1950; *Journal and Guide*, May 21, 1949.
43. Richard O. Davies, *Housing Reform during the Truman Administration* (Columbia, Mo., 1966), p. 107.
44. *Chicago Defender*, May 7, 14, 28, 1949; *Call*, May 6, July 8, 1949; Davies, *Housing Reform*, pp. 107–8.
45. Davies, *Housing Reform*, pp. 136–37.
46. Murphy Papers, HSTL: C. S. Murphy to Truman, June 28, 1949.
47. *C. Q. A., 1949*, pp. 266, 268; *Call*, May 13, 1949.
48. *Call*, May 20, 1949; Truman Papers, HSTL: Roy Wilkins to D. K. Niles, June 20, 1949, PPF 393; Murphy Papers, HSTL: C. S. Murphy to Truman, June 28, 1949.
49. *C. Q. A., 1949*, pp. 269–70.
50. NAACP, *Annual Report, 1949*, pp. 20–21; Congressional Quarterly Service, *Congress and the Nation, 1945–1964* (Washington, 1965), p. 1617; *C. Q. A., 1949*, p. 591; *Call*, June 10, 17, 1949; *Afro-American*, June 18, 1949; Truman Papers, HSTL: Roy Wilkins to D. K. Niles, June 20, 1949, PPF 393.
51. *Call*, Sept. 23, 30, 1949; *Public Papers, 1949*, pp. 479–80.
52. NAACP, *Annual Report, 1949*, p. 15; *New York Times*, Aug. 31, 1949; *C. Q. A., 1949*, pp. 455–56.
53. NAACP, *Annual Report, 1949*, p. 15; *Washington Daily News*, Oct. 3, 1949; *New York Times*, Oct. 4, 1949; *Call*, Oct. 14, 1949; *Courier*, Oct. 15, 1949.
54. *Journal and Guide*, July 9, 1949; *Afro-American*, Oct. 29, 1949.
55. *Chicago Defender*, Apr. 30, 1949; *Journal and Guide*, Aug. 20, 1949.
56. *Amsterdam News*, Oct. 1, 1949.
57. *Public Papers, 1949*, pp. 499, 501, 527, 541, 552; *Call*, Nov. 11, 1949.
58. *Public Papers, 1949*, pp. 560–63.
59. Ibid., pp. 564–66.
60. Truman Papers, HSTL: Proclamation of United Nations Human Rights Day, OF 85NN.
61. Spingarn Papers, HSTL: S. J. Spingarn to Clark Clifford, Nov. 22, 1949; Spingarn to C. S. Murphy, Nov. 28, 1949; Spingarn Memorandum for Civil Rights File, Dec. 1, 1949.
62. *Public Papers, 1950*, pp. 102–3; *The Budget of the United States Government for the Fiscal Year Ending June 30, 1951* (Washington, 1950–1951), pp. 911–12.

63. *Public Papers, 1950*, pp. 9–10.

64. A. B. Spingarn Papers, Library of Congress: NAACP Report of the Acting Secretary for the February 1950 Meeting of the Board; NAACP, *Annual Report, 1949*, pp. 4–5; Truman Papers, HSTL: Roy Wilkins to Clark Clifford, Dec. 20, 1949, OF 596B.

65. Truman Papers, HSTL: S. J. Spingarn to Clark Clifford, Dec. 19, 1949; Roy Wilkins to Clifford, Dec. 20, 1949, OF 596B; Spingarn to Clifford, Dec. 21, 1949, Clifford Files.

66. A. B. Spingarn Papers, Library of Congress: NAACP Report of the Acting Secretary for the February 1950 Meeting of the Board.

67. *Crisis*, LVII (Feb. 1950), 100.

68. NAACP, *Annual Report, 1950*, p. 6; *Public Papers, 1950*, p. 115.

69. Murphy Papers, HSTL: D. E. Bell to C. S. Murphy, Jan. 16, 1950; Wadsworth Papers, Library of Congress: Diary, Jan. 17, 1950.

70. *Public Papers, 1950*, pp. 115, 117; Murphy Papers, HSTL: D. E. Bell to C. S. Murphy, Jan. 16, 1950; Murphy to Truman, Jan. 16, 1950; NAACP, *Annual Report, 1950*, p. 7; *Crisis*, LVII (Feb. 1950), 100–101; *C. Q. A., 1950*, pp. 384, 544; Wadsworth Papers, Library of Congress: Diary, Jan. 20, 1950.

71. *New York Times*, Jan. 14, 18, 21, 23, 1950; Truman Papers, HSTL: A. C. Powell, Jr., to Truman, Jan. 19, 1950, OF 596A; *C. Q. A., 1950*, pp. 376–77.

72. *New York Times*, Jan. 24, 26, 1950; *Journal and Guide*, Feb. 4, 1950; *Public Papers, 1950*, pp. 141, 143.

73. Murphy Papers, HSTL: S. J. Spingarn to C. S. Murphy, Jan. 12, 1950; *Washington Star*, Jan. 26, 1950; S. J. Spingarn Papers, HSTL: Spingarn to C. S. Murphy, Jan. 18, 1950; *Public Papers, 1950*, pp. 133–35.

74. *Public Papers, 1950*, p. 149; S. J. Spingarn Papers, HSTL: Address of the President to the Attorney Generals Conference on Law Enforcement Problems, Feb. 15, 1950.

75. *New York Times*, Feb. 7, 1950.

76. Ibid., Feb. 7, 8, 1950; *Afro-American*, Feb. 18, 1950.

77. *Call*, Feb. 10, 17, 1950.

78. *C. Q. A., 1950*, pp. 377–79; *New York Times*, Jan. 26, Feb. 22, 23, 1950; Hays, *A Southern Moderate Speaks*, p. 60.

79. *Crisis*, LVII (Mar. 1950), 170.

80. *Afro-American*, Mar. 25, 1950; *Public Papers, 1950*, p. 177; *Call*, Mar. 3, 1950.

81. *Call*, Feb. 17, Apr. 7, 1950; *Journal and Guide*, Mar. 11, 1950; S. J. Spingarn Papers, HSTL: Spingarn to C. S. Murphy, Mar. 16, 1950; *New York Times*, Apr. 12, 1950.

82. Truman Papers, HSTL: Roy Wilkins to Truman, Apr. 12, 1950; D. K. Niles to Wilkins, Apr. 20, 1950, OF 413; *Public Papers, 1950*, pp. 251, 253.

83. *Courier*, Apr. 22, 1950; *Call*, May 5, 1950.

84. *Call*, May 19, 1950; Ruchames, *Race, Jobs & Politics*, pp. 210–11; *Crisis*, LVII (June 1950), 374–75; S. J. Spingarn Papers, HSTL: Roy Wilkins to Walter White, May 23, 1950; *Afro-American*, May 27, 1950; *Call*, May 26, 1950; *Chicago Defender*, June 3, 1950.

85. S. J. Spingarn Papers, HSTL: Philleo Nash to C. G. Ross, May 18, 1950; Nash to Spingarn, May 22, 1950; *Public Papers, 1950*, pp. 431, 439.

86. *C. Q. A., 1950*, pp. 296–98.

87. S. J. Spingarn Papers, HSTL: Philleo Nash to Spingarn, June 21, 1950; Spingarn and C. S. Murphy to Truman, July 3, 1950.

88. Green Papers, Library of Congress: S. W. Lucas to Green, June 15, 1950; W. M. Boyle, Jr., to Green, July 8, 1950; S. J. Spingarn Papers, HSTL: Spingarn Memorandum for the FEPC File, July 5, 1950; Democratic National Committee News Release, July 9, 1950.

89. *Journal and Guide*, July 12, Aug. 5, 1950; *Afro-American*, Sept. 23, 1950.

90. Lehman Papers, Columbia University: H. H. Lehman to William Benton, May 18, 1950; Green Papers, Library of Congress: L. S. Perry to Green, Aug. 4, 1950; *New York Times*, July 18, Sept. 9, 11, Oct. 16, 1950.

91. *C. Q. A., 1950*, p. 429; U.S. Congress, Senate, Subcommittee of the Committee on Appropriations, *Hearings, Departments of State, Justice, Commerce, and the Judiciary Appropriations for 1951*, 81st Cong., 2d sess., 1950, pp. 169–79; Murphy Papers, HSTL: C. S. Murphy to Truman, May 23, 1950.

92. 64 Stat. 319; *Public Papers, 1950*, p. 772; S. J. Spingarn Papers, HSTL: Spingarn to Truman, Sept. 8, 1950.

93. *Public Papers, 1950*, pp. 624–25.

94. R. A. Schermerhorn, "America's Disadvantaged Minorities: The American Indian," *Journal of Negro Education*, XX (Summer 1951), 294.

95. *Amsterdam News*, Dec. 10, 1949; Murphy Papers, HSTL: M. J. Connelly to C. S. Murphy, Nov. 8, 1947; Murphy to Truman, Nov. 10, 1947.

96. *Public Papers, 1947*, pp. 502–4; Truman Papers, HSTL: J. L. Krug to Truman, Feb. 6, 1948; Truman to Krug, Mar. 13, 1948, OF 6c.

97. Truman Papers, HSTL: J. L. Krug to J. W. Martin, n.d., OF 6c; Carey McWilliams, "Power Politics and the Navajo," *Nation*, CLXVII (July 17, 1948), 73–74.

98. Oliver La Farge, "To Set the Indians Free," *New Republic*, CXXI (Oct. 3, 1949), 12–13.

99. Truman Papers, HSTL: O. L. Chapman to Truman, July 8, 1948, OF 121A; Felix S. Cohen, "Our Country's Shame," *Progressive*, XIII (May 1949), 9–10.

100. McGrath Papers, HSTL: J. E. Curry to R. M. Bronson, Jan. 28, 1949; Truman Papers, HSTL: S. J. Spingarn to C. S. Murphy, Jan. 10, 1950, Nash Files.

101. Schermerhorn, "The American Indian," p. 292; Truman Papers, HSTL: Oliver La Farge to Truman, Oct. 8, 1949, Nash Files.

102. Truman Papers, HSTL: S. J. Spingarn to C. S. Murphy, Jan. 10, 1950; Philleo Nash to Spingarn, Apr. 19, 1950, Nash Files; *Public Papers, 1949*, pp. 514–17; *Public Papers, 1950*, p. 259.

103. *Public Papers, 1949*, pp. 544–45; William A. Brophy and Sophie D. Aberle, eds., *The Indian, America's Unfinished Business: Report of the Commission on the Rights, Liberties, and Responsibilities of the American Indian* (Norman, Okla., 1966), pp. 170–71.

CHAPTER 10

1. *Call*, Jan. 21, 1949; Jay Franklin, "What Truman Really Thinks of Negroes," *Negro Digest*, VII (June 1949), 10.

2. S. J. Spingarn Papers, HSTL: Spingarn to C. M. Clifford, May 16, 1949; Truman Papers, HSTL: D. H. Davis to Truman, Aug. 11, 1949, OF 93 Misc.

3. *Tribune* (Philadelphia), Aug. 9, 1949; Truman Papers, HSTL: OF 208M Endorsements, Aug. 1949.
4. Truman Papers, HSTL: Truman to W. H. Hastie, Nov. 9, 1948, PPF 2583.
5. Truman Papers, HSTL: OF 41A Endorsements, July, Sept., 1949; OF 209C and 209C Endorsements, Aug., Sept., Oct., 1949; *Call*, Oct. 14, 1949; *Courier*, Oct. 22, 29, 1949.
6. Truman Papers, HSTL: F. J. Myers to M. J. Connelly, Sept. 23, 1949, OF 208M; Truman to Francis Biddle, Oct. 5, 1949, OF 209C; *Call*, Oct. 14, 1949.
7. Truman Papers, HSTL: unsigned note, Oct. 13, attached to J. H. McGrath to Truman, Oct. 13, 1949, OF 209C.
8. *Chicago Defender*, Oct. 29, 1949.
9. *Washington Post*, July 18, 1950; Truman Papers, HSTL: S. J. Spingarn to Donald Dawson, May 1, 1950; Dawson to Peyton Ford, May 16, 1950; Truman to Alben Barkley, May 6, 1950; Spingarn Memorandum for the Files, May 8, 1950; John Gunther to Spingarn, n.d.; Spingarn to Truman, May 12, 1950, OF 209C.
10. *Courier*, Feb. 19, 1949; *Call*, June 3, 1949; *Washington Times-Herald*, June 3, 1949; Chapman Papers, HSTL: Walter White to Chapman, Memorandum of telephone conversation between White and Chapman, both Dec. 19, 1949.
11. Truman Papers, HSTL: T. L. Dodson to Truman, Oct. 20, 1949, OF 41L; J. H. Sengstacke to Truman, Mar. 21, 1950; D. K. Niles to Sengstacke, Apr. 20, 1950, OF 93 Misc.
12. *Chicago Defender*, Aug. 12, Sept. 2, 1950; *Journal and Guide*, Nov. 11, 1950; *Courier*, Aug. 5, 1950; Truman Papers, HSTL: D. K. Niles to S. C. Brightman, July 26, 1950, Nash Files.
13. *Courier*, July 17, 1954; *Call*, July 21, 1950; Editors of *Ebony*, *The Negro Handbook* (Chicago, 1966), p. 319.
14. 245 U.S. 60; Charles Abrams, *Forbidden Neighbors: A Study of Prejudice in Housing* (New York, 1955), pp. 229–33.
15. Vose, *Caucasians Only*, pp. 82, 113–15, 128, 158–60; *Chicago Defender*, June 22, 1946; *Call*, Apr. 4, 1947; *Afro-American*, Dec. 13, 1947.
16. Chapman Papers, HSTL: O. L. Chapman to T. C. Clark, Sept. 11, 1947; President's Committee on Civil Rights, *To Secure These Rights*, pp. 169, 171; Vose, *Caucasians Only*, pp. 169–70; *Afro-American*, Nov. 22, 1947.
17. Vose, *Caucasians Only*, pp. 193–99.
18. Tom C. Clark and Philip B. Perlman, *Prejudice and Property: An Historic Brief against Racial Covenants* (Washington, 1948), pp. 39, 75, 68–73, 30–38, 86 ff., 12–14.
19. Vose, *Caucasians Only*, pp. 205–10; *Shelley* v. *Kraemer*, 334 U.S. 1; *Hurd* v. *Hodge*, 334 U.S. 24. The other two cases were *Urciolo* v. *Hodge* and *McGhee* v. *Sipes*.
20. *Afro-American*, May 8, 15, Jan. 31, 1948; *Chicago Defender*, May 1, 8, 15, 1948.
21. Vose, *Caucasians Only*, pp. 211–12, 230–37; Weintraub, *How Secure These Rights?*, p. 17; John Hope Franklin, *From Slavery to Freedom: A History of Negro Americans* (3d ed., rev. and enl.; New York, 1967), p. 610; Carey Papers: Charles Stanley to A. J. Carey, Jr., Sept. 6, 1948; Cannon, *Gentle Knight*, p. 190; Arvarh E. Strickland, *History of the Chicago Urban League* (Urbana, Ill., 1966), pp. 158–63.
22. U. S. Commission on Civil Rights, *1961 Report, Housing*, IV (Washington,

1961), 24; Murray, *States' Laws on Race and Color*, p. 11; *Courier*, Mar. 5, 1949.

23. Davies, *Housing Reform during the Truman Administration*, pp. 107–8, 111; *Amsterdam News*, July 16, 1949.

24. Davies, *Housing Reform during the Truman Administration*, p. 124; Truman Papers, HSTL: D. K. Niles to Truman, Oct. 31, 1949, OF 63; Abrams, *Forbidden Neighbors*, p. 259; AJC and NAACP, *Balance Sheet, 1949*, pp. 38–39; Jack Greenberg, *Race Relations and American Law* (New York, 1959), pp. 391–94; Martin Meyerson and Edward C. Banfield, *Politics, Planning and the Public Interest: The Case of Public Housing in Chicago* (Glencoe, Ill., 1955), p. 23.

25. Truman Papers, HSTL: D. K. Niles to Truman, Oct. 31, 1949; Truman to C. R. Gray, Jr., Nov. 1, 1949; R. M. Foley to Truman, Nov. 18, 1949, OF 63; S. J. Spingarn Papers, HSTL: Statement by Solicitor General Philip B. Perlman, Dec. 2, 1949; Commission on Civil Rights, *Housing*, IV, p. 25; Murray, *States' Laws on Race and Color*, pp. 599–607.

26. Abrams, *Forbidden Neighbors*, pp. 224–26, 378–79; Guzman, *Negro Year Book, 1952*, pp. 175–76; Harriet H. Dexter, *What's Right with Race Relations* (New York, 1958), pp. 80–81.

27. McGrath Papers, HSTL: Walter White to McGrath, Jan. 30, 1951; *Chicago Defender*, Feb. 16, 1952; Truman Papers, HSTL: White to Truman, June 12, 1952; R. C. Weaver to Truman, June 12, 1952, OF 1282C; Philleo Nash to Truman, June 23, 1952, Nash Files.

28. *American Jewish Year Book, 1954* (New York, 1955), p. 42; *Chicago Defender*, Oct. 25, 1952; Truman Papers, HSTL: R. C. Weaver to Truman, Jan. 5, 1953; M. Foley to Philleo Nash, Jan. 15, 1953, Nash Files.

29. Robert C. Weaver, "Habitation with Segregation," *Crisis*, LIX (June–July 1952), 350; Guzman, *Negro Year Book, 1952*, p. 184; B. T. McGraw, "The Housing Act of 1954 and Implications for Minorities," *Phylon*, XVI (Second Quarter 1955), 180–81; Vose, *Caucasians Only*, p. 227 and chart following p. 44.

30. *Public Papers, 1952*, pp. 422, 799; Robert C. Weaver, "Integration in Public and Private Housing," *Annals*, CCCIV (Mar. 1956), 87; Abrams, *Forbidden Neighbors*, p. 309.

31. Guzman, *Negro Year Book, 1952*, pp. 171, 174; *American Jewish Year Book, 1954*, pp. 42–43; Abrams, *Forbidden Neighbors*, pp. 244–46, 344–45; Weaver, "Habitation with Segregation," pp. 347–53, 402–3; McGraw, "The Housing Act of 1954," p. 181; Strickland, *History of the Chicago Urban League*, p. 158.

32. *Brunson v. North Carolina*, 333 U.S. 851; *Bob-Lo Excursion Co. v. Michigan*, 333 U.S. 28; *Sipuel v. Board of Regents*, 332 U.S. 631; *Oyama v. California*, 332 U.S. 633; Guzman, *Negro Year Book, 1952*, pp. 286–88.

33. Guzman, *Negro Year Book, 1952*, p. 288; *Afro-American*, Feb. 4, 1950.

34. Murray, *States' Laws on Race and Color*, pp. 676–94; McGrath Papers, HSTL: "Argument by Honorable J. Howard McGrath . . . before the Supreme Court of the United States in the Case of Elmer W. Henderson vs United States of America . . . April 3rd, 1950."

35. NAACP, *Annual Report for 1947*, pp. 22–25; Henry Allen Bullock, *A History of Negro Education in the South: From 1619 to the Present* (Cambridge, Mass., 1967), pp. 262–63; Weintraub, *How Secure These Rights?*, pp. 62–63.

36. *Afro-American*, Feb. 18, 1950; *Call*, Apr. 14, 1950. Although Perlman aggressively sought the reversal of the separate-but-equal doctrine, he apparently did not believe that the court would invalidate it in the *Henderson*, *Sweatt*, or *McLaurin* cases. S. J. Spingarn Papers, HSTL: Spingarn to C. S. Murphy, Mar. 1, 1950.
37. *Henderson v. United States*, 339 U.S. 816; *Sweatt v. Painter*, 339 U.S. 629; *McLaurin v. Oklahoma State Regents*, 339 U.S. 637; *Afro-American*, June 17, 1950.
38. Greenberg, *Race Relations and American Law*, pp. 121–22; *Chicago Defender*, Apr. 12, 19, 1952; Jacob K. Javits, *Discrimination—U. S. A.* (New York, 1960), p. 237.
39. Bullock, *A History of Negro Education in the South*, pp. 262–63; *Call*, July 7, Sept. 22, Nov. 10, June 16, 1950; *Chicago Defender*, June 17, 1950; *Afro-American*, Sept. 16, 1950.

CHAPTER 11

1. Nichols, *Breakthrough on the Color Front*, pp. 89–90.
2. RG 335: K. C. Royall to the secretary of defense, Sept. 22, 1948; Royall to Truman, Sept. 17, 1948; Reddick, "Negro Policy of the American Army since World War II," p. 208.
3. Fahy Committee Papers, HSTL: secretary of defense Memorandum for the secretaries of the army, navy, and air force, Oct. 21, 1948; Richard M. Dalfiume, "The Fahy Committee and Desegregation of the Armed Forces," *Historian*, XXXI (Nov. 1968), 4; Nichols, *Breakthrough on the Color Front*, p. 90; *Public Papers, 1948*, p. 422; Truman Papers, HSTL: Meeting of the President and the Four Service Secretaries with the President's Committee on Equality of Treatment and Opportunity in the Armed Services, Jan. 12, 1949, OF 1285F.
4. Fahy Committee Papers, HSTL: Louis Johnson Memorandum for the secretaries of the army, navy, and air force, Apr. 6, 1949. For the background to Johnson's order, see Dalfiume, "Fahy Committee and Desegregation of the Armed Forces," pp. 7–8.
5. Fahy Committee Papers, HSTL: E. W. Kenworthy to C. H. Fahy, Apr. 20, 1949.
6. President's Committee on Equality of Treatment, *Freedom to Serve*, p. 36; Truman Papers, HSTL: Meeting of the President and the Four Service Secretaries with the President's Committee, Jan. 12, 1949, OF 1285F.
7. President's Committee on Equality of Treatment, *Freedom to Serve*, pp. 37–38; Monroe Billington, "Freedom to Serve: The President's Committee on Equality of Treatment and Opportunity in the Armed Forces, 1949–1950," *Journal of Negro History*, LI (Oct. 1966), 264.
8. RG 330: Department of the Air Force Letter, May 11, 1949; Murray, *States' Laws on Race and Color*, pp. 586–87.
9. President's Committee on Equality of Treatment, *Freedom to Serve*, pp. 38, 43; Truman Papers, HSTL: Fahy Committee Interim Report to the President, July 27, 1949, Nash Files; Fahy Committee Papers, HSTL: E. W. Kenworthy to D. R. G. Palmer, Feb. 2, 1950; Kenworthy to Emanuel Celler, Mar. 16, 1950.
10. President's Committee on Equality of Treatment, *Freedom to Serve*, p. 43.

11. RG 330: Captain Herbert D. Riley, Memorandum on the Secretary of the Army's Proposal Concerning Experimental Non-Segregated Units in the Armed Forces, Dec. 6, 1948.

12. President's Committee on Equality of Treatment, *Freedom to Serve*, pp. 19–24; RG 330: D. A. Kimball to the chairman of the Personnel Policy Board, May 2, 1949; Fahy Committee Papers, HSTL: "Report on Gillem Board Policy and Implementation," n.d., p. 156.

13. Fahy Committee Papers, HSTL: Interim Report to the President, July 27, 1949; President's Committee on Equality of Treatment, *Freedom to Serve*, pp. 24–27; RG 330: D. A. Kimball to the secretary of defense, May 23, 1949.

14. President's Committee on Equality of Treatment, *Freedom to Serve*, p. 27; RG 330: D. A. Kimball to the chairman of the Personnel Policy Board, Dec. 22, 1949.

15. President's Committee on Equality of Treatment, *Freedom to Serve*, pp. 21, 28; Fahy Committee Papers, HSTL: E. W. Kenworthy to Emanuel Celler, Mar. 16, 1950.

16. Fahy Committee Papers, HSTL: W. S. Symington to J. V. Forrestal, Dec. 22, 1948; J. N. Brown to the secretary of defense, Dec. 28, 1948; "Report on Gillem Board Policy and Implementation," pp. 154–56; President's Committee on Equality of Treatment, *Freedom to Serve*, pp. 58–59.

17. Fahy Committee Papers, HSTL: Interim Report to the President, July 27, 1949.

18. Ibid.: "Report on Gillem Board Policy and Implementation," p. 157.

19. Ibid., pp. 159–61; President's Committee on Equality of Treatment, *Freedom to Serve*, p. 55; E. W. Kenworthy, "The Case against Army Segregation," *Annals*, CCLXXV (May 1951), 27–33; Dalfiume, "Fahy Committee and Desegregation of the Armed Forces," pp. 2, 5, 6, 12.

20. Fahy Committee Papers, HSTL: C. H. Fahy to Truman, Sept. 26, 1949.

21. RG 330: Department of Defense News Release, Sept. 30, 1949; Truman Papers, HSTL: D. K. Niles to Truman, Oct. 5, 1949, Nash Files; Fahy Committee Papers, HSTL: Further Interim Report to the President, Oct. 11, 1949.

22. RG 330: T. R. Reid to the secretary of defense, Apr. 14, 1949; Dalfiume, *Desegregation of the U.S. Armed Forces*, pp. 191–92.

23. On interservice rivalry, see Timothy W. Stanley, *American Defense and National Security* (Washington, 1956), pp. 94–95; Lawrence J. Legere, Jr., "Unification of the Armed Forces," Ph.D. diss., Harvard University, 1950, pp. 372–79.

24. *Call*, Oct. 14, 1949; *Amsterdam News*, Oct. 8, 1949.

25. *Chicago Defender*, Dec. 31, 1949; *Amsterdam News*, Jan. 7, 1950; *Call*, Oct. 14, 1949.

26. *Public Papers, 1949*, p. 501; Truman Papers, HSTL: C. H. Fahy to Truman, Oct. 20, 1949; Truman to Fahy, Oct. 27, 1949, OF 41H.

27. Fahy Committee Papers, HSTL: "Report on Gillem Board Policy and Implementation," pp. 171–72; RG 330: Department of Defense News Release, Nov. 3, 1949; Nichols, *Breakthrough on the Color Front*, p. 93.

28. Fahy Committee Papers, HSTL: C. H. Fahy to Gordon Gray, Nov. 8, 1949; Gray to Fahy, Nov. 17, 1949.

29. Ibid.: E. W. Kenworthy Memorandum for the President's Committee, Nov.

18, 1949; Kenworthy to C. H. Fahy, Nov. 22, 1949; Kenworthy Memoranda for the Record, Nov. 28, Dec. 9, 1949.

30. Ibid.: C. H. Fahy Memorandum for the President's Committee, Dec. 27, 1949.

31. Ibid.: C. H. Fahy to Truman, Jan. 16, 1950; *Crisis,* LVII (Feb. 1950), 101; *Amsterdam News,* Jan. 21, 1950.

32. S. J. Spingarn Papers, HSTL: Clark Clifford to Truman, Jan. 23, 1950; Truman Papers, HSTL: D. K. Niles to Truman, Feb. 7, 1950; C. H. Fahy Memorandum for the President's Committee, Feb. 1, 1950, Nash Files.

33. Leo Bogart, ed., *Social Research and the Desegregation of the U.S. Army* (Chicago, 1969), p. 19.

34. Truman Papers, HSTL: Gordon Gray to Truman, Mar. 1, 1950, OF 1285-B.

35. Fahy Committee Papers, HSTL: C. H. Fahy Memorandum for the President's Committee, Mar. 8, 1950; Fahy to D. K. Niles, Mar. 13, 1950; RG 319: Gordon Gray to Truman, Mar. 24, 1950; President's Committee on Equality of Treatment, *Freedom to Serve,* p. viii.

36. *Public Papers, 1950,* p. 431; Truman Papers, HSTL: "Report of Distribution of *Freedom to Serve,*" D. K. Niles to Truman, May 22, 1950; Truman to C. H. Fahy, July 6, 1950, Nash Files.

37. *Amsterdam News,* July 22, 1950; Truman Papers, HSTL: Lester Granger to Truman, Sept. 28, 1950, OF 1285o.

38. Truman Papers, HSTL: E. W. Kenworthy to C. H. Fahy, July 25, 1950, Nash Files.

39. RG 319: Homer Case to W. H. Haislip, May 15, 1950; E. H. Brooks to Haislip, Oct. 6, 1950; Nichols, *Breakthrough on the Color Front,* pp. 108–11.

40. *Afro-American,* July 22, 1950; *Call,* Oct, 13, 20, 1950; Reddick, "Negro Policy of the American Army since World War II," pp. 213–14; *Amsterdam News,* Oct. 7, 1950.

41. Operations Research Office, Johns Hopkins University, *Utilization of Negro Manpower in the Army: A 1951 Study* (Washington, 1963), p. A-IV-11; Nichols, *Breakthrough on the Color Front,* pp. 111–12.

42. Nichols, *Breakthrough on the Color Front,* pp. 114–15.

43. *Amsterdam News,* July 29, Aug. 5, 1950.

44. Ibid., Sept. 16, 1950; *Call,* Sept. 29, Oct. 27, 1950; *Courier,* Sept. 9, 16, 1950.

45. *Call,* Jan. 5, 1951; *New York Times,* Dec. 17, 1950.

46. Nichols, *Breakthrough on the Color Front,* pp. 113–14; *New York Times,* June 4, 1951; *Call,* Apr. 20, 27, June 8, 1951.

47. *Afro-American,* July 29, 1950; *Call,* Aug. 4, 18, 25, Oct. 6, 20, 1950.

48. *Amsterdam News,* Aug. 26, 1950; *Call,* Sept. 8, 1950.

49. *Courier,* Sept. 16, 1950; *Call,* Sept. 22, 1950; Harold H. Martin, "How Do Our Negro Troops Measure Up?," *Saturday Evening Post,* CCXXIII (June 16, 1951), 30, 31, 139, 141.

50. *Call,* Oct. 20, Nov. 3, 17, 24, Dec. 1, 22, 1950, Jan. 26, 1951.

51. NAACP, *Annual Report, 1951,* p. 49; *Call,* Nov. 17, 1950, Jan. 5, 19, Feb. 2, 9, Mar. 2, 1951; *New York Times,* June 4, 1951.

52. *Call,* Feb. 16, 23, Mar. 2, 9, 1951; NAACP, *Annual Report, 1951,* p. 49.

53. *Call,* Apr. 20, 27, May 4, 1951; *Amsterdam News,* Aug. 8, 1953.

54. *Call,* Jan. 19, Mar. 9, 1951; *Chicago Defender,* May 24, 1951; *Courier,* Mar. 31, 1951; *Amsterdam News,* May 19, 1951.

55. Nichols, *Breakthrough on the Color Front,* p. 137; *Call,* Aug. 17, 1951;

Operations Research Office, *Utilization of Negro Manpower in the Army*, p. 34; *New York Times*, Mar. 19, 1951.

56. Truman Papers, HSTL: Frank Pace, Jr., to D. K. Niles, Feb. 21, 1951, OF 93B; Operations Research Office, *Utilization of Negro Manpower in the Army*, p. C-I-14; RG 319: D. A. D. Ogden to the assistant chief of staff, Mar. 3, 1951; RG 335: E. D. Johnson to the secretary of the army, Apr. 26, 1952.

57. RG 319: E. H. Brooks to the chief of Staff, Dec. 18, 1950.

58. Operations Research Office, *Utilization of Negro Manpower in the Army*, pp. C-I-12, 26–27.

59. RG 319: W. H. Haislip to the secretary of the army, May 31, 1951.

60. RG 319: W. H. Maris to director, Operations Research Office, Mar. 29, 1951; Bogart, *Social Research and the Desegregation of the U.S. Army*, p. 22.

61. Operations Research Office, *Utilization of Negro Manpower in the Army*, pp. S-4, 5, 6.

62. Nichols, *Breakthrough on the Color Front*, pp. 136, 140–41; *C. Q. A., 1951*, pp. 282–83.

63. Matthew B. Ridgway, *The Korean War* (Garden City, N.Y., 1967), pp. 192–93; RG 330: G. C. Marshall to H. H. Lehman and H. H. Humphrey, July 20, 1951; *Call*, Aug. 17, 1951; *Chicago Defender*, Aug. 4, 1951.

64. Operations Research Office, *Utilization of Negro Manpower in the Army*, pp. B-III-5, 6, 7; RG 330: A. M. Rosenberg to H. H. Humphrey, Oct. 6, 1952; Mark W. Clark, *From the Danube to the Yalu* (New York, 1954), pp. 197–98.

65. *Call*, June 8, 15, 22, 29, July 20, Aug. 3, 10, Sept. 21, 28, Oct. 5, Dec. 28, 1951, Jan. 4, 11, 1952.

66. RG 319: A. C. McAuliffe to J. M. Swing, Sept. 17, 1951; McAuliffe, "Summary Sheet," Dec. 29, 1951; Nichols, *Breakthrough on the Color Front*, pp. 132–33.

67. Nichols, *Breakthrough on the Color Front*, pp. 127–28.

68. Ibid., pp. 128–29; Dalfiume, *Desegregation of the U.S. Armed Forces*, pp. 216–17.

69. Dalfiume, *Desegregation of the U.S. Armed Forces*, p. 217.

70. *Call*, Feb. 22, 29, 1952; *Afro-American*, Feb. 23, 1952; *Chicago Defender*, Mar. 1, 1952.

71. Nichols, *Breakthrough on the Color Front*, p. 129; *New York Times*, Sept. 8, 1952.

72. *Call*, June 1, 22, Oct. 26, 1951.

73. Truman Papers, HSTL: administrator of the Federal Security Agency to F. J. Lawton, Oct. 26, 1951, Nash Files; RG 330: C. E. Wilson to D. D. Eisenhower, May 29, 1953.

74. Truman Papers, HSTL: I. M. Labovitz to Roger Jones, Oct. 26, 1951, Nash Files.

75. Ibid.: W. C. Foster to F. J. Lawton, Oct. 29, 1951; administrator of the Federal Security Agency to F. J. Lawton, Oct. 26, 1951, Nash Files; *C. Q. A., 1951*, p. 194.

76. *Public Papers, 1951*, pp. 616–17.

77. *Call*, Oct. 24, 1952; RG 330: A. M. Rosenberg to E. J. McGrath, Jan. 10, 1953; Nichols, *Breakthrough on the Color Front*, p. 197.

78. *Call*, Apr. 3, Sept. 4, 1953.

79. RG 330: C. E. Wilson to D. D. Eisenhower, May 29, 1953; *Call*, Sept. 4, 1953; *Amsterdam News*, Feb. 13, 1954.

80. Truman Papers, HSTL: W. McL. Hauge to Clarence Mitchell, Feb. 4, 1952; Clarence Mitchell to D. A. Kimball, Feb. 8, 1952, Robert L. Dennison Files.

81. Ibid.: Lester Granger to D. A. Kimball, May 22, 1952; Kimball to Granger, June 18, 1952, Dennison Files.

82. Ibid.: Lester Granger to D. S. Dawson, June 30, 1952; M. J. Connelly, Memorandum, June 28, 1952; Walter White to Truman, June 27, 1952, Dennison Files; Philleo Nash to Commander Rigden, July 11, 1952, Nash Files; *Chicago Defender*, July 5, 1952.

83. *Call*, June 5, Aug. 28, 1953; *Charleston News and Courier*, Aug. 21, 1953; *Amsterdam News*, Nov. 28, 1953.

84. *Call*, Sept. 25, Oct. 9, 1953; *Courier*, Oct. 10, 1953; *Amsterdam News*, July 31, 1954.

85. *Amsterdam News*, July 31, 1954; *New York Times*, Oct. 31, 1954; *Courier*, Aug. 7, 1954; U.S. Commission on Civil Rights, *Civil Rights '63* (Washington, 1963), p. 180.

86. Frank Pace, Jr., Papers, HSTL: Pace to Walter White, Jan. 19, 1953; *Call*, Sept. 11, 1953; *Amsterdam News*, July 10, 1954; *New York Times*, Oct. 31, 1954.

87. Commission on Civil Rights, *Civil Rights '63*, pp. 175–76, 221.

88. Nichols, *Breakthrough on the Color Front*, p. 97; Office of the Assistant Secretary of Defense, *Integration and the Negro Officer in the Armed Forces of the United States of America* (Washington, 1962), pp. 25–26; Richard J. Stillman, II, *Integration of the Negro in the U.S. Armed Forces* (New York, 1968), p. 68; *Courier*, June 7, 1969.

89. *New York Times*, Oct. 31, 1954; *Kansas City Star*, May 5, 1969.

90. *Kansas City Times*, Apr. 1, 1969; Commission on Civil Rights, *Civil Rights '63*, pp. 180–83, 192–202, 216.

91. *New York Times*, Oct. 31, 1954; Stillman, *Integration of the Negro in the U.S. Armed Forces*, p. 85; *Courier*, Aug. 10, 1968.

92. Stillman, *Integration of the Negro in the U.S. Armed Forces*, pp. 95–107, 115.

93. Commission on Civil Rights, *Civil Rights '63*, p. 221.

94. Stillman, *Integration of the Negro in the U.S. Armed Forces*, p. 65; *Courier*, July 27, Aug. 10, 1968; *Los Angeles Times*, May 14, 1971.

95. *New York Times*, July 27, 1968; *Courier*, Aug. 10, 1968.

CHAPTER 12

1. *Call*, Oct. 22, 1948; Truman Papers, HSTL: Guy Moffett to the Civil Service Commission, Sept. 30, 1949, OF 2F.

2. Truman Papers, HSTL: Guy Moffett to the Civil Service Commission, Sept. 30, 1949, OF 2F.

3. Ibid.

4. Samuel Krislov, *The Negro in Federal Employment: The Quest for Equal Opportunity* (Minneapolis, Minn., 1967), p. 117; Truman Papers, HSTL: J. L. Houghteling to the Civil Service Commission, n.d., OF 2F.

5. Truman Papers, HSTL: J. L. Houghteling to D. S. Dawson, June 6, 1951, OF 2F.

6. Ibid.: J. L. Houghteling, "Fair Employment Board Information Bulletin No. 6," Mar. 31, 1952, OF 2F; Fair Employment Board, U.S. Civil Service Com-

mission, *Fair Employment in the Federal Service* (Washington, 1952), p. 10; Krislov, *The Negro in Federal Employment*, p. 133.

7. *Washington Times-Herald*, Oct. 8, 1948.
8. Truman Papers, HSTL: D. K. Niles to D. S. Dawson, Dec. 12, 1950; M. L. Friedman to Dawson, Dec. 18, 1950, and enclosed "Summary of Report of Fair Employment Board," n.d., OF 2F.
9. Ibid.: D. S. Dawson to Truman, Dec. 28, 1950; Philleo Nash to M. L. Friedman, Nov. 8, 1951, OF 2F.
10. Ibid.: Guy Moffett to the Civil Service Commission, Sept. 30, 1949, OF 2F.
11. Ibid.: W. R. Vawter to J. O. Garber, Feb. 15, 1950, OF 596.
12. Ibid.: J. L. Houghteling to D. S. Dawson, May 26, 1950, OF 596.
13. Fair Employment Board, *Fair Employment in the Federal Service*, pp. 5–6.
14. Ibid., pp. 8–11; Truman Papers, HSTL: J. L. Houghteling to the Civil Service Commission, n.d., OF 2F.
15. Fair Employment Board, *Fair Employment in the Federal Service*, pp. 3–4; Fair Employment Board, "Complaints of Discrimination in the Federal Service," *Informational Bulletin No. 10* (Washington, Aug. 1, 1954).
16. *New York Times*, Jan. 27, 1948; *Courier*, Jan. 8, 1949; NAACP, *Annual Report, 1948*, p. 54; *American Jewish Year Book, 1951*, p. 31.
17. *Afro-American*, July 30, 1949; *Chicago Defender*, Aug. 6, 1949; *Journal and Guide*, July 30, 1949.
18. Truman Papers, HSTL: Taft Feiman to W. D. Hassett, Dec. 16, 1948, OF 2F Misc.; Green, *Secret City*, p. 286; National Archives and Records Service, Washington, D.C., Record Group 16, Records of the Secretary of Agriculture: C. A. Barnett to C. F. Brannan, Mar. 2, 1951; Truman Papers, HSTL: A. A. Clemons to O. L. Chapman, June 28, 1952, OF 400 Alaska.
19. *Afro-American*, May 20, 1950; *Courier*, Oct. 23, 1948; Truman Papers, HSTL: W. F. Ryan to D. S. Dawson, July 25, 1949, OF 252; Graves, *Fair Employment Practice Legislation*, p. 14.
20. *Call*, Feb. 18, 1949; Truman Papers, HSTL: J. L. Houghteling, Memorandum, "Basis of Appeal," Feb. 23, 1950, Nash Files.
21. *Call*, Feb. 18, 1949; Truman Papers, HSTL: Thomas Richardson to D. K. Niles, Jan. 26, 1949; J. L. Houghteling, Memorandum, "Basis of Appeal," Feb. 23, 1950, Nash Files; Fair Employment Board, *Fair Employment in the Federal Service*, pp. 7–8.
22. *C. Q. A., 1950*, pp. 415–16; Truman Papers, HSTL: E. H. Foley, Jr., to D. K. Niles, July 7, 1950, Nash Files.
23. Truman Papers, HSTL: E. H. Foley, Jr., to D. K. Niles, July 7, 1950, Nash Files; S. J. Spingarn Papers, HSTL: R. L. Neustadt to Spingarn, July 15, 1950.
24. *American Jewish Year Book, 1952*, pp. 100–101; Guzman, *Negro Year Book, 1952*, p. 120; *Courier*, Nov. 21, 1953.
25. *Courier*, Apr. 15, 22, 29, 1950.
26. *Call*, Mar. 9, 1951; Truman Papers, HSTL: D. S. Dawson to C. E. Wilson, Oct. 4, 1951, OF 93.
27. Department of State, Office of Personnel: P. W. Condon to Mr. McDermott, Apr. 16, 1951.
28. Ibid.: A. P. Randolph to Dean Acheson, Mar. 28, 1952.
29. Ibid.: E. N. Montague to T. E. Brown, May 22, 1952; Montague to J. C.

Green, Mar. 13, 1953; Truman Papers, HSTL: D. W. Kuhn to Philleo Nash, June 10, 1952, Nash Files.

30. Department of State, Office of Personnel: E. N. Montague to C. M. Mitchell, Mar. 31, 1953, and enclosed "Progress Report on the Employment of Colored Persons in the Department of State."

31. *Call*, Sept. 7, Nov. 2, 1951.

32. *Chicago Defender*, Dec. 16, 1950; *Courier*, Apr. 28, 1951; *Call*, July 27, 1951.

33. *Chicago Defender*, Sept. 22, 1951; *Call*, Oct. 5, 26, 1951, Mar. 21, June 13, 1952.

34. *Chicago Defender*, Apr. 28, 1951; *Call*, May 11, 1951; William Seal Carpenter, *The Unfinished Business of Civil Service Reform* (Princeton, N.J., 1952), p. 39; Herbert Hollander, *Crisis in the Civil Service* (Washington, 1955), pp. 67, 69; Paul P. Van Riper, *History of the United States Civil Service* (Evanston, Ill., 1958), pp. 344–47, 469.

35. *Afro-American*, Jan. 6, 1951; *Amsterdam News*, Feb. 3, 1951.

36. *Courier*, Mar. 24, 1951; *Amsterdam News*, Feb. 3, Apr. 14, 1951; *Chicago Defender*, Jan. 27, 1951; *Afro-American*, Jan. 6, 1951; *Call*, May 11, 1951.

37. *Call*, Mar. 2, 1951; *Chicago Defender*, Apr. 28, 1951; *Afro-American*, Apr. 21, 1951.

38. *Afro-American*, May 5, 1951; *Call*, Apr. 20, 1951; *Amsterdam News*, May 12, 1951.

39. *Chicago Defender*, June 9, 1951; *Courier*, June 2, 1951; *Call*, Aug. 24, 1951; Truman Papers, HSTL: D. S. Dawson to W. J. Hopkins, June 12, 1951, Nash Files.

40. *Chicago Defender*, Mar. 3, June 30, 1951; *Courier*, Dec. 8, 1951.

41. For example, see Eleanor Bontecou, *The Federal Loyalty-Security Program* (Ithaca, N.Y., 1953).

42. *Afro-American*, Mar. 29, 1947; *Amsterdam News*, June 28, 1947; *Call*, Aug. 29, 1947; Truman Papers, HSTL: Truman to Philip Murray, Apr. 15, 1947, OF 252K; Walter White to Truman, Nov. 12, 1947, OF 2E.

43. Truman Papers, HSTL: J. L. Thurston to J. R. Steelman, Nov. 13, 1947, OF 596A; C. S. Murphy Papers, HSTL: S. J. Spingarn to Clark Clifford, Apr. 6, 1949; S. J. Spingarn Papers, HSTL: Spingarn to Clifford, Dec. 30, 1949.

44. *Courier*, Oct. 30, 1948; *Call*, Oct. 29, 1948; *Amsterdam News*, Dec. 25, 1948.

45. Bontecou, *The Federal Loyalty-Security Program*, p. 141; Truman Papers, HSTL: Abram Flaxer to Truman, Nov. 24, 1948; Walter White to Truman, Nov. 26, 1948, OF 252K.

46. Truman Papers, HSTL: Abram Flaxer to Truman, Nov. 24, 1948, OF 252K; *Chicago Defender*, Mar. 22, 1952.

47. *Courier*, Jan. 22, 1949; Truman Papers, HSTL: Andrew Jacobs to Truman, Mar. 25, 1949; M. J. Connelly to Jacobs, Apr. 15, 1949, OF 252K.

48. Truman Papers, HSTL: Carl Murphy to Truman, Apr. 10, 1950; D. S. Dawson to Murphy, June 7, 1950; S. W. Richardson to H. B. Mitchell, May 23, 1950, OF 93 Misc.

49. *Public Papers, 1950*, p. 184.

50. *American Jewish Year Book, 1952*, p. 95.

51. National Archives and Records Service, Washington, D.C., Record Group 174, General Records of the Department of Labor (hereafter cited as RG 174): Walter White to W. S. Symington, Aug. 10, 1950; Symington to Maurice Tobin, Aug. 25, 1950; White to Symington, Sept. 12, 1950;

Symington to Tobin, Sept. 15, 1950; National Archives and Records Service, Washington, D.C., Record Group 304, Records of the Office of Defense Mobilization (hereafter cited as RG 304): Lester Granger to W. S. Symington, Aug. 22, 1950; Arnold Aronson to Walter White, Oct. 18, 1950; White to Aronson, Oct. 19, 1950; White to Symington, Oct. 19, 1950.

52. RG 304: W. S. Symington to Walter White, Oct. 21, 1950; Symington to Michael Gavin, Oct. 21, 1950; V. Laird to Symington, Oct. 24, 30, 1950; R. L. Memorandum, Oct. 30, 1950.

53. Truman Papers, HSTL: G. L. P. Weaver to W. S. Symington, Dec. 1, 1950; A. P. Randolph to Truman, Dec. 14, 1950, Nash Files; *Public Papers, 1950,* pp. 741–47.

54. Truman Papers, HSTL: Maurice Tobin to D. K. Niles, Dec. 27, 1950, Nash Files; *Chicago Defender,* Jan. 6, 1951; *Amsterdam News,* Jan. 20, 1951.

55. RG 304: Walter White to W. S. Symington, Jan. 5, 1951; White to C. E. Wilson, Jan. 4, 1951; Truman Papers, HSTL: White to D. K. Niles, Jan. 5, 1951, Nash Files.

56. Truman Papers, HSTL: M. McL. Bethune et al. to Truman, Jan. 9, 1951; D. K. Niles to A. P. Randolph, Jan. 10, 1951; Randolph to Niles, Jan. 15, 1951, OF 93; "Statement by the President," Jan. 16, 1951, Nash Files.

57. *Public Papers, 1951,* pp. 108–12.

58. *Afro-American,* Jan. 27, 1951; *Chicago Defender,* Feb. 3, 1951; *Crisis,* LVIII (Feb. 1951), 102; Truman Papers, HSTL: D. K. Niles to M. J. Connelly, Jan. 17, 1951; A. P. Randolph to Niles, Jan. 18, 1951; M. McL. Bethune et al. to Truman Jan. 25, Feb. 9, 1951, OF 93; G. L. P. Weaver to W. S. Symington, Mar. 30, 1951, Nash Files.

59. Federal Register Division, National Archives and Records Service, *Code of Federal Regulations: Title 3—The President, 1949–1953 Compilation* (Washington, 1958), pp. 390–91, 732, 739, 741, 752, 781–84, 828–29.

60. Truman Papers, HSTL: J. R. Steelman to H. H. Lehman, Oct. 26, 1950, OF 264.

61. Ibid.: G. L. P. Weaver to W. S. Symington, Mar. 30, 1951, Nash Files; Undated Memorandum filed by W. J. Hopkins, June 11, 1951; A. P. Randolph to Truman, Feb. 28, 1951, OF 93.

62. Ibid.: W. J. Hopkins Memorandum (and notations), Feb. 6, 1951, OF 40.

63. Ibid.: Memorandum, "President's Fair Employment Practices Committee," Jan. 3, 1951, Nash Files.

64. *American Jewish Year Book, 1952,* p. 96; *Congressional Record,* Feb. 23, 1944, 78th Cong., 2d sess., p. 1963.

65. Truman Papers, HSTL: G. L. P. Weaver to W. S. Symington, Dec. 1, 1950; Maurice Tobin to D. K. Niles, Dec. 27, 1950; Memorandum, "President's Fair Employment Practices Committee," Jan. 3, 1951, Nash Files.

66. *Chicago Defender,* Jan. 27, 1951; *Courier,* June 2, 1951; *American Jewish Year Book, 1952,* pp. 95–96; U.S. Commission on Civil Rights, *1961 Report, Employment* (Washington, 1961), pp. 20, 56; C. S. Murphy Papers, HSTL: J. C. Duggan to Murphy, Dec. 3, 1951.

67. *Call,* Mar. 30, Apr. 6, 1951.

68. C. S. Murphy Papers, HSTL: J. E. Webb to Truman, Dec. 9, 1950.

69. *Public Papers, 1951,* pp. 6–13.

70. Truman Papers, HSTL: President's Appointments Books, May 21, 1951, M. J. Connelly Files; Philleo Nash to G. M. Elsey, May 23, 1951, Nash Files.

71. *C. Q. A., 1951,* pp. 116, 337–38. Throughout early 1951 the White House also toyed with the idea of issuing an executive order establishing the President's Commission on the Exercise of the Right to Vote. According to George Elsey, the proposal "died a slow death" because of the opposition of Chairman William Boyle and other members of the Democratic National Committee. Elsey also noted that the Budget Bureau saw "some risk in proposing another Presidential Commission to be paid out of emergency funds at this time, inasmuch as the Congress is in a bearish mood on Presidential Commissions." G. M. Elsey Papers, HSTL: Memorandum for the File, June 30, 1951; Elsey to D. D. Lloyd, Apr. 2, 1951.

72. *The Budget of the United States Government for the Fiscal Year Ending June 30, 1952* (Washington, 1951), p. 48; *Afro-American,* May 19, 1951; *Call,* May 18, 1951.

73. Ibid.; *Public Papers, 1951,* pp. 79–80; *C. Q. A., 1951,* p. 116.

74. Truman Papers, HSTL: Walter White to Truman, Mar. 20, 1951, OF 413; S. M. Cavert to Truman, June 25, 1951, OF 2953; *Call,* Apr. 6, May 11, 1951; *Courier,* May 12, 1951; *Crisis,* LVIII (Apr. 1951), 258; *Crisis,* LVIII (June–July 1951), 395.

75. *Public Papers, 1951,* pp. 347–48; Truman Papers, HSTL: P. M. Malin et al. to Truman, June 24, 1951, OF 40 Misc.; *American Jewish Year Book, 1952,* pp. 96–97.

76. Nash Papers, HSTL: Truman to C. S. Murphy, attached to William Benton to Truman, Oct. 20, 1951; Murphy Papers, HSTL: C. S. Murphy to Truman, Dec. 1, 1951; Truman Papers, HSTL: Walter White and A. P. Randolph to Truman, Nov. 30, 1951, Nash Files.

77. *Public Papers, 1951,* pp. 640–41.

78. *New York Times,* Dec. 4, 1951; Murphy Papers, HSTL: J. C. Duggan to C. S. Murphy, Dec. 3, 1951.

79. Paul H. Norgren and Samuel E. Hill, *Toward Fair Employment* (New York, 1964), p. 157.

80. Ibid., p. 158; *New York Times,* Dec. 4, 1951; *Courier,* Mar. 29, 1969.

81. Murphy Papers, HSTL: C. S. Murphy to Truman, Dec. 1, 1951; *New York Times,* Dec. 4, 1951; Truman Papers, HSTL: Truman to D. R. G. Palmer, OF 526B.

82. *Washington Post,* Dec. 4, 1951; *Afro-American,* Dec. 15, 1951; *Call,* Dec. 14, 1951.

83. *Courier,* Dec. 15, 1951; *Afro-American,* Dec. 15, 1951; *Amsterdam News,* Dec. 15, 1951.

84. Clarence Mitchell, "President Truman's 'FEPC,'" *Crisis,* LIX (Jan. 1952), 5; *Public Papers, 1952,* p. 19.

85. *Chicago Defender,* June 21, 1952; National Archives and Records Service, Washington, D.C., Record Group 325, Records of the Committee on Government Contract Compliance (hereafter cited as RG 325): Minutes of the CGCC, Feb. 19, Mar. 10, Nov. 12, 1952; Agenda for Meeting of CGCC, May 20, 1952.

86. President's Committee on Government Contract Compliance, *Equal Economic Opportunity* (Washington, 1953), p. 3.

87. Ibid., pp. 15, 17–18, 42–46; RG 325: Minutes of the CGCC, Oct. 7, Nov. 12, 1952.

88. President's Committee on Government Contract Compliance, *Equal Economic Opportunity*, pp. 26–27; RG 325: R. R. Granville to D. R. G. Palmer, June 9, 20, 23, July 9, 30, 1952.
89. President's Committee on Government Contract Compliance, *Equal Economic Opportunity*, pp. 28, 31–32; RG 325: R. R. Granville to D. R. G. Palmer, July 30, 1952; CGCC Summary of Complaints, May 16, 1952.
90. *Courier*, Mar. 29, 1969.
91. President's Committee on Government Contract Compliance, *Equal Economic Opportunity*, pp. 63–76; Commission on Civil Rights, *1961 Report, Employment*, pp. 14–16.
92. Commission on Civil Rights, *1961 Report, Employment*, pp. 65–66.
93. *Courier*, Mar. 1, 29, 1969; *Kansas City Star*, May 22, 1969.

CHAPTER 13

1. *Afro-American*, Nov. 11, 1950.
2. *Chicago Defender*, Oct. 21, 1950.
3. *Call*, Nov. 3, 1950; *Chicago Defender*, Nov. 4, 1950; *Public Papers, 1950*, p. 702.
4. *Call*, Nov. 3, 1950.
5. Guzman, *Negro Year Book, 1952*, p. 301.
6. *C. Q. A., 1950*, p. 736.
7. *Afro-American*, Nov. 18, 1950; *Journal and Guide*, Nov. 25, 1950; *Chicago Defender*, Nov. 18, 1950.
8. *New York Times*, Jan. 4, 1951.
9. *Public Papers, 1950*, p. 714; S. J. Spingarn Papers, HSTL: Philleo Nash to Spingarn, June 21, 1950; Memorandum, "Civil Rights Votes, 1949–1950."
10. *Call*, Jan. 12, 1951; *Afro-American*, Jan. 20, 1951; *Chicago Defender*, Jan. 13, 1951; *Amsterdam News*, Jan. 13, 1951.
11. *Public Papers, 1951*, pp. 1, 5.
12. Ibid., pp. 6–13, 22.
13. Ibid., p. 80.
14. *Journal and Guide*, Jan. 20, 1951.
15. *Afro-American*, June 30, 1951.
16. *Call*, Apr. 6, 1951; RG 16: C. A. Barnett to Wesley McCune, Nov. 29, 1950.
17. *American Jewish Year Book, 1952*, p. 97; *New York Times*, June 26, 1951; *Chicago Defender*, Sept. 22, 1951.
18. *C. Q. A., 1951*, pp. 333–34; A. B. Spingarn Papers: Report of the Secretary to the June 1951 Meeting of the Board of Directors of the NAACP.
19. 65 Stat. 151.
20. *Chicago Defender*, Apr. 28, 1951; *Call*, May 4, 18, 1951.
21. *Chicago Defender*, June 2, 1951; A. B. Spingarn Papers: Opening Remarks of Walter White at Civil Rights Conference in Washington, May 22–23, 1951; Report of the Secretary to the June 1951 Meeting of the Board of Directors of the NAACP.
22. American Jewish Committee, *45th Report, 1952*, pp. 38–39; AJC and NAACP, *Balance Sheet, 1951*, pp. 7–8.
23. *Amsterdam News*, Jan. 27, 1951.
24. *C. Q. A., 1951*, pp. 282–83; *Afro-American*, Mar. 31, 1951.

25. *C. Q. A.*, *1951*, p. 296; A. B. Spingarn Papers: Report of the Secretary to the June 1951 Meeting of the Board of Directors of the NAACP.

26. *Public Papers, 1951*, pp. 616–17; *Chicago Defender*, Nov. 17, 1951.

27. Guzman, *Negro Year Book, 1952*, p. 297.

28. *Public Papers, 1950*, p. 116, n. 1; *New York Times*, Feb. 4, 24, Mar. 9, 22, Apr. 18, May 7, 11, 25, 27, 1950; Truman Papers, HSTL: E. H. Pruden to Truman, May 31, 1950; Truman to Pruden, June 6, 1950, OF 76B. See also the correspondence in Truman Papers, OF 76B, OF 76B Myron Taylor Misc., OF 76B Personal Representative to the Vatican.

29. Truman Papers, HSTL: E. H. Pruden to Truman, n.d. (filed Sept. 23, 1950), OF 76B Personal Representative to the Vatican.

30. Ibid.: OF 76B.

31. *Public Papers, 1951*, pp. 601, 603; S. J. Spingarn Papers, HSTL: G. M. Elsey to C. S. Murphy, Feb. 16, 1950; Truman Papers, HSTL: W. J. Williams to W. J. Hassett, Nov. 1, 1951, OF 76B; *New York Times*, Oct. 30, 1951.

32. *Public Papers, 1951*, pp. 603, 645; *C. Q. A.*, *1951*, p. 689.

33. *New York Times*, Oct. 20, 1951.

34. *Chicago Defender*, Oct. 6, Dec. 8, 1951; *Courier*, Sept. 22, 1951; *Chicago Tribune*, Nov. 14, 1951.

35. *Courier*, Sept. 15, 1951; *Chicago Defender*, Oct. 6, 27, 1951.

36. *Chicago Defender*, Oct. 6, 1951; *Courier*, Sept. 29, 1951.

37. See the numerous clippings in Democratic National Committee Papers, HSTL, Clipping File.

38. *Call*, July 20, 1951; *New York Times*, July 13, 1951; NAACP, *Annual Report, 1951*, pp. 55–57.

39. *Call*, July 20, Aug. 10, 1951.

40. NAACP, *Annual Report, 1951*, pp. 56–57; *New York Times*, Dec. 14, 1951, June 5, July 29, 1952; *Public Papers, 1952–53*, p. 799.

41. *Call*, July 20, 1951; *Journal and Guide*, Jan. 19, 1952; *New York Times*, Dec. 11, 1952; *Chicago Defender*, Mar. 22, 1952.

42. *Crisis*, LIX (Jan. 1952), 34; *Call*, Jan. 11, 1952; McGrath Papers, HSTL: Walter White Address to the Emergency Conference at Jacksonville, Florida, Jan. 21, 1952.

43. McGrath Papers, HSTL: Walter White to McGrath, Jan. 3, 4, 14, 1952; McGrath to White, Jan. 11, 1952; M. E. Fanebust to White, Jan. 3, 1952; *Journal and Guide*, Jan. 19, 1952; *New York Times*, Dec. 11, 1952; Truman Papers, HSTL: Philleo Nash to Truman, Jan. 3, 1952, Nash Files.

44. *New York Times*, Mar. 2, 1951.

45. *Public Papers, 1951*, pp. 314–16, 370–74.

46. *New York Times*, Aug. 30, 1951; *Washington Post*, Aug. 30, 1951; Truman Papers, HSTL: H. H. Vaughan to Herman Feldman, Sept. 11, 1951, OF 471B.

47. See correspondence in Truman Papers, HSTL: OF 471B, and H. H. Vaughan to Harry Wilson, Jan. 18, 1952, OF 471B; *Journal and Guide*, Sept. 8, 1951; *New York Times*, Jan. 13, 1952.

48. Edward A. Richards, ed., *Proceedings of the Midcentury White House Conference on Children and Youth* (Raleigh, N.C., 1951), pp. 29, 35, 36, 39, 48.

49. *Public Papers, 1952–53*, p. 3; President's Commission on the Health Needs of

the Nation, *Building America's Health* (5 vols.; Washington, 1952–1953), I, iii–viii.
50. President's Commission on the Health Needs of the Nation, *Building America's Health*, III, 26–27.
51. Ibid., V, vii–viii, 172, 175, 179–80.
52. Ibid., I, 21, 28, 48, 52, 70.
53. *Public Papers, 1952–53*, pp. 1087, 1166–67.
54. Truman Papers, HSTL: J. H. McGrath to Truman, Dec. 6, 1951; C. W. Sawyer to Truman, Nov. 30, 1951, Nash Files.
55. *Public Papers, 1952–53*, pp. 16, 94.
56. *Afro-American*, Jan. 19, 1952; *Call*, Jan. 25, 1952; *Chicago Defender*, Jan. 19, 1952.
57. *Crisis*, LIX (Mar. 1952), 170; *New York Times*, Feb. 18, 1952.
58. *Public Papers, 1952–53*, pp. 225, 325–26, 346; *Call*, May 16, 1952, *Amsterdam News*, May 24, 1952; *C. Q. A., 1952*, pp. 235–37.
59. *Public Papers, 1952–53*, pp. 303, 409; *C. Q. A., 1952*, p. 233; Congressional Quarterly Service, *Congress and the Nation*, p. 1514.
60. *Chicago Defender*, Mar. 29, 1952; *Amsterdam News*, May 31, 1952.
61. *Public Papers, 1952–53*, pp. 441–47.
62. *Amsterdam News*, July 5, 1952; *Afro-American*, July 5, 1952.
63. *C. Q. A., 1952*, pp. 154–60, 184.
64. *New York Times*, Apr. 14, 1952; *New Republic*, CXXVI (June 23, 1952), 8; Harold L. Ickes, "The Indian Loses Again," *New Republic*, CXXV (Sept. 24, 1951), 16.
65. Truman Papers, HSTL: Oliver La Farge to Truman, Aug. 27, 1951; N. B. Johnson to Truman, Aug. 27, 1951, OF 296.
66. *New York Times*, Dec. 15, 1951, Jan. 25, 1952; Harold L. Ickes, " 'Justice' in a Deep Freeze," *New Republic*, CXXIV (May 21, 1951), 17; Chapman Papers, HSTL: H. L. Ickes to O. L. Chapman, Aug. 28, 30, 1951; Lehman Papers, Columbia University: Rex Lee to H. H. Lehman, Nov. 19, 1951.
67. *C. Q. A., 1952*, p. 501.
68. *New York Times*, Nov. 1, 3, 1951; *Public Papers, 1951*, p. 478.
69. Chapman Papers, HSTL: H. L. Ickes to the Editor of *New York Herald Tribune*, Sept. 8, 1950; Ickes to O. L. Chapman, Sept. 9, 1950; Lehman Papers, Columbia University: John Collier to H. H. Lehman, Nov. 20, 1950; Dillon S. Myer Papers, HSTL: Speech by Commissioner of Indian Affairs Dillon S. Myer before the Annual Meeting of the Association on American Indian Affairs, Mar. 26, 1952; 67 Stat. 277, 280, H. Con. Res. 108.
70. *New Republic*, CXXIX (Nov. 2, 1953), 3; John Collier, "Back to Dishonor?," *Christian Century*, LXXI (May 12, 1954), 578–80; Commission on Civil Rights, *1961 Report, Justice*, pp. 123–24; Brophy and Aberle, *The Indian*, pp. 180–93.
71. *Public Papers, 1952–53*, p. 106; D. S. Myer Papers, HSTL: Speech by . . . Dillon S. Myer . . . Mar. 26, 1952.
72. Commission on Civil Rights, *1961 Report, Justice*, p. 159; Fey and McNickle, *Indians and Other Americans*, pp. 150–53; *Los Angeles Times*, May 2, 1971.
73. Truman Papers, HSTL: J. L. Sundquist to R. W. Jones, Mar. 30, 1950, OF 407D; J. H. McGrath to Truman, Dec. 6, 1951, Nash Files.
74. Ibid.: J. L. Sundquist to R. W. Jones, Mar. 30, 1950; C. P. Anderson to Truman, May 26, Aug. 24, 1949, OF 407D; David H. Stowe Papers, HSTL:

P. R. Kibbe, Report to Members of the Good Neighbor Commission of Texas, April 17–27, 1947.

75. Edward D. Garza, "LULAC (League of United Latin American Citizens)," Master's thesis, Southwest Texas State Teachers College, 1951, pp. 14, 29, 36, 41–43, 49–51; *Afro-American,* June 5, 1948; Truman Papers, HSTL: H. P. Garcia to Civil Rights Commission, May 5, 1948, OF 596 Misc.; W. Y. Herrara to Truman, Oct. 20, 1948, OF 407D.

76. Truman Papers, HSTL: J. L. Sundquist to R. W. Jones, Mar. 30, 1950; Roy Wilkins to Truman, OF 407D; *New York Times,* June 26, 1951; Peter Matthiessen, "Profiles," *New Yorker,* XLV (June 21, 1969), pp. 42, 46, 48.

77. Truman Papers, HSTL: Truman to C. P. Anderson, June 2, Aug. 26, 1949; Truman to H. L. Mitchell, Nov. 5, 1949, OF 407D.

78. Stowe Papers, HSTL: Byron Mitchell to J. O. Garber, Feb. 17, 1949; Truman Papers, HSTL: D. K. Niles to Truman, June 8, 1949; Truman to Roy Wilkins, Nov. 8, 1949; J. L. Sundquist to R. W. Jones, Mar. 30, 1950, OF 407D.

79. *Public Papers, 1950,* pp. 452–53.

80. President's Commission on Migratory Labor, *Migratory Labor in American Agriculture* (Washington, 1951), pp. vii, 56–59, 177–85; *New York Times,* Apr. 8, 1951.

81. Commission on Migratory Labor Papers, HSTL: Varden Fuller to M. T. Van Hecke, Apr. 11, 1951; *C. Q. A., 1951,* pp. 95–98; Truman Papers, HSTL: William Green to Truman, July 3, 1951; Philip Murray to Truman, July 5, 1951; H. L. Mitchell to Truman, July 3, 1951, OF 407D.

82. Stowe Papers, HSTL: Stowe to Truman, July 8, 1951.

83. *Public Papers, 1951,* pp. 389–93.

84. Stowe Papers, HSTL: Truman to Miguel Aleman, July 14, 1951.

85. *New York Times,* Aug. 12, 1951; *C. Q. A., 1952,* pp. 113–14, 117–18, 160–61, 189–90; Truman Papers, HSTL: R. W. Jones to W. J. Hopkins, Mar. 18, 1952, OF 407D; Ellis W. Hawley, "The Politics of the Mexican Labor Issue, 1950–1965," *Agricultural History,* XL (July 1966), 162, 174–76.

86. Stowe Papers, HSTL: F. J. Lawton to Truman, Jan. 4, 1952; "Summary of Task Force Report on Migratory Labor in Agriculture," n.d.; *Public Papers, 1952–53,* pp. 94–95, 102; *New York Times,* May 11, 1952.

87. *C. Q. A., 1951,* p. 213; *C. Q. A., 1952,* p. 270.

CHAPTER 14

1. *Public Papers, 1952–53,* pp. 220–25.

2. *Chicago Sun-Times,* Feb. 23, 1952; *Christian Science Monitor,* Apr. 7, 1952; Democratic National Committee Papers, HSTL, Clipping File.

3. *Journal and Guide,* Apr. 5, 1952; *Call,* Apr. 18, 1952; *Courier,* Apr. 19, 1952. See also Truman Papers, HSTL: Walter White News Release, Apr. 3, 1952, OF 413.

4. *Afro-American,* Feb. 9, 1952; *Chicago Defender,* Feb. 9, 1952; *Call,* Apr. 4, 1952; *New York Times,* May 4, 1952.

5. Truman Papers, HSTL: Walter White News Release, Apr. 3, 1952, OF 413; *Afro-American,* Feb. 9, 1952; *Chicago Defender,* Apr. 5, 1952; *Call,* Apr. 4, 1952; *Courier,* Apr. 19, 1952.

6. *New York Times,* Mar. 31, 1952; Noel F. Busch, *Adlai E. Stevenson of Illinois: A Portrait* (New York, 1952), pp. 94–95, 203.

7. *New York Times*, May 4, 14, 18, June 17, 25, 1952; *Call*, June 27, July 4, 1952.
8. *Journal and Guide*, June 2, 1951; *Afro-American*, June 2, 1951.
9. *Call*, Feb. 15, 1952; *Afro-American*, Mar. 29, 1952.
10. *Afro-American*, Oct. 27, 1951, Apr. 5, 1952; *Call*, Nov. 16, Dec. 14, 1951; Guzman, *Negro Year Book, 1952*, p. 302.
11. *New York Times*, Apr. 21, 1952; *Crisis*, LIX (Mar. 1952), 171; *Afro-American*, June 7, 1952.
12. *Call*, May 9, 1952; Truman Papers, HSTL: Walter White News Release, Apr. 3, 1952, OF 413; *New York Times*, Apr. 21, 1952; *Afro-American*, Apr. 26, 1952.
13. *New York Times*, June 6, 1952; *Call*, June 13, 1952.
14. *C. Q. A., 1952*, pp. 493–94; *New York Times*, July 9, 10, 11, 1952; *Call*, July 18, 1952.
15. *Call*, July 18, 1952; *Chicago Defender*, July 19, 1952; *Journal and Guide*, July 19, 1952; *Courier*, July 19, 1952; *Afro-American*, July 19, 1952.
16. *New York Times*, May 18, June 6, 1952.
17. *Public Papers, 1952–53*, pp. 341–47.
18. *New York Times*, May 18, 1952; *Washington Star*, May 19, 1952.
19. *Public Papers, 1952–53*, pp. 420–24.
20. *Chicago Defender*, June 21, 28, 1952; *Courier*, June 28, 1952; *Afro-American*, June 21, 1952; *Amsterdam News*, June 21, 1952; *Call*, June 20, 1952; Truman Papers, HSTL: Thurgood Marshall to Truman, June 14, 1952, M. McL. Bethune to Truman, June 16, 1952, PPF 200 Speeches.
21. *Public Papers, 1952–53*, p. 435.
22. Truman Papers, HSTL: C. S. Murphy to J. W. McCormack, June 28, July 8, 1952, Murphy Files; Paul T. David, Malcolm Moos, and Ralph M. Goldman, *Presidential Nominating Politics in 1952: The National Story* (Baltimore, Md., 1954), p. 111.
23. Murphy Papers, HSTL: C. S. Murphy to Truman, July 16, 1952; Elsey Papers, HSTL: Draft of Democratic Platform, July 18, 1952.
24. *Call*, Aug. 1, 1952; Hays, *A Southern Moderate Speaks*, pp. 74, 79–80; David, Moos, and Goldman, *Presidential Nominating Politics in 1952*, pp. 131–36.
25. *Public Papers, 1952–53*, pp. 505, 507.
26. *Call*, Aug. 1, 1952; *Chicago Defender*, Aug. 2, 1952; *Amsterdam News*, Aug. 2, 1952.
27. *Crisis*, LIX (Aug.–Sept. 1952), 413.
28. *C. Q. A., 1952*, pp. 495–502.
29. Hays, *A Southern Moderate Speaks*, pp. 80–81.
30. *New York Times*, July 27, Aug. 5, Sept. 3, 1952.
31. Ibid., Aug. 5, 10, 1952; *Public Papers, 1952–53*, p. 512.
32. *Call*, Sept. 5, 19, 1952; *New York Times*, Aug. 30, Sept. 3, 10, 1952.
33. *New York Times*, July 27, 30, 1952.
34. *Amsterdam News*, Aug. 2, 1952; *Afro-American*, Oct. 4, 25, 1952; *Call*, Oct. 3, 17, 24, 31, 1952.
35. *Afro-American*, Aug. 9, 1952; *Call*, Sept. 3, Oct. 17, 24, 31, 1952; C. A. Bacote, "Negro Vote in the Southeast," *Crisis*, LIX (Oct. 1952), 501–4.
36. *New York Times*, Sept. 19, 1952; Val J. Washington, "The Republican Case for 1952," *Crisis*, LIX (Oct. 1952), 487–91, 539; Bacote, "Negro Vote in the Southeast," p. 503; *Call*, Oct. 24, 1952.

37. *New York Times*, Oct. 1, 26, 28, 31, 1952; *Call*, Oct. 10, 1952.
38. *Public Papers, 1952–53*, pp. 535, 544.
39. Ibid., pp. 770–74, 785–86, 797–801, 862, 887, 897, 906–7, 909, 974, 977, 986–88, 990, 1006–12, 1030–31, 1046.
40. Ibid., p. 799.
41. Ibid., pp. 800, 887–88, 897.
42. Ibid., pp. 906, 986–88.
43. Ibid., pp. 1008–12.
44. Ibid., p. 1047.
45. *Call*, Sept. 19, 1952.
46. Ibid., Nov. 14, 1952.
47. *Courier*, Oct. 25, 1952.
48. *Call*, Sept. 26, Oct. 3, 10, 17, 24, 1952; *Afro-American*, Oct. 11, 1952; *Chicago Defender*, Oct. 18, 1952; *Journal and Guide*, Oct. 4, 1952; *Amsterdam News*, Oct. 25, 1952.
49. *Call*, Oct. 3, 24, 1952; *Afro-American*, Oct. 11, 1952; *Amsterdam News*, Oct. 25, 1952.
50. S. J. Spingarn Papers, HSTL: K. W. Hechler to Spingarn, Nov. 14, 1952; *Afro-American*, Jan. 10, 1953; Henry Lee Moon, "Election Post-Mortem," *Crisis*, LIX (Dec. 1952), 616–17.
51. Helen L. Peterson, "American Indian Political Participation," *Annals*, CCCXI (May 1957), 123–24; *New York Times*, Nov. 2, 1952.
52. *Call*, Nov. 14, 1952; *Journal and Guide*, Nov. 15, Dec. 6, 1952; *Crisis*, LIX (Dec. 1952), p. 646.
53. *Call*, Nov. 21, 28, 1952; *Amsterdam News*, Jan. 24, 1953; *Journal and Guide*, Jan. 24, 1953; *Afro-American*, Jan. 31, 1953; *Chicago Defender*, Jan. 24, 1953; Truman Papers, HSTL: Roy Wilkins to Truman, Jan. 12, 1953, OF 596.
54. *Public Papers, 1952–53*, p. 1050; *Call*, Jan. 2, 1953; *Afro-American*, Mar. 28, 1953.
55. *Amsterdam News*, Oct. 4, 1952; *Public Papers, 1952–53*, pp. 1050–51, 1062–64.
56. *Public Papers, 1952–53*, pp. 1117, 1174, 1202.
57. Ibid., pp. 897, 1090.
58. Green, *Secret City*, pp. 274, 278, 283–84.
59. Ibid., p. 275.
60. Chapman Papers, HSTL: Charles Alldredge to O. L. Chapman, Jan. 9, 1947; acting director of National Park Service to Chapman, June 12, 1947; Truman Papers, HSTL: J. A. Krug to Truman, Apr. 4, 1949, OF 93B; RG 330: Krug to Louis Johnson, Apr. 19, 1949; Johnson to Krug, Apr. 23, 1949; Gordon Gray to Johnson, May 2, 1949.
61. RG 330: G. R. Young to the secretary of defense, June 3, 1949; S. J. Spingarn Papers, HSTL: Spingarn to Clark Clifford, June 6, 1949.
62. Truman Papers, HSTL: S. J. Spingarn to Clark Clifford, June 15, 1949, Clifford Files; A. G. Klein to H. S. Wender, May 3, 1949, OF 93B; *Afro-American*, June 25, 1949; *Washington Post*, June 15, 1949; Chapman Papers, HSTL: "Steps in Progressive Elimination of Segregation in Recreation," May 4, 1950, enclosed in Russell Young to D. S. Dawson, May 5, 1950.
63. Truman Papers, HSTL: Urban League Statement to Truman, July 8, 1949, OF 93B; *Call*, July 15, 1949; Green, *Secret City*, p. 292.
64. Chapman Papers, HSTL: A. E. Demaray to O. L. Chapman, Apr. 4, 1950;

Truman Papers, HSTL: J. A. Krug to E. O. Melby, July 29, 1949, OF 93B; *Call*, Oct. 21, 1949.

65. *Call*, Oct. 21, 1949; Truman Papers, HSTL: J. D. Lohman to Philleo Nash, Feb. 13, 1950; Chapman Papers, HSTL: Department of the Interior News Release, Apr. 7, 1950.

66. RG 48: Oscar Chapman Form Letter, n.d.; Truman Papers, HSTL: Chapman to Truman, Sept. 6, 1950; Truman to Chapman, Sept. 8, 1950, OF 6P.

67. *Washington Post*, Sept. 10, 1950; Truman Papers, HSTL: E. J. Kelly to O. L. Chapman, Sept. 4, 1951, OF 6P; *Chicago Defender*, Oct. 7, 1950.

68. *Washington Post*, Mar. 14, 1952; AJC and NAACP, *Balance Sheet, 1952*, pp. 117–18; Green, *Secret City*, p. 295.

69. *Washington Post*, July 26, 1950; *Chicago Defender*, Oct. 20, 1951; AJC and NAACP, *Balance Sheet, 1951*, pp. 103, 118–19; Green, *Secret City*, pp. 294, 316–17.

70. AJC and NAACP, *Balance Sheet, 1952*, pp. 119–20; Department of State, Office of Personnel: R. A. Rose to J. A. Davis, May 1, 1953.

71. Landis, *Segregation in Washington*, p. 18; *Amsterdam News*, May 28, 1949.

72. Chapman Papers, HSTL: O. L. Chapman to M. G. White, Feb. 6, 1950; *Chicago Defender*, July 22, 1950.

73. *Chicago Defender*, Nov. 15, 1952; Green, *Secret City*, p. 297.

74. RG 48: O. L. Chapman to P. B. Perlman, Oct. 3, 1950; Perlman to Chapman, Oct. 5, 1950.

75. Ibid.: P. B. Perlman to O. L. Chapman, June 28, 1951; *Afro-American*, July 7, 1951.

76. *Chicago Defender*, July 14, 1951; *Afro-American*, July 7, 1951; *Call*, Sept. 28, 1951.

77. *Journal and Guide*, Jan. 31, 1953.

78. RG 48: Douglas McKay to Herbert Brownell, Jr., Feb. 13, 1953; *Afro-American*, Mar. 21, May 9, June 20, 1953; *District of Columbia* v. *John R. Thompson Company*, 346 U.S. 100.

79. *Afro-American*, June 20, 1953; H. H. Lehman Papers, Columbia University: Frances Williams to Tommie Brunkard, Dec. 9, 1953.

80. Green, *Secret City*, pp. 299–300.

81. President's Committee on Civil Rights, *To Secure These Rights*, p. 90; Landis, *Segregation in Washington*, pp. 75–81; AJC and NAACP, *Balance Sheet, 1951*, p. 106, *Balance Sheet, 1952*, p. 121; Irene Osborne and Richard K. Bennett, "Eliminating Educational Segregation in the Nation's Capital— 1951–1955," *Annals*, CCCIV (Mar. 1956), 101.

82. Kenneth B. Clark, *Prejudice and Your Child* (2d ed., enl.; Boston, 1963), pp. vi, 11, 12.

83. *Afro-American*, Feb. 9, Mar. 22, 1952; *Courier*, Aug. 18, 1951; *Journal and Guide*, Mar. 22, 1952; *Call*, June 13, 1952; Truman Papers, HSTL: Philleo Nash to Elmer Staats, Nov. 25, 1952, Nash Files.

84. Hugh W. Speer, *A Historical and Social Perspective on "Brown v. Board of Education of Topeka" with Present and Future Implications* (Washington, 1968), pp. 149–50.

85. Daniel M. Berman, *It Is So Ordered: The Supreme Court Rules on School Segregation* (New York, 1966), pp. 51, 59–60; interview with Mrs. James P. McGranery, Oct. 20, 1967.

86. *Brief for the United States as Amicus Curiae, in the Supreme Court of the*

United States, Oct. Term, 1952, Oliver Brown, et al. v. Board of Education of Topeka, et al.; Berman, *It Is So Ordered*, p. 60.
87. Berman, *It Is So Ordered*, p. 61; J. F. Davis (Clerk of the Supreme Court) to R. T. Ruetten, July 29, 1969.
88. Berman, *It Is So Ordered*, pp. 76–77, 79–81; *Courier*, Sept. 19, 1953; Speer, *A Historical and Social Perspective*, p. 205.
89. Berman, *It Is So Ordered*, pp. 83–86.
90. *New York Times*, Nov. 28, 1953; *Washington Star*, Dec. 8, 1953.
91. *New York Times*, Dec. 9, 1953; *Washington Star*, Dec. 9, 1953.
92. *Brown v. Board of Education of Topeka*, 347 U.S. 483; *Bolling v. Sharpe*, 347 U.S. 497.
93. Milton R. Konvitz, *Expanding Liberties: Freedom's Gains in Postwar America* (New York, 1966), pp. 254–55.
94. *Chicago Defender*, Nov. 29, 1952.
95. *Journal and Guide*, Feb. 7, 1953.

CHAPTER 15

1. Morroe Berger, *Racial Equality and the Law: The Role of the Law in the Reduction of Discrimination in the United States* (Paris, 1954), p. 48; U.S. Congress, Senate, Subcommittee of the Committee on Labor and Public Welfare, *State and Municipal Fair Employment Legislation*, 82d Cong., 2d sess., pp. 20–21; Norgren and Hill, *Toward Fair Employment*, p. 115; *American Jewish Year Book 1954*, pp. 34–41.
2. *American Jewish Year Book 1952*, p. 93; *The American Negro Reference Book*, pp. 232, 235, 259, 220.
3. Guzman, *Negro Year Book, 1952*, pp. 188–91, 121–22; *Jewish Year Book 1954*, p. 46; *Courier*, July 19, 1952; AJC and NAACP, *Balance Sheet, 1953*, p. 154; United States Bureau of the Census, *Historical Statistics of the United States*, p. 25.
4. United States Bureau of the Census, *Historical Statistics of the United States*, p. 213; U.S. Congress, Senate, Subcommittee of the Committee on Labor and Public Welfare, *Employment and Economic Status of Negroes in the United States*, 82d Cong., 2d sess., pp. 8–9; President's Committee on Government Contract Compliance, *Equal Economic Opportunity*, p. 105; Carter G. Woodson and Charles H. Wesley, *The Negro in Our History* (Washington, 1962), p. 690; Guzman, *Negro Year Book, 1952*, p. 207; Harry S. Ashmore, *The Negro and the Schools* (Chapel Hill, N.C., 1954), p. 62.
5. Department of Labor, *The Economic Situation of Negroes in the United States, Bulletin S-3* (Washington, 1952), p. 24; Norgren and Hill, *Toward Fair Employment*, p. 189.
6. Donald R. McCoy, Richard T. Ruetten, and J. R. Fuchs, eds., *Conference of Scholars on the Truman Administration and Civil Rights, April 5–6, 1968* (Independence, Mo., 1968), pp. 65–70.
7. *The American Negro Reference Book*, pp. 235, 232, 259.
8. See Numan V. Bartley, *The Rise of Massive Resistance* (Baton Rouge, La., 1969).

Bibliography

ARCHIVAL AND MANUSCRIPT MATERIALS

Harry S. Truman Library (Independence, Mo.)

William A. Brophy
Oscar L. Chapman
Will L. Clayton
Clark M. Clifford
Democratic National Committee
George M. Elsey
Raymond M. Foley
Michael J. Galvin
John W. Gibson
Melvin D. Hildreth
Frederick J. Lawton
David D. Lloyd
J. Howard McGrath
Francis P. Matthews
Charles S. Murphy
Dillon S. Myer

Philleo Nash
Frank Pace, Jr.
President's Commission on Migratory Labor
President's Committee on Civil Rights
President's Committee on Equality of Treatment and Opportunity in the Armed Services
John M. Redding
Samuel I. Rosenman
Charles G. Ross
Stephen J. Spingarn
David H. Stowe
Harry S. Truman
A. Devitt Vanech
Joel D. Wolfsohn

Library of Congress (Washington, D.C.)

Clinton Anderson
Harold H. Burton
Tom Connally
Democratic Caucus
Charles Fahy
Theodore F. Green
League of Women Voters

National Association for the Advancement of Colored People
Robert P. Patterson
Lewis B. Schwellenbach
Arthur B. Spingarn
Mary Church Terrell
Harry S. Truman
James Wadsworth

Franklin D. Roosevelt Library (Hyde Park, N.Y.)

Harley M. Kilgore
Franklin D. Roosevelt

Aubrey Williams

National Archives and Records Service (Washington, D.C., and Suitland, Md.)

Adjutant General's Office. Record Group 94.
Army Staff. RG 319.
Bureau of Indian Affairs. RG 75.
Bureau of Naval Personnel. RG 24.

Committee for Congested Production Areas. RG 212.
Committee on Fair Employment Practice. RG 228.

Committee on Government Contract Compliance. RG 325.
Department of Commerce. RG 40.
Department of Labor. RG 174.
Department of the Navy. RG 80.
Housing and Home Finance Agency. RG 207.
Office of Community War Services. RG 215.
Office of Defense Mobilization. RG 304.
Office of Education. RG 12.
Office of the Secretary of Agriculture. RG 16.

Office of the Secretary of Defense. RG 330.
Office of the Secretary of the Air Force. RG 340.
Office of the Secretary of the Army. RG 335.
Office of the Secretary of the Interior. RG 48.
Office of the Secretary of War. RG 107.
Office of War Information. RG 208.
Office of War Mobilization and Reconversion. RG 250.
War Department General and Special Staffs. RG 165.
War Relocation Authority. RG 210.

Federal Executive Agencies (Washington, D.C.)

Civil Service Commission.
Department of Justice.
Department of State. Office of Personnel.

Department of the Navy.
Department of the Treasury.
Operational Archives Branch. Naval History Division.

Chicago Historical Society (Chicago, Ill.)

Brotherhood of Sleeping Car Porters
Archibald J. Carey, Jr.
Corneal A. Davis

Friendship House
Independent Voters of Illinois

Others

Arthur Capper. Kansas State Historical Society, Topeka, Kan.
James V. Forrestal. Princeton University, Princeton, N.J.
Herbert H. Lehman. Columbia University, New York, N.Y.

William Pickens. New York Public Library, Schomburg Collection, New York, N.Y.
Henry L. Stimson. Yale University. New Haven, Conn.

ORAL HISTORY TRANSCRIPTS

Columbia University

Will Alexander
Joseph A. Gavagan
Ernest Rice McKinney
Benjamin McLaurin

George S. Schuyler
J. Waties Waring
Roy Wilkins

Harry S. Truman Library

John E. Barriere
William L. Batt, Jr.
Kenneth M. Birkhead
Samuel C. Brightman

John Franklin Carter
Jonathan Daniels
Martin L. Friedman
Harry H. Vaughan

PUBLIC DOCUMENTS

Brief for the United States as Amicus Curiae, in the Supreme Court of the United States, Oct. Term, 1952, Oliver Brown, et al. v. Board of Education of Topeka, et al.

The Budget of the United States Government for the Fiscal Year Ending June 30, 1951, June 30, 1952. Washington, 1950–51.

Department of Commerce. *3rd Report of Insurance Companies Owned and Operated by Negroes.* Washington, 1949.

————. *3rd Report of Savings and Loan Institutions Operated by Negroes.* Washington, 1948.

————. *4th Annual Report of Banking Institutions Owned and Operated by Negroes.* Washington, 1944.

————. *5th Annual Report of Banking Institutions Owned and Operated by Negroes.* Washington, 1947.

Department of Labor. *The Economic Situation of Negroes in the United States, Bulletin S-3.* Washington, 1952.

Ewing, Oscar R. *The Nation's Health: A Report to the President.* Washington, 1948.

Fair Employment Board. U.S. Civil Service Commission. "Complaints of Discrimination in the Federal Service." *Informational Bulletin No. 10.* Washington, Aug. 1, 1954.

————. *Fair Employment in the Federal Service.* Washington, 1952.

Fair Employment Practices Committee. *Final Report.* Washington, 1946.

Federal Register Division. National Archives and Records Service. *Code of Federal Regulations: Title 3—The President, 1949–1953 Compilation.* Washington, 1958.

Geis, Margaret L. *Negro Personnel in the European Command: 1 January 1946 to 30 June 1950.* European Command, Historical Division. Washington, 1952.

Hutchins, Clayton D., and Munse, Albert R. *Expenditures for Education at the Midcentury.* Washington, 1953.

————. *Supplement—Expenditures for*

Education at the Midcentury. Washington, 1954.

Johnson, Campbell C. *Special Groups.* 2 vols. Washington, 1953.

Lee, Ulysses. *The United States Army in World War II: Special Studies: The Employment of Negro Troops.* Washington, 1966.

Office of the Assistant Secretary of Defense. *Integration and the Negro Officer in the Armed Forces of the United States of America.* Washington, 1962.

Operations Research Office. Johns Hopkins University. *Utilization of Negro Manpower in the Army: A 1951 Study.* Washington, 1963.

President's Advisory Commission on Universal Training. *A Program for National Security: The Report of the President's Advisory Commission on Universal Training.* Washington, 1947.

President's Commission on Higher Education. *Higher Education for American Democracy.* 6 vols. New York, 1947–1948.

President's Commission on Immigration and Naturalization. *Whom We Shall Welcome.* Washington, 1953.

President's Commission on Migratory Labor. *Migratory Labor in American Agriculture.* Washington, 1951.

President's Commission on the Health Needs of the Nation. *Building America's Health.* 5 vols. Washington, 1952–1953.

President's Committee on Civil Rights. *To Secure These Rights: The Report of the President's Committee on Civil Rights.* New York, 1947.

President's Committee on Equality of Treatment and Opportunity in the Armed Services. *Freedom to Serve.* Washington, 1950.

President's Committee on Government Contract Compliance. *Equal Economic Opportunity: A Report by the President's Committee on Government Contract Compliance.* Washington, 1953.

Public Papers of the Presidents of the

United States, Harry S. Truman. 8 vols. Washington, 1961–1966.

Speer, Hugh W. A Historical and Social Perspective on "Brown v. Board of Education of Topeka" with Present and Future Implications. Washington, 1968.

United States Bureau of the Census. Historical Statistics of the United States, Colonial Times to 1957. Washington, 1960.

United States Commission on Civil Rights. Civil Rights '63. Washington, 1963.

———. 1961 Report. 5 vols. Washington, 1961.

United States Congress. Congressional Record. 1940–1954.

United States Congress. House. Subcommittee of the Committee on Education and Labor. Hearings, Federal Fair Employment Practice Act. 81st Cong., 1st sess., 1949.

United States Congress. Senate. Subcommittee of the Committee on Appropriations. Hearings, Departments of State, Justice, Commerce, and the Judiciary Appropriations for 1951. 81st Cong., 2d sess., 1950.

United States Congress. Senate. Subcommittee of the Committee on Labor and Public Welfare. State and Municipal Fair Employment Legislation. 82d Cong., 2d sess., 1952.

———. Employment and Economic Status of Negroes in the United States. 82d Cong., 2d sess., 1952.

United States Housing and Home Finance Agency. Housing of the Nonwhite Population, 1940–1947. Washington, 1948.

———. Housing of the Nonwhite Population, 1940–1950. Washington, 1952.

United States Office of Education. Biennial Survey of Education in the United States, 1946–48, 1952–54. Washington, 1951, 1959.

United States Senate Library. Presidential Vetoes. Washington, 1961.

United States War Liquidation Unit. Department of the Interior. People in Motion: The Postwar Adjustment of the Evacuated Japanese Americans. Washington, 1947.

United States War Relocation Authority. WRA: A Story of Human Conservation. Washington, 1946.

NEWSPAPERS

Afro-American (Baltimore), 1939–1953.

Afro Magazine (Baltimore), 1947–1948.

Amsterdam News (New York), 1940–1954.

Call (Kansas City, Mo.), 1934–1954.

Charleston News and Courier, 1953.

Chicago Defender, 1940–1953.

Chicago Sun-Times, 1947–1948, 1952.

Chicago Tribune, 1951.

Christian Science Monitor (Boston), 1952.

Daily News Bulletin (Jewish Telegraphic Agency), 1945.

Daily Worker (New York), 1948.

Daily World (Atlanta), 1948.

Inquirer (Philadelphia), 1947–1948.

Journal and Guide (Norfolk), 1940–1953.

Kansas City Star, 1969.

Kansas City Times, 1969.

Los Angeles Times, 1971.

New York Herald Tribune, 1945–1953.

New York Post, 1948.

New York Sun, 1948.

New York Times, 1939–1954, 1968.

People's Voice (New York), 1947.

Philadelphia Evening Bulletin, 1948.

Pittsburgh Courier, 1939–1954, 1968–1969.

PM (New York), 1947.

Providence Evening Bulletin, 1948.

Raleigh News and Observer, 1948.

St. Louis Argus, 1944–1945.

St. Louis Post-Dispatch, 1948.

Tribune (Philadelphia), 1948–1949.

Washington Daily News, 1945, 1949.

Washington Post, 1946–1953.

Washington Star, 1946–1953.

Washington Times-Herald, 1948–1949.

UNPUBLISHED STUDIES

Bureau of the Budget, Press Intelligence. "Summaries of Editorials and Column Comment from 9 Negro Weeklies." Mimeographed. Washington, Jan. 11, 1946.

Byers, Jean. "A Study of the Negro in the Military Service." Mimeographed. Washington, Department of Defense, 1950.

Garza, Edward D. "LULAC (League of United Latin American Citizens)." Master's thesis, Southwest Texas State Teachers College, 1951.

Hamby, Alonzo. "Harry S. Truman and American Liberalism, 1945–1948." Ph.D. dissertation, University of Missouri, 1965.

Kifer, Allen F. "The Negro Under the New Deal, 1933–1941." Ph.D. dissertation, University of Wisconsin, 1961.

Lawrence, Charles R. "Negro Organizations in Crisis: Depression, New Deal, World War II." Ph.D. dissertation, Columbia University, 1952.

Legere, Lawrence J., Jr. "Unification of the Armed Forces." Ph.D. dissertation, Harvard University, 1950.

National Housing Agency. "Negro Share of Priority War Housing—Private and Public, As of Dec. 31, 1944." Mimeographed. Washington, 1945.

Schmidtlein, Eugene F. "Truman the Senator." Ph.D. dissertation, University of Missouri, 1962.

BOOKS

Abrams, Charles. *Forbidden Neighbors: A Study of Prejudice in Housing.* New York, 1955.

Allport, Gordon W. *The Nature of Prejudice.* Cambridge, Mass., 1954.

American Jewish Committee. *American Jewish Year Book 1948–1949, 1950, 1951, 1952, 1954.* Philadelphia and New York, 1949, 1950, 1952, 1953, 1955.

————. *Annual Report, 1945, 1948, 1949, 1952.* New York, 1946, 1949, 1950, 1953.

American Jewish Congress and National Association for the Advancement of Colored People. *Civil Rights in the United States in 1949, 1951, 1952, 1953: A Balance Sheet of Group Relations.* New York, 1950, 1952, 1953, 1954.

Anderson, Patrick. *The Presidents' Men: White House Assistants of Franklin D. Roosevelt, Harry S. Truman, Dwight D. Eisenhower, John F. Kennedy, and Lyndon B. Johnson.* Garden City, N.Y., 1968.

Anti-Defamation League of B'nai B'rith. *Anti-Semitism in the United States in 1947.* New York, 1948.

Ashmore, Harry S. *The Negro and the Schools.* Chapel Hill, N.C., 1954.

Atwood, J. Howell. *The Racial Factor in YMCAs.* New York, 1946.

Bailey, Stephen K. *Congress Makes a Law: The Story Behind the Employment Act of 1946.* New York, 1950.

Bartley, Numan V. *The Rise of Massive Resistance.* Baton Rouge, La., 1969.

Becker, Gary S. *The Economics of Discrimination.* Chicago, 1957.

Benedict, Ruth. *Race: Science and Politics.* New York, 1940.

Berger, Morroe. *Racial Equality and the Law: The Role of Law in the Reduction of Discrimination in the United States.* Paris, 1954.

Berman, Daniel M. *It Is So Ordered: The Supreme Court Rules on School Segregation.* New York, 1966.

Berman, William C. *The Politics of Civil Rights in the Truman Administration.* Columbus, Ohio, 1970.

Bernstein, Barton J., ed. *Politics and Policies of the Truman Administration.* Chicago, 1970.

Blanshard, Paul. *American Freedom and Catholic Power.* Boston, 1949.

Blood, Kathryn. *Negro Women War Workers.* Washington, 1945.

Bloom, Leonard, and Riemer, Ruth. *Removal and Return: The Socio-*

Economic Effects of the War on Japanese Americans. Berkeley, Calif., 1949.

Bogart, Leo, ed. *Social Research and the Desegregation of the U.S. Army.* Chicago, 1969.

Bone, Robert A. *The Negro Novel in America.* New Haven, 1958.

Bontecou, Eleanor. *The Federal Loyalty-Security Program.* Ithaca, N.Y., 1953.

Brock, Clifton. *Americans for Democratic Action: Its Role in National Politics.* Washington, 1962.

Broderick, Francis L. *W. E. B. DuBois.* Stanford, Calif., 1959.

Broom, Leonard, and Kitsuse, John I. *The Managed Casualty: The Japanese-American Family in World War II.* Berkeley, Calif., 1956.

Brophy, William A., and Aberle, Sophie D., eds. *The Indian, America's Unfinished Business: Report of the Commission on the Rights, Liberties, and Responsibilities of the American Indian.* Norman, Okla., 1966.

Brown, Earl, and Leighton, George R. *The Negro and the War.* New York, 1942.

Bullock, Henry Allen. *A History of Negro Education in the South: From 1619 to the Present.* Cambridge, Mass., 1967.

Burma, John H. *Spanish-speaking Groups in the United States.* Durham, N.C., 1954.

Busch, Noel F. *Adlai E. Stevenson of Illinois: A Portrait.* New York, 1952.

Caliver, Ambrose. *Education of Negro Leaders: Influences Affecting Graduate and Professional Studies.* Washington, 1949.

Cannon, Poppy. *A Gentle Knight: My Husband, Walter White.* New York, 1956.

Carpenter, William Seal. *The Unfinished Business of Civil Service Reform.* Princeton, N.J., 1952.

Carr, Robert K. *Federal Protection of Civil Rights.* Ithaca, N.Y., 1947.

Carter, Dan T. *Scottsboro: a Tragedy of the American South.* Baton Rouge, La., 1969.

Chalmers, David M. *Hooded Americanism: The First Century of the Ku Klux Klan, 1865–1965.* Garden City, N.Y., 1965.

Clark, Kenneth B. *Prejudice and Your Child.* 2d ed., enl. Boston, 1963.

Clark, Mark W. *From the Danube to the Yalu.* New York, 1954.

Clark, Tom C., and Perlman, Philip B. *Prejudice and Property: An Historic Brief against Racial Covenants.* Washington, 1948.

Conference of Negro Writers, 1st. *The American Negro Writer and his Roots: Selected Papers.* New York, 1960.

Congressional Quarterly News Features. *Congressional Quarterly Almanac, 1948, 1949, 1950, 1951, 1952.* Washington, 1949, 1950, 1951, 1952, 1953.

Congressional Quarterly Service. *Congress and the Nation, 1945–1964.* Washington, 1965.

Corrigan, Joseph M., and O'Toole, G. Barry, eds. *Race: Nation: Person: Social Aspects of the Race Problem: A Symposium.* New York, 1944.

Dalfiume, Richard M. *Desegregation of the U.S. Armed Forces: Fighting on Two Fronts, 1939–1953.* Columbia, Mo., 1969.

Daniels, Jonathan. *The Man of Independence.* Philadelphia, 1950.

David, Paul T.; Moos, Malcolm; and Goldman, Ralph M. *Presidential Nominating Politics in 1952: The National Story.* Baltimore, Md., 1954.

Davies, Richard O. *Housing Reform during the Truman Administration.* Columbia, Mo., 1966.

Davis, John P., ed. *The American Negro Reference Book.* Englewood Cliffs, N.J., 1966.

Dexter, Harriet H. *What's Right with Race Relations.* New York, 1958.

Dorsett, Lyle W. *The Pendergast Machine.* New York, 1968.

Drake, St. Clair, and Cayton, Horace R. *Black Metropolis: A Study of Negro Life in a Northern City.* New York, 1945.

Editors of *Ebony. The Negro Handbook.* Chicago, 1966.

Ellis, John Tracy. *American Catholicism.* Chicago, 1956.

Fey, Harold E., and McNickle, D'Arcy.

Indians and Other Americans: Two Ways of Life Meet. New York, 1959.

Forrestal, James. The Forrestal Diaries: The Inner History of the Cold War. Edited by Walter Millis. London, 1952.

Forster, Arnold, and Epstein, Benjamin R. The Trouble-Makers: An Anti-Defamation League Report. Garden City, N.Y., 1952.

Foster, William Z. The Negro People in American History. New York, 1954.

Franklin, John Hope. From Slavery to Freedom: A History of Negro Americans. 3d ed., rev. and enl. New York, 1967.

Freidel, Frank. F.D.R. and the South. Baton Rouge, La., 1965.

Garfinkel, Herbert. When Negroes March: The March on Washington Movement in the Organizational Politics for FEPC. Glencoe, Ill., 1959.

Gossett, Thomas F. Race: The History of an Idea in America. Dallas, 1963.

Graves, W. Brooke. Fair Employment Practice Legislation in the United States: Federal—State—Municipal. Washington, 1951.

Green, Constance McLaughlin. The Secret City: A History of Race Relations in the Nation's Capital. Princeton, N.J., 1967.

Greenberg, Jack. Race Relations and American Law. New York, 1959.

Griffith, Winthrop. Humphrey: A Candid Biography. New York, 1965.

Grodzins, Morton. Americans Betrayed: Politics and the Japanese Evacuation. Chicago, 1949.

Guzman, Jessie P., ed. Negro Year Book: A Review of Events Affecting Negro Life, 1941–1946. Tuskegee, Ala., 1947.

———. Negro Year Book, 1952: A Review of Events Affecting Negro Life. New York, 1952.

Hagan, William T. American Indians. Chicago, 1961.

Handel, Leo A. Hollywood Looks at Its Audience: A Report of Film Audience Research. Urbana, Ill., 1950.

Handlin, Oscar. Adventure in Freedom: Three Hundred Years of Jewish Life in America. New York, 1954.

———. The Newcomers: Negroes and Puerto Ricans in a Changing Metropolis. Cambridge, Mass., 1959.

Harte, Thomas J. Catholic Organizations Promoting Negro-White Race Relations in the United States. Washington, 1947.

Hartmann, Susan M. Truman and the 80th Congress. Columbia, Mo., 1971.

Hayes, Laurence J. W. The Negro Federal Government Worker: A Study of His Classification Status in the District of Columbia, 1883–1938. Washington, 1941.

Hays, Brooks. A Southern Moderate Speaks. Chapel Hill, N.C., 1959.

Higbee, Jay A. Development and Administration of the New York State Law Against Discrimination. University, Ala., 1966.

Hollander, Herbert. Crisis in the Civil Service. Washington, 1955.

Horton, David S., ed. Freedom and Equality: Addresses by Harry S. Truman. Columbia, Mo., 1960.

Hutchinson, E. P. Immigrants and Their Children, 1850–1950. New York, 1956.

Ichihashi, Yamato. Japanese in the United States: A Critical Study of the Problems of the Japanese Immigrants and Their Children. Stanford, Calif., 1932.

Isaacs, Harold R. The New World of Negro Americans. New York, 1963.

Javits, Jacob K. Discrimination—U.S.A. New York, 1960.

Johnson, Charles S. et al. Into the Main Stream: A Survey of Best Practices in Race Relations in the South. Chapel Hill, N.C., 1947.

Kesselman, Louis C. The Social Politics of FEPC: A Study in Reform Pressure Movements. Chapel Hill, N.C., 1948.

Key, V. O., Jr. Southern Politics in State and Nation. New York, 1949.

Kingrea, Nellie Ward. History of the First Ten Years of the Texas Good Neighbor Commission and Discus-

sion of Its Major Problems. Fort Worth, 1954.

Konvitz, Milton R. *Expanding Liberties: Freedom's Gains in Postwar America.* New York, 1966.

Krislov, Samuel. *The Negro in Federal Employment: The Quest for Equal Opportunity.* Minneapolis, Minn., 1967.

Krueger, Thomas A. *And Promises to Keep: The Southern Conference for Human Welfare, 1938–1948.* Nashville, 1967.

Kung, Shien-woo. *Chinese in American Life.* Seattle, Wash., 1962.

La Farge, John. *The Catholic Viewpoint on Race Relations.* Garden City, N.Y., 1956.

Landis, Kenesaw M. *Segregation in Washington: A Report of the National Committee on Segregation in the Nation's Capital.* Chicago, 1948.

Lee, Alfred M., and Humphrey, Norman D. *Race Riot.* New York, 1943.

Lee, Rose Hum. *The Chinese in the United States of America.* Hong Kong, 1960.

Levine, Stuart, and Lurie, Nancy O., eds. *The American Indian Today.* Rev. ed. Baltimore, 1970.

Lilienthal, David E. *The Journals of David E. Lilienthal.* 4 vols. New York, 1964, 1966, 1969.

Lind, Andrew W., ed. *Race Relations in World Perspective.* Honolulu, 1955.

Littlejohn, David. *Black on White: A Critical Survey of Writing by American Negroes.* New York, 1966.

Loescher, Frank S. *The Protestant Church and the Negro: A Pattern of Segregation.* New York, 1948.

Logan, Rayford W., ed. *What the Negro Wants.* Chapel Hill, N.C., 1944.

Long, Herman H., and Johnson, Charles S. *People vs. Property: Race Restrictive Covenants in Housing.* Nashville, 1947.

McAvoy, Thomas T. *Roman Catholicism and the American Way of Life.* Notre Dame, Ind., 1960.

McCoy, Donald R.; Ruetten, Richard T.; and Fuchs, J. R., eds. *Conference of Scholars on the Truman Ad-*

ministration and Civil Rights, April 5–6, 1968. Independence, Mo., 1968.

MacDougall, Curtis Daniel. *Gideon's Army.* 3 vols. New York, 1965.

McWilliams, Carey. *A Mask for Privilege: Anti-Semitism in America.* Boston, 1948.

————. *North from Mexico: The Spanish-speaking People of the United States,* Philadelphia, 1949.

Marshall, F. Ray. *The Negro and Organized Labor.* New York, 1965.

Matthews, Donald R., and Prothro, James W. *Negroes and the New Southern Politics.* New York, 1966.

Meier, August, and Rudwick, Elliott M. *From Plantation to Ghetto.* New York, 1966.

Meyerson, Martin, and Banfield, Edward C. *Politics, Planning, and the Public Interest: The Case of Public Housing in Chicago.* Glencoe, Ill., 1955.

Miller, Kelly. *The Everlasting Stain.* Washington, 1924.

Mitchell, Franklin D. *Embattled Democracy: Missouri Democratic Politics, 1919–1932.* Columbia, Mo., 1968.

Moon, Henry Lee. *Balance of Power: The Negro Vote.* Garden City, N.Y., 1948.

Morgan, Ruth P. *The President and Civil Rights.* New York, 1970.

Murray, Pauli, comp. and ed. *States' Laws on Race and Color.* Cincinnati, Ohio, 1951.

Myrdal, Gunnar. *An American Dilemma: The Negro Problem and Modern Democracy.* New York, 1944.

National Association for the Advancement of Colored People. *Annual Report for 1947, 1948, 1949, 1950, 1951.* New York, 1948, 1949, 1950, 1951, 1952.

National Urban League. *40th Anniversary Year Book, 1950.* New York, 1951.

Nelson, Dennis D. *The Integration of the Negro into the U.S. Navy.* New York, 1951.

Newby, Idus A. *Jim Crow's Defense: Anti-Negro Thought in America, 1900–1930.* Baton Rouge, La., 1965.

Nichols, Lee. *Breakthrough on the Color Front*. New York, 1954.

Noble, Peter. *The Negro in Films*. London, 1948.

Norgren, Paul H., and Hill, Samuel E. *Toward Fair Employment*. New York, 1964.

O'Neill, James M. *Catholicism and American Freedom*. New York, 1952.

Osborne, William A. *The Segregated Covenant: Race Relations and American Catholics*. New York, 1967.

Osofsky, Gilbert. *Harlem: The Making of a Ghetto: Negro New York, 1890–1930*. New York, 1966.

Ottley, Roi. *"New World A-Coming": Inside Black America*. Boston, 1943.

Ovington, Mary White. *The Walls Came Tumbling Down: The Autobiography of Mary White Ovington*. New York, 1947.

Phillips, Cabell. *The Truman Presidency: The History of a Triumphant Succession*. New York, 1966.

Ploski, Harry A., and Brown, Roscoe C., Jr., eds. *The Negro Almanac*. New York, 1967.

Porter, Kirk H., and Johnson, Donald B., comps. *National Party Platforms, 1840–1964*. Urbana, Ill., 1966.

Powell, Adam Clayton, Jr. *Marching Blacks: An Interpretive History of the Rise of the Black Common Man*. New York, 1945.

Record, Wilson. *Race and Radicalism: The NAACP and the Communist Party in Conflict*. Ithaca, N.Y., 1964.

Redding, John M. *Inside the Democratic Party*. Indianapolis, 1958.

Redding, Jay Saunders. *The Lonesome Road: The Story of the Negro's Part in America*. Garden City, N.Y., 1958.

Richards, Edward A., ed. *Proceedings of the Midcentury White House Conference on Children and Youth*. Raleigh, N.C., 1951.

Ridgway, Matthew B. *The Korean War*. Garden City, N.Y., 1967.

Riggs, Fred W. *Pressures on Congress: A Study of the Repeal of Chinese Exclusion*. New York, 1950.

Rose, Arnold and Caroline. *America Divided: Minority Group Relations in the United States*. New York, 1948.

Ross, Irwin. *The Loneliest Campaign: The Truman Victory of 1948*. New York, 1968.

Ruchames, Louis. *Race, Jobs & Politics: The Story of FEPC*. New York, 1953.

Rudwick, Elliott M. *W. E. B. DuBois*. Philadelphia, 1960.

St. James, Warren D. *The National Association for the Advancement of Colored People: A Case Study in Pressure Groups*. New York, 1958.

Salmond, John A. *The Civilian Conservation Corps, 1933–1942: A New Deal Case Study*. Durham, N.C., 1967.

Sawyer, Charles. *Concerns of A Conservative Democrat*. Carbondale, Ill., 1968.

Shogan, Robert, and Craig, Tom. *The Detroit Race Riot*. Philadelphia, 1964.

Silberman, Charles E. *Crisis in Black and White*. New York, 1964.

Smith, Stanley H. *Freedom to Work*. New York, 1955.

Spangler, Earl. *The Negro in Minnesota*. Minneapolis, Minn., 1961.

Stanley, Timothy W. *American Defense and National Security*. Washington, 1956.

Steinberg, Alfred. *The Man from Missouri: The Life and Times of Harry S. Truman*. New York, 1962.

Stillman, Richard J., II. *Integration of the Negro in the U.S. Armed Forces*. New York, 1968.

Stokes, Anson Phelps, et al. *Negro Status and Race Relations in the United States, 1911–1946*. New York, 1948.

Stouffer, Samuel A., et al. *The American Soldier: Adjustment during Army Life*. Princeton, 1949.

Strickland, Arvarh E. *History of the Chicago Urban League*. Urbana, Ill., 1966.

Strong, Donald S. *Organized Anti-Semitism in America: The Rise of Group Prejudice During the Decade 1930–40*. Washington, 1941.

tenBroek, Jacobus, et al. *Prejudice, War and the Constitution*. Berkeley, Calif., 1958.

Thomas, Dorothy S. *Japanese-American*

Evacuation and Resettlement: The Salvage. Berkeley, Calif., 1952.

Truman, Harry S. *Memoirs.* 2 vols. New York, 1965, 1966.

Tuck, Ruth D. *Not with the Fist: Mexican-Americans in a Southwest City.* New York, 1946.

University of Chicago Committee on Education, Training and Research in Race Relations. *The Dynamics of State Campaigns for Fair Employment Practices Legislation.* Chicago, 1950.

Valien, Bonita H. *The St. Louis Story: A Study of Desegregation.* New York, 1956.

Van Riper, Paul P. *History of the United States Civil Service.* Evanston, Ill., 1958.

Vose, Clement E. *Caucasians Only: The Supreme Court, the NAACP, and the Restrictive Covenant Cases.* Berkeley, Calif., 1959.

Weaver, Robert C. *Negro Labor: A National Problem.* New York, 1946.

————. *The Negro Ghetto.* New York, 1948.

Weintraub, Ruth G. *How Secure These Rights? Anti-Semitism in the United States in 1948: An Anti-Defamation League Survey.* Garden City, N.Y., 1949.

Wells, Henry. *The Modernization of Puerto Rico: A Political Study of Changing Values and Institutions.* Cambridge, Mass., 1969.

White, Walter. *A Man Called White.* New York, 1948.

Williams, Robin M., Jr., and Ryan, Margaret W., eds. *Schools in Transition: Community Experiences in Desegregation.* Chapel Hill, N.C., 1954.

Wolters, Raymond. *Negroes and the Great Depression: The Problem of Economic Recovery.* Westport, Conn., 1970.

Woodson, Carter G., and Wesley, Charles H. *The Negro in Our History.* Washington, 1962.

Woofter, Thomas J. *Southern Race Progress: The Wavering Color Line.* Washington, 1957.

ARTICLES

Aptheker, Herbert. "Literacy, The Negro and World War II." *Journal of Negro Education,* XV (Fall 1946).

Bacote, C. A. "Negro Vote in the Southeast." *Crisis,* LIX (Oct. 1952).

Bickerton, Ian J. "President Truman's Recognition of Israel." *American Jewish Historical Quarterly,* LVIII (Dec. 1968).

Billington, Monroe. "Freedom to Serve: The President's Committee on Equality of Treatment and Opportunity in the Armed Forces, 1949–1950." *Journal of Negro History,* LI (Oct. 1966).

Bloom, Leonard. "Will Our Nisei Get Justice?" *Christian Century,* LXV (Mar. 3, 1948).

Brown, Sterling A. "Athletics and the Arts." *The Integration of the Negro into American Society.* Edited by E. Franklin Frazier. Washington, 1951.

Cantor, Louis. "A Prologue to the Protest Movement: The Missouri Sharecropper Roadside Demonstra-

tion of 1939." *Journal of American History,* LV (Mar. 1969).

Carr, Robert K. "Screws v. United States, The Georgia Police Brutality Case." *Cornell Law Quarterly,* XXXIII (Sept. 1948).

Caudill, William. "Japanese American Personality and Acculturation." *Genetic Psychology Monographs,* XLV (Feb. 1952).

Clark, Kenneth B. "Candor about Negro-Jewish Relations." *Commentary,* I (Feb. 1946).

Cobb, W. Montague. "Medicine." *The Integration of the Negro into American Society.* Edited by E. Franklin Frazier. Washington, 1951.

Cohen, Elliot E. "Letter to the Movie-Makers." *Commentary,* IV (Aug. 1947).

Cohen, Felix S. "Our Country's Shame." *Progressive,* XIII (May 1949).

Collier, John. "Back to Dishonor?" *Christian Century,* LXXI (May 12, 1954).

Cooke, W. Henry. "The Segregation of Mexican-American School Children in Southern California." *School and Society*, LXVII (June 5, 1948).

The Crisis, 1940–1954.

Cushman, Robert E. "American Civil Liberties in the Mid-Twentieth Century," *Annals*, CCLXXV (May 1951).

Dalfiume, Richard M. "The Fahy Committee and Desegregation of the Armed Forces." *Historian*, XXXI (Nov. 1968).

———. "The 'Forgotten Years' of the Negro Revolution." *Journal of American History*, LV (June 1968).

———. "Military Segregation and the 1940 Presidential Election." *Phylon*, XXX (Spring 1969).

Davis, John A. "Nondiscrimination in the Federal Services." *Annals*, CCXLIV (Mar. 1946).

Davis, Kingsley, and Senior, Clarence. "Immigration from the Western Hemisphere." *Annals*, CCLXII (Mar. 1949).

De Moraes, Vinicius. "The Making of a Document: 'The Quiet One.'" *Hollywood Quarterly*, IV (Summer 1950).

Dorey, Frank D. "Religion." *The Integration of the Negro into American Society*. Edited by E. Franklin Frazier. Washington, 1951.

Doscher, Luelyne. "Notes and Communications: Birth of a Stereotype." *Hollywood Quarterly*, III (Fall 1947).

Ebony, 1945–1954.

Farmer, James. "The New Jacobins and Full Emancipation." *100 Years of Emancipation*. Edited by Robert A. Goldwin. Chicago, 1963, 1964.

Fearing, Franklin. "A Word of Caution for the Intelligent Consumer of Motion Pictures." *Quarterly of Film, Radio, and Television*, VI (Winter 1951).

———. "Influence of the Movies on Attitudes and Behavior." *Annals*, CCLIV (Nov. 1947).

Fey, Harold E. "Can Catholicism Win America?" *Christian Century*, LXI-LXII (Nov. 29, Dec. 6, 13, 20, 27, 1944, Jan. 3, 10, 17, 1945).

Fishel, Leslie H., Jr. "The Negro in the New Deal Era." *Wisconsin Magazine of History*, XLVIII (Winter 1964–1965).

Ford, Nick Aaron. "The Influence of Literature on the Civil Rights Revolution." *Afro Magazine*, Sept. 18, 1948.

Franklin, Jay. "What Truman Really Thinks of Negroes." *Negro Digest*, VII (June 1949).

Glazer, Nathan. "The American Jew and the Attainment of Middle-Class Rank: Some Trends and Explanations." *The Jews: Social Patterns of An American Group*. Edited by Marshall Sklare. Glencoe, Ill., 1958.

Gosnell, Harold F. "Politics." *The Integration of the Negro into American Society*. Edited by E. Franklin Frazier. Washington, 1951.

Granger, Lester B. "Racial Democracy—The Navy Way." *Common Ground*, VII (Winter 1947).

Grossman, Mordecai. "The Schools Fight Prejudice." *Commentary*, I (Apr. 1946).

Haas, Theodore H. "The Legal Aspects of Indian Affairs from 1887 to 1957." *Annals*, CCCXI (May 1957).

Halpern, Ben. "America is Different." *The Jews: Social Patterns of an American Group*. Edited by Marshall Sklare. Glencoe, Ill., 1958.

Handel, Leo A. "Hollywood Market Research." *Quarterly of Film, Radio, and Television*, VII (Spring 1953).

Hardwick, Leon H. "Screen Stereotypes." *Negro Digest*, IV (May 1946).

Hatch, Robert. "Gold Fever." *New Republic*, CXVIII (Jan. 26, 1948).

Hawley, Ellis W. "The Politics of the Mexican Labor Issue, 1950–1965." *Agricultural History*, XL (July 1966).

High, Stanley. "Black Omens." *Saturday Evening Post*, CCX (May 21, June 4, 1938).

Ickes, Harold L. "The Indian Loses Again." *New Republic*, CXXV (Sept. 24, 1951).

———. "'Justice' in a Deep Freeze." *New Republic*, CXXIV (May 21, 1951).

Inter-American, II (Sept. 1943).

Johnson, George M. "Legal Profession." *The Integration of the Negro into American Society.* Edited by E. Franklin Frazier. Washington, 1951.

Jones, Dorothy B. "William Faulkner: Novel into Film." *Quarterly of Film, Radio, and Television*, VIII (Fall 1953).

Kenworthy, E. W. "The Case against Army Segregation." *Annals*, CCLXXV (May 1951).

Knox, Ellis O. "The Negro as a Subject of University Research in 1950." *Journal of Negro Education*, XXI (Winter 1952).

Kong, Walter. "Name Calling." *Survey Graphic*, XXXIII (June 1944).

La Farge, Oliver. "To Set the Indians Free." *New Republic*, CXXI (Oct. 3, 1949).

Lancaster, Emmer M. "Insurance Companies Owned and Operated by Negroes." *Business Information Service*, Nov. 1952.

Lee, Rose Hum. "A Century of Chinese and American Relations." *Phylon*, XI (Third Quarter 1950).

———. "The Hua-ch'iao in the United States of America." *Colloquium on Overseas Chinese.* Edited by Morton H. Fried. New York, 1958.

Lee, Thomas H. "Six Months Since Repeal." *Asia and the Americas*, XLIV (July 1944).

Liveright, A. A. "The Community and Race Relations." *Annals*, CCXLIV (Mar. 1946).

Lovell, John, Jr. "Roundup: The Negro in the American Theatre (1940–1947)." *Crisis*, LIV (July 1947).

Lurie, Nancy O. "The Indian Claims Commission Act." *Annals*, CCCXI (May 1957).

McCoy, Donald R., and Ruetten, Richard T. "The Civil Rights Movement: 1940–1954." *Midwest Quarterly*, XI (Autumn 1969).

McGraw, B. T. "The Housing Act of 1954 and Implications for Minorities." *Phylon*, XVI (Second Quarter 1955).

McManus, John T., and Kronenberger, Louis. "Motion Pictures, the Theater, and Race Relations." *Annals*, CCXLIV (Mar. 1946).

McWilliams, Carey. "America's Disadvantaged Minorities: Mexican-Americans." *Journal of Negro Education*, XX (Summer 1951).

———. "Power Politics and the Navajo." *Nation*, CLXVII (July 17, 1948).

Martin, Harold H. "How Do Our Negro Troops Measure Up?" *Saturday Evening Post*, CCXXIII (June 16, 1951).

Mason, Lucy R. "The CIO and the Negro in the South." *Journal of Negro Education*, XIV (Fall 1945).

Matthiessen, Peter. "Profiles." *New Yorker*, XLV (June 21, 1969).

Mitchell, Arthur W. "The New Deal and the Negro." *Congressional Record*, 76th Cong., 3d sess.

Mitchell, Clarence. "President Truman's 'FEPC.'" *Crisis*, LIX (Jan. 1952).

Moon, Henry Lee. "Election Post-Mortem." *Crisis*, LIX (Dec. 1952).

Nash, Philleo. "An Introduction to the Problem of Race Tension." *The North American Indian Today.* Edited by Charles T. Loram and Thomas F. McIlwraith. Toronto, 1943.

Norford, George. "On Stage. . . ." *Opportunity*, XXV (Summer 1947).

Osborne, Irene, and Bennett, Richard K. "Eliminating Educational Segregation in the Nation's Capital—1951–1955." *Annals*, CCCIV (Mar. 1956).

Paszek, Lawrence J. "Negroes and the Air Force, 1939–1949." *Military Affairs*, XXXI (Spring 1967).

Perl, Arnold. "'To Secure These Rights.'" *Hollywood Quarterly*, III (Spring 1948).

Peterson, Helen L. "American Indian Political Participation." *Annals*, CCCXI (May 1957).

Reddick, L. D. "The Negro Policy of the American Army since World War II." *Journal of Negro History*, XXXVIII (Apr. 1953).

Redding, Saunders. "The Negro Writer and American Literature." *Anger, and Beyond: The Negro Writer in the United States.* Edited by Herbert Hill. New York, 1966.

Reynolds, Grant. "A Triumph for Civil Disobedience." *Nation,* CLXVII (Aug. 28, 1948).

Román, Josefina de. "New York's Latin Quarter." *Inter-American,* V (Jan. 1946).

Rowan, Carl T. "Harry S. Truman and the Negro." *Ebony,* XV (Nov. 1959).

Schermerhorn, R. A. "America's Disadvantaged Minorities: The American Indian." *Journal of Negro Education,* XX (Summer 1951).

Sitkoff, Harvard. "Harry Truman and the Election of 1948: The Coming of Age of Civil Rights in American Politics." *Journal of Southern History,* XXXVII (Nov. 1971).

———. "Racial Militancy and Interracial Violence in the Second World War." *Journal of American History,* LVIII (Dec. 1971).

Smith, William Thomas. "Hollywood Report." *Phylon,* VI (First Quarter 1945).

Stettinius, Edward R., Jr. "Human Rights in the United Nations Charter." *Annals,* CCXLIII (Jan. 1946).

Stevens, Alden. "Whither the American Indian?" *Survey Graphic,* XXIX (Mar. 1940).

Stokes, Frank. "Let the Mexicans Organize!" *Nation,* CXLIII (Dec. 19, 1936).

Time, XLIX (May 19, 1947).

Tuck, Ruth D. "Behind the Zoot Suit Riots." *Survey Graphic,* XXXII (Aug. 1943).

Weekly Analysis of Newspaper Opinion (James S. Twohey Associates), 1944–1948.

Van Auken, Cecelia. "The Negro Press in the 1948 Presidential Election." *Journalism Quarterly,* XXVI (Dec. 1949).

Washington, Val J. "The Republican Case for 1952." *Crisis,* LIX (Oct. 1952).

Weaver, Robert C. "Habitation with Segregation." *Crisis,* LIX (June–July 1952).

———. "Integration in Public and Private Housing." *Annals,* CCCIV (Mar. 1956).

Wechsler, James A. and Nancy F. "The Road Ahead for Civil Rights." *Commentary,* VI (Oct. 1948).

White, William L. "The Report That Stirred America's Conscience." *This Week,* Dec. 17, 1950, reprinted in *Negro Digest,* IX (May 1951).

Wilkins, Roy. "Emancipation and Militant Leadership." *100 Years of Emancipation.* Edited by Robert A. Goldwin. Chicago, 1963, 1964.

Wirth, Louis. "The Unfinished Business of American Democracy." *Annals,* CCXLIV (Mar. 1946).

Wolfenstein, Martha, and Leites, Nathan. "The Study of Man." *Commentary,* X (Oct. 1950).

Woodbury, Clarence. "Our Worst Slum." *American Magazine,* CXLVIII (Sept. 1949).

Yinger, J. Milton, and Simpson, George E. "The Integration of Americans of Mexican, Puerto Rican, and Oriental Descent." *Annals,* CCCIV (Mar. 1956).

Index

414